Understanding Physical, Health, and Multiple Disabilities

Second Edition

Kathryn Wolff Heller
Georgia State University

Paula E. Forney
Georgia Department of Human Resources

Paul A. Alberto
Georgia State University

Sherwood J. Best
California State University, Los Angeles

Morton N. Schwartzman
Joe Dimaggio Cystic Fibrosis and Pulmonary Center

Merrill
is an imprint of

Upper Saddle River, New Jersey
Columbus, Ohio

Library of Congress Cataloging in Publication Data
Understanding physical, health, and multiple disabilities / Kathryn Wolff Heller ... [et al.].-- 2nd ed.
  p. cm.
  Rev. ed. of: Understanding physical, sensory, and health impairments. 1996.
  Includes bibliographical references and index.
  ISBN-13: 978-0-13-240273-6
  1. Children with disabilities. 2. Child development deviations. 3. Children with
disabilities--Education.   I. Heller, Kathryn Wolff
  RJ137.U53 2009
  362.4083--dc   2008001298

Vice President and Executive Publisher: Jeffery W. Johnston
Executive Editor: Ann Castel Davis
Editorial Assistant: Penny Burleson
Senior Managing Editor: Pamela D. Bennett
Production Editor: Sheryl Glicker Langner
Production Coordination: Mary Tindle, S4Carlisle Publishing Services
Photo Coordinator: Valerie Schultz
Design Coordinator: Diane C. Lorenzo
Cover Designer: Ali Mohrman
Cover Image: Fotosearch
Production Manager: Laura Messerly
Director of Marketing: Quinn Perkson
Marketing Manager: Kris Ellis-Levy
Marketing Coordinator: Brian Mounts

This book was set in Garamond by S4Carlisle Publishing Services. It was printed and bound by Courier Corporation. The cover was printed by Courier Corporation.

Chapter Opening Photo Credits: Anthony Magnacca/Merrill, p. 1; Tom Watson/Merrill, p. 18, Anne Vega/Merrill, p. 35; © Ellen B. Senisi/Ellen Senisi, p. 51; Bill Aron/PhotoEdit, p. 72; Richard Hutchings/PhotoEdit Inc., p. 94; David Mager/Pearson Learning Photo Studio, p. 118; Scott Cunningham/Merrill, pp. 139, 249, 316; Zephyr/Photo Researchers, Inc., p. 156; Bart's Medical Library/Phototake NYC, p. 172; Medical-on-Line/Alamy, p. 191; Barbara Schwartz/Merrill, pp. 219, 387; Robin Nelson/PhotoEdit Inc., p. 232; Pascal Alix/Photo Researchers, Inc., p. 261; Michal Heron/PH College, pp. 280, 333; Elizabeth Crews/Elizabeth Crews photography, p. 294; Lori Whitley/Merrill, pp. 349, 399; Robert Brenner/PhotoEdit Inc., p. 368.

Pearson® is a registered trademark of Pearson plc

Merrill® is a registered trademark of Pearson
Education, Inc.
Pearson Education Ltd., London
Pearson Education Singapore, Pte. Ltd.
Pearson Education Canada, Inc.

Pearson Education—Japan
Pearson Education Australia PTY, Limited
Pearson Education North Asia, Ltd., Hong Kong
Pearson Educación de Mexico, S.A. de C.V.
Pearson Education Malaysia, Pte. Ltd.

Merrill
is an imprint of

PEARSON

Pearson Education Upper Saddle River, New Jersey

9 10 V092 15
ISBN 13: 978-0-13-240273-6
ISBN 10:   0-13-240273-4

DEDICATION

To the children, families, teachers, and college students who have taught us so much over the years and to our children and grandchildren—Daniel Bryan, Megan Caitlin, Sarah Elizabeth, Rhonda Beth, Paula Renee, Jon David, Harold Steven, Marissa Leigh, Ari Michael, Lauren Michele, and Alicia Renee—from whom we've learned the most about growth and development and the learning process. Also, to the late Natalie Tumlin, who taught us to look for the capabilities and possibilities in every individual. This book is also dedicated to the memory of Eileen Wolff who always instilled in her children a love of teaching and learning.

PREFACE

In this textbook, we describe various physical, health, and multiple disabilities and their educational implications. Although each student who has one of these conditions is unique, school personnel need to understand the student's disability in order to meet his or her unique needs and to provide an appropriate education. Because it requires a team of individuals to properly educate students with physical, health, or multiple disabilities, a team of individuals wrote this book. Collectively, our backgrounds include education, medicine, nursing, physical therapy, parenting a child with a severe health impairment, and grandparenting a child with severe physical disabilities.

This book is divided into six parts. Part I lays a foundation for the rest of the book. Chapter 1 is a general introduction to physical, health, and multiple disabilities and provides information on working together as a team to provide the best educational services to these students. Chapter 2 provides an overview of the learning and behavioral characteristics of students with physical, health, and multiple disabilities within the context of the Physical and Health Disabilities Performance Model. When students have significant intellectual disabilities, there are unique learning and behavioral characteristics which are described in Chapter 3. Chapter 4 provides an overall picture of motor development, including theories of motor development, atypical motor development, intervention approaches, and lifting and positioning considerations.

"Knowledge to practice" chapters and disability-specific chapters are found after Part I of the book. The "knowledge to practice" chapters are the final chapter in each major section of the book that provides practical information that pertains to that section. For example, Part II, "Neuromotor Impairments," contains a "knowledge to practice" chapter on assistive technology considerations. The disability-specific chapters describe the major physical, health, or multiple disabilities that are often found in school-age populations. Each of these chapters is organized in a similar fashion, containing sections on description, etiology, dynamics, characteristics, detection, treatment, course, and educational implications. Each "educational implications" section is subdivided into the following areas: meeting physical and sensory needs, meeting communication needs, meeting learning needs, meeting daily living needs, and meeting behavioral and social needs.

Part II, "Neuromotor Impairments," describes cerebral palsy, traumatic spinal cord injury, spina bifida, and traumatic brain injury. The "knowledge to practice" chapter on assistive technology considerations provides information on assessment and training considerations as well as different types of assistive technology. Part III, "Orthopedic, Musculoskeletal, and Sensory Disorders" contains information on such conditions as scoliosis, hip displacement, juvenile rheumatoid arthritis, arthrogryposis, osteogenesis imperfecta, vision loss, hearing loss, and deaf-blindness. The "knowledge to practice" chapter on classroom adaptations provides information on identifying the need for adaptations and highlights the Classroom Adaptations Checklist for Students with Physical, Health, or Multiple Disabilities. Part IV, "Degenerative and Terminal Diseases," provides information on muscular dystrophy, spinal muscular atrophy, and cystic fibrosis and has a chapter called "Coping with Degenerative and Terminal Illnesses." Part V, "Major Health Impairments," focuses on commonly encountered impairments such as epilepsy, asthma and diabetes. In the "knowledge to practice" chapter on monitoring students' disabilities and individualized healthcare plans, other health impairments are described, such as sickle cell anemia, hemophilia, attention-deficit/hyperactivity disorder, mitochondrial encephatopathy, Rett syndrome, hereditary degenerative cerebellar disorders, congenital heart defects, childhood cancer, and chronic renal failure. This chapter emphasizes how to monitor for problems with these and other conditions and treatments (e.g., tube feeding). This chapter also has information on how to construct individual health care plans and action plans for school personnel. Part VI, "Infectious Diseases," includes information on acquired infections, AIDS, and congenital infections. The "knowledge to practice" chapter on universal precautions provides useful information on infection control.

ACKNOWLEDGMENTS

We are grateful for the many people who helped us prepare this textbook. We want to extend a special thanks to the following individuals who assisted in reviewing select chapters, taking photographs, and providing support: Edward Heller, Virgil Wolff, Eileen Wolff, Lee Wolff, Larry Forney, Michael Carroll, Marilyn Schwartzman, John Best, Juane Heflin, Shayna King, Calvin Maddox, Richard Couture, and Janie Avant. A special thank you to our outside reviewers: Donna G. Andrews at Piedmont College, Barbara A. Beakley, Millersville University; and Robert Perkins, College of Charleston.

Special thanks go to our editor, Ann Davis, for her feedback and support, and to the rest of the staff at Pearson/Merrill, including Penny Burleson, Sheryl Langner, Valerie Schultz, Carol Sykes, and Robin Holtsberry. Thanks also go to Mary Tindle for her help in the production process.

Finally, we would like to thank the graduate students who took our course on characteristics of severe physical and multiple disabilities and who provided feedback regarding the need for a current, understandable textbook that would help them understand various physical, health, and multiple disabilities and their educational implications. These students' comments over the years prompted the writing and revision of this textbook. Also a special thanks to students who read draft chapters and provided feedback: Corrie Bray, Monique Evans Newsome, Stephanie Herndon, Jessica Morrow, Darlene Muhammad, Courtney Ragsdale, Neeldhara Sharma, Wendell Simpson, and Chris Wood. Students' feedback on draft chapters has assisted us in providing an understandable, interesting, and meaningful textbook that we hope will provide a strong knowledge base for attaining an appropriate education for students with physical, health, and multiple disabilities.

Kathryn Wolff Heller

Paula E. Forney

Paul A. Alberto

Sherwood J. Best

Morton N. Schwartzman

Kathryn Wolff Heller, R.N., Ph.D.

Kathryn Wolff Heller is a professor in special education at Georgia State University and directs the graduate program in physical and health disabilities. She is also the director of two statewide technical assistance projects, the Georgia Bureau for Students with Physical and Health Disabilities, which provides assistance to teachers and families of students with orthopedic impairments, and the Georgia Sensory Assistance Project, which provides assistance to teachers and families of students with deaf-blindness.

Dr. Heller, a registered nurse with experience in pediatric medicine, worked for 5 years in intensive care units and then went on to obtain master's and doctoral degrees in special education. She began her career in teaching as a classroom teacher to students who had orthopedic impairments, severe intellectual disabilities, traumatic brain injury, visual impairments, and multiple disabilities. Dr. Heller has made numerous national presentations, served on several advisory boards, held several offices on national committees and organizations, and coauthored several books, book chapters, and articles pertaining to students with physical and health disabilities, sensory loss, and intellectual disabilities. One of her primary interests is in providing effective educational instruction and health care for students with physical, sensory, health, and multiple disabilities.

Paula E. Forney, M.M.Sc., PT

Paula Forney, technical assistance specialist with Georgia's Part C Early Intervention Program, Babies Can't Wait, located within the Georgia Department of Human Resources/Division of Public Health, provides statewide technical assistance and training to Georgia's 18 district early intervention programs. She is also on the executive board and is past president of the American Association for Home-Based Early Interventionists. Previously, she was therapy coordinator for the Georgia Parent Infant Network for Educational Services, training and supervising therapy consultants to provide supports to families/caregivers of young children with sensory loss and multiple disabilities in natural environments. Ms. Forney has a B.S. degree in physical therapy from Simmons College, Boston, and a M.M.Sc degree in pediatric physical therapy from Emory University, Atlanta, and is certified in both pediatric neurodevelopmental treatment and sensory integration. In addition, she has over 30 years of experience in physical therapy in hospital, school-based, and early intervention settings, including the development of school-based therapy and early intervention programs.

Ms. Forney has made numerous presentations, taught in a variety of settings, and conducted workshops on pediatric physical therapy, children with sensory loss and multiple disabilities, family-centered early intervention, and evidence-based practice in early intervention. She has also coauthored videotapes, articles, curricula, book chapters, and textbooks related to pediatric development/disability, collaborative teaming, and supporting families, caregivers, and teachers in natural and school-based environments. One of Ms. Forney's primary interests is in collaborative teaming to provide appropriate supports and services to children with disabilities and their families, caregivers, and teachers.

Paul A. Alberto, Ph.D.

Paul A. Alberto, a professor of educational psychology and special education at Georgia State University, directs the teacher training program in multiple and severe disabilities. He also directs the Bureau for Students with Multiple and Severe Disabilities, a joint project with the Georgia Department of Education, Division for Exceptional Students, to provide technical assistance to students, parents, teachers, and administrators. He began his career as a classroom teacher of students with mental retardation.

Dr. Alberto coauthored a textbook on applied behavior analysis for teachers. He has written chapters and articles concerning students with multiple and severe disabilities, focusing on instructional prompting and strategies for instruction and behavior management during community-based instruction. He has directed funded projects developing community-based educational strategies and secondary education and transition programs and instructing students with profound disabilities. Currently, he is directing a project on integrated literacy for students with moderate and severe disabilities.

Sherwood J. Best, Ph.D.

Dr. Sherwood J. Best began her professional career as a teacher of students with physical and health impairments in southern California in 1979. After earning three teaching credentials and a master's degree from California State University, Los Angeles (CSULA), Dr. Best taught at CSULA in the Division of Special Education and Counseling while she continued to teach in the public school classroom. Dr. Best completed her Ph.D. in educational psychology/special education from the University of California, Riverside, in 1995. She then became a permanent member of the CSULA faculty, which has been her professional home ever since.

Dr. Best has served as vice president, president-elect, president, and past president of the Division for Physical and Health Disabilities (DPHD) of the national Council for Exceptional Children. During her service to DPHD, she also edited the *DPHD Newsletter*, for a total of 16 years as editor. Dr. Best currently edits the newsletter for the California Association for Physical and Health Impairments and has been active in leadership in that organization, most recently serving as president in 2002–2004.

Dr. Best has presented at numerous local, state, national, and international conferences. In 2002–2003 and 2003–2004, she traveled to Bangalore, India, where she helped establish an early intervention training program at the Vydehi Rehabilitation Centre. She is the author of numerous scholarly articles, and book chapters and is the first author of *Teaching Individuals with Physical and Multiple Disabilities* with Drs. Kathryn Heller and June Bigge.

Morton N. Schwartzman, M.D.

Dr. Schartzman is a pediatrician who specializes in pulmonary diseases. He is the medical director of the Cystic Fibrosis Center affiliated with the Joe DiMaggio Children's Hospital at Memorial, Hollywood, Florida. Dr. Schwarztman, whose previous experience includes working as a practitioner for 40 years, was a medical consultant for the Health Rehabilitative Service Agency, Dade County, Florida. His responsibilities included caring for infants, children, and adolescents with chronic disease, such as neurological disorders, muscular disease and myopathies, and chronic pulmonary diseases. He was also involved with the care and treatment of children with special needs who resided in various group homes. In addition, he has served as medical director for a prescribed pediatric extended care facility for children with medical and physical impairments and has served on many advisory boards, medical boards, and boards of directors, including the American Lung Association of South Florida and the American Lung Association of the State of Florida. Dr. Schwartzman was also a former member of the executive committee of the Joe DiMaggio Children's Hospital. He was past president of the medical staff as well as past chief of pediatrics at Miami Children's Hospital, Miami, Florida. Dr. Schwartzman has lectured to students at local universities and to civic groups and professional organizations and has coauthored several published articles in various medical journals. His interest lies in creating new avenues to improve care for children and adolescents with medical needs and with physical and mental impairments.

BRIEF CONTENTS

CONTENTS

NOTE: Every effort has been made to provide accurate and current Internet information in this book. However, the Internet and information posted on it are constantly changing, so it is inevitable that some of the Internet addresses listed in this textbook will change.

PART **1**

IMPLICATIONS OF PHYSICAL, HEALTH, AND MULTIPLE DISABILITIES

CHAPTER

UNDERSTANDING DISABILITIES AND EFFECTIVE TEAMING

Kathryn Wolff Heller and Paula Forney

What do you do if a child has a seizure? What adaptations do you need to make for a student with juvenile rheumatoid arthritis? What do you do when a child with muscular dystrophy says he is dying? What do you need to know about AIDS? Are children who are deaf-blind totally deaf and totally blind? Educators face questions like these every day as students with physical, health, or multiple disabilities are educated in their classrooms. Knowing the answers to these and other such questions will help prepare teachers to better meet the needs of students with disabilities.

In order to understand physical, health, or multiple disabilities, the teacher must know the characteristics of these disabilities and their educational implications. Sometimes, the teacher should be prepared to provide adaptations for students with severe physical or multiple disabilities. At other times, the teacher should be able to recognize signs and symptoms of distress and know what to do for students with health impairments. Knowing the course of diseases and ways of addressing concerns relating to dying is often needed when dealing with students with degenerative and terminal diseases, as knowing how to implement proper infection control procedures to help maintain a healthy environment for all students, including those with infectious diseases. Regardless of the specific type of disability, the teacher can maximize his or her effectiveness by addressing these various issues using a team approach.

This chapter will provide an introduction to the areas that educators need to have familiarity with in order to meet the needs of students with physical, health, or multiple disabilities. It will begin by giving an overview of different types of disabilities and frequently encountered terminology. Sources for obtaining information and the various team models will be discussed.

CHARACTERISTICS AND TYPES OF DISABILITIES

There are many different causes of physical, health, and multiple disabilities. Some of the most common etiologies are chromosomal and genetic defects, teratogenic causes (i.e., outside causes such as infection and drugs that can produce fetal abnormalities), prematurity and complications of pregnancy, and acquired causes (e.g., trauma, infections, or disease occurring after birth) (Heller, 2006). Some disabilities, such as **cerebral palsy**, have multiple etiologies. Sometimes the exact cause of physical, health, or multiple disabilities is unknown.

The characteristics of individuals with physical, health, or multiple disabilities differ greatly. Even individuals with the same impairment can be affected differently. Severity can range from an obvious, severe physical involvement to no noticeable impairment. Students with disabilities also range from having gifted intelligence to having profound intellectual disabilities, regardless of the severity of the physical disability (e.g., a student with a very severe physical disability could have normal or gifted intelligence). Students also differ in the type of curriculum that is most appropriate for them (e.g., general academic curriculum, adapted curriculum, or functional curriculum), in the types of services they need (e.g., general education only or support from special education), and in their optimal placement (e.g., general education classroom or resource room).

Federal Definitions

There are several different diseases and disorders that make up physical, health, and multiple disabilities. One classification system by the federal government established several categories of disabilities for educational purposes. Four categories that fall under physical, health, and multiple disabilities are orthopedic impairment, other health impairment, multiple disabilities, and traumatic brain injury (see Figure 1-1). State departments of education often use these disability categories, although they may deviate from them or from their definitions. School personnel should be familiar with their own state definitions.

Classifying Physical, Health, and Multiple Disabilities

When studying the different types of physical, health, or multiple disabilities typically encountered in the school system, a different grouping of conditions is often needed. One way

Disability	Definition
Orthopedic impairment (OI)	The orthopedic impairment must be severe enough to adversely affect the child's educational performance. The term includes impairments caused by congenital anomaly (e.g., club foot, absence of some member, etc.), impairments caused by disease (e.g., poliomyelitis, bone tuberculosis, etc.), and impairments from other causes (e.g., cerebral palsy, amputations, and fractures or burns that cause contractures).
Other health impairment (OHI)	The health impairment results in having limited strength, vitality, or alertness, including a heightened alertness to environmental stimuli, that results in limited alertness with respect to the educational environment that (i) Is due to chronic or acute health problems such as asthma, attention deficit or attention deficit hyperactivity disorder, diabetes, epilepsy, a heart condition, hemophilia, lead poisoning, leukemia, nephritis, rheumatic fever, and sickle cell anemia and (ii) Adversely affects a child's educational performance.
Multiple disabilities	Multiple disabilities refers to concomitant impairments (e.g., such as mental retardation, blindness), the combination of which causes such severe educational needs that they cannot be accommodated in special education programs solely for one of the impairments. (This term does not include deaf-blindness.)
Traumatic brain injury (TBI)	TBI refers to an acquired injury to the brain caused by an external physical force, resulting in total or partial functional disability of psychosocial impairment, or both, that adversely affects a child's educational performance. The term applies to open or closed head injuries and results in impairments in one or more areas, such as cognition; language; memory; attention; reasoning; abstract thinking; judgment; problem-solving; sensory, perceptual, and motor abilities; psychosocial behavior; physical functions; information processing; and speech. The term does not apply to brain injuries that are congenital or degenerative, or to brain injuries induced by birth trauma.

FIGURE I–I   Federal categories pertaining to physical, health, and multiple disabilities.
Source. 34 C.F.R. 300.7[c], 1999.

to group the different conditions together, based on medical characteristics and educational implications, is to divide the conditions into six major categories:

1. Neuromotor impairments
2. Orthopedic and musculoskeletal disorders
3. Sensory disorders
4. Degenerative and terminal diseases
5. Major health impairments
6. Infectious diseases

Each of these categories constitutes a major section in this book (except that sensory disorders have been placed in the section containing orthopedic and musculoskeletal disorders since many of these occur concomitantly in multiple disabilities).

Neuromotor Impairments

Neuromotor impairments include disorders that affect the nerves and muscles. Impairments typically found in this category are cerebral palsy, spina bifida, and spinal cord injury and are addressed in Part II of this book. Traumatic brain injury is also included, although the condition varies as to which area is affected (e.g., cognition, motor, sensory, or behavior).

Students with neuromotor impairments often have very involved conditions that can affect several areas of functioning (e.g., movement skills or cognitive skills, perceptual skills, or language skills). Also, it is not unusual for several conditions in this area to have additional impairments (e.g., cerebral palsy with visual impairments and intellectual disability, spina bifida with perceptual impairments, or spinal cord injury with traumatic brain injury). Teachers need to be prepared for the multiple conditions that can occur with neuromotor impairments as well as the diverse educational implications (see Figure 1-2). This may include the need for assistive technology that is discussed in a "knowledge to practice" chapter at the end of Part II.

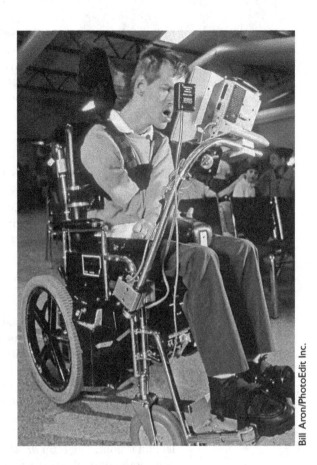

FIGURE 1–2 This student has severe spastic cerebral palsy and a visual impairment and uses an augmentative communication device to communicate.

Orthopedic, Musculoskeletal, and Sensory Disorder

The next grouping is a combination of orthopedic, musculoskeletal, and sensory disorders discussed in Part III of this book. These conditions can occur singularly (e.g., osteogenesis imperfecta) or can occur in combination with other conditions (such as scoliosis and hip dislocation being found in students with cerebral palsy or vision impairments occurring with some types of juvenile rheumatoid arthritis). Since these conditions typically need many classroom adaptations, especially when they occur with other disorders, the "knowledge to practice" chapter at the end of Part III discusses various classroom adaptations.

Degenerative and Terminal Diseases

The degenerative and terminal disease category could technically be included with other sections (e.g., neuromotor or health impairments), but there are special considerations for students with such conditions as muscular dystrophy, spinal muscular atrophy, and cystic fibrosis. Students who have degenerative diseases are faced with a progressive loss of function, and conditions which are terminal may leave the students with issues surrounding death and dying. Teachers should understand not only adaptations but also how to cope and support students with these types of illnesses. A special chapter on coping with degenerative and terminal illnesses is provided to assist with this difficult area at the end of Part IV of this book.

Health Impairments

Several types of impairments are not typically discernible on seeing the student but may severely affect student functioning. These health impairments are discussed in Part V and contain many of the conditions found in the federal definition of other health impairments (e.g., diabetes, asthma, seizure disorders, attention-deficit-hyperactivity disorder). Teachers need to know how to monitor these conditions and what to do if something goes wrong. This will be addressed in the individual chapters as well as a special "knowledge to practice" chapter on monitoring and writing individualized health care plans. This final chapter will also contain pertinent information on other health impairments, such as cancer, hemophilia, sickle cell anemia, and chronic renal failure.

Infectious Diseases

Several types of infectious diseases can be medically devastating to individuals who acquire them. The last category of disabilities on infectious diseases includes both acquired infections (e.g., hepatitis and AIDS), as well as congenital infections (e.g., cytomegalovirus and toxoplasmosis) and is discussed in Part VI of this book. Teachers need to have a good understanding of how infection is transmitted and how to implement proper infection control procedures. This will be discussed in Part VI, with a special emphasis in the last chapter of the book.

Terminology

Teachers may encounter several terms used to describe students with physical and multiple disabilities other than those found in the federal definitions or the terminology used in this text. Some terms try to describe certain attributes of students with physical and health disabilities. Some terminology is inappropriate and insulting to individuals with disabilities.

Three terms that are often encountered are *impairment, disability*, and *handicap*. The term *impairment* refers to the presence of a specific condition that results in an abnormality of psychological, physiological, or anatomical structure or function that affects a specific part of the body (e.g., a visual impairment may refer to a person with a cataract that is affecting vision). The term *disability* refers to a reduction or loss of ability (outside the range considered normal) due to an impairment (e.g., the person with the visual impairment has a disability in reading print). The term *handicap* refers to an impairment or disability that is a disadvantage for that individual and that limits or restricts the individual from doing something (Beadles, 2001; Florian et al., 2006). The term handicap is often based on self-perception or others' perceptions and is focused more on circumstances, than on attributes of the individual (Best, 2005).

The terms *impairment, disability,* and *handicap* may be used to describe the same condition, but the meaning is different, depending on the term that is used. For example, a person with well-controlled asthma has an impairment that causes the airways to constrict. Asthma becomes a disability when it occurs several times a month resulting in a high rate of absenteeism and low grades. It is a handicap when others decide to have the individual with asthma sit on the bench for almost the entire basketball season instead of playing with the team because of the possibility of an asthma attack, whether justified or not (Best, 2005).

This book will use the terms *impairment* and *disability* since it is important to understand a condition when it does not interfere with school (i.e., impairment) as well as when it progresses and impacts student performance (i.e., disability). The term handicap is based on perceptions, so it is not an appropriate term to use.

When referring to individuals with disabilities, it is important to use people-first language. People-first language describes what a person has, not what a person is. A person with a disability may also be an artist, a friend, a student, or many other things that describe people. Therefore, it is appropriate to say a "student with a disability" and inappropriate to say "the disabled student." In the same manner, it is appropriate to say "a person who has cancer" and not refer to him as the "cancerous person."

Other negative terms should also be avoided. For example, it is more appropriate to say the "student uses a wheelchair" than "confined to a wheelchair" or "she's wheelchair bound." Saying "he has a physical disability" is more appropriate than saying "he's crippled." When words are misused, attitudinal barriers are often reinforced, devaluing the individual. The power of the spoken word should not be underestimated; hence, respectful terminology that supports the individual should always be used.

When interacting with students with disabilities, adults (and children) should not engage in the manifestation known as "spread." The concept of "spread" refers to the overgeneralization of unrelated aspects of a disability that leads to stereotyping (Kirshbaum, 2000). Examples of "spread" are seeing a student with a severe physical disability and assuming he has an intellectual disability, raising your voice to talk to someone who is blind, or talking to a young adult who uses an augmentative communication device as if he were a young child. These negative behaviors affect the perception of others and create a negative environment for the student.

Learning About the Student's Disability

Teachers need to learn all that they can about their students' various disabilities. Besides studying textbooks (such as this one), the teacher should use additional resources. Traditional written resources include books, articles, organizational material, and material found on the Internet. Although there is a wealth of information on the Internet, teachers should always consider the source of the information since some information found on the Internet is inaccurate.

It is not unusual for a teacher to have a student with a rare condition. Trying to find information on the condition may be difficult. One organization that specializes in rare disorders is the National Organization for Rare Disorders (www.rarediseases.org). This organization provides understandable descriptions of specific rare disorders as well as an index of organizations related to the disorder. Another good source of information is usually the parents.

Although it is important for teachers to have a good understanding of the various conditions their students have, it is critically important to have a clear understanding of how the condition affects the individual student. Not only are no two students alike, but some students' impairments may affect them differently from what is described in the medical literature. Parents know the child the best and often have valuable information regarding the condition and how it affects their child. The child with a disability may also have important information and a certain perspective about the impairment that teachers should know. Teachers should establish a good rapport with parents as well as their students and learn from them.

When communicating with parents about their child, it is important that teachers strive for a positive orientation and be respectful regarding the family's knowledge and insights about their child and his impairment. Teachers may ask questions such as "What do Jeremy's seizures look like and what do you do when they happen?" or "What are some things I should know about Shelly's cerebral palsy?" or "Tell me about Dan's asthma." or "What have the doctors told you about Ben's muscular dystrophy, and what do you think about it?" To get more of an insight into the whole child, a teacher may ask, "What's Mario's day like from when he gets up until when he goes to bed?" Unexpected issues and concerns may arise from open-ended questions that the teacher may need to address with the student in the school setting.

In order for a teacher to be certain that she understands what a parent is telling her, the teacher should use active listening skills. This occurs when the teacher tries to understand what the parent is feeling and the main message being said by intently listening and stating the message back to the parents in her own words. This assists with clarification and provides confirmation that the teacher is listening and understanding what the parent is saying (Hornby, 2000).

While listening, the teacher may realize that the family has a different perspective on the disability than expected. This may be due to many different factors such as individual viewpoints, religious beliefs, or cultural factors (within the backdrop of such contextual variables as education, acculturation, socioeconomic status, or geographic location). In the area of severe disabilities, the attributes of etiology or importance of the disability can widely differ as well as the extent of the stigma attached to it. For example, some cultural patterns that have been described for certain groups include: the attribution of disability to spiritual reward or retribution among some Asian groups, an emphasis of the wholeness of the spirit in a body that is disabled among some Native American groups, and the belief that conditions like epilepsy are reflections of spirit among some Hmong (Fadiman, 1997; Harry, 2002).

The teacher should develop a regular two-way communication system with parents and others not only to keep others informed regarding the student but also to gain new information

(Christenson & Sheridan, 2001). There are several other individuals besides the parents and student who can assist the teacher in better understanding the student and his impairment. Many of these individuals will be part of the educational team, and the teacher will need to know the best way to collaborate as a team.

EDUCATIONAL TEAM MEMBERS

The composition of any collaborative educational team will vary according to the educational needs of the individual student whom they serve and may change over time as student needs change. Core team members are those individuals who are directly involved with the design and daily implementation of the student's educational program. For example, core team members for a junior high school student with multiple disabilities could include the student, family members, special education teacher, general education teachers, physical and/or occupational therapists, speech-language pathologist, classroom teaching assistant, and community work site representative.

Support team members serve on a consultant basis. Their roles do not as directly support the student's day-to-day educational program. Examples of support team members could include the psychologist, social worker, vision specialist, audiologist, dietician, nurse, orientation and mobility specialist, and physician(s). In some cases, when students have extensive sensory or medical needs, some of the support team members mentioned previously may be part of the core team. For example, if a student had a visual impairment, the vision specialist (see Figure 1–3) and orientation and mobility specialist (see Figure 1–4) would see the student regularly and be part of the core team.

All the team members are important to the student's educational program, but from a practical point of view, individuals who are necessary for the student's program on an ongoing daily basis should be identified as core team members to facilitate the collaborative process. As the number of core team members increases, efficient coordination of team

FIGURE 1–3 Teacher certified in visual impairments showing a student a tactile book that also has braille.

Robin Sachs/PhotoEdit Inc.

FIGURE 1–4 An orientation and mobility (O&M) instructor assisting students with mobility.

efforts tends to decrease because of the inability of all team members to schedule time to communicate with one another.

As students' needs change, the type and amount of individual team member's participation should also change to meet these needs. For example, in the case of a student with severe physical disabilities who is transitioning from a preschool special education program into an integrated kindergarten, the team might decide that, during the first few weeks, the highest priority is that the child's basic physical needs be met. Therefore, the occupational therapist (OT) and physical therapist (PT) might initially intensely follow the child in the classroom to work with the teacher and teaching assistant on positioning, handling, and daily living activities (e.g., feeding and toileting) (see Figure 1–5).

After almost daily involvement for the first few weeks of school, the OT and PT may adjust their schedules to less frequent regular in-classroom consultation. At this time, the speech-language pathologist may need to increase her time in the classroom to expand the student's communication system. Schedules are adjusted so as not to overwhelm the classroom teacher and to meet the student's prioritized needs during functional classroom routines and activities as determined by the total educational team.

FIGURE 1–5 A physical therapist showing the teacher and teaching assistants how to properly position a young girl with cerebral palsy into an adapted chair

All team members share some basic roles and responsibilities, including participating in decision making about each student's educational program, contributing problem-solving strategies to the student's educational program, sharing specific knowledge and skills to facilitate understanding of the student's capabilities and needs, supporting contributions of other team members, and supporting practices that facilitate the student's education and integration into the community (Orelove, Sobsey, & Silberman, 2004; Rainforth, 2002).

Each discipline also brings to the team its own set of knowledge and skills. These discipline-specific roles and areas of expertise are described in Figure 1-6. While there are specific knowledge and skill areas inherent among different disciplines, there are also overlapping areas of knowledge and skill between disciplines as well. Furthermore, different individuals

Team Members	Roles
Adapted physical education teacher (APE)	Provides adaptations to regular PE program to promote student participation Provides specially designed PE programs
Audiologist	Identifies types and degrees of hearing loss and provides equipment guidelines
Family members and student	Has the most knowledge about the student and the greatest stake in the student's future
General education classroom teacher	Brings important information to the team concerning general education curriculum and student participation in this curriculum
Intervener	Provides direct support to a student with deaf-blindness Has specialized knowledge and skills (e.g., sign language)
Nurse	Information source for the educational team concerning students' medical conditions Performs specialized medical procedures (e.g., tube feeding and catheterization); liaison between the educational team and the medical community
Occupational therapist (OT)	Promotes optimal physical functioning, particularly in fine motor skills, visual-motor skills, and self-care activities Provides suggestions or constructs devices to facilitate necessary adaptations to the learning environment
Orientation & mobility instructor (O&M instructor)	Has specialized training in visual functioning as it relates to mobility and travel through specific environments such as home, school, and community
Paraprofessional (teaching assistant)	Plays a vital role in the daily functioning of the classroom and has important personal knowledge about the student
Personal care assistant	Assists with physical and health needs of student with disabilities
Physical therapist (PT)	Provides essential input regarding optimal physical functioning particularly as they relate to gross motor skills and mobility Provides suggestions or constructs devices to facilitate necessary adaptations to the learning environment
Psychologist	Evaluator of a student's intellectual and adaptive abilities and interpreter of the evaluation results for classroom programming May also design strategies for reducing negative student behaviors
Social worker	Facilitates access to services and establishing linkages between the school and community programs
Speech-language pathologist (SLP)	Provides instruction in the area of communications, language, and speech Provides suggestions and instruction with augmentative and alternative communication devices Expertise in oral motor and feeding skills
Special education teacher	Provides specialized knowledge and skills regarding the education of students with disabilities Provide disability-specific content instruction (e.g., assistive technology use) Specialized teaching strategies Provides and implements adaptations

FIGURE 1-6 Examples of team members and their areas of expertise.

within the same discipline may not necessarily have the same knowledge and skills, depending on their training programs and work experiences. When determining who makes up the student's educational team, student needs must be matched with the potential team members who can contribute the necessary knowledge and skills regardless of their title.

TEAM MODELS

The way in which teams are formed and how they operate determine both the educational process and the outcomes for the student with disabilities. Several different team models are described in the literature, representing a hierarchy of increasingly more coordinated approaches (Effgen, 2005; Orelove et al., 2004). These models—multidisciplinary, interdisciplinary, transdisciplinary, and collaborative—are explained next and summarized in Figure 1–7.

Multidisciplinary Team Model

The multidisciplinary team model evolved from a medical approach to service delivery where problems are typically isolated to one particular domain. Within this approach, each professional with expertise in a different discipline evaluates and works with the student individually. No formal effort is made to prioritize the student's needs, and overlap among disciplines is not considered. The professionals working with the student usually do not think of themselves as belonging to a team because they are working in isolation.

In this model, each professional carries out his or her own assessment of the student related to a particular area of expertise. Assessments are typically conducted in isolation, outside the student's natural environment (e.g., therapy room vs. classroom). Since no individual can be an expert in all or even in several fields, no discipline's evaluation takes into account the whole student. Therefore, the likelihood of inaccurate, incomplete, or duplicative assessment results is increased. Recommendations based on these evaluations are also more likely to be discipline specific, conflict with one another, and be extremely difficult for the teacher to synthesize and implement. For example, the speech-language pathologist may recommend activation of a communication device using a movement pattern that the physical therapist has reported is difficult for the child to accomplish.

In this multidisciplinary model, the assumption is that periodic and fragmented "treatment" of the student's problems will eventually result in improved performance that will automatically generalize in meaningful ways to everyday life. Generalization is unlikely when treatment occurs in unrelated settings, contexts, and activities. Prior to the legal mandate for related services in education, therapy services for students were at times discontinued not because the students were unable to make improvement but because the isolated, noncontextualized, and periodic services failed to tap the students' potential (Heron & Harris, 2001). The direct, isolated therapy approach often seen in the multidisciplinary team model is problematic because it focuses on domain-specific, noncontextualized student skills rather than collaboration between professionals to achieve functional student outcomes across various daily settings and activities.

Interdisciplinary Team Model

The interdisciplinary team model represents a somewhat higher level of evolution of team models than the multidisciplinary model. The interdisciplinary approach is similar to the multidisciplinary model in that assessments and implementation of program goals are still discipline specific and still carried out primarily in isolation from other team members. However, the interdisciplinary model does provide a formal structure for interaction and communication among members of the team, encouraging a sharing of information. Programming decisions are made by group consensus, and a formal method for communication among team members is established by assigning a case manager or team leader for each student whose role is to coordinate services for that student.

However, as in the multidisciplinary model, the reality of the interdisciplinary model is that program assessment, planning, and implementation are still separate. The isolated

	Multidisciplinary	Interdisciplinary	Transdisciplinary	Collaborative
Assessment	Team members conduct separate assessments.	Team members conduct separate assessments.	Team members and family conduct joint assessment.	The fewest number of service providers who are needed, along with the family, participate in the assessment across desired settings and learning opportunities.
Parent/teacher participation	Parent/teacher meet with team members individually.	Parent/teacher meet with entire team or a representative of the team.	Parent/teacher are full, active members of the team.	Parent, teacher, and other care providers are equal team members.
Service plan development	Team members develop separate, discipline-specific plans.	Team members develop separate, discipline-specific plans but share them with each other.	Team members and parent/teacher develop a joint plan based on priorities, needs, and resources.	Team members and parent/teacher develop outcomes/goals based on improving student function across activity settings.
Service plan responsibility	Team members are responsible for their own discipline-specific plans.	Team members share information with each other about their part of the plan.	Team members are jointly responsible and accountable for how the primary service provider implements the plan.	Team members are jointly responsible and accountable for how the primary service provider implements the plan.
Service plan implementation	Team members are responsible for their discipline-specific plans.	Team members implement their portion of the plan and incorporate other sections where possible.	A primary service provider implements the plan with the family.	Team members provide coaching to the primary service provider in order to effectively implement the plan across activity settings.
Lines of communication	Informal.	Occasional case-specific staffing.	Regular team meetings to exchange information, knowledge, and skills among team members.	Regular team meetings. Ongoing interaction among team members for reflection and sharing of information occurs beyond scheduled meetings.
Guiding philosophy	Team members recognize the importance of information from other disciplines.	Team members are willing to share and be responsible for providing services as part of the comprehensive service plan.	Team members commit to teach, learn, and work across traditional discipline lines to implement a joint service plan.	Families, teachers, and service providers engage in learning and coaching to develop the necessary expertise to improve the student's participation across activity settings and learning opportunities.
Staff development	Independent and discipline specific.	Independent within and outside own discipline.	A critical component of team meetings for learning across discipline boundaries and for team building.	Team members implement an ongoing team development plan to identify any gaps in skills and knowledge and improve expertise across disciplines.

FIGURE 1-7 Models of team interaction.

Source. Used with permission and adapted from Woodruff and McGonigel (1998). Woodruff, G., & McGonigel, M. J. (1998). Early intervention team approaches: The transdisciplinary model. In J. B. Jordon, J. J. Gallagher, P. L. Huntington, & M. B. Karnes (Eds.), *Early childhood special education: Birth to three* (pp. 63–182). Reston, VA: Council for Exceptional Children and the Division for Early Childhood.

service delivery model, described previously, also still occurs in the interdisciplinary model, with all its inherent problems.

Transdisciplinary Team Model

The transdisciplinary team model was introduced initially to serve the complex needs of high-risk infants who could not tolerate multiple inputs from a variety of professionals. This model recognized primarily that the multiple needs of children are interrelated and that children do not perform skills in isolation; rather, skills are directly related to function and occur in response to the environmental demands.

The transdisciplinary team model is characterized by sharing information and skills across discipline-specific boundaries. In contrast to the multidisciplinary and interdisciplinary models that use a direct intervention approach, the transdisciplinary model uses an indirect or integrative approach where one or two persons (usually the teacher) act as the primary program provider and other team members act as consultants (Snell & Janney, 2000). In this model, all team members provide information and teach intervention techniques to each other, thereby promoting consistency in program implementation for each individual student.

Integrated Therapy

An important additional component of the transdisciplinary team model is the integrated therapy approach. The basic assumptions of an integrated therapy approach are that: (a) assessment of a student's abilities can best be conducted in natural environments (e.g., home, classroom, work site), (b) students are best taught through functional activities that relate to everyday life and occur in natural settings, (c) student supports should occur throughout the day in situations and settings in which the student functions and when natural learning opportunities occur, and (d) learning outcomes should be verified in natural environments (Orelove et al., 2004). By providing therapy services in these real-life situations, generalization of skills to relevant contexts occurs by design rather than by accident, and therapy services do not have to compete with classroom activities but rather support them.

As evidenced by the integrated therapy approach, there are several concepts key to the transdisciplinary team approach. These concepts include: (a) shared goals—all team members' (including the student and family members) efforts are focused on jointly developing and implementing an overall set of objectives as described in the individual individualized education plan (IEP); (b) role release—the roles of each discipline become more flexible, and some functions related to one's own discipline, as appropriate, are "released" to or performed by another discipline or team member; and (c) an active and reciprocal learning process in which team members teach each other new skills and learn new skills from other team members, over time, as determined by student needs.

Collaborative Team Model

The collaborative team model is currently considered as exemplary practice in providing educational support to students with disabilities. A major difference between the collaborative model and other models is that while members of the collaborative team bring their own perspective to the team, these perspectives evolve and change through planned, regular interaction with other team members. This not only increases shared knowledge of each team member's expertise but also puts that knowledge to work in collaborative evaluation, planning, and implementation for students.

The collaborative team model also describes the following:

1. Who is on the team, based on student needs, as well as what core individuals are needed at specific times to support the student's learning
2. A shared conceptual framework about the best way to educate students through provision of learning opportunities in functional contexts
3. Ways to share information and expertise through meetings and written communication

4. Processes for working together as a team including: face to face interactions (including team meetings), commitment to shared values focused on supporting students and other team members, commitment to interpersonal skills necessary for group interaction (e.g., problem-solving, conflict management), and accountability to other team members for accomplishing individual and group goals
5. Student goals, objectives, and implementation strategies agreed to by team consensus

Coaching Approach

The coaching approach is one way to achieve collaborative teaming. Hanft, Rush, and Shelden (2004) describe coaching as a process that evolved from the athletic, business, and education fields. They further define coaching as a voluntary, nonjudgmental, and collaborative learning partnership between two individuals, the coach, and the learner (e.g., a family member and a professional or two professionals).

There are several key elements of the coaching approach. Coaching is based on: (a) conversations of personal discovery about what is known by an individual or team and what new learning is desired; (b) improving a person's performance within a specific context; and (c) a process for improving skills/knowledge, implementing evidence (research)-based practices, experimenting with new approaches, resolving challenges, and building relationships (Hanft et al., 2004).

Two primary goals guide the coaching approach. One goal is to support learners in recognizing what they are already doing that promotes student learning. Another goal is to assist learners in creating ongoing learning opportunities for the student when the coach is not present. Figure 1-8 outlines the five components of the coaching process—initiation, observation, action, reflection, and evaluation—and includes examples of coaching tasks and questions that can be used to support learners and ensure positive outcomes for students.

STRATEGIES TO FACILITATE EFFECTIVE COLLABORATIVE TEAMWORK

The information presented in this section describes strategies for facilitating collaborative teaming that reflect educationally effective practices and can be used as a guide in planning and implementing this approach. The three main areas within the educational setting that are most affected by choosing a collaborative team model for educational services are assessment, development of instructional goals, and actual delivery of instruction and therapy supports.

Assessment

The method used by an educational team to obtain initial assessment information on a student will affect all other subsequent programming for that student. Therefore, the educational team should share in the evaluative process from the onset. The evaluation information should be obtained in settings that are natural for the student. There are several types of information that can be obtained when assessing a student, and all are important to appropriate program development.

Background Information

Important background information on the student should be obtained by one or more team members from the student and/or his family, previous or current service providers, and the student's educational file. The following valuable information can be obtained on the student through this process: current and previous educational goals; special learning characteristics or preferences; student, family, or professional prioritization of needed skills; student preference for learning activities; teaching materials; use of reinforcers and preferences; type of communication the student uses; favorite or regular family activities; and medical problems and precautions. The general background information obtained should be shared with all team members.

Initiation

Coach focuses on learner's goals by helping to:
- Specify the relationship between coach and learner, focusing on the learner's priorities
- Clarify student's and/or coaching partner's abilities and desired outcomes
- Pair outcomes to particular intervention strategies
- Determine evidence for student's and/or learner's progress

Examples of questions to ask:
- What would help you (in your role as parent, teacher, physical therapist, and so on)?
- What supports would be helpful for you/the student?
- What have you thought about doing (or tried)?
- What will indicate to you that the student (or you) is learning?

Observation and Action

Coach gathers data by soliciting information about:
- Student activities, skills, and behavior
- Learner's interactions, strategies, and decisions

Coach may use:
- Firsthand observations, audiotapes, videotapes, and progress reports
- Storytelling, dialogue, and interviews
- Demonstration, guided practice, modeling

Reflection

Coach enhances learner's perception and actions by helping:
- Summarize impressions of actions/events
- Compare planned for and obtained results
- Analyze relationships between student behavior and learner decision/behaviors
- Apply new information and reflect on coaching process

Examples of questions to ask:
- What happened when you . . . ?
- What did you do to influence what happened? How is this different?
- What changes would you make, if any, the next time?
- What have you learned from this process?

Evaluation

Coach reviews the effectiveness of the coaching sessions, either alone or with the learner to:
- Review the strengths and weaknesses of the coaching session
- Analyze the effectiveness of the coaching relationship
- Determine whether progress is being made to achieve intended outcomes, resulting in continuation or resolution of the coaching process

Examples of questions to ask:
- Do I need to make any changes in the coaching process?
- Am I assisting the learner to achieve the intended outcomes?
- Should I continue as the coach or will another teammate have the specialized experience/skills needed at this time?

FIGURE 1–8 Components of the coaching process

Source. Adapted from Rush, Shelden, and Hanft (2003). Rush, D. D., Shelden, M. L., & Hanft, B. E. (2003). Coaching families and colleagues: A process for collaboration in natural settings. *Infants and Young Children, 16*(1), 41.

Student Observation

Traditionally, assessment has been performed in isolation by each discipline, yielding diagnostic information on the student's current physical status and ability to perform certain isolated skills within individual developmental domains (such as communication or motor skills). In the collaborative team model, team members jointly plan for and conduct the assessment that is carried out in the student's natural environment during regular daily activities. Information gleaned from this type of assessment allows the team to plan student goals that are age appropriate, functional, and meaningful to the student and that are integrated with other aspects of the student's daily life.

The collaborative assessment technique is referred to as an ecological inventory and consists of the following steps:

1. Determine the environments in which the student currently functions or is likely to function in the near future.
2. Determine the desired activities and skills necessary to perform in those environments.
3. Determine the professionals who need to be involved in the various areas of the assessment. For example, for the skill of ordering and eating out in a restaurant, the speech-language pathologist might be designated to assess how well an individual student can order food to determine the student's communication needs related to this activity. The occupational therapist may also be involved to assess the student's self-feeding to determine any needed interventions in the areas of positioning or adapted devices.
4. Conduct the actual environmental assessment:
   a. Designated team members go to the natural environments with the student.
   b. Team members record the student's responses during performance of natural activities.
   c. Team members make notes on activities that require further assessment and potential needed adaptations or interventions.

Discipline-Specific Information

Not all needed information about a particular student can always be obtained through the observational assessment method described here. At times, some individual team members may need to use assessment strategies that are more traditional to their respective disciplines. Examples of this type of information, in the case of the physical therapist, might include specific assessment of muscle tone. However, even this type of information can usually be obtained within natural situations, and it should be, as the main purpose of the assessment is to use it to determine relevant educational goals.

Collaborative assessment requires both additional discussion time among various members of the educational team and additional direct contact with the student in order to allow for problem solving, consultation, and training among team members.

Development of Instructional Goals

Following the completion of the assessment process, the collaborative team prioritizes the skills to be taught to the student and jointly writes goals that address these skills. Prioritizing the skills to teach the student in the course of the school year can be a difficult task and must take into consideration the student's and family's preferences as well as which skills are necessary for educational, social, and vocational participation and development.

The student's IEP is developed by the whole team, including the student and his family. The goals and objectives on each student's IEP dictate the physical setup of the classroom, the day's schedule, and the choice of instructional materials and strategies. In the collaborative team model, each discipline does not write its own separate section of the IEP. Such an individual approach would promote development of goals having no function in the real world and would exclude critical objectives related to multiple domains across school and community environments. Instead, the team develops goals that identify environments that are educationally relevant and specific desired activities to be performed within those environments. The goals should address the question "What difference will this make in the student's life?" For example, in the case of an elementary student with multiple disabilities, instead of the PT working on a discipline-specific goal related to "increasing the student's midline control and balance" in isolation in the therapy room, the team might develop a goal related to the student's ability to carry her tray independently in the lunchroom.

Delivery of Instruction and Therapy Support

It has been mentioned that in the collaborative model, an integrated therapy approach is utilized. The common features of this approach are that each discipline's planning and skills are applied to a common set of shared goals. Therapeutic supports are implemented by all members of the team within functional instructional activities.

SUMMARY

This chapter defined the different types of disabilities that will be addressed in this book. Guidelines about terminology and obtaining information about the disability were discussed. In addition, several teaming models were discussed, as were strategies to facilitate collaborative teamwork.

REFERENCES

Beadles, J. J. (2001). How to refer to people with disabilities: A primer for laypeople. *Review, 33,* 4–7.

Best, S. (2005). Definitions, supports, issues, and services in schools and communities. In S. J. Best, K. W. Heller, & J. L. Bigge, (Eds.), *Teaching individuals with physical or multiple disabilities* (pp. 3–29). Upper Saddle River, NJ: Pearson Merrill/Prentice Hall.

Christenson, S. L., & Sheridan, S. M. (2001). *Schools and families: Creating essential connections for learning.* New York: Guilford Press.

Effgen, S. K. (2005). *Meeting the physical therapy needs of children.* Philadelphia: F. A. Davis.

Fadiman, A. (1997). *The spirit catches you and you fall down: A Hmong child, her American doctors, and the collision of two cultures.* New York: Farrar, Straus & Giroux.

Florian, L., Hollenweger, J., Simeonsson, R., Wedell, K., Riddell, S., Terzi, L., et al. (2006). Cross-cultural perspectives on the classification of children with disabilities: Part I. Issues in the classification of children with disabilities. *Journal of Special Education, 40,* 36–45.

Hanft, B. E., Rush, D. D., & Shelden, M. L. (2004). *Coaching families and colleagues in early childhood.* Baltimore: Brookes.

Harry, B. (2002). Trends and issues in serving culturally diverse families of children with disabilities. *Journal of Special Education, 36,* 131–139.

Heller, K. W. (2006). Persons with physical disabilities, health disabilities or traumatic brain injury. In R. M. Gargiulo (Ed.) *Special education in contemporary society* (pp. 562–615). Belmont, CA: Thompson Learning.

Heron, T. E., & Harris, K. C. (2001). *The educational consultant: Helping professionals, parents, and students in inclusive classrooms* (4th ed.). Austin, TX: PRO-ED.

Hornby, G. (2000). *Improving parental involvement.* New York: Cassell.

Kirshbaum, M. (2000). A disability culture perspective on early intervention with parents with physical or cognitive disabilities and their infants. *Infants and Young Children, 13*(2), 9–20.

Orelove, F. P., Sobsey, D., & Silberman, R. K. (2004). *Educating children with multiple disabilities: A collaborative approach* (4th ed.). Baltimore: Brookes.

Rainforth, B. (2002). The primary therapist model: Addressing challenges to practice in special education. *Physical and Occupational Therapy in Pediatrics, 22,* 29–51.

Snell, M. E. J., & Janney, R. (2000). *Teachers' guides to inclusive practices: Collaborative teaming.* Baltimore: Brookes.

CHAPTER 2

LEARNING AND BEHAVIORAL CHARACTERISTICS OF STUDENTS WITH PHYSICAL, HEALTH, OR MULTIPLE DISABILITIES

Kathryn Wolff Heller

Students who have physical, health, or multiple disabilities are at risk of poor school performance. In some instances, this may be the direct result of the specific disability; in other instances it may be due to the student's response to the disability. The student's environment may also influence how well a student performs, spanning across social, physical, technological, learning, and attitudinal environments.

It is important for teachers to have a clear understanding of how physical, health, and multiple disabilities can affect students' learning and behavioral functioning in regard to school performance. This understanding will give teachers a clear idea of the type of interventions that are needed to meet these students' needs. This chapter will provide a foundation for understanding the impact of physical and health disabilities on student performance (including those who have multiple disabilities with one of the disabilities being a physical or health impairment). Although this chapter applies to students with physical, health, or multiple disabilities who have a range of intellectual abilities (from an **intellectual disability** to gifted abilities), additional considerations are present when the student has a moderate, severe, or profound intellectual disability, and these will be addressed in Chapter 3.

PHYSICAL AND HEALTH DISABILITIES PERFORMANCE MODEL

When educating students with physical or health disabilities, there are three major areas that can affect student performance: (a) the type of disability, (b) functional effects of the disability, and (c) psychosocial and environmental factors. These three areas interact and create the Physical and Health Disabilities Performance Model (see Figure 2–1).

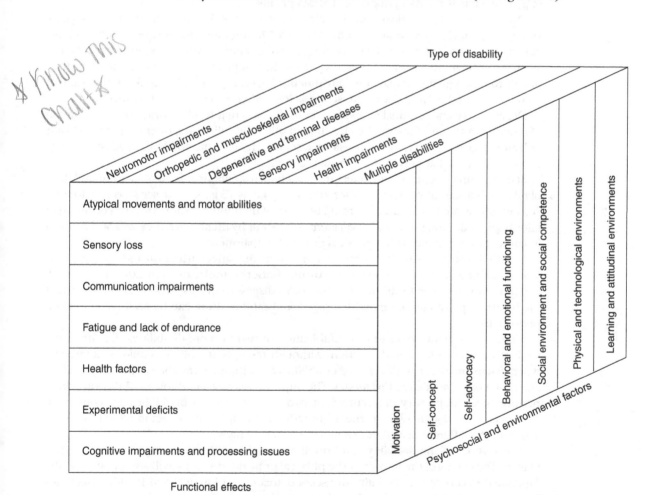

FIGURE 2–1 The Physical and Health Disabilities Performance Model shows the interactive effect of the different variables that can impact on student performance.

Student performance may vary as a result of the type and severity of the disability. However, students who have the same type of impairment may perform differently because of differences in the functional effects of the disability on the individual student. Even when the functional effects are the same, psychosocial and environmental factors vary, and this can create differences in performance between students. The following sections will describe each of the components of the Physical and Health Disabilities Performance Model as to its effect on performance as well as some strategies to improve student performance.

TYPES OF DISABILITY AND STUDENT PERFORMANCE

The first major area in the Physical and Health Disabilities Performance Model is the type of disability. Although there are a number of ways to classify diseases and conditions, we will use a similar classification system that was introduced in Chapter 1 and that is used in this book. In this system, disabilities are divided into: (a) neuromotor impairments, (b) orthopedic and musculoskeletal impairments, (c) degenerative and terminal diseases, (d) sensory impairments, (e) health impairments (which also includes infectious diseases), and (f) multiple disabilities.

Neuromotor impairments refer to conditions that affect the nervous impulses to the muscles, such as **cerebral palsy** and **spina bifida.** Neuromotor impairments are often very involved conditions that can affect several areas of functioning (e.g., motor movement, cognitive functioning, or language skills) and are often accompanied with additional impairments (e.g., visual impairments, epilepsy, or hydrocephalus).

Orthopedic and musculoskeletal impairments consist of disorders that may occur singularly (e.g., **juvenile rheumatoid arthritis**) or with other impairments (e.g., **scoliosis** occurring with cerebral palsy). When occurring alone, students with these impairments usually have normal intelligence. When they occur in combination with other disorders, they often produce a greater impact on daily functioning (e.g., positioning issues with a student who has cerebral palsy and a severe scoliosis impacting sitting ability and movement).

Degenerative and terminal illnesses refer to diseases that result in death or deterioration of function. Although they can be classified in other disability categories (e.g., neuromotor or health impairments), they are considered separately since they often have additional psychosocial factors that need to be considered.

Sensory impairments usually refers to visual impairments, deaf, hard of hearing, and deaf-blindness but can also include other sensory systems (e.g., loss of sensation of touch). Sensory impairments can affect learning because of their interference with the reception of information. Although sensory impairments can occur by themselves, they will be discussed in context of occurring with a physical or health impairment.

Health impairments include chronic conditions that affect attention and stamina. This would include such conditions as **asthma, diabetes mellitus,** and attention–deficit-hyperactivity disorder. In this model, infectious diseases, such as AIDS, is also included. If the health impairment occurs with a physical disability, there can be additive effects on performance.

Multiple disabilities refer to the combination of two or more disabilities that affect the student's ability to learn and function. Although multiple disabilities could be addressed when discussing the specific types of disabilities constituting it (as done in this book), a separate category is needed in this model. The impact of having a multiple disability on school performance can be very different when two or more distinct disabilities are combined. There is usually not an additive effect but rather a multiplicative effect in which the interaction of the different disabilities results in new challenges.

The severity of the disability and how it affects the student can impact school performance. The extent of the impact of the physical or health disability will also depend on the functional effects of the disability, the second area of the Physical and Health Disabilities Performance Model that will be described next.

FUNCTIONAL EFFECTS OF THE DISABILITY
AFFECTING LEARNING AND PERFORMANCE

There are several different functional effects that are associated with the various types of disabilities identified in the Physical and Health Disabilities Performance Model. Not all these effects occur with every disability or with every student. However, each of these should be considered when educating a student with a physical or health impairment. There are seven functional effects that can occur with physical and health disabilities that have the potential to affect student learning and performance: (a) atypical movements and motor abilities, (b) sensory loss, (c) communication impairments, (d) fatigue and lack of endurance, (e) health factors, (f) experiential deficits, and (g) cognitive impairments and processing issues.

Atypical Movements and Motor Abilities

Most students with neuromotor impairments, orthopedic impairments, musculoskeletal impairments, and degenerative diseases will have some type of abnormality in the motor system resulting in atypical movements or atypical motor abilities. Atypical movements refer to any movement that is performed differently than the norm, including uneven or extraneous movements, uncontrolled movements, restricted range of motion, decreased strength of movement, decreased speed of movement, lack of movement, and mobility issues. Atypical motor abilities refer to delayed, absent, or different motor skills that allow a person to perform certain tasks (e.g., eating, brushing one's hair, using a pencil, or manipulating a book).

Atypical movements or motor abilities may affect several aspects of learning and performance. One way learning can occur is through doing the task, or through active participation (Lefrancois, 2000). For students with severe motor impairments, that form of learning may not be possible. For example, a student with cerebral palsy and asthma who uses a nebulizer may need to know how to put it together in order to direct others in its use. However, the student cannot benefit through actually performing the task but rather must learn through observation and instruction. This can also apply to many academic tasks (e.g., moving math manipulatives when counting or science experiments). The teacher will need to be sure that appropriate adaptations are in place as well as appropriate instructional strategies (e.g., breaking down a task into parts, modeling, or having the student respond as to the next steps).

Atypical motor movements or motor abilities may also affect school performance, even when appropriate adaptations are in place. For example, a student with severe spastic quadriplegic cerebral palsy will often lack the motor control to use a pencil or a standard keyboard. In some cases, this student may need to use an on-screen keyboard and scanning program to write out sentences. Depending on the student's capabilities, the student could have a typing speed of five words per minute and not be able to type for very long because of endurance and fatigue issues. Not only does this motor issue result in less writing in a given amount of time, but it may result in the student having less opportunity to learn how to revise his work due to the time it takes for him to complete it (Heller, 2006). Teachers may need to modify students' workload while being sure that an ample amount of time is given to learn the task well (see Chapters 8 and 12 for more information on assistive technology and adaptations).

Sensory Loss

Students with sensory impairments, some types of physical disabilities, and some types of multiple disabilities will have sensory loss. This may be a visual impairment, deaf or hard or hearing, deaf-blindness, tactile deficits (as in a spinal cord injury), or other sensory loss (e.g., **proprioceptive** deficits or olfactory deficits). This may be a partial or complete sensory loss.

A sensory loss may affect several aspects of learning and performance. Not being able to see an activity or hear what is being said will obviously impact how the student performs. Even more subtle sensory losses, such as a lack of the touch sensation, can affect a student's perception of items and certain concepts (e.g., coldness of ice or smoothness of paper). In addition, sensory loss can affect motor ability (see Chapter 4 on motor development). As with atypical motor movements and motor abilities, it will be important that appropriate adaptations and assistive technology be put in place (see Chapters 8 and 12 for more information).

Communication Impairments

Although the majority of physical and health disabilities do not result in communication impairments, some students with conditions such as severe spastic cerebral palsy may have articulation difficulties (**dysarthria**) that makes speech unintelligible or have no speech at all (anarthia) (Hustad, Auker, Natale, & Carlson, 2003). When speech is affected, there may be a significant impact on students' learning and performance. Without speech, students are unable to ask questions, clarify concepts, read aloud, or answer questions using their own words. Although augmentative and alternative communication (AAC) can help students communicate, students may be unable to use the system accurately when they are first learning it. Also, no AAC system contains everything students may want to express unless the students have learned to write out messages using the alphabet.

Other types of communication impairments may also be present. For example, students with spina bifida and shunted hydrocephalus have been shown to have difficulties in word comprehension and pragmatic language (ability to use language in social situations) (Vachha & Adams, 2003). Students with traumatic brain injury can have difficulties with expressive language, receptive language, comprehension, word retrieval, labeling, and verbal organization (Burton & Moffatt, 2004). Students who are deaf or deaf-blind will usually need augmentative communication, as will some students with multiple disabilities. Teachers will need to work systematically with students who have communication impairments to assist them in conveying their thoughts, whether this be through speech or augmentative communication.

Fatigue and Lack of Endurance

Some students with physical and health disabilities will have problems with fatigue and endurance. Individuals with cerebral palsy, for example, have reported higher levels of physical fatigue (Jahnsen, Villien, Stanghelle, & Holm, 2003). Students with severe spastic cerebral palsy who struggle to access adapted keyboards can become fatigued after a period of time, affecting concentration and performance. Students with health impairments such as **sickle cell anemia** may have fatigue and limited stamina and endurance as a result of their condition and the amount of work they are doing. In the area of sensory impairments, students with low vision may fatigue after reading print for a protracted period of time and need to rest their eyes.

Some students with such conditions such as muscular dystrophy will typically have obvious fatigue issues. However, some teachers who have students who experience temporary or gradually increased level of fatigue may not realize that these variables are impacting the student's learning and performance. Close observation for fatigue is important in order to provide appropriate adaptations should it occur.

Several strategies may be used when fatigue is present. If the fatigue is due to repetitive motor movements, alternating with a different motor movement or a different activity can help. Some fatigue problems may be addressed through programming more difficult subjects for times when the student is most alert. In some cases, the student may need a break or a rest time. This is often seen in students with advanced muscular dystrophy. In some cases, the student may need a shortened school day.

Health Factors

Most students with physical and health disabilities have some type of health issues that can interfere with learning and school performance. Health factors can vary widely from pain and discomfort to side effects of medications to frequent school absences due to health problems.

Pain and Discomfort

In some instances, students may experience pain or discomfort because of their impairment (e.g., juvenile rheumatoid arthritis, sickle cell anemia, severe scoliosis, or problems associated with cerebral palsy) (Herring, 2002; Houlihan, O'Donnell, Conaway, & Stevenson, 2004; Jahnsen et al., 2003). Sometimes, pain occurs in conjunction with an activity the student is performing. For example, students with juvenile arthritis can experience pain if they sit too long in one position and then get out of their desk to perform a task.

Students' functioning in the classroom and interactions with peers can be impaired when they experience pain or discomfort (Nabors & Lehmkuhl, 2004). Pain can result in missed work as well as poorer attention to the task. According to Maslow (1954), physiological well-being, including lack of pain or discomfort, is the most basic need that must be met for an individual to reach his potential.

Whether pain is recognized in a student and dealt with will influence the student's performance. Unfortunately, pain in individuals with disabilities, such as spina bifida, is often underestimated and sometimes goes unrecognized (Clancy, McGrath, & Oddson, 2005). Teachers need to be observant for signs of pain and provide appropriate intervention. This may be done through modifying the activity that is causing the pain (e.g., decrease amount student needs to walk or allow student to change positions), taking medication for the pain, taking a short break, having the student go to the nurse, or other similar interventions. In some instances, an older student's preference may be for others to ignore the pain and allow him to work through the pain himself. The teacher may later provide a review of the material that may have been missed because of the distraction of experiencing pain.

Medication and Treatment Side Effects

Another health factor is the effect of medications and treatment that can interfere with learning and performance. For example, fatigue is a common side effect of many antiepileptic medications taken by students with seizures. These medication effects may interfere with attending to relevant information. In addition, some of these medications are associated with affecting cognition by diminishing the speed of information processing (Engelberts et al., 2002). Treatments such as radiation, taken by students with some forms of cancer, can also result in fatigue and **malaise** (i.e., achy feeling).

If medication is not taken properly, problems can result that affect not only school performance but also the student's health. For example, if prescribed **insulin** is not taken by the student who has diabetes, a diabetic emergency can occur, such as diabetic ketoacidosis. It is important that medication be properly administered and side effects and the effectiveness of medication be tracked. In this way, student performance can be enhanced, and medication changes can occur, as needed, when reported to the physician.

Absenteeism

Students with physical and health disabilities may have increased absenteeism from class because of pain, treatments (including surgery), and illness. Difficulty managing some disabilities, such as diabetes, has been associated with greater school absences and lower academic achievement (Yu, Kail, Hagen, & Wolters, 2000). Absenteeism may range from missing 10 minutes of class every day to perform a urinary catheterization procedure by a student with spina bifida to missing many days of school because of frequent hospitalizations associated with cystic fibrosis. Several weeks of school may be missed because of surgeries, pneumonia, or even an extended asthma attack.

Missing part or all of a school day can result in missing crucial information or concepts that are needed to adequately perform in school. How the teacher addresses this missed work can make a difference in how the student performs. At times, it will be important to have home-based instruction or tutoring to help the student not fall too far behind (Nabors & Lehmkuhl, 2004).

Experiential Deficits

Some students who have physical and health disabilities lack experiences or concepts that are important for school performance. For example, some students with physical disabilities may have never been to such common locations as movie theaters or stores with escalators because of transportation issues. Common experiences, such as having a picnic in the grass, may have been missed because of positioning or motoric issues. In the school setting, these students may encounter stories or material containing these common experiences, and they may have difficulty with the material because of comprehension issues.

Students may also have incorrect or missing concepts. For example, an 18-year-old girl who was blind was walking in the dirty snow in Pittsburgh. Her friend said, "The bottom of your cane looks just like applesauce." The girl, who was blind, replied, "How did the snow turn red?" She had been told that apples were red, and no one had thought to explain to her the interior color. Along the same lines, a student with a physical disability who has never held a cotton ball may think it is heavy or rough.

Not only can these misconceptions and lack of experiences place the student at a disadvantage in understanding the academic material but they can also adversely affect testing. For example, one question on a standardized test was "What do you talk with?" and pictures of a telephone, calculator, and two other items were provided. The student selected the calculator because it resembled his augmentative communication device. On a different test, one of the questions was "How do you remove a ring that is stuck on a finger" and the choices were soap and water, pliers, and two other choices. The pliers seemed like a logical choice to the student, who was born with no hands or arms.

Experiential deficits are common to students with physical and health disabilities, but they are often missed. Students do not necessarily tell the teacher when they don't understand something, and some students who lack communication are unable to do so. To address these experiential deficits, teachers should be sure to provide complete information on the topic at hand and not assume that something is common knowledge. Testing results should also take into consideration whether the test items relied on common experiences that the student may not have encountered.

Cognitive Impairments and Processing Issues

A cognitive impairment refers to impairment that affects a person's attention, memory, processing of information, or ability to learn. It covers a wide range of impairments, from those that are more severe, such as intellectual disabilities, to those that are more subtle and that deal with cognitive functioning (e.g., attention and memory). A child may be born with a cognitive impairment or develop one (e.g., **traumatic brain injury**). In other cases, children may have no documented impairment but have delays in reaching cognitive milestones or have barriers in processing information. Learning and academic performance may be affected by the student's intellectual functioning, delays in developmental milestones, and difficulties in information processing.

Intellectual Functioning

Some physical and health disabilities are associated with cognitive impairments. For example, students with cerebral palsy may have a range of abilities from gifted to having severe intellectual disabilities; however, there is a higher incidence of intellectual disabilities with students who have cerebral palsy (Nehring, 2004). Spina bifida with hydrocephalus is associated with problems in perception, motor planning, attention, memory, organization, impulsivity, hyperactivity, and sequencing (Lazzaretti & Pearson, 2004). Individuals with traumatic brain injury may have multiple problems in such areas as attention, memory, naming, word retrieval, comprehension, organization, impulsivity, and poor judgment (Burton & Moffatt, 2004). Students with health impairments, such as poorly controlled **epilepsy,** have been shown to have academic underachievement that does not improve, even when the seizures become more controlled (Austin, Huberty, Huster, & Dunn, 1999). The intellectual ability of the student will affect performance and necessitate the need for enrichment, remediation, or use of specialized learning strategies. (For students with significant intellectual disabilities, refer to Chapter 3 for more information.)

Developmental Milestones

Some developmental milestones may be reached differently, slowly, or not at all in students with physical or health impairments. Children with physical impairments often have delays in reaching cognitive milestones such as concrete and formal operations, as delineated by Piaget's work, because of decreased opportunities to interact with the environment and fewer confrontational interactions with peers (Yoos, 1987). Children of normal intelligence who are blind from birth often take longer to achieve cognitive developmental milestones than their sighted peers because of their lack of sight (Hatwell, 1985). Motor and mobility milestones may also be affected when a physical or visual disability is present (Celeste, 2002). Children who have intellectual disabilities in addition to their physical or health disability may not reach certain developmental milestones. (See Chapter 3 for more information on students with intellectual disabilities.) Regardless of the cause of a developmental delay or absence of certain developmental milestones, teachers will need to take into consideration where their students are functioning and provide appropriate strategies to meet their needs.

Information Processing Issues

Information processing refers to the ways in which information is processed by an individual. This includes such areas as how individuals attend and select relevant information, remember information, rehearse and process information, store and organize information, and retrieve information. There are several different theories as to how these processes occur. Although the effect of a physical or health disability can be applied to most of these theoretical models, we will limit our discussion to one of the early models that is still recognized today, namely, Atkinson and Shiffrin's (1968) memory model.

Memory Mode. Although it is beyond the scope of this chapter to go into detail about information processing, a few key points will be discussed. Atkinson and Shiffrin's memory model consists of three components: the sensory register, the short-term store (short-term memory), and the long-term store (long-term memory). Each of these has unique characteristics, with different storage capacities for memory.

Before information processing can begin, environmental input (or stimuli) must be received by one or more of the sensory systems (e.g., visual, auditory, or tactile) and converted into electrochemical impulses that are transmitted to the brain. For example, in the visual system, the eye receives a visual image via light rays from the environment that travel through various parts of the eye until the image reaches the retina, where it is converted to electrochemical impulses and transmitted by the optic nerve to the visual cortex in the back of the brain. The arrival of this information marks the beginning of the first memory component, known as the sensory register (see Figure 2–2).

The sensory register (also known as sensory memory) is the label used to describe the immediate and initial registration of stimuli that are received from the sensory systems. There are several different sensory registers (e.g., visual and auditory) that receive an overwhelming amount of information that is held in the sensory register for only a very brief period of time (less than a second to a few seconds). People are unaware of most of this information, and it quickly decays (fades away). However, information that the person attends to is moved into short-term memory (see Figure 2–2).

Short-term memory (also known as short-term store or working memory) is an active memory system that can be established by information coming from the sensory register or from internal processes (such as from long-term memory information). Short-term memory consists of numerous stores, also referred to as types of memory (e.g., auditory-verbal-linguistic memory or haptic short-term stores) (Atkinson & Shiffrin, 1968; Shiffrin, 1999). All the work of memory is performed in the short-term system (e.g., decisions, operations used to control short-term systems, and operations used to retrieve from long-term memory).

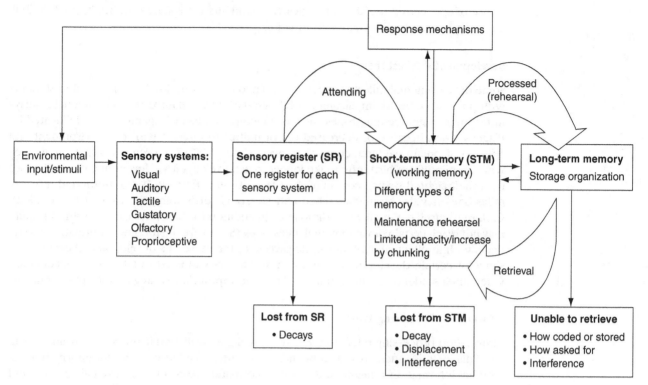

FIGURE 2–2 Adaptation of the Atkinson and Shiffrin (1968) information processing model of memory.

Short-term memory holds information for a limited duration and has a limited capacity. Information can be held in short-term memory for approximately 2 to 20 seconds, but information can be maintained for a longer period of time when the person engages in maintenance rehearsal (i.e., consciously repeats the information). Short-term memory also has a limited capacity (about seven items plus or minus two items for adults), but more items can be held in short-term memory by chunking (grouping) the items together. Because of the limited capacity and the short duration for which information is retained, information can be easily lost (through decay, displacement by new information, or interference of competing stimuli). However, when the information is processed through one of several different mechanisms (e.g., rehearsal of information or encoding of information), it is moved into long-term memory.

Long-term memory (also known as long-term store) refers to a more passive memory system that stores information over a long period of time (Shiffrin, 1999). Being able to use and remember information in long-term memory depends on how it was stored. The better the information has been understood and stored (or organized) with previously learned information, the easier it is retrieved. Forgetting is often attributed to unsuccessful retrieval of information (Ormrod, 1999; Shiffrin, 1999).

The term *executive function* is often found in the field of information processing. Although it is a general term that may include several differing definitions, it typically refers to control processes of each aspect of information processing. For example, the executive aspect of attention is what the person does and does not pay attention to. In short-term memory, the strategic processes used to retain information and move it to long-term memory, such as putting like words together when memorizing a list of words, falls under executive function. Executive functioning is often associated with the frontal (or, more specifically, prefrontal) part of the brain (Denckla, 1996).

Memory Model and Physical and Health Disabilities. Students with physical or health disabilities may have additional impairments that affect their attention, memory, storage, and retrieval of information because of their specific type of disability or concomitant cognitive impairments. For example, students with spina bifida have been found to have deficits in working memory and information processing speed, deficits in attention, poor memory spans, and lack of efficient strategy to remember a list of words (Boyer, Yeates, & Enrile, 2006; Dennis, Landry, Barnes, & Fletcher, 2006; Vachha & Adams, 2005). Students with spastic cerebral palsy have been found to have impairments of executive functioning aspects of memory and learning, although they could use executive strategies to facilitate recall when support was given (White & Christ, 2005). In some cases, the type of cerebral palsy may make a difference, such as the finding that some individuals with dyskinetic cerebral palsy have better working memory (in terms of verbal and immediate visual working memory) than those with spastic cerebral palsy (Roser, Canne, & Vendrell, 2003). Individuals with traumatic brain injury may have difficulty retrieving information from long-term memory (Bourne, 2006). Some individuals with epilepsy have been have found to score lower on test measuring attention, learning, and speed of information processing (Engelberts et al., 2002).

Sometimes students who have physical or health disabilities also have intellectual disabilities. Students with intellectual disabilities consistently perform poorer than children who are the same chronological age across working memory performance (Henry & MacLean, 2002). (For more information on the effects of an intellectual disability on memory, see Chapter 3.)

Information processing can be affected by a severe physical disability, even with students who have normal intelligence. For example, a student with severe spastic quadriplegia cerebral palsy with normal intelligence may have difficulties across each area of the information processing model. In terms of input, one or more of the sensory systems may be impaired (e.g., tactile or visual), resulting in a lack of input into the sensory register that may lead to a loss of information or inaccurate information. In order for the information to proceed to short-term memory, the individual needs to direct his attention to it. This may not occur if the student's attention is being affected by pain, discomfort, or fatigue.

Interference in short-term memory may also occur because of competing tasks, such as when students are having their concentration diverted to moving their arm to a certain location or using new assistive technology while they are trying to simultaneously perform another task (e.g., construct a sentence while they struggle to access an adapted keyboard and locate the appropriate keys). Some mechanisms used to retain information in short-term memory may also be affected, such as subvocal rehearsal of the information. It has been suggested that some individuals with severe physical and speech impairments may have difficulty with subvocal rehearsal, making retention of information more difficult (Sandberg, 2001), although subvocal rehearsal has been taught (Heller, Fredrick, Tumlin, & Brineman, 2002). Subvocal rehearsal problems have not been present in individuals with spastic cerebral palsy who have speech (White, Craft, Hale, & Park, 1994).

Students with physical or health disabilities may have difficulties encoding information into long-term memory when there are experiential deficits that result in a lack of information needed to integrate the new material. When information does move into long-term memory, difficulties in retrieval may occur when the information is not stored among relevant information because of inaccurate input or experiential deficits.

Many individuals with severe spastic cerebral palsy have speech that is not understandable, so the response mechanism in the information processing model may be affected. If the student cannot provide the intended output in an understandable manner, there will be a disruption of the feedback loop in which there is no response mechanism to provide input to the external stimuli (e.g., the student is unable to express confusion to influence the teacher's oral and visual instruction).

Strategies. There are several strategies that may be used to increase attention, memory, and retrieval of information. These strategies are used with students who do not have disabilities as well as with those who do. Some of these strategies include using visual imagery, mnemonic devices, rehearsal strategies, elaboration strategies, advanced organizers, attentional cues (i.e., antecedent prompts), prior knowledge activation strategies, and other learning and metacognitive strategies (Ormrod, 1999; Shiffrin, 1999).

When a physical or health disability is present, teachers will need to use additional specific strategies to meet the needs of these students. For example, to counteract a loss of sensory input (due to impairment), teachers will need to provide additional information utilizing other sensory systems. To maximize attention to the relevant stimuli, teachers will need to control pain, discomfort, and fatigue through appropriate medication, positioning, and rest breaks. To facilitate information being retained in short-term memory, students may be systematically taught subvocal rehearsal strategies. To avoid interference of other tasks, the student's easiest, most reliable response should be used, and new assistive technology should not be learned simultaneously when new information is being introduced in another area (e.g., answering comprehension questions in a science class using a new augmentative communication system that the student has difficulty accessing and locating desired symbols). To make storage and retrieval of information in long-term memory more effective, teachers should provide many experiences and not assume that students have background knowledge in common areas. Since the response mechanism is affected when there is a lack of speech, teachers should systematically check for comprehension and provide a means for the student to communicate.

PSYCHOSOCIAL AND ENVIRONMENTAL FACTORS AFFECTING BEHAVIOR AND PERFORMANCE

There are seven different psychosocial and environmental factors identified in the Physical and Health Disabilities Performance Model that may affect student behavior and performance: (a) motivation, (b) self-concept, (c) self-advocacy, (d) behavioral and emotional functioning, (e) social environment and social competence, (f) physical and technological environments, and (g) learning and attitudinal environments.

Motivation

The extent the student is motivated to learn will influence his performance. Although this varies across individuals and tasks, there are additional considerations when students have physical or health disabilities. For example, disabilities that result in pain, discomfort, or fatigue may decrease a student's motivation to perform a task. Often these need to be directly addressed in order for motivation to increase. Some individuals with physical or health disabilities may become depressed and display a lack of motivation because of despair over their condition. In this instance, counseling, therapy, or medication may be used to improve depression and increase motivation (Nabors & Lehmkuhl, 2004). When there are no physical or health reasons for the motivation, reinforcement may be needed to increase correct responding (see Chapter 3 for more information).

A lack of motivation may also be a direct result of others. Sometimes parents and school personnel may be overprotective of the student or unwilling to wait for the student to slowly attempt a task. In these instances, they may perform tasks for the student that he could do himself. If this goes on for a while, the student will expect others to do the task and he may not attempt to perform it himself. The behavior of not attempting the task as well as expecting to fail, setting lower goals, and reducing the amount of effort needed to perform a task are all characteristics of a condition called **learned helplessness** (Hamill & Everington, 2002; Seligman, 1975). Learned helplessness is the lack of persistence at tasks that could be mastered. For example, if the door is always opened for the student who is a wheelchair user, he may wait by a door for someone else to open it instead of learning how to open it himself. Systematic instruction, errorless learning, reinforcement, promoting positive attitudes in others regarding student abilities as well as the student, and a cessation of doing the task for the student are often needed to combat learned helplessness.

Self-Concept

Student's self-concept can have an effect on student performance. Self-concept refers to the general understanding and ideas we have about ourselves and is closely tied to self-esteem, which refers to how we value ourselves. As early as preschool, children with physical impairments begin to recognize that they are different from others. As young as ages 3 and 4, many children can associate the name of their disability with at least one of its effects

(Dunn, McCartan, & Fuqua, 1988). How a child perceives himself and his needs will be partially determined by what he knows about his disability. Understanding what the child knows and thinks about his disability is an important part of assisting the student in understanding what he needs to optimally function and to promote a positive self-concept.

Some students with physical or health disabilities may have negative concepts about themselves, resulting in low self-esteem and poor academic performance. Negative reactions can include feeling guilt over the disability, feeling like a hindrance, and having feelings of isolation or unhappiness (Rydstrom, Englund, & Sandman, 1999). Impairments that are unpredictable, such as epilepsy, may result in stress, anxiety, and embarrassment, which may interfere with developing a good self-concept and interfere with school learning (Frank, 1985). Students with degenerative conditions that result in death, such as Duchenne **muscular dystrophy,** may have a poor self-concept, such as the teen who said, "I am a snowflake melting in your hand."

Students can have poor self-concept and low self-esteem even when the disability is mild. It has been found in such conditions as cerebral palsy and spina bifida that the perceived significance of the impairment, not the severity of the impairment, affects how individuals respond to their disability (Manuel, Balkrishnan, Camacho, Smith, & Koman, 2003; Zipitis, Markides, & Thedosiou, 2005). Therefore, some students with more mild disabilities may have a poorer self-concept because of their perception of the impairment than those with more severe disabilities.

Several strategies may help to promote a positive self-concept and high self-esteem. First, students should learn about their disability and how it affects them to increase their understanding and ability to know what they need. A positive self-concept may be developed through exposure to other people (either in person or through books) who have similar disabilities and who have positive self-concepts. Finding activities (e.g., sports or leisure activities) that the student finds important and can excel in may promote a positive self-concept and increase self-esteem (Specht, King, Brown, & Foris, 2002; Wind, Schwend, & Larson, 2004). In some instances, counseling may be needed to help the child understand his own problems and achieve some sense of control.

Self-Advocacy

Self-advocacy refers to knowing one's rights and responsibilities and speaking out about them. In the classroom setting, self-advocacy can include such actions as telling a teacher of a needed adaptation or asking a peer to carry a book that is too heavy to class. Effective self-advocacy skills have been tied to increases in academic achievement, positive self-concept, and high self-esteem (Grover, 2005; Stevens, 2005).

Self-advocacy often involves having knowledge of self and knowledge of rights since individuals need to know and understand themselves before they tell others what they need. It is also linked to effective communication skills that are needed to effectively inform others what is needed (Test, Fowler, Wood, Brewer, & Eddy, 2005). In the context of the Physical and Health Performance Model, self-advocacy refers to the student's willingness and ability to inform teachers and others of his needs in order to improve his performance.

Often students with physical or health disabilities have specialized needs that must be addressed in order for the student to succeed at a task. Adults may quickly identify that adaptations need to be made with the student who has limited functional use of his hands in the biology lab. However, other needs may be more subtle and not recognized by the adult. Students will then need to serve as their own advocate and vocalize their needs. For example, a student with a physical impairment may need repositioning of the material in front of him in order to access it. Similarly, a student with a hearing impairment may need the teacher to stop turning away from her while lecturing. Unless the student says something, performance can be affected.

A lack of self-advocacy skills can affect not only a student's academic performance, but also his health and physical well-being. For example, a young student with diabetes may recognize that he needs a snack, but unless he speaks up and reminds the teacher to retrieve it, a medical emergency could result. Even more difficult for some children is disagreeing with the adult over their particular needs. The substitute physical education instructor may tell the student with a **congenital heart defect** to run faster when he has been doing modified walking in the past, and the student may have difficulty explaining the situation or he may have difficulty refusing to do what he is told. In order to promote health and performance, students will need to be systematically taught self-advocacy skills and how to use them in school and other environments (Macdonald & Block, 2005).

Behavioral and Emotional Functioning

Students with physical or health disabilities may be well adjusted or may have behaviors or emotional issues that affect school performance. Students may exhibit a range of behaviors, such as anger, depression, hopelessness, and depression. For example, some students with traumatic brain injury may be very aggressive. Students with Duchenne's muscular dystrophy are at increased risk for emotional disturbance with one of the most common symptoms being depression (Polakoff, Morton, Koch, & Rios, 1998). For students with severe or profound intellectual disabilities, self-stimulatory or self-injurious behaviors may be present (see Chapter 3 for more information on these behaviors). Some individuals with physical or health disabilities may have clinical psychiatric problems. One study found that students with type 2 diabetes had a higher prevalence of depression, attention-deficit-hyperactivity disorder, schizophrenia, and bipolar disorders (Levitt Katz et al., 2005). Depending on the type of behavior or emotional problem and its severity, treatment may range from a behavior plan to therapy and medication.

Social Environment and Social Competence

When determining possible factors that may affect school performance, it is important to take into consideration the student's social environment and social competence. According to some developmental and social learning theories (e.g., Piaget and Vygotsky), active participation is a critical component of learning and development. Students who are able to participate in the social environment and experience successful social interactions with other students will form experiences that will become a basis for cognitive and social growth (Simeonsson, Carlson, Huntington, McMillen, & Brent, 2001) (see Figure 2–3).

Maslow (1954) identified feelings of safety and belongingness as major individual needs that are partly dependent on the social environment. Classmates who tease students with spina bifida due to incontinent problems will create a negative social environment and decrease a sense of belonging (Zipitis et al., 2005). Since the social environment is

FIGURE 2–3   A student with cerebral palsy working with a friend in a classroom activity.

identified as one of the major environmental factors affecting participation (Mihaylov, Jarvis, Colver, & Beresford, 2004), teachers may need to help peers be more supportive of all students. Helping to promote friendships and assisting students to be part of a group will create a positive social environment and higher self-esteem, both of which can positively affect performance (Appleton et al., 1994; Zipitis et al., 2005).

Some students with physical or health disabilities will have social skills deficits or have difficulty being accepted by peers (Nabors & Lehmkuhl, 2004). This can also lead to a negative social environment. Social skill deficits and poor peer relationships may occur for a multitude of reasons. Students with such disabilities as cerebral palsy, traumatic brain injury, and spina bifida may have deficits in initiating and maintaining social interactions or entering into ongoing peer activities (Warschausky, Argento, Hurvitz, & Berg, 2003). Sometimes the impairment may affect social interaction. If a student is blind, she is unable to incidentally observe and model nonverbal interactions (e.g., eye contact and body position) and may encounter social challenges in areas of peer interaction (Msall et al., 2004). Sometimes students with such disabilities as cerebral palsy are at risk for social isolation because of stereotyped perceptions regarding children who are different (Nadeau & Tessier, 2006). Some students with disabilities will benefit from social skills training, and peers may benefit from disability awareness training.

Physical and Technological Environments

Physical and technological environments are two environmental factors that can influence child participation and scholastic performance. In some cases, the physical environment may have architectural barriers (Zipitis et al., 2005) despite regulations concerning having school buildings accessible. In addition, assistive technology devices (ranging from a bent spoon to an accessible computer) may also not be in place, and this can also affect participation and learning. The availability and proper use of assistive devices has been found to have an equalizing effort on participation with students with disabilities (Simeonsson et al., 2001). Teachers, along with the rest of the educational team, will need to make their classrooms and schools physically accessible and be sure the proper assistive technology is in place (see Figure 2–4).

Learning and Attitudinal Environments

The learning environment needs to be conducive to learning and supportive of students with physical or health disabilities in order to promote optimal academic performance. To do this, teachers will need to use appropriate adaptations and specialized instructional strategies. They will also need to set a positive attitudinal environment.

In the learning environment, the attitudinal barrier that students cannot do more complex work will have a negative impact on academic performance, especially when they are capable. Memories of adults with different types of disabilities pertaining to their childhood often involved ridicule, exclusion, and physical abuse by other children as well as more subtle but equally distressing situations, such as having one's ability underestimated by adults (Marshak & Seligman, 1993). Students with severe physical disabilities (e.g., cerebral palsy) and who are unable to speak intelligibly are at risk of being treated as if they have intellectual disabilities, even when they have normal intelligence. Students with severe physical and speech disabilities are reliant on their teachers to teach appropriate material and are at the distinct disadvantage of not being able to demonstrate their ability to master more difficult material when the material is never introduced. It is important for teachers to not limit student learning on the basis of what could be an inaccurate IQ score; rather, they should try more difficult material and see if students can master it when given systematic instruction and appropriate adaptations.

Individual, cultural, and societal beliefs, as well as superstitions, folklore, and mythology regarding individuals with disabilities, can result in a positive or negative attitudinal environment that can affect school performance. Blindness, for example, is surrounded by

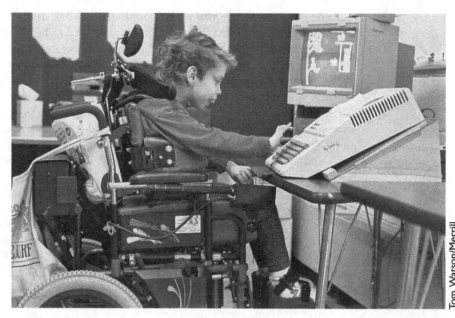

FIGURE 2–4 This student requires an adjustable height desk to accommodate his power wheel chair and to hold his CCTV (that enlarges print) and a typewriter that needs to be positioned on a slant board.

several negative and positive beliefs. Blindness has been viewed as a punishment from God, as worse than being dead, or as a mark of an evil person. Equally damaging, unrealistic positive beliefs include such views that individuals who are blind have "second sight," magical abilities, or a keener sense of the other senses (Wagner-Lampl & Oliver, 1994). Teachers should create positive attitudes in their classroom that are supportive of their students with disabilities.

SUMMARY

This chapter provided a broad overview of the impact of physical and health disabilities on learning, behavior, and performance. The Physical and Health Disabilities Performance Model illustrated the interrelatedness of the disability type, functional effects of the disability, and psychosocial and environmental factors. Physical and health disabilities were divided into six categories that closely follow Chapter 1 and the contents of this book. Functional effects of the disabilities included (a) atypical movements and motor abilities, (b) sensory loss, (c) communication impairments, (d) fatigue and lack of endurance, (e) health factors, (f) experiential deficit, and (g) cognitive impairments and processing issues. The psychosocial and environmental factors included (a) motivation, (b) self-concept, (c) self-advocacy, (d) behavioral and emotional functioning, (e) social environment and social competence, (f) physical and technological environments, and (g) learning and attitudinal environments.

It is the combination of the type of disability, the functional effects of the disability, and the psychosocial and environmental factors that creates a student's unique response to his situation and shapes how he will perform in an academic setting. Although there is no control over the type of impairment that a student has, functional effects and psychosocial and environmental factors can be addressed to improve student functioning. Teachers should take into account each aspect of this model and provide appropriate interventions. Teachers and the other members of the team should work together to address the specific areas found in this model to promote optimal performance.

REFERENCES

Appleton, P. L., Minchom, P. E., Ellis, N. C., Elliott, C. E., Boll, V., & Jones, P. (1994). The self-concept of young people with spina bifida: population-based study. *Developmental Medicine and Child Neurology, 36*, 198-215.

Atkinson, R. C., & Shiffrin, R. M. (1968). Human memory: A proposed system and its control processes. In K. W. Spence & J. T. Spence (Eds.), *The psychology of learning and motivation: Advances in research and theory* (Vol. 2, pp. 89-195). New York: Academic Press.

Austin, J. K., Huberty, T. J., Huster, G. A., & Dunn, D. W. (1999). Does academic achievement in children with epilepsy change over time? *Developmental Medicine and Child Neurology, 41*, 473-479.

Bourne, C. (2006). Cognitive impairment and behavioural difficulties in patients with Huntington's disease. *Nursing Standard, 20* (35), 41-44.

Boyer, K. M., Yeates, K. O., & Enrile, B. G. (2006). Working memory and information processing speed in children with myelomeningocele and shunted hydrocephalus: Analysis of the Children's Paced Auditory Serial Addition Test. *Journal of the International Neuropsychological Society, 12*, 306-313.

Burton, R., & Moffatt, K. (2004). Head injury. In P. J. Allen & J. A. Vessey (Eds.), *Primary care of the child with a chronic condition*, (4th ed., pp. 511-525). St. Louis: Mosby.

Celeste, M. (2002). A survey of motor development for infants and young children with visual impairments. *Journal of Visual Impairment and Blindness, 96*, 169-174.

Clancy, C. C., McGrath, P. J., & Oddson, B. E. (2005). Pain in children and adolescents with spina bifida. *Developmental Medicine and Child Neurology, 47*, 27-34.

Denckla, M. B. (1996). A theory and model of executive function: A neuropsychological perspective. In G. L. Lyon & N. A. Krasnegor (Eds.), *Attention, memory, and executive function* (pp. 263-278). Baltimore: Brookes.

Dennis, M., Landry, S. H., Barnes, M., & Fletcher, J. M. (2006). A model of neurocognitive function in spina bifida over the life span. *Journal of the International Neuropsychological Society, 12*, 285-296.

Dunn, N. L., McCartan, K. W., & Fuqua, R. (1988). Young children with orthopedic handicaps: Self-knowledge about their disability. *Exceptional Children, 55*, 249-252.

Engelberts, N. H., Klein, M., van der Ploeg, H. M., Heimans, J. J., Ader, H. J., van Boxtel, M. P., et al. (2002). Cognition and health-related quality of life in a well-defined subgroup of patients with partial epilepsy. *Journal of Neurology, 249*, 294-299.

Frank, B. B. (1985). Psycho-social aspects of educating epileptic children: Roles for school psychologists. *School Psychology, 14*, 196-203.

Grover, S. (2005). Advocacy by children as a causal factor in promoting resilience. *Childhood: A Global Journal of Child Research, 12*, 527-538.

Hamill, L., & Everington, C. (2002). *Teaching students with moderate to severe disabilities: An applied approach for inclusive environments.* Upper Saddle River, NJ: Merrill/Prentice Hall.

Hatwell, Y. (1985). *Piagetian Reasoning and the Blind.* New York: American Foundation for the Blind.

Heller, K. W. (2006). Physical and health disabilities. In R. Gargiulo (Ed.), *Special education in contemporary society: An introduction to exceptionality* (2nd ed., pp. 562-615). Belmont, CA: Wadsworth.

Heller, K. W., Fredrick, L. D., Tumlin, J., & Brineman, D. G. (2002). Teaching decoding for generalization using the nonverbal reading approach. *Journal of Physical and Developmental Disabilities, 14*, 19-35.

Henry, L. A., & MacLean, M. (2002). Working memory performance in children with and without intellectual disabilities. *American Journal on Mental Retardation, 107*, 421-432.

Herring, J. A. (2002). *Tachdjian's pediatric orthopaedics.* Philadelphia: W. B. Saunders.

Houlihan, C. M., O'Donnell, M., Conaway, M., & Stevenson, R. D. (2004). Bodily pain and health-related quality of life in children with cerebral palsy. *Developmental Medicine and Child Neurology, 46*, 305-310.

Hustad, K. C., Auker, J., Natale, N., & Carlson, R. (2003). Improving intelligibility of speakers with profound dysarthria and cerebral palsy. *Augmentative and Alternative Communication, 19*, 87-98.

Jahnsen, R., Villien, L., Stanghelle, J., & Holm, I. (2003). Fatigue in adults with cerebral palsy in Norway compared with the general population. *Developmental Medicine and Child Neurology, 45*, 296-303.

Lazzaretti, C., & Pearson, C. (2004). Myelodysplasia. In P. J. Allen & J. A. Vessey (Eds.), *Primary care of the child with a chronic condition* (4th ed., pp. 630-643). St. Louis: Mosby.

Lefrancois, G. A. (2000). *Psychology for teaching* (10th ed.). Belmont, CA: Wadsworth.

Levitt Katz, L. E., Swami, S., Abraham, M., Murphy, K. M., Jawad, A. F., McKnight-Menci, H., et al. (2005). Neuropsychiatric disorders at the presentation of type 2 diabetes mellitus in children. *Pediatric Diabetes, 6*, 84-89.

Macdonald, C., & Block, M. E. (2005). Self-advocacy in physical education for students with physical disabilities. *Journal of Physical Education, Recreation and Dance, 76*, 45-48.

Manuel, J. C., Balkrishnan, R., Camacho, F., Smith, B. P., & Koman, L. A. (2003). Factors associated with self-esteem in pre-adolescents and adolescents with cerebral palsy. *Journal of Adolescent Health, 32*, 456-458.

Marshak, L., & Seligman, M. (1993). *Counseling persons with physical disabilities: Theoretical and clinical perspectives.* Austin, TX: PRO-ED.

Maslow, A. H. (1954). *Motivation and personality.* New York: Harper & Row.

Mihaylov, S. I., Jarvis, S. N., Colver, A. F., & Beresford, B. (2004). Identification and description of environmental factors that influence participation of children with cerebral palsy. *Developmental Medicine and Child Neurology, 46*, 299-304.

Msall, M. E., Phelps, D. L., Hardy, R. J., Dobson, V., Quinn, G. E., Summers, G., et al. (2004). Educational and social competencies of 8 years in children with threshold retinopathy of prematurity in the CRYO-ROP multicenter study. *Pediatrics, 113*, 790-799.

Nabors, L. A., & Lehmkuhl, H. D. (2004). Children with chronic medical conditions: Recommendations for school mental health clinicians. *Journal of Developmental and Physical Disabilities, 16,* 1-15.

Nadeau, L., & Tessier, R. (2006). Social adjustment of children with cerebral palsy in mainstream classes: Peer perception. *Developmental Medicine and Child Neurology, 48,* 331-336.

Nehring, W. M. (2004). Cerebral palsy. In P. J. Allen & J. A. Vessey (Eds.), *Primary care of the child with a chronic condition* (4th ed., pp. 327-346). St. Louis: Mosby.

Ormrod, J. E. (1999). *Human learning* (3rd ed.). Upper Saddle River, NJ: Merrill/Prentice Hall.

Polakoff, R. J., Morton, A. A., Koch, K. D., & Rios, C. M. (1998). The psychosocial and cognitive impact of Duchenne's muscular dystrophy. *Seminars in Pediatric Neurology, 5,* 116-123.

Roser, P., Canne, J., & Vendrell, P. (2003). Neuropsychologic differences between bilateral dyskinetic and spastic cerebral palsy. *Journal of Child Neurology, 18,* 845-850.

Rydstrom, I., Englund, A., & Sandman, P. (1999). Being a child with asthma. *Pediatric Nursing, 25,* 589-596.

Sandberg, A. D. (2001). Reading and spelling, phonological awareness, and working memory in children with severe speech impairments: A longitudinal study. *Augmentative and Alternative Communication, 17,* 11-26.

Seligman, M. E. (1975). *Helplessness: On depression, development and death.* San Francisco: Freeman.

Shiffrin, R. M. (1999). 30 years of memory. In C. Izawa (Ed.), *On human memory: Evolution, progress, and reflections on the 30th anniversary of the Atkinson-Shiffrin Model* (pp. 17-33). Mahwah, NJ: Lawrence Erlbaum Associates.

Simeonsson, R. J., Carlson, D., Huntington, G. S., McMillen, H. S., & Brent, J. L. (2001). Students with disabilities: A national survey of participation in school activities. *Disability and Rehabilitation, 23,* 49-63.

Specht, J., King. G., Brown, E., & Foris, C. (2002). The importance of leisure in the lives of persons with congenital physical disabilities. *American Journal of Occupational Therapy, 56,* 436-445.

Stevens, B. E. (2005). Just do it: The impact of a summer school self-advocacy program on depression, self-esteem, and attributional style in learning disabled adolescents. *Dissertation Abstracts International: B. The Physical Sciences and Engineering, 66(6-B),* 3445.

Test, D. W., Fowler, C. H., Wood, W. M., Brewer, D. M., & Eddy, S. (2005). A conceptual framework of self-advocacy for students with disabilities. *Remedial and Special Education, 26,* 43-54.

Vachha, B., & Adams, R. (2003). Language differences in young children with myeolomeningocele and shunted hydrocephalus. *Pediatric Neurosurgery, 39,* 184-189.

Vachha, B., & Adams, R. C. (2005). Memory and selective learning in children with spina bifida-myelomeningocele and shunted hydrocephalus: A preliminary study. *Cerebrospinal Fluid Research, 2,* 10.

Wagner-Lampl, A., & Oliver, G. W. (1994). Folklore of blindness. *Journal of Visual Impairment and Blindness, 88,* 267-276.

Warschausky, S., Argento, A. G., Hurvitz, E., & Berg, M. (2003). Neuropsychological status and social problem solving in children with congenital or acquired brain dysfunction. *Rehabilitation Psychology, 48,* 250-254.

White, D. A., & Christ, S. E. (2005). Executive control of learning and memory in children with bilateral spastic cerebral palsy. *Journal of the International Neuropsychological Society, 11,* 920-924.

White, D. A., Craft, S., Hale, S., & Park, T. S. (1994). Working memory and articulation rate in children with spastic diplegic cerebral palsy. *Neuropsychology, 8,* 180-186.

Wind, W. M., Schwend, R. M., & Larson, J. (2004). Sports for the physically challenged child. *Journal of the American Academy of Orthopaedic Surgeons, 12,* 126-137.

Yoos, L. (1987). Chronic childhood illnesses: Developmental issues. *Pediatric Nursing, 13,* 25-28.

Yu, S., Kail, R., Hagen, J., & Wolters, C. (2000). Academic and social experiences of children with insulin-dependent diabetes mellitus. *Children's Health Care, 29,* 189-207.

Zipitis, C. S., Markides, G. A., & Theodosiou, G. N. (2005). Psychosocial aspects of spina bifida. In M. Zesta (Ed.), *Trends in spina bifida research* (pp. 77-99). New York: Nova.

CHAPTER 3

LEARNING AND BEHAVIORAL CHARACTERISTICS OF STUDENTS WITH SIGNIFICANT INTELLECTUAL DISABILITIES

Paul A. Alberto and Rebecca Waugh

Students' level of intellectual functioning will affect their ability to interact appropriately with others and the degree to which they will interact independently in their environment. In society at large and in educational and professional institutions in particular, we are moving away from use of the term *mental retardation* to terms such as **intellectual disability.** This movement is away from a term that has become a common pejorative that diminishes how these students and adults are valued and educated (Wolfensberger, 1982). As of 2007, the primary professional organization in the field adopted the term *intellectual disability* and changed its name from the American Association on Mental Retardation to the American Association on Intellectual and Developmental Disabilities (AAIDD). A term used in provisions of the legislation No Child Left Behind and therefore increasingly in some literature is *significant intellectual disability*. This term refers to students who constitute the lowest 1% functioning level of the student body. In the main, these are students with moderate and severe intellectual disabilities.

The term *intellectual disability* includes the same students diagnosed previously with mental retardation in number, kind, level, type, and duration of disability (Schalock, et al., 2007). In current federal law (Individuals with Disabilities Education Act [IDEA], 2004) and in most states, in order to be eligible for services as a student with an intellectual disability, three criteria set forth by AAIDD must be met. First is significantly subaverage general intellectual functioning. This is defined as an IQ score, resulting from an appropriate individually administered assessment, of 70 or below. This is then divided into levels of functioning based on standard deviations (about 15 points) from the average score of 100: mild intellectual disability is a score of 70 to 55, moderate intellectual disability is a score of 55 to 40, severe intellectual disability is a score of 40 to 25, and profound intellectual disability is a score less than 25. Second are concurrent impairments in adaptive behavior that are impairments of the student's ability to meet standards of maturity, learning, and personal independence expected of their age and social subgroup. For example, are infants, toddlers and young children meeting expected developmental milestones for sensorimotor, communication, self-help, and social development? Are school-age children demonstrating application of basic academic and social skills in daily life activities and appropriate reasoning and judgment navigating their environment? And are adolescents and young adults able to meet community standards for social responsibility, independence, and employability? Third is that these are manifested during the developmental period (conception to 18 years old).

Intellectual disability is included within the broader category of developmental delay. As defined in the Developmental Disabilities Assistance and Bill of Rights Act of 2000 (Public Law 106-402); the term **developmental disability** means a severe, chronic disability of an individual that (a) is attributable to a mental or physical impairment or combination of mental and physical impairments, (b) is manifested before the person attains age 22, (c) is likely to continue indefinitely, (d) results in substantial functional limitations in three or more of the following areas of major life activity—self-care, receptive and expressive language, learning, mobility, self-direction, capacity for independent living, and economic self-sufficiency—and (e) reflects the individual's need for a combination and sequence of special, interdisciplinary, or generic services, individualized supports, or other forms of assistance that are of lifelong or of extended duration and are individually planned and coordinated (SS 102[8][A][i–v]). A developmental delay implies that students go through the same stages of cognitive, communication, social, and motor development as nondisabled peers; however, because of their disability, they progress through the stages of development at a slower rate (Zigler, 1969). Slower developmental progress is directly correlated to these students' levels of intellectual functioning. This delay in rate of progress is not a difference in the stages through which a student progresses, such as stages of cognitive development. In many instances, intellectual disability is associated as a secondary disability of other developmental disabilities, such as **cerebral palsy** or autism.

All students with moderate and severe intellectual disabilities have a physical cause of their disability associated with brain damage or genetic disorders. For students functioning in the range of moderate to severe disability, their rate and path of development is also influenced by the presence of numerous secondary disabilities due to a physical etiology underlying a syndrome (e.g., Down syndrome). These etiologies result in a heterogeneous and multiply impaired population of students. In addition to their cognitive disability, significant numbers of these students will have sensory, physical, and health impairments. These may include vision and hearing impairments, physical disabilities (e.g., cerebral palsy or **spina bifida**), or health impairments (e.g., **epilepsy** or **asthma**). These various potential combinations of disabilities present a significant challenge to our educational technology and creativity.

Although this is a heterogeneous population of students, certain generalizations can be made about their learning characteristics that result from their cognitive deficits. The following characteristics frame the content of curriculum and influence strategies for instruction.

CHARACTERISTICS THAT AFFECT LEARNING AND INSTRUCTION

Cognitive Characteristics

Cognitive Development

4 stages of Cog develop.

The framework for researching and discussing cognitive development was pioneered by Jean Piaget (Piaget, 1969; Woodward, 1979). In his work and expanded by researchers since then, he describes four stages of cognitive development: sensorimotor, preoperational, concrete operations, and formal operations. It is expected that students with moderate and severe intellectual disabilities will progress through the sensorimotor stage and have cognitive understandings and abilities that include the ability to map their environment visually and auditorily; to reach, grasp, lift, transfer, place, and release objects; to understand that an object exist even if it cannot be seen and will pursue searching until they find it; and to use attached tools (e.g., finger feeding, zippers, pump soap, windup toys, or faucet) and unattached tools (e.g., pencils, TV remote control, or keys). Most students with moderate intellectual disabilities will achieve abilities of the preoperational stages, including classification, generalization, and seriation. It was originally stated by Piaget that cognitive development progressed solely by child exploration and that the sequences of stages and phases was inviolate. However, the work of researchers in the area of mental retardation indicates that these students can systematically and directly be taught the concepts and abilities associated with these stages of cognitive development (Dunst, 1998; Kahn, 1979; McCormick, Campbell, Pasnak, & Perry, 1990; Rogers, 1977).

Attending

Characteristics that affect learning & instruction:
- Cog Dev
- Memory
- Attending
- Synthesizing Info
- Communication
- Verbal lang.

In learning interactions, two forms of attention are necessary for successful learning: selective attention and sustained attention. Selective attention is the ability to attend to the relevant aspects of a task and to ignore irrelevant aspects. Sustained attention is the ability to maintain concentration long enough to process and comprehend information.

Zeaman and House conducted much of the early research on attention, hypothesizing that learners with intellectual disabilities differ from typical learners in their selective attention. Their research found that learners with intellectual disabilities required more trials to learn to select the relevant dimension by which to reliably select a correct answer. For example, when presented with a sweater, the learner with an intellectual disability will take more trials to figure out that by looking for the label on the back, they can reliably select front from back and therefore put on the sweater correctly each time. They concluded that individuals with intellectual disabilities require more time to learn to attend to the relevant dimensions of a task (Mercer & Snell, 1977; Zeaman & House, 1979).

This difference in selective attending and its implication for learning is presented in their Two-Stage Theory of Learning depicted in Figure 3-1. The configuration and number of stages of the learning curves of each of the four categories of learners is the same. The primary difference is that as the intellectual disability is greater, so too is the length of the first stage, which is the trial-and-error period for selecting what to look for in the material or activity in order to reliably select the correct answer. Generally, it has been found that students with significant intellectual disabilities are less able than typical students to perceive, select, and group relevant stimuli and discard irrelevant stimuli (Cha & Merrill, 1994).

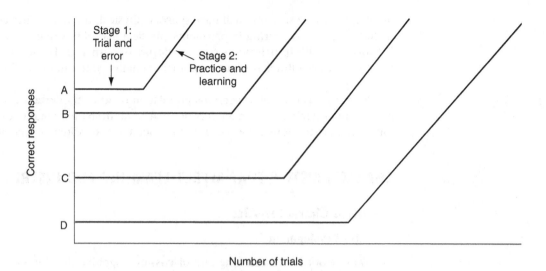

A—learning curve of typical learner
B—learning curve of student with mild intellectual disability
C—learning curve of student with moderate intellectual disability
D—learning curve of student with severe intellectual disability

FIGURE 3–1 Adaptation of Two-Stage Theory of Learning by Zeaman and House (1979).

The results of studies of sustained attention indicate that when required to make a comparison between the relevance of a task and its components, individuals with intellectual disabilities exhibit a more rapid decline in attention and persistence than do typical individuals (Tomporowski & Simpson, 1990). Typically, for a student with significant intellectual disability, the ability to discriminate between relevant and irrelevant stimuli is overwhelmed by the quantity of information in the environment. These students have difficulty learning what is important in the environment or on what part of an object they should focus to get information to make a correct answer or decision, and these learners could not attend to as many dimensions simultaneously as could typical learners (Zeaman & House, 1979). Therefore, the teacher must employ behavioral instructional strategies, such as antecedent prompting, in order to focus student attention. For example, a teacher would draw a student's attention to the first letter of the words "saw" and "was" by making them larger or different color in order for the student to learn to read them correctly; a teacher would draw a student's attention to the label for a sweater by attaching a red ribbon in order for the student to learn front and back for dressing. Without such prompting, there will be long periods of trial and error by the student. There is some disagreement as to whether this represents a difference in the learning of disabled and typical learners or rather a developmental delay (Iarocci & Burack, 1998).

Memory

A central cognitive mechanism critical to learning and instruction is memory function. Various components allow us to remember what is immediately in front of us, enabling a student to hold on to what a teacher is modeling and saying and to remember what was learned yesterday or last month so that it can be used over and over again.

Figure 3–2 depicts an adaptation of an information processing model of memory (Atkinson & Shiffrin, 1968). It has three storage components (sensory register, short-term memory, and long-term memory) in which information is received and held for various amounts of time and purposes and two processes (attending and rehearsal) that enable movement of information between storage components.

The sensory register is made up of the sensory receptors (visual, auditory, tactile (touch), gustatory (taste), olfactory (smell), and **proprioceptive**). Information is received as electrical impulses resulting in chemical reactions. Visual information is held for about 1 second

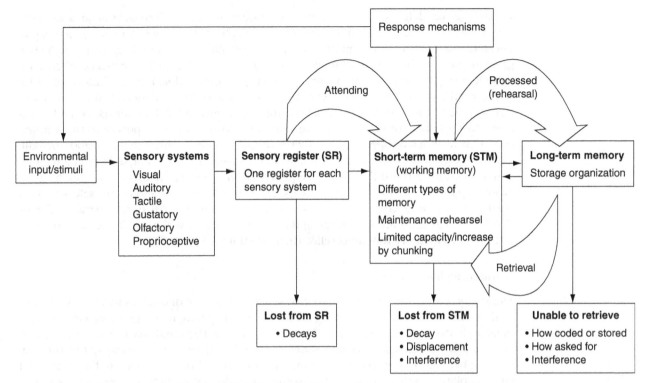

FIGURE 3–2 Adaptation of Atkinson and Shiffrin (1968) information processing model of memory.

[handwritten margin note: Short term mem = working mem; ↓ Info currently being used (Limited capacity)]

and auditory information for about 2 to 3 seconds. This is long enough to interpret impressions but not retain them. Information to which a student attends or takes notice of is passed to short-term memory. Incoming information that is not attended to decays.

Short-term memory is also know as working memory, as it holds the information a student is using at the moment or information the student and teacher are using during a lesson. Information is held between 2 and 20 seconds and is continuously renewed by the rehearsal or use of the information during the lesson. Short-term memory has a limited capacity, with adults able to hold about seven items and a 6-year-old about two or three items. Grouping enlarges the number of items and how long they remain. On tasks requiring low control (e.g., memory for positions of items), students with Down syndrome show impairment on verbal but not visuospatial working memory tasks. As the requirement of control increase, they show greater impairment on tasks and more disparity from typical peers (Lanfranchi, Cornoldi, & Vianello, 2004).

Long-term memory holds information that is transferred from short-term memory by rehearsal (Ellis, Deacon, & Woolridge, 1985). However, these students are not able to generate their own rehearsal strategy; it must be provided by the teacher. Information in long-term memory is stable; if we know the capital of Georgia, then we know it today, tomorrow, and next week. Long-term memory does not appear to have a limited capacity. For students with significant intellectual disabilities, the deficit is in the ability to retrieve stored information. Ability to recall information from long-term memory depends on factors such as (a) the amount of time that passes between the occurrence of the activity and the recall attempt, (b) the amount of time spent in the activity, (c) the number of sessions over which the activity took place, and (d) the amount of enjoyment perceived by the individual carrying out the activity (Boucher & Lewis, 1989).

Students with significant intellectual disabilities may have a variety of deficits that will affect their memory ability. The sensory register is affected by the prevalence of secondary visual and auditory impairments that impair the reception of information and the effects of certain medications. Their noted problem attending to relevant information impairs the movement of information to short-term memory. Short-term memory is impaired by the need for continuous external monitoring of aspects of working memory and the student's verbal language deficits. The inability to generate or monitor rehearsal strategies independently affects the passage of information from short-term memory to long-term memory. In long-term memory, storage is inefficient and thereby hinders retrieval because of ineffective grouping of material. Instead of new information being added to hierarchical classification groupings (e.g., things you eat or things you travel on), individual pieces of information are stored on the basis of how they were first encountered. These deficits result in memory characterized by less reliable information storage, fragmented skill performance, and significant "loss" of information. This may be due to inadequate initial exposure to the learning condition, insufficient opportunity to retrieve and practice or use the information or skill, or learning without appropriate context. For curriculum development, skills selected for instruction must be those that occur frequently in the students' lives so that they have repeated opportunities for practice. For example, reading words should be selected from environmental print encountered in the community rather than from a basal reader or Dolch lists. Skills that are used often and in various settings will naturally occur and therefore enhance memory functions (Ellis, 1970; Westling & Fox, 1995).

Synthesizing Information

The ability of students with moderate and severe intellectual disabilities to synthesize information and skills is limited (Westling & Fox, 1995). They have difficulty perceiving the relationship between parts and whole. This can be seen in their inability to combine parts to create a story or relate a morning's series of activities. They do not initially detect the relationship between one step in a chain and the next. This also is demonstrated in their initial limited ability to anticipate sequential steps that make up self-help, leisure, and vocational tasks. For example, during job training, after spraying window cleaner, the student would not necessarily anticipate the need for wiping the window. This lack of anticipation is seen across behaviors. As a result, a teacher should not teach isolated skills and expect the student to organize the information for use. Skills must be taught within the contexts of and embedded within the environment and activity in which they will be performed. In addition, the acquisition of skills requires an instructional strategy that breaks down task chains into component steps and skills so that each can be taught directly.

Communication Characteristics

Symbolic and Nonsymbolic Communication

The development of language is a complex process made up of many components. While most people view language and communication as the symbolic act of speaking words to express meaning, communication includes both symbolic and nonsymbolic forms. **Symbolic communication** is communicating using specific symbols that represent an object, action, or thought. As noted in Figure 3–3, forms of symbolic communication include speech, manual sign language, pictures, and written language. **Nonsymbolic communication** is communicating using (typical or atypical) movements, gestures, or sounds to represent an object, action, or thought. Forms of nonsymbolic communication include vocalizations, physiological changes, facial expressions, gestures, and behavior. For example, a student may increase muscle tone when presented with a desired activity by using physiological changes to express a want; a different student may slap her face, scream, or push an item away to express rejection or "do not want." While there are common forms of nonsymbolic communication (e.g., smiling and crying), there also can be unique forms that are specific to individuals.

There is a direct correlation between level of intellectual functioning and use of symbolic and nonsymbolic forms of communication. Studies have found that certain groups of students may characteristically use differing amounts of symbolic and nonsymbolic communication. Mar and Sall (1999) examined the communication of 103 children with severe and profound intellectual disabilities and found that the majority of children were nonsymbolic communicators. The majority of children at both levels of functioning used direct behaviors

---

Nonsymbolic communication

Vocal—using sounds and utterances (e.g., laughing, yelling, crying, cooing)

Affect—displaying a feeling or emotion (e.g., facial expressions)

Tactual—using touch (stimulation of passive skin receptors and active manipulation and exploration)

Behavior—(e.g., hitting, throwing, slapping, kissing, stroking, pushing away, clapping)

Body movement—general motion of body such as leaning away from or into, pulling away, or swaying

Gestural—using broad movements of the arms and hands

Physiological—displaying functions of body such as alertness, sweating, and muscle tone

Symbolic communication

Verbal—using words

Sign language—using system of hand and arm gestures

Photographs and pictures—using visual representation or image

Representational objects—using objects to depict activities using miniature objects to depict real objects or activity; using portions of a real object to depict a real object or activity

Graphic system—written words, using a method of symbols (e.g., Mayer & Johnson symbols, logos, Rhebus symbols)

FIGURE 3–3 Examples of nonsymbolic and symbolic forms of communication.
Source. Used with permission and adapted from Stillman and Siegel-Causey (1989).

to communicate (e.g., grabs for toys, pushes away bowl of food, kicks when angry, or reaches toward peer to initiate interaction). Only 12% of children with severe intellectual disabilities and 3% of children with profound intellectual disabilities used symbolic forms of communication. In a similar study of children and adults with severe intellectual disabilities (IQ 25–40), McLean, Brady, and McLean (1996) found that the majority of children were nonsymbolic communicators; while the majority of adults were symbolic communicators with only 20% of the adults using nonsymbolic forms of communication (see Table 3–1). These data suggest the complexity of language development for these children and adults who were symbolic communicators using multiword or multisymbol phrases. McLean et al. suggest several possible explanations for the difference in communicative complexity of children and adults who have severe intellectual disabilities. First, as individuals with intellectual disabilities grow

TABLE 3–1 Types of Communication Used by Individuals with Severe Intellectual Disabilities

	Children*		Adults**	
	%	n	%	n
Nonsymbolic	57	67	20	19
Nonintentional	33	39	6	6
Intentional	24	28	14	13
Symbolic	43	50	80	75
<5 words/symbols	7	8	7	7
>5 words/symbols	9	11	12	11
Combines words/symbols	27	3	61	57
Total	100	117	100	94

*Chronological age 7 to 12 years.
**Chronological age 25 to 35 years.
Source. Used with permission from McLean, Brady, and McLean (1996).

older, they are likely to be reclassified as having profound intellectual disabilities, and therefore a significant number of children who are nonsymbolic communicators may be reclassified as having profound intellectual disabilities. Second, the difference in communicative form between these adults and children may be due to the fact while their diagnosis may be stable, their symbolic communication abilities continue to develop through adolescence and early adulthood in this population, indicating the importance of continued language instruction though their school years.

These studies suggest the diversity in the form of communication used by these students. They report that these students often use multiple forms of communication to express their wants and needs (see Figure 3–4). For example, students may use a combination of gestures, vocalizations, and manual signs to communicate with others.

Verbal Language

For those students with intellectual disabilities who acquire verbal language, as is the case for students with moderate intellectual disabilities, their language development is delayed, not different (Pruess, Vadasy, & Fewell, 1987; Rosenburg & Abbeduto, 1993). However, as they grow older, their language development tends to slow. Despite the delay in language development, individuals with intellectual disabilities appear to follow the same sequence of language development as typically developing peers. Most of the research indicating this was conducted with children with Down syndrome, as they are the largest subpopulation (about 20%) of children functioning at this level. The research suggests that initial babbling occurs at approximately the same age and in the same development sequence as typically developing infants (Smith & Oller, 1981), and they show an emergence of communicative intentions at the same age, but these intentions appear to be less spontaneous and are often the result of elicitation by a caregiver (Fischer, 1987). They develop initial production and comprehension of object names at approximately the same mental age as typical peers, but they accumulate words at a slower rate (Cardosa-Martins, Mervis, & Mervis, 1985).

Individuals with significant intellectual disabilities exhibit several common deficits in their language and communication skills. They have weaknesses and greater delay in the development of expressive skills with relative strength in their receptive skills. They have deficits in production that are greater in syntax (average sentence length and structure) than in vocabulary learning (Chapman, 1997). As part of this, these students with Down syndrome are slower to develop sentence structure and length compared to typically developing peers (Chapman,

FIGURE 3–4   Student using gestures and vocalizations to communicate.

1997; Dykens, Hodapp, & Evans, 1994; Kumin, 2001). Because of the production of shorter and less complex utterances, they may be perceived as understanding less information. Although students with Down syndrome exhibit deficits in expressive language skills, their vocabulary development is more easily acquired than skills involving grammatical structure (Kumin, 2001). They use more simplistic grammatical structure when speaking, producing significantly fewer grammatical and lexical verbs. However, they demonstrate greater diversity in verb production as compared to typical peers matched on utterance length but produced utterances without any verb more often than peers (Hesketh & Chapman, 1998).

Individuals with significant intellectual disabilities exhibit difficulty with pragmatics or the social use of language. Pragmatics includes conversational skills such as turn taking, maintaining communicative content, and responding to requests. The ability to take turns during conversations allows engagement in the reciprocal nature of conversations. These students can learn to appropriately take turns during conversations, though they spend more turns on the same topic because of difficulty following topic shift and will repeat or revise their statements when asked for initial clarification (Brinton & Fujiki, 1996; Rosenburg & Abbeduto, 1993). These students often use less directive language when communicating with nondisabled peers than disabled peers, indicating they may view typical developing peers in higher status than themselves. More subtle aspects of conversational competence are less commonly displayed, for example, they are unable to tailor their language to a particular listener based on difference in social roles (Chapman, 1997; Hatton, 1998). The communicative environment with which these students are acquainted can affect their acquisition of pragmatic skills. Also, the number and extent of communication interactions with peers with and without disabilities can effect pragmatic development (Hatton, 1998). As the number of individuals within a conversational group increases, their appropriate use of pragmatic skills lessens. The ability of these students to interact appropriately through conversations with peers impacts how they are viewed as a member of the community and in the workplace. They are often characterized as exhibiting lower levels of social interactions, fewer interactions with coworkers and increased interaction with support staff, fewer occurrences of involvement in workplace joking, and increased engagement in work-related and inappropriate behaviors (Hatton, 1998).

CHARACTERISTICS THAT AFFECT BEHAVIOR

Social Characteristics

Students with significant intellectual disabilities demonstrate deficits in social skills, most clearly seen as difficulty engaging in appropriate reciprocal relationships with peers. Because of deficits in social skills, these students are often isolated in their school and neighborhood settings. They are socially accepted or rejected on the basis of the quantity and quality of their interactions with nondisabled peers (Siperstein, Leffert, & Widaman, 1996). The quantity of social interactions is affected by the number of opportunities to be in the same locations with nondisabled individuals and the number of nondisabled individuals with whom they must actually engage. The quality of social interactions is affected by the student's inability to accurately interpret social cues of interaction, such as changes in vocal tone, facial expressions, and body language. The quality is also affected by their communications deficits, such as their ineffectiveness at initiating conversations and those that affect the quality of conversations, such as appropriate turn taking, following topic changes, and use and understanding of abstractions, slang, and jokes.

The inability on the part of students with significant intellectual disabilities to accurately detect and interpret social cues in the form of emotions being expressed through facial expressions will likely contribute to their responding inappropriately to the social interaction of others (Hardwood, Hall, & Shinkfield, 1999; Kasari, Freeman, & Hughes, 2001; Wishart & Pitcairn, 2000). Rojahn, Lederer, and Tasse (1995) reported that with increased severity of mental retardation, the ability to identify emotions decreased, supporting the correlation between IQ and social impairments (i.e., interpreting social cues). By the age of 4 children with

Down syndrome made no progress in distinguishing sad, happy, anger, and fear of known and unknown peers and adults (Kasari et al., 2001; Wishart & Pitcairn, 2000).

Play Behavior

Children with moderate and severe intellectual disabilities have deficits in social play and toy play. Of an expected progression of social play from solitary play to parallel play to cooperative play, their social play is characterized predominantly by solitary and parallel play rather than cooperative play (Kasari & Bauminger, 1998). The complexity of their social play improves with the children's developmental level but is not associated with their chronological age (Crawley & Chan, 1982; Odom, 1981; Westling, 1986). Of a progression of the development of play skills with toys from exploratory manipulation to functionally appropriate use to symbolic play with and without objects, their play is characterized primarily as functional play. They are less likely to engage in imaginative or symbolic play. They show fewer different symbolic uses in free play, tending to elaborate the same idea repeatedly (Cunningham et al., 1985). This is in part due to the concrete rather than abstract nature of their cognitive abilities and probably in some part to the emphasis and nature of the overall functional framework of their educational programming and therefore the use of the materials to which they are exposed. They do, however, appear to have a similar development through symbolic play stages as do their typical peers. Children with significant intellectual, disabilities prefer more structured toys that are self-prompting (e.g., peg boards or puzzles) as opposed to more flexible toys that require creativity in their use (e.g., building blocks or clay). They are attracted to reactive toys that provide an external stimulus, especially those that have a sensory feedback for reinforcement (Malone & Langone, 1994; Westling, 1986). Their interactions with toys tend to be more narrow, less exploratory, and less complex. Their play tends to be restricted to single toys rather than multiple toys, and they do not incorporate a variety of toys into play and have limited repertoire for use of toys (Farmer-Dougan & Kaszuba, 1999). With systematic and direct instruction, the children have developed the skills needed for reciprocal social play, skills that include turn taking and waiting, sharing materials and toys, and appropriate social communication skills (Brodin, 1999; Sigafoos, 1999).

Friendships

For many family members, the focus of long-term social acceptance is on the establishment of friendships between their sons and daughters and typical peers. However, for children with intellectual disabilities, the establishment of friendships with age-appropriate peers can be a difficult challenge. Siperstein and Bak (1989) examined the friendships of individuals with mental retardation. Eighty-one percent of adolescents with mental retardation reported persons other than classmates as their friends with 42% of the reported friends being an adult. The adults named as friends included teachers, administrators, neighbors, doctors, and parents. Freeman and Kasari (2002) examined the characteristics of friends of children with Down syndrome during play sessions. The children with Down syndrome brought typically developing peers of the same age, gender, and ethnicity. However, unlike typical children, the friends brought by children with Down syndrome were not matched on developmental level and were from a different classroom setting. Freeman and Kasari (2002) reported that it is difficult to evaluate the longevity of these friendships because of the "increasing discrepancies between age and ability for children with Down syndrome" (p. 26).

Self-Determination and Locus of Control

A focus of education for these students is to build skills associated with self-determination. Self-determination is "a combination of skills, knowledge, and beliefs that enable a person to engage in goal-directed, self-regulated, autonomous behavior" (Field, Martin, Miller, Ward, & Wehmeyer, 1998, p. 2). Self-determination includes skills such as the ability to identify preferences, to evaluate possible options when problem solving, and to monitor and regulate one's own behavior. Students with intellectual disabilities are challenged by the high level of cognitive understanding and processing involved with many of these skills. Despite the challenges they face developing a complete sense of self-determination, by providing these individuals with an opportunity to participate in the decisions that are being made concerning their lives, they are provided with an opportunity to increase their level of self-determination (Wehmeyer, 2002). For example, students with significant intellectual disabilities may be allowed to select the order in which they will engage in morning tasks, the snack they want, the reinforcer for which they will work, or the picture book to be read this morning. Because these students lack complete levels of self-determination, they often view control and choices that affect their lives from the standpoint of an external locus of control (Wehmeyer, 1994). Locus of control refers to where a person sees authority that controls his or her actions. Internal locus of control refers to the reliance on one's self for personal actions and outcomes. External locus of control refers to the reliance on others for direction and guidance. Wehmeyer (1994) examined the locus of control and self-determination of 282 students with intellectual disabilities. He found that these students are more externally controlled than peers without disabilities and "hold perceptions of self-determination which are not conducive to becoming the causal agent in one's life" (p. 16).

Because of the external locus of control experienced by individuals with intellectual disabilities, they are often strategy passive and unable to generate their own strategy to use in social situations (Leffert, Siperstein, & Millikan, 2000). The ability to generate a strategy involves the ability to think of solutions for resolving social problems that are age appropriate and that fit the social situation. The inability of these students to generate strategies forces them to rely on others to assist them to handle situations that occur daily, thereby decreasing their ability to be self-determined.

Challenging Behaviors

Many students with significant intellectual disabilities may exhibit challenging behaviors, especially students with the most severe disability. These behaviors include stereotypic behaviors (e.g., repetitive behaviors such as body rocking and hand flapping), self-injurious behaviors (e.g., head banging and face slapping), and aggressive behaviors (e.g., hitting others and throwing objects). Such behaviors are part of the display of some of the syndromes associated with significant intellectual disabilities; for example, self-injurious behavior is associated with Lesch-Nyhan syndrome and Prader-Willi syndrome. However, it is generally accepted that a significant majority of the occurrences of these behaviors are attempts by students to communicate, resulting from an inability to communicate in a more standard manner (Carr & Durand, 1985). In most instances, these nonsymbolic communicative behaviors serve the function of attempting to gain a person's attention or gain a particular object. Alternatively, they are attempts to escape from a task or social situation by causing its termination because of the unacceptable and possibly dangerous behavior. If the student finds these behaviors successful in fulfilling his or her function, the behavior is strengthened by this naturally occurring reinforcement. For students at more severe and profound levels of functioning, an additional function may be to obtain sensory input (e.g., mouthing objects or finger flicking in front of eyes) or an attempt to escape from some internal pain or discomfort (e.g., head or ear banging because the student does not have a means of stopping a sinus headache or an earache). As indicated by best professional practice and by IDEA, the function of a student's challenging behavior is determined by conducting a functional assessment and/or functional analysis that becomes the basis on which an appropriate alternative standard behavior is selected for instruction (Alberto & Troutman, 2006; Iwata, Dorsey, Slifer, Bauman, & Richman, 1994).

ACADEMIC PERFORMANCE

Skills Learned and Generalized

Students with significant intellectual disabilities learn fewer skills within the time available in school, require more instructional opportunities (trials) to learn those skills and therefore more time to learn, and require more time to recoup lost skills (Brown et al., 1989). These learning characteristics require the careful selection of learning objectives, and those selected must have a direct effect on the student's life. From this is derived the necessary functional characteristic required of the curriculum. For example, teaching a student to put together a peg board has little direct effect on a student's life now or in the future. However, teaching a student to set the table for morning snack has an immediate and long-term purpose.

One of the most significant learning weaknesses of these students is the inability to apply information learned in one situation to another. This is known as a deficit in generalization (Browder, 1991; Haring, 1988). Deficits in generalization will appear when the student attempts to use newly learned skills in contexts other than that in which it was originally taught and learned. Thus, they have difficulty using new skills in different settings (e.g., dressing at home and at school), with a variety of people (e.g., giving correct coins to the teacher, a cashier, and a bus driver), with various materials (e.g., learning to clean the floor in a grocery with a broom and a mop), and across time (maintenance of learned skills). Generalization also involves using skills in other environments and situations in different ways. For example, calculators can be used to do addition in situations other than just grocery shopping. Students without intellectual disabilities would determine a variety of ways addition can be used in everyday life, whereas students with moderate and severe intellectual disabilities would require explicit instruction (Taylor, Richards, & Brady, 2005). Context and environment are critical factors for instruction (Brown et al., 1989). To the extent possible, instruction should take place in the setting(s) in which skills are to be used with natural materials and with a variety of people.

*Generalization
variety of :
· settings · materials
· people · across
                time

Direct and Observational Learning

Years of research and classroom practice make it clear that learning by students with significant intellectual disabilities is a result of systematic, direct instruction. Direct instruction is teacher directed. It involves the use of behavioral instructional strategies (e.g., reinforcement, response prompting, shaping, fading, and task analysis) and management of the learning environment so that it provides opportunities for student errorless responding, systematic movement from partial participation in tasks to increasing independent performance, and decision making based on ongoing data collection. In addition to learning through direct instruction, these students benefit from observational learning. Observational learning employs modeling, in which correct imitation of a model by the student is reinforced. Learning through observation enables group instruction (Collins, Gast, Ault, & Wolery, 1991). The use of adults, peers, and nondisabled peers as models is effective for social, motor, and some communication and problem-solving skills (Mercer & Snell, 1977; Snell & Brown, 2006; Westling, 1986). In both direct and observational learning, instruction is targeted directly to the student. The tendency of these learners to be outer directed or to look to others for cues or guidance in problem solving and their suggestibility indicates that modeling can be effectively used for acquiring or changing behavior (Turnure & Zigler, 1964; Zigler, 1999).

Functional Academics

Literacy

Many students with moderate and severe intellectual disabilities are functioning at the prealphabetic stage of reading. At this stage, students do not understand that letters represent the sounds in words, although they do know that print represents spoken messages. They remember words such as names of family members and signs by configuration and general visual appearance and depend on the context in which words occur to recognize them. They have no strategy other than rote memory of visual patterns or recognition of a word in its physical or environmental context to read it. When students at this stage are observed to read print in their environment, such as walk and fast-food restaurant signs, they do this by remembering configuration or visual cues accompanying the print rather than the written words themselves. For example, they read "McDonald's" on the sign because of the golden arches rather than the initial "M" in the name (Ehri, 1998; Moats, 2000). This is not because they ignored letters in the signs but because they did not store the letters in memory as part of the connections that prompted their reading of the signs (McGee, Lomax, & Head, 1988). These students connect print to ideas and produce and read the idea rather than reading the exact wording, such as reading "Crest" as "brush teeth" or "toothpaste." This indicates that the connections formed are between visual cues and the meaning of words. In later phases the students' knowledge of letter-sound connections restricts the word accessed in memory, to a single pronunciation linked to the word's spelling (Ehri & Wilce, 1987; Harste, Woodward, & Burke, 1984). This deficit of phonemic awareness and bias for remembering words based on the basis of configuration or visual patterns is the basis for the focus of research and instruction on sight-word reading strategies.

The most common instructional practice and the majority of reading research conducted with students with significant intellectual disabilities focuses on sight-word instruction. With sight-word instruction, students learn through repeated practice to recognize/read words on the basis of the configuration of the letters. A sight-word approach is used because of students' articulation difficulties and the complexity and abstraction of letter-sound correspondence in the English language. The words selected for instruction are functional words that will facilitate access to and independence in current and future environments. Students are taught words and phrases in the formats they appear in natural settings. The words and phrases provide information (e.g., signs and product labels), directions (e.g., pull, stop, and exit), safety warnings (e.g., do not enter and caution), and those that affect job performance.

While sight-word instruction can teach individual words, it does not provide word analysis skills that would allow students to read untaught words they encounter (Browder & Xin, 1998; Browder, Wakeman, Spooner, Ahlgrim-Delzell, & Algozzine, 2006; Conners, 1992). For this reason, it is important to consider additional approaches to reading instruction. Phonics instruction is successful with nondisabled students and students with mild mental retardation, and initial studies indicate that it holds promise with some students with significant intellectual disabilities (Bradford, Shippen, Alberto, Houchins, & Flores, 2006; Hoogeveen, Smeets, & Lancioni, 1989). An example of a phonics program that has been used with success is the Distar Program. The Distar Program is a sequential, direct instruction program that requires students to master developmentally sequential skill levels. The program includes explicit step-by-step teaching procedures for student mastery, immediate feedback, practice, and gradual fading of teacher direction. However, even with degrees of success with such a program, students with moderate intellectual disabilities demonstrated fluency levels below those of grade-level expectations. This fluency deficit may affect their reading comprehension as a similar deficit does for typical learners (Bradford et al., 2006; Torgesen & Hudson, 2006).

Some students will achieve reading at the second-grade level through phonics. However, the primary purpose of phonics with these students is not to be able to read books but rather to have a tool with which to confront untaught words and phrases in various environments and thereby increase their independence. The overall programming of reading instruction for these students should provide opportunities at sight-word and phonics instruction. Because of the complexity of the written English language and the various sound combinations, a complete phonics approach to learning to read all words may not be practical. Not all functional words in the environment conform to common phonics rules for decoding. If a phonics approach is not successful, the student will have sight words available.

Arithmetic

The arithmetic ability of students with significant intellectual disabilities is circumscribed by their limited cognitive ability to deal with abstractions. The primary framework for content and process of arithmetic instruction therefore is its concrete application in a functional curriculum. To meet the functional learning needs of these students, arithmetic instruction begins with a foundation of basic skills. The natural occurrence of arithmetic for these students is with manipulations embedded in functional activities rather than being able to recite addition and subtraction facts. In an embedded approach to functional instruction of arithmetic, skills are taught in the context of daily activities such that the priority for instruction is to increase the student's independence in activities (Ford, Schnorr, Meyer, Black, & Dempsey, 1989; Snell & Brown, 2006). Therefore, from the beginning basic skills are taught with manipulatives within applications embedded in the requirements of activities, such as money management for shopping, counting the dots on dice and moving spaces in board games, number recognition of phone numbers, or telling time for breaks on job sites.

Research on instructional strategies with basic skills has demonstrated students with moderate intellectual disabilities learning number identification, rote counting, counting objects, equality and comparison of sets, and basic computation (Butler, Miller, Lee, & Pierce, 2001; Mastropieri, Bakken, & Scruggs, 1991; Vacc & Cannon, 1991; Young, Baker, & Martin, 1990). Successful use of a "dot notation" system, similar to the published TouchMath materials (e.g., Kramer & Krug, 1973), and use of a number line (Sandknop, Schuster, Wolery, & Cross, 1992) have been demonstrated to increase addition and subtraction performance. However, for many students, it is more efficient to teach computation performance by teaching the use of a calculator, which improves efficiency and accuracy of timed performance (Matson & Long, 1986; Snell & Brown, 2006).

SUMMARY

A significant intellectual disability and the underlying etiology will affect most if not all aspects of a student's functioning and therefore their educational programming. While a listing of deficits associated with moderate and severe intellectual disabilities can be intimidating to educators and related professionals, it should not be paralyzing. Over the past 25 years students have been graduating into a more integrated and participatory postschool world. The range and number of options have steadily increased as educators and family members work together to refine and tailor educational programs to desired and now realistic outcomes. The range of postschool residential options no long is limited to the family home or state institution. It now realistically includes group homes and semi-independent apartment living. The range of postschool vocational options no longer is limited to state-run "work centers for the retarded." It now realistically includes working 10 to 30 hours a week on a job in a community business through the availability of support employment programs. These outcomes are providing for a more integrated life in the community in which they and their family and friends live.

REFERENCES

Alberto, P., & Troutman, A. (2006). *Applied behavior analysis for teacher*, (7th ed.). Columbus, OH: Merrill/Prentice Hall.

Atkinson, R., & Shiffrin, R. (1968). Human memory: A proposed system and its control processes. In K. W. Spence & J. T. Spence (Eds.), *The psychology of learning and motivation* (Vol. 2, pp. 89–95). New York: Academic Press.

Boucher, J., & Lewis, V. (1989). Memory impairments and communications in relatively able autistic children. *Journal of Child Psychology and Psychiatry and Allied Disciplines, 30,* 99–124.

Bradford, S., Shippen, M., Alberto, P., Houchins, D., & Flores, M. (2006). Using systematic instruction to teach decoding skills to middle school students with moderate intellectual disabilities. *Education and Training in Developmental Disabilities, 41,* 333–343.

Brinton, B., & Fujiki, M. (1996). Responses to requests for clarification by older and young adults with mental retardation. *Research in Developmental Disabilities, 17,* 335–347.

Brodin, J. (1999). Play in children with severe multiple disabilities: Play with toys. *International Journal of Disability, Development, and Education, 46,* 25–34.

Browder, D. (1991). *Assessment of individuals with severe disabilities* (2nd. ed.). Baltimore: Brookes.

Browder, D., Wakeman, S., Spooner, F., Ahlgrim-Delzell, L., & Algozzine, B. (2006). Research on reading instruction for individuals with significant cognitive disabilities. *Exceptional Children, 72,* 392–408.

Browder, D., & Xin, Y. (1998). A meta-analysis and review of sight word research and its implications for teaching functional reading to individuals with moderate and severe disabilities. *Journal of Special Education, 32,* 130–153.

Brown, L., Long, E., Udvari-Solner, A., Schwarz, P., VanDeventer, P., Ahlgren, C., et al. (1989). Should students with severe intellectual disabilities be based in regular or in special education classrooms in home schools? *Journal of the Association for Persons with Severe Handicaps, 14,* 8–12.

Butler, F., Miller, S., Lee, K., & Pierce, T. (2001). Teaching mathematics to students with mild-to-moderate mental retardation: A review of the literature. *Mental Retardation, 39,* 20–31.

Cardosa-Martins, C., Mervis, C. B., & Mervis, C. A. (1985). Early vocabulary acquisition by children with Down syndrome. *American Journal on Mental Deficiency, 90,* 177–184.

Carr, E., & Durand, V. M. (1985). Reducing behavior problems through functional communication training. *Journal of Applied Behavior Analysis, 18,* 111–126.

Cha, K., & Merrill, E. (1994). Facilitation and inhibition of visual selective attention processes of individuals with and without mental retardation. *American Journal on Mental Retardation, 98,* 594–600.

Chapman, R. S. (1997). Language development in children and adolescents with Down syndrome. *Mental Retardation and Developmental Disabilities, 3,* 307–312.

Collins, B., Gast, D., Ault, M., & Wolery, M. (1991). Small group instruction: Guidelines for teachers of students with moderate to severe handicaps. *Education and Training in Mental Retardation, 26,* 18-31.

Conners, F. A. (1992). Reading instruction for students with moderate mental retardation: Review and analysis of research. *American Journal on Mental Retardation, 96,* 577-597.

Crawley, S., & Chan, K. (1982). Developmental changes in free-play behavior of mildly and moderately retarded preschool age children. *Education and Training of the Mentally Retarded, 17,* 234-239.

Cummingham, C., Glenn, S., Wilkinson, P., & Sloper, P. (1985). Mental ability, symbolic play and receptive and expressive language of young children with Down's syndrome. *Child Psychology, 26,* 255-265.

Dunst, C. (1998). Sensorimotor development and developmental disabilities. In J. Burack, R. Hodapp, & E. Zigler (Eds.), *Handbook of mental retardation and development* (pp. 135-182). Cambridge, UK: Cambridge University Press.

Dykens, E. M., Hodapp, R. M., & Evans, D. W. (1994). Profiles and development of adaptive behavior in children with Down syndrome. *American Journal on Mental Retardation, 98,* 580-587.

Ehri, L. (1998). Grapheme-phoneme knowledge is essential for learning to read words in English. In J. Metsala & L. Ehri (Eds.). *Word recognition in beginning literacy* (pp. 3-40). Mahwah, NJ: Lawrence Erlbaum Associates.

Ehri, L., & Wilce, L. (1987). Does learning to spell help beginners learn to read words? *Reading Research Quarterly, 22,* 47-65.

Ellis, N. (1970). Memory process in retardates and normals. In N. Ellis (Ed.). *International review of research in mental retardation* (Vol. 9, pp. 1-32). New York: Academic Press.

Ellis, N., Deacon, J., & Woolridge, P. (1985). Structural memory deficits of mentally retarded persons. *American Journal of Mental Deficiency, 89,* 393-402.

Farmer-Dougan, V., & Kaszuba, T. (1999). Reliability and validity of play-based observations. *Educational Psychology, 19,* 429-441.

Field, S., Martin, J., Miller, R., Ward, M., & Wehmeyer, M. (1998). A practical guide for teaching self-determination. Reston, VA: Council for Exceptional Children.

Fischer, M. A. (1987). Mother-child interaction in preverbal children with Down syndrome. *Journal Speech Hearing Disorder, 32,* 179-190.

Ford, A., Schnorr, R., Meyer, L., Black, D., & Dempsey, P. (1989). *The Syracuse community-referenced curriculum guide for students with moderate and severe disabilities.* Baltimore: Brookes

Freeman, S., & Kasari, C. (2002). Characteristics and qualities of play dates of children with Down syndrome: Emerging or true friendships? *American Journal on Mental Retardation, 107,* 16-31.

Hardwood, N. K., Hall, L. J., & Shinkfield, A. J. (1999). Recognition of facial emotional expressions from moving and static displays by individuals with mental retardation. *American Journal on Mental Retardation, 104,* 270-278.

Haring, N. (1988). *Generalization for students with severe handicaps: Strategies and solutions.* Seattle: University of Washington Press.

Harste, J., Woodward, V., & Burke, C. (1984). *Language stores and literacy lessons.* Portsmouth, NH: Heinemann.

Hatton, C. (1998). Pragmatic language skills in people with intellectual disabilities: A review. *Journal of Intellectual and Developmental Disability, 23,* 79-100.

Hesketh, L. J., & Chapman, R. S. (1998). Verb use by individuals with Down syndrome. *American Journal on Mental Retardation, 103,* 288-304.

Hoogeveen, F. R., Smeets, P. M., & Lancioni, G. E. (1989). Teaching moderately mentally retarded children basic reading skills. *Research in Developmental Disabilities, 10,* 1-18.

Iarocci, G., & Burack, J. (1998). Understanding the development of attention in persons with mental retardation. In J. Burack, R. Hodapp, & E. Zigler (Eds.), *Handbook of mental retardation and development* (pp. 349-381). Cambridge: Cambridge University Press.

Individuals with Disabilities Education Act (IDEA) P.L. 108-446. (2004). Retrieved on March 10, 2007 from http://frwebgate.access.gpo.gov/cgi-bin/getdoc. cgi?dbname=108_cong_public_laws&docid= f:pub1446.108.

Iwata, B., Dorsey, M., Slifer, K., Bauman, K., & Richman, G. (1994). Toward a functional analysis of self-injury. *Journal of Applied Behavior Analysis, 27,* 197-209.

Kahn, J. (1979). Applications of the Piagetian literature to severely and profoundly mentally retarded persons. *Mental Retardation, 7,* 273-280.

Kasari, C., & Bauminger, N. (1998). Social and emotional development in children with mental retardation. In J. Burack, R. Hodapp, & E. Zigler (Eds.), *Handbook of mental retardation and development* (pp. 411-433). New York: Cambridge University Press.

Kasari, C., Freeman, S. F. N., & Hughes, M. A. (2001). Emotion recognition by children with Down syndrome. *American Journal on Mental Retardation, 106,* 59-72.

Kramer, T., & Krug, D. (1973). A rationale and procedure for teaching addition. *Education and Training of the Mentally Retarded, 8,* 140-144.

Kumin, L. (2001). *Topics in Down syndrome: Classroom language skills for children with Down syndrome: A guide for parents and teachers.* Bethesda, MD: Woodbine House.

Lanfranchi, S., Cornoldi, C., & Vianello, R. (2004). Verbal and visuospatial working memory deficits in children with Down syndrome. *American Journal on Mental Retardation, 109,* 456-466.

Leffert, J. S., Siperstein, G. N., & Millikan, E. (2000). Understanding social adaptation in children with mental retardation: A social-cognitive perspective. *Exceptional Children, 66,* 530-545.

Malone, D., & Langone, J. (1994). Object-related play skills of youths with mental retardation. *Remedial and Special Education, 15,* 177-189.

Mar, H. H., & Sall, N. (1999). Profiles of the expressive communication skills of children and adolescents with severe cognitive disabilities. *Education and Training in Mental Retardation and Developmental Disabilities, 34,* 77-89.

Mastropieri, M., Bakken, J., & Scruggs, T. (1991). Mathematics instruction for individuals with mental retardation: A perspective and research synthesis. *Education and Training in Mental Retardation, 26,* 115-129.

Matson, J., & Long, S. (1986). Teaching computer/shopping skills to mentally retarded adults. *American Journal of Mental Deficiency, 91*, 98–101.

McCormick, P., Campbell, J., Pasnak, R., & Perry, P. (1990). Instruction on Piagetian concepts for children with mental retardation. *Mental Retardation, 28*, 359–366.

McGee, L., Lomax, R., & Head, M. (1988). Young children's written language knowledge: What environmental and functional print reading reveals. *Journal of Reading Behavior, 20*, 99–118.

McLean, L. K., Brady, N. C., & McLean, J. E. (1996). Reported communication abilities of individuals with severe mental retardation. *American Journal on Mental Retardation, 100*, 580–591.

Mercer, C., & Snell, M. (1977). *Learning theory research in mental retardation: Implications for teaching.* Columbus, OH: Merrill.

Moats, L. C. (2000). *Speech to print.* Baltimore: Brookes.

Odom, S. L. (1981). The relationship of play to developmental level in mentally retarded children. *Education and Training of the Mentally Retarded, 16*, 136–141.

Piaget, J. (1969). *The theory of stages in cognitive development.* New York: McGraw-Hill.

Pruess, J. B., Vadasy, P. F., & Fewell, R. R. (1987). Language development in children with Down syndrome: An overview of recent research. *Education and Training in Mental Retardation, 22*, 44–55.

Rogers, S. (1977). Characteristics of the cognitive development of profoundly retarded children. *Child Development, 48*, 837–843.

Rojahn, J., Lederer, M., & Tasse, M. J. (1995). Facial emotion recognition by persons with mental retardation: A review of the experimental literature. *Research in Developmental Disabilities, 16*, 393–414.

Rosenburg, S., & Abbeduto, L. (1993). *Language and communication in mental retardation.* Hillsdale, NJ: Lawrence Erlbaum Associates.

Sandknop, P., Schuster, J., Wolery, M., & Cross, D. (1992). The use of an adaptive device to teach students with moderate mental retardation to select lower priced grocery items. *Education and Training in Mental Retardation, 27*, 219–229.

Schalock, R., Luckasson, R., Shogren, K., Borthwick-Duffy, S., Bradley, V., Buntinx, W., et al. (2007). The renaming of mental retardation: Understanding the change to the term intellectual disability. *Intellectual and Developmental Disabilities, 45*, 116–124.

Sigafoos, J. (1999). The wages of playing are fun and learning. *International Journal of Disability, Development, and Education, 46*, 285–287.

Siperstein, G., Leffert, J., & Widaman, K. (1996). Social behavior and the social acceptance and rejection of children with mental retardation. *Education and Training in Mental Retardation and Developmental Disabilities, 31*, 271–281.

Siperstein, G. N., & Bak, J. J. (1989). Social relationships of adolescents with moderate mental retardation. *Mental Retardation, 27*, 5–10.

Smith, B. L., & Oller, D. K. (1981). A comparative study of premeaningful vocalizations produced by normally developing and Down's syndrome infants. *Journal of Speech and Hearing Disorders, 46*, 46–51.

Snell, M., & Brown, F. (2006). *Instruction of students with severe disabilities* (6th ed.). Columbus, OH: Merrill/Prentice Hall.

Stillman, R., & Siegel-Causey, E. (1989). Introduction to nonsymbolic communication (p. 4). In E. Siegel-Causey & D. Guess (Eds.), *Enhancing nonsymbolic communication interactions among learners with severe handicaps* (p. 4). Baltimore: Brookes.

Taylor, R., Richards, S., & Brady, M. (2005). *Mental retardation: Historical perspectives, current practices, and future directions.* Boston: Allyn & Bacon.

Tomporowski, P., & Simpson, R. (1990). Sustained attention and intelligence. *Intelligence, 14*, 27–38.

Torgesen, J., & Hudson, R. (2006). Reading fluency: Critical issues for struggling readers. In S. Samuels & A. Farstrup (Eds.), *What research has to say about fluency instruction* (pp. 130–158). Newark, DE: International Reading Association.

Turnure, J., & Zigler, E. (1964). Outer-directedness in the problem solving of normal and retarded children. *Journal of Abnormal and Social Psychology, 69*, 427–436.

Vacc, N., & Cannon, S. (1991). Cross-age tutoring in mathematics: Sixth graders helping students who are moderately handicapped. *Education and Training in Mental Retardation, 26*, 89–97.

Wehmeyer, M. L. (1994). Perceptions of self-determination and psychological empowerment of adolescents with mental retardation. *Education and Training in Mental Retardation and Developmental Disabilities, 29*, 9–21.

Wehmeyer, M. (2002). *Promoting the self-determination of students with severe disabilities.* Arlington, VA: ERIC Clearinghouse on Disabilities and Gifted Education. (ERIC Document Reproduction Service No. ED470522).

Westling, D. (1986). *Introduction to mental retardation.* Englewood Cliffs, NJ: Prentice Hall.

Westling, D., & Fox, L. (1995). *Teaching students with severe disabilities.* Columbus, OH: Merrill/Prentice Hall.

Wishart, J. G., & Pitcairn, T. K. (2000). Recognition of identity and expression in faces by children with Down syndrome. *American Journal on Mental Retardation, 105*, 466–479.

Wolfensberger, W. (1982). A brief outline of normalization. *Rehabilitation Psychology, 27*, 131–145.

Woodward, W. (1979). Piaget's theory and the study of mental retardation. In N. R. Ellis (Ed.), *Handbook of mental deficiency: Psychological theory and research* (2nd Ed., pp. 169–195). Hillsdale, NJ: Lawrence Erlbaum Associates.

Young, M., Baker, J., & Martin, M. (1990). Teaching basic number skills to students with a moderate intellectual disability. *Education and Training in Mental Retardation, 25*, 83–93.

Zeaman, D., & House, B. (1979). A review of attention theory. In N. Ellis (Ed.), *Handbook of mental deficiency: Psychological theory and research* (2nd ed., pp. 159–223). Hillsdale, NJ: Lawrence Erlbaum Associates.

Zigler, E. (1969). Developmental vs. differential theory of mental retardation and the problem of motivation. *American Journal of Mental Deficiency, 73*, 536–556.

Zigler, E. (1999). The individual with mental retardation as a whole person. In E. Zigler & D. Bennett-Gates (Eds.), *Personality development in individuals with mental retardation* (pp. 1–16). Cambridge UK: Cambridge University Press.

CHAPTER 4

MOTOR DEVELOPMENT: CHARACTERISTICS AND INTERVENTIONS

Paula E. Forney

Students with physical and multiple disabilities often have motor impairments. Depending on the etiology of the disability and its severity, some students will have difficulty walking, and some will be unable to use their hands to perform everyday tasks. It is important for teachers to understand atypical motor development and its impact in order to meet the needs of their students.

Prior to discussing atypical motor development and potential interventions, teachers should have a basic working knowledge of motor development. This chapter will begin by providing a brief overview of theories of motor development, followed by basic information on joint structure, muscle tone, reflexes, and reactions. This information will lay the foundation for a discussion on atypical motor development, including its impact on a variety of systems. Several different approaches to intervention with atypical motor development will also be provided. Since teachers also need to know how to lift and handle students with motor impairments, the last section will give concrete information on lifting, carrying, and transferring techniques as well as positioning for functional participation.

THEORIES OF MOTOR DEVELOPMENT

Theories of motor development have changed considerably over the years, depending on the different levels of understanding at the time regarding structure and function within the individual and environmental influences on the course of development. Campbell (2006) summarizes the major theories of development as (a) cognitive, (b) neuromaturationist, and (c) dynamical systems. As theories of development have changed, revisions to intervention approaches have followed in order to appropriately facilitate motor development in children.

Cognitive Theories

In cognitive theories of maturation, development is thought to occur in stages when new learning takes place. In classic stage theory, it is assumed that an individual must pass through a certain period of development—or stage—and learn all the adaptive behaviors within that stage before moving onto other stages successfully. As the child assimilates environmental experiences, initially through reflex response to stimuli and later through direct action, cognitive structures are thought to accommodate to the experiences, resulting in new learning (Campbell, 2006).

Neuromaturationist Theories

The neuromaturationist theories assume that development occurs as a result of maturation of the **central nervous system** (CNS), including the brain and spinal cord. According to this model, movement progresses from reflexive control to voluntary control as progressively higher levels of the CNS mature.

This neuromaturationist theory also includes several other assumptions on which interventions for atypical development have been based (Dennis & Schlough, 2004, Forney & Heller, 2004). According to these assumptions, motor development tends to proceed as follows:

In a cephalo-caudal (head-to-tail) direction. Control of head movement occurs first, and subsequent motor control proceeds downward toward the feet. Therefore, children first learn to lift their heads; then to control movement of the upper trunk, arms, and hands; and finally to control their lower trunk and leg and foot movements.

In a proximal-to-distal (central-to-peripheral) direction. Control of movement occurs first at the center of the body and progresses outward to the extremities. Young children initially gain control over the muscles of the trunk, providing the stability necessary to subsequently allow movement of the arms and legs against gravity.

From reflex to volitional. In the first 6 to 9 months of life, many early movements are reflex based. That is, certain incoming sensory stimuli result in predictable patterns of movement responses. Gradually, the infant develops more voluntary control over body movements.

From gross to fine movements. Control of movement is at first more generalized and proceeds to refinement of skilled movement. For example, infants respond very early with widely fluctuating, imprecise movements of the arms when presented with a toy. These movements later become refined into a precise, accurate, visually directed reach toward the toy when it is presented.

From movements toward the body (flexion movements) to movements away from the body (extension movements). Because of the position in utero, the newborn infant is predominantly flexed at all joints of the body, with arms and legs bent and hands fisted. As development proceeds, the infant gains more and more control over extending or straightening the body against gravity. A balance between these two types of movement is necessary for children to gain control of their bodies, to be able to move into upright positions against gravity, and to move out into space.

From stability to mobility to skilled movement. Development of antigravity control over body movements, as described previously, allows the child to proceed from being able to assume and hold a developmental position (e.g., on hands and knees) to moving within that position (e.g., rocking on hands and knees) to performing a skilled action while in the position (e.g., creeping).

Although the previously listed assumptions generally describe the sequence and timing of typical development of motor skills in children and, in addition, still tend to guide therapeutic interventions for children with atypical development, they have been modified by more recent research evidence, leading to the dynamical systems theory of motor development.

Dynamical Systems Theory

Thelen (2000), Shumway-Cook and Woollacott (2001), and others (Goldfield & Wolff, 2004) have described the dynamical systems theory, which is an open, process-oriented, and functional perspective on motor development. Basic to this theory is that movement emerges primarily from the interaction of three factors: the individual, the task, and the environment. The individual generates movement based on incoming sensory stimuli to meet the demands of the task at hand, a task being performed within a specific environment. The individual's functional capability is measured by his ability to successfully meet the combined demands of the task and the environment. For example, a child first learning to walk can successfully respond to her father who is across the room encouraging her to walk only if she (a) has the prerequisite motor skills to accomplish this, (b) can register the sensory elements related to the task (e.g., seeing and hearing Dad), (c) understands the nature of the task from previous walking experiences, (d) is motivated to move to her parent, and (e) does not encounter environmental obstacles such as toys on the floor or a change in the walking surface (e.g., rug to hardwood floor) (Forney & Heller, 2004).

Dynamical systems theory also places all structures and processes that interact to promote motor development on an equal plane. Cooperating systems within the individual include the musculoskeletal system, the senses (vision, hearing, and so on), cognition, and arousal and motivation factors. In the dynamical systems approach, these internal components and the external context of the task are equal because behavior is considered task specific. Therefore, when considering the motor development of the child in the context of the dynamical systems theory, the environment is as important as the child. In the previous example, the factor of the environment being unobstructed and conducive to the task of walking across the room was as important to successful completion of the task as was the child's walking skill.

Constraints or limitations on the performance of any specific motor behavior must also be considered in the context of the various cooperating systems. In the case of the developing child, physical system components that do not develop at the same time, such as those involving muscle strength or postural control against gravity, are seen as limiting to the performance of motor behaviors at certain developmental periods. Additionally, environmental factors, such as the lack of opportunity to practice a particular movement skill, are also considered limiting to the development of specific motor behaviors. For example, a child who is not exposed to practice eating with utensils will be limited in fully developing self-feeding as a skilled movement pattern because of environmental factors (Forney & Heller, 2004).

The dynamical systems theory also describes motor development as occurring at its own rate for each individual, based on spontaneous, active, self-directed movement opportunities, with practice leading to refinement of motor skills. Periods in development when movement patterns are most variable are also thought to be critical periods when intervention might be most effective.

Rate pattern

JOINT STRUCTURE, MUSCLE TONE, REFLEXES, AND REACTIONS

Joint Structure and Muscle Tone

Body movement involves the force of muscles acting on the jointed structures of the skeleton. Normal joint movement occurs within a range that is specific to each joint. The types of movements made at each joint depend on that joint's construction. For example, hinge joints allow the movements of **flexion** (bending) and **extension** (straightening), pivot joints permit rotational movements, and ball-and-socket joints allow body parts to move in a variety of directions such as in flexion and extension, **abduction** (movement away from the midline of the body) and **adduction** (movement toward the midline of the body), internal rotation (turning a limb inward), and external rotation (turning a limb outward). It is important to know what constitutes normal direction and range of joint movement when working with children with motor impairments.

Although the skeleton provides the foundation for movement, the muscles of the body acting on the skeleton provide the force to create body movements. Every muscle in the body is made up of a muscle belly (containing thousands of muscle fibers) and muscle tendons. Muscle fibers are connected to muscle tendons, which are attached to bones. Movement occurs when the brain sends electrical signals through the spinal cord and the nerves to the muscle fibers, causing the fibers to shorten. The force of the shortening muscle fibers, acting on the bones to which they are attached, causes the body part to move.

The spinal cord exerts a certain level of continuous stimulation on all muscles of the body in order to maintain a certain level of muscle tension. This state of tension is called muscle tone. Muscles are thus ready for movement at any time. The physiological state of the body can modify the body's muscle tone. For example, stimulation to the muscles decreases during sleep, allowing relaxation. During times of anxiety, fear, or excitement, stimulation to the muscles increases, preparing the body for "fight or flight."

This normal tension in the muscles is sometimes called **postural tone** and provides the background for normal movement. When there is a breakdown in communication between the brain and the muscles in the developing child because of damage somewhere in the communication pathway (in the brain, spinal cord, nerves, or muscles), muscle tone and body movement will be atypical, and as a result motor development will be affected.

Reflexes and Reactions

Primitive Reflexes

At birth, the typical infant's movements are dominated by primitive reflexes or involuntary movements stimulated by various kinds of external stimuli. These reflexes are genetically preprogrammed. Some function to protect the baby; others form the beginnings of motor skills.

Involuntary should eventually integrate & become voluntary by 6-1yr mo

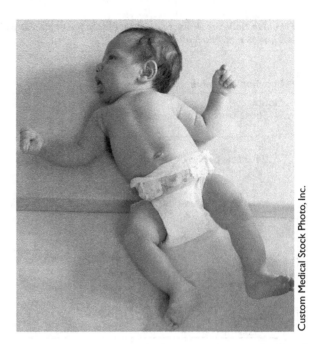

ATNR

FIGURE 4–I In the asymmetrical tonic neck reflex, when the head is turned to one side, the arm on that side extends and the opposite arm becomes flexed.

For example, a baby's initial reflex grasp of an object placed in her hand contributes to the eventual development of voluntary grasp. In another example, when the baby turns his head in response to visual or auditory stimuli, the arm reaches out. This is known as the asymmetrical tonic neck reflex (ATNR) or the fencer position (see Figure 4-1). The reflex is thought to facilitate the infant's development of visually directed reaching as well as contribute to rolling from back to side (see Figure 4-2 for descriptions of other primitive reflexes).

As the central nervous system matures, usually by about 6 months of age, these primitive reflex patterns of movement gradually integrate and are replaced by higher-level automatic postural reactions that continue for life. For example, the ATNR response begins to fade, and the older infant begins to develop postural reactions that allow more mature body movements, such as pushing up into sitting or onto hands and knees (Forney & Heller, 2004).

In the typically developing child, primitive reflexes are never totally obligatory; that is, they do not have to occur. Although automatic responses can be elicited through the appropriate stimulus, the child with normal central nervous system function can always supersede the expected response by responding to other environmental stimuli (Cronin & Mandich, 2005; Hooper & Umansky, 2004). In the example given previously, the reflexive ATNR posturing could be interrupted if a strong environmental stimulus is introduced. If the child's mother were to offer a toy to the child, for example, the child's reaching toward the toy would typically interrupt and override the influence of the ATNR. For any primitive reflex, consistent absence of a response at an expected age, an obligatory response at any age, or persistence of a response beyond the expected age range could all indicate central nervous system immaturity or dysfunction (see Figure 4-2).

Postural Reactions

As the central nervous system matures, higher-level reactions take over from the early primitive reflexes to help regulate postural control against gravity. The postural reactions established at this time are the righting, protective, and equilibrium reactions (see Figure 4-2). Delay or absence of these postural reactions can indicate immaturity or damage to the central nervous system.

Startle Reflex

Location/ Stimulus	Primitive Reflex	Response	Fades/ Integrates
Mouth			
Stroke corner of mouth	Rooting	Movement of the tongue, mouth, and head toward the site of stimulus	4 months
Neck			
Head falls back with sudden neck extension	Moro ✓	Arm extension-abduction (away from the body) followed by arm flexion-adduction (toward the body)	4–6 months
Head turns toward side	Asymmetric tonic neck ✓	Extension (straightening) of the extremities on the face side, flexion (bending) of the extremities on the opposite side (toward back of head)	6–7 months
Neck flexion	Symmetric tonic neck ✓	Arm flexion, leg extension with neck flexion	6–7 months
Neck extension		Arm extension, leg flexion with neck extension	
Hand			
Pressure on the palm	Palmer grasp	Flexion of fingers	5–6 months
Foot			
Tactile contact and weight-bearing on the sole of foot	Positive supporting	Leg extension for supporting partial body weight	3–7 months
Pressure on sole of foot under toes	Planter grasp	Flexion of toes	12–18 months
General position			
Supine (on back)	Tonic labyrinthine ✓	Predominant extensor tone on back Predominant flexor tone on stomach	4–6 months

Postural Reactions: Emerge as Child Matures, Present Throughout Life, Influenced by Intentional Movements, Delay or Absence Seen in CNS Immaturity or Damage

Stimulus	Postural Reaction	Response	Emergence
Visual and vestibular with movement	Head righting	Align face vertical, mouth horizontal	2 months prone 3–4 months supine
Tactile, vestibular, proprioceptive with movement	Body righting	Align body parts	4–6 months
Displacement of center of gravity outside of supporting surface	Protective reactions	Extension of arm or leg toward the side of displacement to prevent falling	5–12 months
General displacement of center of gravity	Equilibrium reactions	Adjustment of total body muscle tone and trunk posture to maintain balance	6–14 months

FIGURE 4–2 Examples of primitive reflexes and postural reactions.

Righting Reactions. These reactions utilize visual information, vestibular information from the inner ear, and information from tactile and **proprioceptive** (or position) receptors in the skin and joints to interact with each other and thus establish normal head and body relationships and alignments in space. They enable the child to learn to roll, get onto hands and knees, and sit up and stand. They also permit the restoration of the normal head position in space when displacement occurs, and they maintain the normal postural

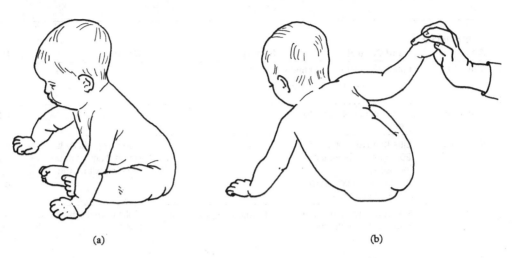

FIGURE 4-3 (a) Protective reaction forward; (b) protective reaction sideways.

relationship of the head, trunk, and limbs during all activities. Righting reactions are present throughout life once they emerge (Dennis & Schlough, 2004; Orelove, Sobsey, & Silberman, 2004).

Protective Reactions. When there is a rapid displacement of the center of gravity outside the supporting surface, the protective reaction occurs through a straightening and outward movement of the arms or legs in the direction of displacement to prevent falling. In the arms, these reactions first develop forward, then sideways, and finally backward (see Figure 4-3). Protective reactions of the arms normally emerge between 5 and 12 months, when the child is first learning to sit. Protective reactions of the legs normally emerge between 15 and 18 months, when the child is first learning to walk.

Equilibrium Reactions. Equilibrium reactions emerge, depending on the developmental position, between 6 and 14 months of age. Equilibrium reactions are elicited when the child's body is displaced off its center of gravity, either when the supporting surface or the body itself moves. They differ in stimulus from protective reactions in that the displacement is neither rapid nor outside the child's area of support but instead is a gradual or subtle movement. Muscles in the head, trunk, arms, and legs contract to adjust the body posture in order to maintain balance.

EARLY MOTOR MILESTONES

During the first few years of life, the young child takes in large amounts of information from the environment and, in response to that information, develops at an amazing rate across all the various domains, with the specific skills of each domain being intradependent as well as interdependent on each another. The need to move and explore the environment is an inherent drive in the newborn and the young child and continues throughout life.

The sequence of typical gross and fine motor development in the first 2 years of life is depicted in Figure 4-4. Having a basic understanding of this development will provide a context to understand the following information about atypical motor development. Although age ranges are used as a frame of reference, the reader is reminded of the individual nature of development in terms of both rate and sequence of development. Increased

Approximate Age	Head Control	Sitting	Moving	Hand Control
1 month	Lifts head while on stomach			Hands mostly fisted (flexor tone predominates)
3 months	Turns head from side to side			Hands mostly open
4 months	Lifts head and upper chest 90 degrees above supporting surface Bears weight on elbows while on stomach		Beginning ability to propel backward by pushing with arms	Looks from object to hand and back (beginning eye hand coordination)
5 months	Bears weight on extended arms while on stomach	Sits with support	Rolls from stomach to back	Voluntarily grasps items Reaches for items (but reach may overshoot item)
6 months		Pulls up to sitting position if hands are held	Rolls from back to stomach Bears weight on legs when held in standing	Increased manipulative skill (holds bottle, grasps feet)
7 months		Sits alone with hands on surface for support	Crawls on stomach	Transfers items from one hand to other
8 months		Sits well unsupported		
9 months		Sits alone with hands free to play	Creeps on hands and knees Pulls to standing Stands holding onto furniture	Uses crude pincer grasp between thumb and index finger
10 months		Gets into sitting from lying on floor		Can pick up small items
11 months			Stands alone Walks holding onto furniture	Neat pincer grasp Puts objects into container and takes out
12 months			Walks with help or alone (with wide base and arms held up)	Builds tower of 2 blocks Scribbles Throws objects
18 months			Walks alone, arms at sides with narrow base Sits self in chair	Hand dominance begins Begins to release objects
2 years			Begins to run Walks up and down stairs	Hand dominance in place Builds tower of 8 blocks

FIGURE 4–4 Major developmental motor milestones (birth to age 2).

control over movement, with refinement of balance and coordination, continues to occur throughout childhood and beyond. Figure 4–5 clarifies motor terminology.

ATYPICAL MOTOR DEVELOPMENT

Students with physical or multiple disabilities often experience atypical motor development. Although these students will learn to move in some fashion and at some level (depending on their degree of physical involvement), movements may or may not be functional for skill development. Some children may experience delays in motor skill acquisition but eventually do develop along a more or less typical sequence. Other children may never develop certain mo-

Motor Terms	Definitions
Abduction	The lateral movement of a body part away from the midline of the body
Adduction	The lateral movement of a body part toward the midline of the body
Asymmetrical	Lack of correspondence in shape, size, and position of the body parts on both sides of the body (e.g., one arm bends while the other straightens)
Bilateral	Pertaining to or affecting both sides of the body
Distal	Point farthest from the central part of the body, the trunk (e.g., the hand is distal to the shoulder)
Extension	Straightening a body part
External rotation	Turning a limb outward, away from the midline of the body
Flexion	Bending a body part
Internal rotation	Turning a limb in toward the midline of the body
Lateral	Pertaining to or relating to the side
Medial	Pertaining to or relating to the middle
Obligatory	Having to occur, as seen in atypical motor development when primitive reflexes cannot be overcome
Prone	Lying on the stomach
Proximal	Point closest to the center of the trunk (e.g., the shoulder is proximal to the hand)
Reaction (or postural reaction)	Subconscious movement that uses visual, vestibular, tactile, and proprioceptive information to establish the normal relationship of the body in space
Reflex	Movement performed involuntarily in response to a stimulus
Supine	Lying on the back
Symmetrical	Correspondence in shape, size, and position of the body parts on both sides of the body
Trunk rotation	Process of turning or twisting the body; movement takes place between the shoulders and hips

FIGURE 4–5   Motor terminology.

tor skills. Although each child with atypical motor development has his or her own pattern of motor strengths and challenges, the following physical characteristics (or combination of characteristics) that can interfere with the acquisition of motor skills may be observed in individual children (Pellegrino, 2007).

Atypical Muscle Tone

A disturbance of muscle tone may occur with damage to the central nervous system. Muscle tone may be lower than expected (**hypotonia**), resulting in decreased power to move body parts against gravity and an interference with postural alignment. Joints may be overly flexible. Muscle tone may also be higher than expected (**hypertonia** or **spasticity**), resulting in labored movement that often occurs in abnormal patterns and within a limited range of motion. Interference with postural alignment and inflexible joints may be present. Timing of muscle contraction may also be atypical (**ataxia**), resulting in uncoordinated movements, especially during activities requiring balance and equilibrium. Muscle tone may also fluctuate in some children (**athetosis**), at times being low and at other times high, making movement imprecise and uncontrolled. Children with atypical muscle tone may also display combinations of the previously mentioned muscle tone problems. Atypical muscle tone may affect the individual's whole body, only one side of the body, or one part of the body. The type and location of the atypical muscle tone is dependent on the location of the damage in the brain.

Disorders of muscle tone may be observed on a continuum from mild involvement that only minimally affects a child's movement and function to severe involvement that makes independent movement and function very difficult without adaptations and supports. The level of involvement will depend on the extent of damage within the brain. Since muscle tone is the basis of the capacity of muscles to act, atypical muscle tone interferes with the child's ability to respond to sensory stimulation in the environment through movement. Therefore, atypical muscle tone may interfere with progression through the various developmental motor milestones and performance of functional tasks (Forney & Heller, 2004). Chapter 5 discusses cerebral palsy and provides additional information on this topic.

Intervention with Atypical Muscle Tone

There are several interventions used to address atypical muscle tone. These include physical and occupation therapy; splints, casts, and orthoses; medication; and surgery.

Physical and Occupational Therapy. Pediatric therapists employ various handling and positioning techniques to attempt to decrease the effects of abnormal muscle tone and increase the normal actions of muscles for postural stability and functional movement at a level that is developmentally appropriate for each individual child. Many of these techniques can be taught to parents and teachers for carryover throughout the child's day (see "Approaches to Intervention" later in this chapter).

Splints, Casts, and Orthoses. Splints, casts, and **orthoses** are all custom-made devices that are sometimes prescribed in order to hold a body part (usually the trunk or an extremity) in a position that makes movement easier for the child, thereby improving mobility and function. These devices can also be used to gradually stretch tight soft tissue. Because of children's rapid growth and the close fit of these devices, careful monitoring and frequent changing of the devices are necessary. Most of these devices are usually made by an orthotist (a professional skilled in custom-making such devices) or by a trained therapist.

Splints are normally made of molded, rigid plastic and are used to position arms and hands. Soft splints may also be used in certain circumstances (e.g., to position the thumb out of the palm). Occupational therapists usually construct custom splints for a child. The splints are removable and may be worn at night only, most of the day, or for part of the day for certain activities.

Casts are normally prescribed to decrease abnormally high muscle tone or stretch out joint contractures caused by shortened muscles (e.g., in legs and feet). Casts are often used for children with more severe disabilities to achieve a functional position so that orthoses/splints can then be prescribed. Casts are usually changed every few weeks as tight muscles gain more length.

About 85% of children with atypical muscle tone use an orthotic device at some time (Campbell, 2006). Orthoses are made of molded, rigid plastic and are used to reduce tone and to position or stabilize the leg or foot. Ankle-foot orthoses (AFO) control the position of the ankle and foot. Knee-ankle-foot orthoses (KAFO) control the position of the knee as well as the ankle and foot. Orthoses are normally prescribed when the child begins weight-bearing activities. Wearing time is gradually increased, usually to include most of the child's waking hours. Parents and professionals must work closely together to ensure proper fit of the orthoses and prevent pressure sores to the child's skin. Frequent adjustments and refitting are often necessary.

Medication. Medications may be used to decrease atypical muscle tone. Oral medications are used, but some do result in sedation and may be avoided for that reason. Some medications may be given by injection or through medication pumps (e.g., Baclofen pump) to decrease high muscle tone.

Surgery. Surgical intervention is usually not considered until every attempt has been made to maintain or improve a child's mobility through more conservative intervention. Various types of surgeries involving the body's soft tissue can be used on the nerves, muscles, or tendons in order to reduce tone and improve joint range and general motor function.

Persistence of Primitive Reflexes

As has been discussed, primitive reflexes normally occur in the first few months of life to protect the baby and form the basis for early motor skill development. However, children with motor impairments may present with a continuation of these primitive reflexes well beyond when they would typically not be present. When this occurs, these reflexes do not promote motor development but can interrupt a child's ability to gain control over body movement. Higher-level postural reflexes described previously are usually also delayed or absent.

Persistent primitive reflexes can interfere with a student's intended movement. For example, if a student with a persistent ATNR is attempting to feed herself with a spoon in her right hand and then turns her head to the right to look at a classmate, an ATNR can occur.

This results in the extension of her right arm, making it difficult for her to bend her arm to get the food to her mouth. A physical or occupational therapist can support the child's parent or teacher in positioning and handling the child and in setting up everyday activities so that the influence of these persistent primitive reflexes is minimized.

Atypical Postural Control and Movement

Children with atypical muscle tone and/or persistent primitive reflexes are unable to make graded movement adaptations to environmental stimuli. They may become fixed in certain positions, held there by the force of gravity or by their own muscle tone. The quality of their movement is also limited by these same tone and reflex factors; the result is decreased efficiency of movement. Since both postural control and movement support children's ability to interact with people and objects, learning and cognitive development may be affected by their inability to explore and interact with the environment (Orelove et al., 2004). To facilitate optimum development of both motor and cognitive skills, early therapeutic and educational intervention that is directed toward improving postural control, movement skills, and environmental exploration is critical for the child with atypical motor development.

IMPACT OF ATYPICAL TONE AND REFLEXES ON FUNCTIONING

Movement and Mobility

As previously discussed, students with atypical tone and reflexes may have difficulty moving their arms and legs in a typical manner. In some instances, students may need a wheelchair to get around or may have limited use of their arms. This will depend on the etiology and severity of their disability. When there are movement and mobility issues, there are several types of assistive technology that may assist the student (see chapter 8 on assistive technology).

Eating Problems

The child with atypical muscle tone and primitive reflex residuals may find sucking, chewing, and swallowing difficult. Either low or high muscle tone in the face and tongue, a persistent bite reflex, a hyperactive or hypoactive gag reflex, or a strong tongue thrust can cause difficulty. Physical, occupational, or speech therapists can help parents and teachers use proper positioning of the child, in conjunction with specific adaptive equipment and techniques, to normalize oral sensitivity, decrease the influence of primitive oral reflexes, and help the child learn how to suck, bite, chew, and swallow more efficiently.

Food in the stomach may also be ejected back into the esophagus, a condition known as **gastroesophageal reflux**. This occurs when the stomach contents escape back up the esophagus (the passageway connecting the back of the throat to the stomach), resulting in frequent vomiting and potential irritation. Upright or semiupright positioning for an hour or so after meals and use of smaller portions or thicker textures of food can sometimes help gastroesophageal reflux, as can certain medications. When more conservative measures do not work, surgery may be needed.

Feeding problems can also make mealtime extremely frustrating, time consuming, and frightening for the parent, teacher, and child and thus create behavioral and socialization problems. Sometimes, the student may have trouble eating enough food to maintain health and growth. If feeding problems prevent a child from growing and gaining weight or if frequent aspiration pneumonias caused by food or drink ending up in the lungs occur, surgery to implant a **gastrostomy tube** (or **gastrostomy button**) may be recommended. During this surgery, a tube is inserted into either the stomach or the small intestine and brought through the abdominal wall. Liquid nutrients may then be introduced directly into the stomach or intestine, bypassing the oral cavity (Heller et al., 2000). In some cases, a nasogastric tube is placed through the nose into the stomach to deliver nutrition as a short-term solution until it is no longer necessary or a gastrostomy tube is surgically inserted (see Figure 4.6).

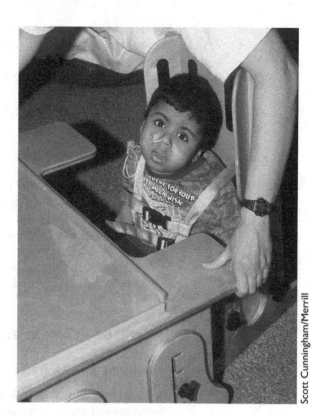

FIGURE 4–6 Student with multiple disabilities who requires a nasogastric tube to deliver nutrition and who needs an adapted chair and table for proper positioning.

Scott Cunningham/Merrill

Bowel and Bladder Issues

Constipation is also a frequent problem for children with atypical muscle tone. Low or high muscle tone, lack of activity, lack of upright positioning, poor sensation, and lack of enough abdominal strength to produce the pressure required for elimination can all contribute to problems with constipation. Changing positions and activity levels, increasing fiber in the diet, and using lubricants and stool softeners can help this problem. Parents, teachers, and professionals (physical and occupational therapists, nurses, physicians, and nutritionists) should work closely together to generate solutions.

Abnormal muscle control and disturbed sensation can also lead to problems with bladder control in children. Bladder control problems, compounded by hygiene difficulties, can lead to urinary tract infections. A hygiene program, antibiotics, and increased fluid intake can help decrease the number of infections. Control over the bladder and bowel can be significantly delayed in children with atypical motor development. Some disabilities also result in medical conditions that preclude the child from ever being able to control bowel or bladder functioning.

Respiratory Problems

Children with atypical muscle tone may not be able to keep saliva and food from being **aspirated** (i.e., inhaled into the lungs). Poor muscle control may make it difficult for these children to cough and thereby to clear aspirated material. When this occurs, chronic congestion can result and can lead to pneumonia if the lungs become infected. Atypical muscle tone may also make it difficult for children to breathe deeply enough to take in adequate oxygen. Not only can this lead to fatigue and health problems, but rib cage formation may be affected as well. The lack of coordination between breathing, sucking, and swallowing may further complicate feeding, and the breath support and control necessary for speech may be inadequate. Speech-language pathologists, physical therapists, occupational therapists, and nurses can work together with teachers and parents to provide proper positioning and facilitation techniques that can decrease aspiration and encourage better respiration patterns in atypical children.

Speech Impairments

Students who have difficulty with feeding may also have difficulty speaking. Speech may be poorly articulated and be difficult to understand (e.g., **dysarthria**). In some cases, speech may not be present at all. Some students will need augmentative communication devices so that they can communicate with others (see chapter 8).

Secondary Orthopedic Changes

Abnormal muscle tone, persistent primitive reflexes, and limitations in positions and movements that the child can use independently can also lead to secondary changes in joints, muscles, and bones. Because the child with atypical motor development is not moving his joints through their normal full range of motion, **contractures** can develop in which muscles shorten and connective tissue tightens around joints. Contractures physically limit the child's ability to move. If intervention to prevent or correct these secondary changes does not occur, atypical muscle tone and the resultant atypical body positions and movement patterns can actually cause changes in bone formation and growth, requiring major orthopedic surgery to correct.

Early therapeutic intervention, with physical and occupational therapists, parents, and teachers all working together to properly position and handle the child with atypical motor development, can help prevent these secondary orthopedic changes. However, once they occur, serial casting of the soft tissue, surgical procedures on tendons, or muscle lengthening may be required to correct soft tissue limitations. In the case of bony changes, surgical procedures on the bones themselves are necessary. These procedures require long-term casting until the bones are healed.

Difficulty with Development of Functional Skills

When children have atypical postural control and movement patterns, they are often unable to make the postural adaptations necessary to independently perform the functional tasks of eating, dressing, washing, and toileting at an age-appropriate level. Additionally, once the child reaches school age, functional tasks necessary for classroom performance, such as writing, may be impaired.

Physical and occupational therapists can assist children, families, and teachers with activities, adapted positions, and adapted equipment that can help increase functional independence. For example, feeding can be improved by training parents and teachers to meet the child's individual needs in the therapeutic preparation of the oral cavity prior to eating or in therapeutic measures to use during eating (e.g., using touch and pressure techniques to either stimulate oral muscles, decrease persistent oral reflexes, or decrease or increase oral sensitivity). A spoon with a curved bowl and a built-up handle may assist the child with independent eating. Allowing the child to use the support of a chair, a wall, or a small bench and adapting clothing with velcro fasteners may improve dressing skills. A wash mitt, an adapted toothbrush, a handheld shower nozzle, or a special bath chair may increase the child's independence with regard to personal hygiene. Special supports or seats on the toilet or individual training in transferring out of a wheelchair onto a toilet may also facilitate more independence. Specially adapted writing equipment or use of a computer to type responses may help the child in classroom activities. Increasing functional skills not only can improve the child's motor performance but also is important to developing cognitive, social, and communication skills.

IMPACT OF SENSORY LOSS ON MOTOR ABILITY

Motor Problems Associated with Hearing Loss

The child who acquires a **sensorineural hearing loss** as a result of a disease process such as meningitis may also experience a loss of motor control and the sense of balance due to damage to the vestibular system in the inner ear. Children who were walking may revert to crawling or may even be unable to sit without support. Postural reactions that were well established before the disease occurred may no longer operate. The amount of damage and, to some extent, the age of the child determine the level of regression. However, with appropriate intervention geared toward balance and equilibrium, the child can develop typically. Balance and equilibrium, however, may continue to be impaired when vision is removed, such as in the dark or with eyes closed (Orelove et al., 2004).

Motor Problems Associated with Vision Loss

Children with vision loss often exhibit developmental delays in many areas, such as language, socialization, self-help skills and motor development (Orelove et al., 2004). Motor development includes the elements of both movement and orientation. Young children with vision loss cannot easily monitor their own movements, nor can they easily copy other people as models of movement. Awareness of their own bodies and their position in space, as well as the relation of other objects in space, can be delayed. Without clear vision, children may experience orientation problems caused by difficulties with creating a mental map of their surroundings. For example, the child with a vision loss may be unable to find his way around obstacles that are in the way of reaching his goal. Vision loss may also remove an important source of motivation for the child to move into and interact with the environment. Reaching or moving toward sound sources, which is possible for children with vision loss, is a more complex task than visually directed reaching. It usually occurs later in motor development (at about 9–12 months), further delaying the motor skills progression of a child with vision loss.

Because the young child with vision loss practices general movements less often than the child with typical vision, postural reactions (righting, protective, and equilibrium reactions) are slower to develop in all positions, resulting in delayed balance. The "stability milestones" (such as sitting and standing) are less delayed than the "mobility milestones" (such as crawling and walking) because the child with vision loss is less motivated to move out into the environment.

When walking occurs, the child with vision loss may exhibit an atypical gait pattern. Stance may be wide based in order to give more support and stability. The child with vision loss may also use a shuffling-type gait pattern, sliding his feet along the floor in order to maintain contact and provide additional cues about the walking surface. Arms are held up for protection in a "high guard" position. There is little trunk rotation, and the gait appears stiff.

The child's fine motor skills may also be delayed. Reaching skills appear later than do those of the child with typical vision. Interpretation of tactile stimulation may also be disordered, creating tactile defensiveness or a reluctance to touch or be touched. The child with a vision loss may have fewer ways to manipulate objects, so he may need hands-on help as well as more time to explore objects with his hands.

APPROACHES TO INTERVENTION

A number of intervention approaches have evolved over the years, the purpose of which has been to support the development of individuals with developmental delays or disabilities. Many of the theoretical foundations of these approaches have not withstood the test of time in light of recent findings in neuroscience, but they continue to be accepted because of assumed clinical effectiveness. Several of the most common current approaches to intervention in the pediatric population will be covered below. However, as has been previously described, current scientific evidence supports a functional and broad-based approach to planning outcomes and activities for children with atypical motor development (Effgen, 2005; Forney & Heller, 2004).

Neurodevelopmental Treatment Approach

In the 1960s, Berta Bobath, a physical therapist, developed an intervention technique that she named neurodevelopmental treatment (NDT). Her husband, Dr. Karl Bobath, explained the scientific rationale for the approach, which was based on the now-questioned neuromaturationist model of motor control. The Bobaths believed that typical child development was characterized by brain maturation that inhibited the early reflex activity and facilitated higher-level skills in a specific developmental sequence, relying on established postural reactions. Their

treatment techniques, focused on children with cerebral palsy and atypical muscle tone, followed these same principles.

In NDT, the therapist uses a "hands-on" approach, placing her hands on specific body parts in order to help align body segments and initiate, guide, or prevent unwanted movement. The ultimate goal of NDT treatment is to inhibit a child's atypical patterns of movement and facilitate typical movement patterns, including requisite postural reactions. Therapy balls are frequently used in treatment sessions to encourage adaptive postural responses to movement. The aim of treatment is to help the child develop new patterns of movement. Although more current treatment includes hands-on facilitation during the child's performance of actual movement activities, this facilitation is expected to carry over into daily functional activities. Training and involvement of other team members (family, therapists, and teachers) is encouraged in the approach in order to plan and execute a well-coordinated treatment program. However, good handling techniques on the part of the therapist are essential to the approach (Effgen, 2005; Montgomery & Connolly, 2003).

Sensory Integration Approach

A. Jean Ayres developed the sensory integration (SI) theory and therapy in the 1960s to address the sensory processing and motor and perceptual problems of children with learning disabilities. According to SI theory, learning is dependent on the child's ability to take in sensory information from the environment and from body movement, process and integrate these sensory inputs within the central nervous system, and use the information to plan and produce organized movement and behavior. SI intervention is currently applied not only to children with learning and attention disorders but also to children with a variety of neurological impairments, such as cerebral palsy.

SI interventions are directed toward better central nervous system organization. The approach facilitates the child's ability to make adaptive responses to specific sensory stimulation (including tactile, vestibular, and proprioceptive stimuli) while engaging in purposeful activity. SI is not directed toward the mastery of specific tasks or skills but rather toward improving the brain's capacity to perceive, remember, and plan motor activity. SI therapy frequently uses activities that provide vestibular stimulation to influence balance, muscle tone, oculomotor responses, movements against gravity, postural adjustments, and arousal or activity level. Suspended equipment, as well as resistive activities, and weighted objects are often used in SI therapy to encourage adaptive postural and movement responses (Effgen, 2005; Montgomery & Connolly, 2003; Smith Roley, Blanche, & Schaaf, 2001).

Mobility Opportunities via Education Approach

The mobility opportunities via education (MOVE) curriculum was developed in the 1990s by Linda Bidabe, an educator, and John Lollar, a physical therapist, to help children systematically develop motor skills. The approach uses a top-down model in which motor goals are based on the identified motor steps of selected functional activities as opposed to a developmental model that would work on motor skills in the sequential order in which they typically occur. The program provides naturally occurring practice of functional motor skills while the child is engaged in educational or leisure activities.

In the MOVE program, activities are selected (e.g., using a public restroom or eating in a restaurant), and they are task analyzed to determine the physical skills needed to do these tasks (e.g., transition from standing to sitting, maintain a sitting position, or walking backward). Each of these physical skills is divided into four levels of success (ranging from skill acquisition with independent mobility to skill acquisition that would improve bone health and functioning). Students target one of these success levels on the basis of testing results. To reach the desired success level, the skill above their current functioning level is targeted, and the amount of prompts needed to perform that skill is determined. A specific prompt reduction program is used in which prompts are given numeric values and systematically faded as the student learns the skill being taught (see Figure 4–7).

FIGURE 4–7 Sample of prompting system used in MOVE curriculum for static seating. Numeric values are assigned in which 0 indicates no prompt and 5 indicates the most prompts. Some skills, such as head control, arrive at a score by counting the number of prompts needed. *Source.* © 1991, 2003 Kern County Superintendent of Schools, reprinted with permission. This publication is licensed to MOVE International.

LIFTING AND POSITIONING CONSIDERATIONS

Some children will need partial or complete assistance in moving from one place to another. Adults who are helping children move should have a good foundation in the basic principles of lifting, handling, and positioning. A nurse, physical therapist, or occupational therapist is a good resource for learning proper techniques.

Considerations Prior to Lifting and Lifting Techniques

Planning prior to lifting children is a step that adults frequently leave out and, by doing so, put themselves and the child at risk for injury. If there is any doubt about whether an individual is too heavy to be safely lifted by one person, a two-person lift or mechanical equipment should be used (see Figure 4–8). The following is a good rule of thumb to use in determining if a child is too heavy for a single adult to lift. If the child weighs more than 35% of the adult's body weight, the adult should not attempt the lift alone. For example, if an adult weighs 120 pounds, she shouldn't lift a child by herself who weighs more than 42 pounds. If the adult weighs 185 pounds, the weight limit for a one-person lift would be 65 pounds (Heller, Forney, Alberto, Schwartzman, & Goeckel, 2000).

Before actually lifting an individual, the adult should determine how much help the individual can provide in being moved, if another adult or special mechanical lift equipment is needed, what should be done to prepare the child to be lifted (e.g., specific handling techniques or specific positions used), and how the environment needs to be adapted to facilitate the transfer.

For the last consideration, the environment should be arranged to minimize the distance the adult must carry the child. This may mean that the child moves himself (e.g., a young child crawls to the changing table) or is moved (e.g., in his wheelchair) to the transfer area. If the child is being lifted into a piece of equipment, such as a stander, the equipment should be close at hand and ready to receive the student. All equipment needed for positioning the child should be brought to the transfer area before lifting. Finally, the area around the transfer area should be free of obstacles to ensure a safe transfer. Figure 4–9

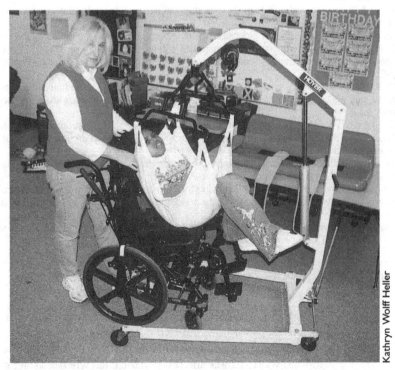

Kathryn Wolff Heller

FIGURE 4–8 A student being lifted from a wheelchair to a side lyer (in the background on the table) using a mechanical lift.

Principles of Lifting

1. Before lifting, take time to think about what you are doing, where you are going, and what you need.
2. Assess the individual's weight to determine how many people are needed to lift.
3. Have the individual bear as much weight as possible and assist as much as possible.
4. Prior to lifting, establish a broad base of support, with one foot slightly ahead of the other and feet apart.
5. Never bend at the waist to lift, instead squat or kneel, bending the knees and keeping the back as straight as possible.
6. Use the large muscles of the arms and legs to lift instead of the small muscles of the back.
7. When lifting or carrying, hold the individual close to your body rather than out in front of you to maintain proper balance and decrease strain on the back muscles.
8. Do not twist your upper body. Turn by moving your feet, keeping your back straight and in line with your feet.
9. When lifting, support the individual's body close to their center of mass (trunk, shoulders, or hips). Never grasp an individual's arms or legs to lift.

FIGURE 4–9 Body mechanics for proper lifting.

One-Person Lift from Floor

1. Bring the equipment as close to the individual as possible or have the individual move as close to the equipment as possible.
2. Kneel on one knee with the opposite foot planted firmly on the floor next to, as close as possible, and facing the individual.
3. Bring the individual into a sitting position, keeping back straight, as instructed by the physical therapist.
4. As instructed by the physical therapist, place one arm under the individual's thighs and the other arm around the back below the armpits. (For some individuals, the therapist may recommend lifting from behind, placing your arms under the individual's arms and grasping the individual's thighs with both hands.)
5. Bring your body close to the individual's body.
6. Communicate to the individual when you are going to lift.
7. Come to a standing position using your leg muscles, keeping your back straight.
8. Carry the individual to the support surface or equipment, keeping the individual at or below your waist level and close to your body.
9. Lower the individual onto the support surface or equipment, bending your knees and keeping your back straight.
10. Be sure the individual is properly positioned.

Two-Person Lift from Floor

1. Bring the equipment as close to the individual as possible or have the individual move as close to the equipment as possible.
2. A. Side-to-Side Method
   a. Two adults kneel on either side of the individual, as close as possible, kneeling on one knee with the other foot planted firmly on the floor.
   b. Bring the individual into a sitting position, keeping back straight, as instructed by the physical therapist.
   c. One person places one arm under the individual's thigh and the other arm around the individual's back. Second person does the same on the opposite side, crossing arms with other adult behind the individual.
   B. Top-Bottom Method
   a. One adult kneels as close as possible to the top of the individual's head (this should be the taller or stronger person since they will be lifting the heavier part of the individual). The other adult kneels as close as possible to the individual's feet.
   b. Bring the individual into a sitting position, keeping back straight, as instructed by the physical therapist.
   c. The adult at the top brings his arms under the individual's arms and around the front of the chest, holding the individual's crossed arms close to the individual's chest.
   d. The adult at the bottom places his hands/forearms on the individual's thighs behind the knees.
3. One person says, "Lift on three. One...two...three."
4. Adults together come to a standing position using their leg muscles, keeping their backs straight.
5. Adults carry the individual to the support surface or equipment, keeping the individual at or below their waist level and close to their bodies.
6. Adults lower the individual onto the support surface or equipment, bending their knees and keeping their backs straight.
7. Be sure the individual is properly positioned.

FIGURE 4–10 One- and two-person lifts from floor.

includes general principles of good body mechanics for proper lifting. Figure 4-10 describes steps for one- and two-person lifts.

The physical or occupational therapist who works with the child can offer suggestions about the best way to handle and position the child when assisting movement. Information about how to prepare the child to move, where to provide support, speed of movement, how to encourage functional movement, and so on can all be important to optimally helping a child move.

Positioning Considerations

Proper positioning for children with physical disabilities is also critical to facilitating typical and functional movement patterns, thereby encouraging child skill development and independence. In selecting optimal positions for a child with physical disabilities, parents, teachers, and therapists should work together to answer the following questions: Is the position developmentally appropriate? Does the position reinforce development of functional skills? Does the position discourage movement patterns that should be avoided (e.g., primitive reflex patterns)? Is the position a realistic alternative that will be used throughout typical home and school routines and activities (Heller et al., 2000)?

Sometimes children with physical disabilities will need special adaptive positioning equipment or devices in order to maintain a functional position during typical activities at home or at school. Positioning devices can be simple such as rolled towels or blankets to help maintain body position. However, some children will need commercially purchased equipment, such as special seating devices, wheelchairs, and wedges, in order to be optimally positioned for functional movement. Positioning devices, such as a prone stander, have additional benefits, such as promoting bone growth (see Figure 4–11). Parents, teachers, and therapists should work together to determine what positioning devices are needed for individual children.

EDUCATIONAL IMPLICATIONS

The educational team must understand typical motor development in children in order to understand where the child with atypical development functions, what concomitant problems may occur, and what secondary problems should be prevented. This understanding will help the team meet the student's needs, determine appropriate educational goals and interventions, and make appropriate environmental adaptations and necessary referrals to support personnel.

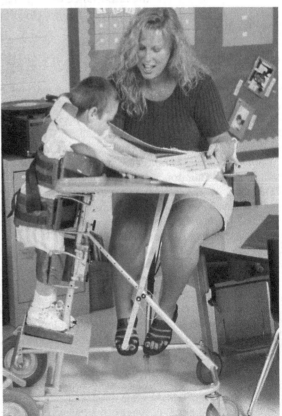

FIGURE 4–11 A young child is doing an activity in her prone stander. The straps around her shoulders help keep her arms forward so she can access the activity.

The child with atypical motor development will require ongoing input from a team of professionals if his physical and sensory needs are to be met and motor development is to reach its maximum potential. Physical and occupational therapists should work together with families and teachers on proper positioning and handling techniques to encourage the student's optimal motor performance and allow for maximum functional independence. Additionally, all team members should be instructed in the use of any adaptive equipment (such as special seating and feeding equipment) or adaptive devices (such as braces and splints) that can facilitate a student's functional motor performance. Ongoing input from the professional team will be important to make necessary changes to motor goals and outcomes as the child develops and changes. Likewise, changes in motor goals are often needed following surgical interventions.

For students with atypical motor development, the educational team may need to adapt how classroom material is presented and how the student is expected to respond. These adaptations will need to consider the individual student's motor strengths and weaknesses. Sometimes alternative movements that the student can accomplish (e.g., switches, eye gaze, and so on) are used. Whatever adaptations are chosen, they should be used across all settings (see chapter 8 on assistive technology and chapter 12 on classroom adaptations).

SUMMARY

This chapter discussed motor development, both typical and atypical. The theoretical framework for discussing development included the following assumptions: (a) development is a collection of processes across domains, (b) development occurs as a process reflective of self-organization of the individual, and (c) development is a transactional process between genetic makeup and the environment. An understanding of typical motor development was cited as critical to understanding atypical motor development. Some of the common problems associated with atypical motor development and their interventions were covered. Motor development as it relates to hearing or vision loss was also discussed. Additionally, information on proper positioning and basic body mechanics for lifting was covered. Finally, the importance of a team approach in the educational evaluation and planning for students with atypical motor development was stressed.

REFERENCES

Campbell, S. K. (2006). The child's development of functional movement. In S. K. Campbell, D. W. Vander Linden, & R. J. Palisano (Eds.), *Physical therapy for children* (3rd ed., pp. 33–76). St. Louis: Saunders/Elsevier.

Cronin, A., & Mandich, M. B. (Eds.). (2005). *Human development and performance throughout the lifespan.* Clifton Park, NY: Thomson Delmar Learning.

Dennis, C. W., & Schlough, K. A. (2004). Gross motor development. In S. R. Hooper & W. Umansky (Eds.), *Young children with special needs* (4th ed., pp. 224–266). Upper Saddle River, NJ: Pearson Education.

Effgen, S. K. (2005). *Meeting the physical therapy needs of children.* Philadelphia: F. A. Davis.

Forney, P. E., & Heller, K. W. (2004). Sensorimotor development: Implications for the educational team. In F. P. Orelove, D. Sobsey, & R. K. Silberman (Eds.), *Educating children with multiple disabilities: A collaborative approach* (4th ed., pp. 193–247). Baltimore: Brookes.

Goldfield, E. C., & Wolff, P. H. (2004). A dynamical systems perspective on infant action and its development. In G. Bremner & A. Slater (Eds.), *Theories of infant development* (pp. 3–29). Malden, MA: Blackwell.

Heller, K. W., Forney, P. E., Alberto, P. A., Schwartzman, M. N., & Goeckel, T. M. (2000). *Meeting physical and health needs of children with disabilities: Teaching student participation and management.* Belmont, CA: Wadsworth/Thomson Learning.

Hooper, S. R., & Umansky, W. (2004). *Young children with special needs* (4th ed.). Upper Saddle River, NJ: Pearson Education.

Montgomery, P. C., & Connolly, B. H. (Eds.). (2003). *Clinical applications for motor control.* Thorofare, NJ: SLACK.

Orelove, F. P., Sobsey, D., & Silberman, R. K. (Eds.). (2004). *Educating children with multiple disabilities: A collaborative approach* (4th ed.). Baltimore: Brookes.

Pellegrino, L. (2007). Cerebral palsy. In M. L. Batshaw, L. Pellegrino, & N. J. Roizen (Eds.) *Children with disabilities* (6th ed.). Baltimore: Brookes.

Shumway-Cook, A., & Woollacott, M. H. (2001). *Motor control: Theory and practical application.* Philadelphia: Lippincott Williams & Wilkins.

Smith Roley, S., Blanche, E. I., & Schaaf, R. C. (2001). *Understanding the nature of sensory integration with diverse populations.* San Antonio, TX: Therapy Skill Builders.

Thelen, E. (2000). Grounded in the world: Developmental origins of the embodied mind. *Infancy, 1,* 3–28.

PART II
NEUROMOTOR IMPAIRMENTS

5

CEREBRAL PALSY

Kathryn Wolff Heller and Jennifer Tumlin Garrett

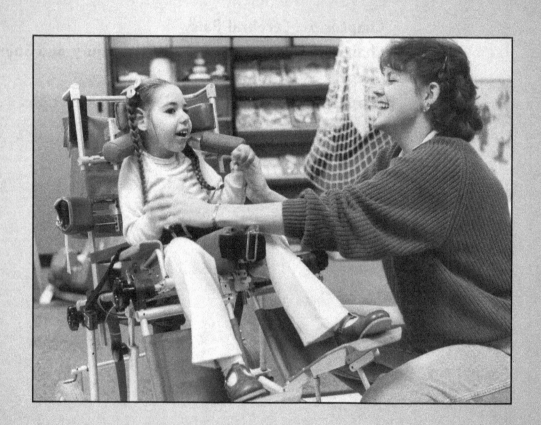

Cerebral palsy means brain (cerebral) paralysis (palsy). It is a loosely descriptive term that refers to a variety of disorders of voluntary movement and posture. Dr. George Little first used the term in the 1860s to describe a form of cerebral palsy that he thought resulted from a lack of oxygen at birth. Since then, however, many new insights into the causal factors of cerebral palsy have evolved.

It is estimated that cerebral palsy occurs in about 1 to 2.4 per 1,000 live births and 15% of premature infants (Beers, Porter, Jones, Kaplan, & Berkwits, 2006; Nelson, 2002). As more low-birth-weight infants have survived premature birth, the prevalence of cerebral palsy has risen, often resulting in additional associated conditions (Nelson, 2003). Depending on the type and severity, children with cerebral palsy present a diverse range of characteristics. Some children's cerebral palsy will be barely noticeable; others will have such severe motor impairment that they will need assistance or adaptations to perform even simple physical tasks. The diversity among children with cerebral palsy requires the educational team to examine the individual characteristics of each child in order to provide optimal treatment and educational support.

This chapter will begin by providing a description of cerebral palsy and its etiology. A brief overview of neuroanatomy is also provided to understand how the various types of cerebral palsy emerge. Characteristics, detection, and treatment options will also be described as well as the educational implications.

DESCRIPTION OF CEREBRAL PALSY

Cerebral palsy (CP) can be defined as a group of nonprogressive disorders characterized by impaired voluntary movement or posture resulting from a brain injury or brain defect occurring before birth, during birth, or within the first few years of life (Beer et al., 2006; Miller, 2005). Another way to conceptualize this is to regard cerebral palsy as a static lesion of the immature brain that causes a permanent motor impairment (Miller, 2005). It has been suggested to add to the definition that cerebral palsy is often accompanied by disorders of sensation, cognition, communication, perception, and/or behavior as well as epilepsy (Bax et al., 2005).

There are several parts of the definition that need further explanation. First, the term *cerebral palsy* refers to a group of disorders. Although they all affect voluntary movement or posture, cerebral palsy has several different etiologies and different types of motor impairments (e.g., spastic and athetoid). Because of this, cerebral palsy may be referred to in the plural (i.e., cerebral palsies) or as cerebral palsy syndromes.

Cerebral palsy is nonprogressive, meaning that the brain lesion does not progress. However, the symptoms of cerebral palsy may get worse (Beers et al., 2006; Blair & Stanley, 1997). For example, movement may become more inhibited over time because of the development of **contractures** (shortening of muscles), or sitting may become difficult because of the development of **scoliosis** (curvature of the spine).

Since cerebral palsy occurs before, during, or within a few years after birth, it influences the way children develop. It is therefore considered a **developmental disability**. It is important to note that several conditions may occur to a child later in life that appears similar to cerebral palsy. For example, a 10-year-old who has a severe brain injury from being hit by a car may have a motor impairment that appears similar to spastic cerebral palsy. However, since it did not occur during the developmental period (i.e., it did not affect the developing brain), it is not considered cerebral palsy but is referred to as spasticity (due to a **traumatic brain injury**).

ETIOLOGY OF CEREBRAL PALSY

Explaining that cerebral palsy occurs from a static brain lesion does not give any information about the etiology. Originally, the etiology was attributed to birth asphyxia (lack of oxygen at birth), but it has been found that prenatal factors and, to a lesser extent, perinatal and postnatal factors can cause cerebral palsy (Griffin, Fitch, & Griffin, 2002; Nelson, 2003). Some prenatal causes of cerebral palsy include brain malformation, genetic syndromes, and congenital infections (see chapter 23) (Nelson, 2003). Perinatal causes include such causes as asphyxia, stroke, and certain infections acquired during delivery. Several postnatal causes have been identified, such as meningitis, ingestion of certain toxins or poisons (e.g., lead), anoxia (as in near drowning or strangulation), and head trauma due to vehicle accidents or child abuse (Griffin et al., 2002; Russman & Ashwal, 2004). Unless the cause is a postnatal factor, determining the precise etiology of cerebral palsy in some children is often difficult.

In addition to these causes, there are also several risk factors for the development of cerebral palsy prenatally, including maternal seizures, toxemia of pregnancy, maternal bleeding, multiple births, placental complications, and maternal chronic infection (Griffin et al., 2002; Russman & Ashwal, 2004; Sankar & Mundkur, 2005). Other risk factors include stroke, thrombosis (blood clot), caesarian delivery, intrauterine growth restrictions, nutritional deficits, low birth weight, and prebirth hemorrhages (Griffin et al., 2002; Nelson, 2003; Reid et al., 2006; Sankar & Mundkur, 2005). It has also been found that in children who experience blood flow reduction prior to 32 to 34 weeks' gestation may have brain damage and hemorrhage (Griffin et al., 2002).

DYNAMICS OF CEREBRAL PALSY

Many minor static lesions in the brain do not result in cerebral palsy (Miller, 2005). However, when static lesions occur in one of the motor areas of the brain, cerebral palsy can result. To gain a better understanding of how cerebral palsy occurs, we still start with an overview of the nervous system and specific motor areas of the brain associated with the different types of cerebral palsy.

Overview of the Nervous System

The nervous system is one of the most complex and fascinating systems of the human body. It has reached a level of complexity that separates humans from all other animals on earth. It provides us with the ability to do such things as think, move, feel, and breathe. It can be divided into three parts: (a) the **central nervous system** (consisting of the brain and spinal cord), (b) the **peripheral nervous system** (consisting of the nerves that connect the spinal cord to the other parts of the body), and (c) the **autonomic nervous system** (which regulates the functioning on internal organs as well as the internal environment). These systems are dependent on transmission of information by the **neurons**, commonly referred to as nerve cells.

The nervous system is composed of more than 100 billion neurons that transmit information between the different parts of the brain as well as between the brain and other parts of the body. Although there are many different kinds of neurons, a typical motor neuron is composed of multiple dendrites (which receive information), a soma (cell body), and a single axon (which sends information) (see Figure 5–1). When several axons are bound together, they form a nerve. Some axons are encased in a fatlike substance known as myelin, which serves as a conductor to speed transmission.

Most neurons in the central nervous system transmit information through electrical-chemical reactions. A neuron is stimulated (fires) and sends an electrical impulse down the axon, which can be as short as a few microns (approximately .00004 of an inch) or several feet in length. The end of the axon has several projections known as (presynaptic) axon terminals, which connect to multiple (sometimes thousands of) other neurons. When the electrical impulse reaches the terminal, it stimulates the release of one of the many different types of **neurotransmitters** (e.g., dopamine or norepinephrine). The neurotransmitter travels across a small gap, known as a synapse, to receptors on the next neuron's dendrite or cell body. As the neurotransmitter binds to a receptor, it will either facilitate transmission of the impulse (excitatory) or decrease the likelihood that the impulse will continue (inhibitory) along that particular neuron. Since thousands of axon terminals may synapse on one neuron's dendrites and cell body, it is the collective action of the neurotransmitters that will determine whether that specific neuron fires an electric impulse. Many medications used to treat such conditions as movement disorders, seizures, and attention-deficit/hyperactivity disorder act on neurotransmitters or their receptors to facilitate or inhibit neurons from firing.

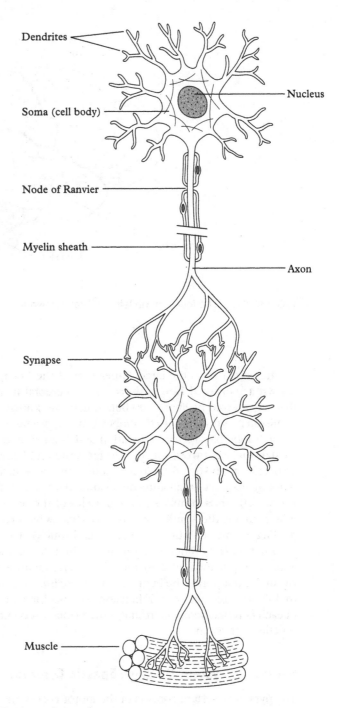

Dendrites

Nucleus

Soma (cell body)

Node of Ranvier

Myelin sheath

Axon

Synapse

Muscle

FIGURE 5–1 Basic anatomy of a neuron.

The central nervous system is composed of three levels: the spinal cord, the lower brain (subcortical), and the higher brain (cortical). The spinal cord allows for transmission of information to and from the body as well as the presence of several types of reflexes. The lower brain (e.g., brain stem, hypothalamus, thalamus, cerebellum, and basal ganglia) controls much of what is referred to as subconscious activity, such as respiration, blood pressure, salivation, and emotional patterns (e.g., reactions to pain and anger). The higher brain has several functions, such as storage of information, making the functions of the lower brain centers more precise, and our thinking processes (Guyton & Hall, 2006). It contains the largest structure of the brain known as the **cerebrum**.

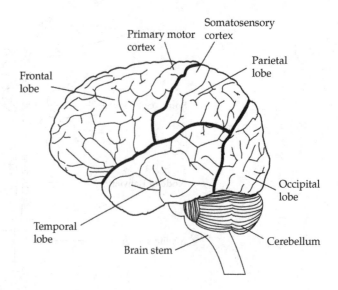

FIGURE 5–2 The lobes of the left cerebral hemispheres and the left cerebellum.

The cerebrum is the large, upper part of the brain, composed of a right and a left side, known as **cerebral hemispheres**. Each cerebral hemisphere has numerous convolutions that are covered by about 100 billion neurons, known as the cerebral cortex. Each cerebral hemisphere is divided into four lobes: frontal, parietal, temporal, and occipital (see Figure 5–2).

Each lobe has a specific location and is attributed to certain functions of the brain, although the areas work together to integrate and interpret information. The frontal lobe is associated with such functions as judgment, personality, elaboration of thought (including working memory), regulating behavior, and movement. It contains the **primary motor cortex** which sends impulses to the muscles of the body, resulting in movement. The parietal lobe contains the **somatosensory cortex**, which receives information from the body regarding simple sensations (e.g., pain and touch). The parietal lobe also integrates sensory information from different modalities. The temporal lobe is the primary receptor area for auditory input and is also attributed to such functions as long-term memory. Located primarily in the temporal lobe in one hemisphere is an area known as Wernicke's area, which has to do with language comprehension. The occipital lobe is located at the very back portion of each cerebral hemisphere and is the primary receptor area for visual input and associated functions of vision.

Pyramidal System Damage: Spastic Cerebral Palsy

The pyramidal system consists of the motor cortex and the pathways from the motor cortex that descend to the spinal cord (known as the pyramidal tract). The motor cortex is located in the posterior one-third of the frontal lobe. It is divided into three sections: the primary motor cortex (also known as the motor strip), the supplementary motor area, and the premotor area. The motor neurons on the primary motor cortex (also known as **upper motor neurons**) control voluntary movement. The supplementary and premotor areas assist in motor functioning, such as supporting complex patterns of movement (e.g., a surgeon's hand movements) (Guyton & Hall, 2006). Specialized areas are also part of the motor cortex, such as Broca's area, which controls the movements needed for speech.

Specific areas of the primary motor cortex control certain body parts. This is often represented using a motor homunculus, which is a distorted upside-down human figure that is drawn over the primary motor cortex to reflect the areas on the cortex that control certain body parts. This is also called "the little man inside the brain" since *homunculus* means "lit-

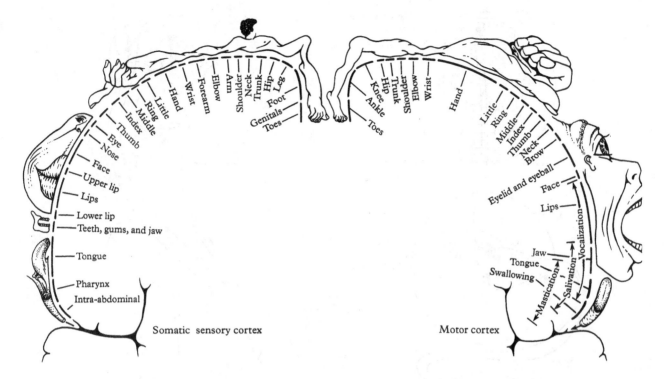

FIGURE 5–3   The motor homunculus and the sensory homunculus that correspond to movement or perception on the primary motor cortex and somatosensory cortex.

tle man" in Latin. As seen in Figure 5–3, the top of the primary motor cortex has neurons controlling the movement of the legs and buttocks, and the bottom has neurons controlling the lips and jaw. The hand on the homunculus is particularly large since there are a great number of neurons on the primary motor cortex that are devoted to all the fine motor movements the hand can make.

The pyramidal tract is composed of the axons from the primary motor cortex. These axons descend through the brain, and at about the level of the brain stem, the majority of them cross over to the opposite side. From that point, this tract continues down the spinal cord and synapses onto neurons in the spinal cord (known as the **lower motor neuron**). From the lower motor neuron, axons leave the spinal cord and go out to the body to where they terminate at various muscles. Because most of the axons cross over, the left side of the brain controls movement on the right side of the body and vice versa.

If a person wanted to move his right leg to kick a ball, for example, the upper motor neurons located on the top part of the left primary motor cortex would be stimulated. Impulses would travel down their axons to the lower motor neurons in the lower portion of the spinal cord (see Figure 5–4). The impulses would exit the spinal cord along the lower motor neuron axons until they ended at the leg muscles and stimulated the leg muscles to contract, making the leg muscles move. In order for the brain to know that the ball has been kicked, another chain of neurons, known as sensory neurons, transmit information from the leg to the somatosensory cortex of the brain informing the brain of the leg movement and the sensation of hitting the ball.

When there is damage to the pyramidal system during gestation or within the first few years of life, **spastic cerebral palsy** may occur. Spastic cerebral palsy is the most common form of cerebral palsy, occurring in over 70% of those with cerebral palsy (Beers et al., 2006). Damage to the pyramidal system results in increased muscle tone to the part of the body corresponding to the location of the damaged neurons on the primary motor cortex. For example, if there is damage near the top of both primary motor cortexes, both legs will have

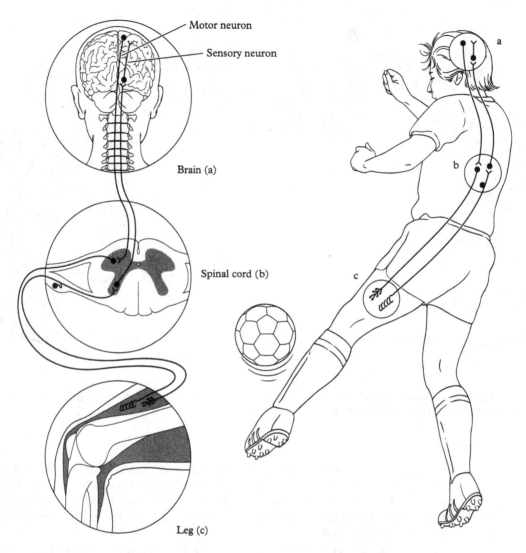

Motor neuron

Sensory neuron

Brain (a)

Spinal cord (b)

Leg (c)

FIGURE 5–4 A chain of motor and sensory neurons sends and receives information.

spasticity (diplegia). If the motor cortex on the left side of the brain is damaged, there would be spasticity on the right side of the body.

Basal Ganglia Damage: Dyskinetic Cerebral Palsy

There are other brain structures and pathways that are outside the pyramidal motor system that also contribute to motor control. One of these is the basal ganglia. If the front part of the cerebral hemispheres were cut off, there would be visible aggregates of cell bodies that resemble gray islands found among the white axons in the middle of the brain. These islands are known as basal ganglia and are part of the extrapyramidal system (meaning "outside the pyramidal system") (see Figure 5–5).

The basal ganglia work in conjunction with the primary motor cortex to make smooth, well-controlled motor movements. The basal ganglia control the intensity, direction, speed, and sequencing of complex movement patterns (e.g., writing the letter "A" in a slow or fast or large or small manner or cutting with scissors) (Guyton & Hall, 2006). The basal ganglia are also attributed to inhibiting muscle tone throughout the body. Because of these different functions, damage to the basal ganglia can result in abnormal patterns of movement or very rigid muscle contractions.

Inhibits muscle tone throughout the body

Damage = abnormal patterns of movement or rigid muscle contraction

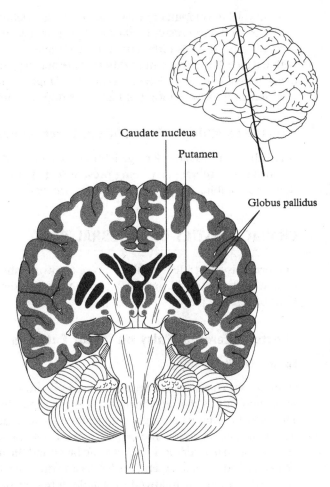

Caudate nucleus

Putamen

Globus pallidus

FIGURE 5–5 The basal ganglia of the brain.

Abnormal development or damage to the basal ganglia results in movement disorders. When they occur during gestation or within the first few years of life, it is referred to as **dyskinetic cerebral palsy**, the second most common form of cerebral palsy, occurring in about 20% of children with cerebral palsy (Beers et al., 2006). Damage to the basal ganglia can interfere with its functions as a relay center that works with the motor cortex to control movement. When these circuits are blocked because of brain damage, the impulses take alternate, deviant routes. This can result in a type of dyskinetic cerebral palsy, known as athetoid cerebral palsy. Athetoid cerebral palsy may present as abnormal, involuntary movements that may be slow and writhing (**athetosis**) or rapid, random, and jerky (**chorea**) (Nehring, 2004). In some rare cases, the part of the basal ganglia that inhibits muscle tone can be affected and result in extremely high muscle tone and can be accompanied by abnormal posturing, known as **dystonia**.

Cerebellum Damage: Ataxic Cerebral Palsy

The cerebellum is an oval-shaped structure located below the occipital lobes of each cerebral hemisphere. The cerebellum significantly contributes to the coordination of movements, including the timing of motor activities (especially rapid movement such as running and playing the piano) and the smooth progression from one muscle movement to the next (Guyton & Hall, 2006). The cerebellum is also involved in the maintenance of balance and equilibrium of trunk and limbs and is part of the extrapyramidal system.

Abnormal development or damage to the cerebellum during gestation or within the first few years of life can result in **ataxia**, also known as **ataxic cerebral palsy**. In this form of cerebral palsy, there is difficulty in the coordination of voluntary movement and problems with balance. It is important to differentiate ataxia associated with cerebral palsy from such degenerative inherited diseases, as ataxia-telangiectasia and Friedreich's ataxia, which may look similar in presentation but have very different prognoses (Gold, 2005).

Damage to Multiple Areas: Mixed Cerebral Palsy

Some children will have damage in multiple areas of the brain. This results in several different forms of cerebral palsy being present (e.g., spastic and athetoid cerebral palsy). When there is a combination of types, the term *mixed cerebral palsy* is often used.

CHARACTERISTICS OF CEREBRAL PALSY

Cerebral palsy may affect a child's motor ability, communication, and cognition. An in-depth look at these areas will provide a better understanding of the characteristics and implications of cerebral palsy.

Effects of Cerebral Palsy on Motor Patterns

Spastic Cerebral Palsy

Students who have spastic cerebral palsy have muscles that are tight, other muscles that are weak, and others that are unaffected. Spastic muscles have increased tone (hypertonia). They usually contract strongly with sudden movement. The motor tone found in spasticity has been called a clasp-knife response or clasp-knife stiffness, which refers to similarity of tension found in opening a pocket knife blade and the initial muscle resistance to movement of a child with spastic cerebral palsy. As an arm or leg begins to move, there is an increased resistance to motion, followed by a sudden release of resistance or tension (Miller, 2005). This abnormality of tone can result in difficulty moving an arm to the intended target, missing the intended target, or being unable to reach the target (the latter being due to contractures that affect how far the arm can move). Fine motor control may be very poor when spasticity is severe, making writing with a pencil impossible.

Certain muscles are more likely to be affected than others. As muscles work together to cause movement, one set causes **flexion** (bending of a body part), and another causes **extension** (straightening). In spastic cerebral palsy, certain muscles tend to have excessive muscle tone, while the opposite muscles will tend to have reduced tone. The excess muscle tone tends to result in flexion of the fingers, wrists, and elbows. The legs are usually extended with hips internally rotated, resulting in the knees being brought together and the legs often crossing (scissoring). There may also be plantar flexion, which causes the child to be on tiptoe. Not all children with cerebral palsy will have all these motor abnormalities. The extent of involvement depends on which body parts are affected.

Spastic cerebral palsy also uses a topographical classification system to connote the location and number of limbs affected. The most common types are **diplegia**, **hemiplegia**, and **quadriplegia** (and when used as adjectives are spelled as *diplegic*, *hemiplegic*, and *quadriplegic*) (see Figure 5–6).

Diplegia.   In spastic diplegic cerebral palsy, the legs are primarily affected, and there is some arm involvement. Depending on the severity, the knees may tend to come tightly together, the legs may tend to cross over each other (scissoring), and the child may walk awkwardly and on tiptoe. Spastic diplegia is caused by damage to the upper part of the primary motor cortex that controls the legs in both the right and the left cerebral hemispheres.

Hemiplegia.   In spastic hemiplegic cerebral palsy, only one side of the body is affected. The arm and the leg on the affected side have increased muscle tone. The leg muscles are tight,

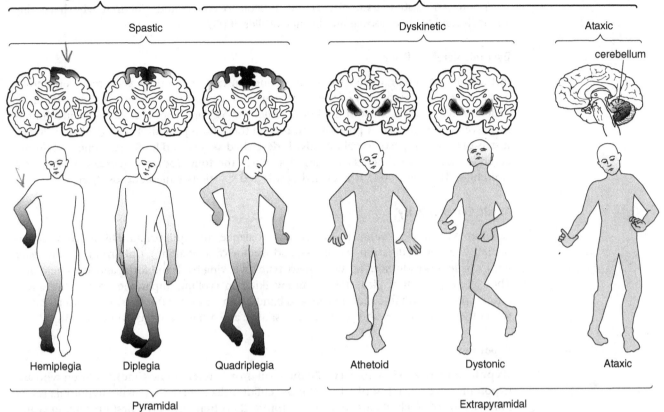

Regional Involvement | **Global (Total Body) Involvement**

Spastic | Dyskinetic | Ataxic

cerebellum

Hemiplegia | Diplegia | Quadriplegia | Athetoid | Dystonic | Ataxic

Pyramidal | Extrapyramidal

FIGURE 5–6 Topographical classification system of the types of spastic cerebral palsy. The darker the shading, the more severe the involvement.

Source. Used with permission from Batshaw (1997).

the child is on tiptoe, and the arm may be drawn into a bent position at the elbow. As discussed earlier, the motor tracts cross at the brain stem. Therefore, when there is hemiplegia on the left side of the body, the primary motor cortex in the right cerebral hemisphere is damaged.

Quadriplegia.   In spastic quadriplegic cerebral palsy, all four limbs are involved—the legs usually more severely than the arms. The trunk and the face may be involved as well. All the conditions described earlier pertaining to the arms, legs, and hips are usually found. Speech is typically affected. For this type of spastic cerebral palsy to occur, there must have been extensive damage to the primary motor cortex and pyramidal tracts on both sides of the brain.

Other Topographical Designations.   There are other types of topographical designations used to describe spastic cerebral palsy, although they are not as commonly encountered. Some of these include monoplegia (one limb), paraplegia (legs only), triplegia (three limbs), and double hemiplegia (arms more involved than the legs).

Athetoid Cerebral Palsy

Individuals with athetoid cerebral palsy have slow, writhing, involuntary movements that are usually more pronounced in the arms (often referred to as **athetosis**). As the individual reaches for an item, there are external rotation and abduction movements in the shoulders (the shoulder causes the arm to be intermittently twisted away from the body) with the fingers often extending and fanning out. This appears as purposeless movements in which the limb rotates back and forth, extends and flexes, and slowly makes its way to the intended destination (sometimes missing the target). The athetoid movements occur when the person tries to voluntarily move or in times of excitement. Walking is also affected, and speech is often poorly articulated (**dysarthria**) and difficult to understand. Children who have only athetosis tend to have normal intelligence (Miller, 2005).

Dystonic Cerebral Palsy

In this form of cerebral palsy, there are strong muscle contractions with recurrent movement patterns. A single area of the body (e.g., a joint) may be affected, or it may be more generalized and affect most of the body (Miller, 2005). For example, a limb may involuntarily move into an abnormal position and remain there for a period of time (Nehring, 2004). Just as the tone in spastic cerebral palsy is described as "clasped knife," the tone in dystonic cerebral palsy is described as a "lead pipe" since the tone does not decrease with gentle stretching (Herring, 2002). However, dystonia and spasticity can occur together.

Ataxic Cerebral Palsy

Children with ataxic cerebral palsy have poor balance and equilibrium. This is often accompanied with incoordination, weakness, and tremor (fine shaking). Children typically walk with a wide unsteady gait, feet wide apart, trunk weaving back and forth, and arms held out. They often appear to walk as if they were walking on a rolling ship in the ocean. Clumsiness is often present with fine motor tasks, and handwriting is often affected. Ataxia often occurs with other types of cerebral palsy such as spastic and athetoid forms (Miller, 2005).

Hypotonic

Hypotonia refers to low tone (while the term *atonia* refers to no tone). Children who are hypotonic have been described as "floppy" children, like rag dolls. Usually, hypotonia refers not to a type of cerebral palsy but to a symptom. It is often one of the first presenting symptoms of an infant with cerebral palsy who may later develop spastic, dyskinetic, or mixed cerebral palsy. For example, an infant born with athetosis may first appear hypotonic, develop some tone over the next few years, and then develop athetosis (Miller, 2005).

Effects of Cerebral Palsy on Movement

Abnormal Movements

No matter which type of cerebral palsy a child has, there will be abnormalities of movement because normal movement requires a coordination of the muscles. A simple movement of bending the arm at the elbow requires using one set of muscles to relax (extensor muscles) and the opposing set to contract (flexor muscles). In a child or adult without disabilities, movement also depends on groups of muscles working together in patterns (Westcott & Goulet, 2005). No single muscle is responsible for the movement. One illustration of how muscles work together is the way a girl goes from a lying position on the floor (with her back against the floor) to a sitting position. As she lifts her head off the floor to sit up, her shoulders assist with the lifting, her arms move forward, her back rounds, and there is bending at the hips. This coordination of movement allows the easy execution of the desired movement. On the other hand, if she pushed her head back, her shoulder would go back, her spine would hollow, and her hips would straighten. This type of muscle coordination would make it almost impossible to sit up.

In the child with cerebral palsy, movements also occur in muscle patterns, but, because of the damage of the motor areas of the brain, the movements are uncoordinated and abnormal. These abnormal movements may be very mild and noticeable only when the child engages in a particular motor activity, such as running, or so severe that the child can move very little independently.

Severity

There is a range of severity of cerebral palsy. Various classification systems have been used, with some describing the severity as mild, moderate, and severe. In this system, mild cerebral palsy indicates very little impairment of movement; often, the fine motor movements are only slightly affected (e.g., difficulty writing). Students with moderate cerebral palsy can still perform the usual activities of daily living, although the motor impairment is quite visible and may result in a longer period of time needed for completion of the activities. Severe cerebral palsy refers to motor involvement so severe that the usual activities of daily living cannot be carried out without extensive adaptations. There has been recent debate, however, about the lack of operational definition and the lack of the reliability of this type of classification system (Bax et al., 2005; Rosenbaum, 2006). Other classifications, using numbers, have also been developed to try to be more precise. For example, the Gross Motor Function Classification System describes a five-level system by which to classify the motor function of children with cerebral palsy, ranging from level I, in which the child can walk but has some limitations in advanced gross motor skills, to level V, in which self-mobility is severely limited even with assistive technology mobility devices (Palisano et al., 1997) (see Figure 5–7).

Primitive Reflexes

In addition to abnormal motor movements, the child with cerebral palsy will have persistent primitive reflexes. As discussed in chapter 4, primitive reflexes are normally present in the first few months of life, and most are integrated into voluntary motor patterns within the first year. Children with cerebral palsy typically have a continuation of these primitive reflexes, which can interfere with maintaining or moving into various positions as well as achieving developmental milestones such as sitting and walking. Abnormalities of the postural reactions also contribute to these problems.

Contractures

Further difficulties in movement are present when contractures occur. Contractures are permanent muscular shortenings in which the muscle length is reduced or there is a fixed resistance to movement. This reduces the child's range of motion and ability to move the limb fully. Contractures can be very debilitating and can result in minimal use of limbs.

Effects of Cerebral Palsy on Communication

The lack of coordinated muscle movement and the persistence of primitive reflexes found in cerebral palsy may also affect the oropharyngeal muscles—those controlling the mouth and throat. Speech may be slurred and poorly articulated (dysarthria), making it difficult to understand. In some cases, it can be so severe that no speech may be present (anarthria).

Cerebral palsy may also affect nonverbal forms of communication. Facial expressions may be strained, and difficulty with head control may impede making eye contact. This may be mistaken for a lack of interest. A student with severe spastic cerebral palsy may want an item and reach for it but knock it away because of abnormal motor movements. This could be mistaken for the student's not wanting the item when the student cannot verbally request it or explain the unintentional motor movement.

Effects of Cerebral Palsy on Cognition

Children with cerebral palsy may be gifted, have normal intelligence, or have intellectual disabilities. Overall, there is a significant incidence of intellectual disability in children with cerebral palsy, with some accounts of up to 60% of individuals with cerebral palsy having intellectual disabilities (Sankar & Mundkur, 2005). Specific learning disabilities, such as those involving visual perception, as well as attention deficit disorders are also present more than would be expected in the general population (Hoon, 2005; Rosenbaum, 2003a). However, it is often difficult to obtain an accurate assessment of intelligence and learning when there is severe motor and speech involvement. This is especially true when the child has no reliable means of responding to questions, that is, has not learned an augmentative or alternative form of communication well enough that it is dependable.

60% of kids w/ CP have intell. disabilities

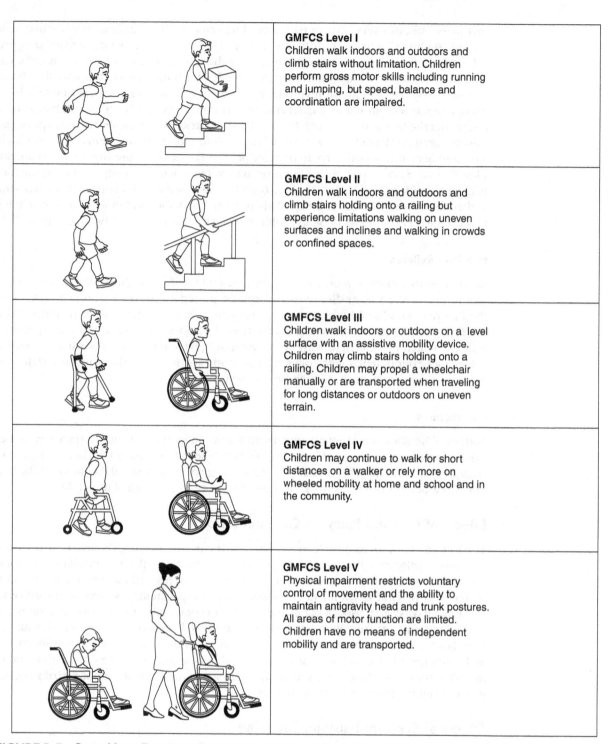

FIGURE 5–7 Gross Motor Functional Classification System (GMFCS) for children with cerebral palsy.
Source. Used with permission from Graham (2005).

Certain types of cerebral palsy have been associated with an increased incidence of intellectual disability. Persons with spastic diplegia and athetoid cerebral palsy may have no intellectual disabilities. Children with spastic quadriplegia, however, have a higher association of intellectual disabilities or learning disabilities than persons with spastic hemiplegia (Russman & Ashwal, 2004).

Additional Impairments

There is an increased incidence of other types of disabilities occurring in children with cerebral palsy. Seizures occur in about 25% of individuals with cerebral palsy (Beers et al., 2006). Sensory impairments also commonly occur. In athetoid cerebral palsy, **sensorineural hearing loss** is often present. Any one of several types of visual impairments may be present, the most common of which are motility defects (defects in moving the eye as in such conditions as strabismus), nystagmus, refractory errors, and optic atrophy (Russman & Ashwal, 2004) (see chapter 11).

Additional disorders may be the result of the cerebral palsy itself. These conditions usually result from abnormal muscle control and unequal muscle pull. One example is hip dislocation in which the hip bone is displaced from the socket. This is most commonly present in spastic cerebral palsy. Another example is scoliosis or other abnormal curvatures of the spine that can occur in cerebral palsy because of poor muscle control on the growing spine (Miller, 2005) (see chapter 9).

DETECTION OF CEREBRAL PALSY

It is difficult to detect cerebral palsy in the newborn. The baby will not display the typical motor characteristics of a child with cerebral palsy. After a few months, very subtle changes can be mistaken for any number of conditions or may even be considered normal. The child may have an excessive or feeble cry. There may be some asymmetry in motion or contour. The infant may appear listless or irritable. There may be some difficulty feeding, sucking, or swallowing. The child may have low muscle tone or abnormal muscle tone.

Near the end of the first year and into the second year, the infant may display persistent primitive reflexes, lagging motor development (with failure to reach motor milestones when typically indicated), and altered muscle tone. Hand preference may also be present, which is abnormal prior to 12 to 15 months of age. Consequently, a particular type of cerebral palsy often cannot be distinguished until after the first 12 to 18 months of life when the specific motor symptoms develop, and often a cause cannot be found (Rosenbaum, 2003a). However, early detection and treatment of at-risk children may promote development and independence and prevent secondary problems.

TREATMENT OF CEREBRAL PALSY

The goal of treating cerebral palsy is to develop maximum independence. There are several treatments that may be used to address the problems associated with voluntary movement or posture. The child with cerebral palsy benefits from physical, occupational, and speech therapy; positioning devices; orthotic devices; medications; and sometimes surgery to improve motor function.

Physical, Occupational, and Speech Therapies

Physical and occupational therapies provide support to children with cerebral palsy. Most therapy attempts to reduce the abnormal movement patterns and encourage normal, purposeful movement in an active and functional manner. Therapy can help the child take in, sort out, and connect information from the environment. Common to the different types of therapy is the emphasis on proper positioning, therapeutic handling, use of automatic reactions, and equilibrium responses (see chapter 4 on the different types of therapies). In addition, speech-language therapy may be able to improve speech production, although augmentative communication will be needed by many individuals with severe spastic quadriplegic cerebral palsy.

Positioning and Mobility Devices

The child with cerebral palsy may need to be positioned in several different types of adaptive equipment. The purpose of this equipment is to promote good body alignment, prevent contractures and deformities, promote movement and comfort, lessen effects of abnormal muscle tone and reflexes, improve circulation, decrease risk of pressure sores (decubitus ulcers), decrease fatigue, and promote bone growth (when weight bearing) (Jones & Gray, 2005). Positioning also provides access to the environment and facilitates performance of certain activities. There is a correspondence between activities and specific positions. For example, a boy with cerebral palsy positioned in a side lyer (equipment that props the person up on his side) may have better use of his left arm, allowing him to participate in the group activity by using a switch.

Specific equipment is prescribed according to the type of motor problem, the child's size and weight, and the nature of the activity. Equipment (such as side lyers, wedges, special seating devices, and prone standers) is commonly used (see chapter 4). Such equipment needs to be specifically adjusted for an individual child by a physical therapist or other qualified professional. There is typically a prescribed period of time the child should spend in the equipment to avoid injury or fatigue; the therapist determines the length of time.

Other equipment, such as scooters, bikes, walkers, and wheelchairs, may assist with mobility (see chapter 8). Often, modifications are made to these mobility devices to allow for proper positioning. Wheelchairs, for example, may have special inserts to keep the knees apart (abductor pad) or the body aligned (lateral supports). Head support may be necessary as well. Some wheelchairs are motorized to allow independent movement for children with upper arm involvement. Again, a physical therapist should help prescribe or modify this mobility equipment, which should help the student be as independent as possible. Since much of the equipment is custom fitted, it is not interchangeable among students.

Orthoses

The child with cerebral palsy may also need to use various braces or splints (**orthoses**). By applying an orthotic splint or brace, the muscle group is placed in a more functional position. This helps maintain proper alignment, improves range of motion, and decreases the development of contractures.

There are many different types of orthoses. To prevent toe walking and the shortening of the Achilles' tendon, a short leg splint may be worn. This is known as an AFO (ankle-foot orthosis) (see Figure 5-8). To help improve hand function, a resting hand splint or hand cone may be used. Since most of these are made specifically for the child, they must be carefully monitored by the therapists for correct fit as the child grows. Staff members should look for and report any reddening of the area or skin breakdown. Also, close adherence to the times the orthosis is supposed to be worn is important if treatment is to be effective (see chapter 4 for more information on orthotics).

Medication

Several medications may be taken to control excess muscle tone and promote relaxation of the muscles. Two commonly prescribed oral medications are Valium (Diazepam) and Dantrium. Side effects may occur, including drowsiness, excessive drooling, and changes in memory, attention, and behavior (Verrotti, Greco, Spalice, Chiarelli, & Iannetti, 2006). Careful monitoring of the side effects and effectiveness are necessary to make any needed adjustments in dosage or to try new treatments.

Baclofen has been found to be useful in the management of spasticity and is often delivered by an implantable pump. Baclofen acts by impeding the release of excitatory neurotransmitters. It is considered to be among the most effective substances in reducing severe spasticity in upper and lower extremities (Verrotti et al., 2006), although it is not effective with everyone. Intrathecal administration consists of inserting a tube into the intrathecal space of the spine. The tube is connected to a battery-operated pump that is implanted in

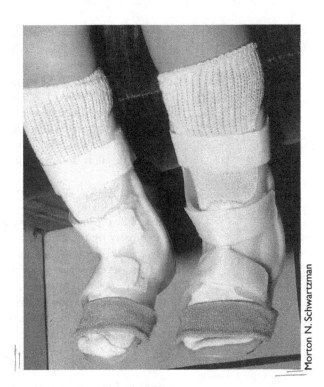

FIGURE 5–8 A child wearing AFOs (ankle-foot orthoses).

Morton N. Schwartzman

the abdominal area. The pump can be programmed by an external radiowave contoller, and the pump reservoir is filled by direct injection through the skin over the device. It may take 3 to 6 months after implantation of the pump before finding a constant level of the drug that will decrease spasticity. Complications can occur with the pump (e.g., infection or catheter [tube] breakage) and side effects of the medication (e.g., hallucinations and psychosis if the medication is suddenly withdrawn) (Miller, 2005).

Another medication that may be used is botulinum toxin, which reduces excessive muscle tone in spasticity and dystonia. Although botulinum toxin is produced by the bacterium that causes botulism, in small quantities is can be safely injected into the spastic muscles (Pellegrino, 2007). Since there is a limit as to how much botulinum toxin can be injected at one time, it works best in children requiring only one or two muscles to be injected (Herring, 2002). It can be effective for up to 3 to 4 months (Verrotti et al., 2006). Side effects include muscle weakness and pain during injection.

Surgery

Surgery may be needed to increase range of motion, decrease discomfort, and/or increase functional use of a body part. Individuals with cerebral palsy are especially at risk of developing contractures, which shorten muscle length and decrease range of motion of a joint. Other impairments may also occur that require surgical intervention.

Orthopedic Surgery

Several different surgical procedures are designed to treat contractures. One common surgery is used to correct the foot deformity of the ankle that results in the child being on tiptoe. In this surgery, the Achilles' tendon (heel cord) is lengthened, resulting in the foot being placed flat on the ground. Because this surgery will allow the child to stand with flat feet, it may assist in walking.

There are many other surgical procedures used to improve the range of motion in the arms and legs due to contractures. The surgical goal of treating children with spasticity in the arms is to release the spastic deformity and reposition the arm to improve its functional use (Kreulen, Smeulders, Veeger, & Hage, 2006). The hamstring muscles in the legs may be released to help with sitting and walking. Surgery to release the tendons and muscle that result in hip deformities may be needed. These surgeries are aimed at preventing hip dislocation and allowing the child to assume a sitting position. If hip dislocation occurs, a more complicated surgical procedure will be needed to correct the dislocation (see chapter 9 on hip dislocation). Cerebral palsy also results in other problems such as curvatures of the spine (e.g., scoliosis). This may be a direct result of the abnormalities of muscle tone on the spinal column. Surgery may be needed to lessen the curve and prevent deformity (see chapter 9 on neuromuscular scoliosis).

Neurosurgery

Neurosurgical procedures have also been used to treat cerebral palsy. These procedures involve surgery on the central nervous system. One such procedure, known as a selective posterior dorsal rhizotomy, involves cutting a certain percentage of specific spinal nerve roots that cause severe spasticity of the legs (McLaughlin et al., 2002). This procedure has resulted in reduced spasticity and improvement in sitting, standing, and moving as well as pain reduction and decreased rate of muscle deformity. However, it has been associated with severe complications, such as spinal deformities and hip abnormalities, and in some cases with functional loss. With the emergence in intrathecal Baclofen as well as positive outcomes in orthopedic surgery, dorsal rhizotomies are not being performed as frequently (Miller, 2005).

Assistive Technology and Adaptations

Although the therapies and medical treatments will improve motor performance, the person with cerebral palsy will usually continue to have abnormalities of tone, movement, or posture. Depending on the severity of the motor impairment, this can affect the person's performance of tasks and activities. Several types of assistive technology and adaptations in the classroom are often needed to improve functioning (e.g., augmentative communication device, adapted keyboard, or adapted toothbrush) (see chapters 8 and 12 for more information).

Other Treatments and Therapies

There are several other treatments used to address the motor problems found in cerebral palsy, but they are not yet supported by the literature. In some cases, the literature base is too small, and additional research is needed. In other cases, the results are mixed. Some treatments are not supported by the literature, but the parents have elected to go ahead with the treatment and feel that they have been beneficial. Some example of these therapies include electrical stimulation, hyperbaric oxygen treatments, equine assisted therapy (hippotherapy), Adeli Suit, conductive education, patterning, craniosacral therapy, Feldenkrais therapy, and acupuncture (Liptak, 2005; Rosenbaum, 2003b).

COURSE OF CEREBRAL PALSY

Cerebral palsy is a chronic condition that will continue throughout the person's life. It is not considered a progressive condition because no further brain damage occurs. However, further impairments (such as contractures, curvatures of the spine, and hip dislocation) may result from abnormalities of tone and movement.

EDUCATIONAL IMPLICATIONS OF CEREBRAL PALSY

It is important that the teacher has a good understanding of cerebral palsy and each student's specific motor involvement and concomitant problems so the student's educational needs can be met.

Meeting Physical and Sensory Needs

Proper positioning of the student is very important since it influences body movement, in turn impacting the student's participation in activities. The teacher must also know the use of adaptive positioning devices (including the child's wheelchair) and be able to verify that the student is positioned in them correctly. To avoid injury to both the teacher and the student, the teacher should be trained in proper body mechanics when positioning a student (see chapter 4). The student's physical therapist and occupational therapist can help with positioning and handling techniques.

Teachers should be familiar with any additional treatment the student is receiving and with their role in providing carryover. The teacher should know the types, dosage, and side effects of medication the student is taking at school. When splints or braces are used, the teacher should be alert for any redness or skin breakdown as well as for poor fit. For the benefit of students in wheelchairs, the teacher should be familiar with minor wheelchair repairs. When the child returns to school after surgery, the teacher should understand any activity restrictions.

Because students with cerebral palsy may have other problems such as seizures, sensory impairments, or cognitive or processing issues, the teacher needs to have a good understanding of the adaptations and assistive technology that is needed for each student as well as how to provide systematic instruction. It is also important that the teacher educate others about the child's disability. Often when a child has severe cerebral palsy, others assume that the child has an intellectual disability, which may not be the case. Sensitivity and support is critical, as is encouragement in being as independent as possible.

Meeting Communication Needs

Children with cerebral palsy have a range of communication skills, from no speech impairments to having no speech. The speech-language pathologist, parent, teacher, and child should work closely together to promote effective forms of communication that may include speech, augmentative communication, or both.

Students with cerebral palsy may benefit from communication devices. Depending on the extent of the cerebral palsy, the student may have a combined system of gestures, signs, and electronic communication device as well as **nonsymbolic communication** (e.g., facial expressions and body movements). It is important that the child be provided an effective means to communicate in order to promote learning, socialization, and fulfilling basic wants and needs (see chapter 8 for more information on augmentative communication). The teacher must keep in mind that when the student is still learning a system of communication, assessments of the student's ability and intelligence may be inaccurate until the system of communication is mastered.

Meeting Learning Needs

Academic instruction for a child with cerebral palsy should be based on the student's cognitive level, not the motor disability level. Depending on the level of severity of the cerebral palsy, special equipment and adaptations may be needed to allow the student to function optimally in the school setting. Some students with very mild cerebral palsy may be slower in writing an assignment and need more time, while students with more severe cerebral palsy may need to use a computer with alternate access to complete an assignment (see Figure 5-9).

Adapted devices, such as use of a pencil grip (either commercially available or made of clay or sponge) and page turners, may be needed. For students unable to hold paper on the desk, the paper may be taped to the desk, or a clipboard may be used. Cutout desks may be used to allow the wheelchair to fit under the table and provide additional arm support. Other tables may need to be lowered for best fit. Whiteboards may also need to be lowered to allow the student access. The need for equipment should not preclude the student from going into the community and to various classes in school.

FIGURE 5–9 Student using a computer that he controls with a switch placed by his head.

Bob Daemmrich/PhotoEdit Inc.

For students who have severe communication problems, the teacher may need to adapt the presentation of material. Material may be presented in a multiple choice format (with numbers for each possible selection) to allow the student to choose the answer, or the student may indicate his response by eye gazing the answer presented in a multiple-choice format or by using a scanning device. Computers with adaptations such as switches, touch windows, alternate keyboards, and specialized software (e.g., on-screen keyboards, word prediction, or speech recognition) often facilitate academic work. These adaptations can either require only minimal movement to activate the device or allow for activation using alternative movement. The adaptations should be used across all settings (see chapters 8 and 12 for more information).

Meeting Daily Living Needs

Depending on the severity of motor involvement, some children will have difficulty with various daily living skills, including eating, dressing, toileting, personal hygiene, and carrying out normal activities of daily living. In the area of eating, the lack of coordination of oral movement, combined with the persistence of primitive reflexes (e.g., asymmetrical tonic neck reflex and bite reflex), may result in severe eating difficulties and drooling. Students may have such difficulties as a tongue thrust (causing food to be pushed out of the mouth), a bite reflex (causing the spoon to be bitten), and choking. Certain feeding techniques, such as those that provide jaw control, may be needed. Children with arm involvement may be unable to bring the spoon to their mouths or be unable to hold utensils. Some devices used for feeding, such as adapted dishes, cups, and utensils, may be necessary (see Figure 5-10). Some students will be unable to eat enough orally because of their oral-motor dysfunction and will need **gastrostomy tube** feedings (feedings through a tube going directly into the stomach) (Sullivan et al., 2005) (see chapter 20 for more information).

Most children with cerebral palsy will be able to use the toilet successfully, although bladder control is usually delayed by many years. Age at which toileting success is achieved is partly dependent on the severity of cerebral palsy and cognitive functioning. In one study by Roijen, Postema, Limbeek, and Kuppevelt (2001), 20% of children with high intellectual capability were still incontinent at 6 years of age, compared with 62% who had lower intel-

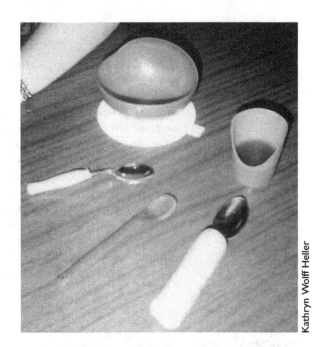

FIGURE 5–10 Examples of an adapted bowl and utensils.

lectual capability. Children with high intellectual ability and spasticity, diplegia, or hemiplegia had a good probability of achieving continence by their eighth birthday. When an intellectual disability is present, the teacher will need to use systematic instruction in toilet use (e.g., trip training strategies) after determining from the physician that there is not any medical reason impeding bladder/bowel control.

Teachers will need to facilitate toilet training by having appropriate adaptations in place. Adaptations such as handrails and a properly fitted adapted toilet are important to decrease fear of falling and allow the child to relax to allow elimination to occur. The student will also need a way to communicate that he needs to use the restroom. It is also important that the student be taught proper transferring techniques and that personnel be trained in correct lifting and handling techniques (see chapter 4).

Activities of daily living may require adaptations or assistive technology to allow the child to participate to the maximum extent possible. For example, toothbrush and toothpaste holders may be used to assist with toothbrushing. A dressing rack and adapted clothing fasteners may help the student dress; push-pull sticks may help with putting on socks. Environmental control devices that allow the child to activate items with a switch (e.g., to turn on lights or a television) may be useful. Switches may also be used for turning on any number of devices, such as electric blenders (see chapter 8 for more information on assistive technology).

Meeting Behavioral and Social Needs

The teacher needs to be alert for any difficulty the student may have with social interactions. Students with visible physical impairments, such as cerebral palsy, may become socially isolated because of their appearance and, often, because of poor social skills. The teacher may need to provide social skills training as well as specific strategies to use in maintaining interactions when communication is slow.

Students with cerebral palsy may also exhibit frustration and have behavioral outbursts when they cannot communicate effectively or are unable to accomplish a task because of their unintentional movements. Teachers need to be sensitive to the student's needs, provide augmented forms of communication, and provide alternate ways of accomplishing tasks.

SUMMARY

Cerebral palsy refers to a variety of disorders of posture and movement and occurs because of a static brain lesion that occurs before, during, or after birth. Several types of cerebral palsy exist, including spastic (pyramidal damage), dyskinetic (basal ganglia damage), and ataxic (cerebellum damage). Cerebral palsy can affect different regions of the body and can be classified as diplegia (legs with some arm involvement), hemiplegia (one side of the body), and quadriplegia (all four limbs affected).

Cerebral palsy can vary in severity, from mild to severe. With mild cerebral palsy, typically only fine motor movements are slightly impaired. In severe cerebral palsy, the student has significant limitations in arm and leg movement and impaired speech and typically needs extensive adaptations for daily living skills. Treatment may include physical, occupational, and speech-language therapy; positioning and mobility devices; use of orthotics; medication; or surgery. The teacher may need to make adaptations to accommodate physical, sensory, communication, learning, and behavioral and social needs of the students. It is important for all professionals to work together to provide best delivery of services possible.

 **Natalie's Story**

Natalie is a bright fourth-grade student who has spastic quadriplegic cerebral palsy. She uses a power wheelchair for mobility, uses an augmentative and alternative communication (AAC) device for communication because she is nonverbal, and has limited daily living skills (needs assistance in the restroom, eating, and accessing school materials). She is unable to write but can produce written work by connecting her AAC device to a computer and typing. At school, Natalie receives weekly physical therapy, occupational therapy, and speech therapy and is seen by the assistive technology specialist each month on a consultative basis to ensure that accommodations are being utilized and/or considered in her educational program. Although she is limited in her verbal ability, Natalie can read on approximately a second-grade level and is learning basic math facts in the resource room for students with physical and health disabilities. She is currently in science and social studies classes with her fourth-grade peers. Natalie's individualized education plan (IEP) committee decided years ago when Natalie entered elementary school that she would attend a school outside her neighborhood district. The committee based the decision on the severity of her disability and the fact that, at the time, her neighborhood school was inaccessible and did not have the proper equipment and support that Natalie needed. Natalie's sisters, however, have always attended their neighborhood school. At her IEP meeting this year, discussion about moving Natalie back to her neighborhood elementary school has arisen again. The IEP team is divided. Natalie's family wants her to be educated in the least restrictive environment in her neighborhood school with her sisters. The family feels that Natalie is entitled to the same supports in her neighborhood school that she is currently receiving. Although Natalie's special education teacher agrees that supports and services could be delivered in her neighborhood school, others on the committee believe that it would be inconvenient because the teachers and students in her current environment know how to interact with her. They also feel that it would be too costly to make environmental modifications in her neighborhood school and therefore too difficult to meet her physical needs. What do you think?

REFERENCES

Batshaw, M. L. (1997). *Children with disabilities* (4th ed.). Baltimore: Brookes.

Bax, M., Goldstein, M., Rosenbaum, P., Leviton, A., Paneth, N., Dan, B.; et al. (2005). Proposed definition and classification of cerebral palsy, April 2005. *Developmental Medicine and Child Neurology, 47,* 571–576.

Beers, M. H., Porter, R. S., Jones, T. V., Kaplan, J. L., & Berkwits, M. (2006). The Merck manual of diagnosis and therapy (18th ed.). Whitehouse Station, NJ: Merck & Co.

Blair, E., & Stanley, F. J. (1997). Issues in the classification and epidemiology of cerebral palsy. *Mental Retardation and Developmental Disabilities Research Reviews, 3,* 184–193.

Burmeister, R., Hannay, H. J., Copeland, K., Fletcher, J. M., Boudousquie, A., & Dennis, M. (2005). Attention problems and executive functions in children with spina bifida and hydrocephalus. *Child Neuropsychology, 11,* 265-283.

Gold, J. T. (2005). Pediatric disorders: Cerebral palsy and spina bifida. In H. H. Zaretsky, E. F. Richter, & M. G. Eisenberg (Eds.), *Medical aspects of disability* (3rd ed., pp. 447-493). New York: Springer.

Graham, H. K. (2005). Classifying cerebral palsy. *Journal of Pediatric Orthopedics, 25,* 127-128.

Griffin, H. C., Fitch, C. L., & Griffin, L. W. (2002). Causes and interventions in the area of cerebral palsy. *Infants and Young Children, 14,* 18-23.

Guyton, A. C., & Hall, J. E. (2006). *Textbook of medical physiology* (11th ed.). Philadelphia: Elsevier/Saunders.

Herring, J. A. (2002). *Tachdjian's pediatric orthopaedics* (3rd ed.). Philadelphia: W. B. Saunders.

Hoon, A. H., Jr. (2005). Neuroimaging in cerebral palsy: Patterns of brain dysgenesis and injury. *Journal of Child Neurology, 20,* 936-939.

Jones, M. J., & Gray, J. (2005). Assistive technology: Positioning and mobility. In S. K. Effgen (Ed.), Meeting *the physical therapy needs of children* (pp. 455-474). Philadelphia: F. A. Davis.

Kreulen, M., Smeulders, M. J. C., Veeger, H. E. J., & Hage, J. J. (2006). Movement patterns of the upper extremity and trunk before and after corrective surgery of impaired forearm rotation in patients with cerebral palsy. *Developmental Medicine and Child Neurology, 48,* 436-441.

Liptak, G. S. (2005). Complementary and alternative therapies for cerebral palsy. *Mental Retardation and Developmental Disabilities Research Reviews, 11,* 156-163.

McLaughlin, J., Bjornson, K., Temkin, N., Steinbok, P., Wright, V., Reiner, A., et al. (2002). Selective dorsal rhizotomy: Meta-analysis of three randomized controlled trials. *Developmental Medicine and Child Neurology, 44,* 17-25.

Miller, F. (2005). *Cerebral palsy.* New York: Springer.

Nehring, W. M. (2004). Cerebral palsy. In P. J. Allen & J. A. Vessey (Eds.), *Primary care of the child with a chronic condition* (4th ed., pp. 327-346). Philadelphia: Mosby.

Nelson, K. B. (2002). The epidemiology of cerebral palsy in term infants. *Mental Retardation and Developmental Disabilities Research Reviews, 8,* 146-150.

Nelson, K. B. (2003). Can we prevent cerebral palsy? *New England Journal of Medicine, 349,* 1765-1769.

Palisano, R., Rosenbaum, P., Walter, S., Russell, D., Wood, E., & Galuppi, B. (1997). The development and reliability of a system to classify gross motor function in children with cerebral palsy. *Developmental Medicine and Child Neurology, 39,* 214-223.

Pellegrino, L. (2007). Cerebral palsy. In M. L. Batshaw (Ed.), *Children with disabilities* (6th ed., pp. 387-408). Baltimore: Brookes.

Reid, S., Halliday, J., Ditchfield, M., Ekert, H., Byron, K., Glynn, A., et al. (2006). Factor V Leiden mutation: A contributory factor for cerebral palsy? *Developmental Medicine and Child Neurology, 48,* 14-19.

Roijen, L. E., Postema, K., Limbeek, V. J., & Kuppevelt, V. H. (2001). Development of bladder control in children and adolescents with cerebral palsy. *Developmental Medicine and Child Neurology, 43,* 103-107.

Rosenbaum, P. (2003a). Cerebral palsy: What parents and doctors want to know. *British Medical Journal, 326,* 970-974.

Rosenbaum, P. (2003b). Controversial treatment of spasticity: Exploring alternative therapies for motor function in children with cerebral palsy. *Journal of Child Neurology, 18*(Suppl. 1), S89-S94.

Rosenbaum, P. (2006). Classification of abnormal neurological outcome. *Early Human Development, 82,* 167-171.

Russman, B. S., & Ashwal, S. (2004). Evaluation of the child with cerebral palsy. *Seminars in Pediatric Neurology, 11,* 47-57.

Sankar, C., & Mundkur, N. (2005). Cerebral palsy—definition, classification, etiology and early diagnosis. *Indian Journal of Pediatrics, 72,* 865-868.

Sullivan, P. B., Juszczak, E., Bachlet, A., Lambert, B., Vernon-Roberts, A., Grant, H. W., et al. (2005). Gastrostomy tube feeding in children with cerebral palsy: A prospective, longitudinal study. *Developmental Medicine and Child Neurology, 47,* 77-85.

Verrotti, A., Greco, R., Spalice, A., Chiarelli, F., & Iannetti, P. (2006). Pharmacotherapy of spasticity in children with cerebral palsy. *Pediatric Neurology, 34,* 1-6.

Westcott, S. L., & Goulet, C. (2005). Neuromuscular system: Structures, functions, diagnoses, and evaluation. In S. K. Effgen (Ed.), *Meeting the physical therapy needs of children* (pp. 185-244). Philadelphia: F. A. Davis.

CHAPTER 6

TRAUMATIC SPINAL CORD INJURY AND SPINA BIFIDA

Kathryn Wolff Heller

When a spinal cord is severely injured or is defective in its development, muscle paralysis and sensory loss is usually present below the level of damage. Two types of spinal cord disorders that can result in paralysis and sensory loss are **spinal cord injury** and **spina bifida**.

Over 10,000 spinal cord injuries occur each year in the United States. Although spinal cord injuries occur at all ages, adolescents are the most represented age-group, with males representing over 80% of the cases (Beers, Porter, Jones, Kaplan, & Berkwits, 2006). When these young people return to school, they often face problems adjusting to their disability and the use of adaptations. This provides special challenges to the educator who must assist the student in adjusting to the physical, psychological, and social impact of this injury.

Spina bifida is one of the most serious congenital disorders affecting the nervous system. Spina bifida is a defect in the spinal column that can affect the spinal cord and result in paralysis and sensory loss. The most serious form of spina bifida, myelomeningocele, occurs in approximately 0.5 per 1,000 live births in the United States (Islam, 2005). Children with the myelomeningocele type of spina bifida often need adaptations and training in such areas as mobility, self-help, social skills, and learning strategies.

This chapter will primarily describe the characteristics of individuals who have a traumatic spinal cord injury and those who have the myelomeningocele type of spina bifida. Although many similarities can be seen between children with these two conditions, there are characteristics and complications that are unique to each of them. These two conditions will be discussed separately, and then the educational implications of both will be discussed together at the end of the chapter.

DESCRIPTION OF TRAUMATIC SPINAL CORD INJURY

The term *traumatic spinal cord* injury refers to damage to the spinal cord that occurs from some type of **trauma** or external force. Depending on the location and severity of the spinal cord injury, the child may have symptoms ranging from weakness of a limb to paralysis of all parts of the body below the neck with ventilator-assisted breathing. Typically, the term implies motor paralysis and loss of sensation for certain parts of the body.

The spinal cord may be adversely affected from causes other than traumatic means. For example, infants can be born with a congenital spinal cord defect, which is a physiological or structural abnormality of the spinal cord that is present at birth (e.g., spina bifida—**myelomeningocele** or tethered spinal cord). In addition, spinal cord disorders may occur from nontraumatic means (e.g., syndromes, tumors, or infections) (see Figure 6-1). This discussion is limited to spinal cord injury from trauma (followed by a discussion on spina bifida later in the chapter).

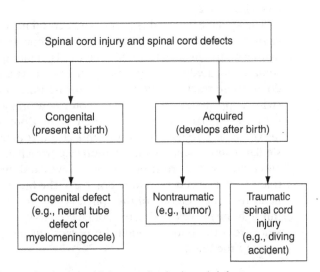

FIGURE 6-1 Types of spinal cord injury and spinal cord defects.

ETIOLOGY OF TRAUMATIC SPINAL CORD INJURY

[handwritten margin note: Accidents are the most common cause: car accidents overall]

There are several common causes of traumatic spinal cord injury in children and adolescents. Some of the most common causes are accidents, physical abuse, traumatic breech delivery, and congenital defects that predispose the child to a traumatic spinal cord injury. Accidents are the most common cause of spinal cord injury, with car accidents as the leading cause overall. Other types of accidents may also result in spinal cord injury, such as falls (e.g., from playground equipment) and sports and recreation accidents (e.g., from diving, soccer, gymnastics, equestrian events, or cheerleading) (Haslam, 2004; Toth, McNeil, & Feasby, 2005).

In addition to accidents, spinal cord injuries may occur during infancy because of a traumatic breech delivery or child abuse. During a breech delivery, the baby is born feet first. As the child passes out of the birth canal, the neck can become hyperextended, resulting in the spinal cord stretching to the point of injury. This can cause paralysis and sensory loss below the neck. Another cause of spinal cord injury is extensive shaking of an infant (known as shaken infant syndrome). The infant's heavy head is violently shaken back and forth and can result in spinal cord damage at the neck. Traumatic brain injury can also occur (see chapter 7).

Certain congenital syndromes may predispose children to spinal cord injuries. Children with Down syndrome, for example, are susceptible to dislocation of the vertebral column because of lax ligaments between the first and second cervical vertebrae (atlantoaxial joint at the top of the spine) (Nader-Sepahi, Casey, Hayward, Crockar, & Thompson, 2005). If dislocation occurs, quadriplegic paralysis can result. Children with this problem are advised not to engage in activities that cause extensive flexion and extension of the neck (e.g., diving and tumbling) (Haslam, 2004).

DYNAMICS OF TRAUMATIC SPINAL CORD INJURY

Overview of Spinal Cord Anatomy

The **spinal cord** is approximately half an inch wide and 18 inches long in the adult male. As with the brain, the spinal cord is surrounded by three **meninges** (membranes known as the dura mater, arachnoid, and pia mater) that assist in protecting the spinal cord. Both the spinal cord and the meninges are enclosed in the spinal vertebrae, providing further protection. The spinal vertebrae are stacked on each other, creating a column known as the spinal column (or vertebral column). The spinal column extends from the bottom of the skull to the coccyx (tailbone). The spinal cord is actually shorter than the spinal column; the end of the spinal cord terminates at about the level of the first lumbar vertebra (see Figure 6–2).

The spinal cord itself is part of the central nervous system and is composed of billions of **neurons** (nerve cells). The spinal cord contains white matter on the outside and gray matter on the inside. The white matter is made up of bundles of axons, known as tracts. Neurons located on the **primary motor cortex** of the brain send impulses (messages) down these tracts, to the lower motor neurons located in the middle of the spinal cord (which appears gray). The lower motor neuron's axons leave the spinal cord, grouped together as spinal nerves, which then branch out and become peripheral nerves. These nerves send impulses to various muscles throughout the body to cause movement. In a similar manner, sensory information (e.g., touch and temperature) from the body's tissues enter the spinal cord from sensory nerves and messages are sent up the spinal cord via tracts to the **somatosensory cortex** in the brain (see chapter 5 for more information on neurons). The function of the spinal cord is to carry impulses (messages) from the brain through the nerves exiting the spinal cord to various parts of the body and to receive messages from the body through the nerves entering the spinal cord and sends these messages to the brain.

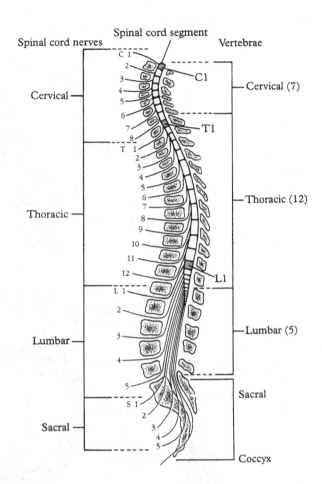

Spinal cord nerves — Spinal cord segment — Vertebrae

Cervical
Thoracic
Lumbar
Sacral

C1
T1
L1

Cervical (7)
Thoracic (12)
Lumbar (5)
Sacral
Coccyx

FIGURE 6–2   The spinal cord with the spinal nerves exiting between the vertebrae.

The gray matter inside the spinal cord are the cell bodies of the neurons. They are arranged in an H pattern (see Figure 6-3). The front section of the H is referred to as the anterior horn and carries motor information that leaves the spinal cord through spinal nerves. The back part of the H is referred to as the posterior horn and carries sensory information that enters the spinal cord through sensory spinal nerves up to the brain for processing.

These spinal nerves are named and numbered according to which vertebrae they exit near. Just as there are cervical, thoracic, lumbar, sacral, and coccygeal vertebrae, so there are cervical, thoracic, lumbar, sacral, and coccygeal nerves. There are eight cervical nerves (referred to as C1–C8), 12 thoracic nerves (referred to as T1–T12), five lumbar nerves (referred to as L1–L5), five sacral nerves (referred to as S1–S5), and one coccygeal nerve. Each of the spinal nerves exit beside the corresponding vertebra (e.g., T1 spinal nerve exits by the T1 vertebra). Since the spinal column is longer than the spinal cord, several spinal nerves extend lower than the cord in order to exit by their corresponding vertebrae. These spinal nerves extending below the spinal cord are referred to as the cauda equina (meaning "horse's tail") (see Figure 6-2).

Each of the spinal nerves exits the spinal cord, branches out into peripheral nerves, and connects with various muscles in the body. These motor nerves exiting the spinal cord transmit impulses that control movement. The sensory nerves that go from the skin and other tissue to the spinal cord carry sensory information (e.g., pain, temperature, pressure, and proprioception). Each motor and sensory nerve corresponds to certain parts of the body. Although there is some overlap, the cervical nerves control primarily the neck and

[handwritten margin notes: Anterior Horn carries info that leaves the spinal cord through spinal nerves. posterior Horn carries sensory info that enters the spinal cord through sensory spinal nerves up to the brain for processing]

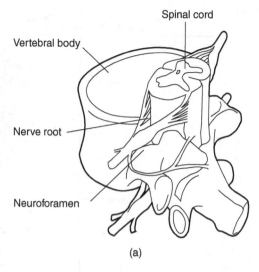

Spinal cord

Vertebral body

Nerve root

Neuroforamen

(a)

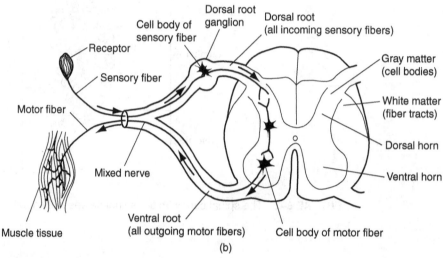

Dorsal root ganglion

Cell body of sensory fiber

Dorsal root (all incoming sensory fibers)

Receptor

Gray matter (cell bodies)

Sensory fiber

White matter (fiber tracts)

Motor fiber

Dorsal horn

Ventral horn

Mixed nerve

Muscle tissue

Ventral root (all outgoing motor fibers)

Cell body of motor fiber

(b)

FIGURE 6–3   Cross section of the spinal cord with the H pattern, surrounded by a vertebra (a) and a section of the spinal cord showing the reflex arc (b).

arm muscles, the thoracic nerves control primarily the chest and abdominal muscles, the lumbar nerves control primarily the leg muscles, and the sacral nerves control some lower leg muscles in addition to bowel, bladder, and sexual function.

   In addition to being a relay between the brain and the body, the spinal cord is responsible for eliciting certain reflexes. For example, when a knee is tapped with a rubber hammer, a sensory impulse is sent to the posterior horn of the spinal cord. The impulse then travels to the motor cell body in the anterior horn of the spinal cord. The impulse then exits the spinal cord via the motor nerve and goes to the leg muscles to cause a kicking motion. All this happens at the level of the spinal cord without brain involvement. A signal is sent from the spinal cord to the brain to let the person know what has happened after the fact.

Spinal Cord Injury

During an accident, the spinal cord is bruised, compressed, crushed, or torn. This may occur from the breakage or dislocation of vertebrae that surround the spinal cord, although damage can occur to the spinal cord even when the vertebrae are not broken (e.g., bleeding occurring at the spinal cord, ligament or disk injury, knife wound to spinal cord, or shaken infant syndrome in which the spinal column is more flexible than the spinal cord)

(Haslam, 2004; Reichert & Schmidt, 2001). The damage to the spinal cord results in the destruction of axons, which compose the tracts that send and receive information to and from the brain.

When the spinal cord injury occurs across the entire width of the spinal cord, a transverse spinal cord injury occurs (also known as complete spinal cord injury). In this type of injury, motor messages traveling from the brain cannot complete their transmission when they come to the area of the spinal cord damage. Because communication is interrupted, the brain is unable to control voluntary muscle movement at and below the point of injury. In the same manner, sensory information traveling from the skin will be unable to reach the brain when encountering the area of the spinal cord injury, resulting in a loss of sensation. If the injury does not transverse across the entire cord, a partial spinal cord injury (formally known as incomplete spinal injury) is present that allows some of the impulses to get through, allowing some movement and sensation.

A transverse spinal cord injury at T2, for example, would mean that none of the nerves below that level (T2 through the sacral nerves) can receive impulses from the brain to move, so there would be paralysis affecting the chest, abdominal, and leg muscles as well as loss of bowel and bladder function. Sensory information from those areas would also be lost since the sensory impulses (from T2 through the sacral nerves) cannot traverse the spinal cord injury to arrive at the brain. However, the neck and arm muscles (which are supplied primarily by the cervical nerves) would be unaffected since those nerves exit and enter the spinal column above the level of injury.

Spinal cord damage is very similar to having a bridge collapse across a major highway. Cars that exit prior to the accident are unaffected and can travel from the highway (spinal cord) to various locations unimpeded. However, the accident prevents cars from continuing down the highway to other locations. Unlike this accident, when the spinal cord is damaged, it presently cannot be fixed and does not regenerate adequately.

When spinal cord injury first occurs, three events may happen affecting the injury. First, the spinal column may be unstable from the injury, and movement of the area may cause further damage (Masri(y), 2006). That is why it is important that the area of damage be immobilized before the person is moved. Second, further damage can occur from the edema (swelling) that occurs at the site of injury. The swelling at the site may cause pressure on adjacent areas of the spinal cord that can damage the cord at that site as well. Medication will often be given to try to reduce the swelling to prevent further damage from occurring. Third, a person may go into spinal shock (i.e., below the level of injury, the muscles become hypotonic and do not function, and the reflexes are often not present). Spinal shock usually lasts days or weeks. After that time, reflexes usually return, and the muscles below the level of injury usually become spastic (meaning they have high muscle tone), and there is no voluntary control of these muscles. However, if a partial spinal cord injury or a less extensive injury occurs, muscle function and sensations may return over the next several months or up to 1 year (Menkes & Ellenbogen, 2002).

CHARACTERISTICS OF TRAUMATIC SPINAL CORD INJURY

The effects of the spinal cord injury will depend on two factors: (a) the level of the injury on the spinal cord and (b) whether it is a transverse or a partial spinal cord injury. The following discussion will first address the effects of a transverse spinal cord injury in regard to muscle paralysis, sensory loss, respiratory complication, bowel and bladder problems, and other specific issues. A separate section will provide some information on partial spinal cord injuries.

Muscle Paralysis

The level of the spinal cord injury will determine which muscles are paralyzed. The spinal cord can be affected anywhere from top to bottom, although one of the most common areas of injury in children is the cervical area (Menkes & Ellenbogen, 2002). As seen

Injury	Possible Effects
C1–C3	Inability to breathe; paralysis of torso, arms, and legs (quadriplegia) Loss of bowel and bladder control
C6–C7	Paralysis of hands, torso, and legs; loss of bowel and bladder control (can bend elbows and move shoulders)
T2	Paralysis of torso and legs (paraplegia); loss of bowel and bladder control
T11–T12	Paralysis of legs; loss of bowel and bladder control
T12–L1	Paralysis below the knee; loss of bowel and bladder control
S3–S5	Loss of bladder and bowel control

FIGURE 6–4 Possible effects that can occur at various levels of a transverse (complete) spinal cord injury.

in Figure 6-4, the higher the spinal cord injury, the more paralysis is present. For example, a C3 injury would result in complete quadriplegia, in which the individual cannot move his arms or legs. However, if the injury occurs a little lower between C6 and C7, the person could move his shoulders and elbows, but the paralysis would remain in his hands, torso, and legs. Injuries at T2, for example, result in paraplegia in which the legs are paralyzed (as well as the torso) but arm movement is normal. A person could have a very low area of injury, such as S3, and be able to walk but have a loss of bowel and bladder function.

When the spinal cord injury occurs to the spinal cord itself (which is above the T12-L1 vertebra level), reflexes are still present below the area of injury. These reflexes are involuntary, and the child may be unaware of them because of absent communication with the brain. Because of the continued presence of reflexes, the reflexes tend to become exaggerated, and the affected muscles become spastic. Muscle contractures often develop in which there is a shortening of the affected muscles.

Muscle paralysis can increase the risk of skeletal abnormalities. For example, individuals with spinal cord injury are at risk of scoliosis (curvatures of the spine) as well as hip dislocation (see chapter 9). The scoliosis tends to be more severe when the spinal cord injury occurs at a young age (Bergstrom, Short, Frankel, Henderson, & Jones, 1999).

Loss of Sensation

The loss of sensation occurs in a similar manner as the resulting muscle paralysis. As described previously, the level of spinal cord injury will determine which areas have a loss of sensation. When there is a transverse spinal cord injury, there will be a loss of sensation at that level and all areas below that level. A loss of sensation would include a loss of touch, pressure, pain, temperature, and proprioception.

A loss of sensation is very serious since sensation provides us with information of whether a body part is hurt and in need of attention. Individuals with spinal cord injury cannot feel below the level of injury and will be unable to determine whether a body part is hurt or damaged (unless there are visual signs of injury).

Because of the paralysis and lack of movement, individuals with spinal cord injury can develop pressure sores (decubitus ulcers) (Dryden et al., 2004). Since there is a loss of sensation, the child will be unable to feel the pressure to indicate the need to move. The child must become aware of the need to move and relieve the pressure based on a timed schedule instead of relying on sensation.

Respiratory Complications

When the spinal cord is injured in the high cervical region, the muscles that control respiration are paralyzed. The diaphragm muscle that is used for breathing is controlled by C3, C4, and C5. A person with an injury at C3 or above will need a mechanical ventilator in order to survive. Because of the partial control of the diaphragm at a C4 or C5 level, a person with spinal cord injury at this level may be able to breathe on his own.

When the spinal cord injury occurs in the high thoracic area, the diaphragm will be functioning, but other respiratory muscles (i.e., the intercostals) that assist with breathing will not be functioning well. Breathing can be compromised as much as 50%, which would increase the susceptibility to respiratory infections and decrease oxygenation. When the spinal cord injury occurs above the lower thoracic area, the person's abdominal muscles will be paralyzed. This may result in a lack of a strong cough that is used to clear respiratory secretions. The lack of an effective cough will also increase the possibility of respiratory infections and pneumonia (Dryden et al., 2004).

Bowel and Bladder Problems and Sexual Dysfunction

The sacral nerves control the bowel and bladder muscles. When an injury occurs at or above this point, the child will be unable to feel a sensation of fullness to indicate a need to void or defecate. Also, in a transverse injury, the child will be unable to control the muscles allowing the emptying of urine and feces. (If there is a partial injury, there is more of a possibility that there will be some control of the bowel and bladder.) In addition, individuals with spinal cord injury are at greater risk of constipation and urinary tract infections (Dryden et al., 2004). Sexual dysfunction is also common (e.g., lack of control over erections).

Partial Spinal Cord Injury

In a partial spinal cord injury, some of the nerves at the site of injury are not damaged. When this occurs, the child may have some functioning in certain areas, at and below the level of injury, because of some unharmed nerves in certain spinal tracts. Because of the variability of which nerves are damaged, individuals with the same level of spinal cord damage may look very different in terms of the extent of their disability based on the type of partial spinal cord injury. Some of the partial spinal cord injuries are Brown-Sequard syndrome, anterior cord syndrome, and central cord syndrome.

Brown-Sequard syndrome refers to spinal cord damage occurring to one side of the spinal cord, often caused by a penetrating object (e.g., knife wound). If there were damage on the right side of the spinal cord, for example, there would be paralysis on the right side of the body, loss of tactile discrimination and proprioception on the right side of the body, and loss of pain and temperature on the left side of the body (Moin & Khalili, 2006). The pain and temperature loss occurs on the other side of the body because the sensory nerves for these senses cross to the opposite side of the body at the level of the spinal cord (instead of crossing at the lower portion of the brain).

The last two syndromes refer to areas of the injury on the spinal cord. In anterior cord syndrome, the anterior (front) of the spinal cord is affected, resulting in paralysis and loss of pain sensation below the level of injury. In central cord syndrome, there is a lesion that damages the central part of the spinal cord, usually in the cervical region. Arm function is usually more impaired than leg function, and sensory loss varies as to the extent of damage (Beers et al., 2006).

Specific Problems in Spinal Cord Injury

Autonomic Dysreflexia

One of the most serious complications is a pathological reflex known as autonomic dysreflexia. This typically occurs in transverse spinal cord injuries occurring above the T6 level. Autonomic dysreflexia is caused by any noxious stimulus that occurs below the area of injury. This includes such problems as a distended bladder, severe constipation, or a pressure sore. Autonomic dysreflexia causes a dangerous rapid elevation of the child's blood pressure. Other symptoms may include pounding headache, sweating (especially around neck and face), blurred vision, nasal congestion, and feeling of anxiety. If treatment is not given immediately, bleeding in the brain (cerebral hemorrhage) can result and the condition can be fatal (Dunn, 2004; Karlsson, 2006).

Complications of Spinal Cord Injury

· pain
· Body temp
· psych reactions

Individuals with spinal cord injury may have several specific problems that will affect the person's quality of life. Some individuals will experience pain that may continue for some time after the injury regardless of the level or completeness of the lesion (Waxman & Hains, 2006). Sometimes this pain will interfere with performance of daily activities and work (Hanley, Masedo, Jensen, Cardenas, & Turner, 2006). Individuals with high-level spinal cord injuries may have problems with body temperature regulation and will need to be sure they are appropriately clothed and protected from extreme temperatures. Some individuals with spinal cord injury may have some psychological reactions (e.g., depression) to having a spinal cord injury after initially being nondisabled (Dryden et al., 2004).

DETECTION OF TRAUMATIC SPINAL CORD INJURY

The physical symptoms of paralysis and loss of sensation will assist the physician in diagnosing a spinal cord injury. Spinal X-rays will show fractures in the spinal column or severe bony changes. However, it is possible to have a normal X-ray and a damaged spinal cord in infants and young children since the spinal column is not formed into solid bone. During this young age, the spinal column can be stretched several inches without damage, while the spinal cord can be stretched only a fraction of an inch. Other imaging techniques, such as computed tomography (CT) or magnetic resonance imaging (MRI) scans will more fully define the spinal trauma and location of injury.

TREATMENT OF TRAUMATIC SPINAL CORD INJURY

Treatment of traumatic spinal cord injury begins by securing proper breathing and circulation. If a high cervical lesion has occurred, a ventilator will be needed to maintain breathing. Treatment will be aimed at preventing any secondary injury from occurring. The spinal cord will be stabilized through splinting, bracing, or surgery on the spinal column. After the emergency phase, a team effort will be needed to assist the child in achieving the fullest recovery and adapting to the paralysis. Team members often include the teacher, physical therapist, occupational therapist, speech therapist, nurse, physician, nutritionist, parent, child, respiratory therapist, social worker, counselor, and psychologist.

Treatment for Muscle Paralysis

Since the muscle paralysis in spinal cord injury is not reversible, the aim will be to assess which muscles are functioning and strengthen those muscles. Physical and occupational therapists will provide therapy to teach functional skills using these muscles. If there is some muscle control in the legs, the therapists will often institute a program aimed at teaching or reteaching the person to walk using the unaffected muscles with braces. If there is control only of the arm muscles, therapy will aim at strengthening these muscles to assist with mobility. In addition, the student may learn to use several different types of adaptive and assistive technology devices in order to perform various activities (see chapter 8).

Therapy will also include management and prevention of contractures and spinal deformity. Contractures can interfere with achieving some functional use of a muscle group.

AT

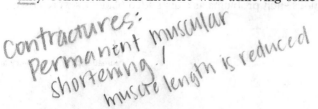
Contractures:
Permanent muscular
shortening.!
musare length is reduced

Children who can walk with braces would be unable to do so with contractures at the knees. Severe contractures may result in hygienic problems due to an inability to be thoroughly cleaned due to the difficulty in extending or moving a limb with a contracture. Assuming different positions such as sitting or lying may be difficult or uncomfortable when contractures are present. Spinal deformities may also occur from the lack of muscular support of the vertebral column. Interventions for both contractures and spinal deformities will include range of motion exercises, splints, braces, and orthotic devices. In some instances, surgery may be necessary to release contractures or manage spinal deformities.

Treatment for Sensory Loss

The loss of sensation from a spinal cord injury can result in further injury. Individuals with sensory loss will be unable to determine if they are getting burned by something hot or if their foot is dragging off the wheelchair support and becoming injured. It is important that the person with the injury as well as the individuals assisting him be attentive to possible problems.

Another frequent problem is pressure sores (decubitus ulcers). Individuals with normal spinal cords typically move around a lot and shift their weight as they sit. This is because after being in a position for a period of time, pressure that is exerted on the skin causes a sensation of discomfort that results in the person moving. A person with a sensory loss does not have a feeling of discomfort below the level of injury. If he does not change positions or relieve the pressure, circulation will be cut off, causing tissue death (necrosis) in the area. This tissue death is a pressure sore and can occur in 2 hours. A reddened area on the skin is often the initial symptom of a pressure sore. When a reddened area is found, the person must be kept off the area completely until the skin returns to normal. If this does not occur, the pressure sore will continue to develop and cause an opening in the skin. What appears as a small open area on the surface of the skin is actually a much larger area of damage below the skin. Pressure sores can become infected and pose a serious health threat.

Pressure sores are completely preventable. The individual needs to change positions often and not stay in one place for extended periods of time. Since sitting causes substantial pressure on the buttocks, it is important that the child not sit for longer than 1 to 2 hours (or for some individuals a shorter period of time) without an assisted position change or a chair lift. Chair lifts can be performed by the child who has arm movement and occurs when the child lifts his buttocks off the chair by pushing down on the armrests with his arms (i.e., a vertical push-up).

Treatment for Respiratory Problems

Students with a high cervical involvement will need the use of a ventilator in order to breathe. A ventilator is a machine that pushes air into the student's lungs. The ventilator is typically placed on the back of a person's wheelchair. Ventilators have alarms that should be continually on to inform people if the ventilator becomes accidentally disconnected or if there is an obstruction (e.g., kink in the tubing) or other problem (Heller, Forney, Alberto, Schwartzman, & Goeckel, 2000). Often students may feel isolated because of the teachers' and students' fears over the ventilator. It is important that the student's overall needs not be overlooked among the machinery. Having someone familiarize school personnel with the ventilator will make it less frightening.

A student on a ventilator will usually have a tracheostomy. A tracheostomy is an artificial external opening into the windpipe (trachea) through which a tube is passed (known as a tracheostomy tube or trach tube). The tube from the ventilator will attach to the tracheostomy tube (see Figure 6-5). The ventilator attachment may be momentarily disconnected if the child receives suctioning (placing a suction catheter [tube] through the tracheostomy tube into the windpipe to remove thick respiratory secretions). Speech can be affected when a tracheostomy is present, with some students having speech that is soft with

Pressure sores

FIGURE 6–5 This student has a spinal cord injury and has a ventilator tube going from his tracheostomy tube (in his neck) to a ventilator located on the back of his wheelchair. The ventilator assists him with breathing.

multiple pauses (Hoit, Banzett, Lohmeier, Hixon, & Brown, 2003) and others requiring augmentative communication devices in order to be understood.

Because of the increased incidence of respiratory infections in children with cervical and thoracic injuries, infection control procedures should be carefully adhered to. This includes good hand washing, disinfecting objects, and sending students home who are sick. (For further information on infection control, refer to chapter 23). If the child with a spinal cord injury acquires a respiratory infection, antibiotics and other forms of treatment will be prescribed.

Treatment for Bowel and Bladder Control

Students with spinal cord injury frequently have no control over their bowel and bladder unless they have a partial lesion. Bowel programs are set up in which the child uses suppositories and other bowel-evacuating medications or procedures that will allow emptying of the bowel at certain times at home. This is important so that constipation or an impaction can be avoided.

Many students with spinal cord injury will have a neurogenic bladder, that is, a bladder whose muscle does not function properly. A neurogenic bladder may not completely empty all the urine, increasing the risk of infection. In some cases, the neurogenic bladder will retain urine, which can back up into the kidneys, causing infection and serious kidney problems. Some individuals will require **clean intermittent catheterization** (CIC) to address these urinary problems. In this procedure, a catheter (a long thin tube) is placed through the urinary opening (or an opening made through the abdominal area into the bladder) to allow urine to be released from the bladder, and then the catheter is removed (Heller et al., 2000). This is a clean procedure (not sterile) that is quick and easy to do and is effective in bladder control. It is performed on a regular basis throughout the day, and most children can learn to do this procedure if hand function is adequate.

Possible New Treatments

At present, the treatment of spinal cord injury is a supportive approach. However, progress is being made with several new innovative treatments that may improve functioning or even

new trials being conducted

cure spinal cord injury. For example, trials are occurring with certain medications that appear to have neuroprotective effects and anti-inflammatory properties to prevent or minimize damage (Baptiste & Fehlings, 2006; Bridwell, Anderson, Boden, Vaccaro, & Wang, 2005). Several regeneration strategies (e.g., growth factors, electrical stimulation, and implants) are being tried to attempt to stimulate nerve cell growth. Cellular transplantation (including stem cell research) appears promising thus far (Bridwell et al., 2005; Garbossa et al., 2006). Further research is needed at this time to determine how well and under what conditions these treatments will work.

COURSE OF TRAUMATIC SPINAL CORD INJURY

Although a spinal cord injury is not a progressive condition, further impairments can occur from the effects of the injury (e.g., contractures or scoliosis). Careful management of the child with a spinal cord injury will aim at minimizing the development of complications and secondary impairments. Even though spinal cord injury cannot be reversed at this time, there is hope that new treatment options will become available soon that will make a significant difference in the outcome of this type of injury.

DESCRIPTION OF SPINA BIFIDA

The term *spina bifida* means "split spine" and refers to a defective closure of the bony vertebral column. There are three types of spina bifida: spina bifida occulta, meningocele, and myelomeningocele.

Spina Bifida Occulta

A common type of spina bifida is spina bifida occulta—a failure of fusion of the back arches of vertebrae that results in malformation of a few vertebrae. In this condition, there is no paralysis or sensory loss. The skin over the malformed vertebrae will often have an abnormality, such as discoloration or tufts of hair. Serious anomalies can be present with this condition (such as a tethered spinal cord) (Beers et al., 2006).

Meningocele

A meningocele refers to the outpouching of the meninges (membranes covering the spinal cord) through the malformed vertebrae. The child is born with a saclike protrusion on the back at the level of malformation. The sac contains the meninges and cerebrospinal fluid. Since the spinal cord and the spinal nerves are unaffected in this condition, there is no paralysis or sensory loss. As with spina bifida occulta, some children may have other associated conditions (e.g., hydrocephalus or tethered cord) (Herring, 2002; Johnston & Kinsman, 2004).

Myelomeningocele

Myelomeningocele, also referred to as meningomyelocele or myelodysplasia, is the most severe form of spina bifida. A saclike protrusion is present on the back at the level of the malformed vertebrae that contains an outpouching of the meninges and the spinal cord (see Figure 6-6). This malformation of the spinal cord results in paralysis and sensory loss at and below the level of the defect. When people refer to a child as having spina bifida, they are usually referring to the myelomeningocele type. Since this is the most significant type of spina bifida, the rest of the chapter will primarily address myelomeningocele.

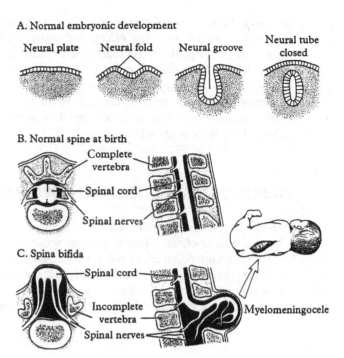

FIGURE 6–6 Normal development of the neural tube, normal spine at birth, and myelomeningocele type of spina bifida.

ETIOLOGY OF SPINA BIFIDA—MYELOMENINGOCELE

Spina bifida is classified as one of several different types of neural tube defect. Within the first 28 days of gestation, a neural tube is formed that develops from the brain and spinal cord. As seen in Figure 6-6, the normal development of the neural tube involves the neural plate evolving into a closed tube. As rapid cell growth occurs and more cells differentiate, the meninges and vertebrae will develop surrounding the neural tube as it develops into a spinal cord. In spina bifida (myelomeningocele type), incomplete closure of the neural tube occurs. Since the neural tube fails to close, the vertebrae also fail to enclose the back portion of the spine in the area that the neural tube defect has occurred. In the myelomeningocele, type, an outpouching of the spinal cord and the meninges occur on the child's back at the level of the defect.

The exact mechanism that causes the neural tube to fail to close is uncertain. There appears to be a genetic predisposition since there is an increased probability of having a second child with a neural tube defect after having one child with this disorder, and this percentage increases if more than one child has a neural tube defect. Nutrition and environmental factors are also thought to play a role in the development of myelomeningocele (Johnston & Kinsman, 2004). Folic acid deficiency, for example, is considered a risk factor for myelomeningocele, and its consumption is recommended in women of childbearing age to reduce the incidence of neural tube defects (Islam, 2005).

DYNAMICS OF SPINA BIFIDA—MYELOMENINGOCELE

The location of the neural tube defect will determine the extent of impairment. If the neural tube defect occurs at the top of the neural tube, there can be an outpouching of part of the brain and the meninges (known as an encephalocele) through an opening in the skull. When the neural tube defect occurs below this point, a myelomeningocele can occur in which the outpouching contains the meninges and spinal cord. This outpouching can occur anywhere along the spinal cord. However, the lumbar and sacral regions account for at least 75% of the cases (Johnston & Kinsman, 2004).

The child with a myelomeningocele has an abnormally formed spinal cord at the level of the outpouching. The spinal cord may be (a) cavitated (hollowed), (b) solid but degenerated and disorganized, and/or (c) grossly proliferated (overgrowth of cells). The nerves coming off the spinal cord appear to be poorly connected to the spinal cord (Herring, 2002). Because of these abnormalities, a child with a myelomeningocele will have good motor and sensory function above the level of the damage, but there is no communication with the brain below this level (similar to a spinal cord injury). This results in paralysis and sensory loss below the abnormality.

CHARACTERISTICS OF SPINA BIFIDA—MYELOMENINGOCELE

Since myelomeningocele involves a damaged spinal cord, some of the characteristics will be similar to spinal cord injury. However, there are also some additional problems associated with this condition: Chiari II malformation, hydrocephalus, cognitive and learning impairments, seizures, musculoskeletal abnormalities, visual impairments, language abnormalities, and latex allergies.

Muscle Paralysis, Sensory Loss, and Bowel and Bladder Problems

As with spinal cord injuries, the level of the myelomeningocele will determine the level of paralysis and sensory loss. Since the level of damage is usually in the lumbar and sacral areas, many of these students will be able to walk, often using a walker or crutches (see Figure 6–7). However, there is a tendency to gain weight (because of inactivity) that can affect the ability to walk.

FIGURE 6–7 Student with spina bifida using a walker to assist with mobility.

Scott Cunningham/Merrill

Exercise is particularly important, as is good nutrition. Proper bladder and bowel care is also important since there will typically be no voluntary control of these areas. Sexual dysfunction is also common (see these sections under "Characteristics of Traumatic Spinal Cord Injury").

Specific Problems in Myelomeningocele

Chiari II Malformation

Children with myelomeningocele are often born with an additional congenital malformation known as Chiari II malformation (also known as Chiari Malformation type II (CMII) and formally as Arnold-Chiari malformation). This malformation involves the displacement of part of the brain stem, cerebellum, and fourth ventricle down into the cervical spinal canal (neck region) out of its normal placement. (Herring, 2002; McLone & Dias, 2003). This malformation can lead to the development of hydrocephalus.

Although an infrequent occurrence, the displaced part of the cerebellum and brain stem in Chiari II malformation can be further compressed down into the neck region (e.g., because of trauma). This results in a Chiari crisis that may present with the following symptoms: choking, difficulty breathing, vocal cord paralysis, pooling of secretions, and arm spasticity. It can lead to death and usually requires surgery (Johnston & Kinsman, 2004).

Hydrocephalus

Hydrocephalus is an abnormal accumulation of cerebral spinal fluid (CSF) in the brain. The CSF is primarily produced by a special group of blood vessels known as the choroid plexus. The choroid plexus secretes CSF into the four ventricles (spaces) of the brain (see Figure 6-8). As CSF is formed and is secreted into the lateral ventricles, the CSF flows from the lateral ventricles to the third and fourth ventricles. The CSF leaves the fourth ventricle through three small openings into a large fluid space that is beneath the cerebellum. The CSF flows between the meninges (subarachnoid space) that surrounds the brain and spinal cord and is reabsorbed near the top of the brain (Guyton & Hall, 2006).

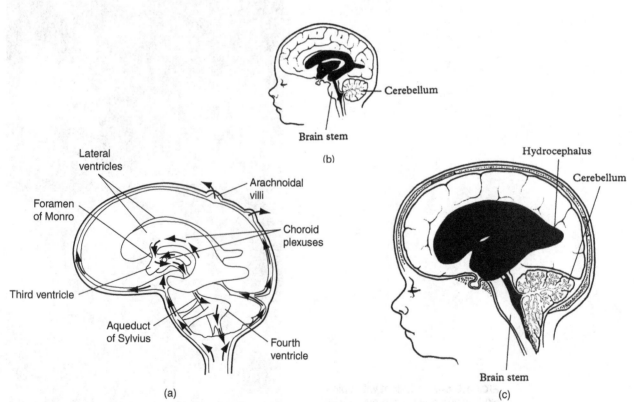

FIGURE 6-8 Flow of cerebral spinal fluid without hydrocephalus (a and b) and with hydrocephalus (c).

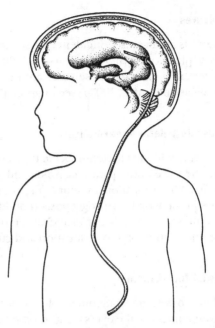

FIGURE 6–9 A ventriculoperitoneal shunt used to divert the excess cerebrospinal fluid found in hydrocephalus.

A common complication of Chiari II malformation is hydrocephalus. In Chiari II malformation, the fourth ventricle and subarachnoid space are displaced, usually resulting in blocking the flow of CSF. This causes an accumulation of excess CSF known as hydrocephalus (meaning "water on the brain"). Although Chiari II is often the main cause of hydrocephalus in myelomeningocele, it should be noted that hydrocephalus can also occur from other types of blockages in the brain or from overproduction of CSF (Chiafery, 2006).

In hydrocephalus, the excess CSF in the brain enlarges the ventricles and puts pressure on the brain. In the infant and young child who still have a "soft spot" on the head (i.e., the sutures of the skull have not closed), the head may expand because of the excess amount of CSF. Some heads may get quite large without intervention, and this can lead to brain damage and in some cases death. The most common intervention consists of inserting a shunt into a ventricle of the brain to move the excess CSF out of the brain to a different part of the body (e.g., peritoneal cavity) where it is absorbed (see Figure 6–9).

Cognitive and Learning Impairments

Children with myelomeningocele who have (shunted) hydrocephalus are at greatest risk for cognitive and learning impairments since the hydrocephalus appears to be primarily responsible for cognitive and learning problems (Barf, Verhoef, Post, Gooskens, & Prevo, 2003; Iddon, Morgan, Loveday, Sahakian, & Pickard, 2006). The majority of children with myelomeningocele and hydrocephalus fall into the low average range of intelligence (Jacobs, Northam, & Anderson, 2001). In addition, there may be learning problems due to deficits in such areas as attention, memory, recall, motor reaction times, visual-perceptual skill, and organizational skills (Houliston, Taguri, Dutton, Hajivassiliou, & Young, 1999; Iddon et al., 2004). An increased incidence of attention-deficit/hyperactivity disorder (ADHD) has also been found with children with myelomeningocele with shunted hydrocephalus (Burmeister et al., 2005).

All these cognitive and learning impairments can negatively impact academic performance. Reading comprehension and writing is often less developed than decoding skills in individuals with spina bifida and hydrocephalus, even when average verbal intelligence is present, and these deficits continue into adulthood (Barnes & Dennis, 1992; Barnes, Dennis, & Hetherington, 2004). The area of math is of particular concern with math scores often being much lower than reading and writing scores (Jacobs et al., 2001; Lazzaretti & Pearson, 2004).

Seizures

There is an increased incidence of seizures with children with myelomeningocele and hydrocephalus (Lazzaretti & Pearsons, 2004). Although any type of seizure may be present, generalized tonic-clonic seizures are the most frequent type. They usually respond well to medication (Liptak, 2007) (see chapter 17 for more information on seizures).

Musculoskeletal Abnormalities

Students with myelomeningocele typically have several types of musculoskeletal abnormalities because of the paralysis. Ankle and foot deformities such as club foot may be present, as may hip dislocation and curvatures of the spine (Verhoef et al., 2004). Since paralysis occurs in the womb, arthrogryposis (condition in which the baby is born with multiple contractures) may also occur (see chapter 10 for information on arthrogryposis and chapter 9 for information on hip dislocation and curvatures of the spine) (Beers et al., 2006).

Visual Impairments

Children with myelomeningocele are at risk of having **strabismus**, which is a deviation in the alignment of the eye(s) (e.g., crossed eyes). This may occur from pressure on the cranial nerves that control eye movements (Lazzaretti & Pearson, 2004). If strabismus is untreated, it may result in **amblyopia** (lazy eye) (see chapter 11 for more information on visual impairments) (Fredrick & Asbury, 2004).

Language Abnormalities

Children with myelomeningocele and (shunted) hydrocephalus may also have language abnormalities. Two areas of particular concern are semantic and pragmatics. In semantics, some of these children have been found to have difficulty comprehending words representing basic linguistic concepts (e.g., size or shape) and abstract concepts. This may play a part in these children's difficulty with word problem-solving abilities. In the area of pragmatics, children with myelomeningocele and shunted hydrocephalus were found to have difficulty using language functionally in social situations (Vachha & Adams, 2003). They may be very talkative, but their conversation may often be noncontextual. These language problems may negatively impact school performance and social interactions.

Latex Allergy Reactions

Many children with myelomeningocele are sensitive or allergic to latex. This can take the form of irritant contact dermatitis (dry, itchy areas), allergic contact dermatitis (e.g., watery eyes or skin eruptions), or an allergic reaction (e.g., wheezing, swelling, or drop in blood pressure) (Lazzaretti & Pearson, 2004). A severe allergic reaction may lead to anaphylaxis, which results in life-threatening respiratory distress and shock. Children with myelomeningocele may need to avoid latex products, such as rubber balls, latex gloves, and toys high in latex.

DETECTION OF SPINA BIFIDA—MYELOMENINGOCELE

Myelomeningocele is easily detected at birth because of the sac on the infant's back. Further medical testing is often performed, such as X-rays, CT or MRI scans, and/or blood analysis to provide further information regarding the myelomeningocele and any associated congenital malformation.

Myelomeningocele can be detected prior to birth. A maternal blood test that checks for alpha-fetoprotein (AFP) is commonly performed as a screening measure. When myelomeningocele is present, AFP leaks from the open spine into the amniotic fluid, after which it enters the mother's bloodstream. Additional tests are typically performed if the blood test is positive.

Ultrasound (or sometimes an MRI) may be used to visualize a myelomeningocele or hydrocephalus in an unborn child (Mavinkurve, Bagley, Pradilla, & Jallo, 2005).

TREATMENT OF SPINA BIFIDA—MYELOMENINGOCELE

When an infant is born with a myelomeningocele, the sac containing the meninges and spinal cord may be open or closed. Sacs that are open have a high risk of introducing infection, which can result in meningitis (inflammation of the meninges). Sacs that are closed can easily rupture when there is a thin layer of skin covering the sac. Whether the sac is open or closed, surgical intervention will occur within the first few hours or days of life. The surgery involves closing the defect by tucking in the meninges and spinal cord. Skin graphs may be necessary to close the site if the sac is large. After surgical intervention, there will no longer be a sac on the child's back. This surgery does not improve function. The damage has been done to the spinal cord and cannot be repaired or improved by surgery with current knowledge and skill.

When the myelomeningocele is detected prior to birth, prenatal surgery may occur in select cases to close the defect so that the spinal cord does not become further damaged by exposure to amniotic fluid, trauma, or pressure (Adzick & Walsh, 2003). Although the damage to the spinal cord cannot be reversed, there is some indication that myelomeningocele repair in utero may reduce the incidence of postnatal hydrocephalus or postpone the development of hydrocephalus (Bruner et al., 2004). In addition, studies are being conducted to correct hydrocephalus in utero. However, there are considerable risks with intrauterine myelomeningocele repair (as well as with intrauterine treatment of hydrocephalus), and further studies are needed to determine if the benefits outweigh the risks (Mavinkurve et al., 2005).

As with spinal cord injury, treatments are available for muscle paralysis, sensory loss, and bowel and bladder control (see the earlier sections on treatment of spinal cord injury for these specific areas). There are also treatments of problems specific to myelomeningocele.

Treatment of Problems Specific to Myelomeningocele

Chiari Type II Malformation and Hydrocephalus

Children will be assessed for Chiari type II malformation and hydrocephalus. As previously mentioned, when the child has Chiari type II malformation, surgical intervention (e.g., Chiari II decompression) will be needed if there is crowding of the brain stem and cerebellum.

When hydrocephalus is present, the most common intervention is the surgical insertion of a ventriculoperitoneal shunt (VP shunt). The shunt consists of a proximal catheter (tube) that goes into the lateral ventricle, a valve (to control the drainage), and a distal catheter that goes under the skin of the neck and chest to end in the peritoneal (abdominal) cavity or alternate site (Chiafery, 2006) (see Figure 6-9). The shunt allows the excess CSF to exit the brain and travel down the tube to the peritoneal cavity, where it is reabsorbed into the body. This prevents a buildup of CSF in the brain and prevents pressure on the brain that could cause brain damage.

Shunts can become infected and blocked. When a blockage occurs, the child may have headaches, blurred vision, nausea and vomiting, lethargy, arm weakness, or uneven dilation of the pupils. If the failure is more intermittent, more subtle signs may be present, such as emotional disturbances (including violence), decreased school performance, or "staring spells" (Mavinkurve et al., 2005). If shunt malfunction is suspected, this is an emergency situation, and the child should go to the hospital for evaluation. If there is a shunt malfunction, a shunt revision is necessary. As children grow, periodic shunt revision may also be necessary to accommodate for growth.

It is important to note that there can also be a malfunction of the valve of the shunt. Some of the shunt valves are programmable, and there is some indication that it may be possible to inadvertently change the pressure setting (e.g., by exposure to a toy magnet), so periodic evaluations are needed (Chiafery, 2006).

Another treatment for hydrocephalus is an endoscopic third ventriculostomy. This is a surgical procedure that creates an opening for the CSF to flow around the obstruction. However, this surgical procedure is still being investigated as to its use in persons with hydrocephalus and myelomeningocele (Mavinkurve et al., 2005).

Treatment of Additional Problems

Other problems that may be present in a child with myelomeningocele may be addressed through bracing, surgery, or medication. Musculoskeletal abnormalities may be corrected or improved through bracing or surgery. Seizures will typically be treated with antiepileptic medication. Strabismus may be surgically managed. Cognitive impairments and learning deficiencies will be addressed educationally.

COURSE OF SPINA BIFIDA—MYELOMENINGOCELE

There is no cure for myelomeningocele, so the symptoms of the disorder will persist throughout the person's lifetime. The prognosis will vary depending on the level of the cord damage and the other associated conditions. One study by Bowman, McLone, Grant, Tomita, and Ito (2001) examined the course of myelomeningocele in individuals over a 25-year period. The study found that 49% had scoliosis, 23% had at least one seizure, 33% had latex allergies, 95% had at least one shunt revision, (with several having 10 or more revisions), 46% continued to walk, 85% used clean intermittent catheterization (with 90% performing their own catheterization), 71% lived with their parents, and 49% attended or graduated from college (36% in high school or recently graduated). The study concludes that at least 75% of those born with myelomeningocele can be expected to reach their early adult years.

Deaths of infants and preschoolers with myelomeningocele have been attributed primarily to Chiari II malformation that resulted in dysfunction of the medulla oblongata (the part of the brain stem that controls respiration, cardiac, and other vital functions). This included those who had decompression to treat Chiari II as well as tracheostomies and/or **gastrostomy tubes**. The most common cause of death in early adulthood is unrecognized shunt malfunction and loss of renal function (Beers et al., 2006; Bowman et al., 2001; Tubbs & Oakes, 2004).

EDUCATIONAL CONSIDERATIONS FOR SPINAL CORD INJURY AND SPINA BIFIDA

To help a child with spinal cord injury or myelomeningocele most effectively, teachers and staff members should know about the medical condition and how it affects the individual student. A child with a high spinal cord injury or high myelomeningocele will have different needs than those of a child with a low spinal cord injury or low myelomeningocele. The challenge of the educational team is to work together to determine how to best meet students' unique needs.

Meeting Physical and Sensory Needs

Depending on the level of damage, muscle paralysis may affect arm and/or leg use. Students may require different types of assistive technology to access the computer, academic material, or daily living items (see chapter 8). Students who do have some muscle paralysis in the legs may use braces, crutches, walkers, and/or wheelchairs. Students who are able to walk with support (e.g., crutches) may fatigue from a lot of walking and need breaks or extra time to go between classes. Depending on the extent of paralysis and the student's vitality, some students may be able to walk only short distances and use a wheelchair for longer distances. Many peers and adults do not understand why a child who is able to walk may need a wheelchair. Education of others is needed to prevent teasing. As a child with myelomeningocele ages, there may be a tendency to become overweight that can result in the child using a wheelchair more often. Sensitivity to this, as well as the importance of diet and exercise, cannot be stressed enough.

Muscle paralysis may also affect such areas as breathing (in a high spinal cord injury) and bowel and bladder control. If the student is on a ventilator, the teacher and other individuals who teach the student will need to become familiar and comfortable with the ventilator and learn what to do if any problems emerge. Students who use clean intermittent catheterization for bladder control will need to have this performed at school at certain specified times. It is important that the team works together regarding sharing information about the procedures, potential problems, and interventions. The team will also need to work together to promote student participation in (or acquisition of) performing certain procedures (e.g., student learning to do his own clean intermittent catheterization). Often the nurse will take the lead in providing information on the procedure, while the teacher will provide instructional strategies (see chapter 20 for more information on health care procedures).

Because of the loss of sensory input, the teacher must be sure to monitor the student for temperature control and for any injuries that may occur to the paralyzed areas. Also, the teacher will need to be observant as to the development of any reddened areas on the skin indicating the development of a pressure sore, especially under splints, braces, and sitting areas. Students should not sit in one position for extended lengths of time. A change of position or chair lifts will need to be encouraged approximately every 1 to 2 hours. Consultation with a physical therapist will be needed to determine proper positioning as well as correct application and removal of splints, braces, or other orthoses.

Teachers and school personnel should be familiar with possible emergencies that can happen with students with spinal cord injury or myelomeningocele. Plans should be in place addressing possible emergencies or problems, including the steps to take should one of them occur (see chapter 20 for health care plans and action plans). For example, a serious complication of a high spinal cord injury is autonomic dysreflexia. Teachers should be aware of the possible triggers of this condition (e.g., distended bladder or constipation), take measures to prevent its occurrence (e.g., urinary catheterizations should occur on time), know its symptoms (e.g., headache), and know what to do if it occurs (e.g., call an ambulance). Plans should be made to address the most common problems found in spinal cord injury and myelomeningocele, such as shunt failure in students with myelomeningocele and hydrocephalus, urinary catheterization problems, and issues surrounding the ventilator or tracheostomy tube (in students with high spinal cord injury).

Meeting Communication Needs

Students with a high spinal cord injury and/or who are on a ventilator may have speech difficulties or be unable to speak. When speech is not understandable, an augmentative communication device should be put in place to allow the student to effectively communicate. These communication devices can be accessed any number of ways, including by eye gaze and switches see (chapter 8).

Students with myelomeningocele may have difficulty with conversational skills because of issues surrounding pragmatics and semantics of language. When pragmatics of language is the problem, conversation can be irrelevant and disorganized and may result in unsuccessful interactions with others, including peers and teachers. In this situation, the teacher may teach the student specific strategies and role-play various situations using appropriate conversation skills. For example, the teacher may teach the student to carefully listen to the thoughts of others, acknowledge thoughts, and respond on the same topic. When semantics of language is an issue, the teacher may provide more systematic instruction on the problematic area.

Meeting Daily Living Needs

Because of the paralysis and sensory loss resulting from spinal cord disorders and myelomeningocele, students will need instruction on daily living skills. Depending on the level of damage on the spinal cord, instruction may be needed in mobility, transferring to a chair or toilet, special feeding devices (e.g., mechanical feeders), and adapted toiletry items (e.g., adapted toothbrush). Putting on clothing may require a push-pull stick or other device to aid in dressing. Many different types of assistive technology devices are used by persons with high spinal cord injuries, often resulting in a positive psychosocial impact and increased independence in a variety of daily living tasks, such as controlling the lights, using a telephone, and accessing a computer (Rigby et al., 2005) (see chapter 8 for more information on assistive technology).

Meeting Learning Needs

The student with a spinal cord injury or myelomeningocele may need adaptations in the educational setting to promote learning. Depending on the level of paralysis, the student may be unable to physically respond to questions, write out answers by hand, or study in the same way as nondisabled peers. The use of various adaptations and assistive technology devices may be needed to allow the student to fully participate.

Students may participate in classroom discussions any number of ways. The student may be able to participate verbally, use an augmentative communication device, eye gaze a response, or respond to a choice that is given in a multiple-choice format. Several different types of switches may also be used for students who are quadriplegic to activate computers, toys, or items in the environment. Some switches can be activated by the movement of a head or contracture of a muscle. Motorized wheelchairs can be controlled by sip and puff switches that are controlled by the child sipping or puffing into a switch that resembles a straw. There are many different types of assistive technology devices and adaptations that may support the student across a wide range of activities (see chapter 8 on assistive technology and chapter 12 on classroom adaptations).

Teachers may also need to present information differently for the student with a high spinal cord injury or a high myelomeningocele. Young children with cervical injuries lose the ability to explore and feel things around them. The teacher needs to take extra care and allow the student to experience things in an adapted manner. For example, the student may need to feel the item with his cheek to receive needed information.

Although students with spinal cord injury usually have the same level of cognitive functioning as they had prior to the accident, students with myelomeningocele may be born with some learning deficits. Depending on the individual student, the regular academic curriculum may be used, or adaptations to the curriculum may be needed to meet individual needs. Specialized instructional strategies may be needed to meet specific learning problems found in many students with myelomeningocele and shunted hydrocephalus. For example, students having difficulty with abstract concepts may need concrete examples, or students with attention and memory issues may need graphic organizers. Extra assistance in learning math concepts is often needed, as is assistance in reading comprehension and writing fluency. Teachers will need to determine specific areas of need of each individual student and determine the best way to systematically teach these areas.

Meeting Behavioral and Social Needs

Students with spinal cord injury or myelomeningocele will vary as to their behavioral and social needs. Students with spinal cord injury may especially have difficulty adjusting to an acquired disability. Unfortunately, former friends and teachers may draw away or avoid the student because of the pain of knowing the student before the injury and seeing his present condition. Teachers and peers need information regarding spinal cord injury and the difficulties in adjustment that sometimes accompany it. Many students adjust well to a spinal cord injury over time and find new enjoyable activities or adapted ways of enjoying old activities (Figure 6-10).

Information about myelomeningocele is also crucial because of its potential impact on student behavior and social skills and the need for teachers to provide social skills training. Teachers need to be aware of their attitudes and actions toward the student with the myelomeningocele and spinal cord disorders. The attitude of the teacher can set the tone for the rest of the class. A warm understanding environment will assist the student emotionally as well as help him achieve his potential. Counseling and support groups may be beneficial.

FIGURE 6–10 Students playing wheelchair basketball.

Bob Daemmrich/PhotoEdit Inc.

SUMMARY

This chapter discussed the etiology and mechanism of spinal cord injury and myelomeningocele. Both conditions involve muscle paralysis and sensory loss and often have additional problems (e.g., respiratory functioning, bowel and bladder control, and sexual functioning). Complications that may occur with a spinal cord injury are autonomic dysreflexia, musculoskeletal abnormalities, pain, and temperature regulation. Individuals with myelomeningocele may have Chiari II malformation, hydrocephalus, seizures, musculoskeletal abnormalities, visual impairments, language abnormalities, and cognitive or learning impairments. Adaptations and assistive technology are often needed in the school setting to allow students with spinal cord injury or myelomeningocele to reach their full potential.

 **Stacy's Story**

Stacy is a 12-year-old girl with myelomeningocele. She has normal intelligence but some learning impairments pertaining to attention, memory, and abstract concepts. She receives instruction from a special education teacher in math. She performs clean intermittent catheterization independently at school but often skips performing the procedure while reporting that she did do it. Stacy has difficulty staying on topic in the classroom and maintaining conversations with her peers. She can ambulate with crutches for short distances (across a room) but otherwise uses a wheelchair for mobility. Her peers don't seem to understand why she needs a wheelchair when they see her walk, and they didn't seem to like interacting with her. As her teacher, what actions should you take to address the identified problems?

REFERENCES

Adzick, S., & Walsh, D. S. (2003). Myelomeningocele: Prenatal diagnosis, pathophysiology and management. *Seminars in Pediatric Surgery, 12*, 168-174.

Baptiste, D. C., & Fehlings, M. G. (2006). Pharmacological approaches to repair the injured spinal cord. *Journal of Neurotrauma, 23*, 318-334.

Barf, H. A., Verhoef, M., Post, M. W., Gooskens, R. H., & Prevo, A. J. (2003). Cognitive status of young adults with spina bifida. *Developmental Medicine and Child Neurology, 45*, 813-820.

Barnes, M. A., & Dennis, M. (1992). Reading in children and adolescents after early-onset hydrocephalus and in normally developing age peers: Phonological analysis, word recognition, word comprehension, and passage comprehension skills. *Journal of Pediatric Psychology, 17*, 445-465.

Barnes, M., Dennis, M., & Hetherington, R. (2004). Reading and writing skills in young adults with spina bifida and hydrocephalus. *Journal of the International Neuropsychological Society, 10*, 655-663.

Beers, M. H., Porter, R. S., Jones, T. V., Kaplan, J. L., & Berkwits, M. (2006). *The Merck manual of diagnosis and therapy*. Whitehouse Station, NJ: Merck Research Laboratories.

Bergstrom, E. M., Short, D. J., Frankel, H. L., Henderson, N. J., & Jones, P. R. (1999). The effect of childhood spinal cord injury on skeletal development: A retrospective study. *Spinal Cord, 37*, 838-846.

Bowman, R. M., McLone, D. G., Grant, J. A., Tomita, T., & Ito, J. A. (2001). Spina bifida outcome: A 25 year prospective. *Pediatric Neurosurgery, 34*, 114-126.

Bridwell, K. H., Anderson, P. A., Boden, S. C., Vaccaro, A. R., & Wang, J. C. (2005). What's new in spinal surgery? *Journal of Bone and Joint Surgery, 87*, 1892-1901.

Bruner, J., Tulipan, N., Reed, G., Davis, G. H., Bennett, K., Luker, K. S., et al. (2004). Intrauterine repair of spina bifida: Preoperative predictors of shunt-dependent hydrocephalus. *American Journal of Obstetrics and Gynecology, 190*, 1305-1312.

Burmeister, R., Hanney, H. J., Copeland, K., Fletcher, J. M., Boudousquie, A., & Dennis, M. (2005). Attention problems and executive functions in children with spina bifida and hydrocephalus. *Child Neuropsychology, 11*, 265-283.

Chiafery, M. (2006). Care and management of the child with shunted hydrocephalus. *Pediatric Nursing, 32*, 222-225.

Dryden, D. M., Saunders, L. D., Rowe, B. H., May, L. A., Yiannakoulias, N., Svenson, L. W., et al., (2004). Utilization of health services following spinal cord injury: A 6 year follow-up study. *Spinal Cord, 42*, 513-525.

Dunn, K. L. (2004). Identification and management of autonomic dysreflexia in the emergency department. *Topics in Emergency Medicine, 26*, 254-259.

Fredrick, D. R., & Asbury, T. (2004). Strabismus. In P. Riordan-Eva & J. P. Whitcher (Eds.), *Vaughan & Asbury's general ophthalmology* (pp. 230-249). New York: Lange Medical Books/McGraw-Hill.

Garbossa, D., Fontanella, M., Fronda, C., Benevello, C., Muraca, G., Ducati, A., et al. (2006). New strategies for repairing the injured spinal cord: The role of stem cells. *Neurological Research, 28*, 500-504.

Guyton, A. C., & Hall, J. E. (2006). *Textbook of medical physiology* (11th ed). Philadelphia: Elsevier/Saunders.

Hanley, M. A., Masedo, A., Jensen, M. P., Cardenas, D., & Turner, J. A. (2006). Pain interference in persons with spinal cord injury: Classification of mild, moderate and severe pain. *Journal of Pain, 7*, 129-133.

Haslam, R. (2004). Spinal cord disorders. In R. E. Behrman, R. M. Kliegman, & H. B. Jenson (Eds.), *Nelson textbook of pediatrics* (pp. 2049-2052). Philadelphia: Saunders.

Heller, K. W., Forney, P. E., Alberto, P. A., Schwartzman, M. N., & Goeckel, T. (2000). *Meeting physical and health needs of children with disabilities: Teaching student participation and management*. Belmont, CA: Wadsworth.

Herring, J. A. (2002). *Tachdjian's pediatric orthopaedics* (3rd ed.) Philadelphia: W. B. Saunders.

Hoit, J. D., Banzett, R. B., Lohmeier, H. L., Hixon, T. J., & Brown, R. (2003). Clinical ventilator adjustments that improve speech. *Chest, 124*, 1512-1521.

Houliston, M. J., Taguri, A. H., Dutton, G. N., Hajivassiliou, C., & Young, D. G. (1999). Evidence of cognitive visual problems in children with hydrocephalus a structured clinical history-taking strategy. *Developmental Medicine and Child Neurology, 41*, 298-306.

Iddon, J. L., Morgan, D. J., Loveday, C., Sahakian, B. J., & Pickard, J. D. (2004). Neuropsychological profile of young adults with spina bifida with or without hydrocephalus. *Journal of Neurology, Neurosurgery and Psychiatry, 75*, 1112-1118.

Islam, K. (2005). Progress in spina bifida research. In M. Zesta (Ed.), *Trends in spina bifida research* (pp. 43-62). New York: Nova Biomedical Books.

Jacobs, R., Northam, E., & Anderson, V. (2001). Cognitive outcome in children with myelomeningocele and perinatal hydrocephalus: A longitudinal perspective. *Journal of Developmental and Physical Disabilities, 13*, 389-405.

Johnston, M. V., & Kinsman, S. (2004). Congenital anomalies of the central nervous system. In R. E. Behrman, R. M. Kliegman, & H. B. Jenson (Eds.), *Nelson textbook of pediatrics* (pp. 1983-1993). Philadelphia: W. B. Saunders.

Karlsson, A. (2006). Autonomic dysfunction in spinal cord injury: Clinical presentation of symptoms and signs. *Progress in Brain Research, 152*, 1-8.

Lazzaretti, D. D., & Pearson, C. (2004). Myelodysplasia. In P. J. Allen & J. A. Vessey (Eds.). *Primary care of the child with a chronic condition* (pp. 630-643). St. Louis: Mosby.

Liptak, G. S. (2007). Neural tube defects. In M. L. Batshaw, L. Pellegrino, & N. Roizen (Eds.), *Children with disabilities* (6th ed., pp. 419-438). Baltimore: Brookes.

Masri(y), W. S. (2006). Traumatic spinal cord injury: The relationship between pathology and clinical implications. *Trauma, 8*, 29-46.

Mavinkurve, G., Bagley, C., Pradilla, G., & Jallo, G. I. (2005). Advances in the management of hydrocephalus in pediatric patients with myelomeningocele. In M. Zesta (Ed.), *Trends in spina bifida research* (pp. 1-29). New York: Nova Biomedical Books.

McLone, D. G., & Dias, M. (2003). The Chiari II malformation: Cause and impact. *Child's Nervous System, 19*, 540-550.

Menkes, J. H., & Ellenbogen, R. C. (2002). Traumatic brain and spinal cord injuries in children. In B. L. Maria (Ed.), *Current management in child neurology* (2nd ed., pp. 442-454). Hamilton, ON: BC Decker.

Moin, H., & Khalili, H. A. (2006). Brown-Sequard syndrome due to cervical pen assault. *Journal of Clinical Forensic Medicine, 13,* 144-145.

Nader-Sepahi, A., Casey, A. T., Hayward, R., Crockar, J. H. A., & Thompson, D. (2005). Symptomatic atlantoaxial instability in Down syndrome. *Journal of Neurosurgery, 103,* 231-237.

Reichert, K. W., & Schmidt, M. (2001). Neurologic sequelae of shaken baby syndrome. *Journal of Aggression, Maltreatment and Trauma, 5,* 79-99.

Rigby, P., Ryan, S., Joos, S., Cooper, B., Jutai, J., & Steggles, E. (2005). Impact of electronic aids to daily living on the lives of persons with cervical spinal cord injuries. *Assistive Technology, 17,* 89-97.

Toth, C., McNeil, S., & Feasby, T. (2005). Central nervous system injuries in sport and recreation: A systematic review. *Sports Medicine, 35,* 685-715.

Tubbs, R. S., & Oakes, W. J. (2004). Treatment and management of the Chiari II malformation: An evidence-based review of the literature. *Child's Nervous System, 20,* 375-381.

Vachha, B., & Adams, R. (2003). Language differences in young children with myelomeningocele and shunted hydrocephalus. *Pediatric Neurosurgery, 39,* 184-189.

Verhoef, M., Barf, H. A., Post, M., van Asbeck, F. W., Gooskens, R. H., & Prevo, A. J. (2004). Secondary impairments in young adults with spina bifida. *Developmental Medicine and Child Neurology, 46,* 420-427.

Waxman, S. G., & Hains, B. C. (2006). Fire and phantoms after spinal cord injury: Na$^+$ channels and central pain. *Trends in Neuroscience, 29,* 207-215.

CHAPTER 7

TRAUMATIC BRAIN INJURY

Sharon Grandinette and Sherwood J. Best

Traumatic brain injury (TBI) is a high-incidence medical disability that affects over 1 million children and adolescents per year (Glang, Tyler, Pearson, Todis, & Morvanta, 2004). Outcomes of traumatic brain injury span a continuum that ranges from death to mild disabilities in cognition and communication or no impairments. Deficits may also occur in physical and psychosocial realms (Ylvisaker, 1998). Although most traumatic brain injuries are mild in nature, individuals who sustain a moderate to severe brain injury are faced with long-term effects that interfere with every aspect of their lives. Traumatic brain injury is more likely to occur in males than females (DiScala & Savage, 2003), and more likely to occur in African American children (Langlois, Rutland-Brown, & Thomas, 2005).

Although the Individuals with Disabilities Education Act added traumatic brain injury as a federal eligibility category in 1991, there appears to be a significant underidentification of children with traumatic brain injury. Every year, approximately 20,000 students reenter school after sustaining a traumatic brain injury. These students require appropriately trained staff to address their persisting disabilities (Ylvisaker et al., 2005). In its 2002 annual report to Congress, the Office of Special Education of the U.S. Department of Education noted that only 14,844 students were served under the category of traumatic brain injury (U.S. Department of Education, 2002). This dynamic occurs because traumatic brain injury is frequently categorized within other federal disability categories, such as multiple, orthopedic, or learning disabilities.

Educators and other professionals who serve students with traumatic brain injury are faced with a daunting challenge. They must try to identify students who have sustained a traumatic brain injury, recognize their deficits, and reintegrate them to school, providing appropriate interventions as the students' needs change over time. While restoration of function in affected areas is the goal of rehabilitation and education, it requires the collaboration of multiple medical specialists, allied health professionals, and educators.

DESCRIPTION OF TRAUMATIC BRAIN INJURY

There are several terms used to describe brain injury. The term *head injury* may be used synonymously with the term *brain injury* but can also include injury occurring only to the scalp or skull. Thus, the term *brain injury* is a more specific term. When brain injury occurs from some type of trauma or external force, it is called **traumatic brain injury** and causes temporary or permanent disruption of brain structure or function (Beers, Porter, Jones, Kaplan, & Berkwits, 2006; Dixon, Layton, & Shaw, 2005).

Traumatic brain injury can be further classified into an open and closed injury. In an open injury, there is penetration of the skull and the underlying brain tissue from sharp objects such as a bullet. A closed injury usually occurs when the head strikes an object, is struck, or is shaken violently (Beers et al., 2006).

The brain may be adversely affected from causes other than traumatic means. For example, infants can be born with congenital brain defects that affect brain development (e.g., encephalocele, microcephaly, anencephaly, or Chiari II malformation). In addition, brain injuries or disorders may occur from nontraumatic means (e.g., stroke, brain anoxia from near drowning, infections, diseases, or tumors) (see Figure 7-1). In this chapter, we will limit our discussion to traumatic brain injury.

ETIOLOGY OF TRAUMATIC BRAIN INJURY

The causes of pediatric brain injury vary by gender, age, and geographic location. Mishandling by caregivers and child abuse are the most prevalent causes of brain injury in infants and toddlers prior to the age of 2. Abuse of infants and young children often occurs in the form of shaking. The condition was originally known as "Shaken Baby syndrome" or "Whiplash Shaken Infant syndrome." Now called "Shaken-Impact syndrome," this form of inflicted head injury is more likely to result in poorer cognitive and motor outcomes (Newton

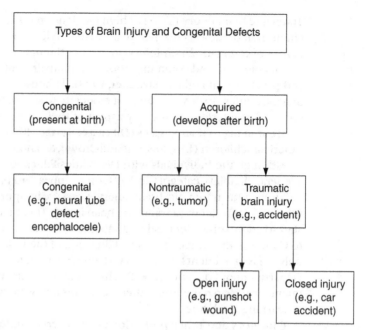

FIGURE 7–1 Types of brain injury and congenital defects.

& Vandeven, 2005) and death (Keenan, Runyan, Marshall, Nocera, & Merten, 2004) than unintentional injury. If infants are premature, developmentally disabled, born to young parents, or live in conditions of poverty or instability, they are more "at risk" for abuse (Duhaime, Christian, Rourke, & Zimmerman, 1998). Infants whose brain injury results from abuse have a worse prognosis than infants whose brain injury is unintentional, perhaps because there is a pattern of repeated abuse (Ewing-Cobbs, Levin, & Fletcher, 1998).

Infants' and toddlers' bodies have heavy heads supported by weak neck muscles. As a result, accidental falls are one of the most frequent causes of traumatic brain injury (DiScala & Savage, 2003). This age-group is also at risk during motor vehicle crashes because the head often becomes the point of impact. Elementary school–age children are more likely to sustain a traumatic brain injury during play, motor vehicle accidents (often as pedestrians), falls, and bicycling accidents. Fortunately, seating restraint systems, air bags in cars, and the use of bicycle helmets have been found to reduce the risk of TBI (Lee, Schofer, & Koppelman, 2005; Michaud, Duhaime, Wade, Rabin, Jones, & Lazar, 2007).

Adolescents are most often involved in motor vehicle accidents (DiScala & Savage, 2003) where, in many cases, drugs and/or alcohol are a contributing factor. Adolescents also sustain injuries from more intensive sports activities, assault, and risk-taking behaviors. Other contributors to adolescent brain injury include gunshot head wounds (Sheehan, Dicara, LeBailley & Christoffel, 1997) and attempted suicide (Michaud, Duhaime, Wade, Rabin, Jones, & Lazar, 2007).

Children who are already diagnosed with special needs in the areas of attention deficit disorder and attention-deficit/hyperactivity disorder (ADHD) or learning or emotional disabilities may be at higher risk of sustaining a traumatic brain injury because of inattention, risk taking, or poor judgment. A traumatic brain injury that occurs in a child with a preexisting condition will usually exacerbate the deficits already present and contribute to additional deficits that often accompany a traumatic brain injury.

DYNAMICS OF TRAUMATIC BRAIN INJURY

The brain is protected by bone, membranes, and fluid. The skull protects and surrounds the brain, except at the base of the brain, where a hole (known as the foramen magnum)

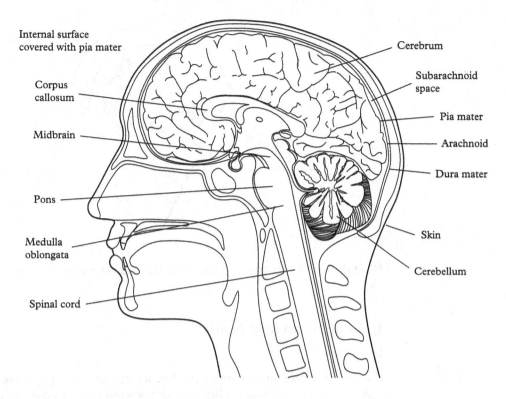

Internal surface
covered with pia mater

Corpus
callosum

Midbrain

Pons

Medulla
oblongata

Spinal cord

Cerebrum

Subarachnoid
space

Pia mater

Arachnoid

Dura mater

Skin

Cerebellum

FIGURE 7–2 Basic anatomy of the brain.

90% of TBI's in children are closed

connects the cranial cavity and the vertebrae. The brain is also surrounded by three layers of membranes: the dura mater (the outermost layer that is next to the skull), the arachnoid (middle membrane), and the pia mater (which is next to the brain) (see Figure 7-2). Together, these three membranes are known as meninges. Finally, the cerebrospinal fluid that surrounds the brain serves as a cushion for the brain within the skull. The brain actually floats in the fluid.

When the brain sustains some type of physical trauma, the type, location, and amount of physical force will determine the kind of injury. In open head injuries, the scalp, skull, meninges, and (usually) the brain are penetrated. Most open head injuries result in focal effects (i.e., effects that are limited to one part of the brain) (Burton & Moffatt, 2004). For example, a bullet wound to the head that goes through the primary motor cortex of the left hemisphere will typically result in paralysis on the right side of the body, leaving the other side unaffected. Although certain types of open head injuries can cause diffuse (generalized or widespread) effects, the primary brain damage in most open head injuries occurs at the site of injury with secondary effects in other areas because of complications.

Closed head injuries, which are nonpenetrating injuries, account for more than 90% of traumatic brain injuries in children (Menkes & Ellenbogen, 2002) and usually result in more diffuse damage. The dynamics of a closed head injury is a combination of deceleration or acceleration, coup-contrecoup injury, and rotational trauma. Since the brain is floating in cerebrospinal fluid, the impact causes the brain to accelerate or decelerate, hitting the inside of the skull. The initial site of impact is known as the coup injury. After the initial impact, the brain rebounds and hits the opposite side of the skull, resulting in injury on that side of the brain, known as the contrecoup injury (see Figure 7-3). As the brain moves back and forth, it may also strike against bony protrusions at the base of the skull (located at the undersurface of the frontal and temporal lobes), resulting in further damage. Rotational trauma may also occur in which the brain twists during acceleration or deceleration. Several other injuries and complications may occur.

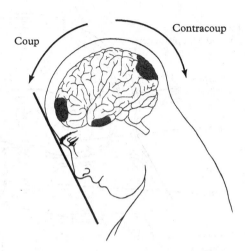

Coup

Contracoup

FIGURE 7–3 Traumatic brain injury showing coup and contrecoup damage.

Types of Intracranial Injuries

Concussion

During a traumatic brain injury a mild injury may occur to the nerve fibers, resulting in a concussion. A concussion is a brief loss of consciousness or amnesia that lasts from seconds up to 6 hours. Usually the child will return to normal after that time. A concussion is considered the least serious type of traumatic brain injury with no gross structural brain injuries being present. However, children should be observed for several weeks after the injury for postconcussion syndrome (e.g., headache, irritability, poor judgment, or poor concentration) (Burton & Moffatt, 2004; Roth & Farls, 2000).

Least serious →

Diffuse Axonal Injury

When a loss of consciousness occurs for more than six hours, a more serious injury is present, known as diffuse axonal injury (DAI). Diffuse axonal injury is the general shearing (breaking) of axons from the violent acceleration or deceleration of the brain that occurs in a closed injury. These axons are responsible for transmitting information between neurons (nerve cells) in the brain and to parts of the body (see chapter 5). Diffuse axonal injury results in widespread neurological dysfunction due to impaired communication between neurons. This is often further complicated by ensuing cerebral edema (swelling of the brain) and other complications (e.g., hypertension or breathing difficulties). Recovery can take weeks to years with possible long-term impairments in motor, communication, cognitive, and behavioral functioning.

Scalp and Skull Injuries

A traumatic brain injury may result in scalp and skull injuries. A scalp injury may cause a lot of bleeding, but it does not affect brain functioning. A skull fracture is often a sign that significant force was involved in the injury, and its effect will depend on the type of fracture. For example, a crack in the skull (known as a linear fracture) usually heals with little consequence. However, a depressed skull consisting of a broken skull that presses on the brain, often results in lacerations (tearing) of brain tissue and hemorrhage (bleeding) and can be often associated with significant brain injury.

Cerebral Contusion

Cerebral contusions are often associated with skull fractures or from the brain hitting the inside of the skull. A cerebral contusion is a bruise on the surface of the brain. It may be accompanied by cerebral edema. Effects of the contusion depend on its size and extent of damage to the brain.   (Swelling)

Hematomas and Cerebral Hemorrhage

Open or closed injuries may result in bleeding in the brain (known as cerebral hemorrhage). When the blood collects in an area, it is referred to as a hematoma. A traumatic brain injury may result in a subdural hematoma (blood between the dura mater and pia-arachnoid mater), an epidural hematoma (blood between the skull and dura mater), or an intracerebral hematoma (blood within the brain itself). Depending on the size, location, and type of hematoma, it may cause an increase in the pressure inside the brain, possibly leading to serious impairment or death.

Cerebral Edema

Any type of traumatic brain injury can cause edema, or swelling of the brain. Edema usually peaks at about 72 hours after the injury and resolves within a few weeks. When the brain swells, it has nowhere to go since it is surrounded by the skull, hense there is an increase in intracranial pressure (ICP). This can compromise blood flow and result in neuronal tissue hypoxia (lack of oxygen to the brain cells) and death of more brain tissue. If the edema continues and is not medically controlled, a cerebral herniation can occur in which the increased pressure forces the brain down the foramen magnum (hole in the base of the skull) and result in death (Burton & Moffatt, 2004).

Severity of Traumatic Brain Injury

After sustaining a traumatic brain injury most children lose consciousness and/or have amnesia. The severity of the traumatic brain injury is often based on the period of unconsciousness or memory loss. Several scales are used to determine severity based on these factors.

After the initial symptoms of a traumatic brain injury, the child may range from being alert to having confusion to being in a coma. (A coma is a lack of responsiveness in which the person cannot be aroused.) Various scales are used to rate the severity of the traumatic brain injury based on the level of consciousness. One of these scales is the Glasgow Coma Rating Scale (GCS), which examines eye openings (none, opens eyes to painful stimuli, opens eyes to speech, spontaneous), verbal responses (none, makes sounds, uses inappropriate words, confused conversation, oriented), and motor responses (none, various abnormal motor responses, obeys commands). Each of these three areas is given a score and upon adding them together, the final score ranges from 3 to 15 (Jennett & Teasdale, 1981). A mild traumatic brain injury is rated as a score of 13 to 15, a moderate TBI has a score of 9 to 12, and a severe TBI has a score of 8 or less (Jaffe et al., 1992). Modified versions of the GCS for infants and children are available but are not used consistently.

The duration of a coma and the duration of amnesia are other predictors of severity of the traumatic brain injury. For example, a coma lasting more than 7 days has been associated with a decrease in IQ in children (Burton & Moffatt, 2004). However, the length of posttraumatic amnesia (PTA) (the time elapsed from injury until the recovery of full consciousness and the return of ongoing memory) is considered a better indicator of the severity of injury. The classification is as follows: mild brain injury has a PTA of less than 1 hour, a moderate injury from 1 to 24 hours, a severe injury from 1 to 7 days, and a very severe injury over 7 days (Dixon et al., 2005).

It is important to note that the level of severity of traumatic brain injury as determined from these various scales does not perfectly correlate with the outcome for all people. Although a severe injury usually indicates a poor outcome, a favorable outcome is possible in an individual case. Likewise, a score indicating a mild traumatic brain injury may result in a poor outcome in a specific individual. Additional factors may also influence the outcome of a traumatic brain injury (e.g., injury location, pre-injury status, treatment effectiveness).

CHARACTERISTICS OF TRAUMATIC BRAIN INJURY

The characteristics of a traumatic brain injury will vary depending on the severity of the injury. The majority of traumatic brain injuries in children are designated as mild. Children with mild traumatic brain injury may have no consequences or may have a variety of vague and subjective problems that fall under the category of postconcussive syndrome. Symptoms may include headaches and dizziness, irritability, poor judgment, emotional liability, poor learning and organizational skills, poor cognitive/communication skills, difficulties maintaining concentration for school or work, and psychosocial difficulties (Blosser & DePompei, 2003; Burton & Moffatt, 2004). These effects may last for hours, days, weeks, or years.

More severe characteristics may be present in a moderate or severe traumatic brain injury. Following a moderate traumatic brain injury, the child may experience physical weakness, cognitive/communicative impairments, difficulty learning new information, and psychosocial problems. Severe traumatic brain injury can result in multiple cognitive, communicative, physical, emotional, social, and behavioral problems that continue throughout life, requiring intensive and ongoing supports and services in school, home, and community settings (Blosser & DePompei, 2003).

Cognitive Effects

The most common cognitive deficits following traumatic brain injury in children include memory impairments and disorders in attention. After an injury, a child may not remember what happened before the accident (retrograde amnesia) or what happened after (anterograde amnesia). However, memory functions, in general, may be affected for some time following the injury. Memory deficits include short-term memory loss that interferes with new learning, long-term memory loss that involves forgetting what was previously learned, and difficulty returning to tasks after interruption and confusion. Additional deficits often do not surface until the child ages, specifically in the area of executive functioning skills. Executive functions include domains such as cognition (decision making and planning), self-regulation (motivation and modulation of emotion), metacognition (self-appraisal and implementation of self-management skills), and social cognition (processing the intent of others) (Levin & Hanten, 2005). Deficits in executive functioning can be a significant challenge for students as they try to fit into academic and social settings. A child may be easily distractible and have poor concentration skills, perhaps leading to difficulty following instructions and shifting attention between tasks. Cognitive deficits, including poor generalization skills, limited abstract thinking, and a decrease in the speed of processing, have detrimental effects in the classroom and in social situations. Other cognitive deficits include poor information organization and problems with retrieval, sequencing, and generalizing. Perceptual and attention deficits, poor judgment, and deficits in processing information may also occur (Savage, DePompei, Tyler, & Lash, 2005). All these cognitive deficits will have a significant effect on the acquisition of new knowledge.

A decline in all academic areas, including reading comprehension, spelling, math, written language, and vocabulary, have been found to occur following traumatic brain injury. While decoding skills may remain intact, reading comprehension is one of the most impaired abilities for many students (Tyler & Mira, 1999). Splinter skills may also be present, in which a child performs on grade level in certain specific areas and below grade areas in others.

Reading comp – most impaired ability

Communication Effects

The ability to communicate adequately is often one of the major deficits to surface in children and adolescents following a traumatic brain injury. While many educators and school-based speech pathologists recognize and address speech difficulties (production of sounds), language deficits (use of words and sentences to convey ideas) and cognitive/communicative abilities (ability to use language and underlying processes such as attention and memory) often go unnoticed (Savage et al., 2005). School-based speech assessment tools may not detect some of the more subtle language and cognitive/communicative deficits that occur in students with traumatic brain injuries, causing them to be ineligible for school-based language therapy.

Speech Impairments

A number of motor-speech disorders can occur following traumatic brain injury because of neuromuscular dysfunction. The muscles of the lips and tongue may become weaker or less coordinated, causing articulation difficulties and affecting a child's ability to speak clearly (dysarthria). Breathing muscles may become weaker, affecting the ability to speak loud enough to be heard in conversation or to speak at all. Weakened muscles may also cause dysphagia (difficulty swallowing). Other motor-speech problems may include decreased verbal fluency, voice disorders (involving pitch, volume, or voice quality), and impaired prosody (rhythm and intonation of speech). Apraxia of speech, may also occur which is difficulty with the voluntary planning, executing, and sequencing of oral motor movements. Augmentative and alternative communication devices (AAC) may need to be considered to address motor-speech disorders (Russell et al., 1998).

Language Impairments

Language-based impairments fall into three categories—receptive, expressive and pragmatic. Students with poor receptive skills struggle with the ability to understand what is spoken or written, while those with expressive deficits have difficulty with the ability to use verbal or written skills to express an idea. Students with pragmatic language deficits have difficulty engaging in social interactions with peers and adults. Over time, receptive and expressive language skills may appear close to normal in assessment situations and non-stressed conversational exchanges. However, when the individual experiences pressure to perform verbally within a specific time period, or recall information from memory, conversational performance may deteriorate (Savage et al., 2005).

Students exhibiting language deficits may have anomia (word-finding difficulties) or aphasia, a disorder that results from damage to the language centers of the brain and that can result in a decrease in or loss of abilities to communicate through speaking, listening, reading, and writing. As a result, they struggle with reading comprehension and written language as well as with syntax and semantics. When pragmatic language is affected, students have difficulty with topic (selection, introduction, maintenance, and change), turn taking (initiation, response, and conciseness), vocabulary selection (specificity, accuracy, and cohesion), and stylistic variation (context and partner appropriateness). In the classroom, these deficits contribute to a child's inability to be understood, to generate or summarize thoughts, or to take turns in conversation. In some cases, they may not be able to get to the point they are trying to make and will "talk around" subjects (circumlocution). Some students may have difficulty understanding the meaning of a conversation when humor or figures of speech are used (Blosser & DePompei, 2003). Impairments in auditory comprehension of language are less common. However, difficulties in understanding verbal abstraction (metaphor and synonym) and high-level verbally mediated items (main idea) have been reported (Ylvisaker, 1986). Individuals with severe traumatic brain injury may have difficulty processing information conveyed in facial expression, which further impedes communication (Braun, Baribeau, Ethier, Daigneault, & Proulx, 1989).

Physical/Motor and Sensory Effects

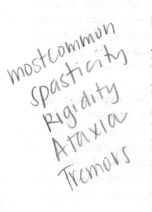

A traumatic brain injury can affect motor abilities and result in severe motor impairments. Examples of motor abilities that can be affected include difficulties with motor speed and precision, balance, muscle weakness, and eye-hand coordination. The most common motor impairments are spasticity (increased muscle tone in parts of the body), rigidity (also a form of increased muscle tone with resistance to movement), ataxia (uncoordinated voluntary movement and with impaired balance), and tremors (Michaud et al., 2007). The type of motor impairment will depend on the location of the traumatic brain injury (e.g., primary motor cortex, basal ganglia, cerebellum). Although there is no cure for the motor impairment, treatment is aimed at increasing functional movement and may include medications, surgeries, orthoses, physical and occupational therapies, and other medical interventions.

Motor impairments may result in secondary problems. For example, individuals with spasticity commonly develop contractures and dislocations. When the traumatic brain injury results in swallowing problems, feeding disorders may occur. In some cases, this may need to be treated with tube feedings (tube placed into the stomach or small intestine to deliver food in liquid form).

Another complication of traumatic brain injury is the development of posttraumatic seizures or posttraumatic epilepsy. This refers to seizures that occur after head injury, and that are attributed to the head injury. Posttraumatic seizures are usually divided into three categories: immediate (occurring when the injury occurred), early (occurring one week after the injury) and late (occurring after one week of the injury). There is an overall occurrence of posttraumatic seizures ranging from 0.2 to 9.8% with early seizures being more common in children than late seizures, and younger children are more likely to have status epilepticus (continuous seizure) (Frey, 2003). These initial seizures may continue and develop into posttraumatic epilepsy (which is more than two unprovoked seizures). Anticonvulsant medications (as well as other treatment options) will be needed to treat the epilepsy. In some cases, a protective helmet is needed when the student falls frequently from a seizure (see chapter 17 for more information on epilepsy).

Sensory impairment may also occur after a traumatic brain injury. Damage to the cochlea may result in sensorineural hearing loss, while middle ear damage may result in conductive hearing loss. Vision problems may occur when the structures of the eye are damaged, as well as when there is damage to the pathways going to the brain (optic nerves and optic radiations) and areas of the brain associated with vision (visual cortex, visual associative cortex area) (Hoyt, 2007). Damage to these areas may result in such problems as visual field deficits, diplopia (double vision), photophobia (sensitivity to light), nystagmus (involuntary oscillations of the eye) and cortical visual impairment (see chapter 11 for more information on sensory impairments). Visual perceptual deficits may also occur that interfere with visual discrimination and visual spatial relations.

Psychosocial/Behavioral Effects

The term *psychosocial* refers to the overall emotional, psychological, and behavioral effects following a traumatic brain injury. Changes in personality, emotions, and behavior often follow severe traumatic brain injury and pose difficult challenges for families, teachers, and friends (Ylvisaker et al., 2005). For example, damage to the frontal lobes can cause lowered inhibitions with accompanying inappropriate behavior and inappropriate reactions to normal situations. Temporal lobe injuries are also common, causing agitation and combative behaviors. Also, behavior problems that were present before the injury are often exacerbated.

There are a wide range of behaviors that can occur from traumatic brain injury, ranging from aggressive and destructive to withdrawn and apathetic. The most common behavior problems found in children with traumatic brain injury are: inattention, verbal outbursts, bolting, property destruction, perseveration, aggression, noncompliance, and inappropriate sexual behavior (Bruce, Selznick-Gurdin, & Savage, 2004). Initially, many of these behaviors may be due to stimulus overload or deficits, such as a student with traumatic brain injury who is sensitive to noise bolts out of the room because people are talking loudly, or a student who is more aggressive in cold weather due to sensitivity to the cold. In addition, verbal outbursts and aggression can occur from frustration related to memory deficits, slow processing, communication issues, or disorientation (Savage, Depompei, Tyler, & Lash, 2005). Over time, stimulus overload and some deficits may decrease, but behavior problems may continue, worsen, or change due to the damaged brain.

Behaviors may also occur from the child's reaction to the injury. Anxiety, depression, posttraumatic stress, and emotional lability (rapid changes) are often seen as a psychological reaction to the traumatic brain injury. Many have a lack of insight into their newly acquired disabilities and do not understand their deficits. Substance abuse and suicide attempts can also occur, especially in adolescents. Often, students who exhibit psychosocial difficulties following traumatic brain injury become eligible for special education services under the category of emotionally disturbed, especially if the injury occurred in the distant past.

Tragically, there is often little connection to the brain injury that happened in younger years to the psychosocial problems occurring as the student becomes older, and many of these students end up in the juvenile justice system.

Why do students with traumatic brain injury have such difficulty controlling behavior? Behavioral control requires the intact and integrated functioning of brain systems. When attention and memory, physical and emotional regulation, planning and anticipation, and speed of processing are affected, children have difficulty controlling emotions or reactions. Instructions, rules, or consequences are not recalled because of memory problems. Limited executive functioning skills interfere with anticipation and planning. Students may not know how to avoid difficult situations and continue to find themselves in the same problems repeatedly. Limited awareness of expectations as well as communication deficits also contribute to inappropriate behaviors. Students who struggle with slowed language processing misperceive the intent of a message and are often unaware of pertinent social cues. Medications can also affect behavior.

DETECTION OF TRAUMATIC BRAIN INJURY

Several diagnostic procedures are used to detect traumatic brain injury. An overall assessment of injuries is performed as well as a neurological evaluation. If there is impaired consciousness, a Glasgow Coma Scale score of less than 15, neurological findings, seizures, or suspected fractures, imaging is done. However, some doctors perform imaging for anything more than a trivial head injury because of the severe consequences of missing a hematoma (Beers et al., 2006).

Diagnostic imaging devices provide a window into the brain to detect abnormalities, determine the significance of the trauma, and study brain function. Two types of neuroimaging techniques are structural imaging and functional imaging. Structural imaging provides information about the neuroanatomy of the skull, brain tissue, and blood vessels and can indicate edema, intracranial bleeding, and degeneration. Structural imaging devices include X-rays, computerized tomography (CT or CAT) scans, and magnetic resonance imaging (MRI) scans. The CT uses a series of X-rays in different locations of the brain (see Figure 7–4). The MRI (see Figure 7–5) uses magnetic properties of the molecules to produce anatomic detail of the brain (Bigler, 2005).

Olivier Voisin/Photo Researchers, Inc.

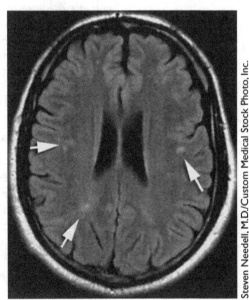

Steven Needell, M.D./Custom Medical Stock Photo, Inc.

FIGURE 7–4   CT scanner (a) with a picture from a CT scanner (b).

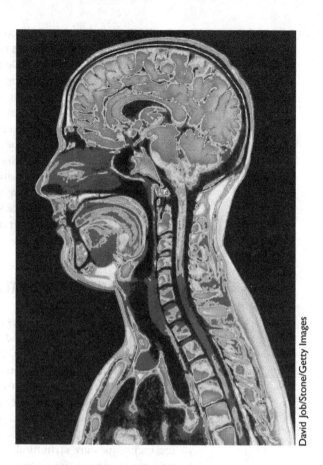

FIGURE 7–5 MRI scan of the head and upper chest.

David Job/Stone/Getty Images

Functional imaging uses newer methods to demonstrate activity in the brain and allows medical personnel to more accurately assess damage to the brain's functional ability and predict potential for rehabilitation through objective brain improvement. Most functional brain imaging in traumatic brain injury is currently performed using a single photon emission computed tomography (SPECT) scan or a positron emission tomography (PET) scan, which provides information on brain metabolism and blood flow. A functional MRI (fMRI) uses the magnetic qualities of oxygenated blood to observe rapid changes in blood flow (Anderson, Taber, & Hurley, 2005). The fMRI, PET, and SPECT scans show particular promise in identifying structural and functional abnormalities following a mild traumatic brain injury that are usually undetected with MRI and CT scans (Belanger, Vanderploeg, Curtiss, & Warden, 2007).

TREATMENT OF TRAUMATIC BRAIN INJURY

Acute Medical Phase

The primary goals of brain injury treatment during the acute care phase are to maintain the airway and secure proper pulmonary gas exchange (which may require a ventilator), stop bleeding, maintain adequate blood flow to the brain, and prevent or control any increase in pressure within the skull. Often surgery is required to treat certain skull fractures, evacuate hematomas, and stop bleeding. Increased intracranial pressure is commonly treated with medications, sedation, and drainage of cerebrospinal fluid (often through a catheter inserted into the brain).

Recovery from Coma

Although the severity of injuries differs between children with traumatic brain injury, there is a certain progression of behaviors that occur during recovery. Initially, the child may be in a coma and unresponsive to any stimuli. As the child begins to emerge from the coma, he may respond to stimuli in an inconsistent or nonpurposeful manner (moving entire body to tap on the arm) to eventually responding in a more localized fashion (moving arm away from stimulus). Next, the child will respond in a confused, agitated state in which he may hit people and try to pull out any medical tubes. As the agitation subsides, the child will begin to follow simple commands more consistently but continues to be confused, often wandering off aimlessly. Gradually, there will be more awareness of the environment with memory of familiar people or objects. Speech will also return, starting with short words or phrases, and behavior will progressively improve. However, deficits in cognition, communication, sensory processes, and behavior will often be present and be addressed in the rehabilitation phase.

Rehabilitation and Long-Term Management

Rehabilitation begins early with the use of therapy to avoid complications from immobilization when in a coma (e.g., muscle atrophy) to augmenting abilities while emerging from a coma (e.g., orientation strategies). Rehabilitation will also play a vital role in maximizing restoration of lost functions and teaching alternative compensatory strategies to promote optimal functioning. Based on assessments, a plan of care will be designed to address motor, communication, sensory, behavioral, and cognitive impairments.

After hospital-based acute rehabilitation, the child may continue to receive rehabilitation on an outpatient basis. Some children will benefit from a post–acute rehabilitation program, while others who are not quite ready for reentry into a school program may receive instruction in the home or may be placed in a transition program that can provide a specialized educational setting, intensive therapy, and assistance from specialists prior to returning to the school setting. Even when a child is discharged from rehabilitation services, the process of recovery often continues.

COURSE OF TRAUMATIC BRAIN INJURY

Children with traumatic brain injury may have minor to devastating deficits from the injury. Typically, recovery occurs rapidly during the first few months. Motor functions usually recover first; communication skills also tend to recover rapidly (although complex language skills may continue to be affected). Recovery of the higher cognitive functions related to attention, memory, and behavior tends to occur more slowly. Typically after rapid progress in the first few months, significant improvement continues over the first year; change will be slower after that, often plateauing after several years.

Research is beginning to determine how the brain heals itself after injury. Animal research has shown that nerve cells may form new connections through the collateral sprouting of dendrites, which restore some lost function. Other research has focused on increased sensitivity of receptor sites so that neuron circuits can function despite the absence of some neurons (see chapter 5 for more information on neurons). Recovery is also enhanced through enrichment of the environment (Dixon et al., 2005). Young children may have a better prognosis for recovery than older individuals due to the resiliency of the immature brain (Burton & Moffatt, 2004). Specific compensatory strategies will also be taught, when indicated, to improve the child's overall functioning. Therefore, improvement in functioning may be attributed to the pediatric brain healing itself and, in some cases, the learning of new compensatory strategies.

EDUCATIONAL IMPLICATIONS OF TRAUMATIC BRAIN INJURY

Transition from Hospital to School

The prescribed course of treatment for students with traumatic brain injury who transition from pediatric trauma centers is a well-prepared discharge plan with referrals to rehabilitation facilities and special education services in their public schools. However, DiScala and Savage

(2003) found that many children and adolescents ages 0 to 19 were discharged without ever being referred for such services. A limited number of rehabilitation programs serving children with traumatic brain injury, as well as inadequate financial resources to fund such programs, causes many students to be discharged home without these services. For those who were discharged home from a trauma center, less than 2% were referred for special education services.

Appropriate school reintegration following brain injury should begin at the time of injury. Many hospitals offer educational services provided by hospital teachers, beginning as soon as the child is medically stable. Parents, with the help of hospital social workers or other medical staff, should make contact with the child's school district to notify them about the child's condition and possible need for special education and support services. Ideally, a staff member from the school district should visit the child to assess possible future needs and confer with hospital staff and parents. A school nurse, psychologist, and special education teacher should become a part of a team that designs and facilitates an individualized school reentry plan based on the child's functioning status. With parental permission, assessments from hospital and rehabilitation placements regarding the child's present levels of functioning should be made available to the school. This will assist in developing the student's IEP and the Individual Health Care Plan (IHP).

Before a student with a traumatic brain injury returns to the school setting, it is important that all teachers and related staff members receive information regarding traumatic brain injury in general as well as about the child's specific deficits. It is important that the school staff employ appropriate assessment and educational strategies that can be used in the classroom to support optimal functioning and that they distinguish students with traumatic brain injury from those with developmental disabilities. Appropriate teacher/staff training, followed by well-designed instruction, will enable the student to experience success in the school program rather than failure. Even with adequate training, developing and sustaining an effective support system for school reentry poses challenges because children with traumatic brain injury are not a homogeneous group with predictable characteristics and needs.

Training and simple explanations regarding traumatic brain injury (with parental permission) should also be provided to the student's peers. Classmates may be under the false impression that the student with traumatic brain injury will be unchanged, especially when there are no apparent physical deficits. Providing the student's peers with accurate information about traumatic brain injury will assist in a smoother school transition.

Meeting Physical/Sensory Needs

Teachers and related staff who have students with traumatic brain injury will need to know how to address any physical or sensory impairments that occur from the traumatic brain injury. Physical and occupational therapists will be involved in promoting motor/sensory function. Adapted equipment and assistive technology is commonly used (e.g., adapted cups, spoons, prone standers, side lyers, and microswitches). At times, various medications may be prescribed to treat spasticity and seizures if they occur and teachers will need to learn about the medications and monitor their effects. For example, some students who have traumatic brain injury and spasticity receive intrathecal baclofen with a baclofen pump (which is implanted in the abdominal area) and teachers will need to be observant for side effects and complications (Ordia, Fisher, Adamski, & Spatz, 2002). In addition, surgical procedures may be used to release contractures or correct dislocations and teachers will need to be familiar with any restrictions following surgery, as well as address absences from school.

Adaptations are often required to address physical deficits. Following a traumatic brain injury, students often fatigue easily and have decreased endurance. Rest breaks and/or a modified schedule can address this issue. Other students may initially reenter school and attend only a partial day. Some students will require accommodations and/or modifications or specialized equipment (such as a closed-circuit TV (CCTV) for low vision) to access the curriculum. Accommodations may include more time to complete tests due to slower motor execution and more time to move between classes. Providing students with an extra set of books (one for home, one kept in each classroom) will assist with transitioning between classes (see chapter 8 on assistive technology and chapter 12 on classroom adaptations for more information).

Retraining or compensatory strategies are often necessary to compensate for existing sensory deficits. For example, a child with left visual neglect was given her reading material with red dots at the beginning of each line of text. She was taught to "find the red dot" to remediate her left visual neglect, which resulted in her ability to read a full page.

Meeting Communication Needs

One of the major consequences of traumatic brain injury can be the inability to communicate adequately. Assessment by a speech-language therapist needs to take subtle cognitive/communicative deficits into account, allowing the speech-language therapist to work on improving any speech disorder as well as language and social/pragmatic deficits. While therapy can be provided individually or in a small group, the therapist should be aware that children with traumatic brain injury often have difficulty generalizing skills learned in therapy to other environments. Services should be offered in the natural environment of the classroom where collaboration with the teacher can take place. The therapist can provide the teacher with interventions and strategies that address expressive and receptive language deficits related to academic functioning. There are a number of effective strategies and interventions, including (a) encouraging communication and allowing ample time for responses; (b) reducing rate of speech, length, and complexity of utterances during conversations; (c) altering the way directions are given (e.g., repeating, reducing complexity of directions, or writing them down); (d) monitoring speech selection (e.g., avoiding sarcasm and puns and limiting humor); (e) organizing and sequencing information; (f) developing memory skills; (g) practicing problem-solving skills to develop higher-level thinking; and (h) structuring communication activities for success (and, in some instances, using AAC systems for communication) (Blosser & DePompei, 2003).

Meeting Learning Needs

Assessment Following TBI

Students with TBI pose a real assessment challenge (Stavinoha, 2005). Although documents such as report cards, standardized test scores, and other information in a student's school record may provide information related to achievement prior to injury, these materials are not always available (Semrud-Clikeman, 2001). Standardized objective assessments may be misleading. For example, a normal IQ score on a standardized intelligence test may indicate achievement at the time of injury but fail to account for deficits in new learning (Mira & Tyler, 1991). Therefore, formal assessment results should always be accompanied by informal assessments such as observation and parental report (Stavinoha, 2005). The guidance of a neuropsychologist adds an important dimension to the assessment process (Semrud-Clikeman, 2001). Finally, teachers should receive appropriate pre-service and inservice training about the impact of brain injury on the assessment process (Savage et al., 2005).

Often, a neuropsychological evaluation will be given to detect deficits in the areas of intelligence, adaptive behavior, problem solving, memory, academics, motor performance, and psychomotor performance. However, to obtain a complete picture of a student's abilities and deficits, assessment information from a variety of sources, including speech pathology, occupational therapy, and physical therapy, must be combined with a functional evaluation of a child's skills in natural settings. Evaluation of a student's ability to perform a task in settings where his adaptive and social skills are called into play is critical. Relying solely on assessments administered in a quiet, one-to-one setting will not provide an accurate indication of how the child will function in a typical classroom and adapt to changes in classroom routines.

Along with data regarding the student's academic functioning, other related information is necessary. Important related information about the student's ability to withstand frustration and changes in routine, understand expectations, sustain attention, and manage fatigue contributes to assessment (Savage, DePompei, Tyler, & Lash, 2005; Semrud-Clikeman, 2001). Because rapid changes in status occur during recovery following a traumatic brain injury, assessment must be an ongoing process. What a child cannot accomplish one day he or she may be able to accomplish the next day, week, or month. Reports often quickly become obsolete.

Learning Problems

Deficits in the cognitive domain, decreased speed of information processing, and executive functioning often cause the most difficulty in the classroom with regard to acquiring new information. Students who may have lost some of their general fund of knowledge may have "holes" in their learning that will need to be filled in. For example, one high school student retained her ability to add, multiply, divide, and solve most fraction, decimal, percent, and algebra problems but was unable to subtract. One common error that is often made when a child returns to school is to have students "catch up" on missed work, putting undue stress on the student as they try to complete tasks they are no longer able to perform. Adult support, accommodations, and modifications may be needed for the student to be successful in the educational program. To determine which teaching methods may be most effective for a student following traumatic brain injury, a well-planned individualized program that addresses all areas of need is still the best approach. When students with brain injury are identified by functional need, a wide range of familiar research-based teaching strategies that teachers are comfortable with becomes available (Figures 7–6 and 7–7). Proven instructional strategies for memory and organization include task analysis, advanced organizational

TBI Characteristic	Strategy	Description
• Fluctuating attention • Decreased speed of processing	Appropriate pacing	Acquisition of new material is increased by delivering material in small increments and requiring responses at a rate consistent with a student's processing speed; assuming familiarity with the teaching routine, pacing may need to be fast, even for a student with slow processing.
• Memory impairment (associated with need for errorless learning) • High rates of failure	High rates of success	Acquisition and retention of new information tend to increase with high rates of success, facilitated by errorless teaching procedures.
• Organizational impairment • Inefficient learning	Task analysis and advance organizational support	Careful organization of learning tasks, including systematic sequencing of teaching targets and advance organizational support (including graphic organizers), increases success.
• Inefficient learning • Inconsistency	Sufficient practice and review (including cumulative review)	Acquisition and retention of new information is increased with frequent review, as well as with both massed and distributed learning trials.
• Inefficient feedback loops • Implicit learning of errors	Errorless learning combined with nonjudgmental corrective feedback when errors occur	Students with severe memory and learning problems benefit from errorless learning. When errors occur, learning is enhanced when those errors are followed by nonjudgmental corrective feedback.
• Possibility of gaps in knowledge base	Teaching to mastery	Learning is enhanced with mastery at the acquisition phase.
• Frequent failure of transfer • Concrete thinking and learning	Facilitation of transfer/generalization	Generalizable strategies, general case teaching (wide range of examples and settings) and content and context embeddedness increase generalization; cognitive processes should be targeted within curricular content.
• Inconsistency • Unpredictable recovery	Ongoing assessment	Adjustment of teaching on the basis of ongoing assessment of students' progress facilitates learning.
• Unusual profiles • Unpredictable recovery	Flexibility in curricular modification	Modifying the curriculum facilitates learning in special populations.

FIGURE 7–6 Research-based cross-population instructional strategies related to characteristics of many students with TBI.
Source. Used with permission from Ylvisaker et al. (2005).

TBI Characteristic	Strategy	Description
• New learning needs • Impaired strategic behavior • Impaired organizational functioning	Metacognitive/strategy intervention	Organized curricula designed to facilitate a strategic approach to difficult academic tasks, including organizational strategies; validated for adolescents with and without specific learning disabilities.
• Decreased self-awareness • Denial of deficits	Self-awareness attribution training	Facilitation of students' understanding of their role in learning; validated for students with learning difficulties.
• Weak self-regulation related to frontal lobe injury • Disinhibited and potentially aggressive behavior	Cognitive behavior modification	Facilitation of self-control of behavior; validated with adolescents with ADHD and aggressive behavior.
• Impulsive behavior • Inefficient learning from consequences • History of failure • Defiant behavior • Initiation impairment • Working memory impairment	Positive, antecedent-focused behavior supports	Approach to behavior management that focuses primarily on the antecedents of behavior (in a broad sense; validated in developmental disabilities and with some TBI subpopulations).
• Frequent loss of friends • Social isolation • Weak social skills	Circle of friends	A set of procedures designed to support students' social life and ongoing social development; validated in developmental disabilities and TBI.

FIGURE 7–7 Integrated approaches to educational, behavioral, and social interventions that have a research base and are applicable to many students with TBI.

Source. Used with permission from Ylvisaker et al. (2005).

supports, the use of visual displays, study guides, and peer tutoring. Appropriate pacing will assist with slowed processing, while teaching to mastery will assist with gaps in student knowledge. Additionally, strategies that are found in commercially produced materials that use a direct instruction approach provide many of the effective strategies, such as advanced organizers, structured lessons, guided practice, immediate feedback, clearly stated expectations, and frequent review, provided in a small group. Direct Instruction (DI) can be highly effective with this population (Tyler & Grandinette, 2003).

When a student first returns to school, teachers should focus on teaching the student the components of cognition (the process of learning) rather than specific content. Time should be spent on developing skills that will assist the student to attend to each task; follow simple directions; use organizational, memory, and problem-solving strategies; and learn to shift from one task to another (Tyler & Grandinette, 2003). Once the student is effective in the process of learning, content can be reintroduced.

Teachers need to ensure that the students with traumatic brain injury truly understand directions and goals. It is important that the teacher never accept silence, impulsive, or incorrect answers at face value, as there may be a processing problem. To determine understanding, the teacher must frequently check the student's comprehension of the directions. It is also helpful if the material and assignments follow a logical progression from simple to complex (Tyler & Grandinette, 2003). Graphic organizers are effective in assisting students to clarify, organize, remember, write, and express thoughts. Compensatory strategies (e.g., use of sentence diagrams, problem-solving guides, and cue cards) are also useful.

The teacher must spend a great deal of time teaching the student how and when to use these strategies and why they are to be used because the goal is eventual independent use by the student. There are many strategies for problems specifically encountered in the cognitive domain. These include decreasing unnecessary distractions and verbalization (e.g., limiting material), providing visual cues (e.g., sign on desk, diagrams using pictures or words, or written or picture list of steps of tasks), and using a tape recorder. Often the student is taught to use metacognition (e.g., cues, verbal rehearsal, and self-questions). This ability to self-monitor and organize tasks is critical to learning. Using a "memory book," checklist, or visual cues are just some of the ways students can organize tasks (Ylvisaker, 1998). Other aids used to increase function include the use of a computer to remediate difficulties with attention. For older students, electronic organizers that show time, allow for calculations, and include a calendar, diary, alarm, memo pad, phone book, and photo capabilities assist with memory deficits (Gillette & DePompei, 2004). Using electronic organizers has the additional benefit of emulating typical adolescent communication behavior, such as text and instant messaging. Whatever the strategy, care must be taken that it is taught to the child so that it will generalize to a number of environments. In addition, there must be reminders and ample opportunity for the student to use the strategies in actual situations in the classroom, home, and community.

School Placement

Depending on the severity of impairment following hospitalization, the student may return to his or her original classroom with minor accommodations with the support of a Section 504 accommodation plan or through special education where he or she will receive supports and services. When placement is being determined during the IEP meeting, it is important to concentrate on where the student's needs can best be met at the present time with appropriate supports and services. Some school districts offer a special transition class for students with traumatic brain injury. Other times, a student may be placed in a self-contained or resource class for students with a learning disability, while those with orthopedic impairments may attend a class with children with similar needs. While a number of these students may present with behavior and emotional issues as their primary problem, placement in a class for students who are emotionally disturbed or behaviorally disordered may not always be the best option. Placement in a class for students with intellectual disabilities may also not be appropriate. Many students will be included in the general education setting with support and collaboration from special education staff. It is important to remember that a child with traumatic brain injury presents unique problems and characteristics that do not typically fit into any single category. Because of the changing nature of the child's deficits throughout recovery, placement changes may occur frequently, and since many of these students are in denial of their deficits and see themselves as they were prior to their injury, they will not identify with disabled students and may resist attendance in classes for children with certain disabilities.

Meeting Daily Living Needs

Because of possible cognitive, behavioral, and physical disabilities resulting from traumatic brain injury, students may have difficulty performing daily living skills. When this is the case, occupational therapy, combined with a functional curriculum that includes instruction of daily living skills, will need to be included in the student's program. Precise areas to be addressed in a functional curriculum will be determined by the student's team and based on the student's individual needs.

Meeting Psychosocial and Behavioral Needs

The classroom teacher needs to be able to provide appropriate intervention for students who manifest emotional, behavioral, and/or social problems due to the effects of their injury. To do this, teachers need to identify the specific behaviors and monitor their occurrence. Taking data on the number of times a specific behavior occurs, or using a checklist with a rating scale can be useful in obtaining a baseline of the severity of the behavior (see Figure 7-8). As an intervention is implemented, continued data collection will provide information regarding the effectiveness of the intervention.

Challenging Behavior Checklist
Rating scale: 1 = never, 2 = some of the time, 3 = unsure, 4 = most of the time, 5 = all of the time

Behavior	Description	Rating
Inattention to task	Students who have difficulty attending to tasks may engage in unrelated tasks or behaviors. *Example: Student may fidget, talk out of turn, leave the room, instigate a fight with a peer, or stare out a window after a task has begun.*	1 2 3 4 5
Failure to initiate tasks	Due to a frontal lobe injury, student may have difficulty starting tasks: *Example: Student may engage in unrelated tasks prior to working on original activity.*	1 2 3 4 5
Aggression	Aggression involves making physical contact with another person. May include hitting, kicking, and punching; may be directed toward teachers, peers, or family members. Student may even hurt himself. *Example: Student may hit teacher because he or she is frustrated by a difficult task or an inability to communicate effectively.*	1 2 3 4 5
Destruction	Destruction includes throwing objects, damaging furniture, walls, etc. *Example: Student may throw object or punch a wall in response to teacher's demand or peer's teasing.*	1 2 3 4 5
Perseveration	Repetitive speech about a particular topic. *Example: Student may talk incessantly about cars, sports, or next visit home.*	1 2 3 4 5
Inappropriate speech and verbal outbursts	Inappropriate speech may occur sporadically or in bursts. *Example: Student may use language that is not appropriate for the setting (i.e., saying, "Hey man, what's up?" to a teacher) or use obscenities.*	1 2 3 4 5
Difficulty waiting	When required to wait (during transitions, before meals, in line at store) he or she may engage in above behaviors. *Example: Student may leave area, hit, kick teacher; start fight with peer.*	1 2 3 4 5
Age-inappropriate behavior	As child gets older, interests may continue to be similar to those of a younger child or may act older than age. *Example: May show interest in sexual activities at earlier age.*	1 2 3 4 5
Inappropriate sexual behavior	May involve making sexual advances to unknown peers, teachers, staff, or family members. *Example: Verbal sexual overtones, non-verbal sexual behavior (touching, groping).*	1 2 3 4 5
Bolting/eloping	Leaving a designated area without permission. *Example: Student leaves school after being reprimanded for verbal outburst.*	1 2 3 4 5
Noncompliance	Refusing to follow instructions. *Example: Student may verbally refuse to do a task or become aggressive.*	1 2 3 4 5

Additional Challenging Behaviors	Description	Behaviors 4 and above
1. _____	1. _____	_____
2. _____	2. _____	_____
3. _____	3. _____	_____
4. _____	4. _____	_____
5. _____	5. _____	_____

FIGURE 7–8 Challenging behavior checklist.

Source. Used with permission. From *Strategies for managing challenging behaviors of students with brain injury.* L & A Publishing, 2003, pp. 23–29.

Some interventions are designed to decrease the likelihood that the behavior will occur. One way this is done is by arranging the physical environment. For example, having organized, uncluttered environments may decrease disorientation and confusion. Having printed or picture schedules prominently displayed may assist students who have difficulty transitioning to the next activity.

One of the most effective approaches to managing behavior problems in students with traumatic brain injury is the use of antecedent-based interventions. Antecedent management addresses the behavior before it happens by managing the environment. For example, once the triggers that set off a student's behavior have been identified, the environment is arranged to promote positive interactions and skill development before the behavior occurs again (Savage et al., 2005). This addresses the child's inability to control his reaction to stimuli or self-monitor his behavior. Examples of antecedent management include removing triggers from the environment, setting up a schedule or routine, preparing the student in advance for schedule changes, being aware of the student's ability to cope with demands, and redirecting the student at the first stage of disruptive behavior.

When behavior problems occur, it is important to provide the students with replacement behaviors that inform students what behavior is expected. They should be told what to do instead of being told what they should not do. An example would be to inform the student who uses a loud voice to use a quiet voice instead of reprimanding him for shouting.

It is important that teachers be firm, fair, and consistent in their application of behavioral interventions. When provided with appropriate supports, students are expected to engage in classroom activities. When a student is apathetic, cannot initiate, or appears depressed, provide controlled choices or attempt to engage a peer to work with the student.

If a student exhibits aggressive behavior, it is important for the teacher to understand that this behavior is not purposeful but more of a reflexive action. Techniques to help deal with aggression include redirecting the student or offering an alternative action. Sometimes having a key word or phrase for the student to say when he or she is beginning to get angry will assist in decreasing impulsive behavior (National Task Force on Special Education for Students and Youths with Traumatic Brain Injury, 1988).

Often students with traumatic brain injury are unaware of their own behavior and lack the internal feedback to self-correct. Social skills training may be helpful if it is adjusted to the processing and memory problems of the student (McGuire & Sylvester, 1987). Use simple interaction rules such as "Leave space between you and others" if the child has boundary issues and "Ask the person if he is done with it" if they tend to grab at items others are using. When there is a lack of structure or appropriate goal setting, frustration and undesirable behavior may result. Structure can be arranged by having a consistent daily schedule, assigning tasks, setting limits, explaining changes in advance, and building in support systems. The teacher needs organization and consistency in the classroom routine and in the administration of any reinforcement programs. Appropriate goal setting should occur with the student, be realistic and measurable, and include short- and long-term goals.

Lack of inhibition is very common in pediatric brain injury. Since this behavior can lead to a reaction by peers and teachers, it is important that all understand this as involuntary (Deaton, 1987). Social skills training and friendship facilitation are recommended.

A lack of adjustment to the newly acquired disability may add to feelings of depression and withdrawal, sometimes causing older students to turn to substance abuse. Many benefit from school-based counseling. Since suicidal ideation can occur, the teacher must be alert to any mention, joke, or threat of suicide. Professional help is needed in these circumstances.

SUMMARY

While children with traumatic brain injury share similar characteristics with students in other disability groups, they also have some very unique differences. Students may change neurologically for months and years after a traumatic brain injury. They may score at misleadingly high levels on tests of academic achievement because of knowledge and skill preserved before the injury. They are susceptible to significant psychosocial difficulties because of poor communication skills, damage to the frontal lobes, and their need to adjust to new disabilities. They often experience difficulty in school and social situations for years following their traumatic brain injury because of damage to parts of the brain that are needed for later maturation (Ylvisaker, 1998). Educators must be aware that if physical disabilities heal, the child is not cured. They must be ready to recognize and provide appropriate interventions for the often subtle cognitive/communicative deficits as well as the psychosocial impairments that can affect students' abilities to function effectively at home, at school, and in the community. Prevention is the best way to decrease the occurrence of traumatic brain injury. Proper identification following injury and appropriate assessment and eligibility for services as a child transitions to school are paramount in a child's outcome.

VIGNETTE Ronald's Story

Ronald is a 15-year-old who sustained a traumatic brain injury in a car crash. At the time of his injury, he was a 13-year-old seventh grader who earned top grades and was very athletic. Ronald has been in hospital and rehabilitation facilities since the time of his accident. Ronald has significant physical and cognitive disabilities as a result of his TBI. He presents with articulation difficulties and poor saliva management. Strength and coordination are moderately to severely impaired, and he is in a wheelchair. Significant short-term memory issues cause difficulty with new learning. He has nystagmus and is fully dependent for his toileting needs. Ronald fatigues easily, is sensitive to loud noises, is demonstrating periods of depression as he mourns his former self, and is engaging in inappropriate social behaviors. Current assessments indicate an IQ of 88, with peaks and valleys in his abilities. Academic achievement scores indicate the following grade-level scores: decoding: 7.5, comprehension: 3.0, spelling: 7.0, and written language: 3.5. In math, Ronald is able to add, multiply, and divide whole numbers but was unable to subtract. He is unable to solve word problems but knows the value of money. Ronald is about to be enrolled in a public school. What assessments, supports, and services need to be put into place for Ronald to successfully reintegrate into a school setting?

REFERENCES

Anderson, K. E., Taber, K. H., & Hurley, R. A. (2005). Functional imaging. In J. M. Silver, T. W. McAllister, & S. C. Yudofsky (Eds.), *Textbook of traumatic brain injury* (pp. 107–129). Washington, DC: American Psychiatric Publishing.

Askainen, L., Kaste, M., & Sarna, S. (1998). Predicting late outcome for individuals with traumatic brain injury referred to a rehabilitation programme: A study of 508 Finnish patients 5 years or more after injury. *Brain Injury, 12*, 95–107.

Beers, M. H., Porter, R. S., Jones, T. V., Kaplan, J. L., & Berkwits, M. (2006). *The Merck manual of diagnosis and therapy* (18th ed.). Whitehouse Station, NJ: Merck & Co.

Belanger, H. G., Vanderploeg, R. D., Curtiss, G., & Warden, D. L. (2007). Recent neuroimaging techniques in mild traumatic brain injury. T*he Journal of Neuropsychiatry and Clinical Neurosciences, 19*, 5–20.

Bigler, E. D. (2005). Structural imaging. In J. M. Silver, T. W. McAllister, & S. C. Yudofsky (Eds.), *Textbook of traumatic brain injury* (pp. 79–155). Washington, DC: American Psychiatric Publishing.

Blosser, J. L., & DePompei, R. (2003). *Pediatric traumatic brain injury: Proactive intervention* (2nd ed.). Clifton Park, NY: Delmar Thompson Learning.

Braun, C., Baribeau, J., Ethier, M., Daigneault, S., & Proulx, R. (1989). Processing of pragmatic and facial affective information by patients with closed head injuries. *Brain Injury, 34*, 5–17.

Bruce, S., Selznick-Gurdin, L., & Savage, R. (2004). *Strategies for managing challenging behaviors of students with brain injuries.* Wake Forest, NC: Lash and Associates Publishing.

Burton, R., & Moffatt, K. (2004). Head injury. In P. J. Allen & J. A. Vessey (Eds.), *Primary care of the child with a chronic condition* (4th ed., pp. 511–525). St. Louis: Mosby.

Deaton, A. (1987). Behavioral change strategies for children and adolescents with severe brain injury. *Journal of Learning Disabilities, 20*, 581–589.

DiScala, C., & Savage, R. C. (2003). Epidemiology of children with TBI requiring hospitalization. *Brain Injury Source, 6*(3), 8–13.

Dixon, T. M., Layton, B. S., & Shaw, R. M. (2005). Traumatic brain injury. In H. H. Zaretsky, E. F. Richter, & M. G. Eisenberg (Eds.), *Medical aspects of disability* (pp. 119–149). New York: Springer.

Duhaime, A. C., Christian, C. W., Rourke, L. B., & Zimmerman, R. A. (1998). Non-accidental head injuries in infants: The "shaken-baby syndrome." *New England Journal of Medicine, 18*, 1822–1829.

Ewing-Cobbs, L., Levin, H. S., & Fletcher, J. M. (1998). Neuropsychological sequelae after pediatric traumatic brain injury: Advances since 1985. In M. Ylvisaker (Ed.), *Traumatic brain injury rehabilitation: Children and adolescents* (2nd ed., pp 11–26). Boston: Butterworth-Heinemann.

Frey, L. C. (2003). Epidemiology of posttraumatic epilepsy: A critical review. *Epilepsia, 44* (Suppl. 10), 11–47.

Gillette, Y., & DePompei, R. (2004). The potential of electronic organizers as a tool in the cognitive rehabilitation of young people. *NeuroRehabilitation, 19*, 233–243.

Glang, A., Tyler, J., Pearson, S., Todis, B., & Morvanta, M. (2004). Improving educational services for students with TBI through statewide consulting teams. *NeuroRehabilitation, 19,* 219-231.

Hoyt, C. S. (2007). Brain injury and the eye. *Eye, 21,* 1285-1289.

Jaffe, K. M., Fay, G. C., Polossar, N. L., Martin, K. M., Shurtless, H., Rivvara, J. M., & et al. (1992). Severity of pediatric traumatic brain injury and early neurobehavioral outcome: A cohort study. *Archives of Physical Medical Rehabilitation, 73,* 540-547.

Jennett, B., & Teasdale, G. (1981). *Management of head injuries.* Philadelphia: F A Davis.

Keenan, H. T., Runyan, D. K., Marshall, S. W., Nocera, M. A., & Merten, D. F. (2004). A population-based comparison of clinical and outcome characteristics of young children with serious inflicted and noninflicted traumatic brain injury. *Pediatrics, 114,* 633-639.

Langlois, J. A., Rutland-Brown, W., & Thomas, K. E. (2005). The incidence of traumatic brain injury among children in the United States: Differences by race. *Journal of Head Trauma Rehabilitation, 20*(3), 229-238.

Lee, B. H., Schofer, J. L., & Koppelman, F. S. (2005). Bicycle safety helmet legislation and bicycle-related non-fatal injuries in California. *Accident: Analysis and Prevention, 37*(1), 93-102.

Levin, H. S., & Hanten, G. (2005). Executive functions after traumatic brain injury in children. *Pediatric Neurology, 33,* 79-93.

McGuire, T., & Sylvester, C. (1987). Neuropsychiatric evaluation and treatment of children with head injury. *Journal of Learning Disabilities, 20,* 590-595.

Menkes, J. H., & Ellenbogen, R. C. (2002). Traumatic brain and spinal cord injuries in children. In B. L. Maria (Ed.), *Current management in child neurology* (2nd ed., pp. 442-454). Hamilton, ON: BC Decker.

Michaud, L. J., Duhaime, A. C., Wade, S. L., Rabin, J. P., Jones, D. O., & Lazar, M. F. (2007). Traumatic Brain Injury. In M. L. Batshaw (Ed.), *Children with Disabilities* (6th Ed., pp. 461-476). Baltimore, MD: Paul H. Brookes Publishing Co.

Mira, M. P., & Tyler, J. S. (1991). Students with traumatic brain injury: Making the transition from hospital to school. *Focus on Exceptional Children, 23,* 1-12.

National Task Force on Special Education for Students and Youths with Traumatic Brain Injury. (1988). *An educator's manual: What educators need to know about students with traumatic brain injury.* Framinham, MA: National Head Injury Foundation.

Newton, A. W., & Vandeven, A. M. (2005). Update on child maltreatment with a special focus on shaken baby syndrome. *Current Opinion in Pediatrics, 17*(2), 246-251. Review.

Ordia, J. I., Fischer, E., Adamski, E., & Spatz. E. (2002). Continuous intrathecal baclofen infusion delivered by a programmable pump for the treatment of severe spasticity following traumatic brain injury. *Neuromodulation, 5,* 103-107.

Roth, P., & Farls, K. (2000). Pathophysiology of traumatic brain injury. *Critical Care Nursing Quarterly, 23*(3), 14-25.

Russell, M. L., Krouse, S., Lane, A. K., Leger, D., & Robson, C. et al. (1998). Intervention for motor disorders. In M. Ylvisaker (Ed.), *Traumatic Brain Injury Rehabilitation: Children & Adolescents* (2nd ed., pp. 61-80). Boston: Butterworth-Heinemann.

Savage, R. C., DePompei, R., Tyler, J., & Lash, M. (2005). Paediatric traumatic brain injury: A review of pertinent issues. *Pediatric Rehabilitation, 8,* 92-103.

Semrud-Clikeman, M. (2001). *Traumatic brain injury in children and adolescents: Assessment and intervention.* New York: Guilford Press.

Sheehan, K., Dicara, J. A., LeBailly, S., & Christoffel, K. K. (1997). Children's exposure to violence in an urban setting. *Archives of Pediatric and Adolescent Medicine, 151,* 502-504.

Stavinoha, P. L. (2005). Integration of neuropsychology in educational planning following traumatic brain injury: *Preventing School Failure, 49*(4), 11-16.

Tyler, J., & Grandinette, S. (2003). Effective teaching strategies. *Brain Injury Source, 6*(3), 38-41, 48.

Tyler, J., & Mira, M. P. (1999). *Traumatic brain injury in children and adolescents: A source book for teachers and other school personnel.* Austin, TX: PRO-ED.

U.S. Department of Education, Office of Special Education Programs. (2002). Implementation of the Individuals with Disabilities Education Act: Twenty-fourth annual report to Congress. Washington, D.C: Author.

Ylvisaker, M. (1986). Language and communication disorders following pediatric head injury. *Journal of Head Trauma Rehabilitation, 1*(4), 48-56.

Ylvisaker, M. (1998). *Traumatic brain injury rehabilitation: Children and adolescents* (2nd ed.). Boston: Butterworth-Heinemann.

Ylvisaker, M., Adetson, D., Wittandino-Braga, L., Burnet, S. M., Glang, A., Feeny, T., et al. (2005). Rehabilitation and ongoing support after pediatric TBI: Twenty years of progress. *Journal of Head Trauma Rehabilitation, 20*(1), 95-109.

CHAPTER 8

ASSISTIVE TECHNOLOGY CONSIDERATIONS

Mari Beth Coleman and Kathryn Wolff Heller

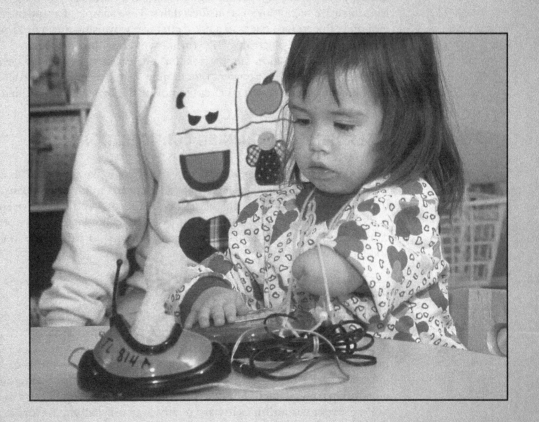

What does a piece of tape have in common with an expensive computer system? Both can be **assistive technology**. When we think about students who have **cerebral palsy**, **spina bifida**, **spinal cord injury**, **traumatic brain injury**, or certain other disabilities, we realize that they may need specialized adaptations, including technology, to perform everyday tasks. Depending on the physical, sensory, and cognitive abilities of the individual with a physical or **multiple disabilities**, anything from toothbrushing to accessing the Internet may require technology. Technology, from simple to complex, that provides an individual with a disability the capability to perform a task that he or she could not perform otherwise is known as assistive technology.

The federal definition of an assistive technology device given in the Individuals with Disabilities Education Act is "any item, piece of equipment, or product system, whether acquired commercially off the shelf, modified, or customized, that is used to increase, maintain, or improve the functional capabilities of a child with a disability" (U.S. Congress, 2004).

There are a few key things to consider from the definition when thinking about assistive technology devices for individuals with physical, health, or multiple disabilities. First, assistive technology does not have to be expensive, specialized equipment. Assistive technology devices can be purchased and used as is, modified, or be homemade. For a student who has **hemiplegic** cerebral palsy and is unable to use one hand to hold his paper, a piece of tape that stabilizes the paper while he is writing is assistive technology. Sometimes there may be several possible assistive technology devices that a student could use, but the most simple, least intrusive technology is considered first. For example, if a student with limited range of motion is able to turn pages in a book effectively by using the eraser on the end of a pencil, then an expensive, electronic page turner would not be considered.

The federal definition emphasizes that the assistive technology device should enhance or maintain the student's current functioning level. The device often allows the person with a disability to perform tasks that could not be performed or performed proficiently.

ASSESSMENT AND TRAINING CONSIDERATIONS

When considering the type of assistive technology that is needed to increase or maintain student performance in a specific task, there needs to be careful consideration of the task requirements and student capabilities. Two students who both have spastic **quadriplegic** cerebral palsy may need very different assistive technologies to perform the same task because of individual differences. The team will need to participate in a careful assessment and have training on the device.

General Assessment Considerations

A thorough assistive technology assessment is important to ensure that the device provides a good setting–person–feature match. Approximately one-third of assistive technology devices are abandoned within the first year because of the lack of careful assessment prior to the purchase of a device (Bryant & Bryant, 2003). Assistive technology assessment must consider individual, environmental, and device factors. Numerous individual factors must be examined, including the student's functional capabilities and functional limitations, preferences, attitudes toward technology use, cultural factors, and motivation. Some factors that must be considered when considering a device are its size, specific usability factors, training time involved, programming time involved, portability, durability, and attractiveness to the user. It is important to consider environmental factors, such as classroom arrangement of the environments in which the technology will be used, personnel to support the technology use, and attitudes and expectations for technology use of the family and school personnel.

Success of an assistive technology device involves looking at the interaction between the individual and specific task within the environment it is performed. Baker's Basic Ergonomic Equation proposes that successful use of assistive technology depends on motivation to perform the task outweighing the student's cognitive effort, physical effort, linguistic effort, and time load that is needed to use the assistive technology device to perform the task (King, 1999):

$$\frac{\text{Motivation of AT user to pursue and complete a task}}{\text{Physical effort} + \text{Cognitive effort} + \text{Linguistic effort} + \text{Time load}} = \text{Successful or unsuccessful AT use}$$

For example, if a student is highly motivated to write using a switch and an on-screen keyboard but it takes a long time to use the assistive technology to construct a sentence, she may persevere if her motivation is higher than the time load issue. On the other hand, if a student has to exert a lot of physical or cognitive effort to use the assistive technology, it may outweigh her motivation to do the task, and the assistive technology is not used. Adjustments would need to be made to decrease the physical or cognitive effort that is needed to encourage assistive technology use.

Because so many factors must be considered, it is vital that assistive technology assessment be a team effort. Input from the user and her family is critical to determine their attitudes and needs regarding assistive technology. Each member of the team will have valuable information to contribute.

AT Analysis of Task and Student Performance

There are many different assessment instruments and procedures that may be used to determine the selection of an assistive technology device. One of the more common processes used to conduct assistive technology assessment is found in the AT Analysis of Task and Student Performance. The AT Analysis of Task and Student Performance is designed to guide the team through a process of examining the task requirements and student performance of the task to determine possible assistive technology solutions.

Current Functioning (Steps 1–3)

The first three steps of the AT Analysis of Task and Student Performance consists of obtaining information on the student's current functioning (see Figure 8-1, which has the steps in bold and gives an example of a student requiring assistive technology). After gathering background information on the student, the first step is to identify the precise task that is being targeted that may require assistive technology or some type of adaptation (see chapter 12 on adaptations). Depending on the task, the task may need to be broken down into steps (task analysis) to pinpoint the precise area of difficulty. The second step is to specify the current assistive technology and adaptations that are being used to support the task. The third step consists of describing how well the task is being performed as well as any specific problems that the student has performing the task.

Discrepancy Analysis (step 4)

After the preliminary steps of describing the task and student performance, the team conducts a discrepancy analysis as the fourth step of the AT Analysis of Task and Student Performance. A discrepancy analysis consists of comparing the student's current performance of the task to the desired (target) performance of the task and determining the cause of the discrepancy. The cause of the discrepancy between the student's current performance (with the assistive technology or adaptations that are presently in place) and the desired performance is determined through student observation, experimentation, and team deliberation. The cause of the discrepancy can usually be attributed to one of the following: (a) atypical movements and motor abilities (which should be broken down into such subcategories as uneven or extraneous movements, uncontrolled movements, restricted range of motion, decreased strength, decreased speed of movement, lack of movement, and mobility issues), (b) sensory loss, (c) fatigue and lack of endurance, (d) health factors, (e) learning or cognitive issues, (f) communication issues (including speech impairments and linguistic problems), (g) motivation, and (h) other (including student driven problems such as interfering self-stimulatory behaviors and external problems such a poor attitudinal environment) (Heller, Forney, Alberto, Schwartzman, & Goeckel,

AT Analysis of Task and Student Performance

Student name: _____Suzie Smith_____ DOB: _____4/8/94_____

School: _____Walker Elementary_____ School system: _____Myer County_____

Background information/student description: Suzie has moderate spastic quadriplegic cerebral palsy, dysarthric speech, and mild intellectual disability. She uses a key guard, slant board, Dycem, enlarged material for easier manipulation, and a scribe. Her speech is understandable to most people with repetition, and AAC is not being considered.

1. Task student needs to do:
Writing (across all subjects.

2. Current AT and adaptations used to support task:
Standard keyboard with key guard on 30-degree slant on slant board with Dycem to prevent slippage. Uses right index finger to type.

3. Describe how well task is currently performed and specific problems:
Slow typing with errors. Types five words a minute. Drags finger across key guard and selects desired target with 60% accuracy. Other fingers sometime push other keys by mistake or index finger gets stuck in wrong hole and pushes an undesired letter. Difficulty reaching letters on far left.

4. Discrepancy analysis: a. atypical movements and motor ability (uneven or extraneous movements, uncontrolled movements, range of motion, strength, speed, no movement, mobility); b. sensory loss; c. fatigue/endurance; d. health; e. learning/cognitive; f. communication; g. motivation; h. other:
For this student, identified discrepancy analysis is:
Atypical movements—upper arm/hand uncontrolled movements, extraneous movements, range of motion limitations, slow speed. Other areas are not a factor (e.g., knows letter locations, understands how key guard works, good motivation).

5. Possible AT/adaptations that could improve performance on task:
Smaller keyboard with a different key guard or
On-screen keyboard with joystick or trackball or other access device.

6. Specify which AT/adaptations team decided to target:
Introduced the options to the student, decided to initially try on-screen keyboard (REACH with joystick and dwell).

7. Describe type of data collection (attach sheet):
Will collect timed writing samples (in which student is copying from print) and determine word per minute and percent correct for 2 weeks. Will compare to earlier samples of standard keyboard with key guard.

8. Results, analysis, and recommendations:
Attached data show great improvement in rate and accuracy. Continue this AT.

FIGURE 8–I AT Analysis of Task and Student Performance completed on a student with spastic quadriplegic cerebral palsy who is having difficulty writing.

2000). It is important that the team determine which area is responsible for the discrepancy since intervention is usually different depending on the area.

In Figure 8-1, the student's task is writing, and she uses a standard keyboard with a key guard and slant board, but she types only five words per minute and selects the desired target with only 60% accuracy. Through careful observation and ruling out other factors, the team decided that the cause of the discrepancy between her current performance and the desired typing speed and accuracy was atypical movements affecting upper arm/hand control, restricted range of motion, and decreased speed. When determining the type of assistive technology she needs, the team bases their recommendations on the discrepancy analysis.

It is important that the team not make an assumption that the discrepancy analysis is due to a motor issue just because the student has a physical or multiple disability. Another student with the exact same physical impairment, writing speed, and error rate as in the example could have a slow and inaccurate typing rate because of a motivation problem in which the student hates writing so she deliberately types slowly and poorly. In this instance, the team would consider ways to make the writing more interesting and possible reinforcement for completion of writing assignments. If the problem was identified as a learning issue in which the student typed slowly because she did not know the location of the keys and was confusing some of the letters, systematic instruction of key location and letter identification may have been the team's solution. If the problem was that the classroom teacher didn't place the keyboard in a consistent location in front of the student (falling into the "other" category), intervention would target teacher training and placing marks on the table for proper keyboard placement along with proper wheelchair placement. If the discrepancy analysis was attributed to a different area, other solutions would need to be explored. If more than one area is thought to be the problem, then all of these will need to be addressed.

AT Selection and Analysis (Step 5–8)

The next four steps of the AT Analysis of Task and Student Performance consist of the team brainstorming possible assistive technology or adaptations that could be used based on steps 1 through 4 and determining which one(s) to target first. The team also needs to determine how the assistive technology will be evaluated and what data will be taken. The last step consists of the team coming back after a trial period to analyze the data taken on the student using the assistive technology and to discuss their follow-up observations of the student. During this time, they will decide if they will continue with the assistive technology, try something different, or take more data (see Figure 8–1 for an example of these last steps).

Training Considerations

No matter how simple and seemingly self-explanatory a device may be, there always needs to be given a rationale for its use and specific training. Lack of appropriate training is a factor in the abandonment of assistive technology devices. The more training that service providers have, the more likely they are to use assistive technology (Wilcox, Guimond, Campbell, & Moore, 2006).

If a device that requires complicated programming is to be used, thorough training must occur for all school personnel (e.g., teachers, paraprofessionals, and related service personnel) as well as for the family if the child will use the device across environments. Training must be done to ensure that the device is learned thoroughly and used properly so that the assistive technology user is able to gain maximum benefit from the device.

Individualized Education Plan Considerations

When the Individuals with Disabilities Act was reauthorized in 1997, assistive technology was mandated as a part of the individualized education plan (IEP) process. For every student who has an IEP, the team must consider whether that student needs assistive technology to benefit from his or her educational program.

One thing to consider regarding assistive technology devices and the IEP is that specific brand-name devices do not have to be identified. This may cause problems if that particular device suddenly is not available. For example, instead of saying that the student will use "the SuperGripper brand pencil grip," the IEP should state that the student will use "a pencil grip." This allows for change and flexibility without having to reconvene the IEP team to change from one device to another.

The federal definition of assistive technology services is "any service that directly assists a child with a disability in the selection, acquisition, or use of an assistive technology device" (U.S. Congress, 2004). The services included in the law include evaluating a student for assistive technology needs, acquiring assistive technology devices, designing or customizing devices, maintaining and repairing devices, coordinating and using therapies or interventions, and training for the child, family, and professionals who work with the child. These services should be documented in the child's IEP.

TYPES OF ASSISTIVE TECHNOLOGY

There are several types of assistive technology devices that may be required for a student to benefit from his education program. These include devices for augmentative and alternative communication, mobility, life management, computer access, academic content areas, and play and leisure. It is beyond the scope of this chapter to provide a comprehensive review of all the various types of assistive technology in each category; rather, an overview will be given with examples to provide the reader with an idea of the types of assistive technology that are available.

Augmentative and Alternative Communication Devices

Augmentative and alternative communication (AAC) refers to communication that is used to enhance a student's existing verbal communication (i.e., augmentative) or serve as the student's primary form of communication (i.e., alternative). Sevcik and Romski (2000) state, "AAC incorporates the individual's full communication abilities and may include any existing speech or vocalizations, gestures, manual signs, and aided communication. AAC is truly multimodal, permitting individuals to use every mode possible to communicate" (p. 5). Individuals with physical and multiple disabilities often use several different types of communication depending on the setting, need, and familiarity of the communication partner (Patel, 2002). For example, a student with severe spastic cerebral palsy who has **dysarthria** may use word approximations and gestures with his family members who understand him well, use an electronic AAC device in the classroom, and use pictures on paper on the playground.

AAC devices may range from the student pointing to pictures on a piece of construction paper to sophisticated electronic devices. Some devices may provide only a single message, whereas others provide hundreds of messages. Some AAC devices may be dedicated devices, which are built only for augmentative communication (see Figure 8-2). Other devices are not dedicated and may provide several functions, such as computer-based AAC systems that provide communication as well as many other computer programs and functions.

In some circumstances, it may be unclear if the team wants to consider AAC for a student. Years ago, it was believed that providing AAC to a young child would inhibit speech production and that AAC should be thought of as a last resort. However, research has demonstrated that AAC does not inhibit spoken communication and may, in fact, enhance a child's development of verbal abilities (Romski & Sevcik, 2005). Even if a student's speech is understandable to those who know him well, AAC should be considered when native listeners cannot understand the student's speech.

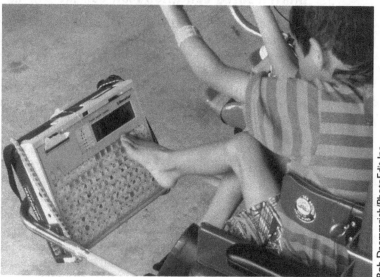

Bob Daemmrich/PhotoEdit Inc.

FIGURE 8–2   Student using an AAC device by making selections with his toe.

Mobility Devices

The ability to move about provides students with the opportunity to interact with their social and physical environment. Students with physical, or multiple disabilities often need some type of mobility device. This may range from devices to assist with crawling to those that assist with transportation. Devices can range in sophistication from a cane for walking support to a car that has been especially adapted for an individual with a severe physical disability.

To assist in crawling or creeping, some children may use scooter boards. Scooter boards are typically small, square pieces of wood covered with plastic and cushioning material that have four casters in the corners of the board to allow the board to move in all directions. Scooter boards may support the trunk (allowing the child's arms and legs to move) or be constructed longer to support the entire body (allowing only arm movement). Children are typically strapped in, lying on their stomach (Heller et al., 2000). Many children will learn to push backward on the scooter board before they learn to move in a typical crawling pattern.

To assist with walking, there are several different mobility devices, including canes, crutches, and walkers. Canes provide the least support and are used for particular physical disabilities and by individuals with visual impairments for mobility purposes. (Canes are constructed differently depending on the purpose.) There are two main types of crutches that may be used: axillary crutches (which are full-length crutches that provide support up to the armpit) and Lofstrand or forearm crutches (which are crutches that extend to the forearm). Students needing more support may use a walker.

Some students may need to use a wheeled device for all of their mobility needs, while others may only need a wheeled device for long distances (and can walk on their own or use a walker for short distances). Some of the most commonly encountered wheeled devices are manual wheelchairs, powered scooters, powered wheelchairs, and powered mobility devices. Although many individuals are in manual chairs for positioning and transportation purposes, they should be encouraged to push themselves in their manual wheelchair whenever possible. The ability to self-propel will result in increased opportunities to explore, interact with the environment, and move to desired locations. There are a wide variety of manual chairs with various shapes, sizes, and features. Some manual chairs are more designed for sport use (e.g., wheelchair basketball and wheelchair races). Individuals with more severe physical impairments may learn to propel themselves using a powered scooter or a powered wheelchair. Some power wheelchairs adjust from a sitting to a standing position (see Figure 8–3).

Children as young as 18 to 24 months of age have been able to operate powered mobility devices (Cook & Hussey, 2002). Often these young children use transitional motorized mobility devices, such as powered toy cars (that they sit in and move) and powered standing frames (Wright-Ott, 1998). Many people now advocate that children who need powered mobility devices should be introduced to them as early as possible (Campbell, McGregor, & Nasik, 1994; Judge & Lahm, 1998). The philosophy is that when children creep and crawl, no prerequisite skills are required; rather, the environment is "childproofed." The same approach is often adopted with mobility devices. Mobility devices are provided to promote movement and development, and then the use of the device is supervised. Mobility devices are now being introduced early because several positive effects have been attributed to the use of powered mobility devices, such as improved head control, truck stability, and arm-hand function; increased motivation in other forms of movement; increases in communication, exploration, social interactions, and self-esteem; and no ill effects on motor development (Judge & Lahm, 1998). There is some evidence of a relationship between self-produced mobility and the acquisition of perceptual and cognitive skills (Bertenthal, Campos, & Barrett, 1984; Kermoian & Campos, 1998).

Life Management

Individuals with disabilities such as cerebral palsy, spina bifida, and other disabilities that limit motor functioning often require assistive technology to perform life management activities, such as self-care, domestic, prevocational, and community activities. Service animals may even be used.

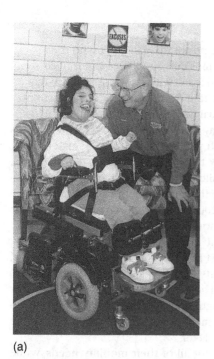  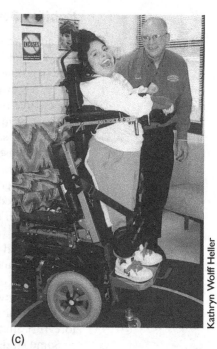

(a) (b) (c)

Kathryn Wolff Heller

FIGURE 8–3 Student using a power wheelchair that can go from a sitting position (a), to a middle position (b), and finally to a full standing position (c).

Self-Care Skills

Self-care skills that may require assistive technology include activities such as eating, drinking, dressing, brushing teeth, and washing. Some assistive technology used for these activities may be very simple solutions that can easily be made by the teacher or parent, while others may draw from the latest technological advances. Often in this area, an occupational therapist plays a key role in providing recommendations along with the rest of the team.

Some individuals with physical disabilities may have difficulty eating with the typical utensils, plates, and cups. Adapted spoons may be necessary to promote success. For example, these spoons may be fitted with a strap to fit around the hand for a person who cannot grip, they may be a different shape, or they may be weighted to steady certain types of abnormal motor movements. Adapted bowls and plates may also be necessary (e.g., scoop dishes or dishes that adhere to the table). Cups may need handles or part of a side of the cup cut out for the nose to fit (when the individual cannot tip his head back). Individuals who have good head control but are unable to use their arms may benefit from a switch-controlled mechanical feeder (see Figure 8–4).

Adapted clothing may be needed for someone with a physical impairment to promote ease of dressing (e.g., clothing with Velcro fasteners). People with limited motor abilities may need to use dressing sticks to help them pull up and pull down their pants. Shoes with Velcro may be easier for individuals with cognitive or physical impairments (Heller, Bigge, & Allgood, 2005). These are only a few examples of the types of adaptations to consider in this area.

There are many types of adapted items that may be used to maintain proper hygiene. For example, toothbrushes may have built-up handles to hold better, or a grip to go around the hand so that the user does not have to maintain a grip. Wash mitts may be used instead of washcloths. Hairbrushes with longer handles may assist individuals with limited movement or shortened limbs. Several of these items are available through companies or can be homemade. As with all technology, careful assessment is needed to determine if the technology is appropriate.

Domestic Tasks

Domestic tasks such as home care and cooking tasks may require the use of assistive technology for individuals with disabilities. While there are commercially available products available for assistance in performing these tasks, often innovative thinking can result in the

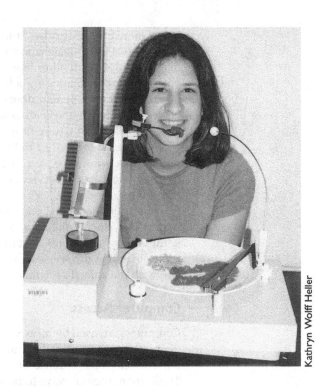

FIGURE 8–4 Student using a switch-controlled mechanical feeder.

Kathryn Wolff Heller

use of an everyday object to serve a different, assistive function. For example, an individual with limited use of one limb may use a plunger held in the limited hand to hold the globes of a ceiling fan while changing lightbulbs with the other hand. Additionally, adaptations to household tools may allow them to be used in an assistive way. For example, a broom may be attached to a power wheelchair to allow the individual to sweep.

Other items around the house also may need to be adapted. Larger telephones make dialing easier for someone with a physical disability or low vision. Some AAC devices allow the person with limited speech to dial the telephone and communicate on the telephone with the device. Sometimes an individual can benefit from the use of an environmental control unit (ECU). This is a system whereby electrical devices are able to be controlled via buttons or spoken commands. Lamps, televisions, stereos, and other devices can be made accessible through an ECU. Special door openers can be attached to doors to allow them to be activated through the ECU. Many other assistive devices are available for environmental control.

There are several assistive technology options for cooking and food preparation. For individuals with cognitive disabilities, the addition of color-coded stickers to the oven or microwave can help provide assistance with setting temperatures or timers. Large-grip utensils, jar openers, and one-handed can openers are just a few examples of assistive technology that may help a person with a physical disability perform food preparation tasks.

Prevocational and Community Tasks

Assistive technology for prevocational and community tasks might include picture schedules, AAC devices programmed with job-specific phrases, and equipment specially adapted for the job task. For example, a student who uses a power wheelchair and works at a grocery store might have a special tray built with a hand basket on the side in which she places items that need to be returned to the shelves. She may move through the store and use a reacher (a long-handled device with a grasping mechanism on one end) to place the items where they belong.

Service Animals

In addition to various types of assistive technology used to promote life management skills, some individuals with disabilities may use a service animal, such as a specially trained dog, horse, monkey, cat, or other animal. Many people initially think of service animals as being used to assist individuals who are blind with mobility; however, service animals are also used to assist people with other types of disabilities and tasks. Service animals may assist students with physical disabilities in such tasks as carrying materials, fetching and returning dropped or needed items, opening doors, turning switches on and off, feeding, and pulling wheelchairs up ramps or across distances (Zapf & Rough, 2002). Service animals have been used with individuals who have hearing impairments to help alert them to noises (e.g., knock on the door, oncoming traffic). Individuals with seizures (or other health impairments) have also used service animals to alert them that a seizure (or other medical problem) is about to occur and, if needed, the service animal may be taught to push a button on a phone to call 911.

Prior to introducing a service animal into a school setting, teachers and students should be taught service animal etiquette. This includes not touching the service animal without permission (since some animals are not to be touched when they are working and in their harness), not making noises at the service animal that might distract the animal from its job, and not feeding the service animal without the owner's permission since that might interfere with the animal's feeding or work schedule.

Computer Access

Computers are used for all aspects of life and can provide opportunities for individuals with disabilities that were never available before. Some people, however, have difficulty accessing the computer because of a motor, health (endurance), sensory, or learning difficulty. There are numerous ways to provide access to computers for individuals with disabilities.

Most computers now come with accessibility features already built into their computer. These features allow the computer display to be modified (e.g., change background color), change the mouse (e.g., mouse speed and cursor appearance), eliminate needing to hold down multikey functions (e.g., holding down control while pressing another key), or ignore repeated keystrokes (e.g., continued pressing down on the "b" key does not result in "bbbbbb"). Several other features are available as standard options, and teachers should investigate what is already available on their classroom computers.

The keyboard itself can also be modified. For example, stickers may be put over the keys with larger letters and higher contrast to improve visibility of the letters. For students who have difficulty isolating a single finger to push a key, a key guard may be used. Key guards are sturdy pieces of plastic with holes cut out above each key that are placed over the standard keyboard to allow a student to rest her hand on the key guard while isolating a single key by pressing her finger into the hole. Students may also access the keyboard differently, such as using a mouth stick to press the keys (see Figure 8–5).

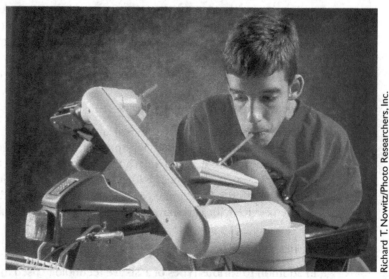

FIGURE 8–5 Student using a mouth stick to access a keyboard.

Many individuals with physical or sensory impairments can benefit from adaptive keyboards. Three types of adaptive keyboards may be considered based on the needs of the individual: expanded, reduced-size, and on-screen keyboards. Expanded keyboards are those that are larger than the standard keyboard. These may be used for someone with a physical disability or vision disability because the larger keys are easier to access. One version of an expanded keyboard is the membrane keyboard, such as IntelliKeys (Intellitools Inc.). This is a flat, sensitive plastic surface that uses several overlays containing different keyboard layouts (ABC, QWERTY, numbers only, and so on) as well as overlays that are designed to be used with academic or learning activities (e.g., sentence writing or cause and effect). Reduced-size keyboards are smaller keyboards that are helpful for students with limited range of motion or who fatigue easily from moving their arms. Another type of keyboard is an on-screen keyboard in which a software program provides a keyboard that covers part of the computer screen. Keys are "pressed" by clicking on them with a mouse or alternative input device.

Alternative input devices are designed to control the mouse cursor on the screen just as the mouse would. Some alternate input devices include joysticks, trackballs (a ball that is rolled around to control cursor movements), and touch screens (a device placed over the computer screen that allows the user to point directly at the item on the screen to make a selection). An example of a more sophisticated alternative input device is a head-controlled mouse. This device has an infrared sensor that sits on top of the monitor that detects head movements by the user wearing a reflective sticker on his forehead. The user is able to move the mouse and make a selection by moving his head.

There are some individuals who do not have enough physical control to operate these various input devices. If a person has one reliable movement, he can access the computer with a switch and scanning. Scanning is when the software program highlights (or verbalizes) one choice at a time in a sequential manner and the student makes the selection by activating a switch. Switches come in various shapes and sizes such as button switches that are activated by pressing, grasp switches that are activated by squeezing, wobble switches that are activated by moving in any direction, or muscle twitch switches that are activated with any small muscle movement, such as raising an eyebrow.

Another input method for computer access is speech recognition software. This type of software allows a user to produce written documents by dictating into a microphone, and the words come up on the computer. This type of program requires a lot of training, and the software may not recognize the speech of individuals who do not have typical speech patterns, such as someone with dysarthric speech or inadequate breath support (Rosen & Yampolsky, 2000). Voice commands can be used for error correction when speech is not recognized accurately as well as for mouse control; however, these processes are tedious and frustrating for some users.

Assistive Technology for Academic Areas

Writing

Writing is an area that poses problems for many individuals with physical, health, and sensory impairments. In the area of handwriting, a felt-tip pen may be needed for students who cannot exert enough pressure using a pencil because of weakness or for students with visual impairments who need ink with high contrast. Some students may need to hold a pencil in their foot or mouth. For individuals who have trouble grasping a pencil, pencil grips or larger writing utensils (fat mechanical pencils or pencils wrapped in pipe insulation) may provide an easier grasping surface. If a student has **athetoid** movements or tremors, a weighted writing utensil may help reduce the extra movements and allow for better writing control. Hand braces may provide extra stability or eliminate the need to grasp the pencil while writing. Adapted paper that has darker or larger lines may be needed. Paper may also need to be stabilized by tape, clipboard, slant board (writing surfaces that change the angle), or nonslip material (e.g., rubber self-liner or Dycem) (see Figure 8–6).

Some students have difficulty writing by hand. These students may benefit from small portable word processors (e.g., AlphaSmart) or laptop computers. The device may also be

FIGURE 8–6   Student using a slant board.
David Grossman/Photo Researchers, Inc.

adapted with different access features or devices to make it accessible. For example, some devices will be equipped with talking word processors that give auditory feedback to what is being typed.

Some students with physical disabilities may benefit from word prediction software that provides a selection of words as the student types in order to decrease the number of keystrokes and increase typing speed. For example, if the student is trying to type *difference*, she begins by typing *d*, and several words that begin with *d* appear in the word prediction list (e.g., *did, do, does,* and *don't*). If her word is not in that list, she types another letter, and word prediction supplies *di* words and so on until the desired word is provided. The student can select the word or continue typing.

Many other forms of assistive technology are available for writing. In some cases, the issue may be not accessibility but difficulty with writing composition. Software is available to assist students with the writing process. Some of these provide graphic organizers or assist the student in outlining the paper.

Reading

Students with physical or multiple disabilities may encounter several problems in the area of reading. Some students with fine motor difficulties have trouble isolating and turning one page at a time. This may be addressed through putting spaces between the pages by attaching paper clips or attaching page fluffers (pieces of material such as sponge or weather stripping) to each page. Some students may use the eraser end of a pencil, a mouth stick, or an electronic page turner to turn pages.

Sometimes the print (or pictures) in the book will need to be enlarged or modified. Other than getting large-print books, teachers can enlarge materials on a copier. Some students may use some type of magnification, such as a handheld magnifier, a software program that enlarges computer text, or a CCTV (closed-circuit television) (see Figure 8–7). A CCTV looks like a television on a stand in which reading materials or other objects (e.g., pictures, stickers, or money) are placed on the tray under the screen and their image is projected onto the screen. The image can be enlarged to various sizes, and the background/foreground color of the items can be changed to improve the students' ability to see the material. Books may also be adapted by having symbols added above the words for students to read when students need symbol support because of age or learning difficulties.

Books can also be accessed electronically through the teacher scanning them into the computer or using commercially produced electronic books. Having books on a computer can provide access for students with physical disabilities who cannot manipulate a book and

FIGURE 8–7 Student using a CCTV to read a book.

help those with reading difficulties. Books can be scanned into the computer using scanning software and pasted into software programs, such as PowerPoint, to produce them in electronic format. Usually pages are presented one page at a time and new pages can be displayed automatically or the student can change them by activating a switch. Copyrighted materials may be adapted in accordance with Public Law 104-197, which allows exemptions for materials to be produced in special formats for individuals with physical or visual disabilities.

Other software that may benefit students for reading includes text-reading and screen-reading software. Text-reading and screen-reading software can be used to read on the computer aloud to the student. These software programs usually have many settings that allow different font sizes and colors, different voices, and various speech speeds that are selected on the basis of the user's needs. Students may use these programs to improve their exposure to text, improve their reading fluency, or provide access when a visual problem is present. Several books can be found free online (through such projects as Project Gutenberg, http://www.gutenberg.org) that can be read using text readers.

Math

Early math skills often involve the use of manipulatives for such things as sorting, counting, and computational skills. Students with poor fine motor control may need larger manipulatives that are positioned within the student's range of motion. Software programs also exist that allow the student to move items on a computer screen with the click of a switch.

Students who are unable to complete math worksheets may benefit from the use of electronic math worksheets that allow the teacher to customize the display (colors, background, and size) and allow the student to complete the problem with a standard keyboard or alternative input device. Several math programs exist that not only assist in practicing new math skills (ranging from counting to algebra) but also provide access to students requiring alternative input devices, alternate output, and screen modifications.

Assistive technology also exists for functional math skills, such as time and money skills. Several software programs address these areas, often with features to make them more accessible. Special money calculators are available that allow the student to select dollars or various coins to come up with the total amount of money.

Science and Social Studies

Many of the assistive technology adaptations that are needed for reading, writing, and math may also be required in other academic areas, such as social studies and science. A CCTV may be used for reading and interpreting graphs or maps or even for dissecting. Adaptive microscopes may be needed for students who need larger images or students with physical disabilities who do not have physical ability to look into a microscope. Special equipment may be used that allows an image such as from a lab experiment or microscope to be projected onto a computer or television screen to make it more accessible to see. As with school tasks, teachers and related service personnel need to think creatively about various assistive technology options to allow each student to participate to the fullest extent of his ability.

Play and Leisure Activities Using Assistive Technology

Play and leisure activities are important aspects of a child's day. At the most basic level, children begin to understand the concept of cause and effect through play. If a child is unable to manipulate toys because of a physical disability, she may have trouble with this concept. Special switch-adapted battery-operated toys can be purchased that allow a child who can access a single switch to operate the toy by pressing the switch (see photo at the beginning of the chapter). Other switch-adapted devices can allow students with disabilities to have control over their leisure activities. For example, a switch-adapted CD player allows a student with a physical disability to control turning music on and off.

Board games may be adapted by using larger play pieces for students with physical disabilities. There are commercially available board games (e.g., Monopoly) that are larger and have Braille writing on the board and cards. Video games may also be adapted for people with disabilities. Adaptive joysticks and other input devices are available that allow people with physical disabilities to participate in gaming.

Sports may require assistive technology for some individuals with disabilities. Students with physical disabilities may need to use larger or softer balls to engage in ball activities. For students with visual impairments, balls with bells or devices that beep help them hear the direction in which it is moving. Bowling alleys have gutter guards that can be raised for young children or children with disabilities to reduce the number of gutter balls. They also have ramps to roll the ball down that can be used by someone who uses a wheelchair (or walker) or cannot perform the physical skills needed to bowl (see Figure 8–8).

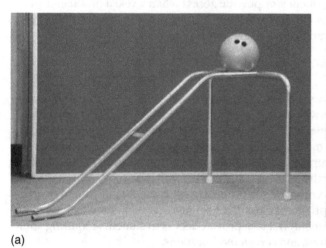
(a)

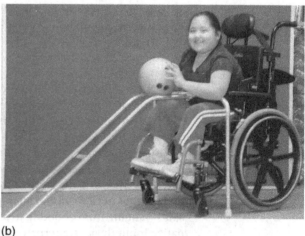
(b)

Janie Avant

FIGURE 8–8 An adapted bowling ramp used for students with physical and multiple disabilities (a) and how a student positions her wheelchair to use the adapted ramp (b).

There are numerous adaptations that allow individuals with disabilities to compete in sports, such as adapted rules, lowered basketball goals, sport-specific prostheses or wheelchairs, and sport-specific equipment, such as seated ski equipment or hand-propelled bicycles. Some individuals with disabilities will participate in organized adapted sports programs. Special Olympics (for individuals with intellectual disabilities who may have accompanying physical or sensory impairments) and Paralympics (for individuals primarily with physical or visual impairments) are very popular events for many individuals with disabilities.

SUMMARY

Assistive technology can be anything that helps an individual with a disability to increase, improve, or maintain the functional capability to perform a task. Many students with disabilities such as cerebral palsy, spina bifida, traumatic brain injury, or other disabilities that result in physical, health, or multiple disabilities may need assistive technology to function in their school, home, and community environments. It is important that teachers and school personnel carefully assess the needs of an individual student in relation to a specific task when considering possible assistive technology. It is also important to be creative and flexible in considering what assistive technology might help the student perform the task more effectively or efficiently. There are numerous commercially available products for assistive technology, but the right assistive technology solution for a student's need may be a common everyday item that is sitting around the classroom.

REFERENCES

Bertenthal, B., Campos, J., & Barrett, K. (1984). Self-produced locomotion as an organizer of perceptual, cognitive and emotional development in infancy. In R. Emde & R. Harmon (Eds.), *Cognitive and emotional development in infancy* (pp. 175–210). New York: Plenum.

Bryant, D. P., & Bryant, B. R. (2003). *Assistive technology for people with disabilities.* Boston: Allyn & Bacon.

Campbell, P. H., McGregor, G., & Nasik, E. (1994). Promoting the development of young children through use of technology. In P. L. Stafford, B. Spodek, & O. N. Saracho (Eds.), *Early childhood special education* (Vol. 5, pp. 192–217). New York: Teachers College Press.

Cook, A. M., & Hussey, S. M. (2002). *Assistive technologies: Principles and practice* (2nd ed.). St. Louis: Mosby.

Heller, K. W., Bigge, J., & Allgood, P. (2005). Adaptations for personal independence. In S. Best, K. W. Heller, & J. Bigge (Eds.), *Teaching individuals with physical and multiple disabilities* (5th ed., pp. 309–336). Upper Saddle River, NJ: Merrill/Prentice Hall.

Heller, K. W., Forney, P. E., Alberto, P. A., Schwartzman, M. N., & Goeckel, T. (2000). *Meeting physical and health needs of children with disabilities: Teaching student participation and management.* Belmont, CA: Wadsworth.

Judge, S. L., & Lahm, E. A. (1998). Assistive technology applications for play, mobility, communication, and learning for young children with disabilities. In S. L. Judge (Ed.), *Assistive technology for young children with disabilities: A guide to family-centered services* (pp. 16–44). Cambridge, MA: Brookline Books.

Kermoian, R., & Campos, J. (1998). Locomotor experience: A facilitator of spatial cognition. *Child Development, 58,* 908–917.

King, T. W. (1999). *Assistive technology: Essential human factors.* Boston: Allyn & Bacon.

Patel, R. (2002). Phonatory control in adults with cerebral palsy and severe dysarthria. *Augmentative and Alternative Communication, 18,* 2–10.

Romski, M. A., & Sevcik, R. A. (2005). Augmentative communication and early intervention: Myths and realities. *Infants and Young Children, 18,* 174–185.

Rosen, K., & Yampolsky, S. (2000). Automatic speech recognition and a review of its functioning with dysarthric speech. *Augmentative and Alternative Communication, 16,* 48–60.

Sevcik, R. A., & Romski, M. A. (2000). AAC: More than three decades of growth and development. *ASHA Leader, 5*(19), 5–6.

Wilcox, M. J., Guimond, A., Campbell, P. H., & Moore, H. W. (2006). Provider perspectives on the use of assistive technology for infants and toddlers with disabilities. *Topics in Early Childhood Special Education, 26,* 33–49.

Wright-Ott, C. (1998). Designing a transitional powered mobility aid for young children with physical disabilities. In D. B. Gray, L. A. Quatrano, & M. L. Lieberman (Eds.), *Designing and using assistive technology: The human perspective* (pp. 285–295). Baltimore: Brookes.

U.S. Congress. (2004). *The Individuals with Disabilities Education Improvement Act of 2004.* Washington, DC: U.S. Government Printing Office.

Zapf, S. A., & Rough, R. B. (2002). The development of an instrument to match individuals with disabilities and service animals. *Disability and Rehabilitation, 24,* 47–58.

PART III

ORTHOPEDIC, MUSCULOSKELETAL, AND SENSORY DISORDERS

CHAPTER 9

NEUROMUSCULAR SCOLIOSIS AND HIP DISPLACEMENT

Kathryn Wolff Heller and Paula Forney

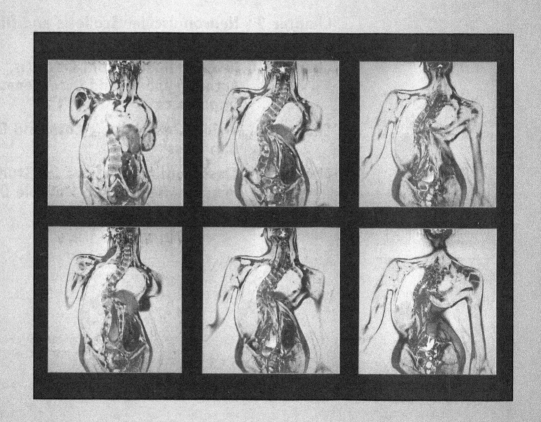

There are several conditions that affect the skeletal system. Two common conditions encountered in children are **scoliosis** and **hip displacement**. Both of these conditions can occur alone, without the presence of any other impairment. However, they are also commonly present in many neuromotor impairments and degenerative diseases. Depending on their severity, scoliosis and hip displacements can interfere with daily functioning and classroom learning. With severe scoliosis, motor impairment occurs to the point that sitting can often become difficult and the lungs can become compromised. Hip displacements may result in pain, decreased range of motion, and difficulty walking. When students have these conditions, their teachers need to have knowledge of proper positioning, therapy, treatment, and adaptations.

Because of the differences between scoliosis and hip displacements, this chapter will begin by describing them separately. At the end of the chapter, the educational implications section will discuss both conditions together.

[handwritten margin note: Alone or w/ neuro-motor & degenerative]

DESCRIPTION OF SCOLIOSIS

One of the most common deformities of the spine that has been recognized since ancient times is scoliosis. The term *scoliosis* is from the Greek word meaning "crooked" (Herring, 2002). Scoliosis is a **lateral** (sideways) curve of the spine. When a person with scoliosis is viewed from the back, the spine appears to curve out to one side or the other instead of appearing straight.

There are several terms used to describe different types of scoliosis. Some of them are based on the location of the curve (e.g., lumbar curve), while others describe the etiology (e.g., neuromuscular). The term *neuromuscular scoliosis* refers to a lateral curve due to a disorder of the muscle or central nervous system (e.g., **cerebral palsy**). Since **multiple disabilities** frequently include cerebral palsy as a disorder, neuromuscular scoliosis is the most common type of scoliosis present in this population of students.

Other curvatures of the spine may also be present in addition to scoliosis or by themselves (see Figure 9–1). A student may have a **kyphosis** or a **lordosis**. Kyphosis refers to an

[handwritten margin note: Most common deformations of the spine]

[handwritten note near figure: Neuromuscular scoliosis is the most common in CP]

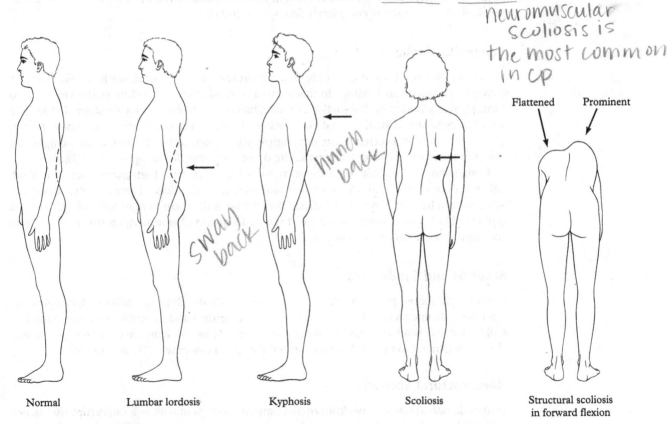

| Normal | Lumbar lordosis | Kyphosis | Scoliosis | Structural scoliosis in forward flexion |

FIGURE 9–1 Normal spine, lordosis, kyphosis, scoliosis, and scoliosis with person bending over.

abnormal **posterior** (convex) curve of the spine. When a person with kyphosis is viewed from the side, the affected section of the spine appears to curve outward more than usual. This usually occurs in the thoracic (upper trunk) section of the spine and has been referred to as a "hunchback" or "humpback." When a kyphosis occurs with a scoliosis, the term **kyphoscoliosis** is often used.

Lordosis is an abnormal **anterior** (concave) curve of the spine. This usually occurs in the lower back. When a person with lordosis is viewed from the side, the small of the back appears to curve farther inward than usual. Lordosis is commonly referred to as "swayback," "hollow back," or "saddle back." When a lordosis occurs with a scoliosis, the term **lordoscoliosis** is often encountered.

ETIOLOGY OF SCOLIOSIS

The exact nature of the scoliosis is determined by its etiology, of which there are many. Most of these causes occurring in the pediatric population can be classified into five distinct categories: **idiopathic**, **congenital**, genetic syndromes, nonfunctional, and neuromuscular (Thompson, 2004).

Idiopathic Scoliosis

Idiopathic scoliosis refers to scoliosis of unknown causes. Idiopathic scoliosis is the most common form of scoliosis, accounting for about 80% of all individuals who have scoliosis (Herring, 2002). It is classified according to age of occurrence: infantile (up to 3 years old), juvenile (between 3 and 9 years old), adolescent (age 10 to maturity), and adult (Lackey & Sutton, 2005).

Idiopathic scoliosis is most frequently seen in adolescents who have no disability, and it is present in about 2% to 3% of children between the ages of 10 and 16 years (Lenssinck et al., 2005). When a mild scoliosis is present in adolescents, it does not typically progress after skeletal maturation is complete (Thompson, 2004).

Congenital Scoliosis

Structural abnormalities of the spine that are present at birth and result in scoliosis are referred to as congenital scoliosis. In this form of scoliosis, there is a failure of the vertebrae to form correctly during gestation. For example, half of one vertebra may be shaped more like a wedge, resulting in an abnormal curve when the other vertebrae are stacked on top of it. In another case, half a vertebra may not completely segment, resulting in one side being wider than the other, and a curve develops as the other vertebrae lie on top of it (see Figure 9–2).

Congenital scoliosis may be present by itself, but there are a high percentage of individuals with congenital scoliosis who also have spinal cord defects. For example, congenital scoliosis can be found in **spina bifida**. This includes the most benign form of spina bifida (spina bifida occulta) as well as the most severe form (**myelomeningocele**), in which neuromuscular scoliosis can also occur.

Scoliosis and Syndromes

Certain syndromes place children at greater risk of developing scoliosis. Examples are Marfan syndrome (which is a connective tissue disorder) and neurofibromatosis (which is a disorder that produces tumors along the nerves). Students who have these types of syndromes will need to be carefully monitored for spinal deformity (Thompson, 2004).

Nonstructural Scoliosis

Nonstructural scoliosis, also known as compensatory scoliosis, is a curvature that is not a fixed deformity and does not result in any permanent changes in the spine. For exam-

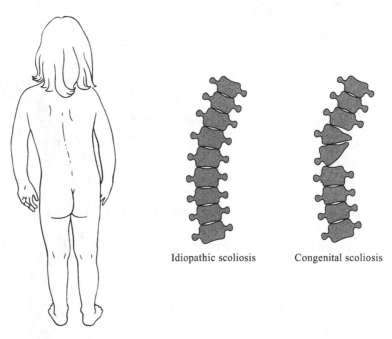

FIGURE 9–2   Idiopathic scoliosis and congenital scoliosis.

ple, different leg lengths may produce a nonstructural curvature of the spine. This type of curvature is usually corrected when the underlying cause is corrected. For example, when an insert is added to the shoe to correct the leg length discrepancy, the scoliosis no longer exists.

Neuromuscular Scoliosis

Neuromuscular scoliosis is scoliosis that occurs in neuromotor disorders and muscle diseases. It is often found as a complication in such conditions as cerebral palsy, **spinal cord injury**, spinal cord tumor, myelomeningocele, poliomyelitis, **arthrogryposis**, **Duchenne muscular dystrophy**, and **spinal muscular atrophy**. These conditions tend to include poor muscle control of the growing spine, muscle imbalances, **contractures**, or progressive weakness that are often attributed to causing the scoliosis.

The severity of neuromuscular scoliosis depends on the severity of the underlying condition, the pattern of weakness, or how far the condition has progressed (Thompson, 2004). For example, a student with severe spastic quadriplegic cerebral palsy will typically have a much more severe scoliosis than a student with a more mild form of cerebral palsy. However, it should be noted that some students with severe spastic quadriplegic cerebral palsy may not develop a scoliosis at all. The rest of this chapter will address primarily neuromuscular scoliosis since it is most commonly seen in individuals with physical and multiple disabilities.

DYNAMICS OF SCOLIOSIS

Overview of the Spinal Column

The spine, also known as the spinal column or vertebral column, is composed of 33 bony units known as vertebrae. Each vertebra is positioned on top of another with pads of fibrocartilage and intervertebral discs between each vertebra. The spinal column runs vertically

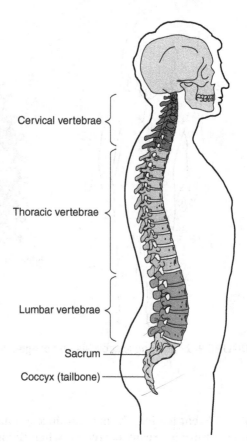

Cervical vertebrae

Thoracic vertebrae

Lumbar vertebrae

Sacrum

Coccyx (tailbone)

FIGURE 9–3   The spinal column.

through the body with the top of the spinal column located at the base of the skull and the bottom part attached to the pelvis (see Figure 9–3).

The vertebrae are named according to their location. The cervical vertebrae are primarily in the neck, the thoracic vertebrae are in the chest, the lumbar vertebrae are in the lower back, and the sacral vertebrae are in the pelvic area. In each group of vertebrae, each individual vertebra is numbered. The seven cervical vertebrae are numbered C1 through C7, the 12 thoracic vertebrae T1 through T12, and the five lumbar vertebrae L1 through L5. The five sacral vertebrae fuse to form the sacrum, and the four coccygeal vertebrae fuse to form the coccyx, or tailbone.

The spinal column serves several functions. As discussed in chapter 6, the vertebral column protects the spinal cord, which runs through the middle of the vertebrae. Exiting between the vertebrae are spinal nerves, which carry impulses to and from the spinal cord. The vertebrae also have a number of muscles attached to them that move either the spinal column or parts of the body in relation to the column.

Another major function of the spinal column is to provide support for the body and posture for the trunk through the spine's own normally curved structure. When viewed from the side, the normal spinal column can be seen to curve forward in the cervical area. This is referred to as a normal cervical lordosis (see Figure 9–3). The spine then curves backward in the thoracic area, which is referred to as a normal thoracic kyphosis. In the lumbar area, the spine curves forward again and is referred to as normal lumbar lordosis or more commonly known as the hollow of the back. When looking at the spinal column from the back, it appears straight.

These normal curvatures of the spine occur within a typical range. When curvatures exceed their normal ranges, larger, abnormal curves are present that are pathological and may cause problems. A larger curve is known as a lordosis or a kyphosis. No sideways curve is normal, and when one is present, it is a scoliosis. When neuromuscular scoliosis is present, it is usually not a simple lateral curve of the spine but is often accompanied by a spinal rotation, a secondary compensatory curve that results from the body's attempt to realign itself in space, and often a kyphosis or lordosis is also present (Herring, 2002; Miller, 2005).

Mechanism of Scoliosis

The exact mechanism causing an abnormal curvature of the spine varies as to its etiology and in many cases is not completely understood. In spastic quadriplegic cerebral palsy, scoliosis is often found to be the primary type of spinal deformity. Although the exact mechanism is not fully known, poor muscle control on the growing spine is thought to be the primary etiology with spasticity, poor balance, and muscle weakness being contributing factors (Miller, 2005).

In spinal cord injuries, a scoliosis is attributed to the accompanying paralysis, which results in a lack of muscle support. Without the muscles supporting the spinal column, the spinal column is unstable and may curve abnormally. Scoliosis has occurred in children regardless of age of injury; however, there have been reports of scoliosis occurring in almost 100% of children who have a cervical spinal cord injury before 10 years of age (Herring, 2002). In spina bifida, scoliosis may result from the paralysis as well as from vertebrae malformation that can be part of the disorder.

Scoliosis is very prevalent in individuals with muscular dystrophy and spinal muscular atrophy (Chng et al., 2003; Herring, 2002). The progressive muscle weakness found in both of these conditions is a major factor contributing to the development of scoliosis. Once the individual loses the ability to walk and begins using a wheelchair full time, scoliosis typically develops and often progresses relentlessly (Alman, Raza, & Biggar, 2004; Herring, 2002).

CHARACTERISTICS OF SCOLIOSIS

Characteristics of curvatures of the spine depend on the type of curvature, the severity of the curve, and its etiology. In scoliosis, the severity of the curve is measured by degrees. A mild curve is usually less than 20 degrees, a moderate curve is 20 to 40 degrees, and a severe curve is more than 40 degrees (Beers, Porter, Jones, Kaplan, & Berkwits, 2006).

Individuals with mild scoliosis usually have very subtle symptoms. One shoulder blade, hip, or breast may appear more prominent or higher than another. Hemlines may appear unequal. In mild scoliosis there is usually no physical discomfort or impact on the person's functioning.

When the scoliosis is severe, there may be a significant impact on walking, sitting, and health. A scoliosis may affect standing balance and make walking difficult for individuals with neuromotor impairments who have unstable or poor walking ability. A severe curvature may result in an inability to sit straight, and the individual may need to use his arms for support to hold the body up. In some instances, as the scoliosis progresses in students with cerebral palsy, they will lose their ability to be independent sitters and will need more sitting support. Students who are wheelchair users may have difficulty achieving a good sitting position and often need to be constantly repositioned to stay in an upright position (Saito, Ebara, Ohotsuka, Kumeta, & Takaoka, 1998). These sitting and positioning problems may predispose the individual to an increased risk of skin breakdown (decubitus ulcers).

Very severe scoliosis found in individuals with neuromotor impairments can result in back pain, deformity, and heart and lung involvement (see Figure 9–4). In terms of back pain, it can sometimes be severe and limit the student's ability to remain in a sitting position. Sometimes the curve is so severe that it is not possible to sit. A very severe curve can distort the rib cage, which in turn presses on the heart and lungs, impairing proper functioning. The lungs may be compromised by decreasing the lung volume capacity (Newton et al., 2005), increasing the risk for respiratory infections and sometimes compounding preexisting respiratory problems (Thompson, 2004).

Depending on the etiology, scoliosis can be present at any time. In individuals with spastic quadriplegic cerebral palsy, scoliosis often develops in early and middle childhood, frequently before the age of 10. There is often a dramatic increase in the curve as the child enters adolescence with the typical growth spurt. The curve may progress at a rate of 2 to 4 degrees a

FIGURE 9–4 A very severe neuromuscular scoliosis.

neuromuscular scoliosis is progressive

mild idiopathic scoliosis may stop © bone maturation.

month and reach a 60- to 90-degree range (Miller, 2005; Saito et al., 1998). A common misconception is that once the adolescent reaches skeletal maturity, the curve becomes stable and progression stops. This can be the case in mild idiopathic scoliosis. However, in neuromuscular scoliosis, the curve often continues to progress into adulthood.

DETECTION OF SCOLIOSIS

Scoliosis may be detected through informal observation of such subtle signs as uneven hip or shoulder height. In the schools, there is also routine screening for a scoliosis, because of the high incidence of idiopathic scoliosis. Screening for scoliosis consists of having the child bend forward and touch his toes with the feet straight while the nurse (or other trained personnel) closely inspects the back (see Figure 9–1 showing scoliosis with a person bending over). (It should be noted that bending over is very important since a mild scoliosis may not be observable when the child is standing or sitting.) While the student is bending over, the nurse will observe for uneven shoulder height, uneven hip height, asymmetrical waist, and a hump in the chest or back area. If any of these symptoms are present, a scoliosis is suspected, and the student is referred for further evaluation (Lackey & Sutton, 2005). Evaluation for scoliosis will typically occur on a regular basis when a child has a known disorder or disease that is associated with a high incidence of scoliosis (e.g., muscular dystrophy or spastic quadriplegic cerebral palsy).

A specialist in orthopedics is often the physician who makes the diagnosis of a scoliosis. X-rays are taken of the spine to confirm an abnormal curve (see Figure 9–5). The degree of curvature is calculated, often by a formula (e.g., the Cobb angle formula), to determine the severity of the curve. Further tests are often performed to determine if there are any underlying causes (e.g., tumor).

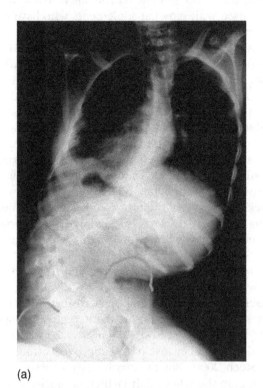

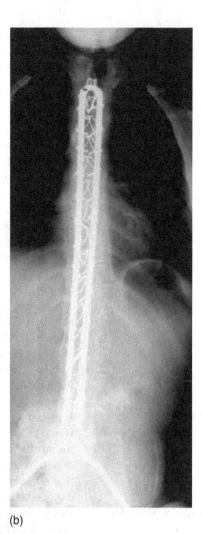

(a) (b)

FIGURE 9–5 X-ray of scoliosis (a) and surgical correction using a rod (b).

Source. Miller, F. (2005). *Cerebral Palsy.* New York: Springer, Figures C9.1.3 and Figure C9.1.4. p. 437, copyrighted material. Reproduced with kind permission of Springer Science and Business Media.

TREATMENT OF SCOLIOSIS

The goal of treatment for individuals with neuromuscular scoliosis is to correct or prevent progression of the spinal distortion that can cause pain, difficulty sitting, or compromise in lung volume and affect other body systems (Miller, 2005). For individuals who have terminal illnesses, such as Duchenne muscular dystrophy, treatment is aimed at maintaining the best quality of life possible for as long as possible, and this may include performing spinal surgery (Harper, Ambler, & Edge, 2004).

There are several different treatments for scoliosis. Some treatments that have been tried have not proven to be successful (e.g., exercise and electrical stimulation). Some treatments that have shown success are very specific to the etiology. For example, steroid treatment in males with Duchenne muscular dystrophy may slow the progression of scoliosis or delay spinal surgery (Alman et al., 2004). The three most common approaches to treating scoliosis include observation, bracing, and/or surgery.

Observation

Once a scoliosis is diagnosed, the only immediate treatment may be observation. Very mild curves may only require close observation and X-rays to determine if the curve is progressing.

This is especially the case when the curve is idiopathic and may not be progressive. Curves that are determined to be progressive may be closely observed until treatment can optimally occur.

Idiopathic before bone maturation

Bracing

The use of a brace (also known as orthosis) to prevent further worsening of an abnormal curvature has shown promising results in some individuals with idiopathic scoliosis in particular. Bracing is typically used with growing adolescents who have not reached skeletal maturity and have a moderate curve (Herring, 2002).

There are many different types of braces that may be prescribed. The Milwaukee brace, for example, provides support from the cervical area to the sacral area. It has a molded plastic pelvic portion of plastic and a metal upright portion going from the pelvic area to a ring that fits around the neck. There are often pressure pads connected to the metal upright portion to assist with correct position. In order for the brace to be comfortable, the child must stand as straight as possible in the brace. By actively pulling away from the pressure pads, the child also strengthens muscles that help to hold the spine straight.

Because of cosmetic reasons, the equally effective thoraco-lumbo-sacral orthosis (TLSO) may be used to provide support to the areas implied in its name. The TLSO consists of a molded plastic jacket. Depending on the type of TLSO, many fit below the breast (and the shoulder blade in the back) to the top of the hips (see Figure 9–6). Although braces were originally worn almost the entire day, research is showing that part time may be just as effective with some students wearing the brace for 16 hours a day. Often students elect not to wear their brace at school (Herring, 2002).

Surgery – primary for neuromuscular scoliosis

Because of the successful response of children with idiopathic scoliosis to bracing, this was tried with children who had neuromuscular scoliosis. Although a few studies have found that bracing is a useful permanent or temporary treatment option, most authorities maintain that bracing does not change the eventual outcome of the spinal deformity and that surgery is the primary option (Miller, 2005; Thompson, 2004). However, parents have expressed satisfaction with bracing because of the improved sitting stability a brace provides (Terjesen, Lange, & Steen, 2000). Bracing may be used to assist with improved sitting when the child is not sitting in the wheelchair (which is usually adjusted for the scoliosis). In this instance, the brace is used only during functional times, and it is expected to assist only with sitting, not with preventing or stopping the scoliosis from progressing (Miller, 2005).

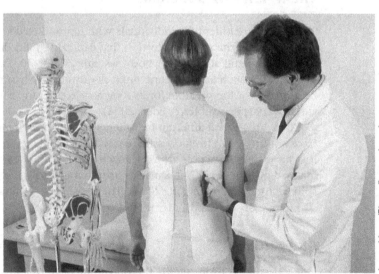

FIGURE 9–6 An orthotist is fitting a teenager with a thoraco-lumbo-sacral orthosis (TLSO) that is worn for the treatment of scoliosis.

Surgery

Students with progressive neuromuscular scoliosis are often candidates for surgery. Determination of whether surgery will be performed will need to take into account the child's age, etiology of the curve, previous treatment, curve magnitude, scoliosis flexibility, effect of the curve on functional living skills and activities, effect of the curve on sitting and mobility, the child's condition, and the family's wishes. For example, an adolescent with an idiopathic scoliosis may be a candidate for surgery once the curve reaches 40 to 50 degrees and is determined to be progressive. However, when a child has a neuromuscular scoliosis, the criteria tend to be different. For example, surgery is often recommended when a curve of 30 degrees is present in boys with Duchenne muscular dystrophy who are no longer ambulatory (Herring, 2002).

There are several different surgical techniques (e.g., posterior fusion and anterior thoracoscopic surgery) and different types of rods (e.g., unit rod) that may be used to treat scoliosis as well as abnormal lordosis or kyphosis (Dabney, Miller, Lipton, Letonoff, & McCarthy, 2004; Lonner, Kondrachov, Siddiqi, Hayes, & Scharf, 2006). All techniques aim at achieving a vertical trunk balanced over a level pelvis.

The most common surgery is a spinal fusion with instrumentation (i.e., rod) and a bone graft. In this surgery, prebent rod(s) are attached to the spine in certain locations by hooks or screws (or other means), and the spine is carefully straightened. Small pieces of bone graft (e.g., from the hip) are placed between the vertebrae to fuse them together, keeping the spine straight. This is referred to as a spinal fusion. The rod(s) keep the spinal column straight while the bone graph grows and makes the spine solid, preventing a curve. The spine remains flexible where it has not been fused.

[handwritten margin note: Spinal fusion w/ instrumentation & bone graft]

COURSE OF SCOLIOSIS

For children and adolescents who receive treatment in the form of surgery, the outcome is generally positive, with most curves being maintained from progressing further or corrected as much as possible. However, in some complicated cases, surgery may not produce the desired effect with regard to functional sitting or ambulation.

In some instances, treatment may not be given because of the child's health, family wishes, or other factors. When there has been no treatment, the neuromuscular curve will typically progress. For example, the scoliosis found in muscular dystrophy usually progresses rapidly if the child is a wheelchair user. Conservative management is often difficult since the sitting position promotes an additional kyphosis. The scoliosis can further progress making any type of sitting difficult, including wheelchair use. Being unable to sit in a wheelchair can severely affect the individual's ability to go out in the community. Many individuals with cerebral palsy who have uncorrected scoliosis lose the ability to sit independently or need more support as the scoliosis advances. More care may be needed in the areas of dressing, positioning, and feeding as the curve becomes more severe (Saito et al., 1998). As previously discussed, additional health issues can also occur (e.g., skin breakdown or decrease in lung volume) as well as pain and discomfort.

DESCRIPTION OF HIP DISPLACEMENT

The hip joint is the largest joint in the body and the joint that can cause the most functional problems in terms or walking, sitting, and lying (Miller, 2005). Although hip problems can occur without any other impairments, they are frequently found in individuals who have neuromotor impairments, such as spastic or athetoid cerebral palsy (Soo et al., 2006), and degenerative conditions, such as spinal muscular atrophy (Herring, 2002).

The three most common hip problems in individuals with cerebral palsy are **hip subluxation**, hip dislocation, and **hip dysplasia.** A hip subluxation refers to an incomplete or partial dislocation of the hip joint from the socket. A hip dislocation refers to a complete separation of the bone ends that normally form a joint. In other words, the end of the thigh-bone (femur) is completely out of the socket, which is part of the pelvis. Hip dysplasia refers to an abnormality of development of the hip.

ETIOLOGY OF HIP DISPLACEMENT

The exact nature of the hip displacement depends on its etiology. Some of the classifications of hip displacements that occur in the pediatric population can be described as follows.

Congenital Hip Dislocation

In congenital hip dislocation, the hip becomes dislocated either before, during, or shortly after birth. If the dislocation is recognized right after birth, the head of the femur can easily be manipulated back into the socket. However, the longer the head of the femur is out of the socket, the more invasive the procedures are to correct the dislocation. A normal hip joint may not be possible if the dislocation persisted for years.

Traumatic Hip Dislocation

Traumatic hip dislocations refers to dislocations that occur from trauma. For example, hip dislocations can occur from accidents such as falls. Many traumatic hip dislocations occur from a severe force to the knee when the hip is flexed, such as against a car dashboard (Beers et al., 2006).

Hip Disorders and Diseases: Slipped Capital Femoral Epiphysis

The most common adolescent hip disorder is slipped capital femoral epiphysis. In this condition, the ball on top of the thighbone slips off the thighbone, usually at the location of the ephiphysis (growth plate). This displacement may occur gradually or suddenly, resulting in mild pain or a limp to severe pain. In 20% of the cases, the adolescent complains only of knee pain (Thompson, 2004). Surgery is usually necessary.

Spastic Hips

The term *spastic hips* is used to describe hip dislocation, hip subluxation, or hip dysplasia that often occurs in children with spastic cerebral palsy. It also includes those children with athetosis and dystonia (Miller, 2005). Although hip problems may also occur with children with low tone (hypotonia), they do not fall under the classification of having spastic hips. This chapter will primarily address hip displacements due to spasticity.

DYNAMICS OF HIP DISPLACEMENT

Overview of the Hip

The hip joint is a ball-and-socket joint. The ball is the rounded head of the femur (thighbone). The ball fits into the pelvic socket, known as the acetabulum (Figure 9–7). Cartilage, ligaments, and capsular structures, as well as the surrounding hip muscles, hold the femoral head in the acetabulum.

The hip is one of the major weight-bearing joints of the body. When movement across the hip joint occurs, such as in sitting and walking, forces much greater than the body weight are generated by the muscles of the hip (Scoles, 1988). The femoral head must fit and move well in the acetabulum for normal growth and development of the hip joint to occur after birth.

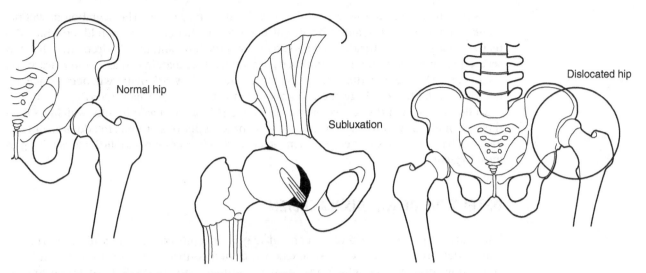

FIGURE 9–7 Normal hip joint, hip subluxation, and hip dislocation.

If the hip joint is not aligned properly, abnormal forces can act on the growing skeleton, changing the shape of the bones around the hip and causing permanent joint deformity. Initially, this deformity may not interfere with the child's function, but with time, if left untreated, the abnormal wear will result in joint degeneration, pain, and loss of function.

Mechanism of Hip Displacement

Dislocation of the hip exists when the femoral head lies outside the acetabulum with no contact between the two articular surfaces. Subluxation of the hip exists when there is partial contact between the two articular surfaces but the femoral head is not completely covered within the acetabulum (see Figure 9-7).

Children with spastic cerebral palsy often develop hip subluxation and dislocation because of a muscle imbalance. The hypertonic (high tone) adductor and flexor muscles of the hip overpower the weaker hip extensors and abductor muscles. Over time, the stronger, spastic muscles pry the femoral head away from the acetabulum (Herring, 2002).

Because of the abnormal forces of the spastic muscles on the developing hip joint in the child with cerebral palsy, the joint itself can become anatomically altered. For example, the neck of the femur can develop at a slightly different angle unless active standing occurs. When hip subluxation begins to occur, the femoral head (the ball) can become flattened. Over time, hip dislocation can occur. Eventually, the acetabulum can become very shallow, and the femoral head can become further deformed (Miller, 2005).

CHARACTERISTICS OF HIP DISPLACEMENT

The characteristics of hip displacement in spastic hip disease depends on the age of the child and progression of the displacement. At birth, infants with cerebral palsy will typically have normal hips (unless they have a different hip abnormality). The spastic hip begins between 1 and 8 years of age, with most occurring between 2 and 6 years of age. Around age 2, most children with spastic cerebral palsy will begin developing spasticity. As the child grows, the muscles are growing stronger and can exert more force as the spasticity worsens. Also, a young child's acetabulum is composed mostly of soft cartilage, which predisposes it to deformity. Over time, the femoral head will be drawn away from the acetabulum, and in the early stages of this subluxation, the child will not have any pain. However, subluxation will continue, often increasing at a rate of about 2% a month (Miller, 2005). As the subluxation progresses, the child will often begin to feel pain.

As the child continues to age, a full hip dislocation may occur. The acetabulum will become shallow, and the femoral head will become misshapen. As the child ages into the teenage years, severe arthritic changes can occur at the hip joint, and children often develop severe pain with motion and sometimes pain at rest. Fortunately, if spastic hip disease has not occurred by the time the child is 8 years old, there is low risk that it will occur since the hip joint has far less cartilage and is composed mostly of bone (Miller, 2005).

Children with hip dislocation may experience pain as well as difficulty walking. Often there is an inability to tolerate sitting or lying for long periods of time. In addition, hip dislocation has several associated problems, such as skin breakdown and difficulties with perineal hygiene.

DETECTION OF HIP DISPLACEMENT

There are several ways hip displacement may be diagnosed. Usually a hip abnormality will be detected during the physical exam and then confirmed by X-rays. Some children and young adults will benefit from having computed tomography (CT) scanning since it can show the direction of the hip dysplasia. Other diagnostics are more commonly used for hip problems other than spastic hips, such as ultrasound for infants, bone scans to evaluate location of unknown pain in children who cannot communicate, arthrography (in which a dye is injected into the hip), and other imaging techniques (magnetic resonance imaging).

TREATMENT OF HIP DISPLACEMENT

The treatment of choice for hip displacement is prevention or early relocation of the hip subluxation in children with spastic cerebral palsy or similar conditions (Ackerly, Vitztum, Rockely, & Olney, 2003). Because of the long-term problems that can occur from hip dislocation, aggressive management to prevent its occurrence is usually a priority, unless the child has an expected life span of only a few years. The hips are usually the second priority of orthopedists for children with spastic cerebral palsy after addressing contractures and deformities of the foot (which is needed for standing or weight bearing).

The treatment goal for hip subluxation is to prevent the subluxation from progressing and resulting in a dislocated hip. Depending on the progression of the spastic hip, there are three types of surgeries: (a) soft tissue release in which the muscles are elongated (e.g., adductor lengthening), (b) reduction and reconstruction of the subluxed or dislocated hip, and (c) salvage surgery for long-term painful dislocations. Typically, children under 5 years of age will have soft tissue releases of the contractures. More extensive surgery is often necessary to treat advanced hip subluxations or dislocations (Herring, 2002).

The goal of hip dysplasia surgery is to provide a painless hip and stable sitting when the child cannot walk. If the child is able to walk, the goal of hip dysplasia surgery is to allow the continuation of walking without groin or hip pain (Herring, 2002). Other treatments specific to hip subluxation are currently under investigation (e.g., intrathecal baclofen and botulinum toxin injections).

COURSE OF HIP DISPLACEMENT

If left untreated, children who develop spastic hips will develop hip subluxation, which may progress to a hip dislocation. This can be associated with problems in several areas, such as walking, tolerating sitting, pain, and skin breakdown. Surgical treatment for spastic hips usually results in a good outcome, with best results occurring with early surgical intervention.

EDUCATIONAL IMPLICATIONS OF SCOLIOSIS AND HIP DISPLACEMENT

Meeting Physical and Sensory Needs

In scoliosis and hip displacement, teachers need to be aware of any adaptations or positioning needs. For students with a severe curve, special adapted seating may be needed to allow the student to sit independently and comfortably with freedom of hand movement. When there is a hip subluxation or dislocation, teachers may also need to be cautious when positioning the student. The physical therapist should work with the teacher in determining appropriate positioning and needed equipment to achieve the best position for students with either type of problem.

Teachers should be alert for any symptoms indicating abnormal curvatures of the spine or hip displacement. When a scoliosis is present, clothes may hang unevenly or jeans may gather in the back. Students may complain of pain when a hip displacement is present. Any suspicion of an abnormal curve or hip displacement should result in notification of the school nurse for further action.

Depending on the severity of the scoliosis or the hip displacement, there may be activity restrictions. Students with severe curves may have lung and heart involvement, which can preclude vigorous exercise. For the student with a hip dislocation who has not received surgical treatment, the teacher will need to be aware of how a hip dislocation may affect the child's mobility, stamina, and participation in certain activities. In some instances, the student may need more time to move from place to place.

Scoliosis and hip displacements may result in a great deal of discomfort or pain. The teacher needs to be aware that decreased endurance accompanied by pain can have an effect on the student's performance. Schedule adjustments and rest times may need to occur. Communication with the student's family, physician, and student will be important if pain management becomes an issue.

Students with scoliosis and hip displacements may have surgery to treat the condition. The teacher may play a part in preparing the student for surgery (e.g., making communication boards to go with the student to the hospital when the student uses augmentative communication). The teacher will also need to be prepared for the student's return to class and have a plan for managing the student's physical needs. Students may require certain modifications. For example, the student may not be allowed to use the standing equipment for a few months that he previously used. Since there may be activity restrictions and adaptations needed after surgery, information should be obtained from the physician regarding any restrictions and their duration.

Some students who have scoliosis may have an orthosis to treat the abnormal curve. Although the orthosis may be uncomfortable at first, discomfort may also occur from improper fit, which may result in skin abrasion. Students should be checked or check themselves for any signs of skin breakdown. This is especially important for students who have such conditions as spinal cord injury who would not feel any pain due to loss of sensation in affected areas. Any type of abrasion or redness on the skin should be reported to the nurse, physical therapist, or parent. The orthosis may need to be reevaluated for proper fit, or the schedule for wearing the brace may need to be adjusted.

Meeting Communication Needs

Students with scoliosis or hip displacements do not have any impairment in the area of language unless there is an underlying condition such as severe spastic quadriplegic cerebral palsy. When that occurs, it is important that teachers are able to understand when the student is in pain. This may occur by observing facial expressions and vocalizations. If possible, having a pain symbol on the student's augmentative communication device and training the student in its use is ideal. Having additional symbols addressing changing positions is often needed.

Meeting Learning Needs

There are <u>no learning deficits associated with scoliosis or hip displacements</u>. Students with scoliosis will need to learn how to wear an orthosis. Students with scoliosis or hip displacement will need to learn how to assist with their care after surgery. Students who have uncorrected severe scoliosis or hip displacements may need to learn how to implement any adaptations or assistive technology that is needed for their activities.

Meeting Daily Living Needs

Students with severe scoliosis, as well as those with hip displacement, may have difficulty in performing certain daily living skills. Dressing, for example, may be difficult when a curve is present or when a hip displacement makes standing difficult when dressing. The teacher may need to teach the student to use various types of adaptations, devices, or alternate positions that would allow the student to be as independent as possible. Specific adaptations would depend on the student's underlying condition (see chapter 8 on assistive technology and chapter 12 on adaptations).

Meeting Behavioral and Social Needs

The teacher also needs to be aware <u>of self-esteem issues</u> related to scoliosis and hip displacements. Deviations in body appearance have been found to be responsible for psychological distress to the point that cosmetic defects that the curvatures produce have been studied (Theologis, Jefferson, Simpson, Turner-Smith, & Fairbank, 1993). Despite recognized effects of curvatures on person's cosmetic appearance and self-esteem, such images in literature and television as "the ugly evil humpback" do not assist the student with a kyphosis in forming a positive self-image. Clothes that do not fit well also may create a negative self-image, especially when the spinal deformity is present during adolescence. In terms of hip displacement, the student with an obvious gait abnormality may be self-conscious about it or be teased by fellow classmates. Students who have scoliosis or hip displacements may need emotional support from the teacher and those in the school setting. Teachers should make themselves available to listen if the student needs someone to talk with.

SUMMARY

Students with multiple disabilities, often have additional disabilities, such as scoliosis or hip displacements. Neuromuscular scoliosis, a lateral curvature of the spine, is caused by muscle imbalances, poor muscle control of the growing spine, contractures, or progressive weakness. If the scoliosis is severe, walking, sitting, and the health of the child can be affected. Hip displacements (including hip subluxation, hip dislocation, and hip dysplasia) may occur in children with such conditions as spastic cerebral palsy because of the abnormal pull of the spastic muscles. If it progresses, it can affect walking, sitting, and lying and result in pain and difficulties with hygiene. In some cases, surgery is needed to correct both conditions.

 **Dushal's Story**

Dushal is a 15-year-old girl who has severe spastic cerebral palsy and profound intellectual disability. She also has untreated severe scoliosis and hip dislocations and needs a wheelchair for mobility. Both conditions are affecting her ability to sit for extended periods of time, and she appears to grimace a lot. What information does the teacher need to acquire to be sure she is meeting Dushal's needs?

REFERENCES

Ackerly, S., Vitztum, C., Rockley, B., & Olney, B. (2003). Proximal femoral resection for subluxation or dislocation of the hip in spastic quadriplegia. *Developmental Medicine and Child Neurology, 45,* 436-440.

Alman, B. A., Raza, S. N., & Biggar, W. D. (2004). Steroid treatment and the development of scoliosis in males with Duchenne muscular dystrophy. *Journal of Bone and Joint Surgery, 86,* 519-524.

Beers, M. H., Porter, R. S., Jones, T. V., Kaplan, J. L., & Berkwits, M. (2006). *The Merck manual of diagnosis and therapy.* Whitehouse Station, NJ: Merck Research Laboratories.

Chng, S., Wong, Y., Hui, J., Wong, H., Ong, H., & Goh, D. (2003). Pulmonary function and scoliosis in children with spinal muscular atrophy types II and III. *Journal of Paediatrics and Child Health, 39,* 673-676.

Dabney, K. W., Miller, F., Lipton, G., Letonoff, E. J., & McCarthy, H. C. (2004). Correction of sagital plane spinal deformities with unit rod instrumentation in children with cerebral palsy. *Journal of Bone and Joint Surgery, 86,* 156-168.

Harper, C. M., Ambler, G., & Edge, G. (2004). The prognostic value of pre-operative predicted forced vital capacity in corrective spinal surgery for Duchenne's muscular dystrophy. *Anaesthesia, 59,* 1160-1163.

Herring, J. A. (2002). *Tachdjian's pediatric orthopaedics* (3rd ed.). Philadelphia: W. B. Saunders.

Lackey, E., & Sutton, R. (2005, October 28). GP clinical: The Basics—Recognizing and identifying a scoliosis. *General Practitioner,* pp. 56-59.

Lenssinck, M. B., Frijlink, A. C., Berger, M. Y., Bierma-Zeinstra, S., Verkerk, K., & Verhagen, A. P. (2005). Effect of bracing and other conservative interventions in the treatment of idiopathic scoliosis in adolescents: A systematic review of clinical trials. *Physical Therapy, 85,* 1329-1339.

Lonner, B. S., Kondrachov, D., Siddiqi, F., Hayes, V., & Scharf, C. (2006). Thoracoscopic spinal fusion compared with posterior spinal fusion for the treatment of thoracic adolescent idiopathic scoliosis. *Journal of Bone and Joint Surgery, 88,* 1022-1034.

Miller, F. (2005). *Cerebral palsy.* New York: Springer.

Newton, P., Faro, F., Gollogly, S., Betz, R., Lenke, L., & Lowe, T. G. (2005). Results of preoperative pulmonary function testing of adolescents with idiopathic scoliosis. *Journal of Bone and Joint Surgery, 87,* 1937-1946.

Saito, N., Ebara, S., Ohotsuka, K., Kumeta, H., & Takaoka, K. (1998). Natural history of scoliosis in spastic cerebral palsy. *Lancet, 351,* 1687-1693.

Scoles, P. V. (1988). *Pediatric orthopedics in clinical practice.* Chicago: Yearbook Medical Publishers.

Soo, B., Howard, J., Boyd, R., Reid, S. M., Lanigan, A., Wolfe, R., et al. (2006). Hip displacement in cerebral palsy. *Journal of Bone and Joint Surgery, 88,* 121-129.

Terjesen, T., Lange, J. E., & Steen, H. (2000). Treatment of scoliosis with spinal bracing in quadriplegic cerebral palsy. *Developmental Medicine and Child Neurology, 42,* 448-454.

Theologis, T. N., Jefferson, R. J., Simpson, A. H., Turner-Smith, A. R., & Fairbank, J. C. (1993). Quantifying the cosmetic defect of adolescent idiopathic scoliosis, *Spine, 18,* 909-912.

Thompson, G. H. (2004). The hip. In R. E. Behrman, R. M. Kliegman, & H. B. Jenson (Eds.), *Nelson textbook of pediatrics* (17th ed., pp. 2273-2280). Philadelphia: W. B. Saunders.

Thompson, G. H. (2004). The spine. In R. E. Behrman, R. M. Kliegman, & H. B. Jenson (Eds.), *Nelson textbook of pediatrics* (17th ed., pp. 2280-2288). Philadelphia: W. B. Saunders.

10

JUVENILE RHEUMATOID ARTHRITIS, ARTHROGRYPOSIS, AND OSTEOGENESIS IMPERFECTA

Kathryn Wolff Heller and Mary Jane Thompson Avant

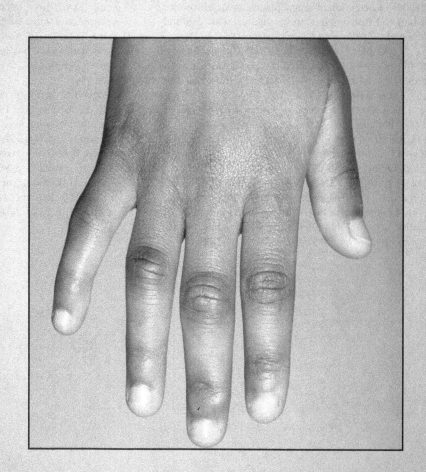

There are several different conditions that can affect the bones and joints and result in a physical disability. Three of these are **juvenile rheumatoid arthritis**, **arthrogryposis**, and **osteogenesis imperfecta**. Each of these conditions is very different, with diverse etiologies, characteristics, treatments, and prognoses. Some of these conditions and their subtypes are not confined solely to the bones and joints but affect other body systems as well. However, the effect of these three conditions on the bones and joints can severely affect movement or physical activity.

Teachers need to have a clear understanding of juvenile rheumatoid arthritis, arthrogryposis, and osteogenesis imperfecta in order to effectively assist students with these conditions. Some students with these conditions may appear to have little to no disability but will need adaptations to make the school environment accessible and safe. Other students with these conditions will have severe physical disability affecting the use of their arms and legs. Even when these conditions are severe, most students with juvenile rheumatoid arthritis, arthrogryposis, and osteogenesis imperfecta will have normal intelligence.

Since these three conditions are different in so many ways, this chapter will discuss the etiology, dynamics, characteristics, detection, treatment, and course for each of the three conditions separately. At the end of the chapter, the educational implications for these conditions will be discussed together.

DESCRIPTON OF JUVENILE RHEUMATOID ARTHRITIS

Juvenile rheumatoid arthritis (JRA) is chronic arthritis that is present in a child or adolescent before the age of 16. Although arthritis is typically thought of as a disease of older adults, it is a major source of disability in children and adolescents. Nearly 300,000 children are diagnosed in the United States with arthritis, with juvenile rheumatoid arthritis being the most prevalent form of connective tissue disease (Labyak, Bourguignon, & Docherty, 2003). Juvenile rheumatoid arthritis is capable of causing significant musculoskeletal changes and pain that can negatively impact on classroom performance. Since this disease is often not readily apparent when looking at the student, the severity of the disease and the impact of the disease may be misunderstood. If this occurs, the resulting lack of adaptations may adversely affect the student's school performance.

Juvenile rheumatoid arthritis is not a single disease but a category of diseases with three major types (and several subtypes). The three major types are pauciarticular (fewer than five inflamed joints), polyarticular (five or more inflamed joints), and systemic (accompanied with characteristic fever). In order for a diagnosis of juvenile rheumatoid arthritis to occur, five criteria need to be met. First, there needs to be chronic joint inflammation that begins before 16 years of age. Second, arthritis needs to be present in one or more joints (i.e., presence of swelling accompanied by two of the following: limited range of motion, tenderness or pain on motion, and/or increased heat). Third, the disease needs to have a duration of 6 weeks or longer. Fourth, the onset needs to be defined by one of the types of diseases in the first 6 months (i.e., polyarticular, pauciarticular, or systemic). Finally, other forms of juvenile arthritis must be ruled out (Miller & Cassidy, 2004).

Some debate still exists regarding the proper terminology to use to refer to these diseases. *Juvenile chronic arthritis* is a European term used to refer to the same condition as juvenile rheumatoid arthritis but also includes some additional diseases. The term *rheumatoid* in *juvenile rheumatoid arthritis* is considered inappropriate by some individuals since few individuals with juvenile rheumatoid arthritis test positive for a rheumatoid factor (antibodies found in the blood of adults with classical rheumatoid arthritis) (Herring, 2002).

ETIOLOGY OF JUVENILE RHEUMATOID ARTHRITIS

The precise etiology of juvenile rheumatoid arthritis is unknown. However, there are several factors that are thought to contribute to the development of this condition. One of these is an altered immune system, which may present as abnormal immunological regulation, T-cell abnormalities, or autoimmune reactions. An autoimmune reaction refers to a reaction to unknown stimuli in which antibodies begin to attack certain normal cells of the body. It has been proposed that an antigen-driven autoimmune process may be at work in which autoreactive T cells play a central role in joint inflammation and destruction (Moore, 1999; Smerdel et al., 2004).

There is thought to be a genetic basis for juvenile rheumatoid arthritis. Certain genes within the HLA (human leukocyte antigen) complex have been shown to contribute to juvenile rheumatoid arthritis. For example, HLA-DR4 is associated with a type of polyarticular juvenile rheumatoid arthritis, and HLA-A2 is associated with pauciarticular juvenile rheumatoid arthritis (Rettig, Merhar, & Cron, 2004). Other factors may also contribute to the development of juvenile rheumatoid arthritis, such as contracting certain viruses (e.g., parvovirus B19) (Oğuz, Akdeniz, Ünüvar, Küçükbasmací, & Sídal, 2002).

DYNAMICS OF JUVENILE RHEUMATOID ARTHRITIS

The human body is composed of more than 500 joints. Some of these joints may normally have limited or no range of movement, such as those found between the bones of the skull or between the bodies of the vertebrae. Other joints may be freely movable, such as those found in the knees and elbows. These are known as synovial or diarticular joints.

Synovial joints have two bone ends that come together with a space between them (known as a joint cavity or joint space) (see Figure 10–1a). The ends of the bones have cartilage on them (known as articular cartilage) and have joint fluid between them. This type of joint is surrounded by a synovium (also known as a synovial lining), which secretes the joint fluid and contains it within the joint. Surrounding the synovium is connective tissue, which has blood vessels within it. This is referred to as the joint capsule.

A joint is moved by the contraction of the surrounding muscles. When a muscle contracts, it causes the bone to move. The cartilage layer of the end of the bone smoothly glides

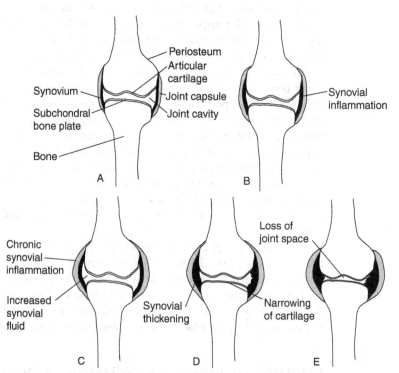

FIGURE 10–1 (a) A normal diarthrodial joint. (b) Early joint inflammation. (c) Chronic joint inflammation. (d) Chronic inflammation of the synovium with protrusion of thickened synovial membrane into the joint space and damage to the cartilage. (e) Cartilage and bone begin to erode, and joint deformity occurs.

Source. Adapted with permission from Jackson and Vessey (2000), p. 608.

over the other cartilage surface of the opposing bone. The joint fluid that nourishes the cartilage also serves as a lubricant that assists in the smooth movement of joint motion.

When there is injury to the joint, an inflammation process begins as part of the defense mechanism of the body as well as part of the healing process. The inflammation process consists of several subprocesses (see Figure 10–1b): (a) dilation of the blood vessel with excess local blood flow; (b) movement of large quantities of fluid to the spaces between the cells; (c) clotting of the fluid in the spaces between the cells; (d) movement of specialized cells into the area, including those that devour destroyed tissues; and (e) swelling in the area (Guyton & Hall, 2006). This process is accompanied by pain and stiffness. The individual usually restricts his own movement of the joint in a protective manner. As the inflammation process subsides, the specialized cells that devour destroyed tissues may at times further injure the still-living tissue cells.

The term *arthritis* is taken from the root *arthro,* meaning "joint," and *itis,* meaning "inflammation." In arthritis, there is no identified area of injury. The inflammation process occurs in the usual manner with swelling of the joint and infusion of blood cells. However, because of the frequency and duration of the inflammation process occurring in the joint, the inflammation process does not serve a beneficial purpose. Initially, the inflammatory process results in chronic inflammation of the synovium (see Figure 10–1c). Over time, projections of thickened synovial membrane form protrusions into the joint space, and the synovium may begin to adhere to the articular cartilage (see Figure 10–1d). Late in the disease, with continued inflammation and proliferation of the synovium, the articular cartilage and other structures (including the bone) may begin to erode and become damaged (Miller & Cassidy, 2004; Rettig et al., 2004). If this occurs, the cartilage on one end of a bone no longer smoothly glides over the other cartilage surface of the opposing bone. Joint deformity and impaired movement may occur (see Figure 10–1e). This process takes a long time in children, and permanent joint damage occurs in only some of the cases.

Joint abnormalities may also develop because of the child's natural tendency to minimize pain. When the joint is inflamed, movement of the joint results in pain. Children will attempt to keep their joints in as comfortable a position as possible. In many cases, this position is a flexed position, and **contractures** can develop rapidly.

CHARACTERISTICS OF JUVENILE RHEUMATOID ARTHRITIS

General Characteristics

Juvenile rheumatoid arthritis most frequently occurs during certain age-groups, with a peak onset at 8 years of age and another peak during puberty (Palmer et al., 2005). When it is present, there are four general symptoms that can occur: (a) stiffness after immobility, (b) pain with joint movement, (c) limitations in joint motion, and (d) in some types, fever. One of the main symptoms of the disease is stiffness. After the child's joint has been inactive for a period of time, such as after sleeping or sitting for a period of time (i.e., half an hour to hours), the joint may become stiff and difficult or painful to move. On moving the joint, it may loosen up within a few minutes or may take hours to do so.

Pain occurs because of the inflammatory process, as it does when inflammation occurs after joint injury. However, in some cases, pain in juvenile rheumatoid arthritis may be underestimated or even missed. Depending on the developmental level of the child, the child's experience with pain, and the child's individual disposition, the child may not verbally express the presence of pain. Often nonverbal expressions of pain predominate. The only signs of pain may be alteration in the joint position and abnormal movement patterns on walking or grasping. Pain may be expressed by the child with juvenile rheumatoid arthritis as having difficulty sleeping and crying during the night. The child may be hesitant to walk because of the pain, and this may be misinterpreted as laziness.

Joint immobility and fever may also occur. Limitations in joint mobility initially occur because of muscle spasms, fluid in the joint, and synovial proliferation. Later, limitations in joint movement occur because of muscle contractures, joint destruction, or ankylosis (immobility of a joint due to disease or injury) (Miller & Cassidy, 2004). Fever may occur as part of the disease and not because of any contagious infection.

Types of Juvenile Rheumatoid Arthritis

Pauciarticular Juvenile Rheumatoid Arthritis

In pauciarticular arthritis (also known as oligoarthritis), fewer than five joints are involved. This is the most common type of juvenile rheumatoid arthritis, with approximately 60% of individuals with juvenile rheumatoid arthritis having this type. The most common subtype, ANA seropositive (antinuclear antibodies seropositive), is most often found in very young girls, with an onset often being between 2 and 4 years of age. In this type, the knee is the most commonly involved joint, followed by the ankle and elbow. Often, only one joint is involved, typically the knee. This can result in leg length discrepancy (with one leg being longer) (Rettig et al., 2004). However, there are other, less frequently occurring subtypes (e.g., rheumatoid factor seropositive and HLA-B27 positive), and the physical findings can vary depending on the subtype. For example, boys more often have the HLA-B27 subtype, which often has an onset after 8 years of age with the large joints of the legs being affected the most.

Children with pauciarticular juvenile arthritis are especially at risk for additional complications affecting the visual system. Uveitis (also known as iridocyclitis) is a serious problem that can be present with the onset of the disease or that can develop during it. Uveitis is the inflammation of the middle layer of the eye (i.e., **uveal tract**), although the term has been used to refer to any inflammation process inside the eye. It occurs in about 10% to 20% of children who have this form of arthritis, especially the ANA subtype (Herring, 2002; Rettig et al., 2004). It can lead to cataracts, glaucoma, and blindness. Symptoms can include red eyes, pain, photophobia (i.e., light causes pain), and blurred vision, or there may be no symptoms (Patel & Lundy, 2002). Children with pauciarticular arthritis need to be evaluated by an ophthalmologist immediately on diagnosis and every 3 to 4 months (if onset was before 7 years of age) or every 6 months (if onset was after 7 years of age) (Rettig et al., 2004).

Polyarticular Juvenile Rheumatoid Arthritis

Polyarticular juvenile rheumatoid arthritis is characterized by involvement of five or more joints, but 20 to 40 joints are often involved (Miller & Cassidy, 2004). Some of the most common joints that are affected are the large joints of the legs, small joints of the hands and feet, the cervical spine, and the jaw. When the hip is involved, walking may be painful or difficult. Involvement of the hand may result in difficulty grasping. When cervical vertebrae are affected, there may be restricted neck movement. Symptoms arising from the jawbones are often described as an earache. The student may describe having chest pain when there is arthritis of the connecting joints of the breastbone, collarbone, and ribs (Herring, 2002).

Polyarticular juvenile arthritis also has several different subtypes. Two main subgroups are rheumatoid factor-negative and rheumatoid factor-positive, depending on whether the rheumatoid factor is present. Children with rheumatoid factor-negative disease often have less involvement of the small joints of the hands and are usually less severe (Herring, 2002). Children with polyarticular juvenile rheumatoid arthritis may also be ANA positive and are at risk of developing uveitis and will need regular ophthalmologic exams.

Systemic-Onset Juvenile Rheumatoid Arthritis

Systemic-onset juvenile rheumatoid arthritis (also known as Still's disease) is the most severe and dramatic form of the disease. Arthritis is only one symptom of this disease, with many organs or systems being involved, such as the liver, spleen, lining around the lung (plura), lining around the heart (pericardium), and skin (Herring, 2002). Organs may be enlarged or inflamed, and a skin rash may be present. Fevers can spike once or twice a day and then go back to normal. Fever can be as high as 102 to 105 degrees Fahrenheit, and during this time the child may appear very ill and listless. Later in the day when the fever is absent, the child may appear very healthy. This pattern of daily fever can occur for weeks or months, then stop for a period of time and begin again. Children with this form of rheumatoid arthritis are at low risk of developing uveitis, but yearly ophthalmologic exams are needed to continue to screen for any eye abnormalities.

DETECTION OF JUVENILE RHEUMATOID ARTHRITIS

There is no singular specific test for juvenile rheumatoid arthritis; rather, diagnosis is made primarily on clinical findings. If juvenile rheumatoid arthritis is suspected in children who are under 16, laboratory tests will be conducted to determine if there is any rheumatoid factor, ANA, or other factors that are present in some types of juvenile rheumatoid arthritis. Since part of the diagnosis is dependent on the continuation of symptoms over a period of time, it may appear that nothing is being done while, in fact, waiting is needed to determine the diagnosis.

Several other diseases may have symptoms similar to juvenile rheumatoid arthritis (especially the systemic type). This includes such diseases as systemic lupus, Lyme disease, trauma, Legg-Calve-Perthes disease, sickle cell disease, and acute leukemia (Siegel & Baum, 1993). Part of the diagnosis of juvenile rheumatoid arthritis will be to rule out other diseases. The child's medical history, physical exam, and laboratory tests will assist with the diagnosis. Other tests, such as X-rays or a biopsy of the synovial lining, may be done to give further information. Additional tests specific to the other suspected diseases will be performed to rule out these diseases. When a diagnosis of juvenile rheumatoid arthritis is made, the physician will determine which type is present.

TREATMENT OF JUVENILE RHEUMATOID ARTHRITIS

Treatment goals of juvenile rheumatoid arthritis include achieving symptom control (e.g., decreased pain), increasing function, and avoiding or minimizing erosive joint damage, with as few adverse events as possible (Lovell, 2004). There are several medications that may be prescribed to try to reduce inflammation and relieve pain. Initial treatment is typically with nonsteroidal anti-inflammatory drugs, progressing to more aggressive therapies. Second-line drugs include disease-modifying antirheumatic drugs (such as sulfasalazine, methotrexate, and cytotoxic drugs) (Hsu, Lin, Yang, & Chiang, 2004; Ilowite, 2002). However, there is a more recent trend of managing juvenile rheumatoid arthritis much more aggressively earlier in the treatment stage to try to prevent joint damage and halt secondary articular damage, especially for those with very active polyarticular or systemic juvenile rheumatoid arthritis (Hsu et al., 2004). The use of systemic corticosteroids is usually avoided, unless severe systemic disease is present, because of their side effects (e.g., growth retardation and osteoporosis). However, localized use of corticosteroid injections into the joint may decrease synovitis and pain, decrease joint deformity, and improve gait (when the legs are involved) (Broström, Hagelberg, & Haglund-Åkerlind, 2004). If uveitis is present, eyedrops will typically be prescribed.

Physical therapy and occupational therapy are often prescribed to decrease the risk of contractures and assist in maintaining the ability to perform certain activities and functions. Treatment modalities include heat–cold treatment, massage, electrical stimulation, ultrasound, therapeutic exercises (e.g., aquatic exercises or isometric exercises), and the use of splints and orthoses (Cakmak & Bolukbas, 2005). If there is hip involvement, additional treatments may be indicated, such as supportive aids for walking, traction (during the evening), or hydrotherapy (therapy implemented in the water) (Jacobsen, Crawford, & Broste, 1992).

It should be noted that if the arthritis is out of control (e.g., joint is painful and hot), the child may need splinting to allow the joint to rest and avoid exercise. When joints are less swollen and painful, exercises may be prescribed as long as they do not cause discomfort. It is important to dispel the idea that pain is gain since there are clearly times when the joints should not be exercised or moved beyond a certain point (Herring, 2002).

Depending on the severity of involvement and complications, surgery may be indicated. Surgery may be needed to release contractures to promote function (e.g., surgical release of severe contractures at the knee and hip may be needed to promote walking). In some cases, joints may be destroyed by the arthritis and need to be surgically replaced. For example, total knee arthroplasty has been effective in terms of pain relief and improvement in function in children with juvenile rheumatoid arthritis (Palmer et al., 2005; Parvizi, Lajam, Trousdale, Shaughnessy, & Cabanela, 2003). **Scoliosis** also occurs with individuals with juvenile rheumatoid arthritis and may need to be treated surgically (Herring, 2002) (see chapter 9).

COURSE OF JUVENILE RHEUMATOID ARTHRITIS

Over time, juvenile rheumatoid arthritis may progress, stabilize, or go into remission. Juvenile rheumatoid arthritis is considered active if there are an increasing number of joints being affected when the child is receiving drug therapy. It is considered active but stable if there is no increase in the number of joints but drug therapy is required. The arthritis is classified as inactive if there is no active inflammation of the synovium or other structures without drugs for less than 2 years. Juvenile rheumatoid arthritis is considered to be in remission if there is no evidence of joint inflammation or other symptoms outside the joint without drug treatment for over 2 years (Gare, Fasth, & Wiklund, 1993).

Although 50% to 75% of treated children with juvenile rheumatoid arthritis go into complete remission, it is estimated that approximately 45% of individuals with juvenile rheumatoid arthritis will have active disease into early adulthood, often with severe limitation in physical functioning (Beers, Porter, Jones, Kaplan, & Berkwits, 2006; Miller & Cassidy, 2004). Although the course of the disease for an individual child is not predictable, there are different prognoses that are based on the type of juvenile rheumatoid arthritis. For example, children with pauciarticular arthritis (ANA-positive type) often have early remission after a few years. However, some may progress to having more joint involvement and resemble polyarticular juvenile rheumatoid arthritis. Also, uveitis may continue and become chronic, even after the arthritis is in remission. Children with polyarticular arthritis usually have a much longer course. The systemic manifestations in the systemic disease may resolve after a few years, but the arthritis may continue and be difficult to control, especially when multiple joints are involved (Herring, 2002; Miller & Cassidy, 2004).

DESCRIPTION OF ARTHROGRYPOSIS

Arthrogryposis, also known as arthrogryposis multiplex congenita (AMC), is a term used to refer to multiple congenital contractures. It is not a disease but a symptom found in several different conditions that have multiple contractures present at birth. The term originated from two Greek words: *arthro,* meaning "joints," and *gryposis,* meaning "curved" or "bent." The first written account of arthrogryposis was made in 1841. It is a very rare condition, with an incidence of about 1 out of 3,000 to 1 out of 10,000 live births (Hall, 1997; Madazli et al., 2002).

ETIOLOGY OF ARTHROGRYPOSIS

Over 150 different conditions have congenital multiple contractures as a predominant sign, and these are categorized as arthrogryposis (Thompson, 2004). Most causes are not genetic, although several genetic patterns have been found, as has an increased incidence in certain genetic conditions (e.g., **spinal muscular atrophy** type 1). Often a specific cause cannot be established.

Five pathogenic categories of arthrogryposis have been identified based on etiology: (a) **neuropathy** (caused by disorders affecting the nervous system, such as spinal muscle atrophy), (b) **myopathy** (caused by disorders affecting the muscles, such as congenital muscular dystrophy), (c) abnormal connective tissue disorders, (d) physical constraints in utero, and (e) maternal illness (such as myasthenia gravis) (Polizzi, Huson, & Vincent, 2000).

The most common form of arthrogryposis is known as amyoplasia or classic arthrogryposis. It accounts for 40% of children with arthrogryposis (Thompson, 2004). This particular type usually has involvement in the arms and legs.

DYNAMICS OF ARTHROGRYPOSIS

Movement of a joint is dependent on an intact nervous system and an intact muscular system. As discussed in chapters 5 and 6, the brain sends electrical impulses down the spinal cord. From the spinal cord, they travel through the peripheral nervous system. When the impulses reach muscle, via the peripheral nerves, the impulse causes the muscle to contract. The ends of the skeletal muscles are attached to bones by tendons and ligaments that are located on opposite sides of a joint. When the electrical impulse causes the muscle to contract, a muscle group shortens (and another muscle group relaxes), causing a pull on the bone across the joint and creating motion of the bone.

In arthrogryposis, there is typically some type of defect or disorder affecting the nerves, muscles, or connective tissues that results in an inability to properly move a joint. This occurs during prenatal development, when the fetus would normally be moving. Without the normal amount of physical movement, certain joints may remain in fixed location or minimally move. When this occurs, contractures and muscle atrophy (wasting away of the muscle) result. Any condition that impairs movement in utero can result in arthrogryposis (Beers et al., 2006).

CHARACTERISTICS OF ARTHROGRYPOSIS

When infants are born with arthrogryposis, they have either flexion (bent) or extension (straight) contractures affecting different joints of the body. In classic arthrogryposis (amyoplasia), the limbs appear thin and may have fat infiltration. There is a characteristic pattern with limited shoulder mobility, elbows in extension, wrists in flexion, and deformity of the thumb and palm. In the legs, the hips are flexed and rotated externally (often with **hip dislocation** being present in one or both hips), the knees are either in flexion or extension, and there is deformity of the feet (e.g., clubfeet) (Herring, 2002; Thompson, 2004) (see Figure 10-2). Although severe physical involvement may be present, intelligence is usually normal.

Kathryn Wolff Heller

FIGURE 10–2 A student with arthrogryposis wears a splint that straightens her wrist, and the splint has a pencil attachment (on the underside of the splint) to help hold the pencil. She is also using a slant board that has Dycem (a nonslip material) underneath it to stabilize the slant board and prevent it from moving.

There may be other conditions associated with the various types of arthrogryposis. Some of these include cleft palate, short stature, scoliosis, and urinary and cardiac abnormalities (Beers et al., 2006). In very rare instances, arthrogryposis may occur in combination with another rare disease. For example, Bruck syndrome is the combination of both arthrogryposis and osteogenesis imperfecta (Berg et al., 2005; Mokete, Robertson, Viljoen, & Beighton, 2005).

DETECTION OF ARTHROGRYPOSIS

At birth, the baby often has dramatic deformities and immobility that results in diagnosis of arthrogryposis. Part of the diagnostic process will be to determine if there is a well-defined disease that has resulted in these multiple congenital contractures. Differential diagnosis may, for example, be used to rule out muscular dystrophy (see chapter 13) or spinal muscular atrophy (see chapter 14). Initial evaluations should include a full history, including maternal history, and examinations by a neurologist and a geneticist. Neuromuscular evaluations are helpful, including nerve conduction studies/electromyography and muscle biopsy. Additional tests may be done to determine etiology.

Diagnosis can occur prenatally, as early as 19 weeks' gestation. Prenatal diagnosis is often based on the detection of diminished fetal movements along with an ultrasound to look for joint contractures. Because of the contractures, some babies will need to be delivered by caesarian section. A few fractures may be present at birth.

TREATMENT OF ARTHROGRYPOSIS

Treatment is aimed at improving the individual's functional ability. Because of the extensive physical involvement that usually occurs in arthrogryposis, only those deformities that interfere with the ability to perform activities of daily living are usually targeted. Ideally, the aim of treatment is to promote independent walking and use of the arms and hands for daily living activities. Traditional orthopedic measures of surgery, casting, bracing (orthoses), and physical and occupational therapy are typically used to try to improve mobility.

A well-planned treatment program is designed to accomplish maximal functional movement with the fewest surgeries. Joint manipulations often occur in the first few months of life. Ideally, the surgeries should be completed by age 6 or 7, with many surgeries occurring early in life (e.g., knee and hip surgeries around 6 months of age) (Herring, 2002).

A careful evaluation is made of each child with arthrogryposis to determine which surgeries would be most beneficial. For example, contractures of the elbows are serious since movement of this joint is necessary to achieve independence in most activities of daily living. Flexion contractures of the wrist also interfere with needed hand use and interfere with finger movement. Surgery may be needed to provide adequate arm use. Contractures of the hip and knees may interfere with standing or walking. Surgery may be performed to correct the contractures in order to allow a stable base and satisfactory gait. If there is hip dislocation, this will need to be corrected at an early age. Foot deformities typically require surgery to allow the child to stand. Other abnormalities, such as scoliosis, may require surgery or bracing (see chapter 9 for information on hip dislocation and scoliosis).

COURSE OF ARTHROGRYPOSIS

The course of arthrogryposis is dependent on the etiology. When there is an underlying condition, such as spinal muscular atrophy, the course will be dependent on that condition. When the term is used to describe the classic form of arthrogryposis, it is a nonprogressive disorder. The child's condition is usually worst when he or she is born, prior to any intervention. Usually, with surgery and other orthopedic treatments, there is some improvement of mobility that may allow limited but independent functioning of the individual.

DESCRIPTION OF OSTEOGENESIS IMPERFECTA

Osteogenesis imperfecta (OI), also known as brittle bone disease, refers to a genetic disorder of connective tissue that results in extreme bone fragility and bone deformity. There are various forms of the disorder. The most severe form of osteogenesis imperfecta usually results in a stillborn delivery or death shortly after being born due to multiple fractures occurring in utero that are not compatible with life (e.g., crumpled rib cage, fragile skull, or multiple bone fractures). On the other extreme, a child with the mildest form of osteogenesis imperfecta may not appear to have any impairment except fractures after mild to moderate trauma. Depending on the form of osteogenesis imperfecta, individuals may have hundreds of fractures in childhood to only a few in their lifetime. Other symptoms may be present, such as short stature, hearing loss, blue sclera (whites of the eyes are blue tinged), hypermobility, and dental fragility (also known as dentinogenesis imperfecta.)

Osteogenesis imperfecta has been around for a long time, with the oldest case first being diagnosed in a mummy in Egypt dating around 1000 B.C.E. (Kuurila, Kaitila, Johansson, & Grénman, 2002). The most colorful description of an individual thought to have osteogenesis imperfecta is "Ivan the Boneless," a Scandinavian prince who reportedly led the invasion of Britain in the ninth century while being carried into battle on a shield by his troops because of his limb deformities (Herring, 2002). Today, osteogenesis imperfecta that is detected at birth occurs at a rate of approximately 1 in 20,000 live births. The mildest form, which may not be diagnosed until later, has a similar incidence (Marini, 2004).

ETIOLOGY OF OSTEOGENESIS IMPERFECTA

Osteogenesis imperfecta is a genetic disorder of connective tissue. Most individuals with osteogenesis imperfecta have a mutation on one of two genes (COL1A1 or COL1A2) on chromosomes 17 and 7 (Pollitt et al., 2006). These genes are responsible for the coding of collagen (i.e., collagen type 1). The mutation may occur in several places on the two chromosomes, resulting in differing characteristics. However, some rare forms of osteogenesis imperfecta have been recently identified that do not have mutations of these genes affecting collagen but do share the characteristic of bone fragility. Research is currently being conducted to investigate these forms.

Most cases of osteogenesis imperfecta are autosomal dominant, especially the mildest forms. More severe forms may be either autosomal dominant or autosomal recessive. As with other conditions, cases have occurred without any clear history, probably because of a spontaneous mutation of the gene.

DYNAMICS OF OSTEOGENESIS IMPERFECTA

Most forms of osteogenesis imperfecta are linked to mutations of genes responsible for the coding of collagen. Collagen is found throughout the body and is essential to bone formation and strength. Bone is a tough, organic matrix that is composed primarily of collagen fibers. Adhering to the collagen fibers are the bone salts calcium and phosphate (Guyton & Hall, 2006). The collagen fibers and organic salts work together to give strength to the bone in much the same way as concrete is reinforced. The steel in reinforced concrete provides tensile strength; collagen fibers do this for bone. In reinforced concrete, the cement, rock, and sand provide compressional strength, much in the same way as bone salts do for bone.

Unlike reinforced concrete, however, bone is not static but is composed of living cells that are constantly changing. New bone is constantly being deposited, while old bone is constantly being reabsorbed. This constant deposition and absorption of bone serves many functions. First, as old bone becomes weak and brittle, new collagen fibers that compose the bone matrix are needed to replace the old matrix as it degenerates. Second, this process allows bones to change their shape and strength in proportion to the amount of stress on the bones. Bones may actually thicken when exposed to heavy loads or thin when there is little weight bearing on them.

In osteogenesis imperfecta, the collagen fibers are defective, and there are less bone salts present in the bone (Cassella & Ali, 1992). This decrease in bone salts is thought to be due not to a defect in the production of the bone salts but to their ability to adhere to the defective collagen fibers. These defects result in the bone being more brittle and subject to breakage.

CHARACTERISTICS OF OSTEOGENESIS IMPERFECTA

General Characteristics

The primary characteristics of osteogenesis imperfecta are the fragility of the bones and the effect of this fragility on bone structures. In some cases, osteogenesis imperfecta may be so severe that a bone may break on picking up a child with osteogenesis imperfecta. In other instances, it may be so mild that it is not diagnosed. Some children with this condition will have additional skeletal abnormalities, such as scoliosis and bowing of the long bones. The effect of osteogenesis imperfecta on bone structure may result in variable degrees of short stature (see Figure 10-3). Some children will be unable to walk independently and will need wheelchairs to achieve independence.

The collagen defects also commonly result in additional abnormalities and may affect the teeth, eyes, hearing, spine, and joints. The teeth may be discolored (ranging from dusky blue to brown) and easily break and wear down, which is known as dentinogenesis imperfecta. The white of the eye, known as the sclera, may appear blue in color because of the thinning of the collagen fibers composing the sclera (resulting in the layer of the eye under the sclera, known as the choroid, to show through as blue). Hearing loss may also occur in childhood or later in life and is often progressive (Kuurila, Grénman, Johansson, & Kaitila, 2000). Curvature of the spine (scoliosis and/or **kyphosis**) often develops, especially in the more severe forms (Engelbert et al., 2003). Other parts of the body that may be affected are the joints and ligaments, which may be lax.

Classification of Types of Osteogenesis Imperfecta

Osteogensis imperfecta has been classified several different ways. Originally, it was classified by the time of birth (i.e., congenital [at birth] or tarda [after birth]). Later it was classified by radio-

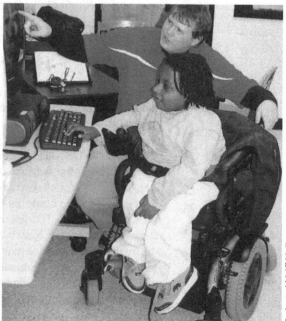

FIGURE 10-3 High school student with osteogenesis imperfecta working with a teacher on the computer.

Kathryn Wolff Heller

Type[a]	Bone fragility and deformity	Stature	Sclera	Hearing loss	Dentinogensis imperfecta (DI)
I	Least fragility Little deformity	Close to normal height	Blue	Loss present 40% loss	IA type—normal IB type—DI present
II	Extreme fragility Crumbled bones Perinatal lethal	Unknown	Blue	Unknown	Unknown
III	Severe fragility Progressive bowing Triangle face	Very short	Blue at birth, white with age	Loss present	DI present
IV	Variable, often moderate to severe	Moderately short	White	Loss— low frequency	IVA type—normal IVB type—DI present
V	Moderate to severe fragility and deformity	Short-mild to moderately	White		Normal teeth
VI	Moderate to severe fragility and deformity	Moderately short	White		Normal teeth
VII	Moderate fragility Early deformities	Mildly short	White		Normal teeth

[a] Types V, VI, and VIII are fairly new and may not be classified as subtypes by some organizations.

FIGURE 10–4 Types of osteogenesis imperfecta.

logical characteristics and then by additional characteristics. A classification system with four main types (I, II, III, and IV) was proposed in 1979 and gained acceptance (Sillence, Senn, & Danks, 1979). Since that time, subsets of these four main types have been proposed on the basis of whether the teeth are involved. Recently, three disease entities (named types V, VI, and VII) have been identified that are not associated with collagen mutations (Rauch & Glorieux, 2004) (see Figure 10-4). However, some researchers believe that only those conditions with mutations of the genes affecting collagen should be considered truly osteogenesis imperfecta (I, II, III, and IV) and consider other conditions with bone fragility as "syndromes resembling osteogenesis imperfecta" (which would include V, VI, and VII and those with names such as Bruck osteogenesis imperfecta) (Plotkin, 2004). Since the classification debate is far from over, we will discuss the seven types with the numerical designation and provide the alternative names. It should be noted that the order of severity does not increase with the number. In fact, the order from least to most severe is type I < types IV, V, VI, and VII < type III < type II (Rauch & Glorieux, 2004).

Type I Osteogenesis Imperfecta (Mild)

Type I is the mildest form of osteogenesis imperfecta and is the most common. There is mild bone fragility and little or no bone deformity. Although fractures may occur from minimal trauma, not all accidents will produce fractures. When deformities occur, they are often a result of fractures, although bowing of the legs can occur without a history of fracture. Fractures often decrease after puberty (Marini, 2004). Sclera of the eyes are distinctively blue throughout life, and 20% develop a curvature of the spine (scoliosis or kyphosis) (Herring, 2002). This type has been divided into type IA and IB on the basis of whether the teeth are normal or have dentinogenesis imperfecta.

Type II Osteogenesis Imperfecta (Perinatal Lethal)

The most severe type of osteogenesis imperfecta is type II, in which the infant usually dies at birth or shortly after. Infants are born with a crumpled (accordion-like) appearance of the long bones with multiple fractures of the ribs. Limbs are usually very short, bent, and deformed, and the skull is soft. In this lethal form of osteogenesis imperfecta, many infants are stillborn. The rest usually die shortly after birth because of difficulty breathing secondary to a defective rib cage.

Type III Osteogenesis Imperfecta (Progressive Deforming)

This type is the most severe, nonlethal form of osteogenesis imperfecta and usually results in significant physical disability. There is severe bone fragility and bowing of the limbs. The newborn or young infant often has multiple fractures, leading to progressively more deformed bones. Fractures occur frequently throughout childhood. Most children have very short stature, and **kyphoscoliosis** (combined scoliosis and kyphosis) is usually present in childhood and progresses to adolescence. Skull deformity often occurs and results in a triangular appearance of the head (Herring, 2002). Hearing loss may occur as well as tooth deformity. By age 10, the majority of children with type III may sit without assistance, but only a few can walk short distances on crutches, with most using wheelchairs (Vetter, Pontz, Zauner, Brenner, & Spranger, 1992). Respiratory complication may result in a shorter life span (Plotkin, 2004).

Type IV Osteogenesis Imperfecta (Moderately Severe)

Type IV has moderate to severe bone deformity. Infants may be born with fractures or bowing of the legs. Fractures may occur with mild trauma; however, like type I, there may be improvement on the onset of puberty with less occurrence of fractures. Motor performance may be delayed or impaired with only about one-third of the individuals able to walk on crutches by age 4. Some will be able to walk without the use of crutches, but some will be able to become independent only with the use of wheelchairs (Vetter et al., 1992). Most children will have short stature. This type has been further divided into two subtypes—IVA, in which the teeth are normal, and IVB, in which teeth abnormality is present.

Type V Osteogenesis Imperfecta (Hyperplastic Callus)

Type V has similar clinical features as type IV. However, it is distinctive because there is an enlarged unorganized meshwork of woven bone (known as a hyperplastic callus) that occurs when a bone is broken. This is often accompanied by hard, painful, and warm swelling over the bone. In addition, the membrane between the two bones in the forearm are often affected, resulting in an inability to rotate the forearm (i.e., pronate and supinate the arm) (Marini, 2004). No mutations of the collagen genes have been identified. Some prefer to classify this as congenital brittle bone with redundant callus formation rather than type V.

Other Types of Osteogenesis Imperfecta

Several other types of congenital brittle bone disease have been found and classified in different ways. Type VI osteogenesis imperfecta, also known as congenital brittle bones with mineralization defect, appears clinically similar to type IV, but the genes affecting collagen production are not affected. Instead, there is a mineralization defect that affects the bone matrix. Type VII, also known as congenital brittle bones with rhizomelia (involving the hip joint and shoulder), presents with short humerus (bone in upper arm) and femur (thighbones). A genetic defect on the short arm of chromosome 3 has been identified (Plotkin, 2004).

DETECTION OF OSTEOGENESIS IMPERFECTA

Osteogenesis imperfecta may be diagnosed through clinical observation, radiological examination, collagen biochemical studies (from a biopsy), and genetic studies. At birth, multiple fractures usually indicate one of the more severe forms. A family history of the disease, dental abnormalities, and blue sclera all provide additional evidence of this disorder. However, skeletal deformities may occur in other types of conditions, such as certain generalized skeletal disorders, so diagnosis is aimed at making a differential diagnosis and determining the type of osteogenesis imperfecta.

As early as 16 weeks of gestation, the more severe forms of osteogenesis imperfecta (type II and type III) can usually be detected by ultrasound (Marini, 2004). Ultrasound will allow visualization of fractures, bowing, and decrease in bone mass. The milder types may not be detected by ultrasound at all.

In most cases, diagnosis of osteogenesis imperfecta is very straightforward. However, in more difficult cases in which the osteogenesis imperfecta is mild, an initial diagnosis may incorrectly be made of child abuse. Some factors that contribute to the misdiagnosis is the failure to recognize that osteogenesis imperfecta can occur without a family history, without blue sclera, without reduced bone mass, without bowed limbs, or without multiple severe fractures (Paterson, Burns, & McAllion, 1993). Many symptoms may appear the same in child abuse and osteogenesis imperfecta. A very careful examination for osteogenesis imperfecta is needed since a misdiagnosis of child abuse can be extremely difficult and damaging to the family. Instances have occurred in which children have been taken from their homes and parents faced criminal charges of child abuse prior to the diagnosis of osteogenesis imperfecta.

TREATMENT OF OSTEOGENESIS IMPERFECTA

There is currently no cure for osteogenesis imperfecta. Orthopedic management aims at managing fractures and correcting deformities in order to improve functioning. Fractures are splinted or casted and typically heal well. Bowing of the long bones may be treated by a surgical procedure known as an osteotomy with rod placement (sometimes called rodding) (see Figure 10–5). In this procedure, wedge-shaped cuts are made through the curved bone, and the resulting fragments are fixed on a rod to straighten the bone and to provide long-term splinting of the fragile bone (Herring, 2002). The rod may be a fixed length or designed to lengthen with bone growth. Important adjuncts to orthopedic management include physical therapy and rehabilitation.

Additional impairments found in osteogenesis imperfecta will often require treatment. For example, curvatures of the spine (e.g., scoliosis and kyphosis) will often need surgery. Some types of hearing loss will improve with surgical intervention on one of the small bones in the middle ear (stapes surgery) (Albahnasawy, Kishore, & O'Reilly, 2001; Kuurila,

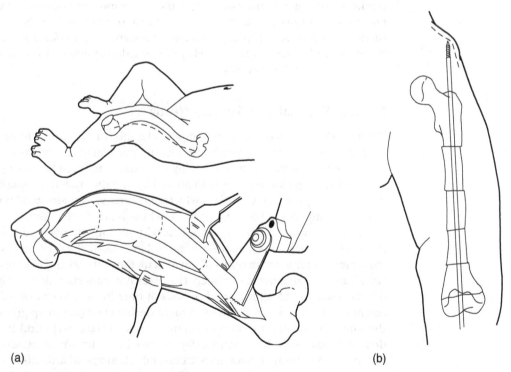

(a)   (b)

FIGURE 10–5 Typical bowing of bones in osteogenesis imperfecta (a) and surgery using rodding (b).

Pynnönen, & Grénman, 2004), and some types of hearing loss have improved with a cochlear implant (Migirov, Henkin, Hildesheimer, & Kronenberg, 2003).

The most encouraging treatment in recent years involves the intravenous use of medications known as bisphosphonates (e.g., pamidronate), given on a cycle of every few weeks to few months. A number of studies involving the use of pamidronate demonstrated a significant reduction in pain and fracture rates and increase in bone density for individuals with moderate to severe osteogenesis imperfecta (Forin et al., 2005; Zeitlin, Rauch, Travers, Munns, & Glorieux, 2006). The long-term effects of this medication are still under investigation, as is the use of other types of medications.

Current research is now targeting possible cellular and gene therapies. The use of bone marrow transplants using marrow mesenchymal cells is being explored, with some limited success (Horwitz, 2001). Gene therapies that would be useful for patients with different mutations of COL1A1 and COL1A2 are being investigated as possible therapy for osteogenesis imperfecta (Millington-Ward, McMahon, & Farrar, 2005; Niyibizi, Wang, Mi, & Robbins, 2004; Rauch & Glorieux, 2005).

COURSE OF OSTEOGENESIS IMPERFECTA

The course of osteogenesis imperfecta depends on its type. The more mild forms of osteogenesis imperfecta, such as type I and type IV, usually do not affect the life span. Infants with type II usually die prior to birth, at birth, or a few months to a year after birth. Individuals with type III may have a reduced life span because of pulmonary causes, and when this is the case, death most frequently occurs during early childhood, in teen years, or in the 40s (Marini, 2004).

EDUCATIONAL IMPLICATIONS OF JUVENILE RHEUMATOID ARTHRITIS, ARTHROGRYPOSIS, AND OSTEOGENESIS IMPERFECTA

When students have conditions that affect their joints or bones, it is imperative that their teachers have a good understanding of the educational implications of these conditions and make the appropriate adaptations to meet these students' needs. In the case of juvenile rheumatoid arthritis, arthrogryposis, and osteogenesis imperfecta, some of the planning will be similar, while other aspects will be different, depending on the characteristics of the specific condition and its severity.

Meeting Physical and Sensory Needs

When a student has osteogenesis imperfecta, the teacher needs to be careful that the student does not engage in activities that would put him at risk of having a fracture. For more severe forms, this may include allowing the student to leave for other classes early to avoid busy hallways and knowing how to lift and handle the student properly. It is also important not to be overprotective, which is why teachers need to understand the specific type of osteogenesis imperfecta the student has and how it is affecting him.

One of the major concerns of students with juvenile rheumatoid arthritis is pain management. The longer a student sits, the more likely he will experience stiffness and pain on movement. After a few minutes of movement, the stiffness and pain usually decrease or dissipate, and he can move more freely. However, it is important that teachers try to avoid having the student sit for prolonged periods of time in the interest of pain management. The teacher may allow for frequent movement during class (e.g., help give out papers) or allow the student to stand for 15 minutes in the middle of the class period. In severe cases, the student may need a modified school day. To avoid missing any more school time than necessary, it is important that students with juvenile rheumatoid arthritis not be sent home when they have a fever (unless they have other symptoms indicating an infection) since fever is a symptom of some forms of this condition.

Students with arthrogryposis—and in some cases severe juvenile rheumatoid arthritis and severe osteogenesis imperfecta—often need assistive technology devices and adaptations. For example, when there are joint limitations affecting hand use as in arthrogryposis and juvenile rheumatoid arthritis, students may need adaptations to writing tools (e.g., built-up pen or alternate access to the computer). For students with more severe forms of osteogenesis imperfecta, activities that require pressing an object with force (e.g., stapling using a manual stapler) may need to be adapted (e.g., electric stapler or using a paperclip) (see chapter 8 on assistive technology and chapter 12 on adaptations).

Physical fitness and activity is important in maintaining health; however, a modified physical education program is usually needed for students who have juvenile rheumatoid arthritis, arthrogryposis, and osteogenesis imperfecta. Because of joint damage or joint pain, students with juvenile rheumatoid arthritis usually need to avoid strenuous games that put extended pressure on the joints or limit the amount of their running. A modified physical education program would take into account whether the student could tolerate light, moderate, or heavy exercise with his upper and/or lower extremities. In arthrogryposis, joint deformity usually requires adaptations to allow the student to participate. Rules of games may be modified, balls may be lightweight, or adapted equipment may be used, such as those in adapted bowling. In osteogenesis imperfecta, physical activity that places stress on the bones is usually contraindicated. Activities may need to be modified that protect the student from being hit or hitting or kicking an object, especially when the student has a more severe type of this disease.

Teachers should be alert to any indications of a sensory problem. Students with certain types of juvenile rheumatoid arthritis can develop a visual impairment, and in osteogenesis imperfecta there is a risk of developing a hearing impairment. If a sensory impairment is found, the teacher will need to work closely with the consulting teacher certified in visual impairments or hearing impairments to determine the appropriate adaptations and/or additional instruction the student may need.

Meeting Communication Needs

There are usually no communication or speech impairments associated with juvenile rheumatoid arthritis, arthrogryposis, or osteogenesis imperfecta. The challenge in communication for these students is then not speech but properly communicating about the disorder to others. It is imperative that school personnel and, in some cases, classmates gain an accurate understanding of the conditions. This is especially crucial in osteogenesis imperfecta in which a playful shove in the hall may result in a broken bone. Depending on the severity, young students may say, "My bones break easy, like glass. I can play with you, I just have to be careful and people have to be careful not to run into me." Young students with arthrogryposis may say to peers, "When I was born my arms and legs would not bend right, and they still don't bend the same as yours." Children with juvenile rheumatoid arthritis may say, "I have children's arthritis. That means my joints hurt me sometimes. I sometimes have to move slowly when I haven't moved around much."

Children with juvenile rheumatoid arthritis may have difficulty expressing whether they are in pain. Pain occurs physiologically the same in children and adults. However, the perception of pain is a subjective, emotional, and individual sensation. Children's stage of development, emotional experiences, and former pain experiences all play a role in how children understand and interpret pain. The teacher should be alert to nonverbal signs of pain, such as lack of movement of a limb, holding a limb in a certain position, or hesitancy in moving about.

Meeting Learning Needs

Students with juvenile rheumatoid arthritis, arthrogryposis, or osteogenesis imperfecta usually have normal intelligence. Often it is important to stress academics when there are physical limitations. However, physical disability and chronic illness often create special problems that may hinder performance at school. Fatigue, absences, low self-esteem, and lack of experiences may all negatively impact on performance. In addition, students with juvenile rheumatoid arthritis may miss information or not be able to do their best work when they are in pain. This is compounded when the student has not slept well because of the pain and discomfort of the disease. These and similar issues need to be closely assessed and addressed in the educational setting to promote a successful experience.

Meeting Daily Living Needs

Students should be encouraged to independently perform daily living skills as much as possible. Students who are mildly affected with juvenile rheumatoid arthritis, arthrogryposis, or osteogenesis imperfecta may require a longer period of time to complete some tasks, or they may require no adaptations at all. However, for some students who are severely affected, adaptations and assistive technology may be needed. For example, adapted pencils, adapted spoons, long shoehorns, or sock aids may be needed. Door handles and faucets with levers on them are easier to manage for students who have affected arms and fingers. An adapted toilet with a raised seat and a grab bar may be needed for students with hip involvement. When there is bone involvement, as in osteogenesis imperfecta, adapted devices are used to minimize stress on the bone structure as well as adapt for any contractures or weakness. Adapted utensils that are lightweight may be helpful. The exact type of adapted device will be individually selected and assessed using a team approach. It is important in each case that the teacher foster as much physical independence as possible and not be overly protective or restrictive (see chapter 8 on assistive technology).

Meeting Behavioral and Social Needs

It is especially important that the educator be aware of the behavioral and social needs of the student with juvenile rheumatoid arthritis, arthrogryposis, or osteogenesis imperfecta. These students may have feelings of frustration, depression, and anger over their condition and need counseling to assist them to cope with it. Social isolation can occur because of the obvious physical deformity that can occur in these conditions. Students with osteogenesis imperfecta may have few friends or playmates because of parents', teachers', or the student's anxiety that playing with others may result in fractures. Students with juvenile rheumatoid arthritis may feel isolated when other students do not understand the pain associated with the condition.

The role of school counselors and, where available, school mental health clinicians can be a vital support for the student and their family. Typical support can include assistance with issues related to the child's disability, frequent absences, adherence to necessary regimes, medical or dietary programs, school reentry after diagnosis or hospitalization, mental health issues such as peer relations and as a facilitator in communicating between the family, health care professionals, and school staff (Kaffenberger, 2006; Nabors & Lehmkuhl, 2004). Assistance may also be given in acquiring needed support through either an individualized education plan or a Section 504 plan

SUMMARY

Students with juvenile rheumatoid arthritis, arthrogryposis, or osteogenesis imperfecta have conditions that affect the joints or bones (and may affect other body systems as well). Juvenile rheumatoid arthritis is a chronic form of arthritis found in children in which one of the main characteristics is joint inflammation that results in painful and stiff joints. In arthrogryposis, the child is born with multiple contractures. Students with osteogenesis imperfecta have excessive bone fragility, which often results in multiple fractures. Teachers need to have a good understanding of these conditions and provide adaptations to school activities to ensure accessibility to the task as well as promote a safe, healthy environment for these students.

Jarrod was diagnosed with polyarticular juvenile rheumatoid arthritis when he was 4 years old. He has severe involvement in several joints, causing him pain and stiffness, fatigue, and fever. He is presently 7 years old and in second grade. He seems to not want to get up to go to the next activity in class, and the teacher feels he is lazy and a behavior problem. What could be some of the issues, and how should the teacher handle the situation?

REFERENCES

Albahnasawy, L., Kishore, A., & O'Reilly, B. F. (2001). Results of stapes surgery on patients with osteogenesis imperfecta. *Clinical Otolaryngology and Allied Sciences, 26,* 473–476.

Beers, M. H., Porter, R. S., Jones, T. V., Kaplan, J. L., & Berkwits, M. (2006). *The Merck manual of diagnosis and therapy.* Whitehouse Station, NJ: Merck Research Laboratories.

Berg, C., Geipel, A., Noack, F., Smrcek, J., Krapp, M., Germer, U., et al. (2005). Prenatal diagnosis of Bruck Syndrome. *Prenatal Diagnosis, 25,* 535–538.

Broström, E., Hagelberg, S., & Haglund-Åkerlind, Y. (2004). Effect of joint injections in children with juvenile idiopathic arthritis: Evaluation by 3D-gait analysis. *Acta Paediatrica, 93,* 906–910.

Cakmak, A., & Bolukbas, N. (2005). Juvenile rheumatoid arthritis: Physical therapy and rehabilitation. *Southern Medical Journal, 98,* 212–216.

Cassella, J. P., & Ali, S. Y. (1992). Abnormal collagen and mineral formation in osteogenesis imperfecta. *Bone and Mineral, 17,* 123–128.

Engelbert, R. H., Uiterwaal, C. S., van der Hulst, A., Witjes, B., Helders, P. J., & Pruijs, H. E. (2003). Scoliosis in children with osteogenesis imperfecta: influence of severity of disease and age of reaching motor milestones. *European Spine Journal, 12,* 130–134.

Forin, V., Arabi, A., Guigonis, V., Filipe, G., Bensman, A., & Roux, C. (2005). Benefits of pamidronate in children with osteogenesis imperfecta: An open prospective study. *Joint Bone Spine, 72,* 313–318.

Gare, B. A., Fasth, A., & Wiklund, K. (1993). Measurement of functional status in juvenile chronic arthritis: Evaluation of a Swedish version of the childhood health assessment questionnaire. *Clinical and Experimental Rheumatology, 11,* 569–576.

Guyton, A. C., & Hall, J. E. (2006). *Textbook of medical physiology* (11th ed.). Philadelphia: Elsevier/Saunders.

Hall, J. G. (1997). Arthrogryposis multiplex congenital: Etiology, genetics, classification, diagnostic approach and general aspects. *Journal of Pediatric Orthopedics, 6,* 159–166.

Herring, J. A. (2002). *Tachdjian's pediatric orthopaedics* (3rd ed.). Philadelphia: W. B. Saunders.

Horwitz, E. M. (2001). Clinical responses to bone marrow transplantation in children with severe osteogenesis imperfecta. *Blood, 97,* 1227–1231.

Hsu, C.-T., Lin, Y.-T., Yang, Y.-H., & Chiang, B.-L. (2004). Factors affecting clinical and therapeutic outcomes of patients with juvenile rheumatoid arthritis. *Scandinavian Journal of Rheumatology, 33,* 312–317.

Ilowite, N. T. (2002). Current treatment of juvenile rheumatoid arthritis. *Pediatrics, 109,* 109–116.

Jacobsen, F. S., Crawford, A. H., & Broste, S. (1992). Hip involvement in juvenile rheumatoid arthritis. *Journal of Pediatric Orthopedics, 12,* 45–53.

Jackson, P. L., & Vessey, J. A. (2000). *Primary care of the child with a chronic condition* (3rd ed.). St. Louis, Mosby.

Kaffenberger, C. J. (2006). School reentry for students with a chronic illness: A role for professional school counselors. *Professional School Counseling, 9,* 223–230.

Kuurila, K., Grénman, R., Johansson, R., & Kaitila, I. (2000). Hearing loss in children with osteogenesis imperfecta. *European Journal of Pediatrics, 159,* 515–520.

Kuurila, K., Kaitila, I., Johansson, R., & Grénman, R. (2002). Hearing loss in Finnish adults with osteogenesis imperfecta: A nationwide survey. *Annals of Otology, Rhinology and Laryngology, 111,* 939–947.

Kuurila, K., Pynnönen, S., & Grénman, R. (2004). Staples surgery in osteogenesis imperfecta in Finland. *Annals of Otology, Rhinology and Laryngology, 113,* 187–193.

Labyak, S. E., Bourguignon, C., & Docherty, S. (2003). Sleep quality in children with juvenile rheumatoid arthritis. *Holistic Nursing Practice, 17,* 193–201.

Lovell, D. (2004). Biologic agents for the treatment of juvenile rheumatoid arthritis: Current status. *Pediatric Drugs, 6,* 137–146.

Madazli, R., Tuysuz, B., Aksoy, F., Barbaros, M., Uludag, S., & Ocak, V. (2002). Prenatal diagnosis of arthrogryposis multiplex congenita with increased nuchal translucency but without any underlying fetal neurogenic or myogenic pathology. *Fetal Diagnosis and Therapy, 17,* 29–33.

Marini, H. C. (2004). Osteogenesis imperfecta. In R. E. Behrman, R. M. Kliegman, & H. B. Jenson (Eds.), *Nelson textbook of pediatrics* (pp. 2336–2338). Philadelphia: W. B. Saunders.

Migirov, L., Henkin, Y., Hildesheimer, M., & Kronenberg, J. (2003). Cochlear implantation in a child with osteogenesis imperfecta. *International Journal of Pediatric Otorhinolaryngology, 67,* 677–681.

Miller, M. L., & Cassidy, J. T. (2004). Juvenile rheumatoid arthritis. In R. E. Behrman, R. M. Kliegman, & H. B. Jenson

(Eds.), *Nelson textbook of pediatrics* (pp. 799–805). Philadelphia: W. B. Saunders.

Millington-Ward, S., McMahon, H. P., & Farrar, G. J. (2005). Emerging therapeutic approaches for osteogenesis imperfecta. *Trends in Molecular Medicine, 11*, 299–305.

Mokete L., Robertson, A., Viljoen, D., & Beighton, P. (2005). Bruck syndrome: Congenital joint contractures with bone fragility. *Journal of Orthopaedic Science: Official Journal of the Japanese Orthopaedic Association, 10*, 641–647.

Moore, T. L. (1999). Immunopathogenesis of juvenile rheumatoid arthritis. *Current Opinions in Rheumatology, 11*, 377–383.

Nabors, L., & Lehmkuhl, H. (2004). Children with chronic medical conditions: Recommendations for school mental health clinicians. *Journal of Developmental and Physical Disabilities, 16*, 1–15.

Niyibizi, C., Wang, S., Mi, Z., & Robbins, P. D. (2004). Gene therapy approaches for osteogenesis imperfecta. *Gene Therapy, 11*, 408–416.

Oğuz, F., Akdeniz, C., Ünüvar, E., Küçükbasmací, Ö., & Sídal, M. (2002). Parvovirus B19 in the acute arthropathies and juvenile rheumatoid arthritis. *Journal of Paediatrics & Child Health, 38*, 358–362.

Palmer, D. H., Mulhall, K. J., Thompson, C. A., Severson, E. P., Santos, E., & Saleh, K. J. (2005). Total knee arthroplasty in juvenile rheumatoid arthritis. *Journal of Bone and Joint Surgery, 87*, 1510–1514.

Parvizi, J., Lajam, C. M., Trousdale, R. T., Shaughnessy, W. J., & Cabanela, M. E. (2003). Total knee arthroplasty in young patients with juvenile rheumatoid arthritis. *Journal of Bone and Joint Surgery, 85*, 1090–1095.

Patel, S. J., & Lundy, D. C. (2002). Ocular manifestations of autoimmune disease. *American Family Physician, 66*, 991–999.

Paterson, C., Burns, J., & McAllion, S. J. (1993). Osteogenesis imperfecta: The distinction from child abuse and the recognition of a variant form. *American Journal of Medical Genetics, 45*, 187–192.

Plotkin, H. (2004). Syndromes with congenital brittle bones. *BMC Pediatrics, 4*, 1471–1477.

Polizzi, A., Huson, S. M., & Vincent, A. (2000). Teratogen update: Maternal myasthenia gravis as a cause of congenital arthrogryposis. *Teratology, 62*, 332–341.

Pollitt, R., McMahon, R., Nunn, J., Bamford, R., Afifi, A., Bishop, N., & Dalton, A. (2006). Mutation analysis of COL1A1 and COL1A2 in patients diagnosed with osteogenesis imperfecta type I-IV. *Human Mutation, 27*, 716–723.

Rauch, F., & Glorieux, F. H. (2004). Osteogenesis imperfecta. *Lancet, 363*, 1377–1385.

Rauch, F., & Glorieux, F. (2005). Osteogenesis imperfecta: Current and future medical treatment. *American Journal of Medical Genetics, 139C*, 31–37.

Rettig, P. A., Merhar, S. L., & Cron, R. Z. (2004). Juvenile rheumatoid arthritis and juvenile spondyloarthropathy. In P. J. Allen & J. A. Vessey (Eds.), *Primary care of the child with a chronic condition* (pp. 582–600). St. Louis: Mosby.

Siegel, D. M., & Baum, J. (1993). Juvenile arthritis. *Primary Care, 20*, 883–893.

Sillence, D. O., Senn, A., Danks, D. M. (1979). Genetic heterogeneity in osteogenesis imperfecta. *Journal of Medical Genetics, 16*, 101–116.

Smerdel, A., Dai, K., Lorentzen, A. R., Flato, B., Maslinski, S., Thorsby, E., et al. (2004). Genetic association between juvenile rheumatoid arthritis and polymorphism in the SH2D2A gene. *Genes and Immunity, 5*, 310–312.

Thompson, G. H. (2004). Arthrogryposis. In R. E. Behrman, R. M. Kliegman, & H. B. Jenson (Eds.), *Nelson textbook of pediatrics* (pp. 2292–2293). Philadelphia: W. B. Saunders.

Vetter, U., Pontz, B., Zauner, E., Brenner, R. E., & Spranger, J. (1992). Osteogenesis imperfecta: A clinical study of the first ten years of life. *Calcified Tissue International, 50*, 36–41.

Zeitlin, L., Rauch, F., Travers, R., Munns, C., & Glorieux, F. (2006). The effect of cyclical intravenous pamidronate in children and adolescents with osteogenesis imperfecta type V. *BONE, 38*, 13–20.

VISION LOSS, HEARING LOSS, AND DEAF-BLINDNESS

Kathryn Wolff Heller, Susan Easterbrooks, Doug McJannet, and Dawn Swinehart-Jones

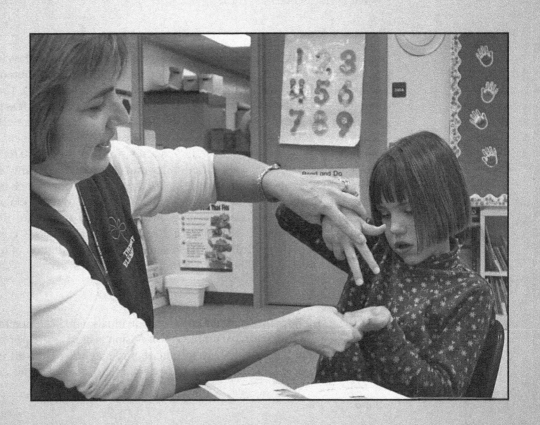

Students with physical and multiple disabilities often have conditions that are accompanied by vision loss, hearing loss, or deaf-blindness. Although a vision or hearing loss can occur alone, each one can be particularly challenging when occurring in combination with other disabilities. Teachers need to have a good understanding of the effect of a vision and/or hearing loss and how to best meet the needs of their students who have these conditions. Given the differences between the sensory systems, each will be described separately, and their educational implications will be described at the end of the chapter.

DESCRIPTION OF VISUAL IMPAIRMENTS

Teachers will typically encounter several different terms used to describe different types of visual impairments. Some of the most common ones are as follows:

Visual Impairment and Visual Disability

The term *visual impairment* encompasses a wide range of vision loss that can include deficits in acuity, field loss, ocular motility, or color perception. The visual impairment may be permanent or temporary. The term *visual disability* is often used synonymously with the term *visual impairment* to refer to a vision loss that adversely affects a child's educational performance.

Legal Blindness

Legal blindness is defined as a central visual acuity of 20/200 or less in the better eye with best correction or the widest diameter of visual field having (subtending) an angle of no greater than 20 degrees (American Optometric Association, 2006). The first part of this definition refers to visual acuity, which is the clarity of one's vision. It is measured in terms of the finest detail that the eye can distinguish from a certain distance. For example, a visual acuity of 20/200 means that the person with the visual impairment can see an object or symbol at 20 feet that a person with unimpaired vision can see at 200 feet. A person with a visual acuity of 20/200 or worse after correction is considered legally blind. The second half of the definition of legal blindness refers to the field of vision, which is the ability to see objects in the center and periphery of one's vision when looking straight ahead. Individuals with unimpaired vision can see objects within a 180-degree arc when looking straight ahead. A person who sees less than a 20-degree arc (or angle) is considered legally blind (since much of one's peripheral vision is missing). The definition of legal blindness is used in many states to determine eligibility for vision services.

Low Vision

This is a broad term that is used to refer to individuals who have significant vision loss (with best correction) but still have usable vision. Vision is used as the primary channel for learning or receiving information. Visual functioning may increase with the use of optical devices, environmental modifications, and/or training (Corn & Koenig, 2002).

Blind

Individuals who are totally without vision or who have light perception only are said to be blind. In education, this term refers to children who use other senses (i.e., hearing and touch) as primary channels for learning or receiving information.

Visual Efficiency

This refers to how well a person uses the vision he or she has. Visual efficiency is considered a learned behavior that is not necessarily reflected by visual acuity. It is possible for a student to have poor visual acuity and good visual functioning and vice versa (Good, Jan, Burden, Skoczenski, & Candy, 2001; Johnson, 1997).

DYNAMICS OF VISUAL IMPAIRMENTS

Anatomy of the Eye

Supporting Structures of the Eye

There are several supporting structures of the eye that assist the eye in proper functioning, including the eyelids, lacrimal apparatus (responsible for tear production), and the six extraocular muscles surrounding each eye. These extraocular muscles allow the eyes to move together in a coordinated manner and provide proper alignment of the eyes so that a single image may be seen (Brodsky, 2005; Johnson, 1997).

The Eye

The outer surface of the eye consists of the sclera and the cornea (see Figure 11–1). The sclera is the white portion of the eye that covers five-sixths of the eyeball, wrapping over the entire eye except where the cornea is located. The sclera consists of rough, dense connective tissue that helps to protect the inner contents of the eye (Young & Young, 1997). The cornea is the transparent portion of the outer surface of the eye that covers the remaining one-sixth of the eyeball. The cornea is the most sensitive tissue of the entire body with the most nerve fibers in an area of its size and is often called "the window of the eye" because light first passes through the cornea as it travels to the inner structures of the eye. As the light passes through the curved shape of the cornea, it refracts (bends) the light, directing it to the back structures of the eye.

As light passes through the cornea, it travels through the fluid known as the aqueous until it reaches the pupil, a black hole that is surrounded by the colored part of the eye, known as the iris. The iris controls the amount of light entering the eye by regulating the size of the pupil. In dim light, certain muscles of the iris will contract, resulting in the pupil becoming larger. With the pupil dilated, more light can enter the eye. In bright light, another set of muscles in the iris contract, causing the pupil to become smaller, allowing less light into the eye.

Behind the pupil is the lens of the eye that further refracts the light rays to focus them properly. Light next travels through a gelatin-like substance known as vitreous that aids in keeping the shape of the eyeball. After the light rays pass through the vitreous, they are

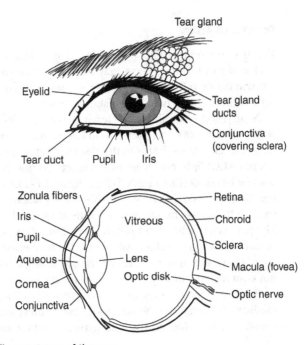

FIGURE 11–1 The anatomy of the eye.

focused on the innermost lining of this cavity, known as the retina. (Underneath the retina is the middle layer known as the choroid, which provides nutrients to the retina, followed by the outermost layer, which is the sclera.)

The retina is composed of approximately 125 million photoreceptors categorized into rods and cones. The rods and cones are responsible for the conversion of light rays to electrochemical impulses (Young & Young, 1997). The rods are sensitive to low intensity illumination (dim light) and can detect gross form and movement. Rods are responsible primarily for peripheral vision and night vision. The cones are sensitive to high-intensity illumination (daylight) and detect fine detail and colors. On the retina there is a small central area in which most of the cones are located. This area is known as the macula. In the center of the macula is the fovea (the area for most distinct vision). The fovea and the macula together are responsible for most central vision.

The Visual Pathways

After the image has been converted into electrochemical impulses by the retina, the impulses leave each eye through the optic nerve, located behind each eyeball. The impulses continue through the rest of the optic tracts to the visual cortex, located in the occipital lobe in the posterior part of the brain.

The Visual Cortex

The visual cortex receives the electrochemical impulses from the eyes and further transmits impulses to higher cerebral centers. In these higher cerebral centers, visual input is integrated with other sensory input to allow a person to interpret or remember perceived images.

Effect of Visual Impairments on Visual Abilities

Visual disorders may negatively impact on one or more visual abilities of the eye. Problems affecting visual abilities include: (a) poor visual acuity, (b) visual field deficits, (c) ocular motility and gaze abnormalities, (d) light and color reception impairments, and (e) abnormalities of the visual cortex and brain functions (Guzzetta, Mercuri, & Cioni, 2001; Madan, Jan, & Good, 2005).

Poor Visual Acuity

Visual acuity refers to how clear or sharp an image is in regard to forms or patterns. Poor visual acuity, or blurred vision, may be due to medical abnormalities of the visual system (e.g., **cataracts**) or refractory errors (e.g., nearsightedness) (Chang, 2004). Visual acuity is described in terms of near and distance acuity.

Near vision is the ability to clearly perceive objects at about 14 inches from the eye (Peters & Bloomberg, 2005). Children who have a refractive error known as **hyperopia** (farsightedness) can clearly see items in the distance, but items near to them are not in focus. Hyperopia occurs when light rays from near objects do not focus on the retina often because of having a smaller eyeball (Chang, 2004) (see Figure 11-2). Individuals may also have poor acuity affecting their distance vision. When this occurs because of a refractory error, they have **myopia** (nearsightedness), in which near items are seen clearly but those farther away are unfocused. Myopia occurs when light rays from distant objects focus in front of the retina often because of having a longer eyeball. Another refractory error is **astigmatism**, in which there is an unequal curvature of the cornea or lens, resulting in blurred or distorted images from the light not coming to a single point of focus on the retina.

Poor visual acuity may not be correctable to 20/20 vision in some cases when it is due to medical abnormalities. When poor visual acuity occurs because of a refractive error, 20/20 vision may be achieved through glasses, contact lenses, or surgery.

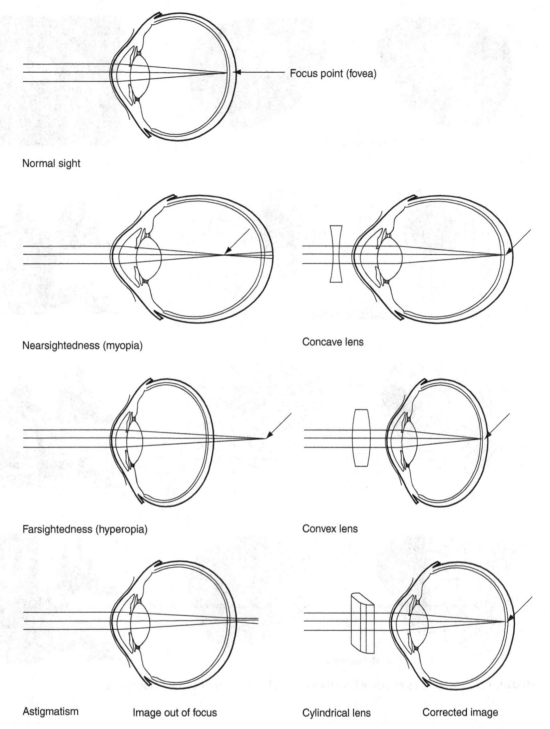

Normal sight

Nearsightedness (myopia)

Concave lens

Farsightedness (hyperopia)

Convex lens

Astigmatism   Image out of focus

Cylindrical lens   Corrected image

FIGURE 11–2 Refractive errors of myopia, hyperopia, and astigmatism that are corrected with different types of lenses.

Visual Fields Deficits

A person's field of vision refers to the entire area that can be seen without shifting one's gaze. Certain visual conditions may result in a loss of vision in certain areas of a person's field of vision. Defects in visual fields may occur in a person's central field of vision, peripheral field of vision, or both (see Figure 11-3).

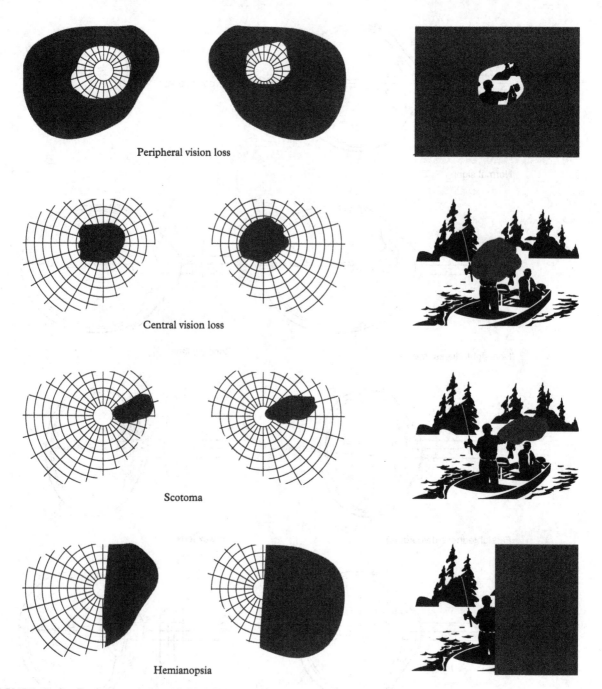

FIGURE 11–3 Examples of visual field deficits that block out part of the person's vision.

Central Field Loss. Central vision refers to the direct line of vision that is essential for discerning details. Certain conditions that damage the macula portion of the retina (e.g., macular degeneration) result in a central field loss. A person with a central field loss may be unable to read print, discern facial features, or perceive objects when looking straight at them (Good et al., 2001). Important information may easily be missed. Often the person will direct his gaze off to the side to see the desired item or person in his peripheral vision. This is known as eccentric viewing and can be mistaken for the individual not looking at the targeted item or person.

Peripheral Field Loss. Peripheral vision refers to the ability to perceive the presence of objects outside the direct line of vision and is necessary for awareness of objects and hazards in the periphery (AGIS Investigators, 2000; Edwards, Fishman, Anderson, Grover, & Derlacki, 1998). When a peripheral field loss exists, the person is unable to see objects in part or all of his peripheral vision. One of the common types of peripheral vision losses involves loss of vision in a ring shape along the periphery that results in a narrower visual field. This is also referred to as "tunnel vision" and results in a reduced angle of vision, limiting how much a person can see at one time across the viewed area. Since the rods are located primarily in the periphery and they permit seeing in dim light, a deficit in this area may be accompanied by loss of night vision. Other types of visual field deficits occur in which sections, parts, or spots of the peripheral field may be missing.

Impairment in Motility and Gaze

Ocular motility refers to the movement of the eye by any of the six extraocular muscles surrounding each eye. Difficulties in ocular motility may occur in individuals with facial paralysis, eye muscle imbalances, cranial nerve damage, or other conditions that may result in diminished or loss of eye muscle movement. Impairments in ocular motility may result in difficulties with tracking, gaze shift, and scanning. Associated with motility and gaze problems are **strabismus**, **amblyopia**, and **nystagmus**.

Strabismus.   Strabismus is a misalignment of the eyes where one or both eyes deviate in a direction (e.g., cross-eyed). When one eye deviates, **diplopia** (double vision) can occur. Often the brain will suppress one image so that only one visual image will be seen instead of a double image. This suppression of an image can lead to amblyopia.

Amblyopia.   Amblyopia, also known as lazy eye, is a reduction of visual acuity in the absence of detectable anatomic defect. It can occur when one eye sees a different image than the other, such as in strabismus, unequal refraction errors, or visual deprivation of one eye during the time the eyes are developing (birth to 6 years) (Bremer et al., 1998). The suppression of images transmitted by one eye can lead to eventual blindness in the unused eye (Johnson, 1997). Blindness can usually be avoided with appropriate intervention at an early age (e.g., patching the good eye or correcting refraction error).

Nystagmus.   Nystagmus is an involuntary, rhythmic oscillation of the eye. The repetitive movement may be vertical, diagonal, or rotary and can be fast or slow, depending on the type of nystagmus. Congenital nystagmus, for example, is often horizontal and occurs within 6 months after birth because of a congenital visual impairment (e.g., congenital cataracts or optic atrophy) or unknown causes (i.e., idiopathic). Children with nystagmus may have reduced visual acuity in the affected eye and tend to tilt their heads to decrease the nystagmus (Riordan-Eva & Hoyt, 2004) and to find the area of clearest vision (null point). Objects usually appear stationary, with the brain adjusting for the movement perceptually.

Impairment in Light and Color Reception

Some children may have difficulty with certain lighting conditions, such as those with photophobia. Photophobia is an unusual sensitivity to light that makes a child uncomfortable in bright or normal lighting conditions. Several eye conditions may result in photophobia (e.g., albinism or cataracts).

The primary impairment in color reception is color blindness. Individuals who are color blind usually cannot see certain colors because of missing or damaged cones (color receptors) in the eye. The most common abnormality is red-green color blindness, in which red and green appear the same color.

Impairment in Brain Function

Damage to the occipital lobe or other areas of the brain may affect visual fixation, fusion, awareness of motion, and changes in the shape of the intraocular lens (Good et al., 2001). In some cases, objects may not be perceived.

Screening Checklist for Visual Impairments

A. Eye appearance
____ Eyes red
____ One eye turns in, out, up, or down
____ Eyes in constant motion (nystagmus)
____ Tears excessively
____ Eyelid crusted

B. Visual abilities
____ No blink reflex
____ Pupils do not react to light
____ Does not fixate on object
____ Cannot track object
____ Does not scan for object
____ Cannot follow moving object toward nose

C. Behaviors
____ Rubs eyes frequently
____ Squints eyes
____ Blinks frequently
____ Closes one or both eye(s) when doing certain tasks
____ Does not look straight at an object (looks from side)
____ Turns or tilts head
____ Approaches items by touch rather than sight
____ Holds items too close or far away

D. Verbal complaints
____ Complains of eye pain, headaches
____ Complains of seeing double
____ Complains of not being able to see well

E. Academic work
____ Cannot copy off blackboard (whiteboard)
____ Makes frequent errors when reading letters that are shaped similarly
____ Rereads or skips words or lines when reading
____ Uses hand to keep place

FIGURE 11–4 Screening checklist for visual impairments.

DETECTION OF VISUAL IMPAIRMENTS

Visual impairments may be noticed by the person having difficulty seeing, or individuals around the person may notice that the person does not appear to be seeing well. It is important that the teacher be alert for any indication that a visual impairment exists. Figure 11–4 contains a list of possible behaviors that may indicate a visual impairment. If a visual impairment is suspected, the teacher should request follow-up investigation by the appropriate personnel, such as the school nurse.

ETIOLOGY, CHARACTERISTICS, COURSE, AND TREATMENT OF COMMON VISUAL DISORDERS

Although students with physical and multiple disabilities may have many different types of visual impairments, some of the most common ones are cataracts, retinopathy of prematurity, optic nerve atrophy, and cortical visual impairment.

Cataracts

A cataract is any clouding of the lens of the eye. Cataracts in children may be present at birth (congenital cataracts) or develop later in life (acquired cataracts). Older adults often develop age-related cataracts.

Etiology

Childhood cataracts may occur from congenital infections (e.g., cytomegalovirus) or genetically transmitted syndromes (e.g., Down syndrome). Cataracts may also occur from severe malnutrition, trauma, or drugs (e.g., steroids) and are associated with several metabolic disorders and diseases (e.g., diabetes) (Harper & Shock, 2004).

Characteristics

Depending on the size and density of the cataract, it may not be noticeable to the naked eye, or in some instances the pupil may appear white. A cataract's effect on vision varies depending on the size, position, and density of the cloudy area. Some cataracts involve pinpoint areas that do not interfere with visual acuity. Other cataracts result in blurred vision. If the cataract is more centrally located, near vision may be affected, and vision may be worse in bright light. Some cataracts become so dense and large that the child can become blind.

Treatment

When an infant has congenital cataracts, surgery is needed to allow for proper development of visual responses. Surgery involves removal of the lens and optical treatment (e.g., glasses, contact lens, or intraocular lens implantation). However, even after surgical and optical treatment of cataracts in infancy, 20% to 30% of children are legally blind (Bashour, Menassa, & Gevontis, 2006; Gillies et al., 1998).

If the cataract has not been operated on, lighting may be adjusted to reduce glare (such as positioning the light behind the person). Also, if the cataract is positioned centrally on the lens, unusual head positions may be observed as the person is "looking around the cataract." This should be encouraged since the person is optimizing his vision. Occasionally, magnification may be helpful to improve vision (Bashour et al., 2006; Good et al., 2001).

Retinopathy of Prematurity (ROP)

Retinopathy of prematurity is an abnormal proliferation of blood vessels that occurs in the immature retina. It is the leading cause of childhood blindness in the United States (Hardy & Shetlar, 2004).

Etiology

Retinopathy of prematurity occurs in the preterm infant, especially those of lowest birth weight. Although it was initially thought to occur to premature infants who were exposed to high levels of oxygen in incubators, the condition has also been present in premature infants not exposed to these oxygen levels (Coe et al., 2006). It is not fully known what causes this disease, but it has been associated with such factors as pregnancy complications, respiratory distress syndrome, and hemorrhage (Coe et al., 2006).

Characteristics

About 90% of the cases are mild and spontaneous regression of these overabundant blood vessels occur with minimal scarring and little to no visual loss (Behrman, Kliegman, & Jenson, 2004). In more severe cases, the abnormal blood vessels extend into the vitreous and may cause retinal detachment, severe visual loss, and/or blindness. In addition, children with retinopathy of prematurity may also have myopia, strabismus, cataracts, or glaucoma.

Treatment

In the majority of cases, regression of the condition will occur, and only monitoring is necessary. However, when retinopathy of prematurity progresses and becomes severe, surgery will often be needed to try to prevent the retina from detaching or to reattach the retina.

Although surgery may prevent vision from worsening, vision may remain poor after surgical intervention. To improve visual functioning, optical devices (e.g., magnifiers or telescopes) may be prescribed. Often a high level of illumination is needed (Corn et al., 2003).

Optic Atrophy

Optic atrophy is the degeneration of the optic nerve and the most common disorder of the visual pathways. It is not a disease itself but rather a disorder that affects the functioning of the optic nerve.

Etiology

Optic atrophy may be congenital and due to hereditary disorders (e.g., Leber's optic neuropathy). It can also occur from acquired causes (e.g., tumors, hydrocephalus, or head trauma). Optic atrophy is sometimes associated with certain metabolic diseases such as diabetes. Depending on the cause, optic atrophy may be progressive.

Characteristics

Optic atrophy results in visual field deficits with the amount of loss typically being roughly proportional to the amount of nerve atrophy. Often both central and peripheral field losses are present but vary as to how much is missing. For example, in some cases, half the visual field may be missing in both eyes. Individuals with optic atrophy may also have a decrease in visual acuity and loss of color vision (Good et al., 2001).

Treatment

There is no current treatment since the degeneration of the optic nerve fibers is irreversible. However, when there are underlying causes, such as from a tumor applying pressure against the optic nerve, early removal of the tumor may result in restoration of vision. Visual functioning may be enhanced by using high illumination and enlarged print. Placement of material is also important.

Cortical Visual Impairment (CVI)

Cortical visual impairment (also known as cortical blindness or neurological visual impairment) is a term used to describe damage to the areas of the brain pertaining to vision. In this condition, the brain is unable to process the incoming visual information because of brain damage in the occipital lobe, while the eye shows no pathology.

Etiology

There are several causes of cortical visual impairment. Some of these include traumatic brain injury, near drowning, prolonged convulsion, meningitis, metabolic disorder, and hypoxia resulting in brain damage. Depending on the cause and extent of damage, cortical visual impairment may be temporary or permanent. Other conditions are often present in children with permanent cortical vision impairment, such as **cerebral palsy**, **hydrocephalus**, **intellectual disability**, and microcephaly.

Characteristics

Children with cortical visual impairment have a range of visual abilities from a mild visual loss to blindness, depending on the cause, the location, and the severity of the damage. Fluctuating vision is common and may create misunderstanding when a child is able to see an item at one moment and unable to see it a short time later. Some children are able to see better using their peripheral vision, which can result in not looking directly at items but off to their side in order to visualize things more clearly. Depending on the severity of the cortical visual impairment, some children will rely on their sense of touch rather than use the vision they have.

Treatment

There is no specific medical treatment at this time, except treating underlying causes when possible. It is often difficult to determine whether visual functioning will improve or remain static. Vision stimulation and environmental arrangement may help with visual functioning.

DESCRIPTION OF HEARING LOSSES

A child who has a hearing loss is at risk for language, social, and academic challenges unless he receives appropriate interventions. Understanding how the ear functions, the common conditions causing hearing losses and their implications in the classroom will help the educator to meet the needs of students with hearing loss. A first step is understanding the common terms used in this field.

Deaf

The term *deaf* refers to a hearing loss so severe that the child is unable to process spoken language through hearing, with or without amplification, and educational performance is adversely affected.

Hard of Hearing

The term *hard of hearing* describes a person who can process some spoken language through hearing, with or without amplification. It is a hearing loss, whether stable or progressive, that affects a child's educational performance.

Conductive Hearing Loss

A conductive hearing loss refers to a hearing loss that is caused by an obstruction, infection, structural abnormality, or other condition in the outer or middle ear that results in failure to conduct the signal to the inner ear.

Sensorineural Hearing Loss

A sensorineural hearing loss refers to an impairment in the inner ear or auditory nerve that results in a hearing loss.

Mixed Hearing Loss

Some individuals will have a mixed hearing loss, which refers to a combined conductive and sensorineural hearing loss.

Central Hearing Loss

A central hearing loss refers to a loss resulting from deficits in the auditory cortex or the pathways going from the brain stem to the auditory cortex.

Congenitally Deaf

When someone is born deaf, they are called congenitally deaf.

Adventitiously Deaf

When deafness is acquired after birth, it is called adventitiously deaf.

Prelingually Deafened

Prelingually deafened refers to a condition where deafness occurs prior to speech or language development.

Postlingually Deafened

Postlingually deafened refers to a condition where deafness occurs after speech and language have developed. As a result of a national trend toward early identification, recent research suggests that 6 months may be the point of demarcation between prelingually and postlingually deafened (Yoshinaga-Itano & Apuzzo, 1998).

DYNAMICS OF HEARING LOSS

Anatomy of the Ear

The Outer Ear

The outer ear is composed of the auricle (pinna) and the external ear (or auditory) canal (see Figure 11–5). The auricle collects sound waves and transmits them through the external ear canal. The external ear canal contains hair cells and cerumen (earwax), which protect the middle ear from foreign objects, such as dust and insects. The hairs "wave" unwanted objects away, while the bitter taste of the cerumen repels insects.

The Middle Ear

The middle ear is bordered on one side by the tympanic membrane (eardrum) and on the other by the oval window. Three connected bones, the malleus (hammer), the incus (anvil), and the stapes (stirrup), are contained in this air-filled space within the temporal bone. The malleus is located adjacent to the tympanic membrane, and the stapes is directly attached to the oval window, with the incus in between. When a sound occurs, air

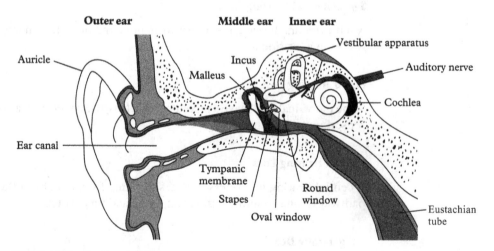

FIGURE 11–5 Anatomy of the ear.

vibrations enter the outer ear and cause the tympanic membrane to move. The tympanic membrane converts sound waves to mechanical vibrations by causing the malleus, incus, and stapes to mechanically vibrate. The vibrations of these three bones result in movement of the oval window.

Because the middle ear is filled with air, it is important that the air pressure in the middle ear is the same as the outside air. If the pressure inside the ear should become greater than the outside air pressure, as can happen in an airplane, the tympanic membrane could rupture. The eustachian tube maintains equal pressure. This tube runs between the middle ear and the pharynx (back of the throat). When a person swallows, the end of the tube located in the pharynx opens and causes air to move between the pharynx and the middle ear, equalizing air pressure.

The Inner Ear

The inner ear consists of two main sections: the cochlea (responsible for the sense of hearing) and the vestibular mechanism (responsible for the sense of balance). Many deaf children have balance problems when they close their eyes (Angelopoulou, Fotiadou, Tsimaras, & Giagazoglou, 1999) because of the interrelationship of the two systems. The cochlea has the appearance of a snail shell and is a system of coiled tubes that are filled with fluid. In the base of the cochlea, located on the basilar membrane, is the organ of Corti, which contains auditory receptor cells (hair cells). When the stapes moves in and out of the oval window, waves (mechanical vibrations) are transmitted within the fluid of the cochlea, causing certain hair cells to bend. The degree and location of movement of the hair cells determines the auditory information that is transmitted out of the inner ear by the eighth cranial nerve (auditory nerve).

The Central Auditory System

The electrical impulses from the end cells of the auditory nerve are transmitted to a relay station in the brain stem and then onward via the central auditory system to the auditory cortex (temporal lobe) in the brain. From here, other higher centers of the brain process the sounds.

Describing Hearing Loss and Severity

Diseases, disorders, or blockages in different parts of the ear and related structures result in a hearing loss. Disorders or abnormalities of the outer or middle ear can result in a conductive hearing loss, called such because sound waves are blocked from continuing to the other structures of the ear. Disease and disorders of the inner ear or auditory nerve result in a sensorineural hearing loss. If there is damage in the part of the brain that receives impulses from the auditory nerve, a central hearing loss is said to occur. The severity of a conductive, sensorineural, and central hearing loss varies.

Impact of Hearing Loss on Hearing Ability

The severity of a hearing impairment is often described in terms of loudness (decibels) and pitch (frequency, or hertz). Loudness is measured in decibels. Zero decibels (0 dB) represent the softest sound a person with normal hearing can perceive; normal hearing occurs generally in the 0- to 15-dB range. Pitch (also known as frequency) refers to the number of repetitions of a complete sound wave (cycle) per second, which can range from a high to a low pitch. A greater number of repetitions per second would result in a high sound, a fewer number of repetitions per second in a lower sound.

Pitch is recorded as cycles per second, or hertz (Hz). The amount of hearing loss may vary across pitch. A person with a high-frequency hearing loss (e.g., 6,000 Hz) may be

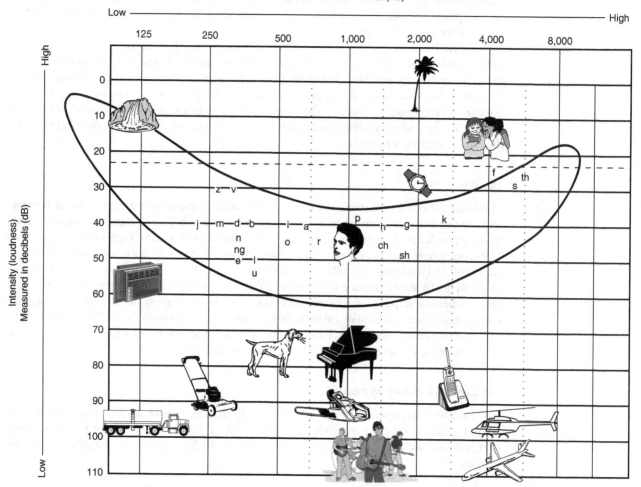

FIGURE 11–6 The frequency and intensity of various environmental and speech sounds.

Source. From The SKI-HI Curriculum by S. Watkins (Ed.), p 426. Copyright 2004 SKI-HI Institute, Utah State University. Reprinted with permission.

unable to hear certain speech sounds, such as /s/ or /th/. A person with a hearing loss that affects all frequencies down to 100 dB at 125 Hz, for example, could feel a truck going by but could not hear it. Figure 11-6 shows a comparison of the frequency and intensity of various sounds.

CHARACTERISTICS OF STUDENTS WITH HEARING LOSS

There is a negative correlation between general knowledge and degree of hearing loss (Most, Aram, & Andorn, 2006). As a hearing loss gets worse, its impact is greater, and the services needed differ. It is therefore important for the teacher to understand the amount of hearing loss that is present. Hearing loss may range from slight to profound, depending on the decibel level needed to hear sounds at various frequencies.

Level of Hearing Loss

Normal

Normal hearing is a hearing level at 0 to 15 decibels.

Slight Hearing Loss

A slight hearing loss is a hearing level at 16 to 25 dB. At this level of hearing loss, vowel sounds are usually heard clearly, but unvoiced consonant sounds may be missed. There is usually difficulty with fast-paced peer interactions, and people will often experience listening fatigue and difficulty hearing in noisy environments. Individuals with a slight hearing loss may miss 10% of the speech signal.

Mild Hearing Loss

A mild hearing loss is a hearing level at 26 to 40 dB. At this level of hearing loss, the person can hear some speech sounds but will have difficulty hearing distant or faint sounds, unvoiced consonants, plurals, and tenses. Individuals with a mild hearing loss may miss 25% to 40% of the speech signal.

Moderate Hearing Loss

A moderate hearing loss is a hearing level at 41 to 55 dB. At this level of hearing loss, the person will miss most speech sounds at conversational levels. Typically, speech problems are present, especially if prelinguistically deafened. Individuals with a moderate hearing loss may miss 50% to 80% of the speech signal.

Moderately Severe Hearing Loss

A moderately severe hearing loss is a hearing level at 55 to 70 dB. At this level of hearing loss, there is usually delayed language and syntax and reduced speech intelligibility. Individuals with moderately severe hearing loss will miss about 100% of speech information. They may require alternative forms of communication.

Severe Hearing Loss

A severe hearing loss is a hearing level at 71 to 90 dB. At this level of hearing loss, the person cannot hear speech sounds of normal conversation but may hear a loud voice at about 1 foot and be able to identify environmental noises. Severe speech problems are present, and alternative forms of communication are needed.

Profound Hearing Loss

A profound hearing loss is a hearing level at 91 dB and higher. At this level of hearing loss, the person cannot hear speech but may react to loud sounds. Also, the person can feel vibrations and may react to that sensation. When a profound hearing loss is present, hearing is not the primary modality used for receptive communication unless a cochlear implant is being used successfully.

ETIOLOGY, CHARACTERISTICS, AND TREATMENT OF COMMON DISORDERS OF HEARING

Hearing losses can be categorized on the basis of where problems exist in the anatomical system. Figure 11–7 provides an at-a-glance look at the location, etiology, characteristics, and treatment of the most common disorders of hearing that are seen in schools today.

Location	Problem	Etiology	Characteristics	Treatment
Outer ear: conductive loss	Obstruction of the external auditory canal	Absence or closure of the external auditory canal due to atresia, impacted cerumen, or foreign bodies.	Usually in one ear. Degree varies. Often turns unobstructed ear toward conversation.	Depends on cause. Most foreign bodies can be removed, restoring hearing to normal. Infections require medicated eardrops. Atresias may be surgically opened.
	Perforation of the tympanic membrane	A hole in the eardrum due to damage from a middle ear infection, a blow to the head, or sudden and severe pressure changes.	Draining ear. Foul odor. May lead to a cholesteatoma (cystic mass), inflammation of the mastoid bone, brain ulcers, or meningitis.	May grow back together; may leave scar. Keep water out of ear; use Vaseline-coated cotton ball in the ear or special ear molds. May require surgical repair or eardrops.
Middle ear: conductive loss	Otitis media	Bacterial or viral infection causing eustachian tube to block. Severe cases may infect temporal bone. Infected or noninfected fluid fills the middle ear cavity, restricting action of the bones. Left untreated, may cause eardrum to burst.	Earache. Temporary loss of hearing. Behavioral changes (irritability, restlessness, fussiness). Fever up to 105°F, nausea, vomiting, diarrhea, dizziness, headache.	Antibiotics commonly prescribed. If otitis media persists, a myringotomy (small incision in tympanic membrane) is made to reduce fluid and prevent perforation. A small tube may be placed in the incision to equalize pressure, allowing the eustachian tube to drain. Tubes typically fall out after several months. Prompt treatment is very important.
	Cholesteatoma	Congenital or acquired cystic mass consisting of pockets of skin located in middle ear or other areas of the temporal bone.	Sequel to chronic or recurrent otitis media. Eardrum is often perforated. Can result in erosion of middle ear structures of facial palsy due to location near a branch of the seventh cranial nerve.	Surgery is performed as soon as possible to prevent spread of mass to other structures.
	Conditions affecting the ossicular chain	Discontinuity of the three middle ear bones. Malleus fixation. Can be congenital or due to head trauma, middle ear disease, or other causes.	Stable conductive loss (discontinuity) or progressive loss (malleus fixation). Tinnitus, or ringing in ears.	Both conditions usually treated surgically; hearing is restored following successful treatment.
Inner ear and auditory nerve: sensorineural loss	Congenital or acquired damage to the cochlea, inner ear hair cells, or auditory nerve	Congenital infections such as Usher syndrome, cytomegalovirus, ototoxic drugs, trauma, noise, meningitis, and genetic causes such as connexin 26.	Hearing loss varies. High frequencies usually affected. Congenital etiologies typically affect both ears. Loss may be constant or progressive.	Use of hearing aids or cochlear implants (see description in this chapter).
Central auditory system: central hearing loss	Auditory neuropathy/ auditory dyssynchrony	Abnormal auditory brain responses and abnormal middle ear muscle functioning. Nerve does not function in the presence of normal cochlea.	Hears but may not understand speech. Intermittent responses to sound.	May not respond well to hearing aids. May or may not benefit from cochlear implant. No definitive protocol of treatment; requires collaborative effort.
	Central auditory processing disorder	Insufficient response to auditory stimuli in the face of normal peripheral hearing.	Hears but has difficulty processing incoming information that impacts spoken and written language and academic performance.	Speech and language intervention; modifications in the classroom to assist with attention, processing, memory, and organization.

FIGURE 11–7 Etiologies of hearing losses.

Sources. Friel-Patti (1999); Isaacson and Vora (2003); Liu (2005); Scott (2003).

```
Screening Checklist for Hearing Loss
─────────────────────────────────────────────────────────

A. Appearance of ears
___ Discharge from ear
___ Excessive wax (cerumen) from ear

B. Behaviors
___ Doesn't respond when spoken to
___ Doesn't turn toward loud sounds
___ Closely watches person's face when spoken to and others' actions
___ Turns one ear toward sound
___ Doesn't follow oral directions well
___ Volume of tape player or radio turned up high
___ Misunderstands what people are saying and confuses similar-sounding words
___ Articulates some words poorly
___ Omits word endings
___ Cannot hear soft sounds

C. Verbal complaints
___ Complains of being unable to hear

D. Academic
___ Doesn't follow oral directions well
___ Frequently asks for directions to be repeated
___ Responds to visual directions faster than when given verbally
```

FIGURE 11–8 Screening checklist for hearing loss.

DETECTION OF HEARING LOSS

New legal mandates, professional guidance, advances in technology (e.g., cochlear implants and programmable hearing aids), and research evidence (Yoshinaga-Itano, Coulter, & Thomson, 2000) have made a significant impact on the early identification of hearing loss. Part C of the Individuals with Disabilities Education Act (1997 and 2004) recommends services to very young children and their families. Newer technologies have made it easy and affordable to screen for hearing loss before a child leaves the newborn nursery.

Once a child is screened and diagnosed with a hearing loss, appropriate early intervention services that include support from a collaborative team at very early ages can significantly ameliorate the effects of a loss. However, services vary from state to state and from district to district within each state (Arehart, Yoshinaga-Itano, Gabbard, Stredler-Brown, & Thomson, 1998), so diligence on the part of case managers, parents, and service providers is crucial to locating and instituting available services.

Several behaviors are commonly indicative of a hearing loss. Examples include tilting the head toward the speaker, asking for frequent repetition, responding one day but not the next, or difficulty mastering phonemic awareness and phonics tasks (see Figure 11–8 for more examples). The teacher should closely monitor students for these behaviors. If a hearing loss is suspected, the teacher should request follow-up investigation by the appropriate personnel, such as the school nurse or audiologist.

DESCRIPTION OF DEAF-BLINDNESS

Contrary to popular belief, most individuals who are deaf-blind are not completely deaf and completely blind. An individual who is deaf-blind has a vision and hearing loss, but functional levels may vary from hard of hearing and partially sighted to profoundly deaf and totally blind. Often there is some residual vision or hearing, but having both distance senses impaired can result in communication, developmental, and learning problems.

Students with deaf-blindness can greatly vary as to their abilities and characteristics. For example, a student born with congenital cytomegalovirus may be deaf-blind and have additional disabilities, such as severe intellectual disability, cerebral palsy, and microcephaly. In another example, a student with Usher syndrome type II may have vision and hearing loss but no other disabilities. Both of these students will have different educational needs.

ETIOLOGIES OF DEAF-BLINDNESS

Prematurity and Small for Gestational Age

Children who are delivered before 37 weeks of gestation are considered premature, and those who weigh less than the 10th percentile are called small for gestational age (or as having intrauterine growth retardation). Children who are born prematurely have immature organs and are at risk for developing complications (e.g., retinopathy of prematurity and apnea). Children who are small for gestational age may have additional impairments due to problems in development. One of the leading causes of deaf-blindness is due to children developing complications from premature birth or having additional impairments associated with being born small for gestational age.

Syndromes and Genetic Conditions

There are many syndromes and genetic conditions that may result in a child having deaf-blindness. One example is Usher syndrome. Usher syndrome is a hereditary condition caused by an autorecessive gene resulting in sensorineural hearing loss and retinitis pigmentosa (an eye disorder causing damage to the retina and often progressive peripheral field loss). In one of the three types of Usher syndrome, children are born deaf and develop a visual field loss in their teens that adversely affects night vision and peripheral vision. This condition may lead to blindness.

Maternal Infections and Diseases During Pregnancy

There are a group of infections, referred to as **TORCH** infections, that are acquired by the pregnant mother and passed on to the fetus, sometimes resulting in severe birth defects (including deaf-blindness). The infections comprising the TORCH infections are toxoplasmosis, other, rubella, cytomegalovirus (CMV), and herpes (see chapter 22). For example, a child born with cytomegalovirus may have multiple disabilities, including profound intellectual disability, cerebral palsy, seizure disorder, severe sensorineural hearing loss, and visual impairments.

Postnatal/Noncongenital Complications

Several additional conditions may occur after birth resulting in deaf-blindness. In some cases, deaf-blindness can occur from an injury, such as **traumatic brain injury** (see chapter 7). Deaf-blindness may also occur from certain infections, such as **meningitis** and **encephalitis** (see chapter 21 on acquired infections). Other causes may also occur after birth (e.g., tumors).

CHARACTERISTICS OF CHILDREN WITH DEAF-BLINDNESS

Children who are deaf-blind miss information that would normally be received by the distance senses of vision and hearing. Distance senses allow individuals to take in information that is farther than arm's reach and are the primary channels through which most people collect information (Prickett & Welch, 1995). Students who are deaf-blind may receive distorted or incomplete information from their distance senses because of the sensory loss. The "near" senses of touch, smell, and taste do provide some information, but they require the student to be in close contact with the item, and these senses may not provide adequate information. For example, it can be difficult to gain an understanding of large items such as a tree or mountain or distant objects like a cloud without the use of distance senses.

Due to the loss of information from the distance senses, children who are deaf-blind receive reduced information that usually results in delays and difficulties in concept development and skill development. The development of these areas is further hampered by the lack of incidental learning that occurs from vision loss. (Incidental learning is unplanned learning that results from seeing or engaging in other activities.) Children with deaf-blindness will need more time to learn concepts with adults providing ample opportunities and systematic instruction.

Children who are deafblind will often have developmental delays in the area of mobility and motor skills. The loss of vision especially makes it difficult for young children to monitor their own movement, or copy other people as models. Milestones such as crawling and walking are usually delayed. In addition, orientation problems can occur due to difficulties in creating a mental map of their surroundings.

One of the major areas that are affected by having deaf-blindness is the area of communication. Communication delays and difficulties typically occur, usually resulting in the need for augmentative and alternative communication. Augmentative and alternative communication can range from the use of gestures and objects to sign language or electronic augmentative communication devices. Because of the hearing loss, augmentative communication needs to take into consideration receptive forms of communication (how the communication partner is communicating with the student who has deaf-blindness) as well as expressive communication (how the student who has deaf-blindness is communicating). When students with deaf-blindness have additional impairments, such as severe cerebral palsy, the student's attempts at communication may be very subtle and easily missed. This difficulty in communication often leads to secondary behavioral challenges (Holte, et al., 2006). Any behavior problems should be assessed to determine if they are from a lack of communication, and if so, communication should be specifically addressed.

The exact characteristics of the child who has deaf-blindness will depend on the etiology, the severity of the sensory losses, and the individual makeup of the child. In addition, many children who are deaf-blind also have additional disabilities, such as cerebral palsy, intellectual disabilities, health impairments, and/or developmental delays. The teacher will need to learn about the unique characteristics of each child with deaf-blindness to determine how to best meet his or her needs.

EDUCATIONAL IMPLICATIONS

Meeting Physical and Sensory Needs

Meeting Sensory Needs of Students with Visual Impairments

Several strategies may be used to optimize the visual functioning of a student with a visual impairment. These include (a) arranging the environment to optimize the visual characteristics of objects, (b) teaching the use of optical devices, and (c) training the use of residual vision (Corn et al., 2003; Wolffe et al., 2002).

Arranging the Environment for Students with Visual Impairments.   There are five major environmental dimensions that can be modified to assist the student with a visual impairment to access his or her environment through the use of vision: (a) color, (b) contrast, (c) time, (d) illumination, and (e) space (Corn et al., 2003). The vision teacher and classroom teacher will need to assess the student to determine how to maximize visual functioning by modifying these environmental dimensions.

Teachers should take into account the color of items being used in the classroom. Some students with low vision may be able to see brightly colored items with greater ease than other colors, while other students with low vision may not see bright colors clearly. Students with color blindness may not benefit from the use of certain colors that appear as the same shade of gray.

The use of contrast should be considered when teaching a student with visual impairments since contrast can make an item easier to visually discriminate. For example, written material clearly and boldly presented on a contrasting colored paper (e.g., black print on white or yellow paper) may assist the student visually. When objects are used in school, such as manipulatives for math or utensils for eating, a contrasting piece of construction paper can be placed under the items to enhance contrast. This is especially needed when the tabletop is a similar color as the item or a clear wheelchair tray has the student's multicolored pants as the background. The teacher needs to be observant of the background color of the walls and carpet areas when holding up an item or putting items on the floor. When the walls or floors are of poor contrast to the item or are not a solid color, the teacher can easily put a piece of contrasting construction paper behind or under the item.

Some students with visual impairments will perform better if given more time to respond. That is because students with visual impairments often need more time to access the item being presented and explore it in order to identify it. In addition, some adaptations will require more time to use, such as reading large print, reading Braille, or using an optical device to read. Some students will benefit if the activity is presented at a slower pace. In addition, many students with visual impairments tire visually and may need to take breaks from activities requiring a lot of use of their vision (e.g., reading text).

Students may benefit from the use of additional light or reduced lighting in order to see items. For example, some students with retinal detachment (where part the retina detaches from the back of the eye) may benefit from increased illumination. Reduced lighting and lighting from behind the student may be needed with students who still have cataracts to reduce glare and promote maximum visual functioning.

Some students with visual impairments will perform better if there are changes in space, specifically how they are positioned in the classroom. For example, a student with poor acuity may perform better in the front row of the classroom because of difficulty seeing the board at a distance. Students with a peripheral field loss (tunnel vision) may be better situated if sitting in the back of the room where more of the classroom can be seen.

Another change in space refers to the size of an item or print. Some students will benefit from having material enlarged (e.g., large print or large items) or using an optical device that enlarges items when looked through. However, enlarging items may be more difficult for students with reduced peripheral fields of vision since an enlarged item may not fit in the student's visual field. The teacher of students with visual impairments should be able to give the classroom teacher guidelines as to the optimal size of print, symbols, and other items and where it should be located (e.g., directly in front of student or within 1 foot).

Optical Devices.   A second major adaptation that assists students to access their environment with their remaining vision is the use of optical devices. Some optical devices, such as the use of magnifiers and telescopes, enlarge normal-sized items and print. These may provide the student with more options of reading material and the ability to better visualize items that are not enlarged. Some optical devices minimize items in order to better visualize them. When optical devices are prescribed by the low-vision specialist, it is important that the teacher has a clear understanding of their proper use and is able to report to the low-vision specialist any difficulties and problems with use of the device. Systematic training by the teacher of students with visual impairments is needed for proper use.

Training to Use Vision and/or Touch.   Students with low vision may be trained to more efficienctly use their vision through the use of vision training programs. These programs are designed to use the systematic presentation of stimuli and instruction to optimize a student's visual functioning. Children who are young and visually inattentive have shown an increase in visual functioning when the programs have been initiated during the time the eye is still developing. This is usually during the first few months of life and especially before age 6. Programs utilizing operant conditioning and the use of highly contrasting stimuli have been effectively used (Nielsen, 2003). The vision teacher along with the rest of the educational team will typically teach the student to use his or her vision to the maximum extent possible.

Students who are unable to use their vision functionally will need to use their sense of touch and other senses. Students will be encouraged to manipulate items and discriminate items on the basis of various features. Discriminations usually start gross (e.g., different in shape and texture and size) and progress to finer discriminations. As the student gains mastery over using the sense of touch, the teacher will need to modify classroom materials (e.g., use actual items, models, or tactile graphics) to allow the student to use this sense to enhance learning.

Meeting Sensory Needs of Students Who Have Hearing Loss

Students with hearing loss may benefit from several environmental and instructional modifications, as well as auditory devices. Environmental and instructional modifications include (a) modifications to the auditory environment and use of listening devices, (b) modifications to the visual environment, and (c) modifications of materials and instruction.

Arranging the Environment for Hearing Loss: Modifications to the Auditory Environment. Typical classrooms can be very noisy places because of background noise and poor acoustics. When sound strikes a surface, it can (a) transmit through the surface, (b) reflect or bounce off the surface, (c) scatter in different directions, or (d) be absorbed. If it is not absorbed, then it bounces around the room, causing reverberation, in turn making things sound noisier. Noise in the room can drown out the message, especially the teacher's voice (or signal). In order to hear the teacher's voice clearly, hearing children require a signal-to-noise (S/N) ratio of +10, where the teacher's voice is at least 10 dB louder than the noise. Children with hearing losses require an S/N of at least +15 (Seep, Glosemeyer, Hulce, Linn, & Aytar, 2000).

To help improve acoustics, the classroom may be modified with carpet(s), drapes, and other sound-absorbing materials on the walls and floor. The classroom should have lower ceilings with sound-absorbing tiles. Double-pane windows and solid doors reduce reverberation as well. The child should be seated away from noisy equipment, such as plumbing, air conditioners, and overhead projectors, as well as from windows where traffic noise is evident.

Arranging the Environment for Hearing Loss: Modifications to the Visual Environment. Deaf and hard-of-hearing students are visual learners (Lane, Hoffmeister, & Bahan, 1996), even those who are benefiting from their listening devices. For this reason, it is as important to manage the visual environment as it is to manage the auditory environment.

Seating arrangement should be considered carefully when a child has a hearing loss. Students should be able to see the teacher as well as classmates easily to allow for speech reading where necessary. Also, having unobstructed visual access to the teacher will allow the student to attend to body language and facial expression, which assists understanding of the message conveyed. Unobstructed views of classmates will facilitate participation in group discussions.

If the student uses sign language, an interpreter may be used in class. This person is usually positioned to the side of the speaker, allowing the student to see both the interpreter and the speaker to promote understanding. The interpreter will repeat what the speaker has said using sign language. There must be sufficient light on the interpreter in order for the student to see the interpreter (e.g., if lights are off to see slides, a small light must remain on the interpreter). Occasionally, the interpreter may need the teacher to slow the pace or momentarily stop instruction, especially when finger spelling complex words. To facilitate the flow of interpreting, only one person should talk at a time since the interpreter cannot interpret several people at one time. It is also important to be respectful of the student by talking directly to the student, not to the interpreter. In addition, the student with a hearing loss often needs extra time to see what is being said as well as to see what is being demonstrated because deaf students process visual information differently from hearing students (Stivalet, 1998). The teacher should be alert for signs of fatigue in the student since attending to the interpreter, using residual hearing, and attending to the material can be tiring. The student's schedule should have nonacademic subjects dispersed among academic ones to reduce fatigue.

Hearing Aids, Cochlear Implants, and Listening Devices.   A very important modification to the auditory environment is the use of hearing aids, cochlear implants, and other listening devices that amplify sound (Amlani, Rakerd, & Punch, 2006). In addition, some devices can improve the signal-to-noise ratio. All hearing aids (a) use batteries, (b) have microphones that pick up sound, (c) have electronic circuitry to process sound and make it louder, and (d) emit louder sounds through speakers. Behind-the-ear aids sit behind the ear, and in-the-canal aids are placed in the ear canal. Sound travels down a tube, through ear molds, and into the ear canal. A snug fit between the ear mold and canal prevents sound from leaking out and causing feedback, a high-pitched squeal (see Figure 11–9 for troubleshooting hearing aid problems).

Hearing Aid Problems and Solutions

Problem: Weak, distorted, intermittent, or no signal

Solutions: Check battery placement
Put in new battery
Clean mold if earwax is present
Check that telephone switch (OTM) is in the on position (not *off* or in telephone position)
Call audiologist

Problem: Squealing or whistling

Solutions: Reinsert ear mold
Push tubing between mold and aid together so it is tight
Call audiologist

FIGURE 11–9 Troubleshooting hearing aid problems.

Cochlear implants are devices that bypass the destroyed hair cells on the cochlea by allowing stimulation of the end nerve fibers to the auditory nerve. Cochlear implants have internal and external components. An electrode array is surgically inserted into the cochlea. A receiver is placed under the skin behind the pinna. A microphone, sound processing computer, transmitter, and batteries are located externally (see Figure 11–10).

There are other assistive listening devices that may be used. Students may use a sound field system that amplifies the teacher's voice via speakers in the room. There are also other auditory devices (e.g., auditory trainers) that can be patched into hearing aids to assist with hearing the teacher in the classroom setting. These devices are available from hearing aid manufacturers.

Modification of Materials. Materials may need to be adapted for the student with a hearing impairment. Tapes used during class or in listening centers should be presented in written form for the student who does not hear speech adequately. Outlines, summaries, written copies of verbal questions, written assignments, homework, and heavy use of visual organizers such as diagrams and charts are helpful (Stoner & Easterbrooks, 2006). Other students can use carbon paper while taking notes to give a copy to the student with a hearing loss.

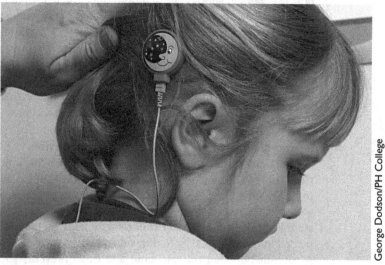

George Dodson/PH College

FIGURE 11–10 Student with a cochlear implant.

FIGURE 11-11 Student using a Brailler for written work.

Arranging the Environment for Students Who Are Deaf-Blind

The individual needs of each student with deaf-blindness will need to be assessed to determine the best way to arrange the environment. Students who are deaf-blind will typically need some combination of the previously mentioned adaptations to meet their needs.

Meeting Communication Needs

Considerations for Students with Visual Impairments

Students with vision impairments who have no additional disability will usually not require any adaptations to promote oral communication but may need adaptations for written communication. These students may need a larger-size print, an optical device to enlarge print (such as a magnifier or closed-circuit TV (known as a CCTV) as shown in Figure 8–6), braille (see Figure 11–11), or a combination. It is important that the student be assessed for the proper reading medium.

When reading or writing print, there may need to be special modifications. Young students with nystagmus, for example, may lose their place as they are reading print. The use of a typoscope (a card with a rectangle cut out of it) or an underliner (a card with a line) may be used. Bold-line paper or raised-line paper may assist some students with low vision writing on the line.

Considerations for Students Who Are Deaf/Hard of Hearing

Teaching relies heavily on communicating, and communication is a significant challenge for children with hearing loss. Teachers need to understand the various languages and options for communicating that a child with a hearing loss may use. There are three communication options commonly used in deaf education (Easterbrooks & Baker, 2004).

One option is spoken language. Spoken language is taught by either auditory-oral or auditory-verbal means. Both rely heavily on the use of listening devices, parent involvement, and training the ear to listen. Auditory-verbal programs tend to work with preschoolers or new cochlear implant users and are more clinically oriented, requiring use of hearing without visual cues. Auditory-oral programs incorporate auditory-verbal techniques into a classroom setting and allow visual enhancement when necessary. Adaptations in the regular classroom for a child using spoken language include having the teacher face the child at all times to promote speech reading and making sure that light is on the teacher's face and not in the child's eyes.

A second option is the representation of English through visual means. Types of visual representation include Signed English, Signing Exact English (SEE), Simultaneous

FIGURE 11–12 Students with hearing loss using sign language to communicate.

Communication (Sim-Com), Conceptually Accurate Signed English (CASE), cued speech, and finger spelling. English signing children may need an interpreter in the general education classroom. Formerly, the use of English signs became known as total communication, but this is not a communication option. Instead, it is the philosophy that one uses regardless of the communication tool needed by a particular child, whether signed, spoken, or written.

The third option for communication and the development of English is through American Sign Language (ASL) (see Figure 11–12). ASL functions both as a primary language and as the language by which to teach English as a second language. This is often referred to as the bilingual-bicultural approach. In the past, it was referred to as "manual communication," which is an antiquated term that neglected to recognize that ASL is seen not only on the hands but also on the face, mouth, and the body in general. For example, specific mouth movements called mouth morphemes can change the meaning of an ASL sentence. Children who are ASL users almost always have an interpreter in the general education classroom.

Considerations for Students Who Are Deaf-Blind

Students who are deaf-blind often need to use augmentative communication for expressive and receptive communication. Communication can take multiple forms, such as gestures, objects, tactile objects, photos, symbols, sign language, and tactile sign language, to name a few. Developing good communication skills is often a priority with this population of students.

Meeting Learning Needs

Depending on the cause of the sensory loss, children may have normal intelligence or cognitive impairments. Infants and young children who have sensory impairments often develop certain developmental milestones (e.g., walking and talking) at slower or different rates than those with intact hearing and vision. This is indicative not of any mental impairment but of the effect of the sensory impairment.

Students with sensory loss usually lack specific knowledge or concepts because of the large amount of information that is typically learned incidentally through visual and auditory experiences. Gaps in information or incorrect information may be present. For example, a child who is blind may think that cooking consists of only stirring since that is the only experience he or she may have had. A student who is deaf or deaf-blind may be unable to converse with his or her peers about rap. Concepts may also be incorrectly generalized when a young child who is blind is given an explanation of how people smile and assume that birds also smile. The teacher must not assume that something is common knowledge to a student with a sensory loss but instead provide meaningful experiences and explanations to address missing information.

In the classroom, children with sensory impairments may need additional information and adaptations to learn a concept. For example, children who have visual impairments may need further verbal description of what they are unable to see. Students with visual impairments or deaf-blindness may need tactile models or tactile graphics to teach concepts through the use of touch. For children who are deaf and hard of hearing, visual strategies are needed (e.g., Venn diagrams or story maps) as well as adaptations such as providing key vocabulary for content area classes, use of captioned media, and having teachers who are skilled communicators (Easterbrooks & Stephenson, 2006).

Meeting Daily Living Needs

Direct instruction in daily living areas is often needed for students who are blind or deaf-blind since incidental learning cannot occur. Instruction often needs to include eating skills, table etiquette, personal grooming, clothing care, food preparation, house care, shopping, and other areas. Specific skills may be taught such as judging the amount of food on a spoon by weight, determining if hair is in place by touch, labeling and storing clothes so that they will match, labeling cans of food to determine what they are, learning how to fold money to determine the denomination of the bills for shopping, and others. There are specific adaptations and strategies for these that will need to be taught.

Students with sensory loss may use several different assistive devices to help with daily living needs. For example, students with hearing loss may use closed-captioned television, a telecommunications device for the deaf (a device with a letter-based keyboard like a typewriter on which the caller types out the message), vibrating or flashing alarm clocks, or flashing door bells. Hearing ear dogs are also available. Students with visual impairments may use special money readers, special devices that buzz when a beverage is near the top of the glass, and others (see chapter 8 on assistive technology and chapter 12 on adaptations).

Orientation and mobility skills are also needed for students with visual impairments or deaf-blindness. Orientation refers to the process of using one's senses to determine one's position in relation to other objects in the environment, and mobility refers to the ability to move about in one's environment (Emerson & Corn, 2006). Orientation and mobility instructors teach students the skills that will enable them to safely and independently move around their environments (see Figure 11-13). Mobility aids may be needed, such as a specially

FIGURE 11-13 Student with deaf-blindness learning to use a cane with an orientation and mobility instructor.

Katelyn Metzger/Merrill

designed cane, dog guides, electronic travel devices, and/or another person (sighted guide). Some students with additional physical disabilities will learn mobility techniques using their wheelchairs or walkers.

Meeting Behavioral and Social Needs

Teachers need to create accepting environments for students with sensory loss that will promote interactions with peers. Students with sensory impairments may need instruction to promote effective social interactions. Without effective sight, students with visual impairments will need instruction on smiling, facing the person who is talking, and other nonverbal forms of communication. Without intervention and peer education, peers may misinterpret the student's lack of smiling or other nonverbal behavior as a lack of interest and not interact with the student.

When a mild hearing loss is present, there may be some misinterpretations of what is being said that may result in exclusion or ridicule by other children. When the hearing loss is severe and the student communicates using signs (or other forms of communication), the student may not be able to communicate with hearing peers without an interpreter. Appropriate adaptations, social skills, and communication modalities need to be in place to facilitate social interactions.

Students with severe visual impairments or deaf-blindness may exhibit stereotypic behaviors. Stereotypic behaviors are motor behaviors such as body rocking and eye rubbing that occur in excessive quantity, frequency, and intensity. A careful assessment is needed to determine the extent to which these behaviors interfere with learning, inhibit social interaction, or cause physical damage to the student. The teacher may permit certain stereotypic behaviors to occur in certain locations (such as rocking in a rocking chair) and inhibit others (such as eye rubbing). Stereotypic behavior may be managed in any number of ways from simple verbal reminders to the implementation of a behavioral plan that is agreed on by the educational team to ensure consistent implementation across settings.

SUMMARY

There are several different types of visual impairments, hearing losses, and deaf-blindness. Visual impairments can vary in terms of visual acuity, field of vision, motility and gaze, light and color reception, and impairment in brain function. Hearing losses are defined in terms of loudness (decibels) and pitch (hertz) and categorized as slight, mild, moderate, moderately severe, severe, and profound. Children with deaf-blindness have a range of sensory impairments from mild hearing loss and low vision to profound deafness and total blindness. Children with sensory impairments may also have additional disabilities, such as cerebral palsy. The unique needs of each individual child will need to be determined with appropriate adaptations, assistive technology devices, and systematic instruction.

 **VIGNETTE** | **Terrill's Story**

Terrill is a 7-year-old boy with cortical visual impairment and a moderate bilateral sensorineural hearing loss. He also has cerebral palsy, a severe intellectual disability, and epilepsy (generalized tonic-clonic seizures). He communicates with teachers and peers through sign approximations and a communication board with objects. When teachers hold up his favorite toy kiosh ball, Terrill is not touching the foam circle on his communication board to request it. What does the teacher need to do, and how could the communication board be modified?

REFERENCES

AGIS Investigators. (2000). The advanced glaucoma intervention study 6: Effect of cataract on visual field and visual acuity. *Archives of Ophthalmology, 118,* 1639-1652.

American Optometric Association. (2006). *Low vision.* Retrieved August 28, 2006, from http://www.aoa.org/x760.xml

Amlani, A. M., Rakerd, B., & Punch, J. L. (2006). Speech-clarity judgments of hearing-aid-processed speech in noise: Differing polar patterns and acoustic environments. *International Journal of Audiology, 45*(6), 319-330.

Angelopoulou, N., Fotiadou, E., Tsimaras, V., & Giagozoglou, P. (1999, September). *Assessment of dynamic balance in deaf children: A comparative study.* Paper presented at the Movement and Health International Conference, Colomouc, Czech Republic.

Arehart, K. W., Yoshinago-Itano, C., Gabbard, S., Stredler-Brown, A., & Thomson, V. (1998). State of the states: Status of universal newborn hearing screening, assessment and intervention in 17 states. *American Journal of Audiology, 7,* 101-111.

Bashour, M., Menassa, J., & Gevontis, C.C. (2006). *Congenital cataract.* Retrieved August 28, 2006, from http://www.emedicine.com/oph/topic45.htm

Behrman, R. E., Kliegman, R. M., & Jenson, H. B. (2004). *Nelson textbook of pediatrics* (17th ed.). Philadelphia: W. B. Saunders.

Bremer, D. L., Palmer, E. A., Fellows, R. R., Baker, J. D., Hardy, R. J., Tung, B., et al. (1998). Strabismus in premature infants in the first year of life. *Archives of Ophthalmology, 116,* 329-333.

Brodsky, M. C. (2005). Visuo-vestibular eye movements. *Archives of Ophthalmology, 123,* 837-842.

Chang, D. (2004). Ophthalmologic exam. In P. Riordan-Eva & J. P. Whitcher (Eds.), *Vaughn and Asbury's general ophthalmology* (pp. 29-61). New York: Lange Medical Books/McGraw-Hill.

Coe, K., Butler, M., Reavis, N., Klinepeter, M. E., Purkey, C., Oliver, T., et al. (2006). Special Preemie Oxygen Targeting (SPOT): (A program to decrease the incidence of blindness in infants with retinopathy of prematurity. *Journal of Nursing Care Quality, 21,* 230-235.

Corn, A. L., Bell, J. K., Anderson, E., Bachofer, C., Jose, R., & Perez, A. (2003). Providing access to the visual environment: A model of comprehensive low vision services for children. *Journal of Visual Impairment and Blindness, 97,* 261-272.

Corn, A. L., & Koenig, A. J. (2002). Literacy instruction for students with low vision: A framework for delivery of instruction. *Journal of Visual Impairment and Blindness, 96,* 305-321.

Easterbrooks, S. R., & Baker, S. (2004). *Language learning in children who are deaf and hard of hearing: Multiple pathways.* Boston: Allyn & Bacon.

Easterbrooks, S. R., & Stephenson, B. (2006). An examination of twenty literacy, science, and mathematics practices used to educate students who are deaf and hard of hearing. *American Annals of the Deaf, 151,* 385-397.

Edwards, A., Fishman, G. A., Anderson, R. J., Grover, S., & Derlacki, D. J. (1998). Visual acuity and visual filed impairment in Usher syndrome. *Archives of Ophthalmology, 116,* 165-168.

Emerson, R. S. W., & Corn, A. L. (2006). Orientation and mobility content for children and youths: A Delphi approach pilot study. *Journal of Visual Impairment and Blindness, 100,* 331-342.

Friel-Patti, S. (1999). Clinical decision-making in the assessment and intervention of central auditory processing disorders. *Language, Speech, and Hearing Services in Schools, 30,* 345-352.

Gillies, M., Brian, G., La Nauze, J., Le Mesurier, R., Moran, D., Taylor, H., et al. (1998). Modern surgery for global cataract blindness: Preliminary considerations. *Archives of Opthalmology, 116,* 90-92.

Good, W. V., Jan, J. E., Burden, S. K., Skoczenski, A., & Candy, R. (2001). Recent advances in cortical visual impairment. *Developmental Medicine and Child Neurology, 43,* 56-60.

Guzzetta, A., Mercuri, E., & Cioni, G. (2001). Visual disorders in children with brain lesions: 2. Visual impairment associated with cerebral palsy. *European Journal of Paediatric Neurology, 5,* 115-119.

Hardy, R. A., & Shetlar, D. J. (2004). Retina. In P. Riordan-Eva & J. P. Whitcher (Eds.), *Vaughn and Asbury's general ophthalmology* (pp. 189-211). New York: Lange Medical Books/McGraw-Hill.

Harper, R. A., & Shock, J. P. (2004). Lens. In P. Riordan-Eva & J. P. Whitcher (Eds.), *Vaughn and Asbury's general ophthalmology* (pp. 171-181). New York: Lange Medical Books/McGraw-Hill.

Holte, L., Prickett, J. G., Van Dyke, D. C., Olson, R. J., Lubrica, P., Knutson, C. L., et al., (2006). Issues in the management of infants and young children who are deaf-blind. *Infants & Young Children, 19,* 323-337.

Isaacson, J. E., & Vora, N. M. (2003). Differential diagnosis and treatment of hearing loss. *American Family Physician, 68*(6), 5-32.

Johnson, M. H. (1997). Vision, orienting, and attention. In M. H. Johnson (Ed.), *Developmental cognitive neuroscience* (pp. 68-97). Malden, MA. Blackwell.

Lane, H., Hoffmeister, R., & Bahan, B. (1996). *A journey into the deaf-world.* San Diego: DawnSign Press.

Liu, X. Z. (2005). Audiological features of GJB2 (connexin 26) deafness. *Ear and Hearing, 26,* 361-369.

Madan, A., Jan, J., & Good, W. V. (2005). Visual developments in preterm infants. *Developmental Medicine and Child Neurology, 47,* 376-380.

Most, T., Aram, D., & Andorn, T. (2006). Early literacy in children with hearing loss: A comparison between two educational systems. *Volta Review, 106*(1), 5-28.

Nielsen, L. (2003). Learning object perception. In L. Nielsen (Ed.), *Space and self: Active learning by means of the little room* (pp. 44-48). Copenhagen: Norhaven Books.

Peters, B. T., & Bloomberg, J. J. (2005). Dynamic visual acuity using "far" and "near" targets. *Acta Oto-Laryngologica, 125,* 353-357.

Prickett, J. G., & Welch, R. R. (1995). Deaf-blindness: Implications for learning. In K. M. Huebner, J. G. Prickett, T. R. Welch,

& E. Joffee (Eds.), *Hand in hand: Essentials of communication and orientation and mobility for your students who are deaf-blind* (pp. 25–60). New York: AFB Press.

Riordan-Eva, P., & Hoyt, W. (2004). Neuro-ophthalmology. In P. Riordan-Eva & J. P. Whitcher (Eds.), *Vaughn and Asbury's general ophthalmology* (pp. 261–306). New York: Lange Medical Books/McGraw-Hill.

Scott, T. M. (2003). Auditory neuropathy in children. *ASHA Leader, 8*(3), 17–18.

Seep, B., Glosemeyer, R., Hulce, E., Linn, M., & Aytar, P. (2000). *Classroom acoustics: A resource for creating learning environments with desirable listening conditions.* Melville, NY: American Acoustical Society.

Stivalet, P. (1998). Differences in visual search tasks between congenitally deaf and normally hearing adults. *Cognitive Brain Research, 6,* 227–232.

Stoner, M., & Easterbrooks, S. R. (2006). Using a visual tool to increase descriptors in writing by students who are deaf or hard of hearing. *Communication Disorders Quarterly. 27,* 95–109.

Watkins, S. (Ed.). (1993). *Graphics to accompany the SKI-HI resource manual.* Carol Stream, IL: Hope.

Wolffe, K. E., Sacks, S. Z., Corn, A. L., Erin, J. N., Huebner, K. M., & Lewis, S. (2002). Teachers of students with visual impairments: What are they teaching? *Journal of Visual Impairment and Blindness, 96,* 293–304.

Yoshinaga-Itano, C., and Apuzzo, M.L. (1998). Identification of hearing loss after 18 months is not early enough. *American Annals of the Deaf, 143,* 380–387.

Yoshinaga-Itano, C., Coulter, D., & Thomson, V. (2000). The Colorado newborn hearing screening project: Effects on speech and language development for children with hearing loss. In M. K. Philbin, S. N. Graven, & A. Robertson (Eds.), The influence of auditory experience on the fetus, newborn, and preterm infant: report of the sound study group of the national resource center: The physical and developmental environment of the high risk infant. *Journal of Perinatology, 20* (8:2), S132–S137.

Young, P. A., & Young, P. H. (1997). The visual system: Anopsia. In P. A. Young & P. H. Young (Eds.), *Basic clinical neuroanatomy* (pp. 153–158, 162). Baltimore: Lippincott Williams & Wilkins.

CHAPTER 12

CLASSROOM ADAPTATIONS FOR STUDENTS WITH PHYSICAL, HEALTH, AND MULTIPLE DISABILITIES

Kathryn Wolff Heller and Mari Beth Coleman

Students who have physical, health, or multiple disabilities often require **adaptations** in order to optimally function in school settings. These may range from stabilizing material on a slant board to using an augmentative communication device. It is important that the educational team accurately determines the most appropriate adaptations for each individual student and accurately convey this information to all teachers and related staff who teach the student. This chapter will provide an overview of various types of adaptations that are commonly needed for students with physical, health, and multiple disabilities and how an adaptation checklist may be used to communicate this information to others.

IDENTIFYING THE NEED FOR ADAPTATIONS

Adaptations are alterations to a task (or materials used in the task) that provide access to a task or facilitate participation in a task for which an individual does not have the requisite abilities (Bryant & Bryant, 2003). Adaptations include modifications and accommodations. Accommodations refer to changes to the task to accommodate for a disability that does not alter the performance standards, whereas modifications refer to changes where the content, level, or number of skills is altered (Beech, 2002). Adaptations also encompasses assistive technology (see chapter 8) and alternate performance strategies that are nontypical ways of performing a task, such as a student who writes by holding a pencil with his or her teeth.

In order to meet the needs of students with physical, health, or multiple disabilities, it is important that appropriate adaptations are identified. This begins by examining the target performance of the task and the student's performance of the task. Any discrepancy between the target outcome and the student's performance is examined in terms of the reason for the discrepancy (e.g., atypical motor movements and motor abilities resulting in restricted range of motion, vision loss affecting access to the task, poor physical endurance, health issues regarding frequent discomfort resulting in inattention to task, learning difficulty regarding understanding task requirements, lack of appropriate communication, or poor motivation) (Heller, Forney, Alberto, Schwartzman, & Goeckel, 2000). Based on the reason identified for the discrepancy between target performance of the task and student performance, appropriate adaptations are selected using a team approach. This is the same process used in the AT Analysis of Task and Student Performance (see chapter 8).

Although the AT Analysis of Task and Student Performance was originally developed to guide in the selection of assistive technology, it can also be used to identify the need for adaptations. When using the AT Analysis of Task and Student Performance, the team should consider all types of adaptations. There are several general considerations the team should take into account when selecting and implementing an adaptation.

General Considerations

Individualization and Increasing Independence

Adaptations must be individualized for the student. Individualization of the adaptation is necessary to adequately meet the student's unique characteristics and should aim at promoting effective student participation and increasing student independence. Adaptations cannot be made for a group or category of students because in the area of physical disabilities, two students with the same diagnosis may have significantly different physical abilities.

Correct Use

It is important for the teacher to be certain that the use of assistive technology devices and activities are not being misused as replacements for teacher–learner interactions (Garner & Campbell, 1987). Adaptations can hinder student progress when they supplant effective teaching practices. In addition, it is important that the teacher be familiar with the adaptation and implements it correctly. Some adaptations may be made due to health or medical concerns (e.g., activity limitations, positioning considerations, or monitoring for a condition), so a thorough understanding of the rationale of the adaptation and factors surrounding its use is important.

Time to Learn the Adaptation

Sufficient time must be given to determine if an adaptation is effective. It is unlikely that an adaptation will be effective after one trial (Baumgart et al., 1982). For example, the student may need some time to adjust to a new physical adaptation or to learn to use an assistive technology device. However, if no positive increase in the targeted behavior is seen after a sufficient period of time, there will need to be a reevaluation of the appropriateness of the adaptation (as well as an examination of the various factors surrounding implementation).

Effectiveness of the Adaptation and Periodic Reevaluation

Adaptations need to be thoroughly evaluated as to their effectiveness with the student. Data should be taken to determine if the adaptation is having its intended effect or if it needs to be changed to something more effective. Adaptations also need to be periodically reevaluated. Some adaptations may not be necessary any longer and can be eliminated, while other adaptations will remain a permanent part of the task. If the student can function as well without the adaptation or go to a simpler form of adaptation, then this should occur. Less complex adaptations are more likely to be systematically used and properly implemented. Thus, when considering adaptations, teachers should always look for the least intrusive, least expensive, and least complex options that result in efficient task performance first. However, some students with conditions such as muscular dystrophy may need more complex adaptations as their condition progresses, so frequent evaluations regarding the effectiveness of the adaptations are important.

Examined Across Environments

Adaptations must be reevaluated as students go to different environments. For example, changes from elementary school to middle school involve differences in such areas as the number of teachers, number of environments, and distances between environments. Changes may need to be made to the adaptations because of the differences in environments.

Team Approach

The teacher will need to involve the related staff (e.g., occupational and physical therapists and speech-language pathologist), parents, and the student in selection of the adaptations as well as the evaluation of their effectiveness. It is important that all individuals working with the student understand the adaptations and work together to consistently implement them. Getting input from all team members while planning adaptations and making sure that proper training of each adaptation takes place helps to get the right adaptation-user match and helps reduce the possibility that adaptations are unnecessarily abandoned (Bryant & Bryant, 2003). After discussing the adaptations with all involved school personnel, a checklist containing the information can be very helpful to have as a reminder of what needs to be done.

CLASSROOM ADAPTATIONS CHECKLIST

There are many different checklists available for the teacher to use in the school system to document adaptations. Unfortunately, very few are in sufficient detail to contain all the adaptations typically needed by many students with physical, health, or multiple disabilities. Ideally, a checklist should be as inclusive as possible so that all areas requiring adaptations can be addressed. Having a detailed checklist also prompts discussions by team members of areas that perhaps were not initially considered.

One checklist designed specifically for students with physical, health, or multiple disabilities is the Classroom Adaptations Checklist for Students with Physical, Health, or Multiple Disabilities (see Figure 12-1). This checklist can be used to document adaptations and kept as a record to compare how adaptations have changed over time (e.g., documentation of what was done last year, and what is being done this year). It can be given to all the student's teachers and related

1. Student Information

Name: Date of birth: Educational placement:

Type of disability: Restrictions (e.g., activity, diet, allergies):

Mobility: Communication:

2. Physical/Health Monitoring

____ Monitor for health problems (e.g., seizure, asthma, shunt malfunction)
____ Monitor for a decline in motor ability or mobility (e.g., falls, difficulty writing)
____ Monitor for need for repositioning
____ Monitor for pressure sores (decubitus ulcers)
____ Monitor for pain and discomfort
____ Monitor for fatigue and low endurance
____ Monitor for medication and treatment effects (including healthcare procedures)
____ Other:
Description and actions to take for checked areas:

3. Environmental Arrangement: Across School Environments and Scheduling

____ Modified day
____ Transportation (bus) modifications
____ Arrival/departure issues
____ School navigational issues (e.g., requires elevator, railings, help with stairs or ramps)
____ Leaves early for next class (specify how early)
____ Close proximity of classrooms needed
____ Classrooms must be near an exit
____ Locker adaptations needed
____ Assistance needed with putting on or taking off outer clothing
____ Bathroom adaptations or assistance needed
____ Lunchroom adaptations or eating assistance required
____ Playground adaptations or assistance needed
____ Assembly adaptations
____ Specialized emergency evacuation plan
____ Scheduling adaptations needed (e.g., trip training, healthcare procedures, positioning)
____ Other:
Description and actions to take for checked areas:

4. Environmental Arrangement: Within Classrooms

____ Widened aisles needed
____ Assistance needed in mobility
____ Assistance needed in getting into or out of a chair, or moving chair up to desk
____ Preferential seating required
____ Special chair, desk, other
____ Work surface adaptations needed (e.g., slant, height)
____ Materials need to be stabilized
____ Materials specially positioned (e.g., location, spacing, target size)
____ Assistance manipulating materials (e.g., alternate access, modify material)
____ Scheduled rest breaks or rest breaks as needed (specify when, how long)
____ Other:
Description and actions to take for checked areas:

FIGURE 12–1 Classroom Adaptations Checklist for Students with Physical, Health, and Multiple Disabilities.

Source. Reproduced with permission from Heller (2007).

5. Communication

_____ Uses AAC (specify type)

_____ Reliable means of response: _____

_____ Communicates correct answer with multiple-choice format

_____ Longer time to respond (specify length)

Description and actions to take for checked areas:

6. Areas Needing Adaptations and Assistive Technology

_____ Computer adaptations needed for access

_____ Writing or keyboarding

_____ Spelling

_____ Reading

_____ Math

_____ Specific content areas _____ (Specify)

_____ Life management/daily living

_____ Recreation or leisure

_____ Physical education

_____ Prevocational areas

_____ Specials (art, music)

_____ Other areas:

Description and actions to take for checked areas:

7. Class Participation

_____ Dependent upon teacher to prompt participation

_____ Give student question(s) to answer in advance

_____ Uses modified response/communication system

_____ Gains teacher attention by: ___ raising hand, _____ signalling device, ___ AAC system

_____ Works best: ___individually, ___ peer, ___ small group, ___ large group

_____ Other:

Description and actions to take for checked areas:

8. Instruction and Curricular Adaptations

_____ Modified curriculum (e.g., lower grade level, adapted curriculum, direct instruction)

_____ Benefits from antecedent prompts (e.g., highlighting relevant feature, modeling, sample)

_____ Benefits from preview types of strategies (e.g., advance organizers)

_____ Benefits from response prompt strategies (e.g., time delay, least prompts)

_____ Benefits from learning strategies (e.g., mnemonics, key words, song)

_____ Benefits from student-directed strategies (e.g., self-monitoring and recording, self-talk)

_____ Requires teacher reinforcement or more feedback

_____ Provide extra repetition

_____ Directions should be: _____ written down, _____read orally, ___demonstrated

_____ Modify activity (e.g., more time, shorter segments, different response, different outcome)

_____ Modify material (e.g., lower grade level, modified books for access)

_____ Requires note taker and/or lectures recorded

_____ Requires textbook on CD

_____ Requires extra set of books

_____ Requires additional personnel support

_____ Requires implementation of behavioral plan

_____ Other:

Description and actions to take for checked areas:

FIGURE 12–1 _(continued)_

9. Assignments and Tests
____ Needs an assignment notebook or organizational binder
____ Abbreviate assignments/tests
____ Requires study guide
____ Break up assignments/tests into shorter segments
____ Provide extended time
____ Reduce paper/pencil tasks
____ Allow computer use for assignments
____ Allow alternate responding
____ Alternate test/assignment format (e.g., word bank on test, multiple-choice format)
____ Omit or use alternate for physical activities (e.g., coloring, cutting, building project)
____ Peer helper for assignments
____ Alternate grading needed
____ Other:
Description and actions to take for checked areas:

10. Sensory and Perceptual Adaptations
____ Need to decrease visual clutter
____ Needs extra lighting or low lighting
____ Needs material to be high contrast
____ Materials need to be modified visually or tactually (specify font type and size)
____ Student uses an LVD (low-vision device), CCTV, other
____ Student needs everything described orally
____ Student uses hearing aids or cochlear implants, or other devices
____ Student requires adapted environment (e.g., sound-absorbing material on floor, walls)
____ Student requires visual presentation
____ Student requires an interpreter
____ Student requires class notes in appropriate format
____ Other:
Description and actions to take for checked areas:

OTHER:

Name of Person Completing Checklist: _____
Title: _____   Date: _____

FIGURE 12–1 *(continued)*

staff to be sure there is consistency across persons in implementing the adaptations. It can also assist a substitute teacher who is unfamiliar with the student. Because of the checklist's breadth and specificity, it can also be used to examine areas of need. Since no checklist can provide all the information, it also has room for additional information. For the checklist to be helpful, it is important that the teacher provide a detailed description of the checked areas at the end of each section (under "Description and actions to take for checked areas") to assist others in understanding the precise adaptation. When reproducing this checklist for use, more space is often needed in the description areas.

The Classroom Adaptations Checklist is composed of 10 sections: (a) student information, (b) physical and health monitoring, (c) environmental arrangement: across environments, (d) environmental arrangement: within classrooms, (e) communication, (f) areas needing adaptations and assistive technology, (g) class participation, (h) instruction and curricular adaptations, (i) assignments and tests, and (j) sensory and perceptual adaptations. Since students with physical, health, and multiple disabilities have a range of intellectual abilities, most sections are designed to be applicable to all students by having a range of adaptations that can be used for academic and functional skill. Each of these sections will be discussed separately.

Student Information

The first section of the Classroom Adaptations Checklist for Students with Physical, Health, or Multiple Disabilities consists of identifying information about the student. It also includes information on any type of restrictions (e.g., activity restrictions or special diet). For quick reference, mobility and communication needs are also included in this section and expanded on later in the checklist.

Physical and Health Monitoring

Teachers need to maintain a safe, healthy environment for all their students. For students with physical, health, or multiple disabilities, this often includes monitoring for specific health problems (e.g., **seizure** or respiratory distress) (Wadsworth & Knight, 1999). In addition, some students may need to be watched for repositioning (e.g., falling to one side of their wheelchair or head coming off a headrest and can't get back). Other students may have problems with pain and fatigue. The teacher should specify at the end of the section specifics about the problem (e.g., where does the student typically have pain or typical medication side effects to watch for) and what needs to be done should any of these be detected (e.g., notify nurse or give a rest break). More extensive information, such as what to do should a seizure occur, should be written up on a separate page and attached at the end of the checklist (more information on monitoring health impairments is given in chapter 20).

Environmental Arrangement: Across Environments

The third section concentrates on adaptations the student may need going to classrooms, as well as specialty areas (e.g., lunchroom, bathroom, assembly, or locker area). When one of these is checked, the teacher should specify the type of adaptation that is needed in the space at the end of the section. For example, some students may need to leave early for the next class for mobility or health reasons (e.g., **juvenile rheumatoid arthritis** or **osteogenesis imperfecta**.) When this is the case, the teacher should specify how early the student needs to leave. Some students will need help going through a lunch line or may need an adapted spoon and scoop dish for lunch, and this can be specified on the checklist.

Environmental Arrangement: Within Classrooms

The fourth section examines the possible adaptations that will be needed in a classroom to assist the student who has a physical or multiple disability. These adaptations fall into several areas: (a) mobility and seating arrangement, (b) student positioning to optimize movements, (c) adaptations to work surfaces, (d) special positioning of materials on the work surface due to restricted range of motion, (e) assistance or adaptations to materials, and (f) modifying activities or tasks in the classroom because of fatigue.

Some students with physical or multiple disabilities will have mobility problems and have difficulty getting to their desks (or areas in the classroom). To address this issue, aisles may need to be widened, or assistance may be needed (including assisting the student in transferring into a chair or moving a chair up to a desk). The team may need to carefully consider the layout of the room and how the student will move to different locations. Seating arrangements should take into account assistive technology devices used by students and the ability to access all classroom areas (Wadsworth & Knight, 1999). For example, some students may need preferential sitting and be near the front of the class to optimize viewing the board or near the side of the room where a computer with adaptations is set up.

Proper positioning is critical for students with physical disabilities since good positioning can maximize movement (e.g., better arm movement can occur when proper positioning is in place for students with severe cerebral palsy). Good positioning is also important

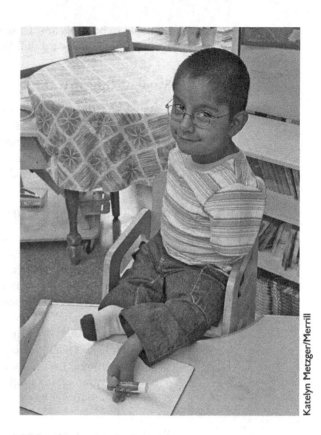

FIGURE 12–2 Student using his foot to write with a marker on a writing board with his chair adjusted to the height of the desk.

Katelyn Metzger/Merrill

to decrease health problems (e.g., skin breakdown in a student with severe scoliosis). To accomplish good body positioning, some students will need an adapted chair or wheelchair that provides the proper support and positioning. Some students may be able to use a regular chair, but their feet dangle, resulting in a lack of stability for some students. In this case, students may need their feet stabilized by having them rest on a box or phone books (or similar material). These adaptations will need to be specified on the checklist.

Once the student is properly positioned, the student may have difficulty accessing the work surface because of atypical arm or hand movements. In this instance, the work surface may need to be adapted. First, it should be determined if the work surface is the proper height. Very often the student's desk is too high for him to effectively use his arm movements (or other body movement) to access items or materials on the desk. When this occurs, the desk needs to be lowered, or an adapted desk may be needed. Some students will have improved movements if the work surface is slanted through use of a slanting tabletop, slant board, or three-ring binder. If the material slides all over the work surface, it will need to be stabilized (e.g., using tape, Dycem, or a rubber shelf liner). It is important to realize that the work surface area includes not only the desk but also the height, slant, and size of work surface areas that students may access using other parts of their body, such as their feet (see Figure 12–2).

Once the work surface is correctly adjusted, the best placement of the materials or items the student is to use will need to be determined on the basis of the student's range of motion. Range of motion refers to the distance the student is able to reach with his hand, foot, mouth stick, or other body part to access materials. This is important to know since materials should be placed within the student's range of motion. One way to assess this is using a grid (see Figure 12–3) or by having the student touch the various areas on the work surface (or other items such as a keyboard or pictures on an augmentative or alternative communication [AAC] device). Once the range of motion is determined, it is important to determine the size and spacing of the target since some students may appear to select two items if they are too close together or too small because of decreased motor coordination or vi-

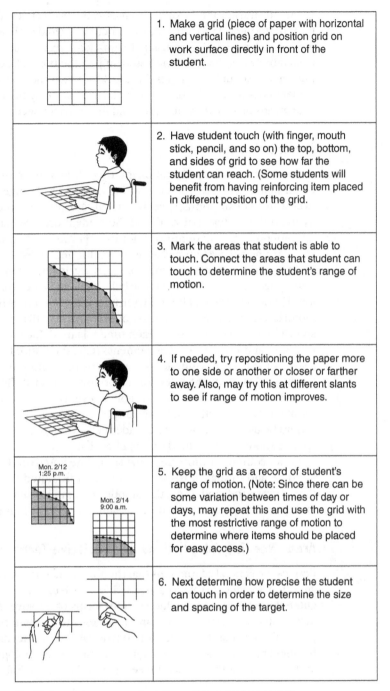

	1. Make a grid (piece of paper with horizontal and vertical lines) and position grid on work surface directly in front of the student.
	2. Have student touch (with finger, mouth stick, pencil, and so on) the top, bottom, and sides of grid to see how far the student can reach. (Some students will benefit from having reinforcing item placed in different position of the grid.
	3. Mark the areas that student is able to touch. Connect the areas that student can touch to determine the student's range of motion.
	4. If needed, try repositioning the paper more to one side or another or closer or farther away. Also, may try this at different slants to see if range of motion improves.
	5. Keep the grid as a record of student's range of motion. (Note: Since there can be some variation between times of day or days, may repeat this and use the grid with the most restrictive range of motion to determine where items should be placed for easy access.)
	6. Next determine how precise the student can touch in order to determine the size and spacing of the target.

FIGURE 12–3   Determining range of motion using a grid approach.

sual impairment. It should also be noted that the slant of the work surface may affect the range of motion and should be adjusted accordingly.

Some students will have atypical movements that are uneven that are uncontrolled, and/or that have extraneous movements. The atypical movements may be slow, lack strength, or be absent. In each of these cases, the student may be unable to manipulate or access the material. It should be specified on the checklist if the student will need to have materials handed to him, if he requires alternate access, or if the materials need to be modified to make them easier for the student to manipulate them.

Some students will experience fatigue or lack endurance as they manipulate materials or engage in an activity. Sometimes the fatigue can be attributed to their physical disability (e.g.,

Duchenne muscular dystrophy), to medication side effects (e.g., some seizure medications), or from performing a repetitive movement (e.g., a child with severe spastic cerebral palsy activating a switch over and over again). By providing rest breaks, the student may be able to accomplish more work than pushing a student past the point of exhaustion. If rest breaks are needed, the teacher should specify on the checklist when they occur and for how long and what the student does during the break. Other adaptations may be needed as well, such as having alternate means of accessing materials, and these would need to be specified on the checklist.

Communication

Some students with physical or multiple disabilities require augmentative and alternative communication (AAC). Since AAC includes the full range of communication abilities (such as gestures, vocalizations, speech, manual signs, objects, and symbols), it is important to specify the different types of AAC that the student uses (Sevcik & Romski, 2000).

Sometimes the student does not use his AAC system in a reliable fashion because he is still learning the system or has some motor access issues. In order for the teacher to accurately determine what the student knows, it is important for the student to be able to answer questions (e.g., "Which is the ball?" "Which is the word 'cat'?") in the most reliable fashion. This allows the teacher to determine if the student is making learning errors rather than motoric errors. A reliable means of response (RMR) is the most motorically accurate response that is also consistent each time it is used. Ideally, the RMR is also the least fatiguing response and uses isolated movements (e.g., the entire body does not move). For example, a student may be learning to use an electronic communication device for communication, but he makes frequent selection errors because of difficulty with motor planning. When given four choices, the student is able to eye gaze the correct answer, thus avoiding his motor planning difficulties. In this example, eye gaze is the most reliable means of response and should be used when assessing student knowledge. The student's most reliable means of response should be specified on the checklist.

Other communication areas that should be noted on the checklist include those concerning time and format of responses. It should be noted whether the student needs a longer time to respond, and, if so, the amount of time should be specified. If the student uses a multiple-choice format, the optimal number of choices for the student should be given.

Areas Needing Adaptations and Assistive Technology

Besides the general adaptations that the student needs within and outside the classroom, there are often specific adaptations needed for particular academic and functional content areas. Often these adaptations include various forms of assistive technology. For example, some students will need alternate keyboards to access the computer, while others may need an adapted pencil for writing. Examples for functional life management skills include adapted toothbrushes and washmitts. Specific types of assistive technology and adaptations can be specified in this section of the checklist (see chapter 8 for more information on assistive technology).

Class Participation

Sometimes it is difficult to promote student participation in a group setting. This section of the Classroom Adaptation Checklist provides several adaptations that may be necessary to promote participation. This can range from the teacher needing to prompt participation to having the teacher provide questions to the student in advance that can be answered during class time. Some of these adaptations may especially be needed if the student is an AAC user who needs time to prepare or if the student tends to be passive.

Instruction and Curricular Adaptations

The eighth section of this checklist addresses the curricular or instructional adaptations that many students with physical and multiple disabilities will need. Some students with physical, health, or multiple disabilities will be able to access the general education curriculum with appropriate adaptations (such as assistive technology). Other students may need a more simplified curriculum or one at a lower grade level. An adapted curriculum or specialized curriculum (e.g., direct instruction) may also be used. Types of instructional adaptations to support the curriculum may include level of support, difficulty, participation, time, size, input, output, alternative curricular goals, or a substitute curriculum (Gunter, Denny, & Venn, 2000; Gunter, Reffel, Rice, Peterson, & Venn, 2005).

Students also differ as to how they respond to various instructional strategies. It is important to document the type of instructional strategies that are usually most effective for the student. Many students benefit from antecedent prompts, such as highlighting addition signs or putting a mark on a dryer to learn where to turn the knob. Prelearning strategies such as advanced organizers, relationship charts, or graphic organizers may help the student pay attention to the relevant information (Bos & Vaughn, 2002). Response prompts (e.g., time delay or graduated guidance) and learning strategies (e.g., mnemonics or the alphabet song) are also effective strategies for many students (Heller et al., 2000). In some cases, the student does best when the instructional activity is modified (e.g., broken up into shorter segments) or when the material is modified (e.g., symbols added to reading material or lower reading grade level) (Alberto, Taber, & Cihak, 2006). Additional material, such as an extra set of books (e.g., one at school and one at home), may also be needed for students who have endurance or mobility issues. The checklist contains only a few of many types of instructional modifications, so the teacher may need to add the specific strategy under the "other" category.

Assignments and Tests

Assignments and tests often need to be adapted to accommodate the needs of students with physical disabilities. Some students with physical or health disabilities (e.g., myelomeningocele and shunted hydrocephalus or attention-deficit/hyperactivity disorder) have organizational issues and need assignment notebooks and organizational binders to organize their assignments and work (Biddulph, Hess, & Humes, 2006). Because of fatigue or the length of time for completion, some assignments or tests may need to be abbreviated or broken up into shorter segments. Providing extended time is a common adaptation for the same reasons. Difficulty with accessing the materials may require reducing paper-and-pencil tasks, computer use, or alternate responding. Some students will require alternate test and assignment formats or need a helper for assignments. Alternate grading may be needed.

Sensory and Perceptual Adaptations

Many students have vision impairments, hearing loss, deaf-blindness, or perceptual issues that require adaptations. For example, students with vision impairments may need more contrast of materials, special lighting, items with tactile cues (or tactile graphics), verbal descriptions of classroom activities, and low-vision devices. Students with hearing impairments may use hearing aids, sign language interpreters, sound-dampening material on the floors and walls, and an extra set of notes since the student cannot watch an interpreter (or speech read) and take notes at the same time. Other adaptations that are applicable to sensory issues (e.g., preferential seating or organizers) are found earlier in the checklist and should be explained as needed for sensory issues when motor issues are not involved.

Evaluation of Adaptations

After an adaptation is selected and implemented, its effectiveness must be evaluated with systematic observation and data collection. The effectiveness of the adaptation must be verified in the environment in which it is to be used since different environments may result in different adaptations (Baumgart et al., 1982). If a least complex adaptation has not been successful after enough time has been allotted to assess its effectiveness, another type of adaptation in the same category may be selected, or the teacher may need to progress to a more complex adaptation. If many types of adaptations in one discrepancy category have been systematically applied with little success, reexamination of the possible cause of the discrepancy must occur. Another discrepancy category with differing types of adaptations may be selected (see chapter 8 for information on discrepancy analysis).

Once an adaptation is in place, periodic reexamination of the adaptation is needed to determine if the adaptation will be faded (gradually removed) or if the adaptation will remain permanently. As the student's skill changes over time, the adaptation may no longer be needed or may be supplanted by a more appropriate one.

SUMMARY

Students with physical, health, or multiple disabilities typically need adaptations to effectively function in the school setting. Careful selection, documentation, and evaluation of each student's adaptations by the educational team is necessary to ensure successful use of any adaptation. One way to document and track adaptations is through the use of the Classroom Adaptations Checklist for Students with Physical, Health, and Multiple Disabilities. This checklist provides detailed information regarding the student's adaptations and can serve as a valuable tool to communicate among school personnel as well as serve as a discussion point when considering appropriate adaptations to meet a student's individual needs.

REFERENCES

Alberto, P., Taber, T., & Cihak, D. (2006). Students with moderate and severe mental retardation. In R. Colarusso & C. O'Rourke (Eds.), *Special education for all teachers* (4th ed., pp. 347-393). Dubuque, IA: Kendall/Hunt.

Baumgart, D., Brown, L., Pumian, I., Nisbet, J., Seet, M., Nessina, R., et al. (1982). Principle of partial participation and individualized adaptations in educational programs for severely handicapped students. *Journal of the Association for Persons with Severe Handicaps, 7,* 17-27.

Beech, M. (2002). Accommodations and modifications for students with disabilities in vocational education and adult general education. Retrieved December 24, 2006 from http://ezproxy.gsu.edu:2048/login?url=http://search.ebscohost.com/login.aspx?direct=true&db=eric&AN=ED473735&loginpage=Login.asp&site=ehost-live&scope=site

Biddulph, G., Hess, P., & Humes, R. (2006). Help a child with learning challenges be successful in the general education classroom. *Intervention in School and Clinic, 41,* 315-316.

Bos, C., & Vaughn, S. (2002). *Strategies for teaching students with learning and behavior problems* (5th ed.). Boston: Allyn & Bacon.

Bryant, D. P., & Bryant, B. R. (2003). *Assistive technology for people with disabilities.* Boston: Allyn & Bacon.

Garner, J. B., & Campbell, P. H. (1987). Technology for persons with severe disabilities: Practical and ethical considerations. *Journal of Special Education, 21,* 122-132.

Gunter, P. L., Denny, R. K., & Venn, M. L. (2000). Modification of instructional materials and procedures for curricular success of students with emotional and behavioral disorders. *Preventing School Failure, 44,* 116-121.

Gunter, P. L., Reffel, J. M., Rice, C., Peterson, S., & Venn, M. L. (2005). Instructional modifications used by national board-certified teachers. *Preventing School Failure, 49,* 47-52.

Heller, K. W., (2007). Classroom Adaptations Checklist for Students with Physical, Health, or Multiple Disabilities. In K. W. Heller, M. B. Coleman, P. Mezei, & D. Swinehart-Jones (Eds.), *Literacy strategies for students with physical and health disabilities* (4th ed., pp. 1-3). Atlanta: Georgia Bureau for Students with Physical and Mental Disabilities.

Heller, K. W., Forney, P., Alberto, P., Schwartzman, M., & Goeckel, T. (2000). *Meeting physical and health needs of children with disabilities.* Belmont, CA: Wadsworth/Thomson Learning.

Sevcik, R. A., & Romski, M. A. (2000). AAC: More than three decades of growth and development. *ASHS Leader, 5*(19), 5-6.

Wadsworth, D. E., & Knight, D. (1999). Preparing the inclusion classroom for students with special physical and health needs. *Intervention in School and Clinic, 24,* 170-175.

PART

DEGENERATIVE AND TERMINAL DISEASES

13

MUSCULAR DYSTROPHIES

Kathryn Wolff Heller, Peter Mezei, and Morton Schwartzman

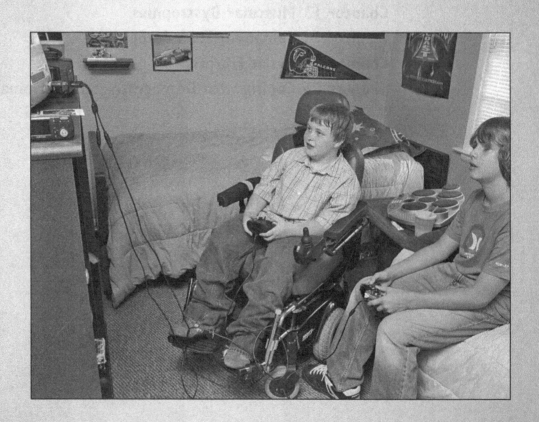

The muscular dystrophies refer to a heterogeneous group of degenerative diseases that result in progressive muscle weakness and a wasting away of the affected muscles. Muscular dystrophies vary as to their etiology, characteristics, and course. Some muscular dystrophies are slowly progressing over decades of life, while others result in a rapid decline and early death. Some types of muscular dystrophy result in being born with severe disability, while other types do not result in symptoms until late in life. The most common type of muscular dystrophy is Duchenne muscular dystrophy (DMD), and it is one of the most common lethal human genetic disorders, affecting approximately 1 in 3,500 live male births (Lovering, Porter, & Bloch, 2005; Van Deutekom & Van Ommen, 2003). Because of the severity of this type of muscular dystrophy and its affect on school-age children, this chapter will primarily concentrate on Duchenne muscular dystrophy, and then there will be another section later in the chapter that will discuss other types of muscular dystrophies.

DESCRIPTION OF MUSCULAR DYSTROPHY

Muscular dystrophy (MD) can be broadly defined as a group of inherited disorders that have progressive muscle weakness due to primary degeneration of muscle fibers (Lovering et al., 2005). So far, there have been over 34 clinical disorders classified as muscular dystrophy, and they have been mapped to over 29 different genetic locations (Dalkilic & Kunkel, 2003; Lovering et al., 2005). For a disorder to be classified as a muscular dystrophy, there are four main criteria: (a) it is a primary **myopathy** (i.e., a disease of the muscle), (b) it is genetically based, (c) it has a progressive course, and (d) there is degeneration and death of the muscle fibers occurring at some stage in the disease process (Behrman, Kleigman, & Jenson, 2004). This definition does not include such diseases as **spinal muscular atrophy** or **cerebral palsy,** which affect primarily the nervous system, in turn affecting the muscles.

ETIOLOGY OF MUSCULAR DYSTROPHY

In 1851, Edward Meryon, an English physician, originally described what is known as Duchenne muscular dystrophy, although the name is derived from a French neurologist, Gullaume Duchenne, who later described this disease in the 1860s. In those early times, this disease was thought to be genetically based, but little information regarding the exact gene responsible for the disease could be determined. It was not until a century after the descriptions of Duchenne muscular dystrophy that the gene defect responsible for Duchenne muscular dystrophy was identified (Ansved, 2001). Since the early 1990s, genes responsible for other forms of muscular dystrophy continue to be identified (Lovering et al., 2005).

Duchenne muscular dystrophy is caused by an abnormal gene on the X chromosome at the Xp21 locus. It is classified as an X-linked recessive disorder, meaning that the defective gene is carried by the mother and may be passed on to her sons (see Figure 13–1). Hence, daughters may be carriers of the defective gene but are rarely affected by the genetic defect. This is not the case in some other types of muscular dystrophy in which both girls and boys can acquire the disease because of the involvement of different defective genes (e.g., a defective gene on chromosome 19q results in myotonic muscular dystrophy, which has an autosomal dominant trait).

There are some variations in the inheritance pattern of Duchenne muscular dystrophy. Although it is X-linked recessive, approximately 30% of the affected children are new mutations in which the mother was not a carrier (Behrman et al., 2004). Although girls are usually symptomless carriers of Duchenne muscular dystrophy, some girls have been found to have mild symptoms to the full expression of the disease. This may be attributed to an inactivation of one of the X chromosomes that occurs in such rare situations as having the defective gene for Duchenne muscular dystrophy and also having Turner syndrome (in which a girl has only one full X chromosome present). Other rare chromosomal events can also result in girls having Duchenne muscular dystrophy (Herring, 2002).

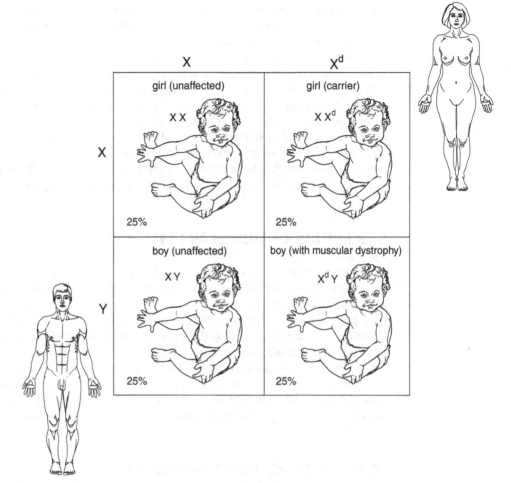

FIGURE 13–1 Inheritance pattern for Duchenne muscular dystrophy.

Genetic (progressive (handwritten margin note)

Absence of dystrophin = degeneration (handwritten margin note)

DYNAMICS OF MUSCULAR DYSTROPHY

Approximately 50% of the body is composed of muscles. These muscles can be classified into three major types: skeletal, cardiac, and smooth. Skeletal muscles are muscles that can be voluntarily moved (e.g., bicep muscle in the arm). The second type of muscle is the cardiac (heart) muscle. Both skeletal and cardiac muscles are striated, which refers to the transverse striations in the muscle that can be seen under a microscope. The third muscle type is smooth muscles; these include all the involuntary muscles except the heart (e.g., muscle layers of the blood vessels and intestines). Smooth muscles do not have transverse striations and are classified as unstriated muscles. The type of muscular dystrophy determines which types of muscles are affected. The striated muscles are often the only muscles affected in most of the muscular dystrophies, including Duchenne muscular dystrophy.

Duchenne muscular dystrophy is classified as one of the dystrophin-deficient dystrophies. The defective gene found in Duchenne muscular dystrophy results in an absence of dystrophin, which is a protein in the muscle cell's membrane (Beers, Porter, Jones, Kaplan, & Berkwits, 2006). When dystrophin is absent or nonfunctional, the muscle degenerates. Unlike healthy people who can regenerate muscle cells, the cells do not regenerate or regenerate ineffectively in individuals with muscular dystrophy. As the disease progresses, fat cells replace the muscle cells, resulting in loss of muscle structure and function (Lovering et al., 2005).

proximal muscles are most severely affected (handwritten)

Ages & Musc. Dys. (handwritten)

As compa...   ...nenne muscular dystrophy typically has   ...cular strength, endurance, and
function.   ...f one's body) are most severely
affected. ...   ...elvis area and progresses to the
shoulder   ...ning affected. Finally, the respiratory mu...   ...dysfunctional and fail to function prop...

Infants a...

Infants ar...   ...ic and early motor milestones
(e.g., rolli...   ...thin the normal time frame or
are slight...   ...t between 2 and 5 years of age
with the   ...difficulty walking, running, or
climbing   ...o fall, and toe walking may be
present b...

Weakn... of a hip waddling gait known as a Trendelenberg gait. In a Trendelenberg gait, the child brings the weight of the upper body over the leg that is on the ground so that the trunk sways back and forth over each limb while walking (Herring, 2002). Weakness in the gluteal, trunk, and hip muscles also results in the child standing with the pelvis tilting forward and an abnormal anterior curve of the lower back (lordosis). The child may lock his knees to prevent buckling due to leg weakness.

Two major signs of muscular dystrophy develop at this time, known as **Gower's sign** and **pseudohypertrophy**. Gower's sign, also known as Gower's maneuver, is seen when the child with Duchenne muscular dystrophy tries to stand up from sitting on the floor. Typically he must begin by placing his hands and feet on the floor with the feet placed widely apart. He then uses his hands to push up on his knees and thighs to get into a full standing position. This occurs due to muscle weakness (see Figure 13-2). Gower's sign is not usually present until around 3 years of age but has occurred as early as 15 months of age (Herring, 2002). Pseudo-hypertrophy is derived from the words *pseudo,* meaning "false," and *hypertrophy* meaning "enlarged." It refers to an enlarged calf that appears as a muscular leg but is actually the result of the infiltration of fat cells and connective and fibrous tissues into the muscle tissue.

Ages 5 to 10

Between the ages of 5 and 10, muscle weakness continues to progress with a steady decline in strength. Children will have increasing difficulty walking. Contractures will continue to develop (especially affecting the ankles, knees, hips, and elbows over time). **Scoliosis** (lateral curvature of the spine) may begin to appear because of the weakening of the back muscles.

As the child enters school, questions arise about intellectual functioning. The majority of children with Duchenne muscular dystrophy have IQs in the lower range of normal, with the mean full-scale IQ score being around 80.2 (Cotton, Voudouris, & Greenwood, 2001). Only 20% to 35% have IQs in the intellectual disability range (Behrman et al., 2004; Cotton et al., 2001). It is speculated that impairments in intellectual ability may be a result of the biological effect of the missing dystrophin in the brain (Hinton, DeVivo, Fee, Goldstein, & Stern, 2004). However, some children have IQs in the high normal to gifted range. In addition, approximately a third of the boys with Duchenne muscular dystrophy experience learning disabilities. It is important to note that the intellectual and learning ability of the child does not change as the disease progresses.

Ages 10 to 12

Between the ages of 10 to 12, most children will lose the ability to walk and need a manual wheelchair. Up to this point, they may have had orthopedic intervention to promote walking (e.g., bracing, physical therapy or Achilles' tendon lengthening), but this treatment only

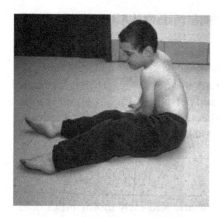

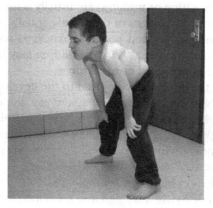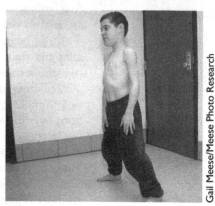

FIGURE 13–2 Gower's sign.

2 major signs

delays the eventual loss of ambulation (walking). It should be noted that children differ as to when they lose walking ability, with some children as young as 7 years of age requiring a wheelchair. Maintaining the ability to walk for as long as possible is important, even it if is only for an hour a day, since scoliosis often becomes rapidly progressive once a wheelchair is used on a permanent basis (Behrman et al., 2004).

Teenage Years and Beyond

Throughout the teenage years, muscle weakness continues to progress. As the arms become weaker, the adolescent will often need to move from a manual wheelchair to a power wheelchair. The muscles of the fingers usually retain enough strength to allow the person to continue to use a pencil, keyboard, and food utensils. However, arm strength will eventually decline to the point that the child cannot raise his hand high enough to bring food to his mouth and will require assistance with eating and drinking. Fatigue will also increase. As time passes, the muscles of the neck, shoulder, and back lose strength, and it will be difficult for the adolescent to hold his head upright. The voice may take on a "breathy," nasal quality. Scoliosis my continue to progress, and other orthopedic problems, such as **hip subluxation** or **hip dislocation,** may occur in some individuals (Chan, Galasko, & Delaney, 2001) (see chapter 9 for more information on hip displacement).

what muscles are affected?

As the disease progresses, severe heart and lung changes occur. Since the cardiac muscle is a striated muscle, changes occur within the heart muscle's tissue. By the age of 15, more than 50% of adolescents will have cardiomyopathy (heart disease) (Ames, Hayes, & Crawford, 2005). Because of the progressive weakening of the respiratory muscles for breathing and diminished ability to cough, the adolescent becomes more prone to respiratory infections. In addition, adolescents can develop restrictive lung disease (which is characterized by reduced lung volume secondary to weakness of the respiratory muscles and commonly occurs in most neuromuscular diseases, often compounded by spine deformity). Over time, respiratory failure can ensue because of the effect of respiratory muscle weakness on lung volume, changes to the mechanical properties of the lungs (e.g., decrease elasticity of the lungs), changes in mechanisms of the chest, changes in the ventilator drive to breathe, and an impaired coughing mechanism. Most adolescents with Duchenne muscular dystrophy will die from heart or respiratory failure, most often as a result of lung infections or cardiomyopathy in their late teens or early 20s.

DETECTION OF DUCHENNE MUSCULAR DYSTROPY

The first signs and symptoms of muscular dystrophy may initially be dismissed as clumsiness or lack of coordination. When muscular dystrophy is suspected, a tentative diagnosis can be made on the basis of the person's history, family history, clinical findings, and lab tests. Often, the first test is to determine the amount of creatine kinase (CK) in the blood. Creatine kinase is an enzyme that is released when muscle cells are damaged, either through normal use or through abnormal wasting, as in muscular dystrophy. Creatine kinase levels above 400 are abnormal, but people with muscular dystrophy sometimes have levels in the thousands. Some of the further diagnostics that may be conducted are electromyographic studies (which test the electrical properties of the skeletal muscles), muscle biopsy, and genetic testing. An electrocardiagram (EKG) or echocardiogram may be utilized to test heart function.

The first genetic tests available were for dystrophin-based dystrophies such as Duchenne muscular dystrophy (Lovering et al., 2005). Later, tests for other forms of muscular dystrophy were developed that tested for the mutated genes. For parents who are known carriers of the disease (or who have the disease), a prenatal diagnosis may be made (through amniocentesis, chorionic villus sampling, or fetal blood sampling).

TREATMENT OF DUCHENNE MUSCULAR DYSTROPHY

There is no specific medical treatment and no cure for muscular dystrophy at this time. The early goal of treatment is to help the child walk and be functional for as long as possible. When walking is no longer possible, the goal is to manage the complications and symptoms of muscular dystrophy as they arise and to promote optimum physical independence and a good quality of life. Treatment efforts are typically carried out through a team approach that frequently includes the student, family, medical personnel, therapists, teachers, assistive technology specialists, dieticians, psychologists, and others.

Orthopedic Management

Physical and Occupational Therapies

Children with Duchenne muscular dystrophy usually receive physical therapy to prolong mobility and stretch the muscles to prevent or minimize contractures (Herring, 2002). Braces and orthotics may be prescribed either to assist with walking or for positioning to prevent contractures. Short leg braces are common (e.g., ankle-foot orthosis (AFO)). Instruction in wheelchair use and transfers will also ensue.

The occupational therapist can suggest techniques and tools to compensate for the loss of dexterity and strength. For example, modified handles and adapted utensils may be used to assist with academics skills as well as daily living skills. The physical therapist and occupational therapist will need to work together to determine compensatory positioning to allow for optimum access to various material. Many other assistive devices may be implemented by the physical or occupational therapist to assist with mobility, academics, and daily living skills, such as eating, dressing, or using the restroom (see chapter 8).

Surgery of the Lower Limbs in Duchenne Muscular Dystrophy	
Early extensive ambulatory approach	Release at hip, hamstrings, heel cords, and posterior tibialis transfer before onset of significant contractures.
Moderate ambulatory approach	Rarely includes hip abductor releases, and surgery is performed while child is still able to walk but is experiencing increasing difficulty.
Minimum ambulatory approach	Correction of only the equinus? (foot) contractures.
Rehabilitative approach	Operative intervention after child ceases walking, but surgery is pursued with goal of reestablishing ambulation.
Palliative approach	Surgical correction of equinovarus (foot deformity in which the heel is elevated and turned outward from the midline of the body). Surgery occurs after full-time wheelchair use has begun, with goal of pain relief and improved ability to wear shoes.

FIGURE 13–3 Shapiro and Specht's classification of contracture surgery of the lower limbs in Duchenne muscular dystrophy.

Source. Used with permission from Herring (2002).

Surgery

Surgery is often performed to improve walking and prolong the ability to walk. Surgery on the legs can include releasing contractures at the hip, hamstrings, heel cord, and/or other parts of the leg. However, there is variability as to when this is done and to what extent. As seen in Figure 13–3, surgery may range from releasing early contractures at multiple locations before the contractures become severe (early extensive ambulatory approach) to correcting only foot contractures from shortening of the heel cord (minimum ambulatory approach). Surgery is not usually performed to correct contractures that may develop in the hand, elbow, or shoulder.

Scoliosis, with or without a **kyphosis**, can become a very serious, life-shortening problem in many cases of Duchenne muscular dystrophy (Alman, Raza, & Biggar, 2004). Scoliosis is usually progressive in this population and may result in curves greater than 90 degrees. A spinal curve of this magnitude can interfere with sitting, lead to skin breakdown, and affect heart and lung function. Therefore, aggressive strategies, such as spinal surgery (e.g., fusion of vertebrae and rod placement), may be performed at a much lower degree of curvature to prevent progression of spinal deformity and maintain the highest quality of life (Harper, Ambler, & Edge, 2004) (see chapter 9 for more information on scoliosis).

Exercise and Diet

Exercise is important for individual's with Duchenne muscular dystrophy since inactivity can be detrimental and accelerate the individual's decline. However, the wrong type of exercise or too strenuous exercise can be harmful. Present research suggests that muscle training for Duchenne should begin early in the disease process but should be limited to low-resistance training to reduce muscle tissue damage and cardiopulmonary fatigue (Ansved, 2001). Exercise programs will also assist in maintaining strength and preventing contractures for as long as possible. Swimming is an excellent form of exercise since individuals with Duchenne are more buoyant in the pool because of decreases in muscle cells and increases in fat cells. For all daily activities, not just exercise regimens, care should be taken to avoid overactivity, fatigue, and strenuous exercise to avoid muscle damage.

A dietician may be needed to assist with providing a balanced diet, and care providers may need to assist the person to make healthy food choices. There is a tendency for obesity, which needs to be controlled. Obesity may decrease the amount of time a person with muscular dystrophy will be able to walk and increase the onset and progression of scoliosis. Gastrostomy tubes are also occasionally used for feeding to maintain nutrition (see chapter 20 for more information on gastrostomy feeding).

Medications

Pharmacological methods are sometimes used to treat Duchenne muscular dystrophy. Several corticosteroids, including prednisone and deflazacort, have been reported to slow the decline in muscle strength and perhaps delay the onset and severity of scoliosis (Alman et al., 2004). However, there is no consensus on the long-term effectiveness of these medications, especially since the complications of these medications (e.g., weight gain and osteoporosis) may offset their advantages. In addition, greater weakness may occur over the long term than would have appeared with the natural progression of the disease (Behrman et al., 2004). Other medications are currently being investigated.

Medications may also be prescribed to combat lung and heart problems. Since there is an increased incidence of respiratory infections in Duchenne muscular dystrophy, medications will be prescribed to combat infections that are bacterial. Universal precaution techniques that prevent the spread of infection are important to implement to decrease the risk of infection to the person with muscular dystrophy. Depending on the type of heart condition that may develop from the muscular dystrophy, medication may be prescribed to decrease extra heartbeats (arrhythmias) or increase the effective contractions of the heart.

Respiratory Treatment and Ventilator Management

When respiratory problems and/or respiratory infections are present, the child may receive chest physiotherapy to help clear the secretions. Chest physiotherapy can involve placing the child in different positions (known as postural drainage) to allow gravity to assist with moving the secretions out of the lung. While that is being done, a trained individual performs a hand-administered therapy known as clapping (or cupping), in which a cupped hand repeatedly slaps the chest and back to loosen respiratory secretions so that they can be coughed out. This may also be done with a machine or Vest clearance system, which consists of an inflatable vest that is worn for a short time each day that rapidly inflates and deflates (5–20 times per second), loosening the mucus from the lungs (see chapter 15 for a picture of a Vest clearance system). Some individuals will have breathing exercises that need to be done on a periodic basis and may use an assisted cough machine (e.g., a machine in which a face mask is held over the mouth and nose and blows a few seconds of positive pressure, followed by negative pressure that sucks the secretions out) (see chapter 14 for a picture of an assisted cough machine).

In the later stages of Duchenne muscular dystrophy, typically years after the person has become dependent on a wheelchair for mobility, respiratory function becomes very impaired from weakening diaphragm and respiratory muscles, resulting in decreased inspiratory and expiratory force (force of breathing in and out). At this point, breathing cannot continue unassisted. Mechanical ventilation may be chosen to prolong the life of the adolescent or adult with Duchenne muscular dystrophy (Gibson, 2001). This may begin by providing noninvasive nasal ventilation at night and progress to the use of a tracheostomy to deliver mechanical ventilation 24 hours a day.

In Denmark, for example, almost all adults with Duchenne muscular dystrophy who are candidates for mechanical ventilation decide to have mechanical ventilation. This has resulted in a whole generation of adult men living with Duchenne muscular dystrophy using mechanical ventilation. One study (Rahbek et al., 2005) examined these Danish adults (ages 18–42) and found that, overall, they were severely limited in their ability to move the hands and fingers or sit unsupported, and they often experienced physical pain. However, they continued to operate their wheelchairs, write and play on the computer, live in their own residence, and go out in the community and reported having an excellent quality of life.

Denmark is a generous welfare society in which personal assistants (provided 24 hours a day), adapted vans, housing, and other supports are available. In other countries, such as the United States, controversy exists regarding the benefits of prolonged life versus quality of life. The decision to use or to forgo assisted ventilation can be one of the most difficult decisions for individuals with muscular dystrophy and their families, and these personal decisions need to be respected.

Gene Therapy and Other Innovative Treatments

Gene therapies to treat Duchenne muscular dystrophy are on the horizon. However, the size and complexity of the dystrophin gene has been a challenge, resulting in difficulties in deriving a replacement or clone of dystrophin that can be injected into the body or placed inside a virus (e.g., adeno-associated virus) to be delivered to the muscles (Athanasopoulos, Graham, Foster, & Dickson, 2004; Klunkel, 2005). Problems in delivering the dystrophin gene exist not only because of its size but also because of unwelcome immunological responses, cellular toxicity, and the need to deliver the new gene to numerous sites in the body in order to be effective (Van Deutekom & Van Ommen, 2003). However, advances in gene therapy make this a likely treatment in the near future.

Other treatments for Duchenne muscular dystrophy are also in the experimental stages. For example, transplantation (by injection) of normal immature muscle cells (myoblasts) are being attempted to provide the missing dystrophin protein and replace the fatty tissue. Rejection of the myoblasts has been problematic, but new methods of myoblast transplantation in mice are looking promising (Camirand, Rousseau, Ducharme, Rothstein, & Tremblay, 2004).

DESCRIPTION OF OTHER FORMS OF MUSCULAR DYSTROPHY

Although Duchenne muscular dystrophy is the most common type of muscular dystrophy found in the schools, there are several other types of muscular dystrophy that may occur in school-age children. The following provides a brief overview of some of the more common types that appear in children and adolescents. As with Duchenne muscular dystrophy, there is no cure, but symptoms are treated with much the same interventions (e.g., physical therapy, diet, and exercise).

Becker Muscular Dystrophy

Becker muscular dystrophy is a dystrophin-deficient dystrophy just like Duchenne muscular dystrophy. Unlike Duchenne muscular dystrophy, in which no dystrophin is present, Becker muscular dystrophy has small amounts of dystrophin present, or the dystrophin is in an abnormal, less effective form (Ansved, 2001). Becker muscular dystrophy typically has the same progression as Duchenne muscular dystrophy, beginning with weakness in the pelvis and legs. However, Becker muscular dystrophy is milder than Duchenne muscular dystrophy and begins much later.

The onset of Becker muscular dystrophy is typically between the age of 5 and 15 but is known to appear as late as the fourth decade of life (Lovering et al., 2005). It can be mild or severe, depending on the amount of dystrophin present (i.e., the greater amount of dystrophin, the less severe the symptoms). In a severe form of Becker muscular dystrophy, ambulation may be lost in adolescence, while in the more mild form, individuals may be able to walk until they are in their 40s. Contractures and severe scoliosis do not typically occur in this type of muscular dystrophy. Depending on the severity of the muscular dystrophy, individuals with Becker muscular dystrophy may die in their 30s or 40s or sometimes live a normal life span. Cardiomyopathy (heart disease) and arrhythmias (abnormal heart rhythms) occur more commonly in Becker muscular dystrophy.

Congenital Muscular Dystrophy

Although all forms of muscular dystrophy are congenital, the term *congenital muscular dystrophy* refers to a group of several distinct disorders in which there are a common set of symptoms present at birth. Unlike other muscular dystrophies, these children are born with severe involvement, but the symptoms progress very slowly or not at all. Although the characteristics and course differ depending on the exact type of congenital muscular dystrophy, infants are generally born with severe proximal weakness (weakness of muscles closest to the middle, or the trunk, of the body) and hypotonia (low tone). They often have arthrogryposis (multiple contractures at birth; see chapter 10) due to the fetus lacking the strength to move in the uterus. Intelligence is usually normal. However, in one variety of congenital muscular dystrophy that occurs primarily in Japan (Fukuyama-type congenital muscular dystrophy), there is accompanying malformation of the brain, intellectual disability, seizures, and early death (Girgenrath, Dominov, Kostek, & Miller, 2004).

Emery-Dreifuss Muscular Dystrophy (Scapulohumeral or Scapuloperoneal Muscular Dystrophy)

This form of muscular dystrophy usually begins in middle childhood and has a slow progression. The name "scapulohumeral" or "scapuloperoneal" muscular dystrophy indicates the location of muscle weakness that appears in the areas of the shoulder (scapula), upper arm (humerus), and outer leg (peroneal). Most individuals retain the ability to walk and have normal intelligence. There are two different genetic forms: X-linked and autosomal dominant (Lovering et al., 2005). While some individuals with Emery-Dreifuss muscular dystrophy may live late into adulthood, life expectancy is often tied to cardiac involvement (Wessely, Seidl, & Schomig, 2005).

Facioscapulohumeral Muscular Dystrophy (Landouzy-Dejerine Disease)

Facioscapulohumeral muscular dystrophy encompasses a group of disorders that vary in severity. Muscle weakness begins in the face (facio), shoulders (scapulo), and upper arms (humeral) (Finsterer, Stollberger, & Meng, 2005). Facial weakness results in the mouth appearing puckered because of the protrusion of the lips. The individual may be unable to whistle, drink from a straw, lift the arms up, or close his eyes completely. The disorder may progress to the pelvic and leg area. There is a wide range of severity, and several systems can be affected, resulting in such problems as cardiac, cognitive, visual, and auditory impairments. Most forms are slowly progressive with the first signs occurring in early adolescence and death occurring at a normal or near normal age (Lovering et al., 2005).

Limb-Girdle Muscular Dystrophy

Limb-girdle muscular dystrophy is a heterogeneous group of diseases that can be autosomal dominant (known as type 1 LGMD) or autosomal recessive (known as type 2 LGMD). These are further divided into six subtypes of type I LGMD and 10 subtypes of type 2 LGMD (Laval & Bushby, 2004). Limb-girdle muscular dystrophy results in weakness in the muscles of the shoulder and pelvic area and spreads to other muscles. Depending on the type of limb-girdle muscular dystrophy, symptoms can emerge at birth to middle age. Symptoms range in severity depending on the type, with most having a mild progression with a loss of ambulation occurring about 20 years after the onset of the disease. However, type 2 LGMD is usually more severe, with a few of the subtypes resembling Duchenne muscular dystrophy (Lovering et al., 2005).

Myotonic Muscular Dystrophy (Steinert's Disease)

Myotonic muscular dystrophy is the second most common type of muscular dystrophy found in North America and the type most commonly found in adults (Behrman et al., 2004; Ranum & Day, 2004). In this type of muscular dystrophy, muscle weakness is accompanied by myotonia, which is a slow relaxation of a muscle after contraction, hence its name "myotonic" muscular dystrophy. Although it may be present in infancy or early childhood, symptoms may not occur until young adulthood (e.g., 20 years) or beyond.

2nd Most Common Found in Adults in N America (handwritten margin note)

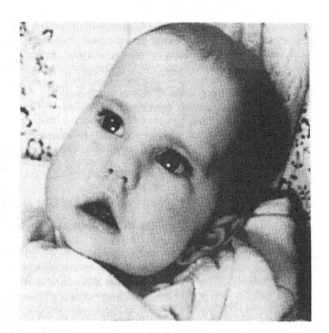

FIGURE 13–4 Facial weakness and inverted-V-shaped upper lip are characteristics of myotonic muscular dystrophy, even in infancy, as seen in this 8-month-old girl.

Source. From *Nelson textbook of pediatrics,* 17th edition, Behrman, R.E., Kleigman, R. M., & Jenson, H.B., p. 2065, Copyright Elsevier/Saunders (2004).

Myotonic muscular dystrophy affects the striated muscles (voluntary muscles and the heart) and the smooth muscles of the gastrointestinal tract. This results in slow emptying of the stomach and often causes constipation. Lack of bowel control may be present as well. There also tends to be multiple system involvement, including endocrine abnormalities (e.g., diabetes), cataracts, cardiac abnormalities, immunological deficiencies, and other abnormalities.

Individuals with myotonic muscular dystrophy have characteristic inverted-V-shaped upper lips, thin cheeks, and facial weakness that may even be present during infancy or develop later (see Figure 13–4). Dropping eyelids (ptosis) may also be present. Speech may be poorly articulated because of the involvement of the face and tongue, and there may be some difficulty with swallowing. Weakness initially occurs in the lower part of the arms and legs and spreads to the shoulder and neck muscles. Gower's sign is usually present, and most individuals do not lose the ability to walk. About half of those with myotonic muscular dystrophy have average or above-average intelligence (Behrman et al., 2004).

Clinically, there are two distinct types of myotonic muscular dystrophy: myotonic dystrophy type 1 (DM1) is associated with a genetic abnormality on chromosome 19 and myotonic dystrophy type 2 (DM2) with an abnormality on chromosome 3 (Ranum & Day, 2004). Both MD1 and MD2 affect the heart, endocrine system, and eye similarly. In terms of muscle weakness, DM1 may sometimes be indistinguishable from DM2. However, the more classic form of DM1 usually has more distal weakness (i.e., muscles away from the trunk of the body), whereas DM2 usually has more proximal weakness (i.e., muscles close to the trunk) (Lovering et al., 2005). DM1 also has a severe neonatal form with many infants dying in their first year of life (Ranum & Day, 2004).

EDUCATIONAL IMPLICATIONS OF MUSCULAR DYSTROPHY

Students with degenerative diseases such as muscular dystrophy have multiple, unique, and evolving needs in the educational environment. As the student's physical abilities decrease, the educator must make increasing adaptations to allow for physical participation in academic and nonacademic activities. The teacher must also be ready to provide emotional support to a student with muscular dystrophy and cope emotionally with having a student with a degenerative disorder.

The teacher must also deal with other people's attitudes. For example, some people think that having a child with a terminal disease go to school, do homework, and expend energy on academic work is unkind when the child may not have long to live. The teacher may have to explain that school is a great normalizing factor for all children. One of the major goals of treatment is to normalize life and prolong living. To have a child quit school may give the impression that all is lost (Simmons, 1994). A caring attitude and collaborative effort will help the teacher make a positive school experience for the student.

Meeting Physical and Sensory Needs

It is important that the teacher have a thorough understanding of the type of muscular dystrophy and its typical progression. Duchenne muscular dystrophy usually has a fairly rapid progression as compared to Becker muscular dystrophy, and the rate of progression can vary greatly for two individuals with the same form. This knowledge will assist the teacher, together with the parents and the team, to make realistic goals for the student as well as proactively plan for the future physical needs of the student.

To adequately meet the physical needs of a student with muscular dystrophy, the teacher and team members must carefully monitor the student's physical ability and be alert for changes in mobility, motor ability, fatigue, and stamina that occur as the disease progresses. The Classroom Adaptation Checklist for Students with Physical, Health, or Multiple Disabilities can be a very useful tool to providing baseline information as to the student's needs (see chapter 12). Specific information should be monitored in such areas as mobility (e.g., walks independently, uses furniture for support, wears braces, needs assistance walking, uses a manual wheelchair, or uses a power wheelchair), going up steps (e.g., independent, uses railing, needs assistance, or needs elevator), going down steps, and chair use (e.g., independent or needs assistance sitting down, getting up, or moving chair to desk). Since arm and hand involvement occurs in many types of muscular dystrophy, teachers should also monitor the student's ability to use writing utensils, type on a keyboard, and manipulate classroom material. An anecdotal record form should be completed by teachers and other team members on a periodic basis (and when a problem is detected) to document and inform others of areas that may need further adaptations (see Figure 13-5).

Students with muscular dystrophy will need adaptations and assistive technology. Depending on the type of muscular dystrophy, adaptations and assistive technology may need to be updated frequently as the condition worsens. If a problem is found on close monitoring of the student, the AT Analysis of Task and Student Performance can help guide the team through a process of examining the task requirements and student performance of the task to determine possible adaptations or assistive technology solutions (see chapter 8).

When the student uses a wheelchair, there are several factors to consider regarding the location of the student in the room and making the items in the room accessible. The student and any accessible furniture (e.g., wheelchair accessible desk) should be located in an area of the room, allowing for interaction with the teacher and fellow students. The student will need to be able to see maps, displays, material on the whiteboard, and/or other items used for demonstration. As the disease progresses, the student will lose his ability to reposition himself in his chair, turn his head, or reposition the chair, so viewing of these materials may be difficult when something is blocking his way. In locating a proper position in the classroom, attention must be given to the possibility of having to remove the student quickly in case of an emergency. When the student uses a resource room for some of his instruction, the room may be set up near an emergency exit when a student is in a very advanced stage of the disease.

Physical fatigue and decreased endurance can be problematic for students with muscular dystrophy (especially Duchenne muscular dystrophy). The teacher should be aware of this potential problem and make any needed adaptations (e.g., shorter tests or shorter writing and homework assignments). As the condition progresses, students often need to take rest breaks and lie down. It is not unusual for special educators to have a cot or special table in their room for this purpose. Students may eventually require a modified school schedule that includes a shortened day.

NAME: _____ DATE: _____

TEACHER: _____

Please give progress report. Stress difficulties as well as assets.

_____ Getting about and being mobile (in the classroom, halls, stairs, cafeteria, restroom, etc.)

_____

_____

_____

_____ Ease with using special equipment (braces, writing devices, eating utensils)

_____

_____

_____

_____ Classroom skills (writing skills, energy level, participation, need for adaptive equipment)

_____

_____

_____

_____ Academic skills (in comparison with expectations, need for special evaluations or ancillary help, such as physical therapy, occupational therapy, speech therapy, psychological testing)

_____

_____

_____

_____ Special notations: (include whether or not a conference is indicated)

_____

_____

_____

FIGURE 13–5 Anecdotal record to be completed by school personnel on periodic basis and as needed for students with degenerative diseases.

Source. Used with permission and adapted from Fithian (1984, pp. 209–212).

Some types of muscular dystrophy have sensory involvement. Students with cataracts that have not been removed or other visual impairments or hearing loss will need appropriate adaptations (see chapter 11 for more information on sensory loss).

Students with muscular dystrophy often die as a result of respiratory infections and respiratory failure. It is imperative that the teacher, staff, and students use good infection control in the classroom (see chapter 23 for universal precaution procedures). Students and staff with minor respiratory infections should be careful not to spread their infection and should avoid direct contact with the student with advanced muscular dystrophy. Students who are sick should be sent home. The teacher should be alert for wheezing, coughing, sniffling, or fever on the part of the student with muscular dystrophy and should report this to the parents or school nurse. If there are difficulties breathing, emergency procedures should be initiated on the basis of a predetermined emergency plan.

Meeting Communication Needs

Verbal communication is usually not problematic with most individuals with muscular dystrophy. In myotonic muscular dystrophy, there can be articulation problems, and in advanced Duchenne muscular dystrophy, the voice can sound weak and breathy. However, these problems are usually not so severe that augmentative communication is needed.

Much communication takes place through body language and other nonvocal forms, so students with advanced Duchenne muscular dystrophy or other forms affecting facial muscles may be misunderstood. In Duchenne muscular dystrophy, facial muscles may become dysfunctional and show a flat affect that can be interpreted as a lack of interest or awareness. Teachers and others should be aware that a lack of expression does not necessarily mean that the student is not interested.

Meeting Learning Needs

As previously discussed, students have a range of intellectual ability from intellectual disabilities to normal or gifted abilities. However, the majority of children with Duchenne muscular dystrophy have IQs in the lower range of normal, with the mean full-scale IQ score being around 80.2 (Cotton et al., 2001), and only 20% to 35% have IQs in the intellectual disability range (Behrman et al., 2004; Cotton et al., 2001). In addition, a greater impairment in verbal areas has been found, such as expressive verbal abilities as well as short-term memory deficits, which include poor verbal working memory (Hinton, DeVivo, Nereo, Goldstein, & Stern, 2000; Leibowitz & Dubowitz, 1981). Reading, writing, and calculating learning disabilities have also been found (D'Angelo & Bresolin, 2006; Dorman, Desnoyers, & D'Avignon, 1988; Sollee, Latham, Kindlon, & Bresnan, 1985). Teachers need to use systematic teaching strategies to assist these students to reach their potential. It is important that teachers provide appropriate, systematic instructional strategies to meet these students' needs and remember that their intellectual ability is not linked to the severity of the muscular dystrophy, nor does it decline as the disease progresses.

Students may fail to perform tasks not because they are unable but because of other factors. In some instances, academic performance may be affected when adaptations are not put into place in a timely fashion. Fatigue can also affect performance. Also, if the student is physically not feeling well, he will have more difficulty learning. Absences due to respiratory infections such as pneumonia or doctor's and outside therapy appointments may also cause the student to fall behind. Additional instruction as well as homebound services and summer school may be needed.

Meeting Daily Living Needs

As the disease progresses, adaptations will also be needed in daily living skills to allow the student to be as independent as possible in such areas as eating, dressing, and toileting. As arm function declines, eating may become difficult and require the student to use his elbows for support or use adapted arm supports. At this point, chewing and swallowing muscles may become affected, so the teacher should observe if food needs to be cut in smaller pieces or if a straw is needed. Later, a mobile arm support (device that assists with arm movement) or a mechanical feeder may assist the student to feed himself, or he may need to be fed by another person. Others may be needed to assist with setup, retrieval from the lunch line, and cleanup. Peer helpers should be used instead of adult personnel to the maximum extent appropriate.

In the area of dressing, clothes that are easy to put on and take off may be selected by the parent. Adaptive clothing with Velcro may be created or purchased, and adaptive devices that easily button shirts are possibilities. The teacher and occupational therapist should serve as a resource for the parent about these options.

Most students with muscular dystrophy usually do not have any incontinence (loss of bowel or bladder control) problems. However, as the student weakens, he will eventually need assistance transferring from the wheelchair to the toilet. Transfers of heavy students can also be facilitated with manual or powered lifts to reduce injury to the student and staff. Another option is to use a urinal. Restroom assistance can often be embarrassing for the student and result in his not asking for assistance. The student may also drink minimal fluids in order to avoid using the restroom. This can result in being uncomfortable throughout the day, having problems with constipation, and possibly becoming dehydrated. The teacher must be sensitive to the student's situation, and whenever possible, the student's preferences should be taken into consideration. An arrangement needs to be worked out where someone with whom the student is comfortable will assist him in toileting needs in a dignified, private, and supportive manner.

Meeting Behavioral and Social Needs

There are several identified stages of disability for an individual with muscular dystrophy (especially the Duchenne type). These are the early and late walking phases, wheelchair use, and dying/death (Hsu & Lewis, 1981), and perspectives may vary in each stage. In the early and late walking phase, there may be a great deal of concern regarding the student falling and injuring himself. At what point the student should begin using a wheelchair can become a sensitive matter in which the student plays an active role in the decision making along with the team. When the student moves on to a wheelchair, responses may range from relief that the student will not be falling to despair that the student is declining. The practical and emotional concerns regarding how the student will carry out daily living skills and the rigors of academics will emerge as weakness continues. Ways of fostering independence using adaptations become important. Finally, as the student is rapidly declining, intensification of issues regarding death and preparing for dying come to the forefront (Gossler, 1987).

A range of behaviors may be exhibited by the student with a terminal illness as well as his family, friends, and school personnel. It is common for those who are dying or who know of someone with a terminal disease to go through the Kübler-Ross's (1969) five stages of death and dying: denial, anger, bargaining, depression, and acceptance. Sometimes a broader range of responses may occur. No matter what the response, it is common for there to be some denial. Denial occurs when something actually perceived is treated as if it did not exist (Gossler, 1987). Denial can be healthy in that it prevents incapacitating anxiety and depression but can be detrimental if it prevents individuals from acting on something that needs immediate attention. Denial should be perceived as a beneficial reaction unless it negatively interferes with the student's functioning or creates negative responses to those interacting with the student. Counseling is recommended when this occurs (and for any emotional or behavioral disorder, such as clinical depression).

It is important that the teacher let the student know that she or he is available if there is anything that the student would like to discuss. Sometimes a student with muscular dystrophy wants a supportive listener to discuss his feelings or problems he is encountering (ranging from difficulties using the water fountain to concerns about dying). Teachers can be invaluable in providing support and brainstorming solutions to minor problems. Often all that is needed is for the teacher to be a supportive listener. If the conversation turns to the area of death, the teacher needs to keep in mind that the student may perceive death differently from the teacher because of developmental levels, cultural differences, or religious beliefs. Teachers should not make assumptions of what the child thinks or believes but should listen carefully to the student and provide support. (For more information, see chapter 16 on coping with degenerative and terminal illness.)

SUMMARY

The muscular dystrophies refers to a group of degenerative diseases that have progressive muscle weakness and a wasting away of the muscles. There are several types of muscular dystrophy, with Duchenne muscular dystrophy being the most common in children, and it is also one of the most severe types of muscular dystrophy. This type of muscular dystrophy first occurs with leg and pelvis weakness that eventually progresses to severe weakness of the legs, trunk, arms, and neck. How rapidly this disease progresses can vary, although many individuals with Duchenne muscular dystrophy will die in their late teens or 20s from respiratory or cardiac complications. Other forms of muscular dystrophy progress differently and often involve different muscle weakness patterns. Although no effective treatment is in place at present, great strides are being made in finding a cure, and there are several treatments aimed at increasing the quality of life. The educator needs to be knowledgeable about the disease in order to effectively meet the student's needs and make appropriate adaptations. Providing emotional support is especially crucial.

VIGNETTE   Bob's Story

Bob is a 16-year-old boy with Duchenne muscular dystrophy. He has lost most mobility in his legs and uses a power wheelchair. The muscles in his torso and arms are weak. He needs to take a rest break during the day because of fatigue. Other adaptations that have been implemented include shorter lessons, use of a computer instead of handwriting his assignments, and a modified exercise program. A peer takes notes for Bob and helps him get his lunch tray. He is involved in a chess club after school and has several supportive and understanding friends. Bob is well informed regarding his disease. He had an older brother with Duchenne muscular dystrophy who died of respiratory complications 5 years ago. However, Bob did become very upset in biology class when he learned that the heart was a muscle. In his next class period with his special education teacher, he began to cry. What should the special education teacher do?

REFERENCES

Alman, B., Raza, N., & Biggar, D. (2004). Steroid treatments and the development of scoliosis in males with Duchenne muscular dystrophy. *Journal of Bone and Joint Surgery, 86-A*, 519-524.

Ames, W., Hayes, J., & Crawford, M. (2005). The role of corticosteroids in Duchenne muscular dystrophy: A review for the anesthetist. *Pediatric Anesthesia, 15*, 3-8.

Ansved, T. (2001). Muscle training in muscular dystrophies. *Acta Physiolojica Scandinavica, 171*, 359-366.

Athanasopoulos, T., Graham, I. R., Foster, H., & Dickson, G. (2004). Recombinant adeno-associated viral (rAAV) vectors as therapeutic tools for Duchenne muscular dystrophy (DMD). *Gene Therapy, 11*, S109-121.

Beers, M. H., Porter, R. S., Jones, T. V., Kaplan, J. L., & Berkwits, M. (2006). *The Merck manual of diagnosis and therapy* (18th ed.). Whitehouse Station, NJ: Merck & Co.

Behrman, R. E., Kleigman, R. M., & Jenson, H. B. (2004). *Nelson textbook of pediatrics* (17th ed.). Philadelphia: W. B. Saunders.

Camirand, G., Rousseau, J., Ducharme, M., Rothstein, D. M., & Tremblay, J. P. (2004). Novel Duchenne muscular dystrophy treatment through myoblast transplantation tolerance with anti-CD45RB, anti-CD154 and mixed chimerism. *American Journal of Transplantation, 4*, 1255-1265.

Chan, K. G., Galasko, C. S., & Delaney, C. (2001). Hip subluxation and dislocation in Duchenne muscular dystrophy. *Journal of Pediatric Orthopaedics B, 10*, 219-225.

Cotton, S., Voudouris, N. J., & Greenwood, K. M. (2001). Intelligence an Duchenne muscular dystrophy: Full-scale, verbal and performance intelligence quotient. *Developmental Medicine and Child Neurology, 43*, 497-501.

D'Angelo, M. G., & Bresolin, N. (2006). Cognitive impairment in neuromuscular disorders. *Muscle and Nerve, 34*, 16-33.

Dalkilic, I., & Kunkel, L. M. (2003). Muscular dystrophies: gene to pathogenesis. *Current Opinion in Genetic Development, 13*, 231-238.

Dorman, C., Desnoyers, H., & D'Avignon, J. (1988). Language and learning disorders in older boys with Duchenne muscular dystrophy. *Developmental Medicine and Child Neurology, 30*, 316-327.

Finsterer, J., Stollberger, C., & Meng, G. (2005). Cardiac involvement of facioscapulohumeral muscular dystrophy. *Cardiology, 103*, 81-83.

Fithian, J. (Ed.). (1984). *Understanding the child with a chronic illness in the classroom.* Phoenix, AZ: Oryx Press.

Gibson, B. (2001). Long-term ventilation for patients with Duchenne muscular dystrophy. *Ethics in Cardiopulmonary Medicine, 131,* 940-946.

Girgenrath, M., Dominov, J., Kostek, C., & Miller, J. (2004). Inhibition of apoptosis improves outcome in a model of congenital muscular dystrophy. *Journal of Clinical Investigation, 114,* 1635-1639.

Gossler, S. (1987). A look at anticipatory grief: What is healthy denial. In L. Charash, R. Lovelace, S. Wolf, A. Kutsher, D. Royce, & C. Leach (Eds.). Realities in coping with progressive neuromuscular diseases. New York: Charles Press Publishing.

Harper, C., Ambler, G., & Edge, G. (2004). The prognostic value of pre-operative predictive forced vital capacity in corrective spinal surgery for Duchenne muscular dystrophy. *Anesthesia, 59,* 1160-1162.

Heller, K. W., Alberto, P. A., Forney, P. E., & Schwartzman, M. N. (1996). *Understanding physical, sensory, and health impairments.* Pacific Grove, CA: Brookes/Cole.

Herring, J. A. (2002). *Tachdjian's pediatric orthopaedics.* (3rd ed.). Philadelphia: W. B. Saunders.

Hinton, V., DeVivo, D., Fee, R., Goldstein, E., & Stern, Y. (2004). Investigating of poor academic achievement in children with Duchenne muscular dystrophy. *Learning Disability Research and Practice, 19,* 146-154.

Hinton, V., DeVivo, D., Nereo, N., Goldstein, E., & Stern, Y. (2000). Poor verbal working memory across intellectual level in boys with Duchenne dystrophy. *Neurology, 54,* 2127-2132.

Hsu, J., & Lewis, J. (1981). Challenges in the care of the retarded child with Duchenne muscular dystrophy. *Orthopedic Clinics of North America, 12,* 72-82.

Klunkel, L. (2005). Cloning the DMD gene. *American Journal of Human Genetics, 76,* 205-214.

Kübler-Ross, E. (1969). *On death and dying.* New York: Macmillan.

Laval, S., & Bushby, K. (2004). Limb-girdle muscular dystrophy—From genetics to molecular pathology. *Neuropathology and Applied Neurobiology, 30,* 91-105.

Leibowitz, D., & Dubowitz, V. (1981). Intellect and behavior in Duchenne muscular dystrophy. *Developmental Medicine and Child Neurology, 23,* 557-590.

Lovering, R., Porter, N., & Bloch, R. (2005). The muscle dystrophies: From genes to therapies. *Physical Therapy, 85,* 1372-1388.

Rahbek, J., Werge, B., Madsen, A., Marquardt, J., Steffensen, B. F., & Jeppesen, J. (2005). Adult life with Duchenne muscular dystrophy: Observations among an emerging and unforeseen patient population. *Pediatric Rehabilitation, 8,* 17-28.

Ranum, L., & Day, J. (2004). Myotonic dystrophy: RNA pathogenesis comes into focus. *American Journal of Human Genetics, 74,* 793-804.

Simmons, J. (1994). Practical issues. In A. Goldman (Ed.), *Care of the dying child* (pp. 115-131). Oxford: Oxford University Press.

Sollee, N. D., Latham. E. E., Kindlon, D. J., & Bresnan, M. J. (1985). Neuropsychological impairment in Duchenne muscular dystrophy. *Neuropsychology, 7,* 486-496.

Van Deutekom, J., & Van Ommen, G. J. (2003). Advances in Duchenne muscular dystrophy gene therapy. *Nature Reviews: Genetics, 4,* 774-783.

Wessely, R., Seidl, S., & Schomig, A. (2005). Cardiac involvement in Emery-Dreifuss muscular dystrophy. *Clinical Genetics, 67,* 220-223.

CHAPTER 14

SPINAL MUSCULAR ATROPHIES

Alison Stafford, Kathryn Wolff Heller, and Morton Schwartzman

Over 100 years ago, Werdnig and Hoffmann described a condition characterized by pelvic weakness, progressive muscle weakness and atrophy (wasting away), and death by age 7 (Hardart & Truog, 2003; Wirth, 2002). This condition is presently identified as spinal muscular atrophy (SMA). Since that time, several different types of spinal muscular atrophies have been identified. It has become the second most common autosomal recessive disorders in humans (after cystic fibrosis). It has an incidence of about 1 in every 6,000 to 10,000 newborns (Nicole, Diaz, Frugier, & Melki, 2002) and a carrier frequency of about 1 in 35 people to 1 in 50 people. It is the most frequent genetic cause of infant death (Monani, 2005).

The most prevalent forms of the disease are the proximal spinal muscular atrophies. Others are so rare in comparison that the term *spinal muscular atrophy* is generally used when referring to only the proximal forms of the disease. Because of the prevalence of proximal spinal muscular atrophy and their affecting children rather than adults, this chapter will concentrate on the proximal spinal muscular atrophies.

DESCRIPTION OF SPINAL MUSCULAR ATROPHY

The spinal muscular atrophies are a group of degenerative diseases characterized by progressive weakening and atrophy of the skeletal muscles due to degeneration of motor **neurons** (nerve cells). There are over a dozen different types and variant forms of spinal muscular atrophy that affect different muscle groups. There are three main types of proximal spinal muscular atrophies that affect children: Type I, Type II, and Type III.

Although these spinal muscular atrophies have different characteristics and courses, they all meet the following criteria: (a) they are primary neuropathies (i.e., affect the nerves first); (b) they are genetically based; (c) they have a progressive, degenerative course; and (d) the motor neurons in the spinal cord are affected (or, in a rare variant form, the motor neurons in the brain stem are affected) (Behrman, Kleigman, & Jenson, 2004). This definition does not include the muscular dystrophies that are primary myopathies (affecting the muscles first) or cerebral palsy that affects the upper motor neurons in the motor cortex of the brain (or the basal ganglia or the cerebellum).

ETIOLOGY OF SPINAL MUSCULAR ATROPHY

The spinal muscular atrophies are genetically based diseases. Depending on the type of spinal muscular atrophy, there are different genes and chromosomes responsible for their occurrence. All the proximal spinal muscular atrophies found in children are caused by a mutation of the survival of motor neuron 1 (SMN1) gene on the short arm of chromosome 5q (more specifically at 5q 11.2–13.3).

SMN1 normally produces the SMN protein, which is an essential protein for cell survival. The defect in SMN1 results in no functional SMN protein from this gene. However, there is a second, almost identical gene known as SMN2, but it is unable to completely compensate for the loss of the SMN protein (Eggert, Chari, Laggerbauer, & Fischer, 2006). The SMN2 is thought to be responsible for the severity or type of proximal muscular atrophy (Monani, 2005; Wirth, Brichta, & Hahnen, 2006). For example, in one study, the majority of individuals with Type I spinal muscular atrophy had one to two copies of SMN2, individuals with Type II had three copies, and individuals with Type III had three to four copies of the gene (Feldkotter, Schwarzer, Wirth, Wienker, & Wirth, 2002). The more copies of SMN2 gene, the more SMN protein is present and the milder the disease. Despite the increased replications of SMN2, the SMN protein level continues to be below normal in individuals with spinal muscular atrophy. Low levels of the SMN protein have a detrimental effect on the motor neurons in the spinal cord, causing cell death (Monani, 2005).

The inheritance pattern for these proximal spinal muscular atrophies is autosomal recessive. Autosomal inheritance indicates that the gene is not sex linked and hence can be passed down from either the mother or the father to either a son or a daughter. When the gene is autosomal recessive, both parents must be carriers and pass on the affected gene for a child to be affected. Other types of spinal muscular atrophy are autosomal dominant, meaning that only one parent passes on the affected gene to his or her offspring, and that parent would also be affected by spinal muscular atrophy. There are also some rare forms that are X linked.

DYNAMICS OF SPINAL MUSCULAR ATROPHY

Proximal spinal muscular atrophies affect the anterior horn cells of the spinal cord. The anterior horn cells are the part of the spinal cord that send motor information to the muscles. Motor information travels from the primary motor cortex area of the brain down the spinal cord. When the impulses reach the anterior horn cells, they leave the spinal cord along the spinal nerves and travel through the peripheral nervous system. When the impulse reaches the muscle via the peripheral nerve, the muscle moves (contracts) (see Figure 14–1). Sensory information, on the other hand, travels in the reverse direction along the sensory nerves of the peripheral system until it reaches the spinal cord, where the impulses enter the posterior horn cells. From there, sensory information travels up the spinal cord to the somatosensory cortex.

As a primary neuropathy affecting the motor cells of the spinal cord, spinal muscular atrophy negatively impacts the function of the spinal cord. Since part of the function of the spinal cord is to carry messages to various parts of the body, including the muscles, the degeneration of the anterior horn cells in the spinal cord blocks motor information from reaching the muscles. The individual then is unable voluntarily to move the corresponding

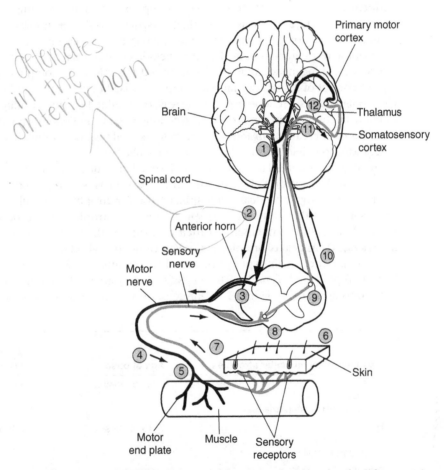

deteriorates in the anterior horn

FIGURE 14–1 Anatomical picture of the motor signal leaving the primary motor cortex (in the brain) via the upper motor neurons and crossing to opposite side (1) and traveling down the spinal cord (2) where it synapses on the lower motor neuron (3) in the anterior horn cells of the spinal cord which transmits the signal out to the muscles (4 & 5). Sensory signals (of pain) travel from the skin (6) to the spinal cord (8 & 9), up the spinal cord (10), and to the somatosensory cortex of the brain (11).

muscles, and weakening, **hypotonia** (low muscle tone or flaccidity), and **atrophy** (wasting away) of the muscles occurs (Wirth, 2002).

Unlike muscular dystrophy, a primary myopathy in which muscle cells are affected, the muscles of an individual with spinal muscular atrophy are unable to react because the messages from the brain are no longer being transmitted to them through the nerves. There is no actual change in the muscle tissue; however, muscle tissue will waste away because of disuse (atrophy), resulting in hypotonia in the affected muscles (Brzustowicz et al., 1990). The progressive loss of physical function due to the lack of physical activity can result in joint **contractures** (Wang, Ju, Chen, Lo, & Jong, 2004).

Spinal muscular atrophy affects only the anterior horn cells, which carry motor information, and not the posterior horn cells, which carry sensory information. Because of this, spinal muscular atrophy does not cause sensory loss. Thus, while children with spinal muscular atrophy experience progressive loss of muscle use, they retain full sensation in the affected areas.

CHARACTERISTICS/COURSE OF PROXIMAL SPINAL MUSCULAR ATROPHY

The proximal spinal muscular atrophies represent several forms of the disease that are characterized by a progressive hypotonia, weakness, and muscle atrophy. The **proximal** muscles, those muscles closest to the center of the body, are affected more than the **distal** muscles. Orthopedic problems are common, such as contractures, **scoliosis**, **hip subluxation**, or **hip dislocation** (see chapter 9 on scoliosis and hip displacement). Although there is virtually no heart involvement, individuals with spinal muscular atrophy are at risk of respiratory involvement (El-Matary, Kotagiri, Cameron, & Peart, 2004). Respiratory involvement can affect several areas of the respiratory system. This can include (a) abnormal oral-motor function and coordination, resulting in swallowing difficulties and possible aspiration pneumonia risk; (b) inadequate control of respiratory muscles with decreased cough reflex and decreased ability to clear pulmonary secretions from the airway; (c) retained sections leading to infections and pulmonary compromise; and (d) decreased lung volume and poor inspiratory and expiratory force (force of breathing in and out) due to weakened respiratory muscles, restrictive lung disease, and/or possible deformed thorax (from scoliosis).

Intelligence is normal in individuals with spinal muscular atrophy and is not affected by the progressive deterioration of the disease. In the past, it has been reported that the IQ tended to be higher in many individuals with spinal muscular atrophy, especially the verbal IQ. It has been suggested that children with spinal muscular atrophy tend to develop effective and useful strategies to compensate for their disability by the acquisition of cognitive skills and knowledge (D'Angelo & Bresolin, 2006; Von Gontard et al., 2002).

There are three main types of proximal spinal muscular atrophy that occur in children: Type I, Type II, and Type III. This classification system is based on the age at which the symptoms appear (see Figure 14–2). Age of onset, while not an absolute predictor, plays a

Proximal spinal muscular atrophies	Age of onset	Approximate life expectancy

Type I
    Acute infantile
    Werdnig-Hoffmann disease
	Birth–6 months	Early infancy–2 years

Type II
    Intermediate
    Chronic infantile
	7–18 months	> 2 years

Type III
    Juvenile
    Kugelberg-Welander
	> 18 months	Near normal to normal life span

FIGURE 14–2 Three types of proximal spinal muscular atrophies found in children.

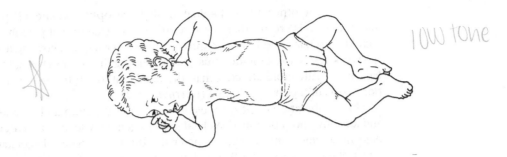

low tone

FIGURE 14–3 Typical frog-leg position of child with Type I spinal muscular atrophy.

role in the rate of progression, severity of symptoms, and life expectancy. A younger age of onset generally indicates a more rapid progression and more severe symptoms. Each of these are described in more detail next.

Type I: Acute Infantile Spinal Muscular Atrophy (Werdnig-Hoffmann)

Acute infantile spinal muscular atrophy, also known as Werdnig-Hoffmann disease, is the most severe of the proximal spinal muscular atrophies, with rapid degeneration and early presentation of symptoms. While some cases of acute infantile spinal muscular atrophy begin during the prenatal period (with less movement than normal), almost all show evidence of muscle weakness between 3 and 6 months of age (Jablonka & Sendtner, 2003; Nicole et al., 2002).

The baby with Type I spinal muscular atrophy is characterized by hypotonia, generalized weakness, absent deep reflexes, and thin muscle mass. The infant is often inactive with movement of the extremities generally being limited to the hands and feet (Wessel, 1989). The infant often assumes a distinctive frog-leg position (see Figure 14–3). These infants usually do not achieve independent head control or the ability to maintain a sitting position without outside support (Merlini et al., 1989). In addition, infants with Type I spinal muscular atrophy generally have an underdeveloped chest wall and lungs, weak cough, and weak cry. This may lead to respiratory difficulties. They also have tongue involvement and excessive drooling and swallowing difficulties, in turn causing feeding difficulties relating to choking and possible aspiration pneumonia (Hardart & Truog, 2003). **Tube feeding** is sometimes necessary.

Children with Type I spinal muscular atrophy typically do not have a long life expectancy because of the severity of symptoms and rate of progression. Rapidly weakening muscles eventually affect respiratory functioning. Degeneration of neurons at the brain stem (bulbar dysfunction) causes swallowing difficulties and contributes to respiratory complications (e.g., aspiration pneumonia). Bulbar dysfunction and respiratory complications typically result in death prior to two years of age, making spinal muscular atrophy Type I the leading cause of infant death from inherited conditions (Hardart & Trug, 2003; Sumner, et al., 2003; Wang et al., 2007). In some instances, survival of infants with spinal muscular atrophy Type I may be prolonged with the use of mechanical ventilation, although there is an ethical debate regarding the use of mechanical ventilation for infants with Type I due to quality of life issues (Bach, Saltstein, Sinquee, Weaver, & Komaroff, 2007).

Type II: Intermediate (or Chronic Infantile) Spinal Muscular Atrophy

Intermediate spinal muscular atrophy (also referred to as chronic infantile spinal muscular atrophy, or Type II spinal muscular atrophy) has a slower rate of progression than Type I spinal muscular atrophy. Onset of Type II spinal muscular atrophy is generally between 7 and 18 months (Wang et al., 2007). Because of the slightly later onset, infants with Type II spinal muscular atrophy may develop the ability to sit but usually cannot stand or walk without assistance (Jablonka & Sendtner, 2003; Wang et al., 2004). Some children will have poor weight gain due to swallowing difficulties (Wang et al., 2007).

As with the other types of spinal muscular atrophy, weakness is progressive, and proximal weakness is greater than distal weakness. An example of proximal weakness would be a child who has good muscle control in his or her hands, allowing a spoon to be held, but has weakness in the shoulder muscles, preventing the spoon's being lifted to the mouth. The legs are usually more affected than the hands, although the hands may have a fine tremor (known as minipolymyoclonus) (Herring, 2002).

The combination of progressive loss of motor function and increased muscle weakness and atrophy with continued skeletal growth generally leads to the development of skeletal deformities and contractures (Wang et al., 2004). Two types of skeletal deformities that can affect children with Type II spinal muscular atrophy are scoliosis and kyphosis (a forward curvature of the upper part of the spine, i.e., humpback). Hip subluxation or dislocation and contractures can also occur. These skeletal deformities can further impair general functioning ability (see chapter 9).

The course for infants diagnosed with Type II spinal muscular atrophy is variable and difficult to predict. The progression of the disease may be slow and steady over a period of years, or the child may experience long periods of stability. Either of these courses may be interrupted by periods of rapid deterioration. Prognosis depends largely on the degree of respiratory involvement due to increased susceptibility to respiratory infection resulting from weakened respiratory muscles (due to hypotonia) and difficulty coughing and clearing respiratory secretions. Life expectancy can range from 2 to 30 years of age (Eggert et al., 2006).

Type III: Juvenile Spinal Muscular Atrophy (Kugelberg-Welander)

Type III spinal muscular atrophy, also known as Kugelberg-Welander disease, is the mildest form of the spinal muscular atrophies affecting children. The onset of these symptoms occurs after 18 months of age (Wang et al., 2007). Most children can stand and walk but may have difficulty running or climbing stairs. Some individuals lose the ability to walk in childhood, while other individuals remain able to walk until their mid-30s, at which time they generally require the use of a wheelchair (Wirth, 2002). A fine tremor of the hands may also occur in Type III. While mild cases of scoliosis are common in individuals still able to walk, once an individual loses the ability to walk, scoliosis can become a severe problem. Many individuals have near normal or normal life spans, depending on respiratory complications and lung disease.

This type of spinal muscular atrophy has been mistaken for muscular dystrophy, particularly in boys. This is because some of the symptoms can be similar (e.g., weakness). Also, about 25% of individuals with Type III develop **pseudohypertrophy** of calf muscles instead of atrophy, which appears similar to the pseudohypertrophy found in Duchenne muscular dystrophy (Behrman et al., 2004; Herring, 2002). A thorough evaluation will distinguish between these conditions.

Other Forms of Spinal Muscular Atrophy

There are many other forms of spinal muscular atrophy. For example, there is a Type IV spinal muscular atrophy that has an adult onset and a Type 0 that refers to an embryonic lethal form of spinal muscular atrophy (Eggert et al., 2006). **Arthrogryposis** (multiple contractures at birth) is present in X-linked infantile spinal muscular atrophy and congenital spinal muscular atrophy (see chapter 10 for more information on arthrogryposis). In addition, there are several different types of spinal muscular atrophy that have more distal muscle weakness (e.g., distal spinal muscular atrophy, distal spinal muscular atrophy—IV, and facioscapulohumeral muscular atrophy). Each of these types of spinal muscular atrophy differs as to onset, rate of progression, and involvement of different muscles.

DETECTION OF SPINAL MUSCULAR ATROPHY

Depending on the type of spinal muscular atrophy, this disease may escape detection for some time or be misdiagnosed because of the range in age of onset and severity of symptoms associated with the different types of the disease. The more severe the spinal muscular atrophy (i.e., Type I), the earlier the diagnosis is typically made.

In most cases of Type I spinal muscular atrophy, infants appear at birth with severe hypotonia and generalized weakness, with about one-third of mothers noticing a change in strength of fetal movements during the third trimester. Children affected with Types II and III spinal muscular atrophy are usually suspected of having some type of problem because of the failure to reach major motor milestones (Wirth, 2002).

A diagnosis is usually made by genetic testing for the SMN gene through a blood test in addition to the child's history and physical exam. Other tests may be performed, especially when the genetic test is negative. Electromyography, nerve conduction tests, and muscle biopsies may be performed that assess the health of the muscles and/or the nerves controlling the muscles. Certain blood tests may also be performed (e.g., creatine kinase (CK or CPK), which indicates damage to the heart, brain, or skeletal muscles, or antiganglioside antibodies, which indicate the presence of certain neurological disorders).

Although carriers of the disease do not have any symptoms, a family history and testing may have made a parent aware of the carrier state. A diagnosis of spinal muscular atrophy can be made prenatally through amniocentesis (in which amniotic fluid is examined) or chorionic villus sampling (a procedure in which placental [chronic] tissue is extracted and examined).

TREATMENT OF PROXIMAL SPINAL MUSCULAR ATROPHY

At this time, there is no specific treatment and no cure for any of the spinal muscular atrophies. Medications that are prescribed tend to be more supportive in nature, although experiments are under way to try to increase muscle strength through drug use (Caruso et al., 1995). Currently, treatment is centered on minimizing the symptoms of the disease and providing appropriate adaptations to maintain a good quality of life. Treatment focuses on orthopedic management, respiratory management, nutritional care, and research for new innovative treatments.

Orthopedic Management

Children with proximal spinal muscular atrophy will often receive physical therapy and occupational therapy. Physical therapy will help maintain a normal range of motion and slow the development of contractures. For children who are unable to sit or stand, adaptive equipment may be used, such as adapted chairs or standers. Depending on the type of spinal muscular atrophy, some children are able to walk independently or need a brace, walker, or wheelchair. A physical therapist will provide training in their use. Occupational therapy may also be used to assist the student in accessing academic materials and daily living tasks.

Surgical intervention may be needed for some children with spinal muscular atrophy. Although contractures develop, surgical release of contractures is controversial since it does not usually improve the function of the nonambulatory (nonwalking) child, and the contractures will reoccur. When the child is a wheelchair user, the development of hip subluxation or dislocation is common. Although surgery is also controversial for hip subluxation or dislocation, the hip displacement may result in pain, and surgery may be able to relieve this.

Scoliosis can have a deleterious effect on sitting posture and respiratory function, especially when it is severe. In these cases, surgery may occur if the child is able to tolerate sitting. The use of rod insertion and/or spinal fusion may be recommended (see chapter 9 for more information on scoliosis and hip displacement). However, spinal surgery may result in a loss of motor function and the loss of ability to perform activities of daily living that the child was able to do before surgery. The rigid and upright spine makes it difficult for the child with proximal spinal muscular atrophy to bring the hands up against gravity to eat, drink, and perform hygiene tasks because of the proximal weakness in the upper arms (Herring, 2002). If surgery is performed, an occupational therapist is needed to provide appropriate adaptive equipment along with physical therapy.

Respiratory Management

Early respiratory management is important to limit pulmonary complications of the progressively worsening course of respiratory insufficiency and improve the quality of life. Weakness in the muscles located between the ribs that aid in inhalation (intercostal muscles) are primarily responsible for respiratory insufficiency in most types of spinal muscular atrophy. A few rare types affect the functioning of the diaphragm.

Frequent respiratory infections can develop, resulting in blockage of the air passages. When an air passage is blocked, the air in the small air sacs of the lungs (aleveoli) is absorbed into the bloodstream, and with the inability to receive more air because of the blockage, the air sacs shrink or collapse (known as **atelectasis**). This can lead to pneumonia, decreased air exchange, and possibly pulmonary failure. The respiratory infections are often treated with antibiotics and respiratory medications (such as bronchodilators like Albuterol) to avoid pulmonary complications.

Periodic chest percussion, assisted cough machines, and inflation of the lungs with positive pressure can limit the risk of pulmonary congestion and atelectasis (Ioos, Leclair-Richard, Mrad, Barois, & Esournet-Mathiaud, 2004). Chest percussion is performed as part of chest physiotherapy in which the child is placed in specific positions to allow for drainage of respiratory secretions (known as postural drainage) and there is tapping (percussion) over the lung area with a cupped hand (or mechanical device) to loosen the respiratory secretions (Wessel, 1989). Sometimes a Vest clearance system is used in which an inflatable vest is worn for a short time each day that rapidly inflates and deflates (5–20 times per second), loosening the mucus from the lungs so that it can be coughed out (see chapter 15 on cystic fibrosis for a picture of the Vest). Assisted cough machines are portable devices that alternately blow positive pressure into the airway alternating with negative pressure (vacuum that sucks out the air) to assist in coughing and secretion removal (see Figure 14–4). Inflation of the lungs can occur with noninvasive inspiratory aids in which a person inhales through a device via a mouthpiece (or nasal oral interface) and air is delivered under pressure. This is known as intermittent positive pressure ventilation (IPPV). Some individuals may need an inspiratory aid only at night (e.g., nasal nocturnal ventilation) because of inadequate oxygenation. The use of a mechanical ventilator can extend the life of a child with spinal muscular atrophy, but there is great variability in the practice of using this form of respiratory support (Hardart & Truog, 2003).

Nutritional Care

Nutrition can be an issue when sufficient food is not being eaten. This is due to the loss of motor function, swallowing difficulties, and poor oral feeding. This may be addressed by

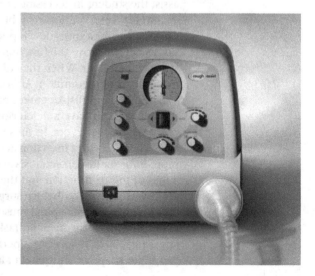

FIGURE 14–4 An assisted cough device used to help a person cough up secretions.

Source. 2007 © Image courtesy of Respironics, Inc. and its affiliates. All rights reserved.

changing food consistency, such as a semisolid diet and thickened liquids. Oral intake will also be optimized. When the child can no longer take enough food orally, nutritional supplementation is needed. This is usually done using gastrostomy tube feedings (Wang et al., 2007) (see chapter 20 for more information on tube feeding).

Gene Therapy and Other Innovative Treatments

Although there is not currently a cure for spinal muscular atrophy, there have been tremendous advances in understanding the genetics and molecular biology of these diseases, making it likely that an effective treatment or cure will be found (Winkeller, 2005). Several experimental and pharmacological treatments are being tried to regulate the SMN2 gene to increase the amount of SMN protein. For example, drugs such as valporic acid or 4-phenylbutyrate have been shown to increase SMN2-derived RNA and protein levels (Wirth et al., 2006). In addition, several studies are under way investigating gene therapy (e.g., gene splicing correction and gene transfer systems). Studies using stem cell replacement therapy to restore neurons following degeneration have also looked promising (e.g., delayed disease progression, spared motor neurons, and increased life span in animals) (Corti et al., 2006).

EDUCATIONAL IMPLICATIONS OF SPINAL MUSCULAR ATROPHY

Students with degenerative diseases, such as spinal muscular atrophy, have evolving needs because of their declining physical ability. As the student's condition deteriorates, adaptations will be needed so that the student may continue to participate in as many activities as possible. The teacher must also be prepared to provide emotional support. Many of the educational needs of a student with spinal muscular atrophy are similar to those needed by a student with muscular dystrophy (see chapter 13).

Meeting Physical and Sensory Needs

In order to appropriately meet the physical needs of the student with spinal muscular atrophy, the teacher must have an understanding of the particular type of spinal muscular atrophy. Rate of progression will depend on the type of spinal muscular atrophy as well as the child's individual physiological reaction to the disease. Students with Type II spinal muscular atrophy will usually physically deteriorate at a much more rapid rate and will therefore require more adaptations sooner than a student with Type III spinal muscular atrophy. The Classroom Adaptation Checklist can be a useful tool in providing specific areas to monitor (see chapter 12). Since different teachers may observe varying problems as time goes on, using an anecdotal record form, such as the one found in chapter 13 on the muscular dystrophies, can also be helpful.

The student should be encouraged to participate in physical activity for as long as possible, adapting activities as necessary. Because individuals with Type III spinal muscular atrophy generally do not lose the ability to walk until adulthood, these students will still be able to walk when they reach school age, and fewer adaptations will be needed for participation in physical activities. However, since weakness will be greater in the legs than in the arms, activities involving strenuous use of the legs will be the first in need of adaptations, possibly placing the student in a less physically active role.

Assistive technology will be needed to allow the student access to academic and nonacademic activities. As the students' arms become more affected, students will need academic tools (e.g., keyboard or lab equipment) positioned within their range of motion and, over time, may need the use of assistive technology to promote access to the equipment or tasks (e.g., alternate keyboard, scanned books, or projection of microscope image). Nonacademic areas (e.g., lunch and restroom use) will also require assistive technology and adaptations (e.g., switch-controlled mechanical self-feeder or assistance with transfers to the toilet) (see chapters 8 and 12 for more information).

Meeting Communication Needs

Communication is usually not severely affected in spinal muscular atrophy. However, if the individual is placed on a ventilator to provide respiratory support, he or she may need an alternative form of communication. Writing messages is often physically taxing, so a communication device may be needed.

Meeting Learning Needs

Students with spinal muscular atrophy are generally of average or above-average intelligence (Hardart & Truog, 2003). Because of the progressive nature of the disease, some teachers may expect a decrease in cognitive ability to accompany the decrease in motor function and consequently have a low expectation of the student's academic ability. This is not the case. Teachers should have a good understanding of the disease process so that unrealistic expectations, either too high or too low, can be avoided.

Some students may fail to perform well because of factors other than academic ability (see chapter 2). In some instances, this can occur when adaptations are not put into place in a timely manner. For example, over time, the student may lose the ability to quickly take notes and need notes to be provided. An unobservant teacher may miss the student's declining ability to take notes until it affects academic performance. Close observation and checking in with the student are needed to keep up with the numerous adaptations that will be needed. Fatigue can also affect performance as well as feeling poorly. Absences due to respiratory infections, outside therapy, or surgery can cause the student to fall behind, and further instruction will be needed to help the student remain on grade level.

Meeting Daily Living Needs

As the student's muscle weakness progresses and functioning level deteriorates, assistance may be necessary in the areas of feeding, dressing, and toileting. The teacher should carefully monitor these aspects of the student's day so as to intervene when necessary while still allowing the student as much independence as possible.

At mealtimes, the teacher should be aware of any modifications that may become necessary, such as support for elbows or arms or the need for food to be cut up for the student. The need for adaptive equipment, such as adaptive plates, utensils, or cups, should also be monitored. Assistance from an occupational and/or physical therapist will be necessary to evaluate needs and suggest adaptations.

Parents and teachers need to establish a good line of communication that will allow them to keep each other informed of any changes in such areas as dressing and toileting. For example, if the student begins having difficulty with removing or putting on clothing, he or she may be embarrassed to ask for help and be unable to take off a jacket at school, resulting in being uncomfortably warm throughout the day. In another example, loss of motor function may result in the inability to transfer from wheelchair to toilet. In the home setting, parents may begin providing assistance in this area, or the student may be able to make adaptations. In the school setting, the student may be embarrassed to ask for help and instead limit drinking to avoid going to the bathroom. This can cause the student discomfort, thus affecting school work, and is not healthy for the student. The teacher may be totally unaware of these problems unless good communication occurs between the home and school settings. It should be noted that toileting is a particularly sensitive situation, and the teacher needs to be discrete when planning to meet this need so as to maintain the student's privacy, dignity, and respect.

Meeting Behavioral and Social Needs

The teacher should also be aware of the student's emotional needs. Because spinal muscular atrophy does not affect the intelligence of the child, he or she will be fully aware of what is happening to his or her body. The teacher should be available to the student and check in with the student on a regular basis. Problems may emerge that the student and teacher can solve together. In some instances, the student may just need someone to talk to and the teacher may fulfill this role. The school counselor can also be very helpful, but the student usually selects whom he or she is most comfortable talking with about various issues dealing with having a degenerative and terminal disease (see chapter 16 for more information on coping with degenerative or terminal illnesses). Sometimes professional counseling is needed.

SUMMARY

Spinal muscular atrophies are a group of degenerative neuromuscular diseases affecting infants to adults. They are characterized by progressive hypotonia, weakness, and muscle atrophy due to a degeneration of the motor neurons in the spinal cord (and sometimes the brain stem). The proximal muscles are more affected than the distal muscles. Intelligence does not deteriorate, and most individuals have normal or above intelligence. There are three main types of proximal muscular atrophies present in childhood: Type I (acute infantile spinal muscular atrophy or Werdnig-Hoffmann disease), Type II (intermediate or chronic infantile spinal muscular atrophy), and Type III (juvenile spinal muscular atrophy or Kugelberg-Welander disease). While there is currently no cure or medical treatment for spinal muscular atrophy, students with spinal muscular atrophy can function productively in the classroom with appropriate adaptations.

 **Jeff's Story**

Jeff is a 10-year-old student who is currently in fifth grade. When he was about 7 months old, his parents began to notice that he was not reaching the developmental milestones at the same age as his siblings. In fact, they felt that he was quite significantly delayed. After seeing several physicians, a diagnosis of chronic infantile spinal muscular atrophy (Type II) was reached. Jeff is a bright student who has little trouble keeping up with his assignments. Jeff gets around with the aid of leg braces (for short distances) and a wheelchair. Because of his progressive muscle weakness, his teacher has made some adaptations for Jeff that have enabled him to fully participate in all of the classroom activities. Jeff's desk is situated so that he has plenty of room to maneuver in his braces or wheelchair and is able to see and hear what is going on throughout the room. Because of his progressive muscle weakness, he cannot complete all his assignments as rapidly as the other students and sometimes needs the opportunity to utilize nontraditional methods. Some of the adaptations that his teacher has made for Jeff include allowing him more time to complete assignments, allowing him to dictate instead of writing some assignments, providing him with copies of assignments that are to be copied from the board, and providing him with a buddy who shares notes and assists Jeff in making sure that he has all the materials he may need. Jeff's teacher collaborated with the occupational and physical therapists to determine what type of adaptive equipment would be appropriate. Some of the adaptive equipment that is being used includes a computer, a book rest and page turner, a larger desktop, and a tape recorder. Jeff is also using a special spoon, plate, and cup at lunchtime that help him eat independently. What else should the teacher be doing to assist Jeff with this progressive degenerative disease?

REFERENCES

Bach, J. R., Saltstein, K., Sinquee, D., Weaver, B., & Komaroff, E. (2007). Long-term survival in Werdnig-Hoffman disease. *American Journal of Physical Medicine & Rehabilitation, 86*, 339–345.

Behrman, R. E., Kleigman, R. M., & Jenson, H. B. (2004). *Nelson textbook of pediatrics* (17th ed.). Philadelphia: W. B. Saunders.

Brzustowicz, L. M., Lehner, T., Castilla, L. H., Penchaszadeh, G. K., Wilhelmsen, K. C., Daniels, R., et al. (1990). Genetic mapping of chronic childhood-onset spinal muscular atrophy to chromosome 5q 11.2-13.3. *Nature, 344*, 540–541.

Caruso, J. F., Signorile, J. F., Perry, A. C., LeBlanc, B., Williams, R., Clark, M., et al. (1995). The effects of albuterol and isokinetic exercise on quadriceps muscle group. *Medical Science Sports Exercise, 27*, 1471–1476.

Corti, S., Locatelli, F., Papadimitriou, D., Donadoni, C., Del Bo, R., Strazzer, S., et al. (2006). Transplanted ALDH[hi] SSC[lo] neural stem cells generate motor neurons and delay disease progression of *nmd* mice, an animal of SMARD1. *Human Molecular Genetics, 13*, 167–187.

D'Angelo, M. G., & Bresolin, N. (2006). Cognitive impairment in neuromuscular disorders. *Muscle and Nerve, 34*, 16–33.

Eggert, C., Chari, A., Laggerbauer, B., & Fischer, U. (2006). Spinal muscular atrophy: The RNP connection. *Trends in Molecular Medicine, 12,* 113–121.

El-Matary, W., Kotagiri, S., Cameron, D., & Peart, I. (2004). Spinal muscle atrophy type 1 (Wernig-Hoffmann disease) with complex cardiac malformation. *European Journal of Pediatrics, 163,* 331–332.

Feldkotter, M., Schwarzer, F., Wirth, R., Wienker, T. F., & Wirth, B. (2002). Quantitative analysis of SMN1 and SMN2 based on real-time LightCycler PCR: Fast and highly reliable carrier testing and prediction of severity of spinal muscular atrophy. *American Journal of Human Genetics, 70,* 358–368.

Hardart, M. K. M., & Truog, R. D. (2003). Spinal muscular atrophy—type I: The challenge of defining a child's best interest. *Archives of Disease in Childhood, 88,* 848–850.

Herring, J. A. (2002). *Tachdjian's pediatric orthopaedics* (3rd ed.). Philadelphia: W. B. Saunders.

Ioos, C., Leclair-Richard, D., Mrad, S., Barois, A., & Esournet-Mathiaud, B. (2004). Respiratory capacity course in patients with infantile spinal muscular atrophy. *Chest, 126,* 831–837.

Jablonka, S., & Sendtner, M. (2003). Molecular and cellular basis of spinal muscular atrophy. *ALS and Other Motor Neuron Disorders, 4,* 144–149.

Merlini, L., Granata, C., Bonfiglioli, S., Marini, M. L., Cervellati, S., & Savini, R. (1989). Scoliosis in spinal muscular atrophy: Natural history and management. *Developmental Medicine and Child Neurology, 31,* 501–508.

Monani, U. R. (2005). Spinal muscular atrophy: A deficiency in a ubiquitous protein; a motor neuron-specific disease. *Neuron, 48,* 885–896.

Nicole, S., Diaz, C. C., Frugier, T., & Melki, J. (2002). Spinal muscular atrophy: Recent advances and future prospects. *Muscle and Nerve, 26,* 4–13.

Ryan, M. M., Kilham, H., Jocobe, S., Tobin, B., & Isaacs, D. (2007). Spinal muscular atrophy type I: Is long-term mechanical ventilation ethical? *Journal of Paediatrics and Child Health, 43,* 237–242.

Von Gontard, A., Zerres, K., Backes, M., Lauferswelier-Plass, C., Wendland, C., & Melchers, P., et al. (2002). Intelligence and cognitive function in children and adolescents with spinal muscular atrophy. *Neuromuscular Disorders, 12,* 130–136.

Wang, C. H., Finkel, R. S., Bertini, E. S., Bertini, E., Schroth, M., Simonds, A., Wong, B., Aloysius, A., Morrison, L., Main, M., Crawford, T., Trela, A., et al. (2007). Consensus statement for stand of care in spinal muscular atrophy. *Journal of Child Neurology, 22,* 1027–1049.

Wang, H. Y., Ju, Y. H., Chen, S. M., Lo, S. K., & Jong, Y. J. (2004). Joint range of motion limitations in children and young adults with spinal muscular atrophy. *Archives of Physical Medicine and Rehabilitation, 85,* 1689–1693.

Wessel, H. B. (1989). Spinal muscular atrophy. *Pediatric Annals, 18,* 421.

Winkeller, V. (2005). *A review of spinal muscular atrophy literature.* Spinal Muscular Atrophy Foundation. New York, New York.

Wirth, B. (2002). Spinal muscular atrophy: State-of-the-art and therapeutic perspectives. *ALS and Other Motor Neuron Disorders, 3,* 87–95.

Wirth, B., Brichta, L., & Hahnen, E. (2006). Spinal muscular atrophy: From gene to therapy. *Seminars in Pediatric Neurology, 13,* 121–131.

CHAPTER 15

CYSTIC FIBROSIS

Kathryn Wolff Heller and Morton Schwartzman

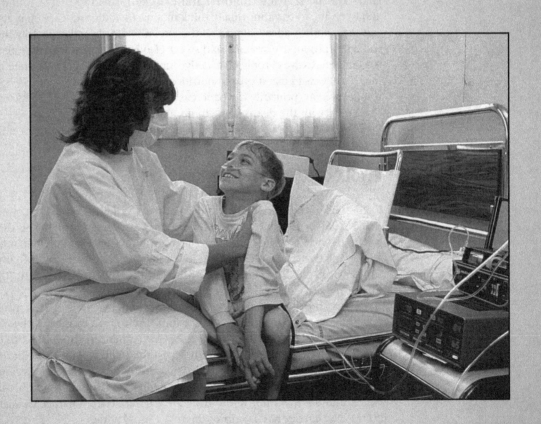

Cystic fibrosis (CF) is the most common life-shortening autosomal recessive genetic disease in whites, occurring in approximately 1 out of 3,300 white births (compared to 1 out of 15,300 births in the black population or 1 out of 32,000 births in the Asian American population) (Beers, Porter, Jones, Kaplan, & Berkwits, 2006). Although a multisystem disorder, it especially results in digestion problems and severe lung disease. In the 1950s, many children with cystic fibrosis died prior to reaching school age, while many will now live into their 30s and beyond.

Although coughing may be the most observable symptom in students with cystic fibrosis, several other organs are involved. Students with cystic fibrosis who are receiving treatment do not typically look ill, and hence cystic fibrosis is often considered one of the "invisible" diseases. However, the gravity of this disease and its impact on the student's overall functioning require that the educator be familiar with this disease, its characteristics, and its course of progression and know how to provide appropriate support in the educational environment.

DESCRIPTION OF CYSTIC FIBROSIS

Cystic fibrosis is a disease of the exocrine glands (glands secreting through ducts). The affected glands often secrete excessive, abnormal secretions that tend to be thick and viscous. This thick mucus can cause obstructions. In fact, the term *cystic fibrosis* is derived from the characteristic scarring (fibrosis) and cystlike formation that is found within the pancreas and liver due to the abnormally thick mucus. In addition, scarring is also found in the lungs.

Cystic fibrosis affects almost all the exocrine glands and especially the respiratory, gastrointestinal, reproductive systems, and sweat glands. In the respiratory system, the thick mucus results in progressive chronic obstructive lung disease that can lead to pneumonia and a collapsed lung. Problems in digestion and nutrition occur because of the disease's effect on the gastrointestinal system (primarily the pancreas and its digestive enzyme, the liver, and the gallbladder). Most men with the disease are sterile, and women can have decreased fertility (McMullen & Bryson, 2004). Also, a characteristic high concentration of salt occurs in the sweat.

ETIOLOGY OF CYSTIC FIBROSIS

Cystic fibrosis is a genetic disease. The defective gene that causes cystic fibrosis was identified in 1989 on chromosome 7 (Grossman & Grossman, 2005). This defective gene encodes a protein known as the cystic fibrosis transmembrane conductance regulator (CFTR), which affects the transport of chloride and sodium. There are over 1,100 different mutations that can occur in CFTR to cause cystic fibrosis, although approximately 70% of the cases of cystic fibrosis are caused by one specific defect (ΔF508) (Cutting, 2005).

Cystic fibrosis is an autosomal recessive genetic disease. This means that both parents must be carriers of the gene in order for there to be a chance of the child getting the disorder. When two parents who are carriers have children, there is a 25% chance that the child will have cystic fibrosis, a 50% chance that the child will be a carrier, and a 25% chance that the child will be totally unaffected. The odds of two carriers marrying are fairly high since an estimated 7 million to 10 million individuals carry the cystic fibrosis gene in the United States, and many do not know they are carriers (Grossman & Grossman, 2005; Robinson, 2001). The carrier rate is approximately 1 in 30 adults.

DYNAMICS OF CYSTIC FIBROSIS

Overview of the Exocrine Glands

Exocrine glands are tubes of epithelial cells that bud off a surface and secrete fluids via ducts. They empty their fluids directly outside the body (e.g., sweat) or to a body cavity that will empty to the outside (e.g., bile to the intestine that exits the anus). Because of this, these glands are known as glands of external secretion (as opposed to endocrine glands, which secrete internally and directly into the bloodstream [ductless], as discussed in chapter 19 on diabetes). Exocrine glands are located throughout the body in such areas as the pancreas, intestines, lungs, sweat glands, liver (hepatobiliary tract), and vas deferens (in the male reproductive system). A brief review of three of these major systems (pancreas, gastrointestinal, and respiratory systems) will be provided to help build an understanding of their function to later promote an understanding of how they are affected by cystic fibrosis.

The pancreas is an elongated organ (about 6–10 inches in length) that is located below the stomach. It has both exocrine and endocrine glands. The exocrine glands secrete pancreatic juice containing digestive enzymes that are important in breaking down food into parts that can be digested. These exocrine glands consist of many small ducts that eventually combine together and empty into the small intestine (see chapter 19 to learn more about the endocrine glands in the pancreas).

The gastrointestinal tract begins with the mouth, which connects to the back of the throat (pharynx), then continues down a long tube, known as the esophagus (see Figure 15–1). The esophagus connects to the stomach, which connects to the narrow, winding small intestine, which is approximately 20 feet in length (and divided into three parts: the duodenum, the jejunum, and the ileum). The small intestine then connects to the wider (but shorter) large intestine and ends at the anus. The purpose of the gastrointestinal tract is to receive food and break it down and absorb the nutrients into the body while expelling waste matter (feces).

Most digestion occurs in the small intestine, where exocrine glands secrete mucus that promotes movement and the effective diffusion of gut contents. Digestive enzymes from the pancreas and bile from the liver and gallbladder empty into the small intestine to aid in digestion and absorption.

The respiratory system consists of a series of airways that carry air from the environment to the lungs when we inhale and that carry unwanted gases to the environment when we exhale. These airways resemble an upside-down tree in which a single airway, known as the trachea (or windpipe), splits into two main branches, known as bronchi, which further divide

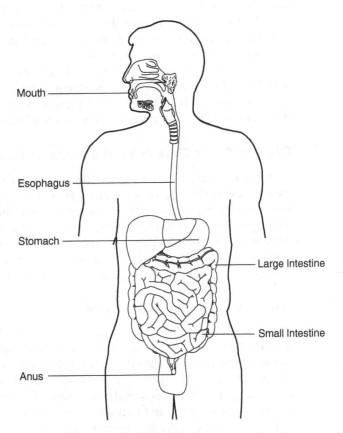

FIGURE 15–1 Anatomy of the gastrointestinal tract.

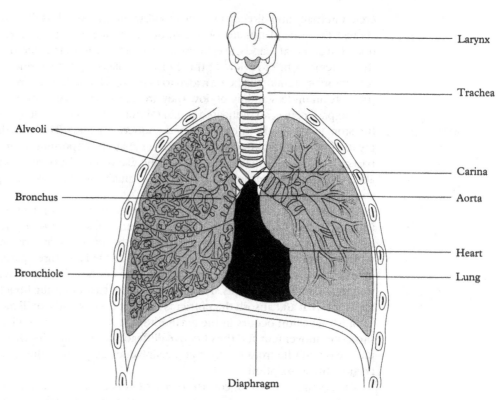

FIGURE 15–2 Anatomy of the respiratory system.

multiple times into smaller and smaller tubes known as bronchioles (see Figure 15–2). The bronchioles eventually end in about 300 million air sacs (alveoli), which have capillaries (small blood vessels) surrounding them. The exchange of gases occurs between the respiratory and circulatory systems at the air sacs.

In the respiratory system, epithelial cells (exocrine glands) secrete mucus in the trachea, bronchi, and some bronchioles. The mucus traps unwanted debris that enters the airway when we breathe. Hairlike projections, known as cilia, sweep the mucus that has trapped the debris from the airways until it can be expelled or swallowed.

Effect of Cystic Fibrosis on the Exocrine Glands

Cystic fibrosis affects the exocrine gland secretions, resulting in four major effects: (a) a paucity of water in mucous secretions, (b) thick mucous secretions that are difficult to clear, (c) elevations of sodium and chloride primarily in the sweat, and (d) chronic infections of the respiratory tract (Behrman, Kliegman, & Jenson, 2004). The role of the abnormal CFTR protein in cystic fibrosis can explain most of these effects as well as the role of inflammation and proinflammatory agents (agents capable of promoting inflammation) that can lead to infections, thickened mucus, and obstruction of the airways.

CFTR Protein and Cystic Fibrosis Gene

The defective gene that causes cystic fibrosis adversely affects the functioning of the CFTR protein. There are different theories of how this occurs, but the role of salt (NaCl, or sodium chloride) absorption is considered key (Marcet & Boeynaems, 2006). Normally, the CFTR protein allows the transportation of sodium and chloride ions across the cells that line the exocrine glands. Water follows the direction of salt transportation, causing the mucous secretions to be hydrated and thinned (Grossman & Grossman, 2005).

In cystic fibrosis, there are several types of errors of production (and migration within the cells) of CFTR that result in CFTR being absent or altered (see Figure 15–3). The absent or al-

Type	Error
I	Zero CFTR is produced.
II	CFTR is not processed correctly, so no protein gets to the cell membrane.
III	The CFTR chloride pathway is regulated differently than normal, but transfer of CFTR occurs.
IV	The chloride current is not conducted properly, so transfer of CFTR is slowed.
V	Synthesis of CFTR is abnormal; however, CFTR is transferred.

FIGURE 15–3 Types of errors in production of the protein cystic fibrosis transmembrane regulator (CFTR) in individuals with cystic fibrosis.

Source. Used with permission from Grossman and Grossman (2005, p. 47).

tered CFTR protein results in an altered chloride channel in the cell membranes, resulting in chloride ions being trapped within the cells. Because of this, sodium ions and water diffuse back into the cells, resulting in the mucus not being properly hydrated (Connors & Ulles, 2005; Shulman & Elias, 2001). This paucity of water in the mucus results in thick and viscous mucus that is difficult to clear. This can lead to blockages, organ damage, and chronic infections in the respiratory system with bacteria embedding themselves within the obstructed mucus (Cutting, 2005).

In many cases, the severity of cystic fibrosis appears to be linked to the amount of CFTR activity (Grossman & Grossman, 2005). For example, those with a 99% loss of CFTR often have pancreatic insufficiency and lung disease, while those with a 95% loss of CFTR functioning will often have pancreatic functioning, although lung disease will be present (Behrman et al., 2004).

Although the amount of CFTR functioning appears to be important in determining the characteristics of the disease, some mutations of the cystic fibrosis gene appear to share common characteristics. For example, the most common form of cystic fibrosis, known as ΔF508, has most of the CFTR missing and usually has pancreatic insufficiency. Some other rare mutations tend not to have pancreatic involvement. Almost all individuals will have the overproduction of thick mucus, leading to chronic pulmonary obstructive lung disease, except in some rare mutations, such as R117H, in which the lungs are less involved (Behrman et al., 2004). However, not all characteristics are linked to the type of genetic mutation, such as liver disease (cirrhosis), which occurs independent of genotype.

 *Most common form →*

In the most common type of cystic fibrosis (ΔF508, which 70% of individuals with cystic fibrosis have), there are particular organs that are typically damaged. The damaged organs can include the pancreas, gastrointestinal tract, respiratory system, and other organs (e.g., liver, gallbladder, and reproductive organs).

Dynamics of Cystic Fibrosis on the Pancreas and Gastrointestinal Tract

As previously discussed, the pancreas contains several exocrine glands that secrete digestive enzymes that are important in breaking down food into parts that can be digested. In cystic fibrosis, there is thick mucus that blocks the small ducts that secrete the digestive enzymes. When the ducts become completely obstructed, the glands continue to secrete and swell and then develop cysts with scarred fibrous tissue around them (hence the name cystic fibrosis).

As there is a decrease in the amount of pancreatic secretion that reaches the intestine, proteins, carbohydrates, and fats are not properly broken down for absorption. Although other enzymes from other organs (such as the small intestine) will assist with the breakdown of food, the decrease in or lack of pancreatic secretions can result in weight loss, malabsorption, and poor nutrition.

Digestion problems can also occur if the intestines become blocked with thick fatty mucus. The stools tend to be fatty and odorous from lack of fat absorption. In addition, bile can be obstructed, resulting in cirrhosis of the liver and gallbladder disease.

Dynamics of Cystic Fibrosis on the Respiratory System

The secretion of mucus in the airways in the respiratory tract is excessive and unusually thick in individuals with cystic fibrosis. The cilia cannot move the mucus effectively, and the lungs have difficulty clearing the mucus. The inability to properly clear out the mucus sets the stage for the emergence of respiratory infections (with such pathogens as *Pseudomonas aeruginosa* and *Staphylococcus aureus*). These infections are difficult to completely eliminate from the respiratory tract.

Chronic infection and inflammation results in a cycle of tissue destruction, chronic dilation of the bronchi (brochiectasis), and airway obstruction. In addition, the small air sacs (alveoli) can collapse because of the mucus obstructing the smaller airway passages (bronchioles) leading to the air sacs. When mucus blocks the bronchioles, air becomes trapped in the alveoli. The air left in the alveoli becomes absorbed into the body, and the affected air sacs shrink or collapse (known as atelectasis) (see Figure 15–4). This chronic obstructive pulmonary dis-

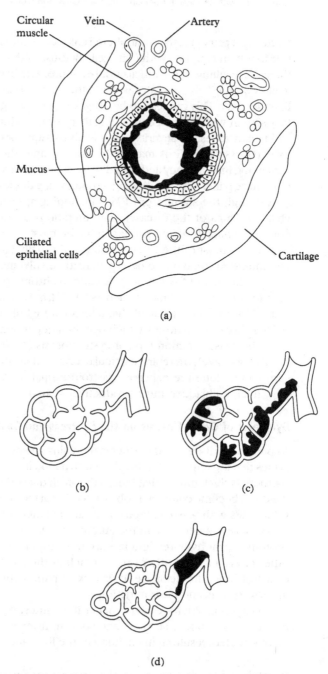

(a)

(b)   (c)

(d)

FIGURE 15–4 In cystic fibrosis, there is an excess of mucus in the respiratory system that may cause the bronchioles to become partially obstructed. (a) A normal alveoli (air sac) (b) may become obstructed, especially during infection (c) and collapse (known as atelectasis) (d).

ease will result in a decline in pulmonary function. Progressive lung injury slowly occurs, with episodic pulmonary exacerbations and periods of disease stability (Rowe & Clancy, 2006). Individuals usually die from respiratory infections (pneumonia) and complications.

Dynamics of Cystic Fibrosis on Other Systems

The characteristic thick mucus can also affect other systems. For example, in the reproductive system, women may have thick cervical secretions that disallow sperm penetration, while men may have obstructions resulting in the absence of sperm transportation or production.

In cystic fibrosis, there are also abnormalities in salt concentrations. Unlike most of the other exocrine glands, the sweat gland cells absorb rather than secrete chloride; hence, salt is not transported into the cells. This results in a characteristic increase of salt in the sweat, especially chloride.

CHARACTERISTICS OF CYSTIC FIBROSIS

There is great variability as to characteristics of cystic fibrosis as well as the onset, duration, and severity of the disease. Some individuals will be born with the symptoms of cystic fibrosis present, while others will not develop symptoms until early childhood, adolescence, or even adulthood. The characteristics of each of the major systems of the body will be discussed next.

Obstruction and Digestion Problems in the Gastrointestinal System

When symptoms of cystic fibrosis are present at birth, they are usually those affecting the gastrointestinal tract. Fifteen to 20% of infants will be born with an obstructed bowel (known as meconium ileus) (Beers et al., 2006). The obstructed bowel occurs because of the mucous stool becoming clogged in the loops of the small intestines. When this occurs, the infant will usually have stomach distention, vomiting, and no bowel movements occurring within the first 1 to 2 days of life. In these cases, testing for cystic fibrosis is indicated since 99% of infants that have meconium ileus have cystic fibrosis. An X-ray is taken to diagnose meconium ileus, and surgery will typically be necessary to remove the blockage, although oral medications and enemas are sometimes successful.

Digestion problems are usually present and result in fatty appearing stools that may occur more frequently. Stools have a characteristic foul odor due to undigested fats in the stool, and frequent gas may be present. Since calories are being lost in the stool because of malabsorption from the decrease in pancreatic digestion secretions, the infant or child may have a large appetite to try to get the caloric intake needed for proper nutrition. Additional problems may also occur, such as constipation, acid reflux, rectal prolapse, peptic ulcer disease, and intestinal obstruction (McMullen & Bryson, 2004).

Pancreatic Insufficiency

In some individuals, symptoms of pancreatic insufficiency will occur during infancy or early childhood. For infants who did not have an obstructed bowel, the symptoms of pancreatic insufficiency may be the first indications that the infant has cystic fibrosis. The pancreatic insufficiency that occurs in cystic fibrosis prevents food from being properly metabolized from the gastrointestinal tract. This problem in digestion can result in a failure to gain weight, and growth may be impeded in infants or young children. If proper intervention is not given (e.g., pancreatic enzyme supplementation), the infant or young child can become emaciated, and long-term lung growth can be affected as well.

Children with cystic fibrosis are often smaller and grow more slowly. This is in part due to nutritional problems that may occur when pancreatic insufficiency is present. Because of poor food absorption and other factors (e.g., chronic respiratory infections), children with cystic fibrosis need an increased amount of caloric intake, even when they take medication to improve food absorption. It is recommended that they attain an overall daily energy intake of 120% to 150% of the Recommended Dietary Allowance (RDA) (Borowitz et al., 2002; Powers, Patton, & Rajan, 2004). Unfortunately, studies examining infants and toddlers with cystic fibrosis have found deficiencies in their diet, with 89% not meeting the daily recommendation of food intake (Powers et al., 2002, 2004). Preadolescent children and some adults with cystic fibrosis have also been found to not meet their dietary recommendations (Schall, 2006). Consequences of this attribute to poor growth and health problems (including respiratory infections).

Additional complications have also been found to occur with the pancreatic involvement. Individuals who have cystic fibrosis with pancreatic insufficiency are at risk of developing **diabetes mellitus** later in life (Hadjiliadis et al., 2005) (see chapter 19 on diabetes). This type of diabetes is referred to as cystic fibrosis–related diabetes. It shares features for both type I and type II diabetes (Spence, 2005). Pancreatitis is another complication.

Respiratory Damage and Cardiac Complications

Respiratory involvement often begins in infancy, although it may not develop until later. For some individuals, there may initially be no symptoms except that respiratory infections are of longer duration than usual or the child has frequent episodes of bronchitis or pneumonia. Many individuals will exhibit their first symptom of respiratory involvement as a cough. It may start as a dry cough, but eventually it will become moist and productive (i.e., accompanied by thickened mucus, usually yellow-green colored). Wheezing may be present as well (indicating reactive airway components).

As the disease progresses, the lungs become increasingly damaged and scarred, and the chest enlarges (barrel chest). Digital clubbing may also occur, which is an enlargement of the ends of the toes and fingers due to hypoxia (decreased oxygen) (Grossman & Grossman, 2005) (see Figure 15-5). Because of the increasing lung damage, the individual becomes unable to tolerate exercise and becomes short of breath (and may require oxygen supplementation.) There continues to be frequent respiratory infections resulting in bronchitis and pneumonia.

Several other respiratory complications can occur, affecting the respiratory and cardiac systems. Some respiratory complications include sinus infections, coughing up blood (hemoptysis), pneumothorax (collapsed lung), and pulmonary hypertension (high blood pres-

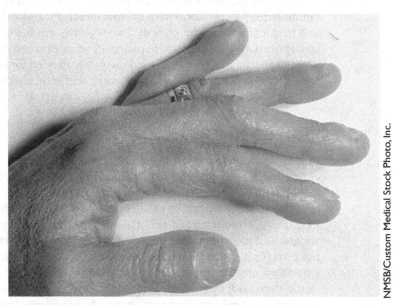

NMSB/Custom Medical Stock Photo, Inc.

FIGURE 15–5 A lack of oxygen causes an enlargement of the ends of the fingers and is known as digital clubbing.

sure in vessels in the lung). Pulmonary hypertension causes an increased pressure in the right side of the heart. The right side of the heart pumps blood into blood vessels that go to the lungs; over time, pulmonary hypertension can cause an enlargement of the right side of the heart as well as other structural changes (known as cor pulmonale). The structural changes in the heart adversely affect the heart's ability to function properly. Often the person with cystic fibrosis dies from a combination of respiratory failure and heart failure.

Dehydration and Loss of Electrolytes in Sweat

As previously described, individuals with cystic fibrosis have a high salt content in their sweat. Children can experience excessive salt loss from hot weather, fever, or extensive exercise. This may first by noticed by the skin having a "frosting" appearance (which is salt crystal formation) or a salty taste being present when the child is kissed (Behrman et al., 2004). Sodium and chloride deficits can occur. In addition, dehydration or heat prostration can also occur and is characterized by lethargy, weakness, and a loss of appetite (Grossman & Grossman, 2005). Extra salt intake is indicated orally.

Liver and Gallbladder Complications

In cystic fibrosis, the bile ducts can become obstructed from thickened bile. As previously discussed, bile is excreted by the liver and leaves through tubelike structures (bile ducts). These ducts go to and from the gallbladder and also to the small intestine. Neonates may present with jaundice due to the thickened bile in the duct. (In jaundice, the skin and sclera of the eyes become yellow because the bile is not transported from the liver to the small intestine; instead an accumulation of bile [bilirubin] occurs in the blood.)

Young adults with cystic fibrosis can present with an enlarged liver (hepatomegaly) due to essential fatty acid deficiency and fatty replacement as well as possible malnutrition. Cirrhosis of the liver may occur in which liver tissue is replaced by fibrotic scar tissue that can lead to a loss of liver function. Portal hypertension (high blood pressure in blood vessels of the liver) can also occur because of the cirrhosis, and this can lead to further complications. In addition, the thickened bile can result in disorders of the gallbladder, including gallstones and shrunken gallbladder.

Sterility and Reproduction System Problems

Generally, there is a delay in sexual development by a couple of years that is difficult emotionally for many adolescents. Males are usually sterile because of an obstruction of the tubes that carry sperm or the failure of these tubes to form during development (known as congenital bilateral absence of the vas deferens). However, sexual functioning is unimpaired. Some women may have decreased fertility but can usually tolerate pregnancy if their lung condition is good and stable.

Other Complications from Cystic Fibrosis

In cystic fibrosis, other systems of the body may be involved. For example, children and young adults can get osteopenia of their bones (a decrease in bone mineral density). Although this can be a precursor condition for osteoporosis, it rarely develops in individuals with cystic fibrosis.

DETECTION OF CYSTIC FIBROSIS

Cystic fibrosis is usually diagnosed in infancy or early childhood. However, approximately 10% are not diagnosed until after age 10 or adolescence. This is especially the case when

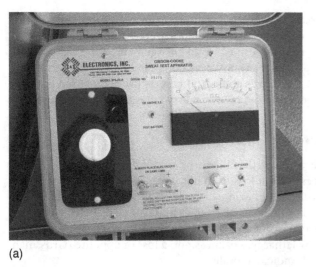

(a)

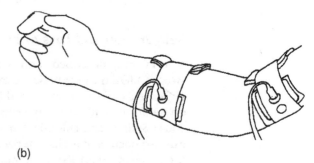

(b)

FIGURE 15–6 Machine used to perform a sweat test (a) and the electrodes that attach to the arm from the machine (b).
Source: Courtesy of C&S Electronics–Columbus, Nebraska

the symptoms are mild or there is delayed onset. Carriers of cystic fibrosis can also be diagnosed as carrying the mutant gene even though they have no symptoms of cystic fibrosis.

Cystic fibrosis has traditionally been diagnosed through the use of a sweat test (known as pilocarpine iontophoresis). This painless test consists of stimulating a small area of the skin (usually on the forearm) to sweat with the use of a small electric current and medication (see Figure 15–6). The sweat is collected by filter paper or a capillary tube that is placed on the stimulated skin. The sweat is then analyzed for salt. If the chloride is over 60 mEq/L, the test is positive (or highly suggestive of cystic fibrosis when over 40 mEq/L in infants younger than 3 months old). Although there are a few other conditions that may result in a high chloride measurement (e.g., severe malnutrition or hypothyroidism), they usually have very different characteristics. A diagnosis of cystic fibrosis is made when the sweat test is accompanied by pulmonary disease, sinus disease, pancreatic insufficiency, or a positive family history, and it is definitely made when genetic testing for cystic fibrosis is positive.

Although the sweat test is considered a very accurate test and the most reliable one, the results are occasionally in a moderately high range or sometimes normal when cystic fibrosis is present. Young infants may have unreliable results using the sweat test, and some mild forms of cystic fibrosis may test normal. In these instances, genetic testing should be used to determine a diagnosis. Also, genetic testing will determine if the sweat test is falsely positive.

Cystic fibrosis may be diagnosed early, either prenatally or soon after birth. Prenatal diagnosis uses DNA genetic testing. This is accomplished through amniocentesis (in which amniotic fluid is examined) or chorionic villus sampling (a procedure in which placental [chorionic] tissue is extracted and examined). Some states routinely perform newborn screening for cystic fibrosis through a blood test immunoreactive trypsin (IRT) at the same time they screen for other disorders (Green, Siobhan, & Thomas, 2006). Although early detection and intervention can prevent nutritional deficiency and improve growth, the long-term outcome due to respiratory complications may be altered to some degree.

Additional tests are available to assist with the diagnosis of cystic fibrosis. Pancreatic function may be tested by analysis of stool samples (e.g., fat analysis or pancreatic elastase 1) or less commonly by more invasive procedures. The lungs and sinuses may be examined by X-rays and computed tomography (CT) scans. Pulmonary functions tests that measure the amount of air exchange and capacity of the lungs may also be performed (see Figure 15–7). These supplementary tests may provide more information and help track lung and pancreatic functioning but in and of themselves are not totally diagnostic of cystic fibrosis.

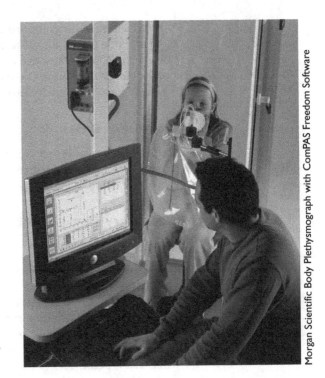

FIGURE 15–7 A child having a pulmonary function test performed and the results are displayed on a pulmonary function graph on a computer screen.

Morgan Scientific Body Plethysmograph with ComPAS Freedom Software

TREATMENT OF CYSTIC FIBROSIS

Individuals with cystic fibrosis typically require comprehensive and intensive treatment from a team of experienced individuals. The goals of treatment are to provide appropriate nutritional support, to prevent or treat respiratory infections, and to provide emotional support to the person with cystic fibrosis and the family (Beers et al., 2006). The protocol of cystic fibrosis treatment is to prevent complications. However, if complications occur, they are treated as they arise.

Nutritional Management

Pancreatic Enzyme Supplementation and Vitamins

For individuals who have pancreatic insufficiency, there is pancreatic enzyme replacement medication that the child will take before each meal and snack. However, this does not completely replace the loss of the child's natural pancreatic enzyme. Fats are not completely absorbed; hence, stools will continue to be fatty if not adequately treated. Vitamins that are fat soluble (e.g., vitamins A and D) will not be absorbed. Because of this, vitamin and mineral supplements are usually needed.

High-Calorie Diet

Most children with cystic fibrosis require higher than usual amounts of calories because of the basic defect or increased pulmonary energy requirements and malabsorption of food. Weight loss is a common problem, especially when there is a respiratory infection or poorly treated malabsorption. Children should be encouraged to eat and take as many helpings as they want. This is especially needed to meet the recommended overall daily energy intake of 120% to 150% of the Recommended Dietary Allowance (RDA).

Nutritional supplementation is often used with children with weight loss issues. This may occur orally with special high-calorie supplements or in some instances through a **gastrostomy**

tube (which is a feeding tube that goes directly into the stomach or small intestine through which liquid nutrition can be administered) (see chapter 20 for information on feeding tubes). In some cases, children may receive extra nutrition parenterally, which consists of a catheter going directly into the circulatory system in which a high-calorie preparation (known as total parenteral nutrition [TPN] or hyperalimentation) is administered.

Salt Supplementation

Abnormal amounts of salt can be lost through the sweat, especially when a fever, hot temperatures, or strenuous exercise occurs. This may result in sodium and chloride deficits. Salt supplementation will often be needed during these times.

Respiratory Management

Airway Clearance

Efforts to clear excessive thick mucus are one of the primary objectives of cystic fibrosis treatment. Two to four times a day, the child may participate in **chest physiotherapy**, which is the removal of respiratory secretions (mucus) from the lungs through physical means, such as postural drainage, clapping, vibropercussion, or the Vest clearance system (McMullen & Bryson, 2004; Rowe & Clancy, 2006). In postural drainage, the child is placed in different positions to allow gravity to assist with moving the secretions out of the lungs. While that is being done, a trained individual performs a hand-administered therapy known as clapping (or cupping), in which a cupped hand repeatedly slaps the chest and back. Instead of or in addition to clapping, a vibropercussion technique uses fine vibratory movements of the hand (or a vibrator) on the chest and back. In both clapping and vibropercussion, the hand (or vibrator) is placed systematically over various parts of the lung to break up the mucus so that it can be coughed up (see Figure 15–8).

Another technique that may be used to clear the airway is the use of a Vest clearance system, also known as high-frequency chest wall oscillation (HFCWO) (see Figure 15–9). In this system, the person wears an inflatable vest for approximately 20 to 30 minutes a few times a day (depending on what the physician ordered). The vest is attached to an air-pulse generator. The air-pulse generator creates air pulses (oscillations) that cause the vest to rapidly inflate and deflate against the chest (e.g., 5–20 times per second). These air pulses mobilize the mucus away from the walls of the airway, allowing the person to cough the secretions out of the lungs (Darbee, Kanga, & Ohtake, 2005).

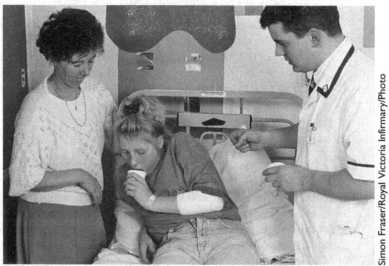

Simon Fraser/Royal Victoria Infirmary/Photo Researchers, Inc.

FIGURE 15–8 A respiratory therapist performing chest physiotherapy (clapping) on an adolescent, after which she is encouraged to cough out the respiratory secretions.

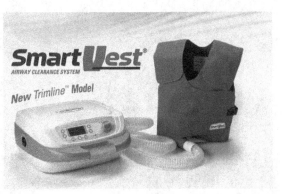

(a)   (b)

FIGURE 15–9 The Vest clearance system (a) and a child using a Vest clearance system to break up secretions so that they can be coughed out (b).

Source: Photos courtesy of Electromed, Inc., makers of the SmartVest® Airway Clearance System

Other airway clearance techniques may also be used by school-age children and adolescents that allow independence in clearing the airways of mucus (e.g., active cycle of breathing or forced expiration techniques). Special handheld airway clearance devices may also be used to loosen mucus and allow it to be coughed out. These devices are usually about the size of a small, fat pipe and have a mouthpiece (e.g., FLUTTER® mucous clearance device or Acapella™ device). There is a slight resistance blowing into these devices which results in an increase in lung pressure (positive expiratory pressure), and the exhalation is rapidly interrupted, resulting in oscillations (vibrations) that help loosen mucus in the lungs. These techniques and devices may be used as an adjunct to traditional chest physiotherapy (McMullen & Bryson, 2004; Rowe & Clancy, 2006).

Medications

Medications aimed at improving respiratory function may be administered orally or in aerosol form, such as with an inhaler or a nebulizer. An inhaler consists of a small handheld pressured canister encased in a plastic container that has a mouthpiece. A nebulizer is a machine that converts liquid medication into aerosol form, and it is breathed into the lungs through a mask or mouthpiece (see chapter 18 on asthma for more information).

Medications may be given to improve mucus clearance or facilitate breathing. Some of these include bronchodilators and anti-inflammatory medication. Bronchodilators are used to increase the diameter of the airways to promote improved breathing (e.g., albuterol). Anti-inflammatory drugs are used to decrease the inflammation occurring in the airways to attempt to slow the lung damage (e.g., ibuprofen). Saline, such as nebulized 7% hypertonic saline (extra salty water that is sterile), has been very effective in increasing the expectoration of mucus, decreasing pulmonary infections, and improving lung function.

Early and aggressive treatment of respiratory infections is believed to be responsible for the improvement in life expectancy in individuals with cystic fibrosis. Although antibiotics are often successful in treating infections, bacterial infections are rarely completely eliminated. More resistant forms of infections make antibiotic therapy problematic. There is some evidence that early antibiotic treatment against the early presentation of infection (such as *P. aeruginosa*) may delay the onset of chronic colonization of the infection and slow the progression of lung disease (Ratjen, 2006; Starner & McCray, 2005).

Exacerbations of chronic lung infections may need more than oral or aerosol forms of antibiotics to treat the infection. In these cases, medications may need to be given intravenously. In these instances, treatment may be initialized in the hospital or home setting in which intravenous antibiotics are given as well as increased respiratory treatments and nutritional support. This is referred to as a pulmonary "tune-up" or "clean out" (McMullen & Bryson, 2004). Differences do exist between cystic fibrosis centers and across countries for providing these

FIGURE 15–10 Student receiving oxygen through a nasal cannula attached to a portable oxygen tank.

pulmonary tune-ups. In European countries, for example, regularly scheduled intravenous antibiotic therapy (e.g., every 3 months) is often given for individuals with chronic infections, while centers in the United States tend to provide aggressive treatment only when pulmonary exacerbations occur (Doring et al., 2000; Rowe & Clancy, 2006).

Oxygen Therapy

When the lung disease is very advanced, there may be insufficient oxygenation occurring (hypoxia). In some instances, oxygen may need to be given on an intermittent basis (e.g., when short of breath or when sleeping) or throughout the day. Oxygen can be easily administered through the use of a portable oxygen tank and a delivery system, such as a nasal cannula (which is a plastic tube that goes from the oxygen source, around the ears, and below the nose with two short prongs placed in the nose) (see Figure 15–10).

Lung Transplant

Some individuals with advanced cystic fibrosis who meet certain criteria may be candidates for a lung transplant. Currently, about 50% to 60% of individuals with cystic fibrosis are alive 5 years after the lung transplant (McMullen & Bryson, 2004). A lung transplant can be a difficult family decision. Even if the family and physicians decide to go forward with a transplant, current shortages result in many people unable to obtain them. Individuals who receive a lung transplant will need to adhere to a strict daily regime of medications to prevent rejection and infection.

Treatment of Associated Problems

Since cystic fibrosis is a systemwide disease affecting the exocrine glands, several other disorders may occur that require treatment. For example, if diabetes develops, the individual will typically need medication and possible dietary and exercise modifications (see chapter 19 on diabetes). Cirrhosis of the liver can occur and may require medication or surgery.

Growth hormones have been given to some children when height has been a concern (Hardin et al., 2005). Infertility problems occur with most men, while the extra demands of pregnancy put women with cystic fibrosis at risk for complications (especially respiratory complications). Concerns also arise over having a child with cystic fibrosis, so genetic and reproductive counseling is recommended (Conners & Ulles, 2005).

New and Innovative Treatments

There are several newer, experimental therapies that are presently under examination to treat cystic fibrosis. Some of these are exploring new medications that would manipulate the faulty chloride transportation occurring at the cellular level. Others have been investigating the regulation of the mutated CFTR.

An exciting new area of investigation is gene therapy for cystic fibrosis. Although still in the early experimental stages, the aim of gene therapy is correcting certain cells to function normally (by replacing the affected gene by its healthy counterpart or adding the healthy counterpart to the affected gene). Current experiments have focused on airway gene therapy as well as gene delivery to human sweat glands (Lee et al., 2005). Although several obstacles remain in place, such as effective transfer of genes into the airways and host immune barriers, the promise of an eventual cure looms on the horizon (Parsons, 2005).

COURSE OF CYSTIC FIBROSIS

Cystic fibrosis continues to be a life-shortening illness with no cure. However, there have been advances in treating and identifying cystic fibrosis. These advances have resulted in a longer life. In 1969, the median age of survival was 14 years, but in 1990 it doubled to 28 years, and in 2006 the median survival rate is 35 to 37 years. Longevity continues to be on an upward trend.

For the most part, children with cystic fibrosis are fairly healthy during childhood and adolescence. During the course of the disease, complications such as intestinal obstructions, diabetes, cirrhosis, and pneumothorax (collapsed lung) may occur. Respiratory infections are common (with *P. aeruginosa* being the most frequently identified respiratory infection). Over time, this progressive disease will result in increasing amounts of lung damage. Eventually, the amount of lung damage will limit the individual's activity tolerance. The individual with cystic fibrosis usually dies from respiratory failure and right-side heart failure. With the discovery of the cystic fibrosis gene and new treatments being investigated and utilized, it is estimated that individuals with cystic fibrosis will continue to live longer lives with a better quality of life. It is hoped that new treatments will eventually be found that will cure this disease.

EDUCATIONAL IMPLICATIONS OF CYSTIC FIBROSIS

Cystic fibrosis does not directly affect the student's academic achievement. However, because of the unique characteristics of the disease, teacher and peer education is important. Some adaptations will be needed to meet the student's physical needs.

Meeting Physical and Sensory Needs

Nutritional Needs and Elimination Issues

Students with cystic fibrosis usually have large appetites due to the loss of calories in the stool as well as high metabolic activity. It is important that students be allowed to eat as much as they want. This includes having seconds, thirds, or fourths at lunch as well as any snacks. Gaining sufficient weight is often difficult for some students, and it is detrimental for the student not to eat as much as he or she needs.

To maintain proper health, students will often need to take medication prior to eating. Pancreatic enzymes need to be taken to help with the absorption of food. In addition, other medications, such as vitamins, may be prescribed. It is important that there is strict adherence to taking these medications to maximize food absorption and proper nutrition.

Digestion problems cause foul-smelling bowel movements and frequent gas. The student may need to leave class to go to the bathroom more frequently than other students and should be allowed to do so. Since bowel movements tend to have a foul odor, the student may be ridiculed by other students. To avoid this from occurring, arrangements should be made to allow the student to use the faculty restroom, and a deodorizer can be made available for the restroom.

Respiratory Needs

The most prominent symptom of cystic fibrosis is a frequent cough. However, students with cystic fibrosis may try to suppress coughing because of embarrassment. The teacher needs to stress to the students that coughing is an important mechanism to clear unwanted secretions. The teacher should explain that not coughing when needed can be harmful since the secretions would remain in the lungs. Having secretions remain in the lungs results in obstruction of some of the smaller airways and promotes infection. The importance of coughing cannot be overstressed since in the early 1980s, four to six children with cystic fibrosis died each year from taking cough suppressants (Umbreit, 1983). Students with cystic fibrosis may need to be allowed to step out of the classroom to cough and get a sip of water. It may be helpful for the student to keep a box of tissues to use when coughing up mucus in class and have a bag for disposal of the tissues.

Since most individuals associate a cough with an infection, the teacher needs to educate others that the cough is not infectious and that a person cannot "catch" cystic fibrosis. The teacher should also maintain good infection control to prevent the student with cystic fibrosis from acquiring new organisms (Rowe & Clancy, 2006). Washing hands, cleaning environmental surfaces, disposing of wastes properly, and sending sick children home are some of the steps that should be taken to promote infection control (see chapter 23 for more information). Maintaining proper infection control is actually important for all students to decrease the spread of infection.

Students with cystic fibrosis may require aerosols, oral medication, and airway clearance techniques during the school day (e.g., High Frequency Chest Wall Oscillation). Ideally, the student's schedule should permit these respiratory treatments to occur when they do not conflict with an academic class. However, if that is not possible and the student misses class, provisions should be made to help the student catch up on missed work. In addition, some students with advanced lung disease may be using a portable oxygen tank. It is important that teachers are familiar with the safe handling of oxygen since it is flammable. See Figure 15–11 for safety tips for oxygen management.

Exercise

Regular exercise is beneficial to the child with cystic fibrosis. Although there is no indication that pulmonary function is improved by regular exercise, it can improve maximal oxygen use, exercise tolerance, and psychological well-being. Encouraging exercise is considered an important treatment goal (Beers et al., 2006).

Some studies have shown students with cystic fibrosis to have a lower level of fitness than their same-age peers (Loutzenhiser & Clark, 1993). In some instances, the student with cystic fibrosis may not have the same stamina as the other students and not be able to compete as well in strenuous sports. In other instances, the student with cystic fibrosis may have had a lack of fitness training and have been socialized into a role of inactivity. Any activity restrictions or limitations should be obtained from the physician and closely monitored.

One caution regarding exercising in the hot summer months or warmer weather is that the student may lose a lot of salt in the sweat. This disturbs the delicate balance of the electrolytes in the body. This can be very serious and in some instances life threatening. Students may need to take additional salt on those hot days when physical activity is expected to oc-

Oxygen Management Tips	Examples
1. Learn how the oxygen systems works	• How to turn oxygen on and off • Remove and attach regulator • Read the settings and amount of oxygen left in tank
2. Know the prescribed settings and do not change them without a doctor's order	• Increasing flow could result in overoxygenation • Decreasing flow could result in hypoxia
3. Know what to do if something is not working properly, such as a decreased flow or no flow of oxygen	• Check tubing for kinks • Be sure oxygen tank is turned on and be sure the regulator is turned on • Check amount of oxygen in tank
4. Decrease risk of obstructing flow of oxygen or disconnection	• Do not put anything over oxygen source • Do not put tubing under clothes
5. Secure tank properly to prevent injury	• Keep oxygen tank in upright, secured position • Place the oxygen tank where it cannot fall since a falling tank can break, causing the tank to propel through the air from the escape of pressurized oxygen • Transportation on school buses requires special safety precautions • Never transport oxygen in the trunk of a car
6. Prevent fires	• Keep oxygen tank at least 5 to 10 feet from heat source and electrical appliances • Do not use electric blanket, heating pads, toys that spark, or certain electrical equipment near oxygen • All cotton clothing or sheets should be used to avoid static electricity • No moisturizers, oil-based products, or other flammable products should be used • Oxygen should be kept off when not in use • No smoking near the oxygen tank • Fire department should be notified when oxygen is being used in the school or home • Post "oxygen in use" sign • Keep a fire extinguisher nearby
7. Check oxygen tank settings on arriving at school and as needed throughout the day	• Be sure the flow rate is set correctly • Check amount of oxygen in tank • Check that oxygen is flowing to the student • Know how to contact parents and oxygen supply company should oxygen tank become empty • If oxygen leaks into classroom by mistake, open a window and follow school procedures

FIGURE 15–11   Guidelines for using oxygen.

cur. There is also a risk of dehydration and a need for increased fluid intake. The teacher should have discussed this with the family, nurse, or physician and have an understanding of any activity restrictions and the need for salt tablets and increased fluids.

Medications

The student with cystic fibrosis may be taking several medications. As already discussed, there may be several pills or capsules taken prior to each meal because of pancreatic insufficiency as well as antibiotics and other medication. It is important that the person dispensing the medication know what the medication is for and adhere to the time schedule. Observing the student taking the medication and proper documentation is important to be able to say with certainty that the medication was taken on a particular day.

Meeting Communication Needs

Cystic fibrosis does not affect the individual's vocal mechanism, so there will be no difficulty in the area of speech. However, students with cystic fibrosis often need to communicate to peers about their condition. The teacher or parents may help the child in deciding what to say to other people.

Meeting Learning Needs

Students with cystic fibrosis are typically of normal intelligence. There is no intellectual disability or learning disability associated with the condition. Cognitive disability may be present as they are in the regular population but not because of the disease.

Tutoring may be needed because of the time missed in school for treatments or from absences due to illness. Students may also have good days and bad days because of their disease that can affect their academic performance. Teachers will need to be sensitive to this and provide any needed adaptations.

In addition, as the disease advances, there is usually a lack of endurance, and adaptations may need to be put in place. Endurance and stamina may become so poor that it becomes difficult to carry books to class or to walk to class within the time given. In these instances, extra books may need to be at home, someone may need to carry books that stay at school to class, and extra time may need to be given to get from class to class. Other adaptations may be needed as well (see chapter 12 for more information on adaptations).

Meeting Daily Living Needs

Daily living needs are similar to other students without disabilities. Modifications and adaptations are not necessary until the disease is advanced. At that time, there are usually significant stamina problems, and adaptations will be necessary.

Meeting Behavioral and Social Needs

As with all chronic disease, it is important that the teacher be aware of the emotional and social needs of the student. The student may have a pattern of **learned helplessness** due to overprotection. The teacher will then need to assist the student in learning to be independent. The student may also have difficulties socializing because of the characteristics of the disease. Education of peers and providing a positive school environment will help in addressing these needs.

Since cystic fibrosis is eventually terminal, the child or adolescent may be faced with questions regarding death or dying. Because of the advances made in the past several years, most students will not normally be faced with the prospect of dying until they are in their 30s (or beyond). However, in some cases, the student may be burdened by the knowledge of the prognosis of the disease or may have an advanced case. Either way, the teacher should be available to provide support to the student, as should other appropriate personnel (e.g., counselor or psychologist) (see chapter 16 for more information on coping with degenerative and terminal illnesses).

SUMMARY

Cystic fibrosis is a terminal illness that affects the exocrine glands of the body. The respiratory system is affected with increased amounts of thick, infected mucus and subsequent lung damage. The gastrointestinal tract is affected by not being able to break down food because of a lack of pancreatic secretions (natural enzymes). Other systems are affected as well. Students with cystic fibrosis will present with frequent coughing and a voracious appetite (although with advancing illness, the appetite can be suppressed). Advances have been made in the area of treatment, with life expectancy in the 30s. It is expected that life expectancy will further increase with new treatments. Progress is also being made toward finding a cure, hopefully in the near future.

VIGNETTE Mary's Story

Mary is a 16-year-old with cystic fibrosis. She moved to a new school this year. Although the homeroom teacher received information on cystic fibrosis and it was discussed by the parents, there has been some breakdown in communication among the school faculty. Mary's peers tend to avoid her because of her coughing, even though she says she is not sick. She has begun to try to suppress coughing because of the stares of her classmates. She is embarrassed to use the restroom and has already been ridiculed. She is going through the cafeteria line only once. What should you do?

REFERENCES

Beers, M. H., Porter, R. S., Jones, T. V., Kaplan, J. L., & Berkwits, M. (2006). *The Merck manual of diagnosis and therapy* (18th ed.). Whitehouse Station, NJ: Merck & Co.

Behrman, R. E., Kliegman, R. M., & Jenson, H. B. (2004). *Nelson textbook of pediatrics*. Philadelphia: W. B. Saunders.

Borowitz, D., Baker, R. D., & Stallings, V. (2002). Consensus report on nutrition for pediatric patients with cystic fibrosis. *Journal of Pediatric Gastroenterology and Nutrition, 35*, 246-259.

Connors, P. M., & Ulles, M. M. (2005). The physical, psychological, and social implications of caring for the pregnant patient and newborn with cystic fibrosis. *Journal of Perinatal Neonatal Nursing, 19*, 301-315.

Cutting, G. R. (2005). Modifier genetics: Cystic fibrosis. *Annual Review of Genomics and Human Genetics, 6*, 237-262.

Darbee, J. C., Kanga, J. F., & Ohtake, P. J. (2005). Physiological evidence for high-frequency chest wall oscillation and positive expiratory pressure breathing in hospitalized subjects with cystic fibrosis. *Physical Therapy, 85*, 1278-1289.

Doring, G., Conway, S. P., Heijerman, H. G., Hodson, M. E., Hoiby, N., Smyth, A., et. al. (2000). Antibiotic therapy against *Pseudomonas aeruginosa* in cystic fibrosis: A European consensus. *European Respiratory Journal, 16*, 749-767.

Green, N. S., Siobhan, D., & Thomas, M. (2006). Newborn screening: Complexities in universal genetic testing. *American Journal of Public Health, 96*, 1955-1959.

Grossman, S., & Grossman, L. C. (2005). Pathophysiology of cystic fibrosis implications for critical care nurses. *Critical Care Nurse, 25*(4), 46-51.

Hadjiliadis, D., Madill, J., Chaparro, D., Tsang, A., Waddell, T. K., Singer, L. G., et al. (2005). Incidence and prevalence of diabetes mellitus in patients with cystic fibrosis undergoing lung transplantation before and after lung transplantation. *Clinical Transplantation, 19*, 773-778.

Hardin, D., Ferkol, T., Ahn, C., Dreimane, D., Dyson, M., Morse, M., et al. (2005). A retrospective study of growth hormone use in adolescents with cystic fibrosis. *Clinical Endocrinoloy, 62*, 560-566.

Lee, H., Koehler, D. R., Pang, C. Y., Levine, R. H., Ng, P., Palmer, D. J., et al. (2005). Gene delivery to human sweat glands: A model for cystic fibrosis gene therapy. *Gene Therapy, 12*, 1752-1760.

Loutzenhiser, J. K., & Clark, R. (1993). Physical activity and exercise in children with cystic fibrosis. *Journal of Pediatric Nursing, 8*, 112-119.

Marcet, B., & Boeynaems, J. (2006). Relationships between cystic fibrosis transmembrane conductance regulator, extracellular nucleotides and cystic fibrosis. *Pharmacology and Therapeutics, 112*, 719-732.

McMullen, A. H., & Bryson, E. A. (2004). Cystic fibrosis. In P. A. Allen & H. A. Vessey (Eds.), *Primary care of the child with a chronic condition* (pp. 404-425). St. Louis: Mosby.

Parsons, D. W. (2005). Airway gene therapy and cystic fibrosis. *Journal of Paediatric Child Health, 41*, 94-96.

Powers, S. W., Patton S. R., Byars, K. C., Mitchell, M. J., Jelalian E., Mulvhill, M. M., et al. (2002). Caloric intake and eating behavior in infants and toddlers with cystic fibrosis. *Pediatrics, 109*, 75-80.

Powers, S. W., Patton, S. R., & Rajan, S. (2004). A comparison of food group variety between toddlers with and without cystic fibrosis. *Journal of Human Nutrition and Dietetics, 17*, 523-527.

Ratjen, F. (2006). Treatment of early *Pseudomonas aeruginosa* infection in patients with cystic fibrosis. *Current Opinion in Pulmonary Medicine, 12*, 428-432.

Robinson, P. (2001). Cystic fibrosis. *Thorax, 56*, 237-241.

Rowe, S. M., & Clancy, J. P. (2006). Advances in cystic fibrosis therapies. *Current Opinion in Pediatrics, 18*, 604-613.

Schall, J. (2006). Meal patterns, dietary fat intake and pancreatic enzyme use in preadolescent children with cystic fibrosis. *Journal of Pediatric Gastroenterology and Nutrition, 43*, 651-659.

Shulman, I., & Elias, S. (2001). Cystic fibrosis. *Clinical Perinatology, 28*, 383-393.

Spence, C. (2005). Cystic fibrosis-related diabetes: Practice challenges. *Paediatric Nursing, 17*, 23-25.

Starner, T. D., & McCray, P. B. (2005). Pathogenesis of early lung disease in cystic fibrosis: A window of opportunity to eradicate bacteria. *Annals of Internal Medicine, 143*, 816-822.

Umbriet, J. (1983). *Physical disabilities and health impairment: An introduction*. New York: Merrill.

CHAPTER 16

COPING WITH DEGENERATIVE AND TERMINAL ILLNESS

Sherwood J. Best

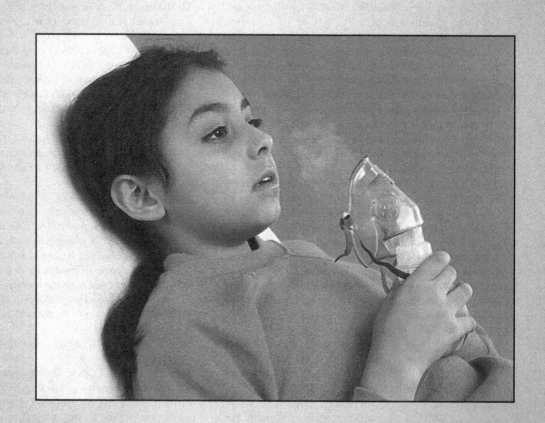

Most students with physical, health, or multiple disabilities have conditions that are chronic in nature. **Chronic illness** is defined as "a condition which lasts for a substantial period and/or persists for more than 3 months in a year or necessitates a period of continuous hospitalizations for more than a month" (Thompson & Gustafson, 1996, p. 4). The number of students with chronic illness has risen dramatically in recent years because of several factors. Conditions such as **asthma** and **diabetes mellitus** are increasingly common in the pediatric population, perhaps as a result of environmental risk factors, including pollution and obesity (Shiu, 2001; Stein & Silver, 1999). Advances in medical science and improvements in early diagnosis and illness management have resulted in increased longevity of children with conditions such as **cystic fibrosis**, **muscular dystrophy**, **cancer**, and **sickle cell anemia** (Hodgkinson & Lester, 2002; Tak & McCubbin, 2002; Thies & McAllister, 2001). Improvements in technologies such as the use of urinary **catheters**, ventilators, and medication delivery support has increased attendance in neighborhood school programs for students with chronic illness (Lehr, 1990; Mukherjee, Lightfoot, & Sloper, 2002).

Although more children with chronic illness live to enjoy school, family life, and the promise of adulthood, chronic illness poses cognitive, social/emotional, and behavioral challenges. The need for special diets, adherence to medication regimens, hospital treatments, and outpatient therapies all disrupt the student's life at home and school. If surgery or medication results in altered appearance or reduced cognitive functioning, the student must contend with additional academic, social, and emotional pressures. Having a chronic illness is a reminder to students that they are dependent on medical support, that they are different from their peers in some ways, and that they must remain vigilant in managing their condition without anticipation that this increased attention and energy will lead to a cure, even when the illness is stabilized.

Some chronic conditions cannot be permanently stabilized by medical treatment. These conditions may be **degenerative** in nature; they follow a downward progression in which abilities such as ambulation or even cognitive function may be gradually lost. Some degenerative conditions, such as Duchenne muscular dystrophy and spinal muscular atrophy, follow a predictable medical course (trajectory) (see chapters 13 and 14 for more information on these conditions). Other degenerative illnesses are less predictable and follow a pattern of exacerbation (acute or extreme illness) followed by a plateau. Degenerative illnesses, such as Duchenne muscular dystrophy, are usually diagnosed early in life, while other illnesses, such as childhood leukemia, have a sudden onset that can occur at any time. With some terminal illnesses, the child will appear ill, while with others, it will not be apparent that the child has a terminal illness until it is advanced (e.g., cystic fibrosis) (see chapter 15 on cystic fibrosis). A **terminal condition** is one that ends in the person's death.

Students with degenerative or terminal conditions and their families face unique stressors. Failure by education professionals to appreciate and support the needs of students with degenerative or terminal illness only adds to their academic and social/emotional burden (Institute of Medicine of the National Academies, 2003; Shiu, 2001; Stillion & Papadatou, 2002).

STRESS AND COPING WITH DEGENERATIVE AND TERMINAL ILLNESS

When a child is diagnosed with a degenerative or terminal illness, the entire family is faced with stressful events with which they need to cope. McCubbin and McCubbin (1993) define **coping** as "a specific effort (covert or overt) in which an individual family member, or the family as a whole, attempts to reduce or manage a demand on the family system and bring resources to bear to manage the situation" (p. 55). Families of children with degenerative and terminal illness must cope with stressors that (a) occur at the time of diagnosis, (b) relate to the child's medical needs, (c) revolve around hospitalizations and illness exacerbations, and (d) occur during developmental transitions, such as puberty (Melnyk, Feinstein, Moldenhouer, & Small, 2001). These stressors may continue for months or even years as family members strive to understand a child's diagnosis, follow medical regimens, communicate with medical personnel, and cope with their own feelings of grief, fear, and loss.

In addition to their personal stress related to the diagnosis and care needs of a child with a degenerative or terminal illness, parents must also cope with the reactions and stress of siblings (Cox, Marshall, Mandleco, & Olsen, 2001) and those of their own sick child. It is important for parents and professionals who support them to understand that children understand illness and death in different ways at different ages and developmental levels.

Developmental Conceptions of Death

Children do not view illness and death as adults do. Their perceptions of their illness and its threat to their lives depend on their age and level of cognitive development. Achieving a mature concept of death occurs over time (Speece & Brent, 1992) and means that the child has an understanding of the following subcomponents of death:

- Irreversibility (death is permanent with no return or recovery)
- Finality (death is a state where there are no life functions)
- Universality (all living things eventually die)
- Causality (death is caused by external or internal forces and is not the result of thinking, magic, and so on) (Stillion & Papadatou, 2002)

Death is perceived differently at different ages (see Figure 16–1). As seen in the figure, infants and toddlers have little real understanding of death. Any anxiety about death is expressed as fear of separation. Young children may not see the finality of death and may even believe that dead people can be made to come alive again (Sourkes, 2000). However, even when their understanding of death is still immature, children with terminal illness may exhibit increased anxiety, fear, and loneliness (Waechter, 1987). Older children become capable of thinking about the meaning of experiences in life, which leads to a more mature concept of death. It is not until adolescence that children acquire all the subcomponents that make up a truly mature concept of death. However, even adolescents may not perceive death as something that happens to them.

In addition to their cognitive understanding of illness and death, children's psychosocial understanding changes with time and experience. The work of Erikson (1950) is instructive in understanding this developmental change. Infants and very young children learn to trust that people in their world will provide them with the components of a supportive life, including food, shelter, and love. If the child is seriously ill, basic trust may be threatened. Reducing the pain of treatments, staying physically close, and surrounding the infant or young child with a sense of security are important psychological supports. Children are less afraid when their parents are close to them, and protocols have changed so that now parents can stay with their children during many medical treatments and hospitalizations.

Older children have developed a sense of trust in the world and in significant persons in their lives. They become involved in tasks of independence and initiative. Children with degenerative and terminal illness may experience fatigue or actual physical restrictions that make task exploration difficult. Their parents' wish to protect them may evolve into overprotection that stifles normal psychosocial development. Parents need to allow their child to play and explore their environment whenever health and stamina permits.

Stage	Age	Perception of Death
1	< 3 years	Little understanding; experience grief due to separation.
2	3–5 years	Death is a departure; death is temporary, reversible; death does not happen to oneself; think they can wish someone dead.
3	6–9 years	Death is final and irreversible; death happens to old people (early in the stage, belief that one never grows old); death may be viewed as a person.
4	>10 years	Death happens to anybody at any age; death is inevitable, universal, final, and irreversible; anxiety about death; adolescent may engage in dangerous activities, feeling invincible.

FIGURE 16–1 Children's concept of death.

When children leave infancy and young childhood, they enter a time of great productivity. They become interested in knowledge and social relationships outside their families. School provides important structure for all children at this time. However, physical fatigue, pain, and altered appearance (e.g., hair loss, cognitive changes from chemotherapy and/or radiation, and so on) may interfere with school attendance and peer relationships. It is important to support the student's sense of self-esteem through involvement in school and extracurricular activities to the extent of the student's ability. Great sensitivity is required to allow children to be involved without sacrificing existing strength and health.

Adolescents become involved in the process of identity development and intimate relationships. This is a time when family conflict may arise from the adolescent's increasing need to assert this emerging identity with values that can be different from their families. They may avoid opportunities for intimacy based on feelings of physical inferiority, further distancing them from critical peer relationships. They must search for life meaning when life expectancy is shorter and characterized by many threats to their health (Stillion & Papadatou, 2002).

Emotional Reactions to Death and Dying

A pioneer in the research on reactions to death and dying was Elizabeth Kübler-Ross (1969, 1974). Kübler-Ross's extensive work with adults who were diagnosed with terminal disease led her to develop a therapy of stages of adjustment to death, consisting of five stages: (a) denial, (b) anger, (c) bargaining, (d) depression, and (e) acceptance.

Denial

The first stage is characterized by denial and isolation, in which the individual believes that the terminal diagnosis cannot be true. During the initial stage, individuals might go "shopping" for alternative diagnoses or declare that test results were "mixed up" (Kübler-Ross, 1969). Denial gives the person time to adjust to the diagnosis.

Anger

Denial eventually gives way to the second stage of anger, which may be displaced to surrounding family and support personnel. The best response to this behavior is respect, time, and attention (Kübler-Ross, 1969). Attempts should be made not to take angry statements personally, as they reflect feelings of fear and anxiety.

Bargaining

The third stage is bargaining, in which the individual attempts to manipulate reality by offering good behavior in exchange for a change in extension of life (Kübler-Ross, 1969). This behavior is a psychological attempt to postpone the terminal outcome and gain control over the illness situation.

Depression

Eventually, bargaining is replaced by depression, in which the individual comes to truly realize the inevitability of death. Depression may occur at a time of relapse accompanied by symptoms of the disease, further hospitalization, and need for treatment. Individuals become worried that they are a burden to family members and can no longer effectively function and in other ways react toward their illness with a sense of extreme negativity (Kübler-Ross, 1969). Trying to cheer up someone is an inappropriate approach since depression represents the anticipation of the loss of loved ones. Rather, allowing the individual to express sorrow is the best approach.

Acceptance

Finally, depression is replaced by acceptance. According to Kübler-Ross, this time is not characterized by happiness but is a time of reduced feelings and increased sleep. The individual may withdraw from social encounters and prefer nonverbal company rather than reassurance.

Parents of children with degenerative or terminal illness may also experience intense emotional reactions. In fact, one parent may experience denial feelings while another is angry or depressed. Individuals do not "move through" emotional stages in predictable time sequences, and they do not necessarily go through the stages in the same order or in a strictly linear fashion. The individual who is disabled or sick or a member of their family could move between intense feelings of anger, depression, bargaining, and/or denial when their life circumstances change.

There are several considerations to take into account regarding the complex nature of reacting to terminal illness beyond the stage theory. Temperament and individual experiences must also be considered. Children and adolescents with degenerative or terminal illness may have heightened awareness and sophisticated knowledge about death based on hospital and treatment experiences and interactions with terminally ill peers (Schonfeld, 1999). Although their knowledge may be greater than their peers, this does not exempt them from the psychological disruption that comes from the burden of their illness while meeting the challenges of normal development. The teacher is instrumental in helping them navigate these experiences and meet their challenges.

SUPPORTING STUDENTS WITH DEGENERATIVE AND TERMINAL ILLNESS IN EDUCATIONAL SETTINGS

For many students with degenerative or terminal illness, school becomes the most "normal" aspect of their lives. Even when they are hospitalized, undergoing treatment, or feeling acutely ill, students with degenerative or terminal illness usually appreciate the distraction afforded through involvement in school activities. Every effort should be made to provide educational services to students, including in the home and hospital.

Hospital and Home Teaching

Hospital-based educational services may be provided in a special classroom in the hospital or at the student's bedside, while home-based services are provided at the student's home. The location of hospital education services is determined by the student's susceptibility to infection, level of mobility and pain, and other factors. Home and hospital services are usually contracted through the student's home school district or the school district where the hospital is located.

Hospital teaching is a unique form of educational service delivery that demands special skills from teachers. Since hospital school programs are based at medical facilities, activities related to medical treatment have priority over educational services. Teachers have to be flexible when they arrive at a student's bedside with teaching materials at hand, only to discover that the student is sleeping or has just left to have X-rays or even a bath. Rescheduling the school session will be required. Hospital teachers also provide services to students across ages and levels of academic achievement. They must be very organized and maintain an array of materials that are age appropriate and easy to transport among hospital rooms. Teachers must also be aware of materials that are contraindicated for some students. For example, wooden pencils may contain bacteria that are dangerous to students who are immunosuppressed and must be replaced by other writing materials. Teachers who work in hospital schools must have excellent communication skills because they will interact frequently with parents, nurses, doctors, respiratory therapists, hospital spiritual support personnel, and many others. Finally, hospital teachers must be prepared for an unusually high level of deaths among their students. Many teachers never experience the death of a student in their entire career, but the hospital teacher may have to cope with this loss several times a year.

Maintaining Academic Focus

As stated earlier, school is a "normal" experience for students with degenerative or terminal illness. For that reason, teachers must make the school experiences as typical as possible for these students and their peers. It is inappropriate to take the attitude of "What difference does it make if the student learns geometry in my class?" or "I don't need to discipline him. He has so much to worry about already." Making special exceptions for the student fosters hopelessness and despair. They send out a negative message of "You're dying, so it doesn't matter." This can be tremendously negative to students and their families. Maintaining the same expectations for academic success and appropriate behavior in school and maintaining the normal routine of going to school provides hope, socialization, and a feeling of accomplishment that every child and adolescent needs.

Teachers must be sensitive to the negative impact of degenerative and terminal illness on students' academic learning. Fatigue and medication may reduce alertness and the ability to focus on tasks. Physical limitations may have resulted from treatments such as surgical intervention or radiation. In these cases, teachers need to provide adaptations in curriculum content, teaching strategies, and scheduling. For example, a student who becomes very fatigued after lunch should receive more academic work earlier in the day. Perhaps a half-day schedule or less homework is appropriate. Teachers must monitor students carefully and evaluate whether transfer to home instruction is a better service delivery option. In all cases, communication with parents is a key ingredient to successful outcomes for students with degenerative or terminal illness.

Sometimes the academic aspect of school learning includes discussions on death. If the teacher is in the position to explain about death, it is best to have simple explanations surrounding the life cycle. Examples of planting a flower or having a classroom aquarium, watching the flower or fish live and then naturally die, helps explain this natural process to younger children. Older children and adolescents may benefit from a more sophisticated approach.

Bibliotherapy

One important educational tool for explaining illness and death is bibliotherapy. Berns (2003–2004) defines bibliotherapy as "the use of any kind of literature by a skilled adult or other interested person in an effort to normalize a child's grief reactions to loss, support constructive coping, reduce feelings of isolation, and reinforce creativity and problem solving" (p. 324). Many books are available that address illness, death, and dying with great sensitivity for a student's developmental level. Books provide a safe avenue to explore feelings, gain insight, and develop positive coping strategies for students with degenerative and terminal illness. In addition, their content can be used to validate students' feelings and assist them to feel less isolated as they come to identify with book characters (Berns, 2003–2004). The object of bereavement can be a family member, a neighbor, or even a pet (Corr, 2003–2004). Fiction, folktales and fairy tales, poetry, biography, and other forms are all acceptable. Berns (2003–2004) cautions against the use of literature that relies on euphemisms such as "passed away" or analogies such as death as sleep, which can be confusing or fear producing. It is acceptable to use straightforward terminology such as "dead," "grief," and "funeral." The adult who uses bibliotherapy must be well acquainted with children's developmental understanding of death and aware of behaviors that indicate termination of a bibliotherapy session or activity. Professionals with expertise in counseling, medical social work, or child life training can assist the teacher in implementing bibliotherapy sessions.

Treatment Adherence

One very important issue for teachers who provide services for students with degenerative and terminal illness is helping the student comply with treatment regimens. When there is lack of adherence, the effectiveness of medications are reduced and even lost (Abbott & Gee, 1998). Other outcomes of failure to adhere with medication regimens include swifter progression of the disease, more frequent medical emergencies, and reliance on additional medications. Sawyer and Aroni (2003) state that as many as 50% of patients with chronic illness do not adhere to medication or therapy regimens.

Blaming students with chronic illness or their families for lack of medication or therapy follow-through will not produce the desired results. Teachers need to appreciate that factors such as time requirements for adherence to regimens, conflicting family priorities, diet restrictions, cultural beliefs about medications, or fear of introducing a new treatment with possible negative side effects are powerful reasons why families may not adhere to treatment. Teachers can assist students and their families by appreciating the stress that occurs when a new medication or therapy treatment is introduced. Sawyer and Aroni (2003) recommend specific strategies that health care personnel can use for promoting treatment adherence, including reducing daily medication doses, combining medications where possible to reduce the total number, and providing reminders for medication refills and appointments. Teachers can provide additional assistance by following these guidelines:

- Become thoroughly acquainted with the dynamics of students' illnesses and symptoms.
- Communicate with family members to discover their knowledge about and support for medication and therapy treatments.
- Become acquainted with students' medical regimens so that adherence problems are recognized sooner rather than later.
- Ask families to report if the student's medical treatment changes.
- Work with family members to develop an action plan for adherence to treatment. This action plan can include short- and long-term goals and objectives for treatment completion, assessment points for evaluating medication effects, providing opportunities for students to make treatment decisions (within appropriate and approved medical parameters), and providing incentives for compliance.
- Incorporate the action plan into students' school-based individual health care plans, including appropriate scheduling of treatments that occur in school. For example, denying a student the opportunity to enjoy recess or lunchtime with peers because it is more convenient to administer medication at that time is insensitive and may be perceived as punishment.
- Reduce noncompliance at school by educating other teachers, administrators, and peers about the illness and its treatment.
- Remember that adolescence is a time when students question authority, including medical treatment adherence. Peer support groups can be especially helpful for the adolescent who is learning to take more responsibility for managing her medical treatment. Individual and/or family counseling may be indicated to reduce anxiety, stress, or acting out related to treatment adherence (Rosina, Crisp, & Steinbeck, 2003; Sawyer & Aroni, 2003).

PROVIDING EMOTIONAL SUPPORT TO STUDENTS WITH DEGENERATIVE AND TERMINAL ILLNESS

Students with degenerative and terminal illness require enhanced planning and support when they return to school from a period of hospitalization. In addition to becoming well acquainted with their disability and treatment regimens, meeting their academic needs, and providing adaptations, teachers who work with students with degenerative and terminal illness will encounter many emotional challenges to their students, their parents, their colleagues, and themselves.

School Reintegration

Students with degenerative and terminal illness may have psychological difficulty returning to school after a period of hospitalization (Sexson & Madan-Swain, 1995; Shiu, 2001). School phobia is a critical problem that can lead to excessive absenteeism. Fears about peer rejection, altered appearance, and decrease in academic performance may all contribute to this dynamic. It is desirable that school reintegration be planned for while the student is still in the hospital (Prevatt, Heffer, & Lowe, 2000; Nabors & Lehmkuhl, 2004). An individual or coordinating team can act as the liaison to school personnel. Rynard, Chambers, Klinck, and Gray (1998) suggested the following roles for transition personnel:

- Helping children cope with absences
- Providing counseling and support to students and their parents
- Teaching coping strategies for dealing with medical fears
- Teaching coping to deal with medication side effects
- Developing classroom emergency plans and interventions

- Assisting with plans for medication and other treatment compliance
- Assessing ongoing academic and psychosocial functioning
- Providing counseling for emotional and behavioral problems.

Teachers who receive students with degenerative or terminal illness in their classrooms are often not provided with information about their roles and responsibilities in ongoing monitoring of students with chronic conditions (Harrison, Faircloth, & Yaryan, 1995; Mukherjee et al., 2002) (see chapter 20 on monitoring students). Another issue is the provision of critical information while remaining sensitive to confidentiality. Although informing classmates about a peer's degenerative or terminal illness can result in a stronger and more sensitive support system, care should be taken about the nature of such teaching. Younger children may prefer that information be provided by their parents and school personnel, while older students may wish to be part of peer discussion. It is important to honor the wishes of individual students and their parents. Frequent and honest communication between school personnel and family members is important to the success of school reintegration.

Long-term follow-up to assess the student's academic and psychosocial well-being is an important component of school reintegration. Thies and McAllister (2001) stress a family-centered approach to school reintegration that recognizes the importance of family members as consistent care providers whose emotional well-being is critical to positive outcomes for students with degenerative and terminal illness.

Psychosocial Needs

Students with degenerative and terminal illness may experience elevated depression and reduced self-esteem (Key, Brown, Marsh, Spratt, & Recknor, 2001). Perception of the severity of a specific chronic condition has been associated with a phenomenon called **learned helplessness**, in which the individual relies inappropriately on others and displays reduced initiative for everyday tasks. In response, teachers need to find ways to give students a way to feel useful and valued. Creating tasks that are age appropriate, valued by others, and achievable can enhance feelings of self-worth. Maintaining focus on skill development or expertise in certain areas may also enhance the student's feeling of self-worth.

A recent innovation in social support for children with disabilities is use of a companion animal (Spence & Kaiser, 2002). Companion animals provide friendship, play opportunities, and unconditional love. They accept the child's status without reservation or hesitation. Because animals require care, they provide an opportunity for the child with a degenerative or terminal illness to engage in caregiving. Engaging in reciprocal caregiving promotes desirable feeling of self-efficacy, competence, and responsibility. Some companion animals are trained to provide services for their owners, such as fetching objects or pulling a wheelchair. Licensed service animals may accompany their owners to public places, including schools. At school, they can function as a facilitator for peer social interactions (Beck & Meyers, 1996).

Healthy peer relationships are important for all students and provide additional coping support for students with degenerative and terminal illness. When students interact with peers in school settings, they are provided with repeated opportunities for social leadership and imitation that bolsters their self-esteem and problem-solving skills (Shiu, 2001). Peer relationships become increasingly important for adolescents. It is important for parents and teachers to encourage independence and autonomy in peer interactions. For example, a student with a degenerative or terminal illness can attend movies with peers. Establishing ground rules such as "checking in" with parents on a cellular telephone and managing medication regimens independently will allow the student to enjoy time with peers (and without parents) while maintaining health precautions. Another important cultural milestone is operation of motor vehicles. Obtaining a driver's license boosts self-esteem even if the adolescent will not be driving a car for many years or the vehicle requires adaptations.

Changing Status

As the student's health status changes over time, teachers and fellow students may begin to feel uncomfortable around the student and may avoid him. Receiving proper information regarding degenerative and terminal illnesses from individuals in the medical profession and from professional associations, such as the Muscular Dystrophy Association or the Cystic Fibrosis Association, is an important first step in dispelling fear and avoidance. Students need assistance about how to inform others about their disease. For young students, a simple explanation such as "some of my muscles are different and become weak" will assist peers in understanding the condition. Older students can supply more detailed and sophisticated explanations. Teachers should provide information to others to dispel misconceptions, such as being sure that peers do not think this is a disease that is contagious. Teachers can also assist students by fostering positive and interdependent interactions among students. Group activities that use cooperative learning strategies (in which each student assists each other in assignments) may be helpful. Teachers should find things that the student with a degenerative or terminal illness does well and emphasize that to boost self-esteem. Interested peers can be designated in assisting with carrying books or getting the lunch tray. Participation in clubs should be fostered, depending on the student's interests.

Even with proper information, the emotional impact of being around a student with a degenerative disease can be difficult for some students, teachers, and even family members. It is not unusual for close friends and teachers of the student to begin to avoid the student as the disease becomes severe. Some peers and teachers will go through **anticipatory grief**. This is where the individual is grieving for the loss of the ill person before that person has died. The problem with anticipatory grief is that the ill person often becomes isolated since friends are grieving and often avoiding contact. Support may need to be given to the student's friends. Information and availability of a counselor or just someone to talk with may assist students in maintaining contact with the student with a degenerative or terminal illness.

Family Support

Emotional support will be needed for the family, student, friends, teacher, and staff. It is common for there to be some denial in any type of physical impairment. Denial occurs when something actually perceived is treated as if it did not exist (Gossler, 1987). Denial is a coping mechanism that can be healthy when it prevents incapacitating anxiety and depression but can be detrimental if it prevents individuals from acting on something that needs immediate attention. Family members, students, friends, teachers, and other professionals may deny some aspects of the disease and/or its progression. Denial should be perceived as a beneficial reaction unless it interferes with the student's functioning or creates negative responses to those interacting with the student. Counseling is recommended when this occurs.

Discrepancies may occur between the family's attitude and perception of the disease and the student's. At times, family members may be concentrating on the next phase of the disease (moving from a manual to a motorized wheelchair), while the student is coping with the dying/death aspect of the disease. Other discrepancies may arise when there is excessive denial on the part of the family. Family members may deny that the student is dying while the student has reached a state of acceptance. Another possibility is that the family accepts that the student is dying but does not want to "let the student know" or discuss it with the student. Very rarely is the outcome of the disease successfully hidden from the student. Excessive denial by members of the family or hiding this fact from the student only produces isolation on the part of the student and is not beneficial.

Talking About Terminal Illness

The student with a terminal illness may seek out the teacher to talk to because of parental denial, because he does not want to upset his parents, or because he does not want to let them know that he is fully aware of the consequences of the disease. It is important that the teacher let the student know that she is available if there is ever anything that the student would like to discuss. If the student selects the teacher as his confidant, it is important that the teacher be supportive of this. She may be the only person the student feels comfortable with talking to about his disease and about dying.

It is helpful if the teacher knows what has been said to him at home and by physicians. This information should have been obtained prior to the start of each year. If this information is not available, the teacher will need to rely on what the student is saying. The teacher may use reflective listening and questioning techniques in which she summarizes what the student is saying and asks him what he thinks about it. It is not the teacher's responsibility to tell the student he is dying. Typically, the student already knows this, or he may be denying this. He may want to discuss it in detail. The teacher does not need to have any answers for the questions the student is asking. Usually, the student just needs a supportive listener. If there is a question the teacher cannot answer, she can honestly say that she does not know or ask what the student thinks about this.

When discussing death, the teacher should avoid making comments pertaining to his or her own personal beliefs and judgments. It is important that the teacher not bring religion into the discussion since the student's religious beliefs may be very different than the teacher's. Instead, the teacher should be supportive of the coping mechanism used by the student. At no time is it ever appropriate to make judgmental comments to the student about how other family members are coping with the situation. Unless teachers have personally experienced the serious illness or death of a child, they cannot ever completely understand the family's pain. If teachers have the insight that is gained from such personal experience, they can use this knowledge to appreciate and support the student's and family's struggle. However, using personal insight as an instructional tool or model for coping only presents the family with an additional burden of trying to support the teacher's experience.

Teacher Support

Research indicates that teachers frequently lack support from the school system in working with students who were dying (Kliebenstein & Broome, 1995; Smith, Alberto, Briggs, & Heller, 1991). Specifically, teachers have reported the following needs: (a) assistance in obtaining pertinent health-related information about specific students, (b) appropriate dissemination of medical information within and among schools, (c) training to provide emotional support to students, (d) assistance about providing specialized health care to students, and (e) adequate service coordination (Mukherjee, Lightfoot, & Sloper, 2000). A school psychologist and/or counselor should be trained and made available to provide emotional support. The teacher will also need to find support through other teachers who have had a student with terminal illness as well as build or rely on an external support network (e.g., friends, family, or clergy). Teachers need to acknowledge the emotional stress that results from becoming attached to a person who is ill and whose quantity of life is uncertain.

PALLIATIVE AND END-OF-LIFE CARE

Even though students with degenerative and terminal illness are living longer than ever before, there may come a time when all medical treatments are exhausted and the emphasis shifts to comfort instead of cure or remission. At this time, students need special care and consideration. According to the Institute of Medicine of the National Academies (2003), the best practice for individuals with chronic conditions must include good palliative and end-of-life care. Palliative care "seeks to prevent, relieve, reduce, or soothe the physical and emotional distress produced by a life-threatening medical condition or its treatment, to help patients with such conditions and their families live as normally as possible, and to provide them with timely and accurate information and support in decision-making" (p. 2). Sometimes palliative care is also called "comfort care" or "supportive care." Palliative care should occur together with ongoing medical treatment. However, in the event of anticipated death, end-of-life care becomes the focus. This is defined as "preparing for an anticipated death ... and managing the end stage of a fatal medical condition" (p. 2). There are many conditions for providing good palliative and end-of-life care. Among others, these include an understandable and timely diagnosis, clear explanations of treatment, honoring family treatment choices, effective physical and psychological symptom management, providing culturally sensitive bereavement services for all survivors and support personnel, restructuring insurance and hospice benefits to eliminate coverage, and providing appropriate training in palliative and end-of-life care for all service

Principles for Pediatric Palliative, End-of-Life, and Bereavement Care

1. Appropriate care for children with life-threatening medical conditions and their families is designed to fit each child's physical, cognitive, emotional, and spiritual level of development.
2. Good care involves and respects both the child and the family.
3. Families are part of the care team.
4. Effective and compassionate care for children with life-threatening conditions and for their families is an integral and important part of the care from diagnosis through death and bereavement.
5. Professionals caring for children have special responsibilities for educating themselves and others about the identification, management, and discussion of the last phase of a child's fatal medical problem.
6. Both individual change and organizational change are needed to provide consistently excellent palliative, end-of-life, and bereavement care for children and their families.
7. More and better research is needed to increase our understanding of clinical, cultural, organizational, and other practices or perspectives that can improve palliative, end-of-life, and bereavement care for children and families.

FIGURE 16–2 Working principles for pediatric palliative, end-of-life, and bereavement care.
Source. When children die: Improving palliative and end-of-life care for children and their families. (2003). Institute of Medicine of the National Academies. Washington, DC: The National Academies Press, p. 29.

providers (Institute of Medicine of the National Academies, 2003). Figure 16–2 provides the basic principles for good palliative and end-of-life care.

It is extremely important to treat the student throughout this time as a living being whose contributions to self and others remain worthwhile and important. Whenever possible, school in some form should remain an important experience. Flexibility about school attendance and assignments, enhanced communication with family members and health care professionals, knowledge about medications, and appreciation of the individual and changing nature of palliative care is necessary to reduce emotional suffering and maintain the quality of school life.

The Importance of Hope

Throughout the progression of a degenerative and terminal illness, students and their families maintain hope for a variety of outcomes. Hope for one student may be looking forward for a cure. Another student may have the hope of graduating from high school or the hope for maintaining a friendship. Another student with a terminal illness may hope to master calculus, and yet another student may hope that the deterioration slows down. All hope sustains life and is very positive (Gossler, 1987). Hope should be encouraged.

Quality of Life and Quality of Death

A person's quality of life encompasses one's physical, psychological, and social functioning. It includes participation in society, a sense of well-being, and satisfaction. Quality of life is an important goal for all people, including students with degenerative and terminal illness. As death comes near, some life experiences assume less importance as others assume greater importance. Gaining a sense of life meaning and accomplishment, achieving comfort and peace, saying good-byes to loved ones, and even transcendence become central feelings and activities.

Students near the end of life may receive hospice care. Hospice "refers to an organization or program that provides, arranges, coordinates, and advises on a wide range of medical and supportive services for dying patients and those close to them" (Institute of Medicine of the National Academies, 2003, p. 34). Hospice care providers are trained professionals whose knowledge and commitment to comfort care assists the person with a terminal illness, family members, and those who care for them toward quality of death.

Death is inevitable, universal, and final. It is part of the human experience. Even when a person's death is anticipated, survivors may experience intense and long-lasting grief.

Family Support

Family members may often turn to a student's teacher for emotional and practical support at the time of their child's death. Because of their close and caring relationship, it is not unusual for family members to include the teacher in activities such as funeral arrangements and other end-of-life rituals. If teachers tell family members that they will help in any way needed, they must be prepared to provide that help. Sometimes help includes informing other educational professionals and classmates about the student's death, removing the student's personal items from the home for donation, preparing a meal, or even caring for siblings while parents cope with more immediate funeral chores.

The rituals of funerals create situations where people congregate, remember past events and share stories about the person who has died, and eat special foods. However, continuing support is important. Visiting family members and/or remembering the student on the anniversary of his or her death with a special card, letter, or telephone call sends the message of lasting memories that family members deeply appreciate.

Bereavement Outside the Family

Feelings of grief are shared by persons outside the immediate family of the student who has died. It is important that support be given to the student's classmates. The facts surrounding the death should be conveyed to the class in an open and honest manner. The teacher should share her reactions with the class. The students should be given an opportunity to discuss their feelings and concerns as a group. Allowing students to talk, write, or draw about their feelings is often helpful. The availability of a trained counselor or other source of bereavement support is considered ideal. It is important to remember that grief responses vary widely. Individuals may act as if nothing has happened or may crack jokes or be depressed. No response is inappropriate since individuals deal with death in different ways. When a classmate dies, it is always important to inform the parents of the other students in the class that a death has occurred.

Teachers and other educational personnel also experience grief and loss when a student dies. Often they assume a position of emotional support for the family and classmates, ignoring their own need to grieve. Unless personal needs are addressed, they may prevent a healthy continuation of teaching or response to other students with degenerative and terminal illness.

The death of a child is one of the most traumatic experiences that can occur within a family. It is also traumatic for teachers and other educational professionals when a student dies. Knowledge, preparation, and self-exploration can help teachers develop values that allow meaning of life to come from the experience of death.

SUMMARY

Although most students with physical, health, or multiple disabilities have conditions that are chronic in nature, some of these conditions are degenerative or terminal. The uncertainty of illness, complications related to treatment, and coping with pain are only a few of the unique stressors faced by students and their families. It is important for teachers to have a good understanding of these stressors as well as the emotional reactions to death and dying. Teachers need to be able to effectively support students who have degenerative and terminal illnesses in the educational setting and provide appropriate emotional support to the student, family, and classmates.

REFERENCES

Abbott, J., & Gee, J. (1998). Contemporary psychosocial issues in cystic fibrosis: Treatment adherence and quality of life. *Disability Rehabilitation, 20*, 662–671.

Beck, A. M., & Meyers, N. M. (1996). Health enhancement and companion animal ownership. *Animal Review of Public Health, 17*, 247–257.

Berns, C. F. (2003–2004). Bibliotherapy: Using books to help bereaved children. *Omega: Journal of Death and Dying, 48*, 321–336.

Corr, C. A. (2003–2004). Pet loss in death-related literature for children. *Omega: Journal of Death and Dying, 48*, 399–414.

Cox, A. H., Marshall, E. S., Mandleco, B., & Olsen, S. F. (2001). Coping responses to daily life stressors of children who have a sibling with a disability. *Journal of Family Nursing, 9*, 397–413.

Erikson, E. (1950). *Childhood and society*. New York: Norton.

Gossler, S. (1987). A look at anticipatory grief: What is health denial. In L. Charash, R. Lovelace, S. Wolf, A. Kutscher, D. Royce, & C. Leach (Eds.), *Realities in coping with progressive neuromuscular diseases* (pp 48–72). New York: Charles Press.

Harrison, B., Faircloth, J., & Yaryan, L. (1995). The impact of legislation and litigation on the role of the school nurse. *Nursing Outlook, 43*, 57–61.

Hodgkinson, R., & Lester, H. (2002). Stresses and coping strategies of mothers living with a child with cystic fibrosis: Implications for nursing professionals. *Journal of Advanced Nursing, 39*, 377–383.

Institute of Medicine of the National Academies. (2003). *When children die: Improving palliative and end-of-life care for children and their families*. Washington, DC: Author.

Key, J. D., Brown, R. T., Marsh, L. D., Spratt, E. G., & Recknor, J. C. (2001). Depressive symptoms in adolescents with a chronic illness. *Children's Health Care, 30*, 283–292.

Kliebenstein, M. A., & Broome, M. E. (1995). School re-entry for the child with chronic illness: Parent and school personnel perceptions. *Pediatric Nursing, 26*, 579–582.

Kübler-Ross, E. (1969). *On death and dying*. New York: Macmillan.

Kübler-Ross, E. (1974). The languages of dying. *Journal of Clinical Child Psychology, 3*, 22–24.

Lehr, D. H. (1990). Providing education to students with complex health care needs. *Focus on Exceptional Children, 22*, 1–9.

McCubbin, M. A., & McCubbin, H. I. (1993). Families coping with illness: The resiliency model of family stress, adjustment, and adaptation. In C. B. Danielson, B. Hamel-Bissel, & P. Winstead-Fry (Eds.), *Families, health, and illness: Perspectives on coping and intervention* (pp. 21–63). St. Louis: Mosby.

Melnyk, B. M., Feinstein, N. F., Moldenhouer, Z., & Small, L. (2001). Coping in parents of children who are chronically ill: Strategies for assessment and intervention. *Pediatric Nursing, 27*, 548–558.

Mukherjee, S., Lightfoot, J., & Sloper, P. (2000). The inclusion of pupils with a chronic health condition in mainstream school: What does it mean for teachers? *Educational Research, 42*, 59–72.

Mukherjee, S., Lightfoot, J., & Sloper, P. (2002). Communication about pupils in mainstream school with special health care needs: The NHS perspective. *Child: Care, Health, and Development, 28*, 21–27.

Nabors, L. A., & Lehmkuhl, H. D. (2004). Children with chronic medical conditions: Recommendations for school mental health clinicians. *Journal of Developmental and Physical Disabilities, 16*, 1–15.

Prevatt, F. F., Heffer, R. W., & Lowe, P. A. (2000). A review of school reintegration programs for children with cancer. *Journal of School Psychology, 38*, 447–467.

Rosina, R., Crisp, J., & Steinbeck, K. (2003). Treatment adherence of youth and young adults with and without a chronic illness. *Nursing and Health Sciences, 5*, 139–147.

Rynard, D. W., Chambers, A., Klinck, A. M., & Gray, J. D. (1998). School support programs for chronically ill children: Evaluating adjustment of children with cancer at school. *Child Health Care, 27*, 31–46.

Sawyer, S. M., & Aroni, R. A. (2003). The sticky issue of adherence. *Journal of Pediatrics and Child Health, 39*, 2–5.

Schonfeld, D. J. (1999). Children, terminal illness, and death. *Home Health Care Consultant, 6*, 27–29.

Sexson, S. B., & Madan-Swain, A. (1995). The chronically ill child in the school. *School Psychology Quarterly, 10*, 359–368.

Shiu, S. (2001). Issues in the education of children with chronic illness. *International Journal of Disability, Development, and Education, 48*, 269–281.

Smith, M., Alberto, P., Briggs, A., & Heller, K. W. (1991). Special educator's need for assistance in dealing with death and dying. *DPH Journal, 12(1)*, 35–44.

Sourkes, B. M. (2000). Psychotherapy with the dying child. In H. M. Chochinov & W. Breitbart (Eds.), *Handbook of psychiatry in palliative medicine* (pp. 265–272). New York: Oxford University Press.

Speece, M. W., & Brent, S. B. (1992). The acquisition of a mature understanding of the three components of the concept of death. *Death Studies, 16*, 211–229.

Spence, L. J., & Kaiser, L. (2002). Companion animals and adaptation in chronically ill children. *Western Journal of Nursing Research, 24*, 639–656.

Stein, R. E., & Silver, E. J. (1999). Operationalizing a conceptually based noncategorical definition: A first look at U.S. children with chronic conditions. *Archives of Pediatric and Adolescent Medicine, 153*, 68–74.

Stillion, J. M., & Papadatou, D. (2002). Suffer the children: An examination of psychosocial issues in children and adolescents with terminal illness. *American Behavioral Scientist, 46*, 299–315.

Tak, Y. R., & McCubbin, M. (2002). Family stress, perceived social support, and coping following the diagnosis of child's congenital heart disease. *Journal of Advanced Nursing, 39*, 190–198.

Thies, K. M., & McAllister, J. W. (2001). The health and education leadership project: A school initiative for children and adolescents with chronic health conditions. *Journal of School Health, 71*, 167–171.

Thompson, R. J., & Gustafson, K. E. (1996). *Adaptation in chronic childhood illness*. Washington, DC: American Psychological Association.

Waechter, E. H. (1987). Children's reaction to fatal illness. In T. Kurlick, B. Holiday, & I. M. Martinson (Eds.), *The child and the family facing life-threatening illness* (pp. 108–119). Philadelphia: Lippincott.

 # MAJOR HEALTH IMPAIRMENTS

CHAPTER 17

SEIZURES AND EPILEPSY

Kathryn Wolff Heller and Elisabeth Tucker Cohen

Seizures are one of the most common disorders of the nervous system affecting children with physical and multiple disabilities as well as their nondisabled peers. Seizures may occur as a symptom of a known condition, such as an infection or a drug reaction. Seizures may also occur as a chronic condition, known as epilepsy or seizure disorder. The prevalence rate for epilepsy is estimated at between 5 to 10 cases per 1,000 (Theodore et al., 2006).

Throughout history, many misconceptions and prejudices have surrounded individuals with epilepsy. Often people with seizures were thought to be possessed by evil spirits or divine presence. In primitive history, seizures were often attributed to evil spirits, and holes were cut into the skull presumably to let the evil spirits escape. Hippocrates wrote about epilepsy over 2,000 years ago in a work titled "The Sacred Disease." During the Middle Ages, individuals with seizures were burned at the stake as witches or were considered possessed. Before the 20th century, individuals with seizures were frequently locked away in insane asylums or jails based on the belief that they were insane. Because of a belief that epilepsy was inherited, mandatory sterilization of individuals with epilepsy remained the law in several states as late as 1971 (Temkin, 1971).

Even today, many misconceptions and social prejudices regarding individuals with epilepsy persist. Classmates and adults who are not taught about the condition may fear being around a child with epilepsy. Teachers who lack understanding of the condition may not recognize certain behaviors as seizures or may lack the knowledge of what to do when a seizure occurs. As the child with epilepsy grows older, he or she may be denied access to certain extracurricular activities. Later, gaining employment may be difficult because of the same social misconceptions and prejudices. It is clearly important that the teacher have a good understanding of the different types and characteristics of epilepsy, as well as their etiology, detection, treatment, course, and educational implications.

DESCRIPTION OF SEIZURES AND EPILEPSY

A **seizure** is defined as a sudden, involuntary, time-limited disruption in the normal electrical activity of the brain. Seizures typically last only a few seconds to minutes. Depending on the area of the brain that is affected, the seizure will present in a number of different ways. There may be involuntary movements, deviant sensations, altered consciousness, and/or other symptoms (Beers, Porter, Jones, Kaplan, & Berkwits, 2006). Seizures may occur as isolated incidences (isolated seizures) or as part of a chronic condition known as **epilepsy**.

Isolated Seizures

Seizures may occur in the healthy brain as isolated incidents due to a reversible stressor. Some examples of reversible stressors include a lack of oxygen, low blood sugar, high fever, and infection. Isolated seizures are provoked by a stressor, and once the stressor is removed, seizure activity stops.

Epilepsy

Epilepsy, also known as a seizure disorder, refers to a chronic condition in which seizures occur over time and occur spontaneously (unprovoked from other conditions). Epilepsy can be defined as two or more unprovoked seizures that occur at an interval greater than 24 hours apart and are triggered from within the brain (Aicardi, 2002; Johnston, 2004). When a person is diagnosed with epilepsy, seizures may be referred to as epileptic seizures.

Epilepsy Syndromes

In some cases, epileptic seizures will be part of an epilepsy syndrome. An epilepsy syndrome is a cluster of symptoms that usually occur together. For example, in Lennox-Gastaut syndrome, there are multiple types of seizures that do not respond well to therapy, intellectual disability or developmental delay, and a certain electroencephalogram (EEG) pattern.

Seizure Phases

Auras and Predromal Symptoms

There can be several different phases of a seizure. Some individuals who have epilepsy have a warning before their seizure begins. This may occur as an aura or a predromal symptom. An aura is a simple partial seizure that may present as certain visual, sensory, or other phenomena (see the discussion in the section "Partial Seizures"). A predromal symptom (also known as premonitory symptom) is not a seizure but a poorly understood event in which the person knows a seizure is going to occur 30 minutes or hours or days prior to its occurrence. In one study (Schulze-Bonhage, Kurth, Carius, Steinhoff, & Mayer, 2006), the mean occurrence of the prodromal symptom was 90 minutes prior to the seizure, and the most common symptoms were restlessness, headache, malaise, nausea, impaired concentration, dizziness, and tiredness.

Ictal Phase

The ictal (or ictus) phase refers to the seizure itself. There are many different types of seizures with many different characteristics. These will be described later in the chapter.

Postictal State

A postictal state refers to the period of time directly after the seizure activity is over in which the person may experience a period of impaired consciousness or confusion. The individual may also be drowsy, fall asleep, or experience specific behaviors. Certain types of seizures are associated with the occurrence of a postictal state (e.g., complex partial or tonic-clonic). The postictal state may last from a few minutes to several hours. In one study (Allen, Ferrie, Livingston, & Feltbower, 2007), median recovery time of full consciousness in children after a seizure was 38 minutes and after idiopathic seizures was 1.25 hours.

ETIOLOGY OF SEIZURES AND EPILEPSY

Causes of Seizures

Anything occurring in the body that disrupts the normal electrical activity in the brain can elicit a seizure. Conditions such as poisoning, cerebral trauma, heat exhaustion, heatstroke, brain tumors, drug overdose, drug withdrawal, metabolic disorders (such as low or high blood sugar), and infections of the central nervous system (such as meningitis or encephalitis) are among the many potential seizure-causing events (Beers et al., 2006). Recently, even common infections often seen in children in the school setting, such as influenza, have been found to trigger seizures (Newland et al., 2007).

The most common cause of seizures in childhood is an elevated temperature (over 102 degrees Fahrenheit, or 39 degrees Celsius). The term *febrile seizures* is used to describe seizures associated with fever (but not including those due to brain infections). They are usually associated with such infections as upper respiratory infections and ear infections, and they most commonly occur between the ages of 18 months and 4 years (McBrien & Bonthius, 2000). Typically, these seizures are generalized tonic-clonic seizures.

When seizures occur as a symptom of a short-term condition, the person will no longer have seizures once the condition is gone. However, in some instances the condition may result in some type of damage or change in brain tissue resulting in seizures after the primary condition has resolved. The person would then be considered to have epilepsy. For example, some individuals have scars in their brains from traumatic brain injury that could lead to abnormal electrical activity that results in epilepsy. Individuals who have had infections of the central nervous system, such as encephalitis, have been found to develop epilepsy, although the exact mechanism causing the epilepsy is not well understood (Chen, Fang, & Chow, 2006).

[handwritten margin note: febrile = fever (not due to brain infections)]

Causes of Epilepsy

The etiology of a person's epilepsy is considered either symptomatic or idiopathic. Epilepsy that is symptomatic refers to epilepsy that occurs as part of a symptom of a known cause. These causes are usually due to chronic conditions involving abnormalities of the brain. Before the age of 2, epileptic seizures are often symptomatic and are often caused by birth defects, birth trauma, or metabolic disorders. Children and adults with brain tumors commonly develop epilepsy, even when the brain tumor is under control (van Breemen, Pharm, & Vecht, 2007). Aneurysms, abnormalities in the blood system, and congenital abnormalities of brain structures are only a few of the possible brain abnormalities that can result in epilepsy. Such abnormalities may occur during fetal development or later in life. When the etiology is unknown but is thought to be due to some central nervous system abnormality, the term *cryptogenic* epilepsy or *probably symptomatic* epilepsy may be used (Bourgeois, 2002; Engel, 2007).

Epilepsy may also be classified as idiopathic. When discussing epilepsy, idiopathic most commonly refers to a disorder unto itself (as opposed to being symptomatic of another disorder) (Engel, 2007). Although the cause is typically unknown, it is suggested that there is probably a genetic base (Beers et al., 2006). Some idiopathic epilepsies have been mapped to specific chromosomal regions, although the specific gene has often not been identified. For example, partial epilepsy with auditory symptoms (e.g., ringing noise that grows louder) has been found to have a chromosome locus of 10q (Delgado-Escueta, Medina, Alonso, & Fong, 2002; Ottman, Risch, & Hauser, 1995). Research is ongoing in this area.

Epilepsy may occur as a single impairment or in conjunction with other impairments. Most individuals who have epilepsy have no other disability. However, there is an increased incidence of epilepsy in children with conditions such as **cerebral palsy**, **spina bifida**, **traumatic brain injury**, intellectual disability, congenital infections, and Rett syndrome (see chapter 20 for information on Rett syndrome) (Agrawal, Timothy, Pandit, & Manju, 2006; McBrien & Bonthius, 2000; Moser, Weber, & Lutschg, 2007; Yoshida et al., 2006). Children with developmental delays are especially vulnerable to developing epilepsy with 25% of children with severe developmental delays and up to 50% of children with profound developmental delays having epilepsy (Lhatoo & Sander, 2001). As seen in Figure 17–1, the risk of having an idiopathic seizure prior to 5 years of age is particularly high in children with intellectual disabilities and cerebral palsy as compared to those who have intellectual disabilities alone (Hollander, Sunder, & Wrobel, 2005; Nevo et al., 1995).

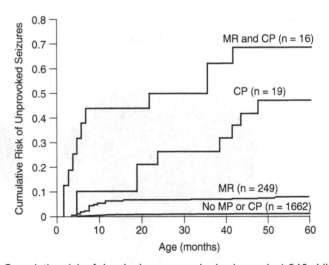

FIGURE 17–1   Cumulative risk of developing unprovoked seizures in 1,946 children referred to the Child Development Center: effect of presence of mental retardation (MR) (intellectual disability) and cerebral palsy (CP) on risk of unprovoked seizures. Kaplan-Meier curves.
Source: Used with permission from Nevo et al. (1995, p. 239).

DYNAMICS OF SEIZURES

As discussed in chapter 5 on cerebral palsy, **neurons** (nerve cells) transport signals between the various areas of the brain as well as between the brain and the rest of the body. Signals are sent and received in an orderly fashion by electrochemical means. During a seizure, there is an abnormal, sudden, excessive, and disorderly electrical firing of neurons in the brain. Some people like to visualize this as an electrical storm. For a seizure to occur, the electrical activity must reach a certain threshold of excitation, often referred to as a **seizure threshold**. Everyone has a threshold of excitation that will result in a seizure under certain circumstances.

There are many different types of seizures. The type of seizure will depend on which part of the brain is involved. Electrical stimulation of certain parts of the brain can result in such symptoms as movement of body parts (including such complex movements as running), tingling sensations, visual images, and certain smells. Anything that the brain can do a seizure may also do. Figure 17–2 illustrates some possible brain locations of some partial and generalized seizures.

Seizures may be more likely to occur in individuals who have epilepsy when certain conditions are present. For example, excess fatigue, lack of sleep, illness, fever, alcohol, illegal drug use, or noncompliance with taking antiepileptic medication may increase the likelihood that a seizure will occur (Beers et al., 2006). There are also certain precipitating factors that may elicit a seizure, known as reflex seizures.

Reflex Seizures

A seizure is considered a reflex seizure if it is evoked by certain precipitating stimuli. Stimuli that can trigger a reflex seizure may be considered elementary or complex. Examples of el-

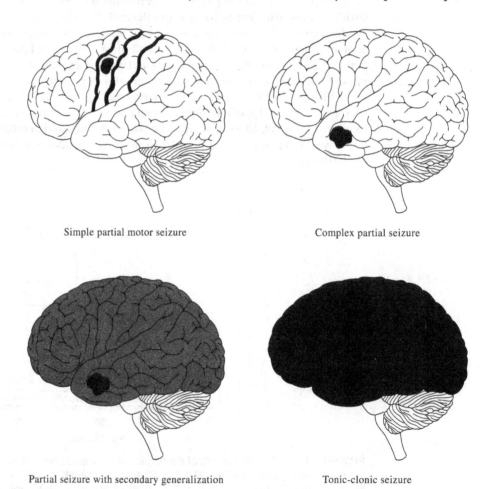

Simple partial motor seizure   Complex partial seizure

Partial seizure with secondary generalization   Tonic-clonic seizure

FIGURE 17–2   Example locations in the brain of different types of seizures.

ementary triggers include flashing lights (e.g., strobe lights), visual patterns (e.g., reflecting geometric designs), certain sounds (e.g., fire alarm), and a startle response. Examples of elaborate stimuli include toothbrushing, reading, chess playing, and thinking of music (D'Souza, O'Brien, Murphy, Trost, & Cook, 2007; Engel, 2007). In some individuals, seizures may be induced on playing certain electronic games on the Internet (e.g., massively multiplayer online role-playing games) (Chuang, 2006). Many different types of seizures (e.g., partial seizure, absence, or tonic-clonic) can occur as reflex seizures.

CHARACTERISTICS OF SEIZURES AND EPILEPSY

There are many kinds of seizures, each with varying characteristics, treatments, and prognoses. The most common classification system of seizures is the Classification of Epileptic Seizures, published in 1981 by the International League Against Epilepsy (ILAE). The classification system is used by several prominent organizations, such the World Health Organization (Theodore et al., 2006). In 2001, the ILAE proposed a revised classification system, although some authorities have found this proposed classification system as having limited daily use (Okuma, 2004).

Both the 1981 and the 2001 classification systems divide seizures into two main classifications: partial (or focal) seizures and generalized seizures. Partial (or focal) seizures begin in a part of one cerebral hemisphere. Generalized seizures begin in both cerebral hemispheres. Some differences exist between the two classification systems in grouping of the seizures and in terminology, which tends to be very descriptive in the proposed classification system. For example, simple partial seizures (with motor signs) are called focal motor seizures with elementary clonic motor signs under the proposed classification system, referring to seizures that are "focal" (initial activation of only part of one hemisphere), have "elementary motor signs" (a single type of contraction of a muscle or group of muscles that is not stereotyped or in phases), and are "clonic" (contraction of muscle group which may be repetitive and often prolonged). Additional subcategories of seizures have been added in the proposed system based on the presence of specific symptoms. Since the 1981 classification system is currently the adopted system, we will use this system to explain the different types of seizures while referencing the 2001 proposed system as appropriate.

Partial Seizures

Partial seizures (also known as focal seizures in the proposed classification system) occur or begin in part of one hemisphere. They account for a large percentage of seizures in children, up to approximately 20% to 40% (Pellock & Duchowny, 2002). Partial seizures are divided into two types: simple and complex. The term *simple partial* refers to seizures that have no impairment of consciousness, and *complex partial* refers to seizures that have impairment of consciousness. A listing of partial seizures based on the current and proposed classification systems is given in Figure 17–3.

Simple Partial Seizures with Motor Signs

Simple partial motor seizures occur from abnormal electrical discharges occurring in a motor area of the brain. Depending on the location of this electrical activity, any part of the body may be involved, although movements of the face, neck, arms, or legs are the most common (Johnston, 2004). For example, if abnormal electrical activity occurs on the part of the primary motor cortex that moves the arm, the arm will make a jerking or stiffening motion during the seizure. If it occurs near the top of the motor cortex where the foot is controlled, the foot will make an involuntary jerking or stiffening movement. Even very small muscles, such as those controlling the movement of a finger or facial muscle, can be affected.

Simple partial motor seizures occurring on the primary motor cortex may involve one select area (such as the foot) or may spread to other motor areas along the primary motor

I. Partial Seizures (ILAE, 1981)	Focal Seizures (ILAE, 2001)
Simple partial	
a. Simple partial seizures with motor signs	Focal motor seizures a. with elementary clonic motor signs b. with asymmetrical tonic motor seizures c. with typical (temporal lobe) automatisms d. with hyperkinetic automatisms e. with focal negative myoclonus f. with inhibitory motor seizures
b. Simple partial seizures with sensory symptoms	Focal sensory seizures a. with elementary sensory symptoms
c. Simple partial seizures with autonomic symptoms	
d. Simple partial with psychic symptoms	b. with experiential sensory symptoms
	Gelastic seizures *
	Hemiclonic seizures **
	Reflex seizures
Complex partial	(Corresponds to focal motor seizures with automatisms)
Partial seizure with secondary generalization	Secondarily generalized seizures

* Gelastic seizure—laughing seizure
** Hemiclonic seizure—seizure occurring on half the body (e.g., right arm and leg)

FIGURE 17–3 Classification of partial (focal) seizures under the current 1981 classification system and the 2001 proposed system.

cortex. When this occurs, the mouth may move, then the neck, and then the shoulder, and then movement continues down to the legs (although it can go in the opposite direction). This sequential involvement of body parts is often referred to as a "Jacksonian epilepsy" or "Jacksonian march" (Guyton & Hall, 2006).

In simple partial seizures, the person is awake and alert as the seizure occurs. These seizures are usually of brief duration, occurring for approximately 10 to 30 seconds. For individuals unfamiliar with seizures, simple partial seizures may be dismissed as nothing important or missed completely.

Simple Partial Seizures with Sensory Symptoms

Simple partial seizures with sensory involvement result from abnormal electrical discharge occurring along the somatosensory cortex or other sensory centers in the brain. Simple partial sensory seizures occurring on the somatosensory cortex may result in feeling of numbness, tingling, pain, or sense of movement on any body part. When the electrical activity occurs on the somatosensory cortex, the resulting seizure may remain in one location or travel to adjacent areas.

Other simple partial sensory seizures may occur from abnormal bursts of electrical impulses occurring in special sensory areas. For example, visual symptoms, such as light flashes, colors, and field defects, may occur from seizures in the occipital lobe of the brain. Simple partial seizures may also cause the individual to smell a certain odor (olfactory symptom) or have a particular taste in the mouth (gustatory symptom). As with simple partial motor seizures, no impairment of consciousness is present. (In the proposed classification system, simple partial seizures with sensory symptoms is known as focal sensory seizures with elementary sensory symptoms, referring to symptoms occurring due to a single phenomena involving primarily one sensory mode such as somatosensory, visual, auditory, or olfactory.)

As previously discussed, a simple partial sensory seizure may occur as an aura. An aura is a simple partial seizure that precedes a more complex seizure. Auras are often present before a complex partial seizure or a tonic-clonic seizure. The aura can serve as a warning to the person that a more severe seizure is about to occur. Any of the simple partial seizures may serve as an aura, although the simple partial sensory seizures are more common.

Simple Partial Seizures with Autonomic Symptoms

Simple partial seizures may also produce autonomic symptoms (or signs) if they involve the autonomic nervous system. Symptoms may include a fast heart rate, dilation of the pupils of the eye, or "goose bumps" (piloerection). Complaints of abdominal pain have occurred, although this is rarely a seizure.

Simple Partial Seizures with Psychic Symptoms

When higher cortical functions are involved, simple partial seizures with psychic symptoms occur. The individual may feel certain emotions, hallucinations, or other disturbances in cognitive functioning. Although psychic symptoms can occur as a simple partial seizure, they are more often associated with more complex seizures. (In the 2001 proposed classification system, these seizures are known as focal sensory seizures with experiential sensory systems.)

Complex Partial Seizures

Complex partial seizures have been formally called psychomotor seizures or temporal lobe seizures (since many occur in the temporal lobe). They often start with an aura, although children are often unable to report them because of not understanding their significance (Pellock & Duchowny, 2002). Being a complex seizure, there is impairment of consciousness in which there is usually some awareness of the environment. Complex partial seizures are often multisymptomatic and usually involve certain motor behaviors and psychic symptoms. They do not usually last longer than a couple of minutes, but they are often associated with a postictal state that lasts over several minutes.

Motor behaviors that occur in complex partial seizures are typically automatisms. An automatism is an involuntary repetitive motor movement. Automatisms may be simple motor behaviors, such as chewing, blank staring, scratching, gesturing, or repeating a phrase. The person may appear dazed and engage in random purposeless activity, such as walking in a circle, picking up objects, or picking at his or her clothes. Automatisms can also be quite complex and appear more purposeful, such as drawing. Whatever form of automatism the person exhibits, the same pattern will typically be repeated with each seizure. Automatisms are also maturationally based. For example, sucking and simple repetitive gestures may be seen in infants as automatisms, whereas more complex motor behaviors occur later in life (Pellock & Duchowny, 2002). (Because of the occurrence of automatisms, the proposed classification system uses the term focal motor seizures with typical (temporal lobe) automatisms.)

Psychic symptoms may be present in complex partial seizures. These may occur prior to the beginning of the seizure as an aura. The child may express a certain emotion such as fear, joy, or embarrassment. Illusions and hallucinations are also possible. Distortions of memory may occur with "flashbacks" to earlier events or déjà vu (sensation that the experience has occurred before). These types of automatism are rarely described by children until near the end of the first decade of life (Pellock & Duchowny, 2002).

Complex Partial Seizures to Generalized Seizures

In this category, the seizure begins with a complex partial seizure and then spreads to other parts of the cerebral cortex, across both hemispheres. This results in a generalized seizure.

Generalized Seizures

Seizures that have abnormal electrical activity occurring in both cerebral hemispheres from the onset are known as generalized seizures. There are many different types of generalized

II. Generalized Seizures (ILAE, 1981)	Generalized Seizures (ILAE, 2001)

Absence
  a. Typical
  b. Atypical
	Typical absence seizures
	Atypical absence seizures
	Myoclonic absence seizures

Generalized tonic-clonic
 	
Clonic
	Clonic seizures
	  a. with tonic features
	  b. without tonic features

Tonic seizures	Tonic seizures

Myoclonic	Myoclonic seizures
	Massive bilateral myoclonus
	Eyelid myoclonia
	  a. without absences
	  b. with absences
	Myoclonic atonic seizures
	Negative myoclonus

Atonic	Atonic seizures
	Spasms Reflex seizures in generalized epilepsy syndromes Seizures of the posterior neocortex Neocortical temporal lobe seizures

FIGURE 17–4 Classification of generalized seizures under the current 1981 classification system and the 2001 proposed system.

seizures, ranging from the subtle absence seizure to dramatic convulsive seizures. Figure 17–4 shows the various types of generalized seizures. The major types of generalized seizures are in both classification systems.

Absence Seizures

Absence seizures were formally known as petit mal (meaning "little bad"). In the typical form of this seizure, the child suddenly loses consciousness, stops what he or she is doing, and either stares straight ahead vacantly or rolls the eyes upward. There is usually no movement or change in tone or posture, except the head may fall slightly forward, and there may be some automatisms. When automatisms occur, they are frequently eye blinking or mouth twitching, although more complex automatisms can occur. These seizures usually last about 5 to 10 seconds, although they can range from 1 second to 1 minute. At the completion of the seizure, the child resumes the previous activity as if nothing occurred. If the seizure occurred in midsentence, the child usually completes the sentence on termination of the seizure. Absence seizures can occur hundreds of times a day (Tovia, Goldberg-Stern, Shahar, & Kramer, 2005).

The onset of these seizures is abrupt and occurs without warning since an aura is not associated with absence seizures. There is no postictal confusion or drowsiness with this type of seizure, so the child can continue with the activity he or she was performing. However, the child may be confused as to what is occurring in class because of the lost time. Frequent absence seizures can make classroom activities incomprehensible, frustrating, or dull, and academic problems can occur (McBrien & Bonthius, 2000). For example, a student who is experiencing several absence seizures during a reading lesson might hear the lesson in this manner:

Today, class, we are going t.............
..............................begins with a
boy who wanted to h................
....
....
............Margaret cried out, I......

Because of the subtlety of the seizures, they are frequently missed. The student may be reprimanded for daydreaming and for not paying attention. Unlike daydreaming, however, the child cannot be brought out of a seizure by touching the student or speaking in a loud voice. Careful observation of the child is needed to detect these seizures. If it is unclear whether an absence seizure is occurring or whether the child is merely staring off into space, teachers may say a word to the child when the questionable episode is occurring and ask the child to recall the word when the episode is over. The child would be unable to recall the word if a typical absence seizure occurred (Bourgeois, 2002). However, some variations exist in which the suspension of consciousness may be less than complete. In these cases, the child continues simple behavior with mild confusion during the seizure without a loss of contact. These seizures may not be detected by observation; instead, a neurological examination with an EEG is needed.

Besides the typical absence seizures that are described here, there are also other forms of absence seizures. In atypical absence seizures, the onset and cessation of the seizure is not as abrupt as a typical absence seizure. This type of seizure is also associated with changes in muscle tone. Certain syndromes, such as the Lennox-Gastaut syndrome, are considered when atypical absence seizures are present. Absence seizures may also have myoclonic seizures (referred to as myoclonic absences in the proposed classification system). In this type of absence, there is a range of consciousness from a complete loss to a partial disruption that is accompanied by severe bilateral myoclonic jerks, usually involving the shoulders, arms, and/or legs (Bureau & Tassinari, 2005).

Generalized Tonic-Clonic Seizures

Generalized tonic-clonic seizures, previously known as grand mal seizures, are the dramatic seizures that people usually think of when they learn someone has epilepsy. It is a convulsive seizure, which refers to a forceful involuntary contraction(s) of the muscles. Some individuals may have an aura or prodromal symptom warning them that a seizure is going to occur. This type of seizure usually has a postictal state after the seizure is over.

When a tonic-clonic seizure occurs, there is a sudden loss of consciousness. A brief cry or scream may occur as the chest and abdominal muscles contract, causing air to be forced out of the lungs. The seizure will progress through a tonic and then a clonic phase. In the tonic (rigid) phase, there is diffuse rigidity of the muscles, with the arms and legs extended. Often the back is arched. (If the student has a medical condition with contractures, this degree of extension may not be present.) If the child is standing, he (or she) will fall and possibly sustain injury from the impact. During this phase, the eyes may deviate upward, and cyanosis (blueness of lips, nail beds, and skin) may occur from lack of oxygen (due to irregular or shallow respirations). The tonic phase usually lasts for a few seconds and evolves into a clonic phase. The clonic (jerking) phase begins with rhythmic jerking motions of the body that gradually decrease in frequency until they end with the body often being limp (Bourgeois, 2002).

Throughout the tonic-clonic seizure, saliva may pool in the mouth and bubble at the lips. Because of inefficient swallowing and the accumulation of saliva, breathing may be noisy and become shallow and irregular, resulting in cyanosis. **Aspiration** of the saliva may occur, unless the person is moved onto his side. The person may bite his tongue, and vomiting is possible. Urinary incontinence (loss of bladder control) is a frequent occurrence, although bowel incontinence may occur as well. The entire seizure usually lasts 1 to 2 minutes (Beers et al., 2006).

After the seizure, the child will be exhausted and typically sleep for 30 minutes to 2 hours (Johnston, 2004). As the child awakens, there may be some confusion and lethargy. Muscle soreness, vomiting, and a headache may also occur.

Tonic Seizures

Seizures may also take the form of having only a tonic phase. In these instances, they are known as tonic seizures.

Clonic Seizures

Some individuals may have only a clonic phase. These are referred to as clonic seizures.

Myoclonic Seizures

Myoclonic seizures are another type of generalized seizure in which there are sudden, brief muscle jerks that may involve part or all of the body. The muscle jerks are so brief (less than half a second) that there is no impairment of consciousness. They occur as isolated events or in clusters (Bourgeois, 2002). The severity of this type of seizure varies, with some myoclonic seizures being very subtle and difficult to recognize and others being severe enough to cause the child to fall. Sometimes the seizures are mistaken for clumsiness. Injury can result if the child falls forward into a desk or other object.

There are multiple kinds of myoclonic movements that are not seizures. Some of these may be normal "sleep starts," other movement disorders, or symptoms of infection. The physician will differentiate these from an actual myoclonic seizure.

Atonic Seizures

Atonic seizures, formerly known as akinetic or drop attacks, consist of a sudden loss of muscle tone. They can almost be considered the opposite of myoclonic seizures in which there is a high degree of muscle tone. In an atonic seizure, the child will suddenly fall to the ground because of a lack of muscle tone and then get back up. Injury can result from the fall.

Unclassified Epileptic Seizures

The current classification system has a category known as "unclassified epileptic seizures." Some seizures do not neatly fit into the partial or generalized categories, so they may fall under this category (e.g., seizure generalized throughout one hemisphere). This category also accommodates some of the unusual seizures that can occur that also do not fit the current system.

Status Epilepticus

Although seizures usually stop within a few minutes without intervention, a dangerous condition known as **status epilepticus** may occur. Status epilepticus is a continuous seizure or recurrent seizures that occur without regaining consciousness. In the past, a seizure would need to last more than 30 minutes to be considered status epilepticus, although some authorities have shortened the times (e.g., more than 5 or 10 minutes for tonic-clonic seizures) to encourage immediate treatment (Lowenstein, Bleck, & Macdonald, 1999; Raspall-Chaure, Chin, Neville, & Scott, 2006). Status epilepticus can occur for any type of seizure, including both generalized and partial forms. It may be divided into partial (focal) and generalized status epilepticus or into convulsive and nonconvulsive status epilepticus. For the purposes of this chapter, the latter will be used because of the differences in consequences between the two types.

Convulsive Status Epilepticus

Convulsive status epilepticus is usually a continuous tonic-clonic seizure or the occurrence of one seizure right after another without gaining consciousness. It is the most serious type of status epilepticus and is associated with causing permanent brain damage or even death. Individuals are at greater risk of having status epilepticus if they have neuromotor retardation (i.e., delays in development in at least two of the following: personal-social, fine motor, language, or gross motor). In addition, abrupt discontinuation of antiepileptic medication is also considered a risk factor (KarasalİhoĞlu et al., 2003).

In a classic study by Aicardi and Chevrie (1970), the effects of status epilepticus (tonic-clonic or clonic type) were examined with 239 children. Eighty-eight children in this study had permanent neurological disorders after the initial episode. These included hemiplegia, diplegia, and other movement abnormalities. About half these children were normal before the status, and the status is attributed as the cause of the neurological problem. (The other half may have had these conditions prior to the status.) After the status, intellectual disability was present in 114 children, with 78 of these children being documented as having normal development prior to their first status. The gravity of status epilepticus is reaffirmed in this study since 13 children's deaths were attributed to the seizures. Fortunately, status epilepticus will usually respond to medication (often given intravenously) that stops the status epilepticus.

Nonconvulsive Status Epilepticus

Nonconvulsive status epilepticus can be defined as a change in mental process or behavior from baseline that is associated with continuous epileptiform discharges in the EEG. Although there is the potential to damage neurons in this form of status epilepticus, the long-term consequences have been difficult to determine because of complications and treatment effects. This condition does not usually result in death, unless the underlying causative medical disorder is fatal (Meierkord & Holtkamp, 2007).

Epilepsy Syndromes

Once the type of epileptic seizure has been identified, the physician will try to determine if the person's seizures is part of a syndrome. Identifying whether the seizure is part of a syndrome will help determine appropriate treatment. There are several epileptic syndromes, each with its own set of characteristics. A few of these syndromes will be described.

Benign Childhood Epilepsy with Centrotemporal Spikes

Two of the most common epileptic syndromes occurring in children from ages 3 to 13 years are benign childhood epilepsy with centrotemporal spikes and childhood absence epilepsy (Tovia et al., 2005). In benign childhood epilepsy with centrotemporal spikes, there are partial seizures with motor signs and often somatosensory symptoms, a certain EEG pattern, and no neurological or intellectual deficit prior to onset, and it usually goes into remission spontaneously during adolescence (Engel & Fejerman, 2005; Loiseau & Duche, 1989).

Childhood Absence Epilepsy

Childhood absence epilepsy syndrome (also known as pyknolepsy) is genetically determined and age related and affects children without disabilities. It usually consists of severe and frequent absence seizures lasting around 10 seconds each and occurring multiple times a day. Childhood absence epilepsy usually disappears by adolescence, although tonic-clonic seizures may develop and continue (Sidenvall, Frogren, Blomquist, Heijbel, 1993; Tovia et al., 2005).

Juvenile Myoclonic Epilepsy (Janx Syndrome)

An epileptic syndrome that occurs in adolescence is juvenile myoclonic epilepsy. This type of epilepsy usually begins between the ages of 12 and 16. Typically, the seizures are mild with involvement of the hand and arms, causing the adolescent to spill or drop objects. Initially, there may only be myoclonic jerks occurring after awakening, causing the adolescent to drop a toothbrush, for example. These seizures are sometimes ignored by the adolescent. However, the adolescent may go on to develop generalized tonic-clonic seizures (Johnston, 2004). Genes and genetic loci have been identified for this epileptic syndrome, although it has a complex pattern of inheritance (Pal et al., 2005).

Progressive Myoclonic Epilepsies

Progressive myoclonic epilepsies consist of a heterogeneous group of rare genetic disorders. For example, in Lafora disease, seizures begin between 10 and 18 years of age with generalized tonic-clonic seizures. Myoclonic jerks appear as the disease progresses. Mental deterioration is a key feature of this disorder (Johnston, 2004).

Lennox-Gastaut Syndrome

As previously described in this chapter, Lennox-Gastaut syndrome occurs in individuals with intellectual disabilities (or developmental delay). This epileptic syndrome consists of multiple types of seizures (such as atypical absences or tonic, atonic, and myoclonic seizures). It is one of the most difficult syndromes to control because of the intractable nature of the seizures. Seizures are usually frequent and may range from approximately 9 to 70 seizures daily. In one study, most seizures occurred while the children were awake and inactive (Papini, Pasquinelli, Armellini, & Orlandi, 1984). A significantly smaller percentage occurred when the children were awake and active. A stimulating environment has been suggested as assisting in reducing the number of daily seizures.

DETECTION OF SEIZURES AND EPILEPSY

Initial diagnosis of a seizure must determine whether a seizure has in fact occurred. Some conditions may closely mimic a seizure and be mistakenly identified as one (e.g., breath-holding spells, fainting, migraine headaches, movement disorders, cardiac arrhythmia, or drug overdose). A medical examination, blood work, and tests are performed to determine if a seizure has occurred and the possible cause. If a seizure is identified, the physician will further try to determine whether it is an isolated seizure or epilepsy, whether it is symptomatic or idiopathic, and whether the seizure is part of an epilepsy syndrome.

One of the best ways to diagnose a new-onset seizure is for the neurologist to directly observe the seizure. Unfortunately, it is unlikely this will occur during the physical examination. A careful description of the seizure (or event) by those observing the incident will assist in diagnosis. In addition, there are usually questions regarding the presence of an aura, clouded consciousness or unconsciousness, understanding or producing language during the seizure, presence of automatisms, and asymmetry of the seizure (to determine if it began on one part or side of the body or both) (Oguni, 2004). This information will help rule out other conditions and help determine the type of seizure.

A neurological exam will be performed to determine any abnormal physical findings. The neurologist will look for anomalies such as abnormal head size, differences in reflexes between the right and left side of the body, balance problems, and ability to detect sensory input. Throughout the examination, the neurologist will assess for signs of other underlying disorders that can cause seizures.

Several laboratory tests are likely to be included in the medical examination. Lab tests may include tests for metabolic disorders, a complete blood count, a serum glucose test, liver function test, or tests for various infections. Other tests, such as a spinal tap, may be performed if meningitis is suspected. In a spinal tap, a needle is inserted into the spinal column to remove cerebral spinal fluid, which is then examined for infection (Beers et al., 2006).

An EEG can provide critical information as to whether epilepsy exists as well as the type of epilepsy (see Figure 17–5). An EEG consists of placing several electrodes (small round discs) in precise places on the scalp (or infrequently on the surface of the brain or within the brain). Wires from the electrodes are connected to the EEG machine, which records the electrical activity of the brain on a graph. Conditions that are known to frequently precipitate a seizure will often be simulated while a child has an EEG, such as encouraging the child to hyperventilate, using strobing lights, or sleep deprivation. Different abnormal wave forms on the EEG indicate different types of seizures.

Abnormalities in the EEG are often present when epilepsy exists, even if a seizure is not occurring at the time of the test. However, a normal EEG does not eliminate the possibility of epilepsy. An EEG may be normal when no abnormal electrical activity occurs between seizures or if the standard positioning of the electrodes does not detect abnormal electrical activity in some obscure place in the brain. As many as 50% of individuals show no indications of epilepsy on a routine EEG (Brodie & French, 2000). When the type of seizure is difficult to diagnose, an ambulatory EEG monitoring system or a prolonged EEG monitoring with simultaneous closed-circuit video recording may be used.

Brain imagery techniques may be used to determine the presence of underlying brain pathology. Brain imagery techniques can detect tumors, atrophy, calcification, aneurysms, and other brain abnormalities. There are several types of imagery techniques. The computerized tomography scan (also known as a CT or CAT scan) takes a series of X-rays at different levels

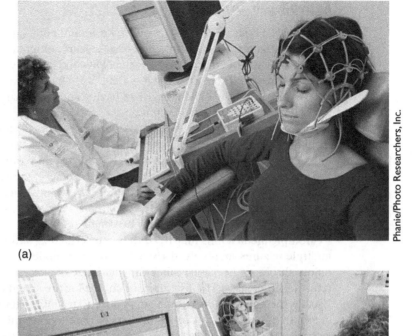

(a)

(b)

FIGURE 17–5 EEG machine with technician monitoring the readout (a) and EEG showing the electrical activity of the brain on the computer monitor (b).

of the brain. A dye may be injected into the bloodstream to enhance visualization of the blood vessels of the brain. Another technique uses magnetic resonance imagery (MRI). Instead of using X-rays, MRI visualizes different parts of the brain through the use of the magnetic qualities of the molecules. This technique can often detect finer detail of the cranial structures. Less frequently used techniques include positron emission tomography (PET) and single photon emission computerized tomography (SPECT). These tests require the injection of a small amount of radioactive material, and the scanners can then detect metabolic activity of the brain to help pinpoint the location of the seizures.

TREATMENT OF EPILEPSY

Treatment for epilepsy may involve medication, vagus nerve stimulation, and possibly surgery. Sometimes a special diet is used. The goal of treatment is to control the seizures and prevent complications. If seizures are symptomatic, control of the underlying condition will be targeted. General treatment precautions may include medical management of the seizure, use of a medical alert bracelet that indicates that the child has epilepsy, use of a protective helmet for frequently occurring seizures that result in falls, avoidance of certain external stimuli that elicit seizures, and providing information regarding seizure management.

Antiepileptic Drugs

Individuals who have epilepsy usually take antiepileptic (anticonvulsant) drugs to help control their seizures. When a child first has a seizure, antiepileptic medication may not be prescribed if there is a normal exam, normal EEG, and negative family history. This is because a single unprovoked seizure has a less than 50% change of reoccurrence (Brodie & French, 2000). However, if the child is at risk of having another seizure (e.g., positive family history), antiepileptic medication will often be prescribed.

There are several different kinds of antiepileptic medications, with some being more effective for certain types of seizures than others. For example, ethosuximide is indicated for absence seizures, while carbamazepine is indicated for partial seizures, generalized seizures, and mixed seizures (but not absence or myoclonic seizures). The goal is to use one drug with the fewest number of side effects (e.g., drowsiness, behavior changes, or gastrointestinal problems). If the side effects become too severe, such as incapacitating drowsiness, the dosage or the medication itself may be changed.

Multiple medications may need to be prescribed in difficult to control seizures or when multiple seizures are involved. Use of multiple antiepileptic medications are usually avoided unless absolutely necessary since the incidence of adverse effects and undesirable drug interactions increases. The first drug of choice for the specific type of epilepsy is tried first. Usually, the child will start on a small dose that will be gradually increased. Blood will be drawn from the child at various periods of time to determine the blood levels of the medication (this will help determine if the child is getting the correct amount). If seizures continue, the amount of medication will be increased until seizure control is reached, observing for undesirable side effects, and avoiding serious toxic blood levels of the drug. If the seizures continue, another medication may need to be added or substituted. Further adjustments may be needed until the seizures are controlled to the maximum extent possible, avoiding severe side effects. Once seizures are controlled as well as possible through medication, the dosage may need to be changed as the child grows and matures.

Daily antiepileptic medication may be successful in eliminating the person's seizures or only in reducing the number of seizures. In addition to the daily medication, some individuals may have medication that is to be given immediately on the start of a seizure (e.g., Diastat via rectal administration). Often careful observation is needed when giving a specific dose of medication to stop a seizure because of potential adverse effects. Effective treatment of seizures requires careful monitoring and reporting of seizure activity to the physician.

Ketogenic Diet

A ketogenic diet may be used in certain circumstances to control seizure activity. This method restricts the amount of carbohydrates and proteins in the child's diet. Instead, most calories are provided by fatty foods (e.g., heavy cream, mayonnaise, or butter). The ratio of fat to carbohydrates is usually four to one. Food must be weighed and each meal carefully calculated. The exact mechanism of how the diet works on decreasing seizures is not fully understood, but it appears to produce an anticonvulsant effect due to the concentration of ketones occurring from the diet.

The ketogenic diet has been found to work on an variety of seizures, including generalized or partial seizures (Maydell et al., 2001). Approximately 30% of individuals become seizure free on the diet, and approximately 60% experience significant benefit (Ma, Berg, & Yellen, 2007; Thiele, 2003). However, in order for the diet to be effective, there needs to be strict compliance. Some parents find the diet too difficult, and many children find the diet unpalatable and engage in sneaking food (McBrien & Bonthius, 2000). Seizure protection has been found to be lost within 10 minutes when "cheating" occurs on the diet (e.g., having a candy bar) (Ma et al., 2007).

Vagus Nerve Stimulation

Individuals whose seizures cannot be controlled by medication may be candidates for vagus nerve stimulation (VNS) (also known as vagal nerve stimulation). A vagus nerve stimulator consists of a generator, about the size of a silver dollar, that is implanted below the skin in the left chest and is programmed externally with a laptop computer (see Figure 17-6). A

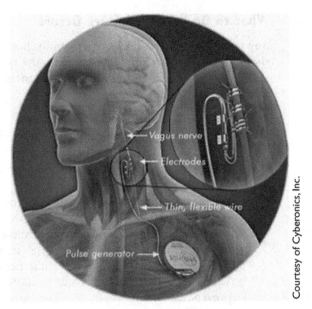

FIGURE 17–6 A vagus nerve stimulator that is implanted under the skin in the left side of the chest and has a wire going up to the vagus nerve.

Courtesy of Cyberonics, Inc.

lead wire is threaded under the skin and goes from the generator to the vagus nerve in the neck area. The device delivers intermittent electrical stimulation to the vagus nerve every few minutes. In addition, a magnet can be passed over the device to provide an extra dose of stimulation prior to the occurrence of the seizure or at the beginning of a seizure. This has been found to be very effective in aborting or shortening the seizure (Wilfong, 2002).

The mechanism of vagus nerve stimulation is poorly understood, but positive responses have occurred in many individuals with minimal to no side effects. Individual responses vary from not being effective to being highly effective; however, more than 40% of individuals have greater than 50% reduction of seizures after 1 or more years of vagus nerve stimulation (Brodie & French, 2000). Adverse effects are usually associated with voice hoarseness, cough, shortness of breath, and infection at the implant site (Wilfong, 2002).

In addition, VNS therapy has been found to be advantageous to those with intellectual disabilities or developmental disabilities who often have difficult-to-control seizures. An added benefit is that less medication may be taken when vagus nerve stimulation therapy is in place, reducing the risk of adverse effects of medication, including some negative effects on behavior with certain antiepileptic medications (Wilfong, 2002).

Surgical Treatment

When other treatment options have failed, surgery may be used to control intractable epilepsy. Surgical interventions used for control of epilepsy are focal excision, hemispherectomy, and corpus callosotomy. Each has a high success rate, with seizures usually being eliminated or reduced.

In a focal excision, a small localized portion of the brain is removed in the area where the seizure originates. It may involve part of a lobe or the entire lobe (lobectomy). This procedure can be used only when the point of origin of the seizure activity is well defined.

In a hemispherectomy, one entire cerebral hemisphere is removed (or in a modified or functional hemispherectomy, parts of a cerebral hemisphere are removed). This type of procedure has shown remarkable results in children and older adolescents. In one study with infants undergoing this procedure, approximately 66% of the infants became seizure free, and another 22% had over 90% reduction of seizure frequency and intensity. Few complications occurred, although there have been reports of infection and hydrocephalus (Gonzalez-Martinez et al., 2005).

A corpus callosotomy consists of severing the corpus callosum or other connecting structures (e.g., anterior commissure) that connect the two cerebral hemispheres. This prevents the spread of the abnormal electrical impulses to the other side of the brain. This type of surgery has been effective in reducing refractory generalized tonic-clonic, absence, and myoclonic seizures (Jenssen et al., 2006).

What to Do When a Seizure Occurs

Any time a seizure occurs, teachers and school personnel should know what steps they should take. This will vary depending on the type of seizure. General guidelines are given for convulsive (e.g., tonic-clonic) and nonconvulsive seizures.

First Aid for Generalized Tonic-Clonic Seizures

When a generalized tonic-clonic seizure occurs, an observer can do several things to assist the child:

1. Stay calm and glance at a clock or watch at the onset of a seizure in order to determine its duration.
2. Do not hold the child down or try to stop the child's movements since this may result in injury.
3. Clear the area around the child of furniture or other hard or sharp objects.
4. Loosen anything around the neck that may interfere with breathing.
5. Put something flat and soft under the head (e.g., jacket).
6. Turn the child on his or her side to allow saliva to drain from the mouth and prevent aspiration.
7. Do not force the mouth open. (People cannot swallow their own tongues.)
8. Stay with the child until the seizure ends.
9. Call an ambulance if
   a. the seizure continues for more than 5 minutes,
   b. there are multiple seizures occurring immediately after each other without the child gaining consciousness,
   c. it is the first time a seizure has occurred,
   d. injury has occurred or the child has **diabetes mellitus**,
   e. breathing difficulties are present, or
   f. the seizure occurs in water (Epilepsy Foundation, 2007).
10. After the seizure is over, the child will be confused and should be reassured. Do not give any liquids during this time since the child may aspirate the fluid.
11. The child should be assessed for injury if there was a fall and first aid given as needed. If a hard blow to the head occurred when the child fell, medical attention is warranted.
12. The child will usually be exhausted after the seizure and should be allowed to rest. Also, it is important that the student's dignity be protected during and after the seizure. If the student's clothes are soiled, for example, arrangements should be made for the clothes to be changed.

First Aid for Nonconvulsive Seizures

Seizures that are not convulsive (e.g., simple partial, absence, or myoclonic) typically do not require any first aid. If the child falls, however, such as during an atonic seizure, the child should be evaluated for injury.

When a child has a complex partial seizure, injuries may occur from running into things (when the child moves around). The observer should gently guide the child away from any obvious hazards. The observer should talk calmly to the child but not expect any verbal instructions to be obeyed. The child should not be restrained. After the seizure is over, confusion often results along with no memory of the events that occurred during the seizure. Thus, reorientation to the environment, reassurance, and support may be necessary.

COURSE OF EPILEPSY

The prognosis of epilepsy depends on the etiology and the type of epilepsy. Some types are better controlled than others. For example, some individuals who have Lennox-Gastaut and brain abnormalities often have seizures that are difficult to control and may continue through adulthood. On the other hand, some individuals who have absence seizures in childhood may outgrow the condition. In general terms, seizures are eliminated in about one-third of individuals receiving treatment and reduced by greater than 50% in another third (Beers et al., 2006).

After being seizure free for a period of time, such as 2 years, the antiepileptic medication may be gradually reduced. Medication should not be abruptly stopped since that increases the likelihood of the occurrence of a seizure or status epilepticus. Approximately 60% of individuals who have their seizures controlled will be able to stop their antiepileptic medications and continue life without seizures (Beers et al., 2006).

Epilepsy typically has no lasting effect on brain functioning. However, individuals who have very prolonged and frequent seizures or those associated with a lack of oxygen or head injury could result in deleterious effects on the brain. There is a greater risk of mortality for individuals with epilepsy as compared with the general population, although this is rare. Epilepsy-related deaths have been found to occur in status epilepticus, sudden unexpected death in epilepsy, suicides, and accidents. Risk factors include generalized tonic-clonic seizures, increased seizure frequency, concomitant learning disability, and the need to take multiple antiepileptic medications. The increased mortality rate is often related to the cause of the epilepsy and is often secondary to acute symptomatic disorders (Hitiris, Mohanraj, Norrie, & Brodie, 2007).

EDUCATIONAL IMPLICATIONS OF SEIZURES

It is important that the school staff be acquainted with the different types of seizures. Sometimes a teacher is the first person to identify a student as having a seizure, especially with the more subtle seizures, such as absence seizures. The teacher may also be the first person on hand to assist a student having a seizure. If a student has a generalized tonic-clonic seizure, for example, the teacher and staff need to know what to do and be ready to act. Information regarding seizure management should be provided to the school staff. In-service training and literature are often available through national or local organizations, such as the Epilepsy Foundation of America.

Meeting Physical and Sensory Needs

When a child with epilepsy enters school, the teacher should obtain some baseline information. Such information should include the type of seizure with a description of what it looks like, any known factors that trigger the child's seizure, presence of any auras or prodromal symptoms, current seizure pattern (e.g., frequency or when they usually occur), and any recent changes in the seizure pattern, typical duration of the seizure, and child's behavior after the seizure. Treatment for the seizure should be specified, including the name of the medications and possible side effects. Any limitations should be noted since certain activities may be restricted until the seizures are under control because of their life-threatening impact when loss of consciousness occurs (e.g., swimming or driving).

It is important that teachers and parents discuss what constitutes an emergency and when the paramedics would be called (e.g., tonic-clonic seizure over 5 minutes, repeated seizures without regaining consciousness, injury, or breathing difficulty). The teacher needs to follow the standard medical guidelines (discussed earlier in the chapter) unless there is something written by the physician indicating otherwise. The school nurse may also want to be involved in these discussions. The Epilepsy Foundation of America has a helpful parent questionnaire on its Web site that may be used by teachers to learn more about the child's seizures and emergency care.

Teachers, paraprofessionals, related staff, and others should receive training regarding what to do when a seizure occurs. An action plan for the student's epilepsy should be in place that outlines the steps and includes what constitutes an emergency (see chapter 20 for more information on action plans).

After a seizure is over, the teacher should document its occurrence along with vital information regarding the seizure. A seizure observation report, like the one in Figure 17–7, should be completed and placed in the student's file with a copy sent home. If the student typically has dozens of seizures a day, the teacher should record how many occurred that day as well as pertinent information regarding daily seizure activity. This information is important to document what the teacher did when a seizure occurred, and it is useful for the physician.

Seizure Observation Record

Student Name:				
Date & Time				
Seizure Length				
Pre-Seizure Observation (Briefly list behaviors, triggering events, activities)				
Conscious (yes/no/altered)				
Injuries (briefly describe)				
Muscle Tone/Body Movements	Rigid/clenching			
	Limp			
	Fell down			
	Rocking			
	Wandering around			
	Whole body jerking			
Extremity Movements	(R) arm jerking			
	(L) arm jerking			
	(R) leg jerking			
	(L) leg jerking			
	Random Movement			
Color	Bluish			
	Pale			
	Flushed			
Eyes	Pupils dilated			
	Turned (R or L)			
	Rolled up			
	Staring or blinking (clarify)			
	Closed			
Mouth	Salivating			
	Chewing			
	Lip smacking			
Verbal Sounds (gagging, talking, throat clearing, etc.)				
Breathing (normal, labored, stopped, noisy, etc.)				
Incontinent (urine or feces)				
Post-Seizure Observation	Confused			
	Sleepy/tired			
	Headache			
	Speech slurring			
	Other			
Length to Orientation				
Parents Notified? (time of call)				
EMS Called? (call time & arrival time)				
Observer's Name				

FIGURE 17–7 Seizure observation record.

Source: Used with permission from Epilepsy Foundation, http://www.epilepsyfoundation.org.

Meeting Communication Needs

Students who have epilepsy will typically have no problems in the area of communication unless there is a secondary disability. When a communication impairment exists, such as in students with severe spastic quadriplegic cerebral palsy, it is important that teachers observe the student carefully for nonverbal forms of communication that may indicate that a seizure is about to occur. If a student does experience an aura prior to seizure, it can be helpful for the student to have a quick way to communicate (e.g., gesture or symbol) that a seizure is about to occur.

Meeting Learning Needs

Students who have epilepsy range in cognitive abilities (from having an intellectual disability to being gifted). However, it has also been suggested that children who have epilepsy often have poor social and educational outcomes. For example, in one study (Schoenfeld et al., 1999), children with complex partial seizures performed worse than their sibling counterparts across verbal memory, nonverbal memory, language, academic achievement, problem solving, motor skills, and mental efficiency, especially when seizures had an early age of onset and were frequent. However, in another study (Berg et al., 2005), it was suggested that behavioral and cognitive abnormalities may pre-date the onset of epilepsy and are not necessarily the consequence of it.

Academic learning may be affected directly or indirectly by all types of seizures. Even minor seizures may result in the student's missing academic content while the seizure is occurring (or afterward if there is a postictal state). Teachers will often need to provide extra instruction on missed information. In the case of frequent absence seizures, the student can be assigned a "buddy" who helps the student find where they are in the lesson after the occurrence of each absence seizure. The use of a buddy is especially useful in a reading group to assist the student in finding where they are on the page after the seizure is over. Learning may also be affected by some seizure medications because of the negative effects some have on alertness and fatigue. The teacher needs to be knowledgeable about the effects of these medications and inform the parents and physician if learning is being affected.

Meeting Daily Living Needs

Typically, the teacher will not need to provide instruction in daily living skills unless the student has disabilities other than epilepsy. The adolescent may feel a loss of independence if driving is contraindicated. Alternate forms of transportation will need to be learned.

Meeting Behavioral and Social Needs

It is the teacher's responsibility to maintain a positive attitude toward the student with epilepsy and assist with promoting social interaction. Students who have epilepsy often encounter stress from this chronic condition, interfering with their interactions with others. The unpredictability of a seizure's occurrence, the need to take medication regularly, and social prejudice can have negative psychosocial effects. Feelings of dependency and loss of control may result in a decreased self-worth or other negative feelings and behaviors. A warm, supporting atmosphere is needed to assist the student. At times, counseling may be indicated.

If a seizure occurs at school, the teacher needs to react in a calm, nonchalant manner. The teacher's tone influences the reaction of the class, and it is important that the class be educated regarding seizures (e.g., through including information during a health class or tying it to famous people who have seizures).

There is much fear and misconception regarding seizures. Some students may falsely think that they can catch seizures from another student. Students on occasion have thought that a student having a convulsive seizure is dying and then dead when the student sleeps afterward. Likewise, nonconvulsive seizures may not be understood as being involuntary. It is important that the teacher be alert to misconceptions and social prejudices and try to properly educate both students and staff members.

SUMMARY

A seizure is a sudden, involuntary, time-limited disruption of the normal functions of the central nervous system. Epilepsy refers to a chronic condition in which seizures occur over time and occur spontaneously (unprovoked from other conditions). There are many types of seizures and epilepsy that can be characterized by altered consciousness, motor activity, sensory phenomena, or inappropriate behavior. Seizures are usually classified as partial seizures and generalized seizures. Partial seizures begin in one area of the brain, while generalized seizures occur in both hemispheres of the brain. Within each category, there are many types of seizures, with each type of seizure having its own characteristics, prognosis, and treatment. Seizures usually last a few seconds to a few minutes and end spontaneously. However, if status epilepticus occurs, medical treatment is needed. The teacher plays an important role in identifying seizures in the classroom and taking the necessary steps to ensure the child's safety and dignity when a seizure occurs in the classroom.

VIGNETTE Calee's Story

Calee, a 12-year-old girl with learning disabilities, has been studying very hard for midterm exams. She has been working hard both in class and out to pass her math exam, an area of difficulty for her. Her mother has called her math teacher, concerned at the amount of stress Calee is under trying both to finish her daily work and to prepare for the exam. She tells her teacher that she is staying up too late to finish the work and is not getting enough rest. The day of the exam, Calee comes into class looking exhausted. As the exam begins, Calee crashes to the floor as convulsions begin. What should the teacher do to help Calee (and her classmates) on this important day? What should the teacher have considered prior to the day of the exam, and what action, if any, should she have taken?

REFERENCES

Aicardi, J. (2002). What is epilepsy? In B. L. Maria (Ed.), *Current management in child neurology* (pp. 86–89). Hamilton: BC Decker.

Aicardi, J., & Chevrie, J. (1970). Convulsive status epilepticus in infants and children: A study of 239 cases. *Epilepsia, 11,* 187–197.

Allen, J. E., Ferrie, C. D., Livingston, J. H., & Feltbower, R. G. (2007). Recovery of consciousness after epileptic seizures in children. *Archives of Disease in Childhood, 92,* 39–42.

Agrawal, A., Timothy, J., Pandit, L., & Manju, M. (2006). *Clinical neurology and Neurosurgery, 108,* 433–439.

Beers, M. H., Porter, R. S., Jones, T. V., Kaplan, J. L., & Berkwits, M. (2006). *The Merck manual of diagnosis and therapy* (18th ed.). Whitehouse Station, NJ: Merck & Co.

Berg, A. T., Smith, S. N., Frobish, D., Levy, S. R., Testa, F. M., Beckerman, B., et al. (2005). Special education needs of children with newly diagnosed epilepsy. *Developmental Medicine and Child Neurology, 47,* 749–753.

Bourgeois, B. (2002). Generalized seizures. In B. L. Maria (Ed.), *Current management in child neurology* (pp. 113–121). Hamilton: BC Decker.

Brodie, M., & French, J. A. (2000). Management of epilepsy in adolescents and adults. *Lancet, 356,* 323–329.

Bureau, M., & Tassinari, C. A. (2005). Epilepsy with myoclonic absences. *Brain and Development, 27,* 178–184.

Chen, Y., Fang, P., & Chow, J. (2006). Clinical characteristics and prognostic factors of postencephalitic epilepsy in children. *Journal of Child Neurology, 21,* 1047–1051.

Chuang, Y. (2006). Massively multiplayer online role-playing game-induced seizures: A neglected health problem in Internet addiction. *Cyberpsychology and Behavior, 9,* 451–456.

Delgado-Escueta, A., Medina, M., Alonso, M. E., & Fong, G. (2002). Epilepsy genes: The search grows longer. In R. Guerrini, J. Aicardi, F. Andermann, & M. Hallett (Eds.), *Epilepsy and movement disorders* (pp. 421–450). New York: Cambridge University Press.

D'Souza, W. J., O'Brien, T. J., Murphy, M., Trost, N. M., & Cook, M. J. (2007). Toothbrushing-induced epilepsy with structural lesions in the primary somatosensory area. *Neurology, 68,* 769–771.

Engel, J. (2007). *A proposed diagnostic scheme for people with epileptic seizures and with epilepsy: Report of the ILAE task force on classification and terminology.* Available: http://www.ilae-epilepsy.or/Visitors/Centre/ctf/overview.cfm#2

Engel, J., & Fejerman, N. (2005). *Benign childhood epilepsy with centrotemporal spikes.* International League Against Epilepsy. Available: http://www.ilae-epilepsy.org/Visitors/Centre/ctf/benign_child_centrotemp.cfm

Epilepsy Foundation. (2007). *First aid.* Epilepsy Foundation. Available: http://www.epilepsyfoundation.org/about/firstaid/index.cfm

Gonzalez-Martinez, J. A., Gupta, A., Kotagal, P., Lachwani, D., Wyllie, E., Luders, H. O., et al. (2005). Hemispherectomy for catastrophic epilepsy in infants. *Epilepsia, 46*, 1518-1525.

Guyton, A. C., & Hall, J. E. (2006). *Textbook of medical physiology* (11th ed.). Philadelphia: Elsevier/Saunders.

Hitiris, N., Mohanraj, R., Norrie, J., & Brodie, M. J. (2007). Mortality in epilepsy. *Epilepsy and Behavior, 10*, 363-376.

Hollander, E., Sunder, T. R., & Wrobel, N. R. (2005). *Management of epilepsy in persons with intellectual/developmental disabilities with or without behavioral problems*. Abbott Park, IL: Abbott Laboratories.

Jenssen, A., Sperling, M. R., Tracy, J. I., Nei, M., Joyce, L., David, G., et al. (2006). Corpus callosotomy in refractory idiopathic generalized epilepsy. *Seizure: The Journal of the British Epilepsy Association, 15*, 621-629.

Johnston, M. V. (2004). Seizures in childhood. In R. E. Behrman, R. M. Kliegman, & H. B. Jenson (Eds.), *Nelson textbook of pediatrics* (pp. 1993-2009). Philadelphia: W. B. Saunders.

Karasalİhoğlu, S., Öner, N., ÇeLtik, C., Çelik, Y., Biner, B., Utku, U., et al. (2003). Risk factors of status epilepticus in children. *Pediatrics International, 45*, 429-434.

Lhatoo, S. D., & Sander, J. (2001). The epidemiology of epilepsy and learning disability. *Epilepsia, 42*, 6-9.

Loiseau, P., & Duche, B. (1989). Benign childhood epilepsy with centrotemporal spikes. *Cleveland Clinic Journal of Medicine, 56*, S17-S22.

Lowenstein, D. H., Bleck, T., & Macdonald, R. L. (1999). It's time to revise the definition of status epilepticus. *Epilepsia, 40*, 120-122.

Ma, W., Berg, J., & Yellen, G. (2007). Ketogenic diet metabolites reduce firing in central neurons by opening K_{ATP} channels. *Journal of Neuroscience, 27*, 3618-3625.

Maydell, B. V., Wyllie, E., Akhtar, N., Kotagal, P., Powaski, K., Cook, K., et al. (2001). Efficacy of the ketogenic diet in focal versus generalized seizures. *Pediatric Neurology, 25*, 208-212.

McBrien, D., & Bonthius, D. (2000). Seizures in infants and young children. *Infants and Young Children, 13*(2), 21-31.

Meierkord, H., & Holtkamp, M. (2007). Non-convulsive status epilepticus in adults: Clinical forms and treatment. *The Lancet Neurology, 6*, 329-339.

Moser, S. J., Weber, P., & Lutschg, J. (2007). Rett syndrome: Clinical and electrophysiologic aspects. *Pediatric Neurology, 36*, 95-100.

Nevo, Y., Shinnar, S., Samuel, E., Dramer, U., Leitner, Y., Fatal, A., et al. (1995). Unprovoked seizures and developmental disabilities: Clinical characteristics of children referred to a child development center. *Pediatric Neurology, 13*, 235-241.

Newland, J., Laurich, V., Rosenquist, A., Heydon, K., Licht, D., Keren, R., et al. (2007). Neurological complications in children hospitalized with influenza: Characteristics, incidence, and risk factors. *Journal of Pediatrics, 150*, 306-310.

Oguni, H. (2004). Diagnosis and treatment of epilepsy. *Epilepsia, 45*(Suppl. 8), 13-16.

Okuma, Y. (2004). International classification of epileptic seizures, epilepsies, and epileptic syndromes. *Rinsho Shinkeigaku, 44*, 970-974.

Ottman, R., Risch, N., & Hauser, W. A. (1995). Localization of a gene for partial epilepsy to chromosme 10q. *Nature Genetics, 10*, 56-60.

Pal, D., Durner, M., Klotz, I., Dicker, E., Shinnar, S., Resor, S., et al. (2005). Complex inheritance and parent-of-origin effect in juvenile myoclonic epilepsy. *Brain and Development, 28*, 92-98.

Papini, M., Pasquinelli, A., Armellini, M., & Orlandi, D. (1984). Alertness and incidence of seizures in patients with Lennox-Gestaut syndrome. *Epilepsia, 25*, 161-167.

Pellock, J., & Duchowny, M. (2002). Partial seizures. In B. L. Maria (Ed.), *Current management in child neurology* (pp. 108-112). Hamilton: BC Decker.

Raspall-Chaure, M., Chin, R., Neville, B. G., & Scott, R. (2006). Outcome of paediatric convulsive status epilepticus: A systematic review. *The Lancet Neurology, 5*, 769-779.

Schoenfeld, J., Seidenberg, M., Woodard, A., Hecox, K., Inglese, C., Mack, K., et al. (1999). Neuropsychological and behavioral status of children with complex partial seizures. *Developmental Medicine and Child Neurology, 41*, 724-731.

Schulze-Bonhage, A., Kurth, K., Carius, A., Steinhoff, B. J., & Mayer, T. (2006). Seizure anticipation by patients with focal and generalized epilepsy: A multicentre assessment of premonitory symptoms. *Epilepsy Research, 70*, 83-88.

Sidenvall, R., Frogren, L., Blomquist, H. K., & Heijbel, J. (1993). A community-based prospective incidence study of epileptic seizures in children. *Acta Pediatrics, 83*, 60-65.

Temkin, O. (1971). *The falling sickness: A history of epilepsy from the Greeks to the beginning of modern neurology* (2nd ed.). Baltimore: Johns Hopkins University Press.

Theodore, W. H., Spencer, S. S., Wiebe, S., Langfitt, J. T., Ali, A., Shafer, P. O., et al. (2006). Epilepsy in North America: A report prepared under the auspices of the Global Campaign Against Epilepsy, the International Bureau for Epilepsy, the International League Against Epilepsy and the World Health Organization. *Epilepsia, 47*, 1700-1722.

Thiele, E. A. (2003). Assessing the efficacy of antiepileptic treatments: The ketogenic diet. *Epilepsia, 44*, 26-29.

Tovia, E., Goldberg-Stern, H., Shahar, E., & Kramer, U. (2005). Outcome of children with juvenile absence epilepsy. *Journal of Child Neurology, 21*, 766-768.

van Breemen, M., Pharm, E., & Vecht, C. (2007). Epilepsy in patients with brain tumors: Epidemiology, mechanisms, and management. *The Lancet Neurology, 6*, 421-430.

Yoshida, F., Morioka, T., Hashiguchi, K., Kawamura, T., Miyagi, Y., Nagata, S., et al. (2006). Epilepsy in patients with spina bifida in the lumbosacral region. *Neurosurgical Review, 29*, 327-332.

Wilfong, A. A. (2002). Treatment considerations: Role of vagus nerve stimulator. *Epilepsy and Behavior, 3*, S41-S44.

CHAPTER 18

ASTHMA

Kathryn Wolff Heller, Morton Schwartzman, and Linda Fowler

The probability that most classroom teachers will at some time instruct a child with asthma is very high due to the fact that the worldwide incidence and prevalence of asthma has reached epidemic proportions (Eder, Ege, & von Mutius, 2006). In 2005, 6.5 million children in the United States were diagnosed with asthma, making it the most common pulmonary condition of childhood. The child with asthma may appear calm and at ease at one moment, then suddenly begin wheezing and require medication. These children may also exhibit a high level of school absenteeism. In view of these findings, teachers need to have an understanding of what asthma is, what can trigger an asthmatic attack, what to do when a child is experiencing symptoms, and the overall effect the condition may have on a student's education.

DESCRIPTION OF ASTHMA

Asthma is a chronic pulmonary condition characterized by episodic inflammation and narrowing of the small airways. The major features include (a) recurrent and variable symptoms, (b) underlying inflammation, (c) airway obstruction, and (d) airway hyperresponsiveness to a variety of stimuli. Hyperreponsiveness is the tendency for the airways to narrow too easily and too excessively to a triggering stimuli (e.g., molds, pet dander, or exercise). This narrowing results in such symptoms as wheezing, chest tightness, coughing, and breathlessness (Kavuru, Lang, & Erzurum, 2005; National Heart, Lung, and Blood Institute, 2007).

ETIOLOGY OF ASTHMA

Because asthma is a complex disease that presents in various forms, many medical practitioners have long believed that it is not a single disease but rather a syndrome. Indeed, a review of research on the topic suggests that the development of asthma is multifactorial and ultimately results from an interaction between genetic predisposition and environmental factors (Beers, Porter, Jones, Kaplan, & Berkwits, 2006; Eder et al., 2006).

Genetic Factors

Asthma is commonly thought of as "running in families." A genetic contribution to the development of the disease is under close examination. Studies with twins have indicated that there is a genetic etiology to asthma. Genetic research has also found more than 22 different locations on 15 different autosomal chromosomes linked to asthma (Liu, Spahn, & Leung, 2004). Variants in 64 genes have been associated with asthma, but only eight genes so far have been consistently associated with asthma-related phenotypes (Hoffjan, Nicolae, & Ober, 2003).

A genetically determined predisposition for hypersensitivity to environmental allergens, known as **atopy**, is often associated with asthma. When exposed to certain environmental allergens, such as molds, animal dander, dust mites, or pollens, people with atopy produce large amounts of IgE antibodies (antibodies that react to allergens that have been breathed into the respiratory system or entered the circulatory system through other means) (Conboy-Ellis, 2006). Asthma with atopy and asthma without atopy have been found in different proportions in different countries, yet the factors that cause these two different forms of asthma remain unknown (Barraclough, Devereux, Hendrick, & Stenton, 2002; Frye, Heinrich, Wjst, & Wichmann, 2001; Russell & Helms, 1997).

Environmental Factors

Although genetic factors may predispose an individual to developing asthma, environmental factors are also thought to be implicated in the development of the disease. This includes household allergens (e.g., dander and dust mites), environmental allergens (e.g., pollen), and viral infections. Some studies have conflicting views as to the effects of household allergens on the development of asthma. For example, exposure to allergens such as cat dander and dust mites has been found to increase a person's risk of developing IgE antibodies (against these allergens), but exposure to dust mites early in life has not been shown to increase the risk for developing asthma (Cullinan et al., 2004; Eder et al., 2006; Layu et al., 2000). Alternately, other studies have reported that early exposure to pets may actually decrease the risk of developing asthma, yet this finding is not yet widely accepted (Ownby & Johnson, 2003; Remes, Castro-Rodriguez, Holberg, Martinez, & Wright, 2001).

Environmental determinants of asthma are also varied. Passive or active exposure to tobacco smoke has been found to be associated with a higher incidence of asthma in children and adolescents (Strachan & Cook, 1998). Air pollution in forms of ozone and particulate matter has also been found to trigger asthma attacks; however, a link between the initial development of asthma and pollutants has not been established (Tatum & Shapiro, 2005).

Other studies have similarly examined the exposure to viral infections early in life and the onset of asthma. These investigations led to the hygiene hypothesis that proposed that the development of asthma is partially due to a lack of exposure to microbial products and infections early in life. A child's risk of developing asthma decreases when the number of older siblings is increased (Karmaus & Botezan, 2002), which may possibly be due to older children passing infections on to their younger siblings, although this has been debated (Eder et al., 2006). Although there appears to be some relationship between infection and the development of asthma, there is some evidence that this relationship is more complex than originally suggested by the hygiene hypothesis (Effros & Nagaraj, 2007).

Certain respiratory viruses that are contracted early in life may be detrimental to the airway and contribute to the development of asthma. Common viral infections of the respiratory tract may result in inflammation of the small passageways of the lungs, possibly leading to pneumonia. This may injure the airway and put infants and toddlers at risk for developing asthma (Liu et al., 2004). Two common respiratory virus that may be contracted during the first year of life is respiratory syncytial virus (RSV) and parainfluenza virus (PIV). There is some evidence to suggest that these two viruses are associated with the initial onset of asthma in high-risk children (Lee et al., 2007).

Additional Factors

Other factors may also play a part in the development of asthma. For example, the status of an infant's lung function may affect the later development of asthma. Research findings have shown that infants with reduced lung function at birth are three times more likely to have asthma by 10 years of age than infants with normal lung function at birth (Haland et al., 2006). Additionally, reduced airway resistance and conductance and reduced ratios of specific respiratory volumes during the first year of life have also been found to be associated with wheezing or recurrent bronchial obstruction as children grow older (Ananth, Savitz, & Williams, 1996; Ananth, Smulian, Demissie, Vintzileos, & Knuppel, 2001; Ananth, Smulian, & Vintzileos, 1999; Ananth & Wilcox, 2001; El-Kady et al., 2004; Miller, Boudreaux, & Regan, 1995). These findings regarding the effects of lung function at birth and early in life suggest that there are certain characteristics in the airways of some infants that predispose them to the later development of asthma.

Several prenatal and perinatal factors have also been linked to asthma. This includes maternal factors such as young maternal age, poor maternal nutrition, and possibly smoking during pregnancy. Infant characteristics such as prematurity and low birth weight have also been linked to a higher incidence of asthma (Beers et al., 2006).

There is recent evidence that the development of asthma may be associated with obesity. A number of studies have shown that weight gain can pre-date the development of asthma. Some studies have shown that the increased effects of body mass index on asthma apply mostly to females, while other studies have seen this apply only to males (Hong et al., 2006). The relationship between obesity and asthma is not well understood; however, proper nutrition and avoidance of becoming overweight may increase lung function among individuals with asthma (Schaub & von Mutius, 2005).

Finally, there may be a link between the increased use of antibiotics and the increased incidence of asthma. Children are often treated with antibiotics for asthmalike illnesses. Antibiotic use can affect the gut by altering the microflora and thus increasing the child's exposure to microbial organisms, which are found in various concentrations in indoor and outdoor environments (Eder et al., 2006).

The preceding discussion exemplifies the disparity of findings regarding the development of asthma. Researchers do not understand all the underlying mechanisms; however, most agree that inflammation and airway reactivity are involved. Asthma has different phenotypes in terms of atopy, suggesting that it is probably not one disease but a syndrome (Eder et al., 2006; Martinez, 2001).

DYNAMICS OF ASTHMA

Overview of the Respiratory System

The major function of the respiratory system is to exchange fresh oxygen from the environment with carbon dioxide within the body. This exchange occurs when the diaphragm and other ancillary muscles contract in a fashion to increase the volume of the lungs. The increased volume causes pressure within the lungs to become negative relative to atmospheric pressure outside the body. Air molecules (oxygen) will flow into the respiratory passages down to the lungs until atmospheric and lung pressures are again equalized.

As air molecules pass through the nose and/or mouth, they travel through the pharynx (throat) down to the trachea (windpipe), where the airway passage splits into two large tubes known as primary bronchi (singular, bronchus) (see Figure 18–1). Each primary bronchus subdivides into secondary bronchi—two on the left and three on the right. The secondary bronchi branch into tertiary bronchi, which divide multiple times into smaller and smaller tubes known as bronchioles. The bronchioles eventually end in small air sacs known as alveoli, where the actual work of respiration and exchange of gases (e.g., oxygen and carbon dioxide) occur.

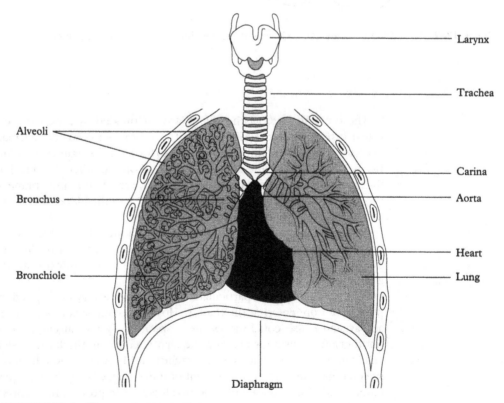

FIGURE 18–1 The respiratory system.

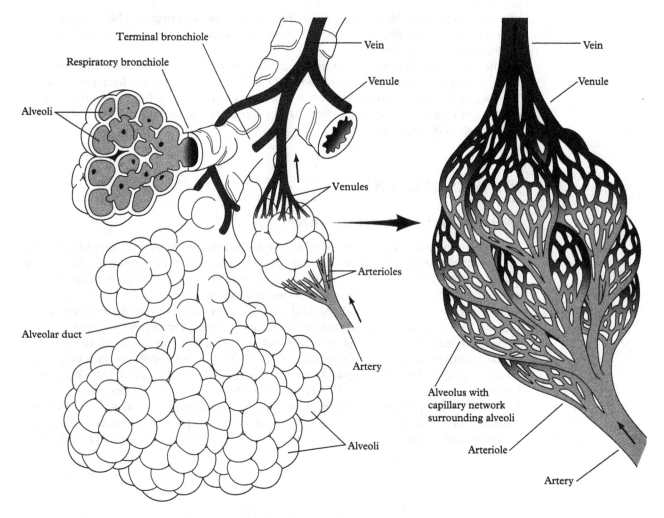

FIGURE 18–2 Exchange of gases occurs between the capillaries and alveoli of the lung.

The outer surfaces of the alveoli are surrounded by a network of small blood vessels called capillaries (see Figure 18-2). The fusion between the alveolar and capillary walls (along with the intervening basal laminae) form the respiratory membrane, an air-blood barrier with gas on one side and flowing blood on the other side. Fresh oxygen that flows to the level of the alveoli easily diffuses across the respiratory membrane—oxygen moves from the alveoli to the blood, and carbon dioxide leaves the blood to enter the alveoli, where it is then expelled from the body during exhalation.

At the completion of an inhalation, the diaphragm and accessory muscles relax, compressing the walls of the lungs and causing an increased or positive pressure in the lungs. The air molecules in the lungs will then flow out of the body (exhalation) until atmospheric and lung pressures are again equalized.

As a person breathes, particulate matter in the air may be trapped in the nasal cavity and prevented from entering the trachea. However, some small pieces of matter may enter the airway and cause coughing as the respiratory system attempts to clear the substance. Another mechanism for clearing the airway comes in the form of small hairlike epithelial cells known as cilia that line the trachea and bronchi. The cilia move back and forth to sweep debris and mucus up and out of the airway to keep it clean (escalator effect). In addition, epithelial cells are tightly joined together to prevent the debris from coming in contact with nerve receptors that lie under the cells.

Asthma and the Respiratory System

Triggers

Individuals with asthma usually have no difficulty breathing until they experience an acute episode, often referred to as an **asthma attack**. Usually, there is a triggering stimulus that causes the asthma attack. Triggers will vary from person to person and commonly include allergens (substances the person is allergic to, such as dust mites, animal dander, or molds); viral or sinus infections; exercise; changes in weather; foods; food additives, such as sulfites; some medications, such as aspirin; air pollutants; reflux disease (stomach acid and partially digested food flowing back up the esophagus); and intense emotions (American Academy of Allergy, Asthma, and Immunology, 2006; Asthma Society of Canada, 2006). In addition, co-existing conditions such as viral disease, sinusitis, and gastroesophageal reflux disease can exacerbate asthma symptoms.

In some instances, hypersensitivity to certain substances may be cyclical. It has been proposed that repeated exposure to allergens in allergic individuals increases airway sensitivity. Further exposure to the allergen may lead to increased airway sensitivity and obstruction, so stimuli that do not produce an asthma attack initially may begin to produce problems later (Hill, Szefler, & Larsen, 1992).

Physical Reaction to Triggers

When exposed to a trigger, a person who has asthma will exhibit airway hyperresponsiveness. Airway hyperresponsiveness is an exaggerated response to a trigger, resulting in the contraction of the bronchial smooth muscles that narrow the airways (known as bronchoconstriction). This results in airway obstruction and can occur from nonallergen and allergen sources (National Heart, Lung, and Blood Institute, 2007).

Inflammation is thought to play a key role in asthma, whether the asthma attack occurs from nonallergen triggers or allergens. In nonallergen reactions, the exact mechanism is not well understood, but the response appears to be related to underlying airway inflammation (National Heart, Lung, and Blood Institute, 2007). Asthma attacks that are triggered by allergens occur in much the same way that other allergic reactions are triggered, such as hives, except that the inflammation occurs in the respiratory system instead of on the skin or in other body systems.

The airway inflammation in allergen-induced asthma results from immunologic processes that increase and activate lymphocytes (specifically T_H2 lymphocytes, which are white blood cells formed in the lymphatic system). These lymphocytes cause inflammation in atopic asthmatics by initiating the synthesis of a large number antibodies (known as IgE antibodies) that bind to receptors called mast cells (as well as other inflammatory cells). Mast cells are very numerous in areas where the body comes in contact with the environment, such as the skin, nose, sinuses, bowel, and lungs. Once the binding has taken place, the person becomes sensitized to the allergen.

When exposed to the trigger, mast cells release chemical substances (such as histamine, neutral proteases, leukotrienes, cytokines, and prostaglandins). These chemical substances cause (a) contraction of bronchial smooth muscle (bronchoconstriction), (b) airway edema (swelling) and inflammatory responses in the bronchiole tubes, (c) secretion of thick mucus in the bronchioles, and (d) formation of mucous plugs (Conboy-Ellis, 2006; Effros & Nagaraj, 2007) (see Figure 18-3). As the bronchiole tubes swell and tighten, the passageways become narrow and partially occluded. This response is further exacerbated when mucus also blocks part of the airway system. These events place extra pressure and obstruction on the bronchioles during expiration, causing the person to have more difficulty breathing out than breathing in. A characteristic wheezing sound occurs as the individual tries to breathe. Stale air becomes trapped in the alveoli, resulting in ineffective air exchange and "air hunger," or the need to breathe. This process may reverse itself spontaneously, or medications and nebulization may reverse it.

There are two different phases of airway obstruction that occur during asthma attacks: the early phase and the late phase. The early phase is the immediate response to a trigger (usually

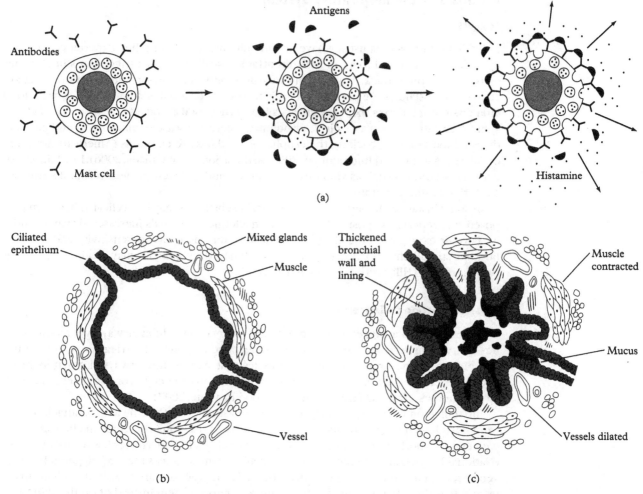

FIGURE 18–3 As allergic substances interact with mast cells (a), the small, usually unobstructed bronchioles (b) constrict and become blocked with mucus (c).

occurring within 15 to 30 minutes of being exposed to a trigger) in which there is bronchoconstriction (narrowing of the passageways in the lungs). The late phase occurs 4 to 12 hours after exposure to the triggering stimuli in which there is tissue inflammation and the immune cellular response. Edema (swelling) of the airways and an excessive production of mucus occurs during this late phase. In addition, this phase also may have hyperresponsiveness of the airway that may persist for weeks after the initial attack (Liu et al., 2004).

In most cases, the overt symptoms that occur in the early phase of an acute attack can be relieved quickly with medication. However, the late phase may result in a serious and sustained episode that can occur hours later (Liu et al., 2004). In some cases, this late phase may result in the continuation of symptoms for days or weeks. In other cases, the symptoms of the asthma attack appear to abate, but days or weeks are needed for a total recovery because the inflammation process damages the epithelial lining of the airways. Time is needed for the epithelial lining to repair, for inflammation to totally subside, and for mucus transport to recover (Suddarth, 1991).

Permanent Lung Changes

Over many years, repeated attacks may result in permanent changes to the lungs referred to as airway remodeling. These structural changes are characterized by permanent narrowing of the airway, especially the bronchioles and the peripheral passages ≥2 mm in diameter. This permanent narrowing increases airway resistance and reduces expiratory airflow rates. The overall functional consequences of these changes can be an increase in the effort needed to breathe, fatigue, exhaustion, and possible respiratory failure if the condition is not treated (Conboy-Ellis, 2006).

CHARACTERISTICS OF ASTHMA

Approximately 80% of children with asthma will experience their first symptoms before the age of 6 years. There are several typical symptoms of an asthma attack, although individuals vary with how many symptoms they have. Besides the characteristic wheezing, there may be coughing (with or without wheezing), shortness of breath, spitting up mucus, a gasping voice, paleness, a cold sweat, bluish nail beds, or feelings of chest tightness. Coughing by itself can be the only symptom of asthma, especially in young children (National Heart, Lung, and Blood Institute, 2007).

Mild asthma attacks usually have few symptoms and may be only mildly stressful to the individual. Moderate and serious asthma attacks may result in a feeling of being suffocated. Some children will be totally disabled during a severe asthma attack and be unable to talk because of severe breathlessness. The child may be consumed by the effort to breathe and be unable to lie flat (and should be allowed to remain in a sitting position). Eating, dressing, and other common activities are often unable to be carried out during a severe acute attack (Bevelaqua, 2005). Symptoms may persist for a few minutes to a few days or longer. It is very important that treatment intervention be instituted early enough to avoid persistence of these symptoms and therefore avoid any detrimental situations. It is very rare, but asthma in extreme cases can be fatal.

Types and Severity of Asthma

There are several different types of childhood asthma that are classified by triggers: (a) allergy-induced asthma, (b) asthma from respiratory infections, (c) asthma associated with obesity with early puberty, (d) occupational asthma, (e) triad asthma, and (f) exercise-induced asthma. The most common type is chronic asthma due to allergy, which usually continues into late childhood and sometimes into adulthood. The second type of asthma is recurrent wheezing triggered by viral respiratory infections in early childhood. A third type of asthma is emerging in obese females who have early puberty (by 11 years of age). A fourth type of asthma, occupational asthma, is sometimes seen in children on farms or in situations in which farm animals are in the home. Although rarely occurring in childhood, triad asthma is associated with some forms of sinusitis/nasal polyposis and hypersensitivity to aspirin and nonsteroidal anti-inflammatory medication (Liu et al., 2004). Asthma attacks that are triggered from exercise are referred to as exercise-induced asthma.

Asthma may also be classified by severity which is based on current impairment and future risk of adverse effects. There are four categories based on severity: (a) intermittent, (b) mild persistent, (c) moderate persistent, and (d) severe persistent (see Figure 18–4). In

Type	Symptoms	Medication use*	Lung function**	Activity
Intermittent	2 or fewer days a week, 2 or fewer nights a month	2 or fewer days a week	Normal between exacerbations Mild restricted airflow	No interference
Mild persistent	More than 2 days a week (not daily), 3 to 4 times a month at night	More than 2 days a week (not daily)	Mild restricted airflow	Minor limitations
Moderate persistent	Daily symptoms, more than 1 night a week (not nightly)	Daily	More airflow obstruction present than in the first two categories	Some limitations
Severe persistent	Throughout the day, often every night	Several times a day	More restricted airflow than the other categories	Extremely limited

*Medication use refers to quick-relief medications.

**Lung function is measured by forced expiratory volume and forced vital capacity to arrive at certain percentages to determine airflow restriction.

FIGURE 18–4 Classification of asthma severity for elementary school-aged children.

the intermittent category, the child has 2 or fewer days a week with asthma symptoms, two or fewer nights a month with symptoms, mild restricted airflow and no interference with normal activity. Each of the subsequent categories reflects an increased frequency of symptoms and use of quick-relief medications and increase in airflow restriction. In the last category, severe persistent, the child has symptoms throughout the day, extremely limited physical activity with frequent exacerbations, frequent symptoms at night, and more restricted airflow than the other categories (Liu et al., 2004; National Heart, Lung, and Blood Institute, 2007). According to this classification system, daily maintenance therapy is started for children falling into the mild persistent category. Medications vary, depending on where the child's asthma is classified and the effectiveness of the treatment. Although this classification system was initially developed to help determine treatment, severity of asthma and its responsiveness to treatment can change over months or years. Because of this consideration, periodic assessment of asthma control is thought to be a more relevant and useful criteria for treatment decisions rather than relying on the classification system (Humbert, Holgate, Boulet, & Bousquet, 2007).

Asthma may eventually be classified on the basis of genotypes, phenotypes, or subphenotypes. However, phenotyping has thus far been difficult, and the contribution of genetic factors has been difficult to determine. Subphenotypes of asthma based on pattern of inflammation (e.g., eosinophilic or neutrophilic) have been proposed as a classification system (Green, Brightling, & Bradding, 2007), and others are being examined. Research is under way to determine if children with different asthma phenotypes need specific therapies (such as individuals with eosinophilic type asthma often having quicker and better responses with inhaled steroid than those with neutrophilic type) (Kiley, Smith, & Noel, 2007).

DETECTION OF ASTHMA

Diagnosis is based on medical history, physical exam, and lab tests, which include specific pulmonary tests. The medical history will include when respiratory symptoms occurred, treatment, and resolution. The information will be examined for any discernible pattern. The physical exam will focus on the respiratory tract, chest, and skin. Laboratory tests are designed to give specific information regarding the possibility of asthma and to rule out other conditions. X-rays and computed tomography (CT) scan may be performed to visualize the sinuses and lungs for any abnormalities. Blood tests will often be performed to rule out infection or anemia. Skin tests are often performed for allergen sensitivity, as are other tests (e.g., blood tests for allergens) to evaluate allergic status. Pulmonary function tests are commonly performed to evaluate lung disease and to provide information on lung capacity, flow rates, timed volumes, and airway reactivity. A sweat test may also be done to rule out cystic fibrosis. Exercise-induced asthma will be evaluated by having the person exercise while respiratory function is monitored.

Asthma in infants and young children is frequently misdiagnosed or underdiagnosed. This is due in part to the difficulty of performing traditional procedures, such as some of the pulmonary function tests. However, there are several tests that show promise for this population, including (a) forced oscillometry, which measures the respiratory system resistance; (b) noninvasive measure of inflammation (e.g., exhaled nitric oxide level, which is elevated in individuals with asthma); and (c) examination of eosinophil cationic protein (Covar, Spahn, & Szefler, 2003; Sterling & El-Dahr, 2006).

TREATMENT OF ASTHMA

There are two major aims in the treatment of asthma: (a) preventing the occurrence of an asthma attack and (b) treating an asthma attack when it occurs. Both require that the child, family, and school personnel have a good understanding of this disease and how to treat it properly.

Controlling Triggers and Conditions that Affect Asthma

In order to prevent the occurrence of an asthma attack, it is important that the triggers be identified. A diagnostic skin test (or certain blood allergen tests) can be given that identifies the allergic substance. Once identified, proper management should begin with avoiding the allergen or irritating substance (Kieckhefer & Ratcliffe, 2004). This is more difficult if dust mites are the triggering substance, whereas if cats or dogs are the trigger item, they can usually be more easily avoided.

Allergy therapy (also known as allergen immunotherapy or hyposensitization therapy) may be given to decrease the person's sensitivity to the triggering item(s). In allergy therapy, the person is injected with very minute amounts of the identified allergen, with subsequently increasing dosages. The body responds by producing certain antibodies that will make the person less allergic to the allergen.

When triggers are in the air (e.g., certain pollens or cat dander), the child with asthma may need additional environmental modifications. Air filtration systems may be placed in certain rooms (e.g., bedroom) to filter out possible triggering substances. The filters used in these systems are typically certified HEPA (high-efficiency particulate air/arresting) filters that capture a minimum of 99.97% of contaminants at 0.3 microns in size. Filters may be placed over air-conditioning/heating ducts to provide further filtration. Bed mattresses and pillowcases may have special covers placed over them to decrease dust mites from entering in the bedding. Vacuum cleaners that use special filtration systems may be used that do not reintroduce dust or other allergens into the air.

Control of environmental factors also includes some general precautions. Individuals with asthma should avoid exposure to tobacco smoke and other respiratory irritants. Also, when the level of air pollution is high, individuals with asthma should avoid exercising outside (National Heart, Lung, and Blood Institute, 2007).

Asthma severity may also be reduced by treating additional conditions that may accompany asthma and worsen its severity. Some of these conditions include sinusitis (inflammation of the sinuses), rhinitis (inflammation of the mucous membranes of the nose), and gastroesophageal reflux (leaking of stomach contents and acid back up into the esophagus). Effective management of these conditions may improve asthma symptoms and decrease the severity of the disease (Liu et al., 2004).

Quick-Relief Medications

Despite all efforts to avoid triggers and control associated conditions, asthma attacks will still typically occur, although they may not be as frequent or severe. Individuals with asthma are taught to identify the signs of the onset of an asthma attack (e.g., chest tightness, wheezing, shortness of breath, or increased coughing) and promptly administer medication. Medications aimed at stopping an asthma attack are referred to as quick-relief, reliever, or rescue medications.

Quick-relief medications are usually short-acting bronchodilators that relax the bronchial smooth muscle, resulting in opening up the bronchial tubes and increasing airflow. This helps relieve wheezing and shortness of breath. There are several quick-relief bronchodilators that may be prescribed for stopping or decreasing the effects of an asthma attack. They typically fall into the classes of short-acting beta agonists bronchodilator (e.g., Albuterol) and anticholinergic bronchodilators (e.g., ipratropium bromide). These quick-relief medications need to be taken at the onset of an asthma attack. For individuals who have exercise-induced asthma, medication (e.g., cromolyn sodium) should be taken prior to exercising.

Quick-relief bronchodilators are often administered in aerosol form with the use of an inhaler (also referred to as a metered dose inhaler). The inhaler is a small device that delivers medication in a premeasured amount. The inhaler consists of a small, pressured canister that is encased in a plastic container that has a mouthpiece. The person places one's mouth over the opening of the inhaler and presses the top while inhaling the medication. In some cases, a spacer (a plastic or metal tube) is placed between the inhaler and the person's mouth for

FIGURE 18–5 Student who has asthma using her inhaler with a spacer attached to it.

proper administration (see Figure 18-5). There are many types of spacers (e.g., accordion-shaped ones that collapse as air is breathed in and spacers with filters that remove unwanted particles), but all have the same purpose of slowing down how quickly the aerosol is received by the person so that more medication gets into the lungs instead of the back of the mouth; hence, less medication is needed. If the inhaler (with or without a spacer) is not used correctly, the person may not get the full amount of medication (see Figure 18-6 for proper inhaler use).

Asthma medication may also be administered using a nebulizer. The nebulizer aerosol machine connects to a mask that fits over the mouth and nose or connects to a mouthpiece that is held in the mouth. The liquid medication is placed in a small cup (nebulizer) that converts the medication to an aerosol form while it is inhaled. (See a young child using a nebulizer in the photo at the beginning of this chapter.)

Other supportive treatments may be prescribed as well. The student may need to drink plenty of fluids and breathe moist air to help rid the body of mucous plugs and ease breathing. If the person is congested, postural draining or clapping (or a high-frequency chest wall oscillation vest) may help dislodge mucus to where it can be coughed up out of the lungs (see chapter 15 on cystic fibrosis for more information on these treatments). Other treatments have been tried to help decrease the anxiety that commonly occurs when an asthma attack begins, such as various relaxation techniques and deep breathing techniques.

Steps for Using an Inhaler with Closed Mouth Technique

1. Shake the inhaler for 2 to 5 seconds.
2. Attach spacer to inhaler if ordered.
3. Position inhaler with mouthpiece on bottom and canister on top. (Usually the student places his index finger on the top and thumb on the bottom.)
4. Have the student exhale completely.
5. Place inhaler (with or without spacer, as ordered) between the student's teeth with the mouth closed around the mouthpiece.
6. Push down on the canister toward the mouthpiece, which will deliver a "puff" of medication as the student starts to breathe in slowly.
7. Continue to have student breathe in slowly for 3 to 5 seconds.
8. Student must hold his breath for about 10 seconds after breathing in the medication and then exhale. (May remove inhaler during this time from mouth.)
9. Wait the prescribed amount of time (per doctor's order) if a second puff is to be given.
10. Student should rinse mouth after using inhaler (to help prevent fungal infections).

FIGURE 18–6 Proper use of an inhaler using a closed mouth technique.

Long-Term Control Medications

Some children and adolescents may not achieve enough control of their asthma only by taking quick-relief medications. In these instances, long-term control medications (also known as controller medications or preventive medications) may also be used along with the quick-relief medications. Long-term control medications are not taken when an asthma attack occurs; rather, they are used on a daily basis or at select times. They help prevent the occurrence of asthma attacks or decrease their severity.

There are many different types of long-term control medications. Some of these include long-acting inhaled beta2 agonists, inhaled corticosteroids, systemic corticosteroids, mast cell stabilizers, leukotriene modifiers, methylxanthines (e.g., Theophylline), and combination drugs. Examples of some newer medications that fall into some of these categories are Ciclesonide (inhaled corticosteroid with fewer side effects), Formoterol (long-acting beta agonist with some anti-inflammatory and bronchodilator effects), and Omalizumab (inhibits binding of IgE to receptors on mast cells).

Monitoring Asthma

Individuals with asthma are taught to monitor their breathing status using a home peak-flow meter (also known as peak expiratory flow testing). A peak-flow meter is a handheld device that the person blows into as hard and fast as possible (after taking a deep breath). It measures the amount of air moving out of the lungs. The person's personal best is determined, and then subsequent peak-flow measurements are taken once or twice a day to determine how well the person is breathing. Medication amounts may be based on the peak-flow reading, and peak-flow measurements also provide information as to how well the medication is working. Individuals are taught to keep diaries of their peak flow to show trends in the disease.

COURSE OF ASTHMA

In most cases, asthma is adequately managed by avoiding triggers and taking the prescribed medication as directed. However, some severe asthma attacks may not respond to quick-relief inhalers, and the person will need to go to the hospital for treatment. Although it is unusual to die from an asthma attack, there are approximately 5,000 deaths a year attributable to asthma in the United States. Most of these could have been prevented with treatment (Beers et al., 2006). Statistically, many of the deaths that occur are the mild persistent and moderate cases because of noncompliance or undertreatment, whereas the severe cases are on continuous treatment and medication.

The majority of children diagnosed with asthma will outgrow the disease. However, about 25% will continue with symptoms of the disease into adulthood or have relapses of the disease later in life (Beers et al., 2006). Some will develop other manifestations, such as chronic sinusitis. If the individual continues to have asthma, certain chronic changes may occur. For example, the shape of the chest may change and become enlarged (known as barrel chest), resulting in an increase in the amount of air left in the lungs after exhalation and affecting endurance.

EDUCATIONAL IMPLICATIONS OF ASTHMA

Asthma is a condition that is full of paradoxes. It is defined by its reversibility yet in a few circumstances may be fatal. It occurs episodically yet is a chronic disease. Several medications are available, yet it is often undertreated. It is recognized as a disease, yet it continues to be perceived by many as an emotional or hysterical condition (which may contribute to its undertreatment). Teachers needs to have a clear understanding of this disease, its symptoms, and the actions to take to properly manage the student's asthma.

Meeting Physical and Sensory Needs

The greatest barrier to quality asthma care in the schools is a lack of education regarding the disease. It has been found that teachers are seldom trained to recognize the signs and symptoms of asthma and often wait until the child is in serious distress to take action (Major et al., 2006). An asthma attack can be more difficult to effectively treat if the student is not promptly given medication. It is important that school personnel be knowledgeable about asthma and know what to do for each individual child.

Detecting an Asthma Attack

The signs of an acute attack will vary with each individual and with the severity of the attack. Some of these signs include coughing, wheezing, shortness of breath, labored breathing, flared nostrils while breathing, complaints of difficulty breathing, difficulty talking, and cyanosis (blue color) of the fingernails or around the lips. It is important for teachers to know what an asthma attack typically looks like for each individual child. For example, many people expect to hear wheezing and complaints of difficulty breathing. This can certainly occur, but some children may look very different. A child having a severe attack who has a very restricted amount of air moving in and out of his lungs may lose the ability to speak and sit motionless at his desk as he concentrates on breathing. What a teacher should look for and what a student will do when an asthma attack occurs need to be known in advance. The teacher also needs to remain calm and allow the student to remain in the position that is most comfortable (which is usually sitting rather than lying down) and implement the individualized health care plan or action plan (more information on these plans is given later in this chapter).

Medications

Students who have asthma need to have their quick-relief medications with them or in a location that is easily accessible to the student at all times. This includes having the medication accessible in different parts of the school as well as on field trips. Having quick access to the medication is important so that it can be used when the asthma attack first begins. Allowing responsible students to have their quick-acting medications with them was supported by the "right to breathe" campaign that stressed that proper breathing was being denied to students who could not access their inhalers in a timely manner.

Teachers should be familiar with the type of medication their students are taking as well as medication side effects, administration procedures, and proper care of the inhaler and nebulizer. The teacher may need to assist the student in taking the medication or observe if the student is self-administering the medication correctly. Part of the proper care of the inhaler is periodically checking the expiration date and checking that the canister in the inhaler is not empty. Shaking an inhaler is not an effective way to determine if medication is available. The canister needs to be taken out of the plastic holder and put in a bowl of water. If it sinks, it is full. If it floats vertically (bobbing up and down in the water), it is half full. If it floats, it is empty (Heller, Forney, Alberto, Schwartzman, & Goeckel, 2000). Some canisters or inhalers come with a counter to help determine the number of doses left.

Teachers should be aware that no medications should be taken without a physician's permission. Some common medications may increase the possibility of an asthma attack and need to be avoided. For example, aspirin should not be given to children with asthma since breathing could be affected and result in the onset of an episode.

Action Plan

Students with asthma need to have an action plan in place that provides information regarding the asthma and its treatment. The action plan should include a listing of possible triggers and any environmental adaptations that are needed. Any activity restrictions (or other restrictions) should also be listed. All medications and their side effects should be included in the plan as well.

The plan needs to describe the student's symptoms of an asthma attack and the steps to take should an asthma attack occur. This includes what medication is given, if it can be repeated, who to notify, and what to document. It is very important that the action plan include the steps to take should the medication not work and symptoms persist. Some doctors will order that if the quick-relief inhaler does not work after one try, 911 should be called and the student taken to the emergency room. It is important that all parties involved with the student know what actions are needed for each particular student and have it documented on an action plan (for more information on action plans, see chapter 20).

Environmental Adaptations

Some adaptations may be necessary to help prevent an asthma attack. Teachers need to know the child's triggers for an asthma attack and make appropriate adaptations so that the child is not exposed to them. For example, if a classroom pet can trigger an attack, then it needs to be kept away from the student.

Environmental adaptations such as the use of HEPA filters may be used in the home or school setting. Some additional environmental precautions include anti–dust mite sheets, special pillowcases, and using only HEPA vacuum cleaners. Dust catchers, such as Venetian blinds, pleated lampshades, and rugs, may need to be eliminated or minimized if dust mites are a trigger for an asthma attack. Pollen exposure may need to be kept to a minimum by keeping the windows shut, not playing outside during times of high pollen, and keeping the lawn mowed frequently to limit the amount of pollen released. Mold can be a trigger for some children, and bathrooms need to be thoroughly cleaned; dehumidifiers may also be used. Many other adaptations may need to be used, depending on the student's triggers and the environment.

Some children will need some adaptations regarding activity. Typically, exercise is encouraged in children with asthma. However, some students with moderate or severe asthma have lower aerobic capacity than healthy children (Alioglu, Ertugrul, & Unal, 2007). This may result in limited stamina that would exclude them from engaging in more vigorous exercise. For example, track may be out of the question, but the student could engage in swimming, gymnastics, or wrestling. Often a warm-up period is helpful prior to exercise to reduce the risk of an asthma attack. If the student has exercise-induced asthma, there may be an activity restriction (e.g., not allowed to engage in vigorous exercise), or extra medication may need to be taken prior to the exercise to help prevent or minimize the reactions. Sometimes the doctor orders activity as tolerated, so the physical education teacher needs to be observant as to the student's condition. It is important that the student know ahead of time what to do when an attack occurs during physical education or sports. For example, one student started to have an asthma attack during a wrestling match and, not knowing what to do, waited until his breathing became very impaired.

Meeting Communication Needs

Communication is only a problem in a few students who are having a severe asthma attack and lose the ability to speak or clearly communicate their needs. If this occurs, it is usually an emergency situation. It is important that the student and teachers have a system worked out that signals the teacher that there is a problem in case it is not immediately evident. For example, one 9-year-old student who would lose his ability to talk during an attack and get very quiet as he concentrated on breathing would reach into his pocket and hand a fellow student a card that said "Help-get the teacher. I [student's name] am having an asthma attack." This was especially critical since the inhaler usually did not stop his asthma attacks. Emergency treatment was printed on the back of the card (although all teachers were informed and had copies of his action plan).

Meeting Learning Needs

Asthma may affect a child's school performance. Asthma is one of the leading causes of absences from school in the United States (Rodehorst, 2003). For some students, this may mean they miss a day here and there because of an asthma attack, whereas some students may miss weeks at a time because of a sustained attack or hospitalizations. In either case, teachers will need to determine how to best assist students to learn missed material.

Some of the asthma medications may have potential side effects that affect school performance. Bronchodilators may cause tremors, resulting in sloppy handwriting. Bronchodilators have also been thought to subtly affect attention and behavior in some students, although this has not been found to always be the case. Teachers should monitor for these side effects and modify instruction accordingly if they should be present.

Students with asthma will need to be taught about the disease and its management. The student will need to learn what stimuli need to be avoided (e.g., pet dander). Students with asthma will also need to be taught the signs and symptoms of an asthma attack and how to properly administer the prescribed medication. This includes how to properly use the inhaler (and nebulizer) and how to take peak-flow measurements.

Meeting Daily Living Needs

Daily living skills are not usually affected by a person with asthma unless they are having a prolonged asthma attack that is lasting days or weeks. In this case, the child may be unable to carry out common activities (e.g., washing or brushing teeth) and may need assistance in the home. In addition, children with asthma should learn how to properly use their inhaler and their nebulizer. This includes proper care and management of the device. For an inhaler, the student should learn how to check if it is full, how to clean around the mouthpiece, the proper care of the spacer, and how to attach it to the inhaler (if one is used). For the nebulizer, the student should learn how to put it together, add medication to the small chamber, use it correctly, and clean it.

Meeting Behavioral and Social Needs

In some instances, asthma has been found to have an adverse effect on student's emotional and social life. Some students have been found to feel restricted socially, perceive themselves as being different, be embarrassed about taking medication, and be afraid of having asthma attacks. Some of these students have been found to worry about death and the side effects of medication (Bloomberg & Strunk, 1992). Children have also been found to be at higher risk for psychological problems, with there being no correlation between the severity of the asthma and the emotional and behavioral symptoms (Goldbeck, Koffmane, Lecheler, Thiessen, & Fegert, 2006). The teacher needs to be sensitive to the student's concerns and maintain good communication with the parents regarding any problems. Students should be referred for help should psychological problems be present.

Social interactions may be adversely affected because of misconceptions that peers have about asthma, the student's absenteeism, and the student's possible activity restrictions. Peers can be educated about asthma and other chronic illnesses as part of their curriculum on health. Since some students with asthma may feel socially isolated, social interactions should be encouraged. There are many clubs and school activities the student may enjoy and easily participate in even when activity restriction has been recommended.

If taking medication is embarrassing to the student, together the teacher, nurse, and student can decide how to best address medication administration. For students who must go to a nurse's office to take the medication, the teacher and student may decide that the student is allowed to get up and leave without interrupting the class. For students who have their medication with them, they may either casually use it in class or freely go to a predetermined private location (with a buddy) in order to increase their comfort level. As discussed, it is important that the medication be taken promptly at the onset of an asthma attack. A method of doing so that causes least embarrassment to the student and maximum compliance will be optimal.

In certain individuals, emotional upset may trigger an asthma attack. Knowledge of this may result in the teacher trying to avoid any unpleasant confrontations with the student as well as the student becoming manipulative. It is important that the teacher not treat the student any differently and expect him or her to comply with the classroom rules or suffer the consequences. Equally important is that the teacher take seriously any complaint that the child is having difficulty breathing or is having an asthma attack.

Students with asthma may be overprotected or overly fearful about their disease. Asthma support groups for the student and the parents can be very beneficial. Additional counseling may be needed in certain circumstances.

SUMMARY

Asthma is a disease that results in acute episodes of inflammation and narrowing of the airways. It may be very mild and not even identified as asthma, or it may be more severe, causing severe respiratory distress. Asthma attacks can usually be effectively treated by medication that is given at the start of an attack. However, an action plan needs to be in place that addresses asthma management as well as the steps to take should the medication be ineffective. The teacher's attitudes, knowledge, and support can make a significant difference in the student's performance.

 **VIGNETTE** | **Ling's Story**

Ling is an 8-year-old with asthma who has behavioral problems. At the beginning of a math test, Ling told the teacher that she was having an asthma attack and could not take the test. She went ahead and used her inhaler but said that she still could not breathe well. The teacher thought she looked fine. What should the teacher do?

REFERENCES

Alioglu, B., Ertugrul, T., & Unal, M. (2007). Cardiopulmonary responses of asthmatic children to exercise: Analysis of systolic and diastolic cardiac function. *Pediatric Pulmonology, 42*, 283-289.

American Academy of Allergy, Asthma, and Immunology. (2006). *Avoid springtime allergens to reduce symptoms of asthma.* Retrieved December 12, 2006, from http://www.aaaai.org/media/news_releases/2006/04/040106.stm

Ananth, C. V., Savitz, D. A., & Williams, M. A. (1996). Placental abruption and its association with hypertension and prolonged rupture of membranes: A methodological review and meta-analysis. *Obstetrics and Gynecology, 88*, 309-318.

Ananth, C. V., Smulian J. C., Demissie, K., Vintzileos, A. M., & Knuppel, R. A. (2001). Placental abruption among singleton and twin births in the United States: Risk factor profiles. *American Journal of Epidemiology, 153*, 771-778.

Ananth, C. V., Smulian, J. C., & Vintzileos, A. M. (1999). Incidence of placental abruption in relation to cigarette smoking and hypertensive disorders during pregnancy: A meta-analysis of observational studies. *Obstetrics and Gynecology, 93*, 622-628.

Ananth, C. V., & Wilcox, A. J. (2001). Placental abruption and perinatal mortality in the United States. *American Journal of Epidemiology, 158*, 332-337.

Asthma Society of Canada. (2006). *About asthma.* Retrieved December 12, 2006, from http://www.asthma.ca/adults/about/whatIsAsthma.php

Barraclough, R., Devereux, G., Hendrick, D. J., & Stenton, S. C. (2002). Apparent but not real increase in asthma prevalence during the 1990s. *European Respiratory Journal, 20*, 826-833.

Beers, M. H., Porter, R. S., Jones, T. V., Kaplan, J. L., & Berkwits, M. (2006). *The Merck manual of diagnosis and therapy* (18th ed.). Whitehouse Station, NJ: Merck & Co.

Bevelaqua, F. A. (2005). Pulmonary disorders. In H. H. Zaretsky, E. F. Richter, & M. G. Eisenberg (Eds.), *Medical aspects of disability* (3rd ed., pp. 543-562). New York: Springer.

Bloomberg, G. R., & Strunk, R. C. (1992). Crisis in asthma care. *Pediatric Clinics of North America, 39*, 1225-1241.

Conboy-Ellis, K. (2006). Asthma pathogenesis and management. *The Nurse Practitioner, 31*(11), 24-37.

Covar, R., Spahn, J., & Szefler, S. (2003). Special considerations for infants and young children. In D. Leung, H. Sampson, R. Geha, & S. Szefler (Eds.), *Pediatric allergy: Principles and practice* (pp. 379-391). St. Louis: Mosby.

Cullinan, P., MacNeill, S. J., Harris, J. M., Moffat, S., Whiste, C., Mills, P., et al. (2004). Early allergen exposure, skin prick responses, and atopic wheeze at age 5 in English children: A cohort study. *Thorax, 59*, 855-861.

Eder, W., Ege, M. J., & von Mutius, E. (2006). The asthma epidemic. *New England Journal of Medicine, 355*, 2226-2235.

Effros, R. M., & Nagaraj, H. (2007). Asthma: New developments concerning immune mechanisms, diagnosis and treatment. *Current Opinion in Pulmonary Medicine, 13*, 37-43.

El-Kady, D., Gilbert, W. M., Anderson, J., Danielsen, B., Towner, D., & Smith, L. H. (2004). Trauma during pregnancy: An analysis of maternal and fetal outcomes in a large population. *American Journal of Obstetrics and Gynecology, 190*, 1661–1668.

Frye, C., Heinrich, J., Wjst, M., & Wichmann, H. E. (2001). Increasing prevalence of bronchial hyperresponsiveness in three selected areas in East Germany. *European Respiratory Journal, 18*, 451–458.

Goldbeck, L., Koffmane, K., Lecheler, J., Thiessen, K., & Fegert, F. M. (2006). Disease severity, mental health, and quality of life of children and adolescents with asthma. *Pediatric Pulmonology, 42*, 15–22.

Green, R. H., Brightling, C. E., & Bradding, P. (2007). The reclassification of asthma based on subphenotypes. *Current Opinion in Allergy and Clinical Immunology, 7*, 43–50.

Haland, G., Carlsen, K. C. L., Sandvik, L., Devulapalli, C. S., Munthe-Kaas, M. C., Pettersen, M., et al. (2006). Reduced lung function at birth and the risk of asthma at 10 years of age. *New England Journal of Medicine, 16*, 1682–1689.

Heller, K. W., Forney, P., Alberto, P., Schwartzman, M., & Goeckel, T. (2000). *Meeting physical and health needs of children with disabilities.* Belmont, CA: Wadsworth/Thomson Learning.

Hill, M., Szefler, S. J., & Larsen, G. L. (1992). Asthma pathogenesis and the implications for therapy in children. *Pediatric Clinics of North America, 39*, 1205–1225.

Hoffjan, S., Nicolae, D., & Ober, C. (2003, December). Association studies for asthma and atopic diseases: A comprehensive review of the literature. *Respiratory Research, 4*, 1–12.

Hong, S., Lee, M., Lee, S., Ahn, K., Oh, J., Kim, K., et al. (2006). High body mass index and dietary pattern are associated with childhood asthma. *Pediatric Pulmonology, 41*, 1118–1124.

Humbert, M., Holgate, S., Boulet, L., & Bousquet, J. (2007). Asthma control or severity: That is the question. *Allergy, 62*, 95–101.

Karmaus, W., & Botezan, C. (2002). Does a higher number of siblings protect against the development of allergy and asthma? A review. *Journal of Epidemiology and Community Health, 56*, 209–217.

Kavuru, M. S., Lang, D. M., & Erzurum, S. C. (2005). *Asthma.* The Cleveland Clinic. Retrieved December 20, 2006, from http://www.clevelandclinicmeded.com/DISEASEMANAGEMENT/pulmonary/asthma/asthma.htm

Kieckhefer, G., & Ratcliffe, M. (2004). Asthma. In P. J. Allen & J. A. Vessey (Eds.), *Primary care of the child with a chronic condition* (4th ed., pp. 174–197). Philadelphia: Mosby.

Kiley, J., Smith, R., & Noel, P. (2007). Asthma phenotypes. *Current Opinion in Pulmonary Medicine, 13*, 19–23.

Layu, S., Illi, S., Sommerfeld, C., Niggemann, B., Bergmann, R., von Mutius, E., et al. (2000). Early exposure to house-dust mite and cat allergens and development of childhood asthma: A cohort study. *Lancet, 356*, 1392–1397.

Lee, K. K., Hegele, R. G., Manfreda, J., Wooldrage, K., Becker, A. S., Ferguson, A. C., et al. (2007). Relationship of early childhood viral exposures to respiratory symptoms, onset of possible asthma and atopy in high risk children: The Canadian asthma primary prevention study. *Pediatric Pulmonology, 42*, 290–297.

Liu, A. H., Spahn, J. D., & Leung, D. Y. (2004). Childhood asthma. In R. E. Behrman, R. M. Kliegman, & H. B. Jenson (Eds.), *Nelson textbook of pediatrics* (pp. 760–774). Philadelphia: W. B. Saunders.

Major, D. A., Clarke, S. M., Cardenas, R. A., Taylor-Fishwick, J., Kelly, C. S., & Butterfoss, F. D. (2006). Providing asthma care in elementary schools: Understanding barriers to determine best practices. *Family Community Health, 29*, 256–265.

Martinez, F. D. (2001). Links between pediatric and adult asthma. *Journal of Allergy and Clinical Immunology, 107*, 449–455.

Miller, J. M., Jr., Boudreaux, M. C., & Regan, F. A. (1995). A case-control study of cocaine use in pregnancy. *American Journal of Obstetrics and Gynecology, 172*, 180–185.

National Heart, Lung, and Blood Institute. (2007) *National Asthma Education and Prevention Program Expert Panel Report 3. Guidelines for the diagnosis and management of asthma* (NIH Publication No. 07-4051). Bethesda, MD: NHLBI Health Information Center.

Ownby, D. R., & Johnson, C. C. (2003). Does exposure to dogs and cats in the first year of life influence the development of allergic sensitization? *Current Opinion in Allergy and Clinical Immunology, 3*, 517–522.

Remes, S. T., Castro-Rodriguez, J. A., Holberg, C. J., Martinez, F. D., & Wright, A. L. (2001). Dog exposure in infancy decreases the subsequent risk of frequent wheeze but not of atopy. *Journal of Allergy and Clinical Immunology, 108*, 509–515.

Rodehorst, T. K. (2003). Rural elementary school teachers' intent to manage children with asthma symptoms. *Pediatric Nursing, 29*, 184–194.

Russell, G., & Helms, P. J. (1997). Trends in occurrence of asthma among children and young adults: Reporting of common respiratory and atopic symptoms has increased. *British Medical Journal, 315*, 1014–1015.

Schaub, B., & von Mutius, E. (2005). Obesity and asthma, what are the links? *Current Opinion in Allergy and Clinical Immunology, 5*, 185–193.

Sterling, Y. S., & El-Dahr, J. M. (2006). Wheezing and asthma in early childhood: An update. *Pediatric Nursing, 32*, 27–34.

Strachan, D. P., & Cook, D. G. (1998). Health effects of passive smoking. 6. Parental smoking and childhood asthma: Longitudinal and case-control studies. *Thorax, 53*, 204–212.

Suddarth, D. (1991). *The Lippincott manual of nursing practice.* Philadelphia: Lippincott.

Tatum, A. J., & Shapiro, G. G. (2005). The effects of outdoor air pollution and tobacco smoke on asthma. *Immunology and Allergy Clinics of North America, 25*, 15–30.

CHAPTER 19

DIABETES

Kathryn Wolff Heller

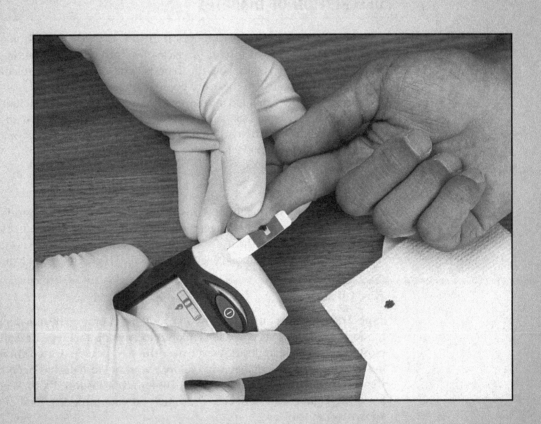

Diabetes consists of several disorders affecting insulin production and use. The most common type of diabetes found in childhood, type 1, is the most common endocrine-metabolic disorder in childhood and adolescence (Alemzadeh & Wyatt, 2004). About 1 in every 400 to 600 children and adolescents have this disorder, and approximately 7% of the entire population have diabetes (American Diabetes Association, 2007a). With proper management, there are typically no outward signs that a child has diabetes. This can make compliance to the treatment regime difficult for children, often resulting in children experimenting with their management program. Emergency situations can arise from noncompliance or from treatment errors. It is important that classroom teachers have an understanding of this disorder and its proper management in order to provide support to the student and to respond to any emergency situations.

Of all the different types of diabetes, approximately 60% to 70% of children and youth with diabetes have type 1. The second most common type in children, type 2, is on the increase with about 30% to 40% of children with diabetes having this type (Boland & Grey, 2004). After a description of different types of diabetes, this chapter will first concentrate on type 1 diabetes because of its prevalence in childhood. Additional information on type 2 diabetes will be provided near the end of the chapter.

DESCRIPTION OF DIABETES

Diabetes, also referred to as **diabetes mellitus**, is a heterogeneous group of disorders in which there is a lack of insulin (or lack of its proper use), resulting in abnormally high amounts of glucose (sugar) in the bloodstream. This high level of glucose, known as **hyperglycemia**, can lead to severe complications unless treated.

Diabetes has been divided into several different types. These include type 1 diabetes mellitus (Type 1 DM), type 2 diabetes mellitus (Type 2 DM), atypical diabetes mellitus, specific types of secondary diabetes, gestational diabetes mellitus, and neonatal diabetes mellitus (Alemzadeh, & Wyatt, 2004; Botero & Wolfsdorf, 2005).

Type 1 Diabetes

Type 1 diabetes was formally known as juvenile-onset diabetes and insulin-dependent diabetes mellitus. These terms are no longer used since children may have other forms of diabetes, and other forms may require the use of insulin. However, type I diabetes is the most common form of diabetes found in childhood. Insulin production is absent in this type of diabetes.

Type 2 Diabetes

Type 2 diabetes was formally known as adult-onset or non–insulin-dependent diabetes. Not too long ago, it was very rare for children to develop this type of diabetes, being found almost exclusively in adults. However, over the past decade or two, there has been an alarming increase in type 2 diabetes in children worldwide. This has been linked to the current trend of increases in childhood obesity (Botero & Wolfsdorf, 2005). When the blood glucose levels are higher than normal but not high enough for a diagnosis of type 2 diabetes, it is known as prediabetes.

Atypical Diabetes

Atypical diabetes has been found in various populations, described primarily in those with African or Asian ancestry. Diabetes falling into this category has been called atypical diabetes mellitus, idiopathic type 1 diabetes, and type 1.5 diabetes. Most of these forms have no autoimmunity present but do have intermittent ketoacidosis (which will be more fully described later in the chapter) (Banerji, 2002; Botero & Wolfsdorf, 2005; Kitabchi, 2003; Winter et al., 1987). However, there is an atypical form found in Japanese children, known as slowly progressing form of type 1 diabetes, in which ketoacidosis does not develop (Ohtsu et al., 2005).

Secondary Diabetes

Secondary diabetes refers to diabetes that has developed because of another disease (e.g., **cystic fibrosis**) or congenital infection (e.g., **congenital rubella**) or that is drug or chemical induced (e.g., thyroid hormone) (Alemzadeh & Wyatt, 2004). Secondary diabetes can also include diabetes associated with certain genetic conditions (e.g., Down syndrome) (Gillespie et al., 2006).

Other Forms of Diabetes

Other forms of diabetes include gestational diabetes and neonatal diabetes. Gestational diabetes is associated with pregnancy. Neonatal diabetes is a rare form of diabetes occurring in the first month of life and has a highly variable course that may resolve or result in the disease permanently (Muhlendah & Herkenhoff, 1995).

ETIOLOGY OF TYPE I DIABETES

Type 1 diabetes is attributed to the destruction of the insulin-producing beta cells of the islets of Langerhans, which are found in the pancreas. The exact mechanism resulting in their destruction is not completely understood. It is hypothesized that there is an autoimmune response due to exposure to an environmental agent in genetically susceptible people (Beers, Porter, Jones, Kaplan, & Berkwits, 2006).

In the diabetic autoimmune response, it is hypothesized that an environmental factor (e.g., a virus or dietary protein) affects the pancreas in genetically susceptible individuals. The beta cells of the islets of Langerhans change structure slightly because of the environmental factor. The body then perceives the islets of Langerhans as foreign bodies and attacks them. There is a gradual destruction of the beta cells with a loss of insulin secretion. Evidence of autoimmune response may be present for quite some time (e.g., months, years, or a decade) before clinical symptoms are present. Clinical symptoms of diabetes begin when approximately 80% to 90% of the cells are destroyed (Alemzadeh & Wyatt, 2004).

There are several hypothesis regarding the types of environmental factors that may trigger an autoimmune response or lead to the development of the disease. The habitual consumption of wheat gluten and exposure to bacterial, viral, or parasitic infections in early childhood have been thought to play an important role in the destructive autoimmune process (Barbeau, Bassaganya-Riera, & Hontecillas, 2007). Other dietary factors, such as protein in cow's milk, high nitrates in drinking water, and low vitamin D consumption, may contribute to the development of diabetes. Viruses such as **rubella**, **cytomegalovirus**, Epstein-Barr, and mumps may also contribute to its development (see chapter 22 for more information on rubella and cytomegalovirus). Additional factors (e.g., chemicals, medications, or seasonal factors) may also be associated with the development of the disease (Alemzadeh & Wyatt, 2004).

Genetic susceptibility is thought to be necessary in order for diabetes to occur. The majority of cases have been associated with the MHC HLA (major histocompatibility complex-histocompatibility leukocyte antigen) class II region on chromosome 6p21. Most individuals with type 1 diabetes have an increased frequency of certain HLA genes (e.g., DR3 or DR4), some of which are thought to be associated with autoimmunity. A unique feature of this disease is that other HLA genes appear to provide protection against the development of diabetes (Alemzadeh & Wyatt, 2004; Boland & Grey, 2004). Genetic studies continue to be conducted to determine how genes affect the development of diabetes. A specific inheritance pattern has not been found to date.

DYNAMICS OF TYPE I DIABETES

Overview of Endocrine Glands

The endocrine system is made up of several ductless glands that secrete hormones directly into the bloodstream. These include the pituitary, thyroid, adrenal, and pineal glands and the

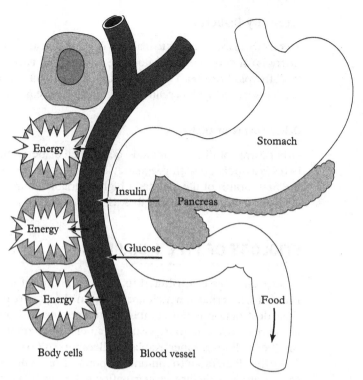

FIGURE 19-1 Insulin transporting glucose from the blood vessel to the body cells.

thymus, ovary, testis, and pancreas. As these glands secrete their hormones, the hormones are transported by the blood to other sites to exert an effect. The hormones are responsible for several diverse functions, ranging from fluid balance to sexual maturation. It should be noted that some of these glands, such as the pancreas, have nonendocrine regions. The pancreas has an exocrine portion that secretes digestive enzymes (see chapter 15 on cystic fibrosis) as well as an endocrine portion that secretes insulin.

The pancreas is located beside the stomach. In the pancreas, there are endocrine cells (beta cells of the islets of Langerhans) that are responsible for the secretion of insulin, which regulates blood glucose levels. When a person eats, food is digested in the stomach, and some of the food is broken down into glucose (sugar), which is then absorbed into the bloodstream. The elevation in blood glucose stimulates the pancreas to secrete insulin into the bloodstream. Insulin is responsible for transporting the glucose from the bloodstream to cells in the body. Once in the cells, glucose serves as the main energy source for the cell (see Figure 19-1). The amount of insulin secreted is closely regulated to correspond to the amount of glucose in the bloodstream. This creates a narrow range of how much glucose remains in the blood, while most is transported to the body's cells.

Effect of Diabetes on the Functioning of the Pancreas

In diabetes, the beta cells of the pancreas are destroyed from an autoimmune process. When a significant portion of the beta cells is destroyed, insulin production will be negatively affected. As glucose increases in the bloodstream after a meal, insulin is not available to transport the glucose into the cells of the body in individuals with diabetes. Instead, the glucose becomes elevated in the blood (hyperglycemia).

With the glucose being trapped in the bloodstream, the body is not receiving the glucose it requires. As the body's cells continue to be deprived of glucose because of the lack of insulin, the body interprets that more glucose is needed. The liver begins to break down fat to obtain further glucose. This process of hepatic production of glucose is usually suppressed by the effects of insulin, but without insulin production, it is not controlled. The production of hepatic glucose results in a by-product of ketones, which are acidic. As the body's cells continue to not receive enough glucose, hepatic production of glucose increases, releasing a quantity of ketones that is too large for the body to dispose of in a timely fashion. This buildup of ketones (as well as other processes affected by it) upsets the acid–base balance in the body, causing acidosis. This is referred to as ketoacidosis. Over time, this can have serious consequences and can lead to coma and death unless it is treated.

CHARACTERISTICS OF TYPE I DIABETES

Hyperglycemia

Hyperglycemia is derived from the words *hyper*, meaning "high" or "excessive," and *glycemia*, meaning the presence of glucose (sugar) in the blood. As the blood glucose rises from the lack of insulin, the initial symptoms of diabetes will emerge, reflecting the developing hyperglycemia.

There are three classic signs that occur as a result of hyperglycemia: polyuria, polydipsia, and polyphagia. Polyuria is the first sign to emerge and is excessive urination. When the body detects a high glucose level in the blood, the body tries to decrease the amount of glucose by having it excreted as a waste product in the urine. The second sign to occur is polydipsia, which is excessive drinking. Since the body is excessively urinating, in order to prevent dehydration, the person becomes thirsty and excessively drinks. Because of an excessive loss of calories in the urine, the third sign, polyphagia (excessive eating) occurs.

If the child's excessive eating is unable to keep up with the loss of calories in the urine, a loss of body fat occurs, resulting in weight loss. For example, an average 10-year-old child with untreated diabetes can lose 1,000 calories or 50% of the daily caloric intake from loss of calories in the urine (Alemzadeh & Wyatt, 2004). In addition, dehydration may occur, resulting in weakness.

Ketoacidosis

If the three classic signs of diabetes do not result in diagnosis and treatment, further symptoms emerge, reflecting the developing ketoacidosis. As previously discussed, the body begins to try to compensate for a lack of glucose in the cells by the liver breaking down fat to obtain glucose. This process causes a by-product of ketones, which are acidic. As the ketones accumulate, the symptoms of ketoacidosis will occur.

Initial symptoms of ketoacidosis include abdominal pain, nausea, and vomiting. Dehydration can accelerate at this time because of the inability to replace lost fluids. As ketoacidosis progresses, the child will develop rapid, deep breathing (known as Kussmaul respirations), fruity odor on the breath (from the excess ketones), and impaired neurocognitive functioning. Drowsiness, unconsciousness, and a diabetic coma can occur. Ketoacidosis requires emergency treatment of fluids, insulin, and close monitoring to return the acid–base balance to normal limits. Almost 20% to 40% of children will progress to diabeteic ketoacidosis before a diagnosis of diabetes is made (Alemzadeh & Wyatt, 2004).

DETECTION OF TYPE I DIABETES

The presence of clinical symptoms of hyperglycemia (and ketoacidosis) will raise suspicion of diabetes, and confirmation of the disease occurs through the measurement of blood glucose. Measurement of blood glucose may be performed after an 8- to 12-hour fast (i.e., fasting plasma glucose) or after ingesting a concentrated glucose solution (i.e., oral glucose tolerance testing). When either test is positive for hyperglycemia, it may be repeated to confirm the diagnosis of diabetes. However, the test may be performed only once when symptoms are present (Beers et al., 2006). Further tests are usually performed to determine if ketoacidosis, dehydration, and/or electrolyte imbalances are present.

Individuals who are at high risk of developing diabetes, such as those with family members who have diabetes, can be tested to determine if they have high levels (titers) of islet-cell antibodies. These antibodies usually precede the clinical onset of the disease. However, there are no effective preventive measures for type 1 diabetes at this time, although research is currently being carried out in this area.

TREATMENT OF TYPE I DIABETES

Treatment of type I diabetes consists of maintaining a balance of medication, diet, and exercise. Glucose monitoring is also necessary to properly adjust the dosage of insulin to keep blood glucose in a normal range. Strict compliance to the prescribed treatment regime is necessary for optimal control of diabetes. Even with strict compliance, some individuals may have difficulty controlling the diabetes. Hyperglycemia (too much glucose) or **hypoglycemia** (too little glucose) can occur and require immediate intervention.

Insulin, Diet, and Exercise

Insulin

Insulin is the medication given to control type 1 diabetes. There are several different types of insulin that are prescribed, depending on the person's exact need. These are classified as rapid acting (e.g., Lispro and Aspart), short acting (e.g., Regular), intermediate acting (e.g., NPH and Lente), and long acting (e.g., Ultralente). Each of these insulin preparations is classified according to how quickly it begins acting. For example, rapid-acting insulin takes effect from 5 to 15 minutes after administration, while long-acting insulin can take 4 to 8 hours to have an effect. The child with diabetes will often take a combination of types (e.g., rapid- and intermediate-acting insulin or rapid- and long-acting insulin) in order to maintain the proper level of glucose. Insulin may be delivered by injection, by insulin pump, orally, or by being inhaled.

Insulin Injections. Insulin may be given through multiple daily injections. A small needle is used to extract the insulin from a vial of insulin and then administered to the child (or self-administered by the child). Insulin injections may also be given using prefilled insulin pen devices (that eliminate having to measure and extract the amount of insulin from a vial) and spring-loaded self-injection devices (that are aimed at reducing the discomfort of regular injections).

Children are taught to give themselves the injections (see Figure 19–2). Injections are given beneath the skin (subcutaneously) in specific areas of the body, such as the abdominal area, upper arm, or thigh. The type of insulin regime the child has prescribed will determine how often injections are needed. For example, the child may have a multiple daily injection regime in which rapid- or short-acting insulin is given before meals to control increases in glucose, while intermediate- or long-acting insulin is taken once or twice during the day for overall control (Boland & Grey, 2004).

Insulin Pump. Insulin may be delivered using an external insulin pump, known as insulin pump therapy or continuous subcutaneous insulin infusion (CSII) (see Figure 19–3). Most insulin pumps consist of three parts: 1) the pump, 2) the insulin reservoir, and 3) the infusion set. The pump itself is about the size of a pager and has several buttons to allow the person to give doses of insulin. The pump is kept on the outside of the body in a side pack, a bra, a pocket, a waistband, a sock, underwear, or in specially designed clothing made specifically to hold the insulin pump. Inside the pump is a disposable reservoir that stores insulin. The reservoir is connected to the infusion set. The infusion set consists of a connecting tube and a small cannula (small tube) that is placed under the skin (subcutaneously) with the help of a very small removable needle. The cannula is usually placed subcutaneously in the abdominal or hip area and is moved to different locations when the infusion set is being changed about every two or three days (or as the doctor advises) (Boland & Grey, 2004). Insulin pumps also have disconnection ports and can allow them to be disconnected during such activities as swimming (although newer pumps that are waterproof eliminate the need to do this).

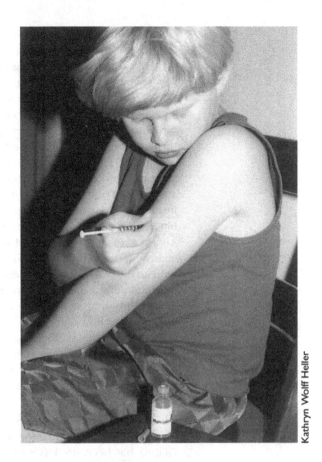

FIGURE 19–2 A student demonstrating how to give an insulin
injection.

Kathryn Wolff Heller

The insulin pump sends insulin from the reservoir through the small narrow connecting
tube, through the cannula and into the body. An insulin pump delivers a small amount of insulin (referred to as the basal insulin infusion) 24 hours a day and is programmed to vary
the amount of insulin delivery based on the child's needs (e.g., exercise, increased eating, or
illness). For example, a child may receive a small dose of insulin every 3 minutes, and to compensate for the increase in glucose with meals, the insulin pump is programmed to give a
larger amount of insulin when eating. If the blood glucose level is high, a correction or sup-
plemental bolus of insulin can be given to achieve the desired blood glucose level.

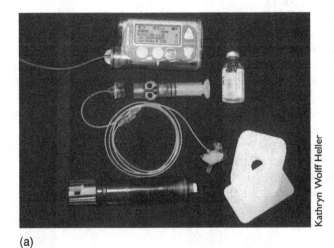

(a)

Kathryn Wolff Heller

(b)

George Dodson/PH College

FIGURE 19–3 From top to bottom, this first figure shows a photo of an insulin pump, a reservoir (taken out of an insulin
pump) with a vial of insulin beside it, an infusion set with two pieces of square tape beside it (to hold the cannula in
place) and the long cylindrical insertion device to assist in inserting the needle and cannula under the skin (a). A young
girl learning to program her insulin pump (b).

Originally, insulin pumps were rarely used with children, but their use increased as the pumps became smaller, easier to program, equipped with a variety of alarms (e.g., tube occlusion and missed meal bolus reminder), programmable in small increments, and easier to access stored information regarding insulin delivery (which may be downloaded to a computer). Insulin pumps continue to advance with new features. Some insulin pumps have added continuous glucose monitoring systems that may assist with providing important information regarding night time glucose levels, as well as monitoring glucose levels during the day (Tamborlane, Sikes, Steffen, & Weinzimer, 2006). In this combined insulin pump and continuous glucose monitoring system, glucose readings are sent every few minutes from a sensor to the insulin pump using wireless transmissions. An alarm sounds if glucose levels are too high or too low. In addition, some insulin pumps are able to calculate the amount of insulin bolus needed when the glucose is high, based on the glucose reading, the target blood glucose, the insulin-to-carbohydrate ratios, as well as other programmed information. Another advance is the recent use of implantable insulin devices.

Insulin pump therapy provides a closer approximation to more typical insulin profiles of individuals who do not have diabetes. It has been associated with improved control of glucose and decreased risk of hypoglycemia (Pickup, 2006; Tamborlane et al., 2006). Unlike earlier insulin pump models, the newer pumps have not seen an increased risk of acute complications with insulin pump therapy in comparison to multiple insulin injections (Guerci, 2006). Parents and youth have reported that insulin pump therapy has given them their former lives back, freeing them from the constraints of diabetes management (e.g., strict schedule of insulin injections, fixed mealtimes, and fixed time to get up in the morning to take insulin) (Tamborlane et al., 2006).

Inhaled, Oral, and Transdermal Insulin Therapies. Insulin may be delivered in forms other than subcutaneous injection or infusion. Oral medication, including oral insulin (e.g., Oralin), has been used as part of the treatment regime but usually in type 2 diabetes. An inhaled form of insulin has been developed and is under evaluation for type 1 and type 2 diabetes. Experimentation is also occurring with the possible delivery of insulin in a transdermal (skin patch) form.

Meal Plan

Administration of insulin will only partly control diabetes. The person's diet also needs to be taken into account. Children with type 1 diabetes need sufficient calories for proper growth and development while maintaining proper glucose levels. The meal plan usually consists of 55% to 60% carbohydrates, 10% to 20% protein, and 10% to 20% fats, with less than 10% saturated fats (Boland & Grey, 2004).

Meal plans are often based on an exchange system or on carbohydrate counting. Exchange systems usually consist of food groups (e.g., fruit, starch, or meat) of which there are a variety of foods in each category that can be substituted or exchanged, depending on the child's preferences. Occasional excesses for parties are usually permissible as long as the food exchange value and carbohydrate content are adjusted in the meal plan. This helps prevent children from rebellion or cheating on their diet (Alemzadeh & Wyatt, 2004).

It is important that the child follow the meal plan and eat at regular times each day. In some instances, it may be important for those who have diabetes to have snacks at certain times of the day to help achieve normal glucose levels. Skipping a meal or a snack can have severe consequences and result in hypoglycemia (low blood sugar) (see the section "Hypoglycemia" later in this chapter). Weight control is also important since being overweight increases insulin needs and can complicate the management of diabetes.

Exercise Considerations

Exercise is important to help with the control of diabetes as well as having good psychological and physiological effects. Exercise affects the insulin–glucose balance by using up glucose and increasing the binding capacity of insulin receptors. This results in insulin being absorbed faster as well as the body needing a decreased amount of insulin. It is therefore important for individuals with diabetes to have a regular exercise regime. However, there are some cautions regarding exercising. If the child with diabetes exercises more than usual, hypoglycemia can occur. In this case, an extra snack may be needed, or insulin should be adjusted prior to exercising as prescribed by the physician. If the diabetes is out of control and hyperglycemia and ketoacidosis are present, it is usually inadvisable to exercise since blood glucose may increase further.

Glucose Monitoring

To maintain near normal levels of glucose, individuals with diabetes will need to routinely monitor their glucose and adjust their insulin based on their glucose level. Typically, the goal is to maintain blood glucose levels between 90 and 130 mg/dl before meals in young adults and adults or at the target that the physician has established (American Diabetes Association, 2007). The physician will have given directions as to how much insulin to give based on the glucose reading. To be sure the blood glucose is being maintained at a correct level, glucose monitoring may occur four times a day as well as when symptoms are present. In addition, the presence of ketones in the urine will occasionally be checked as an additional measure to be sure the diabetes is under control.

Self-monitoring of glucose levels usually consists of sticking the side of the finger with a lancet (a needle) to get a drop of blood (although some meters will allow other sites to be used, such as the forearm or palm). The drop of blood is placed in the glucose meter (often on a test strip). The glucose meter will provide a reading of the amount of blood glucose (see Figure 19-4).

There are several different types of glucose meters. Some variations include the size of the display screen, how quickly results are given (e.g., 5 or 30 seconds), and if they need calibration. There are also some newer meters that check glucose levels transcutaneously (entering

FIGURE 19–4 Student drawing blood from finger to place on glucose monitoring machine to determine blood glucose level.

Roy Ramsey/PH College

the dermis, or skin) as in some continuous glucose monitoring systems. Unfortunately, some erratic readings have occurred with some of these new types of meters requiring high or low readings be confirmed with a fingerstick blood glucose reading. It is thought that they will improve as technology advances.

Preventing Hyperglycemia and Hypoglycemia

Hyperglycemia

A balance must be maintained between the food intake (glucose), amount of insulin, and quantity of exercise. If there is too much glucose and too little insulin, hyperglycemia (high blood sugar) can occur. The symptoms of hyperglycemia occur over hours, days, or weeks. As seen in Figure 19–5, the classic signs of hyperglycemia develop first (polyuria, polydipsia, and polyphagia). As hyperglycemia continues, fatigue and weakness may emerge. Symptoms of ketoacidosis, such as nausea and vomiting, fruity odor on the breath, breathing abnormalities, confusion, and a diabetic coma, may occur. Unless treated, death can ensue.

Hyperglycemia and ketoacidosis can occur when diabetes is not diagnosed, when insulin is not taken (or an inadequate amount is taken), or when there is too much glucose in the diet. Also, different stressors on the body (e.g., illness, injury, or psychosocial stress) can interfere with metabolism, resulting in hyperglycemia (Boland & Grey, 2004).

Treatment of Hyperglycemia.   Hyperglycemia is treated by the administration of insulin. A close examination of the treatment regime is necessary if the person is developing hyperglycemia

Category	Possible Symptoms	Causes	Treatment
Hyperglycemia and ketoacidosis	High glucose levels (and presence of ketones for ketoacidosis)	Insufficient insulin (e.g., did not take insulin or not enough insulin)	Give insulin
	Symptoms occur gradually (hours or days)		Follow plan of action
	Early signs of hyperglycemia: Polyuria Polydipsia Polyphagia Fatigue and weakness	Noncompliance with diet Stressor (e.g., illness, injury, or psychosocial stress)	
	Signs of ketoacidosis: Nausea and vomiting Fruity odor on breath Rapid, deep breathing Inattention or confusion Diabetic coma		
Hypoglycemia (also known as insulin reaction)	Low levels of glucose	Too much insulin	Give glucose (sugar)
	Symptoms occur quickly (minutes)	Delayed eating	Follow plan of action
	Mild Hypoglycemia: Sweating Tremor Hunger Headache Dizziness and light-headedness Behavior change	Strenuous exercise	
	Moderate hypoglycemia: Personality changes Difficulty speaking Drowsiness Confusion		
	Severe hypoglycemia: Seizures Diabetic coma		

FIGURE 19–5   Symptoms, causes, and treatment of hyperglycemia and hypoglycemia.

while being treated for diabetes. Further education may also be necessary if hyperglycemia is developing because of noncompliance, improper diet, or not adjusting insulin intake when stressors are present.

Hypoglycemia

Hypoglycemia is an emergency complication of diabetes in which there is too little glucose (hypoglycemia) and too much insulin in the body. It is also referred to as an **insulin reaction**. The symptoms of hypoglycemia develop very rapidly, often in 15 minutes to an hour. Early symptoms include sweating, tremor, headache, hunger, dizziness, and behavior changes (e.g., apprehension, tearfulness, naughtiness, and aggression). Eventually, this can lead to moderate hypoglycemia in which drowsiness and confusion are present. Without intervention, severe hypoglycemia will occur in which seizures and a diabetic coma can occur, followed by death (Alemzadeh & Wyatt, 2004).

Hypoglycemia occurs when too much insulin is given, insulin is given in preparation for eating and eating is delayed, too little food is eaten, or there is prolonged, strenuous exercise. Teenagers should be aware that alcohol consumption augments the effects of insulin, which can result in hypoglycemia. Since the symptoms of hypoglycemia and alcohol intoxication can appear similar, treatment may be delayed until severe symptoms are present. It is recommended that children and teenagers wear a medical identification so that diagnosis and treatment can be given quickly.

Emergency Treatment of Hypoglycemia.   Treatment for hypoglycemia consists of raising the blood glucose through food, glucose tablets or pastes, emergency glucagon injection, or intravenous glucose. In some instances, the glucose level can be raised by ingesting certain foods high in sugar (e.g., orange juice or soda). Glucose tablets and pastes are also available in a variety of flavors that can be taken for hypoglycemia. These should be with the child at all times should symptoms start to develop.

In cases of severe hypoglycemia (e.g., unconsciousness), an emergency glucagon kit should be available. Glucagon is a hormone (that is naturally secreted by the alpha cells in the pancreas) that can rapidly raise the glucose level in the body by causing the liver to release glucose (that is stored as glycogen and converts to glucose). When glucagon is given for hypoglycemia, it is injected and quickly raises the glucose level. Another treatment of severe hypoglycemia is the intravenous administration of glucose that may be given in emergency situations.

Transplantation and Stem Cell Research

Another possible treatment of diabetes is an islet transplantation, in which the pancreatic islet cells are taken from a donor and transferred into the person with diabetes. Once in place, the islets begin making insulin, resulting in a decrease of blood glucose levels (Sassa et al., 2006). Islet transplantation may eventually become the standard treatment for type 1 diabetes (Kim, 2004). However, further research is needed, and alternate sources, such as stem cells, may need to be developed in order for a large number of people to benefit (Otonkoski, Gao, & Lundin, 2005).

Another possible treatment is whole or partial pancreas transplantation. As discussed later in this chapter, long-term diabetes can adversely affect the kidneys. If a kidney transplant needs to be performed, a simultaneous transplant of the pancreas may also occur. At this time, pancreas transplantations are infrequently performed alone because of the risks of organ transplants (i.e., infection or rejection), problems associated with taking the immunosuppressive medications (e.g., medications not always being effective), and the procedure's high morbidity and mortality rate (Kim, 2004).

COURSE OF TYPE I DIABETES

Individuals may strictly adhere to their insulin therapy, diet, and exercise regime, but normal blood glucose levels cannot be achieved at all times. Because of this, hyperglycemia-related complications often emerge after many years of having diabetes. The complications typically involve damage to (a) large blood vessels, (b) small blood vessels, and (c) nerves.

The large blood vessels that are often damaged from diabetes include those of the heart, brain, and limbs. There is a tendency for the persons with diabetes to develop arteriosclerosis (thickening of the arteries), atherosclerosis (localized accumulations of lipid-containing material in the arteries), and microcirculatory lesions due to high levels of circulating cholesterols and lipids. Coronary artery disease may develop, resulting in increased incidence of heart attacks. Damage to the arteries of the legs and feet can result in circulation problems and gangrene (tissue death due to lack of blood supply). Gangrene can result in amputation, and it is estimated that over 60% of nontraumatic amputations of the lower limb are performed on individuals with diabetes (American Diabetes Association, 2007b). There is also an increase incidence of stroke (blockage of blood vessels in the brain).

Small blood vessels of the eye and kidney may be affected in individuals with diabetes. Damage to the small blood vessels of the eye results in diabetic retinopathy. Diabetic retinopathy is a progressive impairment in retinal circulation that progresses to bleeding in the vitreous, scarring, and sometimes retinal detachment. The effects of diabetic retinopathy ranges from blurred or spotty vision to blindness. It is the most common cause of acquired blindness in adults in the United States. Approximately 98% of individuals with type 1 diabetes are at risk for getting the disease (Alemzadeh & Wyatt, 2004).

When the small blood vessels of the kidneys are affected because of diabetes, a diagnosis of diabetic nephropathy is made. This affects approximately 20% to 30% of individuals with type 1 diabetes (Alemzadeh & Wyatt, 2004). In diabetic nephropathy, the part of the kidney that filters the waste products (glomerulus) is damaged, resulting in chronic renal failure. As the chronic renal failure advances, dialysis will be needed. Diabetic nephropathy is one of the leading causes of acquired end-stage renal disease.

Diabetic neuropathy is another possible complication of diabetes in which the peripheral and autonomic nervous system is affected, producing a variety of different syndromes and symptoms. Often the nerves of the feet and legs are affected with numbness, tingling, loss of temperature perception, loss of touch perception, or occasionally pain. When the autonomic nervous system is affected, there may be low blood pressure, sweating disorders, diarrhea or constipation, and/or impaired bladder and sexual functions (Beers et al., 2006).

It has been estimated that individuals who have type 1 diabetes have a life span that is approximately 10 years shorter than those who do not have diabetes (Alemzadeh & Wyatt, 2004). Complications of diabetes frequently occur, although those individuals who can keep their glucose levels as close to normal as possible are less at risk for developing complications. An earlier death is often attributed to cardiovascular disease or diabetic nephropathy.

TYPE 2 DIABETES

Although type 1 diabetes is more prevalent in children, type 2 diabetes is the most common form of diabetes and is on the rise in the pediatric population. This increase in type 2 diabetes in childhood corresponds to an increase in obesity. Twenty-two percent to 45% of new cases of childhood diabetes are now being diagnosed as type 2, with almost all these children being overweight or obese (Alemzadeh & Wyatt, 2004; Boland & Grey, 2004). Type 2 diabetes has been especially prevalent in youth who are African American but has also been present in youth who are Mexican American, Native American, white, and others (Botero & Wolfsdorf, 2005).

A genetic basis for type 2 diabetes has not been completely identified, but this disease is considered to be aggravated by environmental factors, such as hypercaloric lipid-rich diet or low physical activity. Insulin may initially be present at a normal level, but there is not enough insulin secreted in response to increases in glucose, or there is peripheral insulin resistance (which means the body fails to use insulin properly). In addition to this insulin abnormality, there is usually an increase in hepatic (liver) glucose secretion. All this results in a chronic state of hyperglycemia. Eventually, there is a decline in the functioning of the pancreatic beta cells, resulting in a decrease of insulin (Alemzadeh & Wyatt, 2004; Boland & Grey, 2004).

Type 2 diabetes has many of the same symptoms as type 1 diabetes. The classic signs of polyuria, polydipsia, and polyphagia are often present as well as obesity and sometimes acanthosis nigricans (which is a skin disorder of dark, thick skin found within body creases and skin folds). In some cases, a person with type 2 diabetes may have no symptoms of the disease. It may not be detected until a routine checkup or years later when complications arise (e.g., diabetic retinopathy, nephropathy, or gangrene). Type 2 diabetes is diagnosed in a similar manner as type 1 diabetes.

Dietary management and exercise are important aspects of treating type 2 diabetes. These lifestyle changes may result in improvement in insulin sensitivity and some weight loss (Ludwig & Ebbeling, 2001). If these lifestyle changes are unable to control the diabetes, medication is needed. Sometimes insulin is necessary for initial treatment, but once hyperglycemia is under control, insulin may be reduced or discontinued in some individuals. Other medications may be used to help maintain metabolic control. However, once the pancreatic beta cells no longer function, insulin will be required.

EDUCATIONAL IMPLICATIONS OF DIABETES

Meeting Physical and Sensory Needs

In order to adequately meet the physical needs of students with diabetes, teachers need to have a thorough understanding of the disease and its treatment. This includes all aspects of treatment, including diet, exercise, medication, and glucose monitoring. The teacher should know about the child's meal plan, including the scheduling of a snack, and be sure food is provided when it is supposed to be scheduled. The teacher should alert the parent and child to activities that provide more exercise than usual, such as a field day, in order for food intake or the insulin dosage to be adjusted. The teacher should have a clear understanding when glucose monitoring is to occur and when or how medication is given. If a student has an insulin pump, the teacher also needs a good working knowledge of the pump and the meaning of the various alarms (and what to do should an alarm sound).

All school personnel who are in contact with the student should know the signs and symptoms of hyperglycemia and hypoglycemia and the actions to take should they occur. Usually the student will be able to detect a reaction himself, and inform the teacher of its occurrence. However, its onset could be so quick that the student delays informing the teacher until he is incapacitated (or the student may have additional disabilities, making it difficult to inform a teacher of the situation). Some of the most typical symptoms of these conditions are given in Figure 19–5.

If the student delayed eating, participated in unusually strenuous exercise, or took too much insulin, he may experience hypoglycemia. In the event of hypoglycemia, food or drinks high in sugar (or sugar itself) or glucose tablets or pastes should be on hand for the student to take. (The teacher should always have something available, and the student should also always carry something with him.) An emergency glucagon kit may also be available to treat hypoglycemia, and the teacher will need to know how it is administered and who will be giving it.

If the student did not take his insulin or there is a need for more insulin (which may occur during illness), the student may experience hyperglycemia. A teacher should know the signs of hyperglycemia, and a system should be in place that tracks when the student has taken insulin (e.g., medication log). A medication log will help determine if the student did not take his insulin. When hyperglycemia is present, insulin is needed.

Since individuals who have diabetes are at risk of developing diabetic retinopathy, teachers should be observant for any signs of vision problems. Even when there are no vision problems present, it is recommended that individuals with diabetes have regular eye exams to detect any problems early.

When a student has diabetes, an action plan should be developed that provides information on the appropriate action to take should the student experience problems (e.g., hyperglycemia or hypoglycemia). This plan should be determined at the beginning of each year and planned with the parent, student, nurse, teacher, and physician (see chapter 20 for more information on action plans).

Meeting Learning Needs

Students with diabetes do not have a higher incidence of intellectual disability or learning disabilities; they usually have normal intelligence. However, subtle neuropsychological deficits have been found in children with type 1 diabetes, but they do not necessarily impact school performance (McCarthy, Lindgren, Mengeling, Tsalikian, & Engvall, 2002).

Lower school grades have been associated with poorly controlled diabetes. Hypoglycemia or hyperglycemia may result in difficulty with concentration, and grades may be affected (Boland & Grey, 2004). It is therefore important for teachers to be alert to any changes in school performance and to report this problem so that the parents or nurse can verify if the child's glucose level is being properly assessed. This is especially the case when students are checking their own glucose. Poor management of diabetes has also been associated with a higher absentee rate and lower grades (Yu, Kail, Hagen, & Wolters, 2000).

Meeting Communication Needs

Children who have diabetes do not typically have communication problems. However, young children are not often capable of communicating to others when they are experiencing the signs of hyperglycemia or hypoglycemia. Teachers need to be alert for the symptoms of these glucose abnormalities. Especially important is to observe for a change in behavior, such as tearfulness, naughtiness, and aggression, that is often associated with hypoglycemia.

Meeting Daily Living Needs

Daily living needs are similar as with other students except for the noted modification in the diet, glucose monitoring, insulin (or other medication) administration, and monitoring changes in exercise. It is important that children learn about their diabetes and its proper management. By age 8, children are often able to perform their own finger-stick test for blood glucose, and by age 13, most students can administer insulin with supervision (American Diabetes Association, 1999; Gretch, Bhukhanwata, & Neuharth-Pritchett, 2007). Teachers and school nurses play an important role in helping students learn to be independent in the management of their medical condition.

Meeting Behavioral and Social Needs

Children and adolescents with diabetes may have difficulty coping with the disease. This may result in noncompliance, which can adversely affect their health. Students with diabetes (or any chronic illness) may feel different and lack self-esteem. Information regarding the disease and books about individuals with diabetes may assist the student. Having other significant individuals with whom to discuss concerns can often be helpful. Social interactions may also be hampered because of peers' misunderstanding the disease or restrictions placed on the student. Peer education becomes important to help in providing a supportive environment. Diabetes can be discussed as part of a health class. A special assembly with a person from the American Diabetes Association can often be arranged.

A high degree of responsibility for control of the disease is placed on the student and family. Compliance with the strict management regime of insulin, monitoring blood glucose, diet, and exercise may lapse. This may occur because of a lack of adjustment to the disease and may be influenced by family and social support as well as educational level and age. Adjustment to the disease may also be affected by knowledge of secondary complications and concern over the possibility of becoming blind or losing kidney function regardless of how well the diabetes has been controlled. A higher level of depression has been found in children with diabetes than the general population (Hood et al., 2006). Therefore, counseling is very important so that depression or other behavioral problems can be addressed.

Providing appropriate support or counseling is especially critical when noncompliance is occurring since this can result in life-threatening situations and increase the probability of secondary complications.

SUMMARY

Diabetes consists of several disorders affecting insulin production and use. The most common type of diabetes found in childhood is type 1 diabetes, although type 2 is becoming more prevalent. In both types of diabetes, there is a high amount of glucose in the blood (hyperglycemia). Treatment usually consists of glucose monitoring and administering medication (insulin). Exercise and diet are also important components of the treatment regime. Long-term complications may also occur with individuals with diabetes, affecting several parts of the body (e.g., eyesight or kidney function). Teachers need to help students with diabetes closely follow their treatment plan and know what to do should hypoglycemia or hyperglycemia occur.

VIGNETTE Carlos's Story

Carlos is a 10-year-old boy with type 1 diabetes. He follows a treatment plan of glucose monitoring and is learning to give himself insulin injections. One morning, the substitute teacher had the class involved in a project and put off having snack. Carlos began to develop a headache and feel light-headed but did not want to interrupt the teacher. After a few minutes, Carlos fell off his chair, had slurred speech, and started to lose consciousness. What should the teacher do? How could this be avoided?

REFERENCES

Alemzadeh, R., & Wyatt, D. T. (2004). Diabetes mellitus in children. In R. E. Behrman, R. M. Kliegman, & H. B. Jenson, (Eds.), *Nelson textbook of pediatrics* (pp. 1947-1972). Philadelphia: W. B. Saunders.

American Diabetes Association. (1999). Care of children with diabetes in the school and day care setting—A position statement. *Diabetes Care, 22,* 163-166.

American Diabetes Association. (2007). Standards of medical care in diabetes—2007. *Diabetes Care, 30,* S4-S41.

American Diabetes Association. (2007a). *All about diabetes.* Available: http://www.diabetes.org/about-diabetes.jsp

American Diabetes Association. (2007b). *Type 1 diabetes complication.* Available: http://www.diabetes.org/type-1-diabetes/complications.jsp

Banerji, M. (2002). Impaired beta-cell and alpha-cell function in African-American children with type 2 diabetes mellitus-Flatbush diabetes. *Journal of Pediatric Endocrinology Metabolism, 15,* 493-501.

Barbeau, W. E., Bassaganya-Riera, J., & Hontecillas, R. (2007). Putting the pieces of the puzzle together—A series of hypotheses on the etiology and pathogenesis of type 1 diabetes. *Medical Hypotheses, 68,* 607-619.

Beers, M. H., Porter, R. S., Jones, T. V., Kaplan, J. L., & Berkwits, M. (2006). *The Merck manual of diagnosis and therapy* (18th ed.). Whitehouse Station, NJ: Merck & Co.

Boland, E. A., & Grey, M. (2004). Diabetes mellitus type 1 and 2. In P. J. Allen & J. A. Vessey (Eds.), *Primary care of the child with a chronic condition* (4th ed., pp. 426-444). Philadelphia: Mosby.

Botero, D., & Wolfsdorf, J. I. (2005). Diabetes mellitus in children and adolescents. *Archives of Medical Research, 36,* 281-290.

Gillespie, K. M., Dix, R., Williams, A., Newton, R., Robinson, Z., Bingley, P., et al. (2006). Islet autoimmunity in children with Down's syndrome. *Diabetes, 55,* 3185-3188.

Gretch, Y., Bhukhanwata, F., & Neuharth-Pritchett, S. (2007). Strategies for helping children with diabetes in elementary and middle school. *Teaching Exceptional Children, 39*(3), 46-51.

Guerci, B. (2006). Acute complications of insulin pump therapy. *Diabetes Research and Clinical Practice, 74,* S104-S107.

Hood, K. K., Huestis, S., Maher, A., Butler, D., Volkening, L., & Laffel, L. (2006). Depressive symptoms in children and adolescents with type 1 diabetes. *Diabetes Care, 29,* 1389.

Kim, K. (2004). Islet transplantation: A realistic alternative for the treatment of insulin deficient diabetes mellitus. *Diabetes Research and Clinical Practice, 66*(Suppl.), S11-S17.

Kitabchi, A. E. (2003). Ketosis-prone diabetes—New subgroup of patients with atypical type 1 and type 2 diabetes? *Journal of Clinical Endocrinology Metabolism, 88,* 5087-5089.

Ludwig, D. S., & Ebbeling, C. B. (2001). Type 2 diabetes mellitus in children: Primary care and public health considerations. *Journal of the American Medical Association, 286,* 1427-1430.

McCarthy, A. M., Lindgren, S., Mengeling, M. A., Tsalikian, E., & Engvall, J. C. (2002). Effects of diabetes on learning in children. *Pediatrics, 109,* 1-9.

Muhlendah, K., & Herkenhoff, H. (1995). Long-term course of neonatal diabetes. *New England Journal of Medicine, 333,* 704-708.

Ohtsu, S., Takubo, N., Kazahari, M., Nomoto, K., Yokota, F., Kikuchi, N., et al. (2005). Slowly progressing form of type 2 diabetes mellitus in children: Genetic analysis compared with other forms of diabetes mellitus in Japanese children. *Pediatric Diabetes, 6,* 221-229.

Otonkoski, T., Gao, R., & Lundin, K. (2005). Stem cells in the treatment of diabetes. *Annals of Medicine, 37,* 513-520.

Pickup, J. C. (2006). Long-term use of continuous subcutaneous insulin infusion. *Diabetes Research and Clinical Practice, 74,* S101-S103.

Sassa, M., Fukuda, K., Fujimoto, S., Toyoda, K., Fujita, Y., Matsumoto, S., et al. (2006). A single transplantation of the islets can produce glycemic stability and reduction of basal insulin requirement. *Diabetes Research and Clinical Practice, 73,* 235-240.

Tamborlane, W. V., Sikes, K. A., Steffen, A. T., & Weinzimer, S. A. (2006). Continuous subcutaneous insulin infusion (CSII) in children with type 1 diabetes. *Diabetes Research and Clinical Practice, 74,* S112-S115.

Winter, W. E., Maclaren, N. K., Riley, W. J., Clarke, D. W., Kappy, M. S., & Spillar, R. P. (1987). Maturity-onset diabetes of youth in black Americans. *New England Journal of Medicine, 316,* 285-291.

Yu, S., Kail, R., Hagen, J. W., & Wolters, C. A. (2000). Academic and social experiences of children with insulin-dependent diabetes mellitus. *Children's Health Care, 29,* 189-207.

CHAPTER 20

MONITORING STUDENTS' DISABILITIES AND INDIVIDUALIZED HEALTH CARE PLANS

Kathryn Wolff Heller

Students with physical, health, or multiple disabilities often have conditions that need to be monitored by the teacher. This may entail observing for changes in a condition due to its degenerative nature (e.g., muscular dystrophy) or monitoring the effectiveness of a medication for a particular condition (e.g., attention-deficit/hyperactivity disorder). In some instances, close monitoring is needed to detect medical problems early on and provide appropriate treatment (e.g., hypoglycemia or blocked shunt). Some students may have health care procedures (e.g., clean intermittent catheterization or tube feeding) that can result in problems that the teacher needs to recognize and act on. In each of these instances, the teacher needs to have an understanding of what to look for and have in place a plan of action should a medical problem occur.

MONITOR FOR ACUTE EPISODES AND COMPLICATIONS

There are many conditions that can have a sudden onset of symptoms or complications that require prompt treatment. It is important that school personnel understand the specific student's condition and know what actions to take should symptoms or complications arise. Although the nurse will play an important role, immediate action is sometimes necessary, meaning that the teacher must know what to do. Acute episodes and complications can occur in such conditions as epilepsy, asthma, diabetes, sickle cell anemia, hemophilia, and spinal cord injury.

Epilepsy

There are many different kinds of seizures that can vary in severity and treatment (see chapter 17 on seizures and epilepsy). It is important that the teacher have accurate information regarding the appearance, duration, and frequency of students' seizures. Some seizures, such as absence seizures, may be easily missed without appropriate information regarding their appearance. It is also important to know if there are certain stimuli that elicit a student's seizure (e.g., blinking lights) and if the student has any indication that a seizure is about to occur (e.g., aura).

The treatment for a seizure will vary, from observation to medication. For example, one student who has tonic-clonic seizures may require the teacher to follow the basic guidelines for a convulsive seizure when one occurs (e.g., turn student on his side or monitor him) (see chapter 17 on seizures and epilepsy for all the steps to take should a tonic-clonic seizure occur). Another student may need to have medication given on the onset of a seizure (e.g., Diastat via rectal administration). A student who has a vagus nerve stimulator will need the teacher to wave a magnet over the device when a seizure begins. In each of these examples, the teacher will also need to know when an ambulance should be called (e.g., tonic-clonic seizure lasting more than 5 minutes) and the appropriate actions to take. Students with epilepsy should have an action plan that provides information on the specific actions to take for that child and when an ambulance should be called (more information on action plans will be provided later in the chapter).

Asthma

When a teacher has a student who has asthma in the class, he or she needs to eliminate any potential triggers that can cause an **asthma attack** (e.g., move the gerbil, monitor exercise, or have the student stay inside on high-smog alert days) (Kieckhefer & Ratcliffe, 2004). Teachers also need to be able to recognize an asthma attack and realize that symptoms can vary between students. Some symptoms may include wheezing, coughing, shortness of breath, labored breathing, flared nostrils, gasping voice, paleness, cold sweat, chest tightness, and bluish nail beds. Knowing the steps to take when an asthma attack occurs is important. If quick-relief medication (rescue inhaler) is needed, teachers should know the proper way the inhaler is used to be sure the student is using it correctly. When students continue to have difficulty breathing, an ambulance is called (see chapter 18 on asthma).

Diabetes

Students who have type I diabetes need to maintain a balance between insulin, diet, and exercise. Emergency situations can occur if this balance is not maintained, such as when hypoglycemia occurs. **Hypoglycemia** is a complication of diabetes in which there is too little glucose and too much insulin in the body. This can occur from taking a bolus of insulin and not eating, engaging in strenuous exercise without adjusting the insulin dosage, or taking too much insulin. Some symptoms include sweating, tremor, headache, behavior change, drowsiness, confusion, seizures, unconsciousness, and coma (Alemzadeh & Wyatt, 2004). The rapid onset of this complication makes it imperative that the teacher closely observe the student so that treatment can be given early. Hypoglycemia is treated by giving glucose, which may be delivered through eating foods (or drinking fluids) that have high sugar content, taking glucose tablets or pastes, administering glucagon intramuscularly for an unconscious student, or calling the paramedics who will deliver intravenous glucose. Teachers need to be alert for other problems as well (e.g., hyperglycemia) (see chapter 19 on diabetes).

Sickle Cell Anemia

Sickle cell anemia is one form of sickle cell disease that consists of anemia (fatigue), painful episodes (known as **vaso-occlusive crisis** or **sickling crisis**), and complications (e.g., eye disease, spleen dysfunction, kidney dysfunction, or stroke). In this hereditary disease, an abnormal type of hemoglobin (HbS) is present. This results in some red blood cells being shaped like a sickle (crescent) instead of the normal disc-shaped red blood cells with pinched-in sides (see Figure 20-1). These poorly formed sickled red blood cells have a shorter life span, usually being broken down in approximately 20 days instead of 120 days (Jakubik & Thompson, 2000). This results in chronic anemia and subsequent fatigue.

Teachers need to try to prevent the triggers of a vaso-occlusive crisis and also monitor for its occurrence. A vaso-occlusive crisis can be triggered by events that result in a decrease in oxygen, such as strenuous exercise, cold weather, dehydration, infection, or high altitude. When a vaso-occlusive crisis begins, some red blood cells change into a sickle shape. These deformed cells can plug the small blood vessels in the body, resulting in localized tissue hypoxia (low level of oxygen), which promotes further sickling of the red blood cells. A blockage occurs in the blood vessel, resulting in tissue death (Dorman, 2005).

The major characteristic found in children having a vaso-occlusive crisis is pain. Where the pain is located will depend on where the vaso-occlusive crisis is occurring. Sickling often occurs in the bones with severe pain in the affected area. When a vaso-occlusive crisis occurs in the

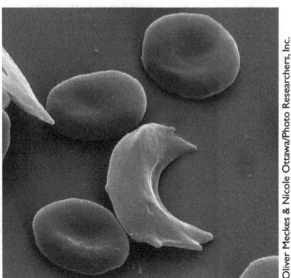

FIGURE 20–1 A sickled red blood cell beside typical red blood cells.

Oliver Meckes & Nicole Ottawa/Photo Researchers, Inc.

liver, spleen, or pancreas, the child usually has severe abdominal pain. Sickling in the lung may result in pain, coughing, and shortness of breath. Especially serious is a vaso-occlusive crisis in the brain that can result in stroke, hemiparesis, and permanent damage. The frequency and severity of these crises vary among individuals. If a vaso-occlusive crisis occurs, the teacher will need to follow the prescribed plan of action, which may include calling an ambulance, especially for a severe crisis. Treatment usually consists of rest, rehydration, pain medication, management of complications, and sometimes blood transfusions (to prevent stroke) (Dorman, 2005).

Hemophilia

Hemophilia refers to a group of hereditary bleeding disorders in which there are inadequate amounts of clotting factor in the blood. Actually, there are several types of clotting factors that together are responsible for stopping bleeding when it occurs. When a clotting factor is missing (or inadequate portions are present), the person has excessive bleeding.

There are several different types of hemophilia that are categorized on the basis of the missing clotting factor. The most common type of hemophilia is hemophilia A (also known as factor VIII deficiency or classic hemophilia). In this type of hemophilia, there is not enough of clotting factor VIII.

The severity of hemophilia depends on the percentage of clotting factor that is present, and it is categorized as being mild, moderate, or severe. Children with mild hemophilia (over 5% of normal clotting factor) usually have prolonged bleeding during surgery or severe trauma. Often it is not realized that they have the disease until they have a procedure such as a tooth extraction and prolonged bleeding occurs. Children with moderate hemophilia (1%–5% of normal clotting factor) usually bleed only after injury or surgery, and fatal bleeding can occur if not treated properly. Children with severe hemophilia (less than 1% of clotting factor) may bleed spontaneously, without any injury. Minor trauma may result in severe, prolonged bleeding. One of the most common places for a bleed is in the joints and may occur because of movement. Over time, severe joint disease can occur from bleeding episodes in the joints.

When a bleeding episode occurs, clotting factor replacement is needed. Usually older children and youth are taught to inject themselves with the clotting factor at the beginning of a bleeding episode. Clotting factor may also be given prophylactically to try to prevent bleeding (Bolton-Maggs, 2006). Although exercise is usually beneficial for individuals with hemophilia, intervention often includes some activity restrictions (e.g., no contact sports).

Teachers need to be alert for a bleeding episode and know the appropriate steps to take if one occurs. It is obvious when bleeding occurs through a break in the skin, but internal bleeding may not be as obvious. When bleeding occurs in the joint, the area initially has a bubbling or tingling sensation, followed by pain and swelling of the joint area, and the area becomes warm to the touch. Pain is often the primary symptom when other areas have a bleed. Clotting factor needs to be immediately administered when bleeding is suspected. If there is any doubt, it is usually recommended to provide the treatment (e.g., a blow to the head could produce life-threatening intracranial bleeding, so treatment is often started before a bleeding episode is established). The teacher should have an action plan in place delineating the exact steps to take.

Teachers should also keep in mind that their students may not always inform them if a bleed is occurring. In one study, fewer than a third of the adolescents treated bleeding episodes within 1 hour because they did not recognize a bleeding episode, they did not think it was serious, or they did not have the clotting factor with them (Nazzaro, Owens, Hoots, & Larson, 2006). Delaying treatment can result in complications, so it is important that teachers, school nurses, parents, and students work together to be sure they understand what a bleeding episode looks like and the actions each person should take should a bleeding episode occur.

Spinal Cord Injury

Some conditions have the potential for complications due to the nature of the disorder. One example is autonomic dysreflexia, which is a dangerous rapid elevation in blood pressure that can occur in individuals with spinal cord injury above the T6 level. Autonomic dysreflexia is caused by any noxious stimulus that occurs below the area of injury (e.g., distended bladder, severe constipation, or pressure sore). Symptoms may include a pounding headache, sweating, blurred vision, nasal congestion, and a feeling of anxiety. Teachers need to know the signs of autonomic dysreflexia and immediately remove the noxious stimuli and follow the action plan. If the teacher does not act immediately, bleeding in the brain (cerebral hemorrhage) can result, and the condition can be fatal (Dunn, 2004; Karlsson, 2006).

MONITOR FOR MEDICATION EFFECTS OR EQUIPMENT MALFUNCTION

Sometimes the teacher needs to be observant for equipment malfunctions. For example, students with spina bifida and hydrocephalus have a shunt inserted to drain excess cerebrospinal fluid. Teachers should know the signs of a blocked or malfunctioning shunt since this can result in an emergency situation (see chapter 6 for more information on blocked shunts). Sometimes the equipment is external to the student, such as a ventilator needed for a student with a high spinal cord injury or advanced muscular dystrophy. In this example, the ventilator (and student) will require monitoring to be sure that the ventilator is properly functioning and that the student is breathing comfortably. The nurse should work closely with the teacher to help identify potential equipment malfunctions that could occur.

Teachers may also be asked to observe if the medication the student is taking is having the intended affect. For example, the proper type and dosage of seizure medication is based primarily on how well the seizures are being controlled. Input from school personnel regarding the number and type of seizures that are occurring while the medication is being regulated is critical for proper dosage adjustment. Medication effectiveness is also important for several other types of disorders (e.g., attention-deficit/hyperactivity disorder).

Attention-Deficit/Hyperactivity Disorder

Attention-deficit/hyperactivity disorder (ADHD) is a common syndrome that consists of three main types: predominantly inattentive type, predominantly hyperactive-impulsive type, and combined type. In the predominantly inattentive type, children have problems focusing on specific tasks. They may be easily distracted by irrelevant stimuli, skip from one uncompleted task to another, or avoid tasks that require focused attention. In the predominantly hyperactive-impulse type, children may seem to be in constant motion (e.g., be fidgety or have difficulty remaining seated) and may have difficulty thinking before they act (e.g., blurting out answers, interrupting others, or making inappropriate comments) (Noorbala & Akhondzadeh, 2006).

Treatment for ADHD often consists of a combination of environmental adaptations, behavioral strategies, and medications. Medications that are most widely used are stimulant preparation (e.g., Ritalin). However, these (and other) medications can have unwanted side effects (e.g., insomnia, depression, or headache). It is important for teachers to monitor the medications to be sure they are having the desired effect with a minimum of side effects (Zentall, 2005). Teachers are in a unique position to observe the child in focused, school tasks and observe their behavior. The teacher's observations regarding the student's behavior is important to share with the parents and physician to help determine if the medication needs to be adjusted.

MONITOR FOR DEGENERATIVE CHANGES

There are several different degenerative diseases that result in declining physical, health, and sometimes cognitive status. Teachers need to closely monitor students who have these degenerative conditions for changes and inform others so that appropriate medical changes (e.g., medications or treatments), educational changes (e.g., adaptations or changes in the curriculum), and technological changes (e.g., alternate computer access or a power wheelchair) can occur. A team approach is especially important when students have degenerative conditions. Some example mitochondrial encephalopathy, diseases with degenerative (or neurodevelopmental) changes are Duchenne muscular dystrophy, spinal muscular atrophy, Rett syndrome, and hereditary cerebellar disorders.

Duchenne Muscular Dystrophy and Spinal Muscular Atrophy

Duchenne muscular dystrophy and spinal muscular atrophy are two types of conditions that result in declining physical ability and an early death. In both of these conditions, there is no decline in mental status, only a physical decline. Teachers need to closely observe students for changes and provide appropriate adaptations and information to the rest of the educational team (see chapters 13 and 14 for more information about these conditions).

Rett Syndrome

Rett syndrome is a neurodevelopmental disorder that is classified as a pervasive developmental disorder. It almost exclusively affects females and is caused by a mutation of the MECP2 gene of the X chromosome (Walker-Date, 2006). There are four stages of Rett syndrome. In stage I, prenatal and early development in infancy is generally normal, except for some possible nonspecific symptoms. Stage II typically occurs between 1 and 3 years of age in which there is stagnation in development, and head circumference falls below the mean. A regressive period occurs at this stage when motor skills and speech are reduced or lost and hand stereotypies appear. Stage III usually begins between 2 and 10 years of age in which there may be some improvement in communication skills, but neuromotor problems worsen with an increase in rigidity and an inability to use the hands for functional purposes (e.g., eating or manipulate toys), although some automatic responses (e.g., scratching) may be retained. Seizures often develop at this stage.

Some children will remain at stage III, while others will progress to stage IV, in which there is further motor deterioration. Girls will lose the ability to walk at this time, if they were ambulatory to begin with. Other problems may also occur, such as poor eye contact (and use of peripheral vision), contractures, breathing irregularities, breath holding, vacant spells (which can be confused with epilepsy), feeding difficulties (including risk of aspiration pneumonia), love of human contact and listening to music, and intellectual disability (Hagberg, 2002; Hagberg & Witt-Engerstrom, 1986; Moser, Weber, & Lutschg, 2007; Walker-Date, 2006). Teachers will need to closely monitor these students and make appropriate adaptations as changes occur.

Mitochondrial Encephalopathy

Mitochondrial encephalopathy is one of the many mitochondrial diseases that occur from failure of the mitochondria, the part of the cell that processes oxygen and converts food into energy. Depending upon which type of mitochondrial disease, only one body system may be affected (e.g., brain) or multiple systems (e.g., muscles, kidneys, heart, eyes, brain). Mitochondrial encephalopathy refers to a wide spectrum of disorders affecting the brain that occur from mitochondrial dysfunction (e.g., Kearns-Sayre syndrome, Leber's hereditary optic neuropathy, and MELAS (mitochondrial myopathy, encephalopathy, lactic acidosis, and stroke-like episodes) (Iizuka & Sakai, 2005).

MELAS is the most frequent genetic mutation occurring in the category of neurodegenerative diseases. Children may be born normal, and symptoms gradually emerge in childhood or young adulthood, leading to complications that will be fatal. Stroke-like episodes typically occur in childhood, but may not occur until adulthood (usually prior to 40 years of age). Lactic acidosis will be present in the blood and/or cerebrospinal fluid. Children with MELAS may develop learning disabilities or intellectual disabilities with a complication of progressive intellectual deterioration (dementia). Neuromuscular impairments often include motor abnormalities (e.g., hemiplegia, ataxia, muscular weakness) and aphasia (inability to produce and/or comprehend language). Health impairments may be present such as seizures, diabetes, severe headaches, and cardiac abnormalities (e.g., irregular heartbeat, cardiomyopathy). Sensory disturbances often occur as well (e.g., cortical visual impairment, sensorineural hearing loss, numbness). Other symptoms such as short stature and exercise intolerance are common (Iizuka & Sakai, 2005; Patel, Sidani, & Zoorob, 2007). Due to the progressive nature of this disease, teachers will need to closely monitor for changes in the student's cognitive, motor, sensory, and health status (including exercise intolerance) and make appropriate adaptations.

Hereditary Degenerative Cerebellar Disorders (Friedreich's Ataxia)

Unlike nonprogressive ataxic cerebral palsy, which results from damage to the cerebellum, there are several different hereditary disorders affecting the cerebellum that are degenerative. They have many different etiologies, such as mitrochonrial (e.g., Friedreich's ataxia), defective DNA repair (e.g., ataxia-telangiectasia), and abnormal protein folding and degradations (e.g., autosomal recessive spastic ataxia Charlevoix-Sagnenay type) (Cocozza, 2004). The most common hereditary ataxia is Fredreich's ataxia.

Friedreich's ataxia typically begins between 5 and 25 years of age (Fogel & Perlman, 2007). The first symptom to emerge is gait unsteadiness. This is followed by progressive ataxia (muscle incoordination) of the arms and legs, resulting in gait abnormalities and difficulty moving the arms in a coordinated manner. Some other symptoms and complications may include severe dysarthria (poor articulation), loss of position and vibration sense, abnormal eye movements (e.g., fixation or nystagmus), vision loss (e.g., optic atrophy), hearing loss (sensorineural), progressive **scoliosis**, and **diabetes mellitus**. Over time, the person will usually lose the ability to walk. A decline in mental functioning may also occur. Most die from cardiomyopathy (enlarged heart) (Alper & Narayanan, 2003; Beers, Porter, Jones, Kaplan, & Berkwits, 2006). Teachers need to closely monitor students with this condition not only for degenerative changes but also for possible complications (e.g., vision loss or hearing loss).

MONITOR FOR FATIGUE OR EXERCISE INTOLERANCE

Some students will have conditions that result in fatigue, or the treatment regime has a side effect of fatigue. Other students may fatigue with exercise or be unable to tolerate physical activity. In each case, teachers may need to observe for fatigue and provide necessary breaks or adaptations when fatigue occurs. Some conditions previously discussed often have fatigue issues (e.g., sickle cell anemia or certain medication used to treat epilepsy). Some other conditions that can result in fatigue include congenital heart defects, childhood cancer, and renal failure.

Congenital Heart Defects

A congenital heart defect (CHD) refers to a variety of conditions in which the heart is structurally impaired at birth. There may be a hole in one of the chambers of the heart, a misshapen valve, misplacement of the vessels of the heart, or any number of abnormalities. The structural abnormality of the heart occurs during fetal development because of genetic factors, syndromes (e.g., Down syndrome), adverse environmental or maternal conditions (e.g., maternal rubella), or other factors that are often unknown. Some defects are minor and will often resolve on their own, while others require surgery.

In a normal heart, unoxygenated blood enters the right side of the heart (the right atrium followed by the right ventricle) and is pumped through the pulmonary arteries to the lungs. From there, the now oxygenated blood goes into the left side of the heart (the left atrium followed by the left ventricle), which pumps the oxygenated blood out to the body via the aorta (see Figure 20–2).

Depending on where the heart defect is located, the defect falls into one of two categories: acyanotic heart defects or cyanotic heart defect (see Figure 20–2). In acyanotic heart defects (meaning heart defects that do not have cyanosis), some oxygenated blood from the left side of the heart is incorrectly pumped to the unoxygenated right side of the heart because of an obstruction or increased blood flow to the lungs (e.g., from a hole between the two sides of the heart). This causes a strain on the heart from pressure or volume overload, which can lead to congestive heart failure (i.e., a severe reduction of blood output from the heart that does not meet the body's demands). In cyanotic heart defects, there is a blue coloration of the mucous membranes and skin (cyanosis) because the defect causes some unoxygenated blood from the right side of the heart to be pumped to the body (Cook & Higgins, 2004).

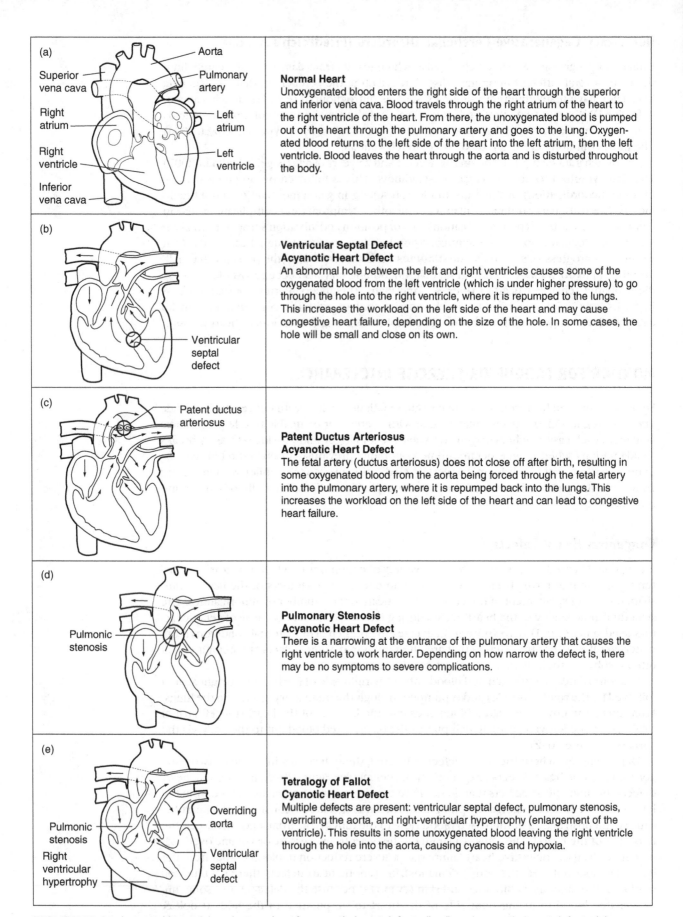

Normal Heart
Unoxygenated blood enters the right side of the heart through the superior and inferior vena cava. Blood travels through the right atrium of the heart to the right ventricle of the heart. From there, the unoxygenated blood is pumped out of the heart through the pulmonary artery and goes to the lung. Oxygenated blood returns to the left side of the heart into the left atrium, then the left ventricle. Blood leaves the heart through the aorta and is disturbed throughout the body.

Ventricular Septal Defect
Acyanotic Heart Defect
An abnormal hole between the left and right ventricles causes some of the oxygenated blood from the left ventricle (which is under higher pressure) to go through the hole into the right ventricle, where it is repumped to the lungs. This increases the workload on the left side of the heart and may cause congestive heart failure, depending on the size of the hole. In some cases, the hole will be small and close on its own.

Patent Ductus Arteriosus
Acyanotic Heart Defect
The fetal artery (ductus arteriosus) does not close off after birth, resulting in some oxygenated blood from the aorta being forced through the fetal artery into the pulmonary artery, where it is repumped back into the lungs. This increases the workload on the left side of the heart and can lead to congestive heart failure.

Pulmonary Stenosis
Acyanotic Heart Defect
There is a narrowing at the entrance of the pulmonary artery that causes the right ventricle to work harder. Depending on how narrow the defect is, there may be no symptoms to severe complications.

Tetralogy of Fallot
Cyanotic Heart Defect
Multiple defects are present: ventricular septal defect, pulmonary stenosis, overriding the aorta, and right-ventricular hypertrophy (enlargement of the ventricle). This results in some unoxygenated blood leaving the right ventricle through the hole into the aorta, causing cyanosis and hypoxia.

FIGURE 20–2   A normal heart (a) and examples of acyanotic heart defects (b–d) and cyanotic heart defects (e).
Source: Used with permission and adapted from Cook and Higgins (2004, pp. 382–403).

Students who have not had their congenital heart defect repaired or who are in the process of undergoing multiple surgeries to repair the defect will need to be closely monitored for signs of distress. Children will often limit activity on their own but can become easily fatigued and breathless if running, climbing stairs, playing for extended periods of time, or, in very severe cases, walking (Cook & Higgins, 2004). Adaptations such as using an elevator instead of stairs may be needed. Some students with cyanotic heart defects will periodically squat after motor activity (e.g., running) to obtain relief and should be allowed to do so. Others may have cyanotic spells (also known as hypoxic spells) in which they become anxious and short of breath, hyperventilate, and have an increase in cyanosis due to their body having a sudden drop in oxygen. Depending on their action plan, these students may need to rest, be given oxygen, or receive emergency care.

Children who have had repair of their congenital heart defect usually do not have any restrictions. However, children who had repair of complex and cyanotic heart defects have shown deficits in exercise capacity with impaired exercise performance (Norozi, Gravenhorst, Hobbiebruken, & Wessel, 2005). Teachers will need to verify with the parents if there has been complete correction of the defect and if monitoring is needed.

Childhood Cancer

Cancer refers to a large variety of diseases in which the cells have the unique trait of unregulated, excessive growth and have the ability to invade local or, sometimes, distant tissue. This can lead to tissue or organ damage that interferes with proper functioning of the tissue or organ being invaded. There are many different types of cancers that vary as to their location in the body and how they spread. Children often get cancer in the brain (brain tumor) and in the bone marrow (leukemia). Some other cancers are those affecting the lymph nodes (e.g., lymphoma such as Hodgkin's disease), kidney (e.g., Wilm's tumor), eye (e.g., retinoblastoma), and bone (e.g., osteosarcoma). The type of cancer will determine how it affects the body, the form of treatment, and the prognosis. Although having a student with cancer usually raises fears about death and dying, it should be remembered that some cancers (such as acute leukemia) have a high cure rate and that others may go into long-term remission.

Students who have cancer that is treated by chemotherapy or radiation therapy may experience side effects that the teacher will need to monitor and provide appropriate adaptations and support. For example, pain, stomach upset, sleep disturbance, and fatigue have been found in children with leukemia following chemotherapy (Gedaly-Duff, Lee, Nail, Nicholson, & Johnson, 2006). Teachers may need to keep track of these symptoms, provide breaks, or repeat instruction at a later time when the student is more alert and comfortable. Fatigue and other symptoms are also often present in children who have end-stage cancer (Mooney-Doyle, 2006), which usually requires some type of adaptations (e.g., rest breaks, shortened day, or homebound services). In addition, children who are undergoing treatment for cancer are usually more susceptible to infections. Teachers need to be alert to sickness in other students and send these students home so that the infection is not transmitted to the student who has cancer.

Chronic Renal Failure

In chronic renal failure, the kidneys no longer function properly. The condition progresses to the point that the kidneys can no longer effectively filter out the waste products from the blood. Other kidney functions may also be affected, such as regulating blood pressure, balancing electrolytes (e.g., sodium and potassium), fluid accumulation, anemia, and disturbance in the acid–base balance (Gerson et al., 2006). Several decades ago, individuals with chronic renal failure would have died. However, individuals with chronic renal failure can presently lead productive lives with the use of dialysis or kidney transplants.

There are different kinds of dialysis, and all have the same aim of imitating what the kidneys would normally do. In hemodialysis (and hemofiltration), the child's blood is pumped through a dialysis machine to clean the blood of impurities and bring its components back

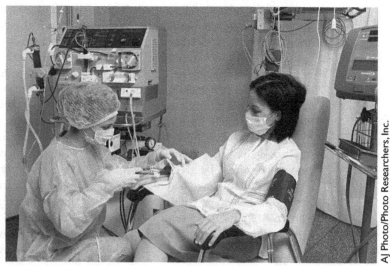

FIGURE 20–3 A hemodialysis machine with a chair for a student to sit in while the procedure is being performed.

into a normal range (e.g., normal levels of sodium and potassium) (see Figure 20–3). In peritoneal dialysis, a sterile solution is placed into the abdominal cavity (peritoneal cavity) through a tube and is left there for a period of time to draw out the waste products, and then it is drained through a tube and discarded. As much as possible, dialysis is scheduled around school and after-school activities, although some school may be missed.

Teachers may need to monitor students' diet and fatigue level. Some students undergoing dialysis may have diet restrictions and/or may eat insufficient amounts of food, and teachers may need to monitor their dietary intake and assist them in meeting their dietary needs. Some students will have fatigue after dialysis treatments (Fishbach, Terzic, Laugel, Helms, & Livolsi, 2004), and their teachers will need to monitor for this and provide appropriate adaptations. Also, if the student has a kidney transplant, the student will need to take immunosuppressive medications that will make him more susceptible to infections. Teachers will need to send sick students home to prevent the spread of the infection not only to the student with the kidney transplant but to all students as well.

MONITOR FOR COMPLICATIONS OF HEALTH CARE PROCEDURES

Students with physical and multiple disabilities sometimes require physical health care procedures. For example, students who have a spina bifida (myelomeningocele) will often need **clean intermittent catheterization**, and students with severe eating and swallowing disorders (often found in students with severe spastic quadriplegic cerebral palsy) may need **tube feeding**. Examples of other procedures found in the school include colostomy care, suctioning, oxygen delivery, and ventilator management.

Health care procedures often need to be provided during the school day. Depending on the school district, the student's physician, the educational team, and various rules and regulations, the procedures may be carried out by the school nurse, student, or qualified school personnel (which can include the teacher, paraprofessional, or other individual who has received appropriate training from a registered nurse on that specific student and is documented as being competent in performing the procedure on the student). Regardless of who administers the procedure, it is important that teachers be familiar with the health care procedure and know what to do should a problem or complication occur. Teachers are also instrumental in teaching students to perform (or participate in performing) their own health care procedure. Of the several different health care procedures that may be performed in the school setting, two of the most common ones for students who have physi-

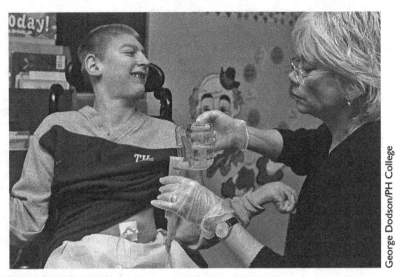

FIGURE 20–4 A student receiving tube feeding through a gastrostomy button.

cal or multiple disabilities are tube feeding and clean intermittent catheterization. A brief description of common complications and problems for these procedures will be provided.

Tube Feeding

Students who are unable to obtain proper nutrition by eating food orally may need to be tube fed. Students receiving tube feedings may have a **gastrostomy tube** (which is a tube that goes directly into the stomach or intestine through the skin) or a skin-level device, such as a gastrostomy button (which is a small round silicon device that goes through the abdominal wall into the stomach and is almost flush with the skin). Liquid nutrition is given through the gastrostomy tube (or through a tube that attaches to the skin-level device) and goes directly into the stomach or small intestine (see Figure 20–4).

Nutrition may be provided on an intermittent basis (e.g., bolus intermittent method, gravity-drip intermittent method, or intermittent feeding using a pump) or on a continuous basis. Although school personnel need to follow the student's specific procedure for tube feeding, a typical procedure for providing tube feeding through an intermittent bolus method is provided in Figure 20–5.

There are several possible problems or complications that can occur while tube feeding or after tube feeding. Some of these include aspiration, tube displacement, nausea, vomiting, cramping, diarrhea, site infection, leaking of stomach contents, and a clogged tube (Heller, Forney, Alberto, Schwartzman, & Goeckel, 2000). Although the action to take will depend on the action plan (as discussed in the next section), there are some standard considerations on how some of these should be addressed.

Aspiration

In regards to tube feeding, aspiration refers to the inhalation of food or water into the lungs. This can occur if the student vomits or has reflux (backward flow of stomach contents) and breathes in the fluid. This can especially occur if the student is fed flat on his back (which is why tube feeding should be performed with the student elevated or sitting).

Depending on how much liquid is aspirated, this can be a life-threatening situation. Subtle signs of aspiration include fast heart rate, shortness of breath, breathing quickly, difficulty breathing, coughing, fever, and wheezing. If a large amount of tube feeding has been aspirated, severe respiratory distress is present with difficulty breathing and cyanosis (bluish color, seen especially around the mouth and fingernails).

If aspiration is suspected, tube feeding should be stopped immediately, and the action plan should be followed (see the discussion later in this chapter). A small amount of aspiration

1. Gather equipment, wash hands, and position the student. The student should never be fed flat on his back because of the risk of aspiration. The student should be in a sitting or elevated position.
2. Attach the syringe barrel.
   a. For G-tube, attach syringe barrel to the feeding tube, keeping the tube clamped by kinking or pinching the tube.
   b. For a gastrostomy button (skin-level device), first attach the extension tube to the syringe barrel and put water into the syringe barrel and allow it to fill the extension tube so it remains full with water. Open the plug of the gastrostomy button and attach the extension tube to the gastrostomy button.
3. Pour fluid/formula into syringe barrel. The syringe barrel should be held approximately 6 inches above the stomach. Unclamp (or unkink) the tube to allow the formula to flow into the stomach.
4. Monitor the flow of the formula and monitor the student, allowing the formula to flow in slowly. (The lower the syringe barrel is held, the slower the formula will flow.)
5. As the level of the formula nears the bottom of the syringe barrel, add more formula. This should be done in such a way that the syringe barrel is never empty so that excess air does not enter the stomach. This is repeated until all formula has been given.
6. When nearing the completion of the formula, add 20 to 30 ml of water to the tube to rinse the tube.
7. Discontinue the feeding.
   a. When the tube remains in place after feeding, some of the water should remain within the tube by plugging (and clamping) the tube with water in it. By allowing some of the water to remain in the tubing, air will not be introduced into the stomach at the next feeding.
   b. For gastrostomy buttons (skin-level devices), remove the extension tube and close the plug.
8. The student should remain elevated after feeding for approximately 30 minutes to help prevent vomiting or aspiration.
9. Document procedure has been completed and observe student for any problems.

FIGURE 20–5 Sample procedure for tube feeding using the bolus (intermittent) method.
Source: Used with permission and adapted from Heller, Forney, Alberto, Schwartzman, and Goeckel (2000, pp. 230–231).

requires an X-ray for confirmation, but a large amount can result in respiratory failure and is associated with a high mortality rate. An ambulance should be called if a large amount of aspiration is thought to have occurred or if there is any difficulty breathing.

Tube Displacement

Gastrostomy tubes and skin-level devices often remain in place even when not in use. The end of the tube or device is prevented from falling out because of the shape of the device or by the inflation of a small balloon on the tip of the tube (or device) within the stomach. However, accidents can happen in which the student or other individual inadvertently pulls out the tube or device. When that occurs, immediate action is needed since some gastrostomies can close within a few hours unless the tube or device is replaced. If it comes out, a clean, dry dressing should be taped over the opening and the tube (or device) kept for visual inspection to be sure that none of it remains in the stomach. The designated person is immediately contacted to replace (or reinsert) the tube or device, or the student may be taken to the hospital or doctor's office. The action plan should specify who is to be contacted and the steps that need to be taken should this occur.

Nausea, Vomiting, and Cramping

Teachers should closely observe for instances of nausea, vomiting, or cramping and follow the action plan to determine the correct steps to take. If it occurs while the feeding is being administered, the feeding needs to be stopped to avoid the possibility of aspiration (when vomiting is present).

Nausea, vomiting, or cramping can occur from procedural errors, such as delivering the tube feeding too rapidly or allowing air to get into the tube and go into the stomach. These symptoms can also occur if the student's stomach is not emptying the food quickly enough or if too much formula is being given. In some instances, it may occur from the formula being given past the expiration date or giving contaminated formula.

Diarrhea

Instances of diarrhea can occur for the same reasons as nausea, vomiting, or cramping. In addition, the formula may need to be modified to have more fiber if that is the cause of the problem. In some instances, diarrhea may have nothing to do with the tube feeding. Teachers need to be sure the student does not become dehydrated when diarrhea is present, and usually the nurse is contacted to help ascertain if the student is sick or if the tube feeding is to blame.

Site Infection

Close observation of the tube feeding site is important to detect any signs of infection early. Redness, irritation, drainage, bleeding, or a foul odor should be reported to the parents and other appropriate personnel (e.g., school nurse) to facilitate the student obtaining the appropriate treatment.

Leaking of Stomach Contents

A feeding tube or skin-level device may leak stomach contents if not securely closed. Feeding tubes typically have a clamping device that needs to be closed. Most skin-level devices have a one-way valve that, when working, prevents stomach contents from coming out. In addition, skin-level devices have a cap that closes over the device to further prevent leakage. If leakage occurs, the teacher should know how to properly secure the tube or device to stop the leakage. A change of clothes may be needed. If most of the feeding was lost, the teacher needs to know whom to contact to determine if it should be repeated. It should also be noted that if there is leakage around the tube (not through the tube), someone will need to be notified.

Clogged Tube

Occasionally, the tube or device may be clogged, and water or other fluid will not flow through the device. This is often due to formula residue, pill fragments, incompatibility of medications, or the formula not being properly mixed. To prevent this from occurring, the tube should be flushed with water after feeding or between giving different solutions. There are several techniques that may be used to open up a clogged tube (e.g., disconnecting the extension tube from a skin-level device and flushing it with water or emptying the syringe barrel and putting water in the barrel and gently pushing and pulling the plunger for a small distance to break up the clog). It is important that the person who is delivering the tube feeding be properly trained as to what to do if a clog occurs. The action plan should specify the best method to use if a clog occurs.

Clean Intermittent Catheterization

Students who have a neurogenic bladder from such conditions as **myelomeningocele** or spinal cord injury may require clean intermittent catheterization. Clean intermittent catheterization is the process of inserting a small tube into the bladder (through the urethra or through a special opening to the bladder) to expel urine. Clean intermittent catheterization is usually scheduled at regular intervals (e.g., every 4 hours) (see Figure 20–6).

There are several possible problems or complications that can occur with clean intermittent catheterizations. Some of these include infection, inability to pass the catheter, omission of catheter, no urine on catheterization, urination between catheterizations, soreness, swelling, discharge, and bleeding (Heller et al., 2000).

Infection

Teachers should be alert to signs of a urinary tract infection. Some of the symptoms include cloudy urine, foul-smelling urine, urination between catheterizations, or change in color of urine. (Burning on urination is often not present in students with myelomeningocele or spinal cord injury when there is a lack of sensation.) If any of these symptoms are present, they will need to be reported to the designated person on the action plan and follow the directions provided on the plan.

1. Gather equipment. Wash hands. Go to a private location (e.g., bathroom stall).
2. Prepare to catheterize. Put on gloves (except for the student). Genital area is usually cleaned, and lubricant may be applied to catheter (e.g., by applying approximately 2 inches of water-soluble lubricant to the end of the catheter).
3. Gently insert the catheter into the urinary opening, and it should easily slide in. (For females, the catheter is tipped slightly upward when first inserting. For males, the penis should be held at 90-degree angle for the entire procedure. If the male is uncircumcised, the foreskin would also have to be gently pulled back and held there.)
4. When urine begins to flow, the catheter is usually advanced another ½ to 1 inch.
5. After the urine stops flowing, slowly remove the catheter. (When catheter is removed, the foreskin of the uncircumcised male should be gently pulled back over the urinary opening.)
6. Student may wipe the genital area with toilet paper after the catheter is removed. The student should dress and wash hands. The person assisting with the procedure should take off gloves and also wash hands.
7. Document procedure has been completed and observe student for any problems.

FIGURE 20–6   Sample clean intermittent catheterization procedure.

Source: Used with permission and adapted from Heller, Forney, Alberto, Schwartzman, and Goeckel (2000, pp. 270–273).

Inability to Pass the Catheter

A catheter should never be forced. A constant, firm pressure may be required when passing the catheter through the bladder sphincter in males; otherwise, the catheter should advance smoothly. If there is resistance, there are several techniques to help pass the catheter (e.g., trying to get the student to relax by taking a deep breath or withdrawing and slightly twisting the catheter and going forward again). However, it is important that the person be trained on what to do should this occur, and the action plan should specify the proper steps to take.

Omission of Catheterization

Catheterization needs to occur at certain times during the day. If it is skipped or forgotten, the bladder can become overdistended, and, in some instances, reflux of the urine back to the kidneys can occur, resulting in serious problems. It is important to adhere to the catheterization times. If catheterization is inadvertently omitted, catheterization should be performed as soon as the omission is discovered.

No Urine on Catheterization

Because the kidneys are constantly producing urine, urine should be present when it is time for catheterization. If no urine is draining from the catheter, it is possible that it has been inserted into the wrong area for females or not inserted far enough for males. The position of the catheter should be rechecked. If urine is still not present, the action plan should be followed.

Urine Between Catheterization

Urination should not occur between catheterization times. It may be a sign of infection or a change in bladder status. The appropriate person should be notified if this occurs.

Swelling, Soreness, Discharge, or Bleeding

Any swelling, soreness, discharge, or bleeding at the entry site may be due to incorrect technique (e.g., not enough lubricant was used) or possibly an infection. In these cases, the appropriate person should be contacted. However, excessive bleeding is an emergency situation in which the student should go to the hospital. In each case, the action plan should be followed.

INDIVIDUALIZED HEALTH CARE PLANS AND ACTION PLANS

In order to maintain a safe, healthy environment for students with disabilities, teachers need to have a good understanding of how to monitor their students and provide appropriate ac-

Action Plan for School Personnel

1. Conditions requiring monitoring
   Specific condition
   Symptoms to watch for
   Actions to take
2. Health care procedures
   Type of health care procedure
   Specific information about procedure (e.g., equipment, schedule, and child-specific procedures)
   Common problems and emergencies

FIGURE 20–7 Components of a typical action plan.

tions should problems arise. To help meet this need, action plans may be developed as part of the individualized health care plan or as a stand-alone document. These plans are typically developed by the educational team or by the school nurse with input from others. It is important that the plans be based on medically sound practices, and directions from the student's doctor or nurse is usually needed. Input from parents and student (when possible) is also important. The plans should clarify what is to be done and by whom.

Action Plans for School Personnel

Action plans should be developed when a student has a condition that needs to be monitored or when the student has a health care procedure that is performed during the school day. Although the student history and student information are often included with the action plan, the action plan itself usually consists of two parts: conditions requiring monitoring and health care procedures (see Figure 20–7).

Conditions Requiring Monitoring

Under the first part of the action plan, the conditions that require monitoring are listed along with their symptoms. The actions to take if the symptoms occur should be outlined next. For example, if the student has diabetes, he should be monitored for hypoglycemia and hyperglycemia. The symptoms of each condition should be listed. The appropriate actions to take for each should be written next. In some circumstances, who should provide the appropriate action will need to be included (e.g., if an insulin injection is needed, the plan should specify if a trained teacher provides it or a school nurse).

Heath Care Procedures

The action plan will contain a second section for students who have health care procedures (e.g., tube feeding or clean intermittent catheterization). This section is usually divided into two parts. First, there is information that is specifically provided about the procedure. For example, for clean intermittent catheterization, information will be given regarding the size of catheter, catheterization schedule, child-specific procedures, and whether the child has a latex allergy. The second part of the health care procedure contains common problems and emergencies, including the actions to take should they occur (as well as a list of symptoms for conditions that are not obvious). For example, if the health care procedure was clean intermittent catheterization, the common problems and emergencies section would include: infection, inability to pass the catheter, omission of catheterization, no urine on catheterization, urination between catheterizations, soreness, swelling, discharge, and bleeding.

Individualized Health Care Plan

In the hospital setting, nurses develop nursing care plans as a way of communicating with other nurses about the specific health needs of their patients. In the school setting, nursing plans have been modified to become individualized health care plans (IHPs). Individualized

Student: _____T.R_____ DOB: _3/12/94_____ Age: _9_____

School: _J.E. Forrest Elementary School_____ Grade: _____3_____

School Phone: _____XXX–XXXX_____ School Fax: ____XXX–XXXX_____

Primary Caregivers: _Joe and Helen Ray____ Daytime Phone: ___XXX–XXXX_____

Other Emergency Contacts: ___George Ray (grandfather)_____ XXX–XXXX___

Physician: _Dr. Green_____ Specialty: _General Practitioner_ Phone: _XXX–XXXX_____

Physician: _Dr. Stanford_____ Specialty: _Neurology____ Phone: __XXX–XXXX____

Person to Contact for Questions Regarding this IHP: _Ms. Smith, R.N._____

Date Plan Approved: ___9/3/02___ Frequency of Review: _annual_____ Last Update: __12/16/03_____

1. Student History and Information

T.R. is a 9-year-old girl who has been diagnosed with cerebral palsy (spastic hemiplegia), seizure disorders (tonic-clonic), and moderate mental retardation. She had a gastrostomy inserted when she was 2 years old because of severe gastroesophageal reflux. Her doctor ordered that she could have very small sips of fluids orally to wet her mouth.

Current Student Information:
a. Medications and procedures: Tegretol (see attached information), tube feeding
b. Allergies: none
c. Diet (dietary issues, feeding techniques): tube feeding
d. Activity restrictions: as tolerated
e. Positioning and mobility needs: manual wheelchair (needs to be pushed), take out of chair at least every 2 hours (see PT report for positioning equipment)
f. Communication: gestures yes/no, uses a Dynavox communication device
g. Transportation needs: wheelchair lift bus, bus driver with cell phone

2. Nursing Plan of Care

Nursing Assessment:
T.R. is tolerating her feedings well and has had only rare episodes of constipation or diarrhea. She is in the 45th percentile for weight and 50th percentile for height. Her diagnosis of gastroesophageal reflux has resulted in an inability to eat by mouth. This has resulted in the need for tube feedings. She has not had a seizure in 2 years.

Nursing Diagnosis:
Risk for aspiration due to gastrostomy tube feeding and seizure activity
Risk for injury due to tonic-clonic movements occurring during seizures or improper delivery of tube feeding

Nursing Goals of Care:
Prevent aspiration during gastrostomy feedings and seizure activity
Minimize occurrence of seizure episodes and injury

Nursing Interventions:
a. Aspiration precautions
    1. Position upright 90 degrees or as far as possible
    2. Avoid feeding if residuals are high
    3. Keep elevated after feeding
b. Tube care
    1. Teach student, family, and designated school personnel how to care for tube, deliver tube feeding, and prevent aspiration
c. Seizure management
    1. Prevent injury
    2. Remain with student during seizure
    3. Administer antiepileptic medication as prescribed by physician

Expected Student Outcomes:
a. Ease of breathing, avoid risk, positions self
b. Family and school personnel learn how to care for tube, deliver tube feeding, and prevent aspiration
c. Seeks medical attention immediately if seizures frequently increase or injury occurs

FIGURE 20–8 Sample expanded individualized health care plan.

Source: Used with permission and adapted from Heller and Tumlin (2004, p. 156, table 1).

health care plans provide important information regarding the health needs of students and can be a good vehicle for planning, managing, and communicating these needs.

Individualized health care plans may be expanded to include action plans for school personnel. This makes the IHPs especially valuable for teachers since they provide infor-

3. Action Plans for School Personnel

Condition(s) Requiring Monitoring:

Condition to monitor: Tonic-clonic seizures

Symptoms: Stiffing of body, followed by shaking. She will be unconscious and may lose bladder control.

Actions to take: Follow seizure plan (attached). If seizure lasts more than 5 minutes (or stops then immediately starts again), call 911.

Health Care Procedure: Specialized Information for Tube Feeding

Tube feeding route: Gastrostomy tube

Type of tube feeding: Bolus method

Formula: 1 can Ensure, 1 can dry baby food with water, extra water as needed for flushing tube and providing hydration

Preparation of formula: Add amount of water specified on baby food box

Schedule of feeding: Every 4 hours (9:00 a.m., 1:00 p.m.)

Child-specific procedure attached: __X__ yes ____no

Actions to Take for Tube Feeding Problems and Emergencies for Student:

a. Aspiration: In this case, this aspiration refers to inhaling the Ensure, dry baby food, or water. Symptoms may include fast heart rate, shortness of breath, breathing quickly, difficulty breathing, coughing, fever, or wheezing. Immediately stop feeding at any signs of aspiration and page school nurse. Call 911 for any breathing difficulty.

b. Tube displacement: Immediately stop tube feeding. Call the mother to come replace the tube. If she cannot be reached, contact school administrator to arrange transportation to hospital for replacement.

c. Nausea, vomiting, and cramping: Stop tube feeding immediately. Check for the following: spoiled formula, tube feeding being delivered too rapidly, excess air entering the stomach, and whether formula is at room temperature. Note signs of illness. Contact nurse.

d. Diarrhea: Follow directions for nausea, vomiting, and cramping.

e. Infection: If site around tube is red or swollen or has suspicious discharge, fill out a health report and send to school nurse and parents. School nurse will follow up regarding appropriate treatment.

f. Leaking of stomach contents: Check to be sure clamp is securely fastened. If stomach contents are leaking from opening or around the tube, call the school nurse.

g. Clogged tube: Follow proper procedure of first "milking" the tube. If this does not work, introduce small amounts of water with the plunger, slowly pulling forward and back with the plunger until clog is cleared (as demonstrated in initial training). If still clogged, call the school nurse.

FIGURE 20–8 *(continued)*

mation regarding monitoring and specific actions to take for various problems and complications. Individualized health care plans that have been expanded to include the action plan usually consist of four sections: (a) student history and student information, (b) nursing care plans (which contains nursing assessment, nursing diagnosis, goals, interventions, and outcomes), (c) action plans for school personnel, and (d) emergency plan. An emergency plan is often a separate document but may be part of the IHP. Emergency plans differ from action plans in that they do not include common problems that are not emergencies (e.g., urination between catheterization). A sample IHP with all four sections is shown in Figure 20–8.

School nurses vary as to whether they construct IHPs on their students who have health concerns. However, in one study, a high percentage of school nurses and special education teachers were in favor of having IHPs, especially if they were expanded to include the action plan for school personnel (Heller & Tumlin, 2004). Because of the usefulness of such a document, it is recommended that action plans are constructed for certain students and, preferably, an entire expanded IHP.

SUMMARY

Teachers need to have a good understanding of their students' disabilities. Several different types of conditions require monitoring. This may include observing for acute episodes and complications (e.g., seizures, asthma attack, or hypoglycemia), medication effects or equipment malfunction (e.g., blocked shunt in student with a myelomeningocele with hydrocephalus), degenerative changes (e.g., difficulty standing up in students with Duchenne muscular dystrophy), and fatigue or exercise intolerance (e.g., difficulty exercising in some students with congenital heart defects). Students may also have health care needs (e.g., tube feeding) that need to be performed in the school setting, and teachers need to be observant for common problems and emergencies that can occur. To assist the teacher in performing the correct action when a problem occurs, action plans or expanded IHPs can be constructed that specify symptoms, problems, and the actions to take for that specific student.

REFERENCES

Alemzadeh, R., & Wyatt, D. T. (2004). Diabetes mellitus in children In R. E. Behrman, R. M. Kliegman, & H. B. Jenson (Eds.), *Nelson textbook of pediatrics* (pp. 1947-1972). Philadelphia: W. B. Saunders.

Alper, G., & Narayanan, V. (2003). Friedreich's ataxia. *Pediatric Neurology, 28,* 335-341.

Beers, M. H., Porter, R. S., Jones, T. V., Kaplan, J. L., & Berkwits, M. (2006). *The Merck manual of diagnosis and therapy* (18th ed.). Whitehouse Station, NJ: Merck & Co.

Bolton-Maggs, P. (2006). Optimal haemophilia care versus the reality. *British Journal of Haematology, 132,* 671-682.

Cocozza, S. (2004). A pathogenetic classification of hereditary ataxias: Is the time ripe? *Journal of Neurology, 251,* 913-922.

Cook, E. H., & Higgins, S. S. (2004). Congenital heart disease. In P. J. Allen & J. A. Vessey (Eds.), *Primary care of the child with a chronic condition* (4th ed., pp. 382-403). St. Louis: Mosby.

Dorman, K. (2005). Sickle cell crisis. *RN, 68,* 33-36.

Dunn, K. L. (2004). Identification and management of autonomic dysreflexia in the emergency department. *Topics in Emergency Medicine, 26,* 254-259.

Fischbach, M., Terzic, J., Laugel, V., Helms, P., & Livolsi, A. (2004). Clinical experiences in daily online hemofiltration: Rescue dialysis modality for children. *Hemodialysis International, 8,* 107.

Fogel, B., & Perlman, S. (2007). Clinical features and molecular genetics of autosomal recessive cerebellar ataxias. *The Lancet Neurology, 6,* 245-257.

Gedaly-Duff, V., Lee, K. A., Nail, L. M., Nicholson, S., & Johnson, K. P. (2006). Pain, sleep disturbance, and fatigue in children with leukemia and their parents: A pilot study. *Oncology Nursing Forum, 33,* 641-646.

Gerson, A. C., Butler, R., Moxey-Mims, M., Wentz, A., Shinnar, S., Lande, M., et al. (2006). Neurocognitive outcomes in children with chronic kidney disease: Current findings and contemporary endeavors. *Mental Retardation and Developmental Disabilities Research Reviews, 12,* 208-215.

Hagberg, B. (2002). Clinical manifestation and stages of Rett syndrome. *Mental Retardation and Developmental Disabilities Review, 8,* 61-65.

Hagberg, B., & Witt-Engerstrom, I. (1986). A suggested staging system for describing impairment profile with increasing age towards adolescence. *American Journal of Medical Genetics, 26,* 47-59.

Heller, K. W., Forney, P. E., Alberto, P. A., Schwartzman, M. N., & Goeckel, T. (2000). *Meeting physical and health needs of children with disabilities: Teaching student participation and management.* Belmont, CA: Wadsworth.

Heller, K. W., & Tumlin, J. (2004). Using expanded individualized healthcare plans to assist teachers of students with complex healthcare needs. *Journal of School Nursing, 20,* 150-160.

Iizuka, T., & Sakai, F. (2005). Pathogenesis of stroke-like episodes in MELAS: Analysis of neurovascular cellular mechanisms. *Current Neurovascular Research, 2,* 29-45.

Jakubik, L. D., & Thompson, M. (2000). Care of the child with sickle cell disease: Acute complications. *Pediatric Nursing, 26,* 373-379.

Karlsson, A. (2006). Autonomic dysfunction in spinal cord injury: Clinical presentation of symptoms and signs. *Progress in Brain Research, 152,* 1-8.

Kieckhefer, G., & Ratcliffe, M. (2004). Asthma. In P. J. Allen & J. A. Vessey (Eds.), *Primary care of the child with a chronic condition* (4th ed., pp. 174-197). Philadelphia: Mosby.

Mooney-Doyle, K. (2006). An examination of fatigue in advanced childhood cancer. *Journal of Pediatric Oncology Nursing, 23,* 305-310.

Moser, S. J., Weber, P., & Lutschg, J. (2007). Rett syndrome: Clinical and electrophysiological aspects. *Pediatric Neurology, 36,* 95-100.

Nazzaro, A., Owens, S., Hoots, K., & Larson, K. L. (2006). Knowledge, attitudes, and behaviors of youths in the US hemophilia population: Results of a national survey. *American Journal of Public Health, 96,* 1618-1622.

Noorbala, A., & Akhondzadeh, S. (2006). Attention-deficit/hyperactivity disorder: Etiology and pharmacotherapy. *Archives of Iranian Medicine, 9,* 374-380.

Norozi, K., Gravenhorst, V., Hobbiebrunken, E., & Wessel, A. (2005). Normality of cardiopulmonary capacity in children operated on to correct congenital heart defects. *Archives of Pediatrics and Adolescent Medicine, 159,* 1063-1068.

Patel, I. B., Sidani, M., & Zoorob, R. (2007). Mitochondrial encephalopathy, lactic acidosis, and stroke-like syndrome (MELAS): A case report, presentation, and management. *Southern Medical Association, 100,* 70-72.

Walker-Date, S. (2006, April 7). Managing the child with Rett syndrome. *General Practitioner,* pp. 38-39.

Zentall, S. S. (2005). Theory and evidence-based strategies for children with attentional problems. *Psychology in the Schools, 42,* 821-838.

PART

VI INFECTIOUS DISEASES

21

ACQUIRED INFECTIONS AND AIDS

Sherwood J. Best and Kathryn Wolff Heller

Individuals typically acquire many types of infections during their lives. Most infections will have no long-lasting effects. Some infections, however, may result in long-term disability or, in extreme cases, death. Because infection is a dynamic process, teachers must be aware of its transmission and effect on individuals. Some of the acquired infections that may have severe consequences include infections of the nervous system (e.g., meningitis and encephalitis), hepatitis, and the human immunodeficiency virus (HIV) infection that results in acquired immunodeficiency syndrome (AIDS). Each of these infections will be described with regard to their etiology, means of transmission, characteristics, detection, treatment, course, vaccination control (where applicable), and infection control. Overall educational implications will be addressed at the end of the chapter.

DESCRIPTION OF ACQUIRED INFECTIONS

The term *acquired infection* refers to any infection that is not transmitted congenitally. The infection is acquired sometime during one's lifetime but not prenatally (before birth) or perinatally (shortly before, during, or shortly after birth). Chapter 22 specifically addresses several congenital infections.

DYNAMICS OF ACQUIRED INFECTIONS

Infection Transmission

In order to have an understanding of how each infection is transmitted, it is important to have an understanding of how infections are generally transmitted. For an infection to be transmitted to a person, three factors must be in place. The infectious agent must have (a) a means of escape from an infected host, (b) a means of transmission, and (c) a means of entry into the body (see Figure 21–1).

Escape from the Infected Host

An infected host may be a person, an animal, or nonanimal material (such as garden soil). In order for the infection to be acquired, it must first have a way to leave the host. An infectious microorganism may escape from an infected host in several different ways; how it leaves is dependent on the type of organism and where it is present. For infections in the respiratory tract, infections may leave the host by a sneeze or cough. Infections in the gastrointestinal tract may leave an infected host through saliva or stool. Infections in the genitourinary system may leave an infected host through urine, semen, or cervical secretions. Infections in the blood may leave through open lesions, a needle stick, blood transfusion, or insect bite.

Infected Host ——————————————————→ New Host

Human   Human

Animal

Nonanimal

Means of Escape	Means of Transmission	Means of Entry
Respiratory tract	Airborne transmission	Respiratory tract
Gastrointestinal tract	Contact transmission	Gastrointestinal tract
Genitourinary tract	Vehicle route transmission	Genitourinary tract
Open lesion	Vector-borne transmission	Direct infection of mucous
Blood from insect bites, needles, or other		membranes; break in skin

FIGURE 21–1 How infection is transmitted.

Means of Infection Transmission

After the infectious organism has left the infected host, it must next have a means of transmission in order to reach another person. Transmission may occur through one of four possible categories: (a) airborne transmission, (b) contact transmission, (c) vehicle route, and (d) vector-borne transmission. Airborne transmission refers to the organisms carried on droplets in the air or dust particles or to organisms shed into the environment from skin or wounds. The second type of transmission is contact transmission, which may occur either directly or indirectly. Examples of direct contact include person to person through sex, fecal–oral transmission, or saliva–oral transmission. Indirect contact transmission refers to transmission through an inanimate object where the infectious organism is on an environmental surface or object. An example is a toy with saliva on it containing a microorganism. The third type of transmission is vehicle route, which occurs when the microorganism is transmitted in infected food, water, drugs, or blood. The last category, vector-borne transmission, occurs when contaminated insects such as mosquitoes, fleas, or ticks transport the infection. However, many infections that are present in blood cannot survive in a mosquito or tick but must migrate to a host that facilitates their life cycle (Munderloh & Kurtti, 2005).

Infection Entry into the Body

Once an organism has left an infected host and has a means of transmission, it can be contracted by another person only if there is a means of entry. Infections that are airborne may enter another person through the respiratory tract by breathing in the infected air droplet. Examples of airborne infections include bacterial strep throat and viral respiratory illness.

Infections that are spread through contact transmission need a mode of entry past the natural barrier of the skin. Contact transmission may be achieved by an infection entering a break in the skin from a cut. Contact transmission may also occur by transporting an infection on one's hands (e.g., from touching infected saliva or stool) and then touching the mucous membranes of the mouth or eye. An example of this type of transmission is hepatitis A. Contact transmission may also occur by infected semen or vaginal secretions entering another person during sexual contact. Syphilis can be contracted through this means.

Infections that are transported by vehicle route transmission may enter through the gastrointestinal tract when a person ingests an organism that is contained in infected food or drink. Diarrheal illnesses are commonly caused through this mode of transmission. An example is salmonella dysentery. Another vehicle route may be through infected blood. Before blood was screened, infections in the blood supply were contracted from receiving a blood transfusion. The HIV virus is an example of this. Transmission may also occur by sharing needles infected with a virus, as in illegal drug use, or by hospital personnel who unintentionally prick themselves with a needle used on an infected patient.

Vector-borne infections occur when one is bitten by an infected tick or mosquito. For example, Rocky Mountain spotted fever and Lyme disease are contracted from infected ticks, and encephalitis is contracted from infected mosquitoes.

Acquiring an Infection

Someone who has an infection cannot pass it on to someone else unless there is a means of leaving the body, a way to transmit the infection, and a way to enter another's body. In order for infection to be transmitted, all three elements must be in place. Even if the infection is transmitted to another person, the person's defense mechanisms may effectively stop the infection. Some defense mechanisms include intact skin, secretions of the mucous membranes that have antimicrobial properties, filter system of the respiratory tract (ciliary ladder), coughing, acid pH of the stomach and vagina, and antibacterial secretions in the gastrointestinal tract. The immune response of antibodies also prevents and fights off infections (Rose et al., 2004).

Although it is common for people to acquire infections all their lives, certain infections may result in significant disability or death. Some of these infections include meningitis, encephalitis, hepatitis, and HIV.

BACTERIAL MENINGITIS

Meningitis is an infection resulting in inflammation of the membranes (meninges) that cover the brain and spinal cord. Meningitis ranges in its effects from no permanent impairments to possible death within hours. Although there are viral forms of meningitis, their symptoms are mild and usually pose no threat to healthy children. Bacterial meningitis, however, can have serious consequences and occurs most frequently in young infants and children (Burns & Zimmerman, 2000).

Etiology of Bacterial Meningitis

There are several different organisms that can cause bacterial meningitis. Some of the most common types of bacteria that may result in meningitis are *Streptococcus pneumoniae, Hemophilus influenzae* type B (Hib), and *Neisseria meningitidis* (meningococcus) (Kanegaye, Soliemanzadeh, & Bradley, 2001). For students who have a shunt to correct hydrocephalus, infection of the shunt may result in meningitis or encephalitis, and in these cases the *Staphylococcus* species are the most common (Livni, Yuhas, Ashkenazi, & Michowiz, 2004). A more recent concern involves risk of bacterial meningitis infection by *Streptococcus pneumoniae* in young deaf children who have had cochlear implants with a positioner that placed the electrode close to the auditory nerve (Boswell, 2003; Van Niel, 2006). Deaf children whose cochlear implants did not include a positioner were not at increased risk of meningitis infection (Biernath et al., 2006). However, deaf children with implants should be monitored for symptoms of meningitis.

Means of Bacterial Meningitis Transmission

Many of the microorganisms causing bacterial meningitis are spread by respiratory transmission. Actually, many healthy children and adults normally carry the Hib bacteria in the back of their throats. This bacterium can be transmitted to susceptible individuals through transmission of respiratory secretions (Burns & Zimmerman, 2000).

Characteristics of Bacterial Meningitis

For children and adolescents, symptoms of meningitis may include a stiff neck (from inflammation of the meninges at the cervical area), fever, sore throat, vomiting, headache, lethargy, seizures, and sensitivity to bright light. A progression through irritability, lethargy, drowsiness, stupor, seizures, and coma is possible (Berkley, Versteeg, Mwangi, Lowe, & Newton, 2004). A nerve that controls the lateral movement of the eye may be affected. Visual impairments, such as cortical visual impairments, may occur when neurological damage is present from a bacterial infection. Hearing loss occurs in approximately 2% to 28% of those who survive bacterial meningitis and is typically sensorineural in nature and permanent (Baraff, Lee, & Schriger, 1993; Kanegaye et al., 2001). Intellectual disability occurs in 15% to 30% of cases (Burns & Zimmerman, 2000).

Detection, Treatment, and Course of Bacterial Meningitis

Meningitis is diagnosed through physical symptoms, lab tests, and lumbar puncture (procedure in which cerebral spinal fluid is extracted and analyzed for infection). Once diagnosed, antibiotics and sometimes corticosteroids are used to treat bacterial meningitis (McIntyre, 2005; Weisfelt, van de Beek, & de Gans, 2006). If seizures are present, antiepileptic drugs will be prescribed as well. Even with antibiotic therapy, some individuals may be left with brain damage, intellectual disabilities, seizures, deafness, blindness, and/or motor impairment (e.g., spasticity or cerebral palsy).

Vaccination Control for Bacterial Meningitis

Vaccines have been developed and are now widely used to prevent infection by Hib and meningococcus bacterium. Before the introduction of the Hib vaccine, Hib disease was the most common cause of meningitis in children under 6 years old. This vaccine has been available since 1985 for older children and since 1990 for infants, resulting in a 97% decline in incidence (Burns & Zimmerman, 2000). The meningococcal vaccine can be administered to children during their preteen years when they receive a diphtheria–tetanus booster or when they enter high school or college (*Child Health Alert*, 2005; *Harvard Men's Health Watch*, 2005). Some colleges now require proof of meningococcal vaccine for college students who will live in dormitories.

Infection Control for Bacterial Meningitis

Since many of the bacteria that cause meningitis transmit the infection through the air, infection control needs to be aimed at decreasing the risk of respiratory transmission. Students need to be taught to cover their mouths when they cough. The best way to cover the mouth is not with the hand, as subsequent contact can then spread bacteria. Instead, the individual should sneeze or cough into the crook of the arm to reduce hand contamination. Students should be taught to use and properly dispose of tissues. However, hand washing remains the single most effective infection control procedure. Proper hand washing includes washing one's hand under warm running water and using pump soap (which reduces the risk of having infectious organisms growing on the soap). After wetting the hands and washing well with soap, the hands should be rinsed and dried. Then the water should be turned off by turning the handles with a paper towel to prevent reinfecting the hands with any microorganism that may have been transferred to the handles. Chapter 23 will specifically address hand-washing techniques as part of universal precautions.

If a student has meningitis caused by *Neisseria meningitidis* or Hib, individuals with close contact to the student should receive antibiotics. Special care should be taken with students who are at high risk for acquiring the infections, such as those with sickle cell anemia or AIDS. In these cases, the compromised student should be separated immediately and the parents contacted regarding the possibility of transmission.

ENCEPHALITIS

Encephalitis is an inflammation of the brain that may result as a primary manifestation of a viral or bacterial infection or as a complication of another infection such as measles, chicken pox, mumps, or rubella. Children who become ill with encephalitis may recover completely, may survive with a variety of disabilities, or may die (Doja et al., 2006).

Etiology of Encephalitis

There are several causes of encephalitis. Encephalitis may be caused by viruses. Viruses causing encephalitis include those that spread person to person (i.e., chicken pox [varicella zoster], mumps, measles [rubella], enteroviruses, herpes, and influenza), viruses that are vector borne (i.e., mosquitoes or ticks), and viruses that are transmitted from warm-blooded mammals to persons (i.e., rabies). A recent concern is West Nile virus, which has traveled throughout many parts of the Western Hemisphere (Hayes & O'Leary, 2004; Yim, Posfay-Barbe, Nolt, Fatula, & Wald, 2004). Although usually transmitted through a tick bite, West Nile virus can be transmitted to the fetus in utero and even through breast milk.

Encephalitis may also occur from nonviral means, including bacterial infections (e.g., streptococcus or *Rickettsia typhi*) or fungal infections. Encephalitis can also ensue from human slow-virus diseases in which the virus was acquired earlier in life but later becomes a chronic neurologic disease resulting in encephalitis (i.e., HIV) (Behrman, 1992).

Of these different types, the most common cause of encephalitis is viruses. The most prevalent viruses causing encephalitis are the respiratory viruses, nonpolio enteroviruses, arboviruses, and herpes viruses (including herpes simplex 1 and 2 and mononucleosis or Epstein-Barr) (Doja et al., 2006; Whitley, 2006).

Means of Encephalitis Transmission

Depending on the etiology of encephalitis, transmission may occur in several ways. The mumps virus is transmitted through respiratory transmission. Enteroviruses are transmitted primarily through infected fecal material (although some of the enteroviruses may result in infectious respiratory secretions for a few days and be transmitted through this route). Arboviruses (such as West Nile virus) are vector borne through infected mosquitoes and ticks. Herpes simplex virus type 1 is transmitted primarily by saliva. Herpes simplex type 2 is usually transmitted by direct sexual contact.

Characteristics of Encephalitis

Symptoms of encephalitis vary. Typically, there is headache, neurologic signs, fever, and altered state of consciousness (Hayes & O'Leary, 2004). At times, there may be a decrease in alertness. More severe symptoms may also be present, such as seizures, paralysis of the arms or legs, or coma (Hayes & O'Leary, 2004; Whitley, 2006).

Detection, Treatment, and Course of Encephalitis

Encephalitis may be diagnosed by the presence of physical signs and symptoms, lab tests, cerebral spinal fluid testing, and brain-imaging techniques. Specific treatment will depend on the cause of the encephalitis. Some children will respond to specific therapy, such as the administration of the medication Acyclovir to individuals with herpes simplex virus. Most viral causes do not have a specific treatment regimen, but treatment is aimed toward controlling symptoms (i.e., seizures or increased intracranial pressure) and preventing complications.

The prognosis of encephalitis varies, depending on the type of virus, the age of the person, and any underlying conditions. Even gravely ill individuals may make a complete recovery. Permanent impairments can occur, and infants and older individuals are particularly at risk, especially when herpes simplex encephalitis is present. Permanent brain damage from the infection can result in intellectual disability, learning disabilities, motor deficits, and seizures. In some cases, especially if untreated, children may die. Approximately 75% of individuals with herpes simplex encephalitis, for example, typically die if not treated, and treatment may be postponed if the condition is not properly diagnosed (Whitley, 2006).

Vaccination Control for Encephalitis

A combined vaccination for measles, mumps, and rubella (MMR vaccine) is recommended between 12 and 15 months and has done much to reduce these viruses and thus associated encephalitis (Ilias, Galanakis, Raissaki, & Kalmanti, 2006; Zimmerman & Burns, 2000a). In some cases, multiple doses of vaccine enhance its effectiveness against disease (Harling, White, Ramsay, MacSween, & Bosch, 2005). Recently, purported connections between the MMR vaccine and autism and/or Crohn's disease have prompted parents to delay or reject vaccination altogether (Seagroatt, 2005; Wallace, Leask, & Trevena, 2006). Numerous laboratory experiments led the American Academy of Pediatrics and the Institute of Medicine to refute claims of links between the MMR vaccine and these disorders (Katz, 2006). Continued delay or rejection of the vaccine may result in a larger pool of children who are susceptible to these viruses, with resulting risk of encephalitis (Alfredsson, Svensson, Trollfors, & Borres, 2004; Dannetun, Tegnell, Hermansson, Torner, & Johan, 2005). Care should be taken to provide complete and updated information to parents to aid in their decision to vaccinate (Wallace et al., 2006).

Infection Control for Encephalitis

Practicing adequate infection control should minimize the risk of transmission of conditions such as encephalitis. As with all airborne infections, it is important that the infected individual cover the mouth when coughing, use tissues (and dispose of them properly), and use proper hand-washing techniques. Students with infectious disease that can easily be transmitted to others should not be allowed to attend school.

To prevent the spread of enteroviruses that could cause encephalitis, proper hand washing and sanitary conditions are critical. Teachers should teach students to wash their hands after using the bathroom and prior to eating to prevent fecal–oral transmission. Proper diapering techniques and disposal of fecal material is important to decrease the risk of infection.

Viruses that are carried by mosquitoes and ticks pose a difficult problem for infection control. Systematic mosquito control programs have been successful in many areas. Insect repellent is recommended and can be applied to exposed skin and clothing. Individuals should avoid scented soaps and lotions, as they attract mosquitoes. Installing screens over windows, wearing appropriate clothing, eliminating standing water close to homes (e.g., in birdbaths and open waste containers), and avoiding exposure during peak hours of dawn and dusk also aid in proper management (Hayes & O'Leary, 2004). If ticks are spotted on students, they should be removed with tweezers or by hands that are protected by gloves. Care should be taken to remove all parts of the tick. Never try to remove the tick by applying a match or other hot object or by attempting to smother the tick with petroleum jelly, alcohol, or other substances (Buckingham, 2005). Wash the affected area and report the incident to the student's parents.

Since herpes simplex virus may develop into herpes simplex encephalitis, infection control should be aimed at reducing the transmission of herpes. Herpes simplex type 1 is often transmitted by saliva. To decrease the risk of transmission, there should be no sharing of food, drinks, utensils, or cups. Teachers should not clean utensils or plates in the classroom, and they should be disinfected in a dishwashing machine with a final rinse of 180 degrees Fahrenheit. Personal care items, such as toothbrushes, should not be shared. Laundry should be done in a washing machine using hot water. Of paramount importance is the cleaning of environmental surfaces. Saliva on classroom items (transferred by drooling or mouthing items) can serve as a form of indirect contact transmission. Toys, mats, school supplies, environmental surfaces, and equipment should be regularly cleansed with 10 parts water to 1 part chlorine bleach. Teachers will often mix this in a spray bottle (like a plant spray bottle or cleaning bottle) each morning in order to quickly and efficiently clean environmental surfaces. Herpes simplex type 2 virus is usually transmitted sexually. Proper education of transmission and prevention is important.

HEPATITIS B

Hepatitis is an inflammation of the liver. There are several different types: hepatitis A (infectious hepatitis), hepatitis B (serum hepatitis), hepatitis C, hepatitis D, and hepatitis E. Each has a diverse etiology and prognosis. Because of the prevalence of hepatitis B and the presence of hepatitis B carriers in individuals with disabilities, only hepatitis B will be discussed.

Etiology of Hepatitis B

Hepatitis B is caused by the hepatitis B virus (HBV). Groups of individuals who are at risk of acquiring this disease are those who receive blood products (i.e., individuals with hemophilia, individuals who have been in accidents and need blood, or those undergoing certain surgical procedures such as organ transplantation), those receiving dialysis, drug users, health care workers, and individuals with disabilities living in institutions or those who have been deinstitutionalized. Hepatitis B is an occupational hazard of teachers and other care providers in schools and day care facilities because the virus survives on environmental surfaces and is transmitted among individuals (Zimmerman & Burns, 2000a).

Means of Hepatitis B Transmission

Although the hepatitis B virus is found in most body secretions, it has been found to be infectious only in blood, saliva, and semen (Armstrong, Mast, Margolis, & Wojczynski, 2001). The most common mode of transmission is through the blood. Hepatitis B can be transmitted through contaminated blood and blood products (although blood screening has greatly decreased this as a mode of transmission) and through intravenous drug use (in which infected blood remains on unclean needles and is transmitted to another person through an injection). The virus can also be transmitted by a bleeding cut in which an unaffected person gets the infected blood on his hands and then puts his hands on his open cut or touches a mucous membrane in his eye or mouth. Direct transmission can also occur during sex or through transfer of saliva from one individual to another (such as saliva entering an open wound). Indirect transmission is also a threat, as the hepatitis B virus can survive on environmental surfaces for up to 7 days and can be transmitted between individuals who share objects such as toothbrushes or washcloths (Armstrong et al., 2001).

Characteristics of Hepatitis B

The symptoms of hepatitis vary greatly from no symptoms or minor flulike illness to fatal liver failure. This depends on the child's immune system response and other factors that are not well understood. Typically, symptoms include fever, nausea and vomiting, weight loss, and an aching feeling. This is often followed by a rash, dark urine, and jaundice (yellowing of sclera of the eye and skin). Up to 90% of infected infants develop chronic HBV infection (Zimmerman & Burns, 2000a), and a quarter of adults who were infected with HBV as children will develop liver disease later in life (Armstrong et al., 2001; Zimmerman & Burns, 2000a).

Detection, Treatment, and Course of Hepatitis B

Hepatitis B is diagnosed by physical symptoms and laboratory data. When there have been no complications, there is no specific treatment. Infected individuals typically stay home until the jaundice is resolved. A few children, however, develop complications (e.g., acute fulminating hepatitis) that can result in death.

In some individuals, the symptoms of hepatitis resolve, but they become chronic carriers of the infection. The hepatitis B virus is found in their blood, saliva, and semen and can be transmitted to others if proper infection control procedures are not followed.

Vaccination Control for Hepatitis B

Before the introduction of the hepatitis B vaccine in 1991, it was estimated that 24,000 children became infected with this virus every year (Shepard, 2005). It is currently recommended that all infants be routinely vaccinated against HBV and that those children and adolescents who were born before the vaccine was available receive vaccination as well (*Morbidity and Mortality Weekly Report*, 2004). In 2002, the HBV vaccine was combined with the DPT (diphtheria, pertussis, and tetanus) and polio vaccines into one injection in a three-dose series (*FDA Consumer*, 2003).

Timely vaccination is important in preventing disease. Unfortunately, many children do not receive the appropriate dosage of vaccine or when it should be administered to ensure maximum protection (Luman, McCauley, Stokley, Chu, & Pickering, 2002). The Centers for Disease Control and Prevention blamed the devastating measles epidemics of 1989 and 1991 on failure to provide vaccines and that reoccurrence of disease is probable without appropriate vaccination (National Vaccine Advisory Committee, 1991). Parental fear of possible adverse reactions and lack of knowledge of the risks of disease, when added to delays in meeting vaccination schedules, contribute to increased risk for disease (Zimmerman & Burns, 2000a). Individuals who are acutely ill, immunosuppressed or pregnant or who have received recent blood products should delay vaccination (Zimmerman & Burns, 2000b).

One important development is the threat of importation of diseases such as hepatitis B through international adoptions, which are becoming increasingly common in the United States (Miller, 2005; Staat & Klepser, 2006). Infants and children who are adopted from orphanages may have been exposed to a variety of infectious diseases, and adoptive families are advised to review their medical records and then plan for travel medication followed by disease screening and treatment on arrival in the United States (Miller, 2005).

Infection Control for Hepatitis B

Proper infection control procedures need to be in place to prevent the spread of infection. Since blood is the primary mode of transmission, proper infection control measures should be in place regarding contact with blood.

As discussed, proper hand washing is the single most important preventive measure. It is recommended that gloves be worn when handling an infected student's blood, as when a nosebleed or cut occurs. However, gloves do not substitute for proper hand washing. When the gloves are removed, the hands still need to be washed. Teaching students to wash their hands is important. Girls should be taught proper menstrual care and proper disposal of menstrual care items since the virus is present in menstrual blood. Open cuts should be covered by a band-aid or gauze to decrease risk of exiting a host or entry into a new host.

Since hepatitis B is also found in saliva, infection control measures should be aimed at preventing sharing of food, drink, or personal care items. Proper cleaning of utensils and equipment is necessary to prevent transmission through indirect contact. Environmental surfaces should be cleaned with 1 part chlorine bleach to 10 parts water, which should be mixed fresh every day.

HIV AND AIDS

Since it was first diagnosed in the pediatric population in 1987, over 10,000 children have been infected with HIV (human immunodeficiency virus) in the United States (Davis-McFarland, 2002). Throughout the world, the incidence has grown to epidemic proportions, with 800,000 new cases of pediatric HIV reported annually (Poirier, Olivero, Walker, & Walker, 2004). It has been suggested that the HIV virus that causes AIDS (acquired immune deficiency syndrome) is the newest chronic illness of childhood and that it is more prevalent in children living in the United States than cystic fibrosis, hemophilia, deafness, acute lymphoblastic leukemia, chronic renal failure, or muscular dystrophy (Meyers & Weitzman, 1991). HIV is more common in children who live in poverty and who acquire HIV through prenatal infection. Among adults, between 800,000 and 900,000 persons in the United States are infected with HIV (Williams, 2003).

Etiology of HIV and AIDS

HIV has been identified as the cause of AIDS. HIV is a member of the lentivirus subfamily of retroviruses. The two major types of the HIV virus are HIV-1 and HIV-2. HIV-1 is most common, and HIV-2 is found in West Africa and India (Hutchinson, 2001).

The immune system is set up to fight incoming infections. White blood cells are responsible for fighting infection and contain both T cells and B cells. One type of T cell, known as CD4+ T cells (which is a helper/inducer T lymphocyte cell), does not attack an invading infection directly but has a vital role in alerting and activating other cells to respond to the incoming infection. CD4+ T cells do this in two ways: (a) by causing the release of proteins (lymphokines) that attract and activate other cells to the area, starting an inflammation response to destroy the invading infection, and (b) by binding to B cells to produce antibodies (which will help fight infections when they return).

When the HIV virus enters the body, it invades the body by typically attaching to CD4+ T cells. When the CD4+ T cells are invaded by the HIV virus, the HIV virus replicates inside the CD4+ T cell and then destroys it. As seen in Figure 21–2, this is a multiple step process involving a strand of RNA leaving the virus and being converted into DNA (reverse transcription), the DNA combining with the CD4+ T cell's DNA (integration), RNA copies being made that result in new viral proteins (transcription), and viral components coming together to bud from the cell and break free to invade other cells. The multiplying virus spreads among CD4+ T cells, increasing in number while decreasing the number of CD4+ T cells. A significant decrease in CD4+ T cells does not allow the body to mount an effective attack against an infection. Instead, the immune system becomes crippled and functions ineffectively against infections, including infections that would not normally harm us. Infections that do

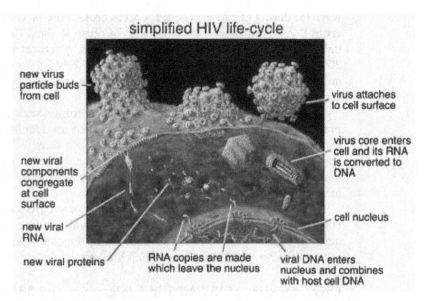

FIGURE 21-2 Simplified life cycle of HIV (starting at upper right and going in a clockwise fashion). Used with permission from Russell Kightley Media.

not normally harm an individual with a healthy immune system but that can cause disease and impairment in those with compromised immune systems are known as **opportunistic infections** (e.g., *Pneumocystic carinii* pneumonia).

HIV can be diagnosed when certain antibodies to the virus are present as well as through other means (e.g., viral culture of bood or tissue). In adolescents and adults, AIDS is diagnosed when the HIV infection causes the CD4+ T cell count to drop to 200 cells per microliter of blood or below (from a normal adult range of 750 ± 250 cells per microliter of blood) or when the HIV infection leads to one of the AIDS-indicator conditions (e.g., opportunistic infections or certain tumors) (Beers, Porter, Jones, Kaplan, & Berkwits, 2006). For infants and children, normal CD4+ T cell counts are age dependent, and the diagnosis of AIDS depends on certain laboratory tests detecting a low CD4+ T cell count for the age of the child, elevation of certain types of Ig (immunoglobulin) antibodies, physical symptoms, recurrent infections, and other abnormalities (Hutchinson, 2001).

Means of HIV Transmission

Although the virus has been detected in several body secretions, it is only infectious in blood, semen, cervical secretions, and breast milk (Spears, 2006). There are typically three modalities of transmitting the HIV infection: through sexual activity, blood exposure, and vertical transmission.

First, HIV may be transmitted during sex (including vaginal intercourse, anal intercourse, or oral–genital contact). Unprotected sexual activity with partners infected with HIV is the most common form of HIV transmission in the United States (Williams, 2003). An increased likelihood of HIV transmission has been reported with anal sex due to the possibility of small tears in the rectal area. Transmission during vaginal sex also occurs. If a sexual partner has herpes simplex virus-2 (genital herpes), the possibility of HIV transmission is further increased because microulcerations cause skin breaks in the genital area and create places for entry of HIV (Celum, Levine, Weaver, & Waid, 2004). There is a low risk of transmission of HIV during oral sex (Campo, Perea, del Romero, Cano, Hernando, & Bascones, 2006).

The second way HIV can be transmitted is through contaminated blood. This can occur from intravenous drug use in which needles are shared. It can also occur from a blood transfusion, but this occurred primarily prior to 1984, when blood screening began. At that time, individuals routinely receiving blood or blood products were at special risk (e.g., those with hemophilia).

The third method of HIV transmission is through vertical transmission, which means from the mother to the infant. This vertical transmission can occur one of the following ways: (a) during gestation where the virus crosses the placenta, (b) during labor and delivery by contact with maternal blood, or (c) by breast feeding. The majority of infants or children under age 13 who have HIV typically are infected by vertical transmission (Davis-MacFarland, 2002; *Morbidity and Mortality Weekly Report*, 2006). Other less common means of transmission in children under 13 are associated with contaminated blood in a blood transfusion and sexually related child abuse.

Adolescents typically acquire the infection through sexual intercourse with an infected person or through contaminated needles typically used for illegal drugs. Both these avenues are examples of horizontal transmission. Substance abuse behaviors appear to place adolescents at greater risk for HIV infection (Howard & Min, 2004). Since blood supplies used for transfusion purposes are now screened, a very small number were infected through contaminated blood.

HIV cannot be transmitted by casual contact or vectors. One study examining preschool children with HIV found no transmission of the virus to their household contacts when sharing beds, toilets, utensils, or toothbrushes or by hugging or kissing (Rogers et al., 1990). Risk of transmission of the HIV virus is therefore extremely low in school settings.

Characteristics of HIV/AIDS in Adolescents and Adults

Classification of HIV

The Center for Disease Control and Prevention (1992) has classified HIV based on the CD4+ T cell level and clinical categories. CD4 levels are divided into three categories: Category 1 is CD4 levels greater than or equal to 500 cells/uL, Category 2 is CD4 levels from 200 to 499 cells/uL, and Category 3 is CD4 levels less than 200 cells/uL. Three clinical categories are also used in this system that describes the symptoms or conditions the person is experiencing. Category A consists of individuals who have a primary HIV infection, are in an asymptomatic stage, or have generalized persistent lymphadenopathy. Category B consists of several symptomatic conditions that are attributed or complicated by HIV. Category C consists of AIDS-indicator conditions (i.e., several conditions that are indicative of AIDS). The CD4 categories and the clinical categories combine to help describe the person's current HIV status in order to assist with determining appropriate treatment. For example, a person who has a symptomatic condition found in Category B and a CD4 level of 300, would have a HIV classification of B2 (AIDS Education and Training Centers, 2007).

Spectrum of HIV Infection

There is a continuum of symptoms associated with HIV, which begin with an initial infection and progresses to late stage or advanced HIV (also known as AIDS) (see Figure 21–3). The first stage of HIV occurs after being infected by the HIV virus and is known as primary HIV infection (also known as seroconversion illness or acute retroviral syndrome). Although a few individuals experience no symptoms, most individuals with primary HIV infection will develop symptoms days or weeks after becoming infected. Individuals experience symptoms that are typically mild and include fever and muscle aches (Stine, 2000) and may develop other symptoms that have been mistakenly diagnosed as mononucleosis or a viral infection. During this time, the immune system is reacting to the virus and developing antibodies. As antibodies become present in the blood, the blood converts from being seronegative to seropositive for HIV (meaning that antibodies for HIV are present in a blood sample). Seroconversion most commonly occurs about 25 days after being infected, and this marks the end of the primary HIV infection stage.

Following the primary HIV infection stage, an asymptomatic state occurs that can last up to 10 years or more. During this time, there are no symptoms, or symptoms are few and mild such as persistent generalized lymphadenopathy (swollen lymph nodes). (This stage as well as the primary infection stage are considered part of Category A in the Center for Disease Control and Prevention's classification system).

As the HIV infection progresses, the person will typically develop symptomatic conditions or symptoms that are due to the HIV infection or complicated by it (Category B conditions). Some

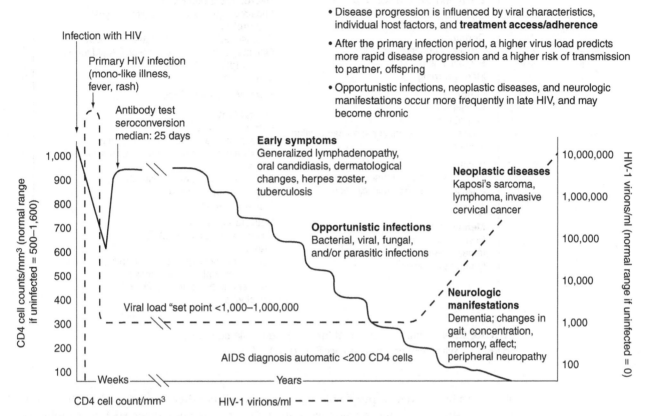

Spectrum of HIV Infection in Adults and Adolescents Without Treatment

- Disease progression is influenced by viral characteristics, individual host factors, and **treatment access/adherence**
- After the primary infection period, a higher virus load predicts more rapid disease progression and a higher risk of transmission to partner, offspring
- Opportunistic infections, neoplastic diseases, and neurologic manifestations occur more frequently in late HIV, and may become chronic

Infection with HIV

Primary HIV infection (mono-like illness, fever, rash)

Antibody test seroconversion median: 25 days

Early symptoms
Generalized lymphadenopathy, oral candidiasis, dermatological changes, herpes zoster, tuberculosis

Neoplastic diseases
Kaposi's sarcoma, lymphoma, invasive cervical cancer

Opportunistic infections
Bacterial, viral, fungal, and/or parasitic infections

Viral load "set point <1,000–1,000,000

Neurologic manifestations
Dementia; changes in gait, concentration, memory, affect; peripheral neuropathy

AIDS diagnosis automatic <200 CD4 cells

CD4 cell counts/mm³ (normal range if uninfected = 500–1,600)

HIV-1 virions/ml (normal range if uninfected = 0)

Weeks — Years

CD4 cell count/mm³   HIV-1 virions/ml – – – – –

FIGURE 21–3 The spectrum of the adult HIV infection.
Used with permission from Sessions (1993).

of these early conditions include oral thrush (which is a yeast infection of the mouth known as oral candidiasis), episodes of shingles (herpes zoster), and peripheral neuropathy (numbness or tingling of feet or sometimes the hands) (Center for Disease Control and Prevention, 1992). As the CD4 cell count continues to fall, more symptoms often emerge or worsen.

When the CD4 cell count falls below 200 or the person has an AIDS-defining illness (Category C conditions), a diagnosis of AIDS is made. AIDS-defining illnesses include opportunistic infections, cancers (neoplasms), and neurological problems (Beers et al., 2006; Hutchinson, 2001).

Symptoms of AIDS

Opportunistic infections usually occur in individuals with AIDS. While they are not a threat to a healthy immune system, they can be fatal to persons with AIDS because of their impaired immune system. Opportunistic infections may be bacterial, viral, fungal, or parasitic and may be mild or severe. **Cytomegalovirus** and **toxoplasmosis** are two examples of opportunistic infections that typically have no significant consequence to healthy individuals when acquired after birth. However, if these are acquired by a person with AIDS (through initial infection or reactivation of a chronic latent infection), they may have devastating results, such as blindness, seizures, encephalitis, and death (Plona & Schremp, 1992; Vidal et al., 2005). One of the most common opportunistic infections is *Pneumocystis carinii* pneumonia (PCP), also known as *Pneumocystis jiroveci,* which is pneumonia caused by a fungal microorganism.

Cancers (neoplastic disease) may also occur in individuals with AIDS. Kaposi's sarcoma is one of the most common forms of cancer in individuals with AIDS that affects mainly the

Clinical Features of the AIDS Dementia Complex	
Early Manifestations	**Neurologic Examination**
Symptoms	Impaired rapid movements (limbs, eyes)
	Hyperreflexia
Cognition	Release reflexes (snout, glabellar, grasp)
Impaired concentration	Gait ataxia (impaired tandem gait, rapid turns)
Forgetfulness	Tremor (postural)
Mental slowing	Leg weakness
Motor	**Late Manifestations**
Unsteady gait	
Leg weakness	**Mental Status**
Loss of coordination, impaired handwriting	Global dementia
Tremor	Psychomotor slowing: verbal responses
	delayed, near or absolute mutism, vacant
Behavior	stare
Apathy, withdrawal, personality change	Unawareness of illness, disinhibition
Agitation, confusion, hallucinations	Confusion, disorientation
Signs	Organic psychosis
Mental Status	**Neurologic Signs**
Psychomotor slowing	Weakness (legs to arms)
Impaired serial 7s or reversals	Ataxia
Organic psychosis	Pyramidal tract signs: spasticity, hyperreflexia,
	extensor plantar responses
	Bladder and bowel incontinence
	Myoclonus

FIGURE 21–4 Clinical features of the AIDS dementia complex.
Source: Used with permission from Butler and Pizzo (1992).

skin (with brown, red, or purple blotches) but can affect other systems, such as the mouth, gastrointestinal tract, and respiratory system. Other forms of cancer, such as lymphomas (cancer of the lymph nodes), can also develop.

Neurologic manifestations and AIDS-associated dementia may occur and include a wide range of symptoms that result from the HIV damage, opportunistic infections, and/or central nervous system lymphoma (Bell, 2004). Some of these include slowed mental functioning, cognitive loss, and hallucinations (Anderson, Zink, Xiong, & Gendelman, 2002). Cognitive decline is usually accompanied by motor dysfunction (Bell, 2004) (see Figure 21–4).

Characteristics of HIV/AIDS in Infants and Children

There are some differences between congenital and acquired HIV/AIDS. Infections in infants and children with congenital HIV/AIDS typically have a shorter incubation, and the disease typically progresses more rapidly in this population. If symptoms appear in infants less than 1 year of age, there is typically a development of opportunistic diseases within the first 12 to 24 months and encephalopathy (neurological involvement) at 9 to 15 months. Early mortality usually occurs without prompt treatment. Children who do not develop symptoms during this time period usually survive beyond 5 years of age, although they may have symptoms of immunosuppression by the time they are 7 to 8 years old (Davis-McFarland, 2002). In some instances, children have remained symptom free for 10 years or more (Warszawski et al., 2007).

Infants and young children with AIDS who acquired the infection congenitally may have variable and nonspecific symptoms. These may include such symptoms as failure to thrive, developmental delay, enlarged liver and spleen, chronic diarrhea, lymphadenopathy, upper respiratory infections, ear infections, thrush, and recurrent pneumonia.

Because of an inefficient immune system, infants and children with AIDS typically develop recurrent bacterial infections and opportunistic infections. Bacterial infections such as *Streptococcus pneumoniae* (strep) and hemophilus influenza often occur. The most common opportunistic infections in children include *Pneumocystis carinii* pneumonia and

Organ System Affected	Signs and Symptoms
General	Fever, malaise, failure to thrive, lymphadenopathy
Respiratory	Otitis, sinusitis, lymphocytic interstitial pneumonitis; pneumonias: bacterial, viral (CMV), protozoal (PCP), and fungal (*Candida* spp., *C. neoformans*)
Cardiovascular	Cardiomyopathy, pericarditis, arrhythmias, arteritis
Gastrointestinal	Anorexia, nausea, diarrhea, wasting, parotitis, oropharyngeal candidiasis, oral hairy leukoplakia, aphthous ulceration, gingivitis, HSV stomatitis, esophagitis (candidal, CMV, HSV), hepatitis, cholecystitis, pancreatitis, enteropathy, colitis (bacterial, viral, protozoal, fungal)
Renal	Nephrotic syndrome, acute nephritis, renal tubular dysfunction
Hematopoietic	Anemia, leukopenia, thrombocytopenia
Endocrine	Short stature, adrenal insufficiency
Central nervous	Loss of developmental milestones, impaired cognitive ability, acquired microcephaly, spastic paraparesis, extrapyramidal tract signs, aseptic meningitis
Ocular	Chorioretinitis (CMV, HSV, VZV, toxoplasmosis), cotton wool spots
Locomotor	Peripheral neuropathy, myopathy
Skin	*Infectious*: bacterial (*S. aureus*); viral (HSV, VZV, *M. contagiosum*, warts); fungal (*Candida* spp., tinea corporis, tinea capitis, *Malassezia* spp.); infestations (scabies) *Inflammatory*: seborrheic, eczematoid, and psoriatic eruptions; drug eruptions
Recurrent bacterial infections	*Sites*: otitis, sinusitis, pneumonia, meningitis, osteomyelitis, bacteremia, urinary tract, cellulitis, bacterial colitis *Common organisms*: S. pneumoniae, H. influenzae, N. meningitides, Salmonella spp., atypical mycobacteria
Malignancy	Lymphoma, Kaposi's sarcoma, leiomyoma, others

FIGURE 21–5 Signs and symptoms of HIV infection in children.
Source: Used with permission from Butler and Pizzo (1992, p. 291).

lymphocytic interstitial pneumonitis (Gill, Sabin, Tham, & Hamer, 2004). Other opportunistic infections, such as cytomegalovirus and toxoplasmosis, may occur in the infant or child with AIDS and adversely affect various organ systems. Figure 21–5 shows the various signs and symptoms that can be associated with each organ affected.

Detection, Treatment, and Course of HIV/AIDS

Detection

Diagnosis of the HIV virus is made through clinical signs and symptoms and lab tests. The ELISA (enzyme-linked immunosorbent assay) test for HIV is the standard screening test that is used to detect HIV exposure. The results of this test are usually confirmed by additional tests (e.g., Western blot assays, which test IgG antibody responses to specific HIV proteins). New rapid tests of the blood or saliva may also be used but will need to be confirmed with a standard test. As previously discussed, a diagnosis of AIDS is made when the CD4 cell count drops below 200 (or the presence of one of the AIDS-indicator conditions when HIV is present).

Infants with HIV are usually more difficult to diagnose. False-positive results may occur in the young infant since the mother's IgG antibodies cross the placenta and may persist in the child. The test results then reflect the maternal infection and not the child's infection status. False-negative results may initially occur in the young infant because of the immaturity of the infant's immune system. Since infants' immune systems are not fully developed at birth, there may be a deficient antibody response that results in an initial negative diagnosis.

Nucleoside Reverse Transcriptase Inhibitors (NRTIs)	Nonnucleoside Reverse Transcriptase Inhibitors (NNRTIs)	Protease Inhibitors (PIs)
Zidovudine—AZT	Nevirapine	Indinavir
Stavudine—d4T	Efavirenz	Saquinavir
Lamivudine—3TC		Ritonavir
Didanosine—ddl		Nelfinavir
Zalcitabine—ddC		Amprenavir
Abacavir		Lopinavir
Tenofovir		

HAART therapy consists of two NRTIs plus either a PI or an NNRTI.

FIGURE 21–6 Drugs used in HAART therapy.
Source: Used with permission from Bell (2004, pp. 549–559).

Treatment

The recent advent of combination therapies known as highly active antiretroviral therapy (HAART) has sharply reduced HIV/AIDS symptoms and even restored immune function (Bell, 2004; Valdiserri, 2004). The success of combination medications lies in their ability to block different aspects of HIV replication, although they do not eliminate the infection. Figure 21–6 indicates the choices of drugs available in the HAART approach. Treatment should be started for asymptomatic individuals who are HIV positive and whose CD4 count is lower than 350 and for individuals with AIDS (DeSimone, 2001). However, HAART does not provide complete protection against AIDS dementia, which may be slowed but not eliminated (McArthur, 2004). Hospital treatment of adults with AIDS is currently less focused on management of opportunistic infections than on treatment of toxic effects of antiretroviral drugs (Morris, 2006), including insulin resistance and cardiovascular disease.

Advances in prevention have substantially reduced the rates of vertical transmission (mother to infant) from 25% to 30% when there is no treatment to less than 2% with appropriate preventive treatment. Examples of intervention include HIV screening during pregnancy, use of antiretroviral drugs, elective Cesarean section, and avoidance of breast feeding (*Morbidity and Mortality Weekly Report*, 2004). Prenatal care should include programs of routine HIV testing during pregnancy and repeat testing for women who are at higher risk for HIV infection (those with a history of sexually transmitted diseases, drug use, and so on), coupled with maternal antiretroviral treatment. However, failure to receive such prenatal support means that infants will continue to be infected with HIV (*Morbidity and Mortality Weekly Report*, 2004). Research toward prevention and cure of AIDS continues.

Course

Although life expectancy for individuals with AIDS has dramatically increased because of new treatments, many individuals will deteriorate and die. Since death is typically not sudden, adults often have time to make final plans and arrangements. However, in the pediatric population, the course can be more rapid. Since the beginning of the epidemic, AIDS has been diagnosed for approximately 8,779 children in the United States from perinatal transmission of the HIV virus, of which 4,982 have died (Centers for Disease Control and Prevention, 2006). As time goes on, more deaths will occur, but fortunately there has been a decline in vertical transmission of HIV, and new treatments are helping to sustain life.

Infection Control for HIV/AIDS

Since the HIV virus is transmitted by blood, semen, vaginal secretions, and breast milk, infection control procedures are aimed at minimizing contact with these secretions. In a school setting, it would be very difficult to acquire the infection. The use of condoms may be discussed for decreasing the risk of transmission of HIV infection during sex. The threat of acquiring AIDS during illegal IV drug use should also be discussed.

Precautions should be taken when cleaning up any blood spills. Gloves should be worn when assisting in the bandaging of bleeding wounds. Getting blood on intact skin, however, will not result in transmission of the infection. After removing the gloves, hands should be washed. If HIV-infected blood drips on an environmental surface, it can be cleaned with 1 part chlorine bleach to 10 parts water.

Prevention of infection transmission to the student with HIV/AIDS is of paramount importance. When a student's immune system is impaired from this virus, infections are easily acquired from others, some of which could be fatal. It is important that the teacher implement infection control procedures and send home children who are sick.

EDUCATIONAL IMPLICATIONS

Many children who have acquired diseases will attend school programs. In order to meet their educational needs, teachers need to have a good understanding of infection, how infections may leave a host, the ways they can be transmitted, and means of entry into unaffected hosts. On a practical level, teachers should always maintain educational environments under strict infection control procedures and employ universal precautions. Unfortunately, many preservice teacher education programs and in-service school-based programs fail to provide this information (Franks, Miller, Wolff, & Landry, 2003).

Meeting Physical and Sensory Needs

To best meet the physical needs of students in the class, the teacher should maintain infection control procedures. Policies should be followed that determine when a student should be sent home because of illness. As a preventive measure, the teacher should follow universal precautions in the classroom. These precautions will be discussed in detail in chapter 23.

The educator must also be aware that students with AIDS are often underweight and may develop wasting syndrome (which presents with progressive weight loss). A positive nutritional program should be in place to assist the student.

If the student is left with physical or sensory disabilities from an infection, teachers will need to incorporate proper adaptations to allow the student to succeed in the classroom. A team approach will be needed to determine individual student needs and methods of implementation of educational goals (see chapter 12 on classroom adaptations).

Meeting Communication Needs, Learning Needs, and Daily Living Needs

Students with chronic infections will need to be given accurate information about their illness. This includes information about transmission, course, treatment, and prognosis. Information should be conveyed by the parents or physician in understandable terms and in a supporting manner. Part of the information should include what the student can do to prevent the spread of infection (i.e., both prevention of transmitting his infection and prevention of acquiring another's infection). The teacher should routinely instruct all students on proper infection control procedures and self-help skills (i.e., hand washing, using band-aid, covering mouth when sneezing and coughing). Health education classes should discuss preventive measures, such as condom use and dangers of drug use.

Students who congenitally acquire the HIV infection are at risk of developing neurological complications, including developmental delays and intellectual disabilities. It is important that these children be closely monitored for the development of any cognitive problems. A team approach is crucial in identifying and implementing proper programming and services needed to meet the individual needs of the student. Providing appropriate emotional support is also crucial when a student is undergoing a change in program due to a change in abilities.

Meeting Behavioral and Social Needs

In addition to knowledge about acquired infections and practice of universal precautions, teachers must become familiar with the psychosocial effects of disease on children and their families and the ethical and legal obligations for maintaining confidentiality (Sileo & Lock, 2005). Students with chronic health impairments, such as a chronic infection, are more likely to have behavioral and educational difficulties than their healthy peers (Scharko, 2006). Specific concerns include a sense of powerlessness and loss of control, inability to reach life goals, and meaning of life (Tsasis, 2000). Students with chronic illness may have increased rates of behavior problems, depression, anxiety, and impaired self-images that may negatively impact on school performance. These problems arise not only from the student's perception of his illness but also from the reactions of teachers, staff, and peers (Meyers & Weitzman, 1991).

It is imperative that students receive proper emotional support. The type of infection and the student's perception of the infection will play a significant role in focusing intervention. For example, students who are chronic carriers of hepatitis B usually have very different concerns than students with the HIV infection. Students with the HIV infection are confronted with a serious infection for which there is treatment but no cure. Students with HIV infection may need someone to talk to regarding issues surrounding the infection as well as issues of death and dying. Teachers should make themselves available to be nonjudgmental, supportive listeners.

Individuals with infections such as HIV may encounter social stigma and hysteria (Ware, Wyatt, & Tugenberg, 2006). In order to provide a culturally and developmentally competent approach to supporting students with acquired diseases, in addition to knowing about the condition, its transmission, and effects on learning, Sileo and Lock (2005) recommend strategies such as role-playing precautionary situations, discussing protective barriers to disease transmission, and using juvenile nonfiction to heighten student awareness and reduce prejudice. Teachers need to be sensitive to the fact that students with acquired infections are more at risk from being infected with illnesses than transmitting their infections to others. In addition, many teachers believe that they have a right to know about a student's disease status, particularly HIV/AIDS. Such disclosure is not required or necessary. Practicing universal precautions will protect everyone in the educational environment.

SUMMARY

There are many different types of infections, most of which do not pose a significant risk to the health and safety of the individual. However, there are some infections that can result in disability or death. Among these are meningitis, encephalitis, hepatitis, and HIV infection. Teachers should implement proper infection control procedures and universal precautions in school environments. Each student's individual needs should be assessed and proper educational and emotional support provided.

 **Mark's Story**

Mark is a 10-year-old boy who has HIV. He has been receiving his education in a regular fifth-grade class with the other students. He has been well liked by his peers and enjoys sports. However, a teacher overheard a parent say that Mark is HIV positive. No one at school knew of Mark's HIV status. His teachers begin to panic and wonder if Mark could be placed in a self-contained class. Mark is feeling uneasy as rumors are going through the hallways about his condition. As a special education teacher, you have been asked what should be done about the situation. How do you respond?

REFERENCES

AIDS Education & Training Centers. (2007). *Clinical Manual for Management of the HIV-Infected Adult, 2006 Edition updated July 2007*. AETC National Resource Center: Newark, NJ.

Alfredsson, R., Svensson, E., Trollfors, B., & Borres, M. P. (2004). Why do parents hesitate to vaccinate their children against measles, mumps, and rubella? *Acta Pediatrica, 93*, 1232-1237.

Anderson, E., Zink, W., Xiong, H., & Gendelman, H. E. (2002). HIV-1-associated dementia: A metabolic encephalopathy perpetrated by virus-infected and immune-competent mononuclear phagocytes. *Journal of AIDS, 31*, S43-S54.

Armstrong, G. L., Mast, E. E., Margolis, H. S., & Wojczynski, M. (2001). Childhood hepatitis B infections in the United States before hepatitis B immunization. *Pediatrics, 108*, 1123-1128.

Baraff, L. J., Lee, S. I., & Schriger, D. I. (1993). Outcomes of bacterial meningitis in children: A metanalysis. *Pediatric Infectious Disease Journal, 12*, 389-394.

Beers, M. H., Porter, R. S., Jones, T. V., Kaplan, J. L., & Berkwits, M. (2006). *The Merck manual of diagnosis and therapy* (18th ed.). Whitehouse Station, NJ: Merck & Co.

Behrman, R. (1992). *Textbook in pediatrics*. Philadelphia: W. B. Saunders.

Bell, J. E. (2004). An update on the neuropathology of HIV in the HAART era. *Histopathology, 45*, 549-559.

Berkley, J. A., Versteeg, A. C., Mwangi, I., Lowe, B. S., & Newton, C. R. J. C. (2004). Indicators of acute bacterial meningitis in children at a rural Kenyan district hospital. *Pediatrics, 114*, 713-719.

Biernath, K. R., Reefhuis, J., Whitney, C. G., Mann, E. A., Costa, P., Eichwald, J., et al. (2006). Bacterial meningitis among children with cochlear implants beyond 24 months after implantation. *Pediatrics, 117*, 284-289.

Boswell, S. (2003). Cochlear implant recipients have increased risk of meningitis. *ASHA Leader, 8*(17), 3-39.

Buckingham, S. C. (2005). Tick-borne infections in children: Epidemiology, clinical manifestations, and optimal management strategies. *Pediatric Drugs, 7*, 163-176.

Burns, I. T., & Zimmerman, R. K. (2000). Haemophilus influenzae type B disease, vaccines, and care of exposed individuals. *Journal of Family Practice, 49*, S7-S14.

Butler, K., & Pizzo, P. (1992). HIV infection in children. In V. Devita, S. Hellman, & S. Rosenberg (Eds.), *AIDS: Etiology, diagnosis and treatment* (pp. 285-312). Philadelphia: Lippincott.

Campo, J., Perea, M. A., del Romero, J., Cano, J., Hernando, V., Bascones, A. (2006). Oral transmission of HIV, reality or fiction? An update. *Oral Diseases, 12*, 219-228.

Celum, C., Levine, R., Weaver, M., & Waid, A. (2004). Genital herpes and human immunodeficiency virus: Double trouble. *Bulletin of the World Health Organization, 82*, 447-453.

Centers for Disease Control and Prevention. (2006). *Mother-to-child (perinatal) HIV transmission and prevention*. Available: http://www.cdc.gov/hiv/resources/factsheets/perinatl.htm

Centers for Disease Control and Prevention (1992). 1993 Revised classification system for HIV infection and expanded surveillance case definition for AIDS among adolescents and adults. *Morbidity and Mortality Weekly Report, Recommendations and Reports*, 41 (RR-17), 1-19.

Child Health Alert. (2005). Vaccine news: New meningitis vaccine approved for children. *Child Health Alert, 23*, 1.

Dannetun, E., Tegnell, A., Hermansson, G., Torner, A., & Johan, G. (2005). Timeliness of MMR vaccination: Influences on vaccination coverage. *Vaccine, 22*, 4228-4232.

Davis-McFarland, E. (2002). Pediatric AIDS: Issues and strategies for intervention. *ASHA Leader, 7*(4), 10-11, 20-21.

DeSimone, G. (2001). Recent developments in antiretroviral therapy. *Clinical Journal of Oncology Nursing, 5*(6), 1-2.

Doja, A., Bitnun, A., Jones, E. I. F., Richardson, S., Tellier, R., Petric, M., et al. (2006). Pediatric Epstein-Barr virus—Associated encephalitis: 10-year review. *Journal of Child Neurology, 21*, 384-391.

FDA Consumer. (2003). Combination vaccine for children. *FDA Consumer, 37*(2), 3.

Franks, B. A., Miller, M. D., Wolff, E. J., & Landry, K. (2003). HIV/AIDS and the teachers of young children. *Early Child Development and Care, 174*, 229-241.

Gill, C. J., Sabin, L. L., Tham, J., & Hamer, D. H. (2004). Reconsidering empirical cotrimoxazole prophylaxis for infants exposed to HIV infection. *Bulletin of the World Health Organization, 82*, 290-297.

Harling, R., White, J. M., Ramsay, M. E., MacSween, K. F., & Bosch, C. (2005). The effectiveness of the mumps component of the MMR vaccine: A case control study. *Vaccine, 23*, 4070-4074.

Harvard Men's Health Watch. (2005). New vaccine may help control a lethal infection. *Harvard Men's Health Watch, 9*(12), 7.

Hayes, E. B., & O'Leary, D. R. (2004). West Nile virus infection: A pediatric perspective. *Pediatrics, 113*, 1375-1381.

Howard, D. E., & Min, Q. W. (2004). The relationship between substance use and STD/HIV-related sexual risk behaviors among U.S. adolescents. *Journal of HIV/AIDS Prevention in Children and Youth, 6*, 65-82.

Hutchinson, J. F. (2001). The biology and evolution of HIV. *Annual Review of Anthropology, 30*, 85-108.

Ilias, A., Galanakis, E., Raissaki, M., & Kalmanti, M. (2006). Childhood encephalitis in Crete, Greece. *Journal of Child Neurology, 21*, 910-912.

Kanegaye, J. T., Soliemanzadeh, P., & Bradley, J. S. (2001). Lumbar puncture in pediatric bacterial meningitis: Defining the time interval for recovery of cerebral spinal fluid pathogens after parenteral antibiotic pretreatment. *Pediatrics, 108*, 1169-1174.

Katz, S. L. (2006). Has the measles-mumps-rubella vaccine been fully exonerated? *Pediatrics, 118*, 1744-1745.

Livni, G., Yuhas, Y., Ashkenazi, S., & Michowiz, S. (2004). In vitro bacterial adherence to ventriculoperitoneal shunts. *Pediatric Neurosurgery, 40*, 64-69.

Luman, E. T., McCauley, M. M., Stokley, S., Chu, S. Y., & Pickering, L. K. (2002). Timeliness of childhood immunizations. *Pediatrics, 110*, 935-939.

McArthur, J. C. (2004). HIV dementia: An evolving disease. *Journal of Neuroimmunology, 157*, 3-10.

McIntyre, P. B. (2005). A population based study of the impact of corticosteroid therapy and delayed diagnosis on the outcomes of childhood pneumococcal meningitis. *Archives of Disease in Childhood, 90,* 391-396.

Meyers, A., & Weitzman, M. (1991). Pediatric HIV disease: The newest chronic illness of childhood. *Pediatric Clinics of North America, 38* 169-194.

Miller, L. C. (2005). International adoption: Infectious disease issues. *Clinical Infectious Diseases, 40,* 285-293.

Morbidity and Mortality Weekly Report. (2004). Acute hepatitis B among children and adolescents: United States, 1990-2002. *Morbidity and Mortality Weekly Report, 53,* 1015-1018.

Morris, A. (2006). Current issues in critical care of the human immunodeficiency virus-infected patient. *Critical Care Medicine, 34,* 42-49.

Munderloh, U. G., & Kurtti, T. J. (2005). The ABCs of Lyme disease spirochaetes in ticks. *Lancet, 366,* 962-964.

National Vaccine Advisory Committee. (1991). The measles epidemic: The problems, barriers, and recommendations. *Journal of the American Medical Association, 266,* 1547-1552.

Plona, R., & Schremp, P. (1992). Nursing care of patients with ocular manifestations of human immunodeficiency virus infection. *Nursing Clinics of North America, 27,* 793-805.

Poirier, M. C., Olivero, O. A., Walker, D. M., & Walker, V. E. (2004). Perinatal genotoxicity and carcinogenicity of antiretroviral neucleoside analog drugs. *Toxicology and Applied Pharmacology, 199,* 151-161.

Rogers, M., White, C., Sanders, R., Schable, C., Ksell, T., Wasserman, R., et al. (1990). Lack of transmission of human immunodeficiency virus from infected children to their household contacts. *Pediatrics, 85,* 210-213.

Rose, M., Hey, C., Kujumdshiev, S., Gall, V., Schubert, R., & Zielen, S. (2004). Immunogenicity of pneumococcal vaccination of patients with cochlear implants. *Journal of Infectious Diseases, 190,* 551-557.

Scharko, A. (2006). DMS psychiatric disorder in the context of pediatric HIV/AIDS. *AIDS Care, 18,* 441-445.

Seagroatt, V. (2005). MMR vaccine and Crohn's disease: Ecological study of hospital admissions in England, 1991 to 2002. *British Medical Journal, 330,* 1120-1121.

Sessions, K. (1993). The spectrum of adult HIV infections. *Emory AIDS Training Network training material.* Atlanta: Emory AIDS Training Network.

Shepard, C. W. (2005). Epidemiology of hepatitis B and hepatitis B virus infection in United States children. *Pediatric Infectious Disease Journal, 24,* 755-760.

Sileo, N. M., & Lock, R. H. (2005). Designing HIV/AIDS prevention education: What are the roles and responsibilities of classroom teachers? *Intervention in School and Clinic, 40,* 177-181.

Spears, E. H. (2006). Students with HIV/AIDS and school consideration. *Teacher Education and Special Education, 29,* 213-224.

Staat, D. D., & Klepser, M. E. (2006). International adoption: Issues in infectious diseases. *Pharmacotherapy, 26,* 1207-1220.

Stine, G. J. (2000). *AIDS update 2000: An annual overview of acquired immunodeficiency syndrome.* Englewood Cliffs, NJ: Prentice Hall.

Tsasis, P. (2000). Health-related quality-of-life measurements in HIV/AIDS care. *AIDS Patient Care and STDs, 14,* 427-438.

Valdiserri, R. O. (2004). Mapping the roots of HIV/AIDS complacency: Implications for program and policy development. *AIDS Education and Prevention, 16,* 426-439.

Van Niel, C. W. (2006). Cochlear implants increase meningitis risk. *Archives of Disease in Childhood, 91,* 619-624.

Vidal, J. E., Hernandez, A. V., Oliveira, A., Dauar, R., Barbosa, S., & Focaccia, R. (2005). Cerebral toxoplasmosis in HIV-positive patients in Brazil: Clinical features and predictors of treatment response in the HAART era. *AIDS Patient Care and STDs, 19,* 626-634.

Wallace, C., Leask, J., & Trevena, L. J. (2006). Effects of a web-based decision aid on parental attitudes of MMR vaccine: A before and after study. *British Medical Journal, 332,* 146-148.

Ware, N. C., Wyatt, M. A., & Tugenberg, T. (2006). Social relationships, stigma, and adherence to antiretroviral therapy for HIV/AIDS. *AIDS Care, 18,* 904-910.

Warszawski, J., Lechenadec, J., Faye, A., Dollfus, C., Firtion, G., Meyer, L., et al. (2007). Long-term nonprogression of HIV infection in children: Evaluation of the ANRS prospective French pediatric cohort. *Clinical Infectious Diseases, 45,* 785-794.

Weisfelt, M., van de Beek, D., & de Gans, J. (2006). Dexamethasone treatment in adults with pneumococcal meningitis: Risk factors for death. *European Journal of Clinical Microbiology and Infectious Diseases, 25,* 73-78.

Whitley, R. J. (2006). Herpes simplex encephalitis: Adolescents and adults. *Antiviral Research, 7,* 141-148.

Williams, P. B. (2003). HIV/AIDS case profile of African Americans. *Family and Community Health, 26,* 289-306.

Yim, R., Posfay-Barbe, K. M., Nolt, D., Fatula, G., & Wald, E. R. (2004). Spectrum of clinical manifestations of West Nile virus infection in children. *Pediatrics, 114,* 1673-1675.

Zimmerman, R. K., & Burns, I. T. (2000a). Child vaccination, part 1: Routine vaccines. *Journal of Family Practice, 49,* S22-S33.

Zimmerman, R. K., & Burns, I. T. (2000b). Child vaccination, part 2. *Journal of Family Practice, 49,* S34-S40.

CHAPTER 22

CONGENITAL INFECTIONS

Sherwood J. Best and Kathryn Wolff Heller

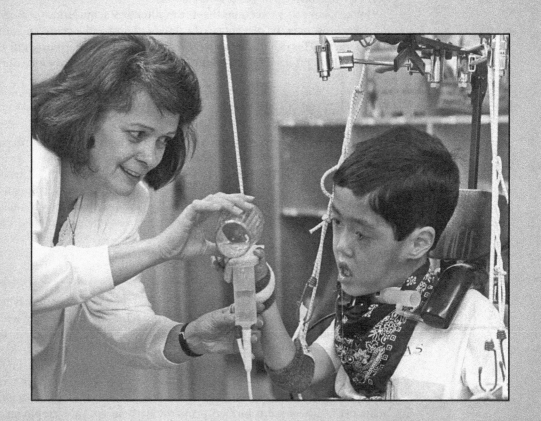

Infection occurs when the body is invaded by viruses, bacteria, or other microorganisms. Transmission of these microorganisms can occur in many ways, including airborne (through droplets or dust particles), vector borne (through a third party such as a tick or mosquito), or through contact with the infectious person or agent. One type of contact is from the mother to the fetus. Although most infections that are acquired during pregnancy are harmless to the mother and her fetus, there is a group of infections that, when transferred to the fetus, may result in multiple birth defects. These infections are referred to by the acronym TORCH.

DESCRIPTION OF CONGENITAL INFECTIONS

TORCH refers to the following group of congenital infections: toxoplasmosis, other, rubella, cytomegalovirus, and herpes. Originally syphilis was included in this grouping, with the acronym being STORCH or TORCHES (with "HE" being herpes and "S" being syphilis). However, there was a decrease of syphilis cases so the "S" was dropped, although some sources keep syphilis in the grouping (or put it in the other category) since it is on the rise in developing countries (Gurleck et al., 2005). The other category traditionally includes such infections as varicella-zoster and parvovirus B19, although it has been suggested that it could be expanded to include the infection that causes Lyme Disease (Borrelia burgdorferi), HIV, and others (Boyer & Boyer, 2004).

Unlike many other infections that the mother may acquire during pregnancy, TORCH infections can cross over the placenta to the fetus and invade the central nervous system and developing organs. This can result in severe fetal impairments or even death. These infections may be transmitted prenatally (before birth) or perinatally (shortly before, during, or after birth).

ETIOLOGY OF CONGENITAL INFECTIONS

The TORCH infections have different causes. Toxoplasmosis is due to a parasite (*Toxoplasma gondii*). Viruses are responsible for rubella (rubella virus), cytomegalovirus, and herpes (herpes simplex viruses type 1 and 2) (Pass, Fowler, Boppana, Britt, & Stagno, 2006; Stanberry et al., 2004; Wicher & Wicher, 2001). Syphilis is caused by a bacterial organism (*Treponema pallidum*). The dynamics of the TORCH infections help explain the variability in their symptoms and the possibility of their overwhelming effects on infants and children.

DYNAMICS OF CONGENITAL INFECTIONS

When a pregnant mother contracts a TORCH infection, it may or may not be transmitted to the fetus. If the infection is transmitted to the fetus, the results vary widely from no clinical damage to multiple impairments. This variability in extent of damage depends partially on the trimester in which the fetus was infected, how long the mother has been infected, and whether the mother has a primary (initial) infection or recurrent infection (Sever, 2002). Infections that occur early in pregnancy are more likely to result in more serious birth defects (Wicher & Wicher, 2001). As seen in Figure 22-1, several organs, such as the heart, brain, eyes, and ears, are formed primarily early in fetal development. Skeletal structures, such as the long bones in the legs and arms, are also formed during early fetal development and may be affected by congenital infections.

TORCH infections, which are transmitted prenatally, cross the placental barrier and may infect developing organs and the nervous system. Infection from mother to her unborn child is called **vertical transmission**. When this occurs early in the pregnancy, there may be extensive damage to the fetal organs and nervous system. Infections such as herpes are transmitted perinatally. If the mother is suffering an active outbreak of the herpes virus during labor, her child may be infected during passage through the birth canal. If not treated quickly, extensive damage to the fetal organs and nervous system can result as the virus attacks the infant's organs.

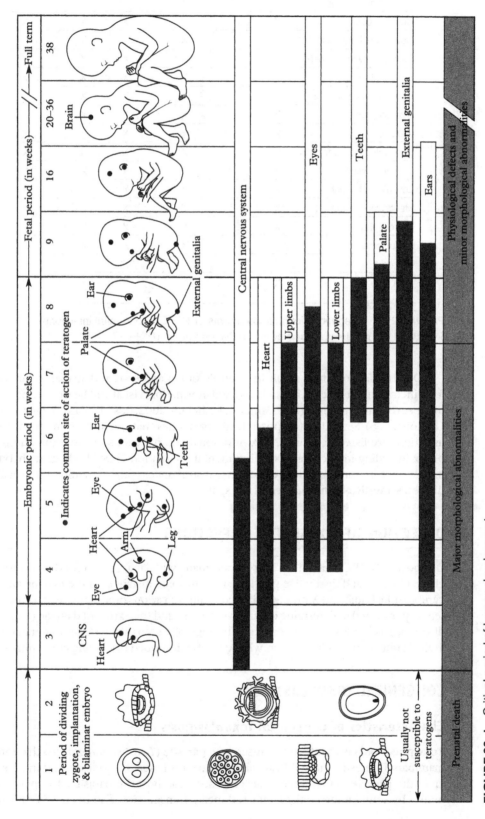

FIGURE 22–1 Critical period of human development.

Source: Used with permission from Moore (1993).

	Toxoplasmosis	Rubella	CMV	Herpes	Syphilis
Anemia	X	X	X	X	X
Brain calcifications	X		X		
Bone abnormalities		X			
Cerebral palsy	X	X	X	X	X
Congenital heart defects		X			
Ear/auditory impairment	X	X	X	X	X
Encephalitis	X	X	X	X	X
Eye/visual impairment	X	X	X	X	X
Hydrocephalus	X	X	X	X	
Jaundice	X	X	X	X	X
Liver/spleen enlarged	X	X	X	X	X
Low birth weight	X	X	X	X	X
Low platelet count	X	X	X	X	X
Mental retardation	X	X	X	X	X
Microcephaly	X	X	X	X	X
Pneumonia		X	X	X	
Seizures	X	X	X	X	X
Skin rash	X	X	X	X	X

FIGURE 22–2 Frequently found impairments of TORCH congenital infections.
Source: Used with permission and adapted from Heller and Kennedy (1994, p. 47).

TORCH infections may result in multiple organ and system damage. Some possible defects include heart defects, brain damage/malformation, visual and hearing impairments, and other severe impairments (Bale, Miner, & Petheram, 2002; Ross, Dollard, Victor, Sumartojo, & Cannon, 2006). Several of the possible abnormalities that occur with many of the TORCH infections are listed in Figure 22–2. Additional complications of these infections may also occur, including intellectual disability (mental retardation), poor body growth, bone deformities, motor abnormalities, endocrine disturbances (e.g., thyroid abnormalities and **diabetes mellitus**), and shortened life span.

DETECTION OF CONGENITAL INFECTIONS

Diagnosis of TORCH infections are typically made with lab tests (such as blood titer analysis), clinical history, and distinctive physical signs. In some instances, there may be an analysis of cerebrospinal fluid and X-rays. Specialized exams of various organs (i.e., eyes or heart) will often be performed to determine organ involvement and the extent of damage (e.g., electrocardiogram, echocardiogram, or computed tomography scan). For a better understanding of the TORCH infections, each infection will be briefly described (including congenital syphilis).

CONGENITAL TOXOPLASMOSIS

Characteristics of Congenital Toxoplasmosis

Toxoplasmosis is an infection caused by a parasite (*Toxoplasma gondii*) that infects most mammals. Domestic and wild cats are primary hosts for the parasite, and infected cats excrete the parasite in their feces. Pigs and cattle also host the parasite. The parasite is transmitted by eating undercooked, infected meat. Transmission also occurs from handling cat feces infected with the parasite and inadvertently ingesting the parasite due to poor hand-washing practices prior to eating. Soil may also contain infected feces so transmission can also occur from such activities as gardening unless proper infection control measures are taken (Lopes, Goncalves, Mitsuka-Bregano, Freire, & Navarro, 2007).

In the healthy adult, symptoms are very mild or nonexistent. However, if a pregnant woman contracts this infection, there is approximately a 40% to 60% chance of the infection being transmitted to the fetus. Maternal toxoplasmosis infection is associated with stillbirth and prematurity (Freeman et al., 2005). Infants who are infected with toxoplasmosis in the first and second trimester and survive will typically have birth defects and severe impairments.

Infants with congenital toxoplasmosis exhibit a large range of symptoms. The classic triad of symptoms include eye abnormalities (retinochoroiditis), hydrocephalus, and intracranial calcification. Some other possible symptoms include seizures, **cerebral palsy**, psychomotor disturbances, and brain abnormalities (e.g., microcephaly). Mental retardation is common in untreated children. Other abnormalities that may occur include enlargement of the liver and spleen, **anemia**, and decreased platelets. Several eye abnormalities may be present, such as retinochoroiditis, **strabismus** and **nystagmus**, and retinal detachment (Bonfioli & Orefice, 2005). Sensorineural hearing loss may also occur. Since sensory abnormalities may be present at birth or develop later, frequent eye exams and hearing tests will be necessary. (Weintraub, 2006). Neurodevelopmental abnormalities from the infection may occur months or years after birth. On the other extreme, congenital toxoplasmosis contracted during the third trimester of pregnancy often results in the infant having no symptoms (Williamson & Demmler, 1992).

Treatment and Outcomes of Congenital Toxoplasmosis

If blood tests are done and the mother is found to have toxoplasmosis, drug treatment may be given to try to reduce the risk of transmission to the fetus although there is limited evidence to its effectiveness (Petersen, 2007). Recent treatment breakthroughs suggest that pyrimethamine plus sulfadizine (among others), when prescribed at birth and continued for the first year of life, can result in normal cognitive, neurologic, and auditory results even in infants who were diagnosed with moderate to severe neurologic impairment (Gilbert, Tan, Cliffe, Guy, & Stanford, 2006; McLeod et al., 2006; Weintraub, 2006). However, these studies have drawn some criticism due to possible selection bias and lack of control groups. Treatment is recommended, but further studies are needed to determine treatment effectiveness. Also, other new medications are currently being examined that appear promising (e.g., atovaquone) (Petersen, 2007).

CONGENITAL RUBELLA

Characteristics of Congenital Rubella

Rubella (also known as German measles) was the most common viral cause of birth defects until a vaccination was developed and a vaccination program implemented, beginning in 1969 (*Pediatric Alert*, 2005). This virus is transmitted to individuals through the respiratory route by infected air droplets. In children and adults who have acquired rubella in this manner, only mild and transient symptoms are typically present. As with the other TORCH viruses, this virus may be transmitted to the fetus across the placenta with adverse effects. There is approximately an 80% risk of transmission to the fetus during the first trimester with the majority of the infected fetuses sustaining damage from the infection. After the 16th week, the fetus may still acquire the infection but usually without sustaining disability.

From the time of the last great rubella epidemic in the United States, which resulted in 10,000 cases in 1969, new cases have declined to 23 in 1998–2000 and 9 in 2004 (Averhoff et al., 2006; *Pediatric Alert*, 2005). In 2004, the CDC declared that rubella was no longer an epidemic in the United States (CDC, 2005). Most of the cases since 1998 were reported in infants born to mothers who were themselves born outside the United States and had not been immunized (*Journal of the American Medical Association*, 2006; *Pediatric Alert*, 2005).

Nevertheless, congenital rubella remains a significant health problem in countries that have less widespread immunization programs (Castillo-Solorzano et al., 2003; Sukonarungsee, Bourquin, & Poonpit, 2006).

Infants with congenital rubella may present with several abnormalities or may be symptomless. Abnormalities that may be present include cardiac defects (patent ductus arteriosus or ventricular septal defects), visual impairments (cataracts, glaucoma, strabismus, pigmentary retinopathy, or optic nerve atrophy), hearing defects (sensorineural loss), and some organ involvement. Additional abnormalities include low birth weight, liver and spleen enlargement, inflammation of the brain, microcephaly, decreased platelets (thrombocytopenia), jaundice, anemia, swelling of the lymph nodes (lymphadenopathy), abnormalities of balance (from vestibular involvement), and inflammation of the lungs (pneumonitis). The kidneys, skin, and bones may be involved as well.

Long-term outcomes for children with congenital rubella exist on a continuum from typical development to significant impairment. Children may have both visual and hearing impairments and be considered deaf-blind. Seizures and cerebral palsy may occur. Although many children with congenital rubella have normal intelligence, intellectual disability and learning deficits have been found in significant numbers of children.

Treatment and Outcomes of Congenital Rubella

At this time, there is no effective antiviral treatment (medication) for congenital rubella. Children with congenital defects from the virus will continue with lifelong disabilities. Surgery may be performed on the eye when cataracts and glaucoma are present, with varied success. Prescriptive lenses and hearing aids may be prescribed. Surgery may also be conducted for any heart defects.

The infant with congenital rubella may excrete the virus for 6 months or much longer. Nonimmunized pregnant women should exercise caution when interacting with infants still shedding the virus. After their pregnancy is concluded, nonimmunized women should be vaccinated. Prevention is the key to controlling the incidence of congenital rubella.

For a variety of reasons, many countries have not been able to institute rigorous vaccination programs against rubella (Castillo-Solorzano et al., 2003; Heininger & Zuberbuhler, 2006). As a result, rubella continues to present a significant worldwide public health problem. In addition, recent allegations of a link between the measles, mumps, and rubella (MMR) vaccine and autism have resulted in decreases in vaccination. Numerous studies have failed to establish this link, and vaccination continues to be endorsed by the American Academy of Pediatrics, the Royal College of Paediatrics and Child Health, the Institute of Medicine, and the World Health Organization (Elliman & Bedford, 2002).

CONGENITAL CYTOMEGALOVIRUS

Characteristics of Congenital Cytomegalovirus

Cytomegalovirus (CMV) is the most common cause of congenital infection in developed countries (Gaytant, Rours, Steegers, Galama, & Sammekrot, 2003; Pass et al., 2006; Rivera et al., 2002). An infection in a healthy individual results in few to no symptoms or related impairments. Approximately 30% of children in the United States have had CMV by the time they reach school age (Sever, 2002).

Cytomegalovirus presents a much different situation when it is contracted prior to birth. Approximately 1% to 4% of women experience a primary CMV infection during pregnancy (Sever, 2002). In the case of infection of pregnant women who have never had CMV, there is a 40% risk of transmission to the fetus. The risk drops to 1% in women who experience a recurrent infection during pregnancy (Gaytant et al., 2003). The virus may or may not invade the fetal central nervous system and cause damage. The likelihood of fetal damage from intrauterine infection is thought to be greater the earlier in the pregnancy the infection occurs (Pass et al., 2005).

There is a wide range of symptoms in the infected infant, ranging from no symptoms or impairments to severe or fatal involvement. Possible symptoms and complication include damage to numerous organs (including brain, liver, spleen, heart, and kidney), decreased platelet count (thrombocytopenia), skin rash, and microcephaly (decreased growth of head and brain). Visual impairments (e.g., retinitis, coloboma, or cataracts) and hearing impairments may occur. Miscarriages and death shortly after birth occur in approximately 2.4% of cases (Sever, 2002).

Long-term outcomes of children born with symptoms of CMV include intellectual disabilities, neuromuscular defects (Sever, 2002), and sensorineural hearing loss (Fowler & Boppana, 2006; Rivera et al., 2002). Seizures can also occur.

Approximately 15% to 20% of congenitally infected children exhibit clinical symptoms, and 5% to 15% are asymptomatic at birth but develop problems later. Sensorineural hearing loss may develop after birth and continue to worsen through middle childhood. It has been suggested that many cases of sensorineural hearing loss with unidentified etiology may actually be due to congenital CMV (Fowler & Boppana, 2006). Other studies have suggested that intellectual disability and cerebral palsy may also develop in some instances.

Although CMV can be detected in fetal amniotic fluid as early as 21 weeks' gestation, the severity of symptoms is not measurable in utero. After birth, congenital CMV is diagnosed by tissue culture or by evaluation of blood, urine, or nasal secretions.

Treatment and Course of Congenital Cytomegalovirus

An important recent breakthrough is the use of ganciclovir to treat potential sensorineural hearing loss in children with congenital CMV (Michaels, Greenberg, Sabo, & Wald, 2003). It has been suggested that widespread neonatal screening for congenital CMV followed by audiological follow-up and appropriate treatment could significantly reduce sensorineural hearing loss (Barbi, Binda, Caroppo, & Primache, 2006). Antiviral medication may be prescribed to treat the initial infection, but it cannot correct the damage. Although surgeries may be performed to correct certain defects (i.e., heart defects), children may continue to have severe disability. Although the Institute of Medicine has prioritized a CMV vaccine as a high public health priority, there are currently no effective vaccines for CMV (Arvin, Fast, Myers, Plotkin, & Rabinovich, 2004; Ornoy & Diav-Citrin, 2006).

One important aspect of CMV is its presence in all liquid bodily secretions, including tears, urine, blood, saliva, stool, cervical secretions, and semen. The virus may be shed by the child with congenital CMV for years. Unless proper infection control measures are used (e.g., proper hand-washing technique, proper disposal of wastes, and cleaning environmental surfaces) persons working with the infant or young child may acquire the infection. If this is the case, symptoms are usually minimal, but a pregnant woman may pass it on to her fetus.

NEONATAL HERPES SIMPLEX VIRUS

Characteristics of Neonatal Herpes Simplex Virus

Herpes simplex is the most common virus in humans (Herpes Simplex Blepharitis, 2004). It is estimated that 60% to 95% of adults have been infected with at least one of the herpes simplex viruses (Brady & Bernstein, 2003). There are two types of this virus: HSV-I (herpes simplex virus type 1), which is associated with mouth disease such as cold sores, and HSV-II (herpes simplex virus type 2), which is associated with genital disease (Brady & Bernstein, 2003). The virus enters the bloodstream through mucous membranes or abraded skin. From there, it travels along peripheral sensory neurons to sites on the skin or mucosal areas, where it remains dormant. Triggers such as ultraviolet radiation, skin trauma, emotional stress, fever, or menstruation (among others) can cause the virus to reactivate with recurrent infection (Brady & Bernstein, 2003).

Most TORCH infections are acquired from the mother by transmission of the virus through the bloodstream to the placenta and then to the fetus. Neonatal herpes, however, is typically acquired during birth as the infant passes through the birth canal of an infected woman or by the infection ascending upward to the fetus after the amniotic membranes have ruptured. Although 60% to 70% of congenital HSV infections are HSV-II acquired during the birth process (Kimberlin et al., 2001), infants can also contract HSV-I via contact from an infected caregiver (Brady & Bernstein, 2003).

Symptoms usually appear between the first and second week after birth but may not appear until the fourth week. Initially, skin vesicles (blisters) appear and often lead to a more serious form of the disease unless treatment is begun. (Approximately 15% of the infected infants will have no skin lesions but will develop encephalitis, which is inflammation of the brain.) Other symptoms that develop include drowsiness, respiratory problems, irritability, lethargy, fever, hypotonia (low tone), hepatitis (inflammation of the liver), and diseases of coagulation (Rudnick & Hoekzema, 2002). Seizures and coma are possible with brain involvement (Frenkel, 2005).

Infants with congenital herpes infection fall into three classifications. The first category consists of skin, eye, and mucous membrane involvement. The second category consists of infants with the disseminated infection with multiorgan involvement. The third category consists of infants with encephalitis, which has its onset usually several days after delivery. This category may be difficult to diagnose through evaluation of the cerebrospinal fluid during early phases of the illness because inflammation may be minimal. Although improved neurologic and motor outcomes have been demonstrated with continuous antiviral drug therapy for infants born with HSV (Tiffany, Benjamin, Palasanthiran, O'Donnell, & Gutman, 2005), mortality for infants with disseminated infection remains high (Kawada et al., 2004; Kimberlin et al., 2001). Infants who survive initial HSV encephalitis may have long-term neurological effects such as spasticity, psychomotor retardation, and seizures that impair intellect and learning (Rudnick & Hoekzema, 2002; van Schoor, Naude, van Rensburg, Pretorius, & Boon, 2005).

Treatment and Outcomes of Neonatal Herpes Simplex Virus

Prompt treatment of HSV using antiviral medication (such as acyclovir and valacyclovir) increases the likelihood of survival as well as increasing the number of infants who will develop normally. Additional medications for HSV continue to be evaluated (Brady & Bernstein, 2003). Prognosis depends on the extent of the disease. Repeat lumbar punctures and cerebrospinal fluid testing is advised for infants suspected of having HSV encephalitis, followed by high-dose intravenous antiviral medication.

If an infected woman is pregnant, transmission to her baby may be prevented if the infant is delivered by cesarean section (Meikle, Steiner, Zhang, & Lawrence, 2005; Rudnick & Hoekzema, 2002). Transmission of HSV is increased if the membranes rupture prior to delivery. The use of a scalp monitor to assess fetal heartbeat during delivery may provide a port of entry for the virus (Rudnick & Hoekzema, 2002). In fact, van der Meijden (2005) reported only a "modest effect" on reduction of HSV transmission using the combination of acyclovir during the last weeks of pregnancy, followed by cesarean section.

Currently, a vaccine has been developed that provides protection against HSV-II in female adolescents and women with no preexisting HSV antibodies (Bernstein et al., 2005). Clinical trials of HSV-II vaccines are ongoing for use with preadolescents and adolescents who have not been sexually active (Gorgos, 2006).

CONGENITAL SYPHILIS

Characteristics of Congenital Syphilis

Syphilis is acquired through sexual contact with another person who has the infection. The infection progresses through a series of stages. In the first stage (i.e., primary syphilis), a localized lesion develops at the site of the initial infection (often the genitals). The pregnant mother who has typically acquired this infection through sexual contact with an infected individual may not realize the significance of the disease and not seek treatment. If left untreated, secondary syphilis may develop, in which the disease may extend to the skin, mouth, genital area, and central nervous system. The maternal infection may progress into the third stage, known as tertiary syphilis, in which the infection spreads to the adult's organ system.

Congenital syphilis is transmitted when an infected woman becomes pregnant or a pregnant woman becomes infected (Wicher & Wicher, 2001). The possibility of fetal transmission increases if the untreated woman has a more recently acquired infection. If the woman suffers from primary or secondary (early) syphilis, transmission to her infant is as high as 50%. However, if she has tertiary (late) syphilis, the rate of transmission may fall to 10% (Wicher & Wicher, 2001). A woman can become infected with syphilis at any time during her pregnancy. The greatest danger to the developing fetus occurs during the first trimester of pregnancy, perhaps because the fetus's immune system is undeveloped early in pregnancy (Wicher & Wicher, 2001). However, the danger of fetal infection is never truly eliminated. In fact, an infant can be asymptomatic at birth but later develop symptoms of syphilis. This was the case with Al Capone, an infamous gangster who was born with congenital syphilis and never exhibited symptoms until adulthood, when he slowly developed mental disability and was insane at the time of his death (Burdick Harmon, 2001).

Congenital syphilis occurs in two forms. In the first form, congenital syphilis may present itself at birth or early infancy. This is known as early congenital syphilis or infantile syphilis. The infant may have skin lesions, lymph node involvement, and blood-stained nasal discharge and have an "old-man" look. Multiple organ involvement may be present. Organs especially affected include the central nervous system, liver, lungs, bones, skin, and kidneys (Gurlek et al., 2005; Peihong, Zhiyong, Rengui, & Jian, 2001). The most characteristic feature of congenital syphilis is skeletal abnormalities (e.g., periostitis, osteochondritis, and osteomyelitis) that often affect the long bones and may inhibit leg movement and growth (Gurlek et al., 2005). Some infants also have seizures, hydrocephalus, meningitis, and intellectual disability. Vision impairments (chorioretinitis or glaucoma) and hearing impairments (sensorineural loss) commonly occur. Approximately 50% of fetuses of women who had primary or secondary syphilis at the time of conception are miscarried, premature, or stillborn or die shortly after birth (Wicher & Wicher, 2001).

Many infants born with congenital syphilis remain in a latent stage where symptoms are not present at birth. This second form is known as late congenital syphilis or congenital syphilis tarda. These individuals usually develop symptoms in childhood, adolescence, or early adult life. Symptoms may include dental abnormalities, skeletal changes (e.g., bone thickening), visual impairments, progressive hearing loss, blood abnormalities, and neurological abnormalities (Gurlek et al., 2005).

Treatment and Outcomes of Congenital Syphilis

If the mother is diagnosed with syphilis during pregnancy, antibiotic treatment can eliminate the infection in the mother and the fetus. If treatment did not occur during pregnancy, antibiotic therapy will be started once congenital syphilis is diagnosed. If organ damage has not occurred, there is usually a good prognosis. However, if severe damage has occurred, treatment will not reverse the effects. The most effective treatment is prenatal screening to prevent congenital syphilis.

Although it has decreased in the United States as a result of recent intensive public health efforts (CDC, 2001), syphilis remains a serious medical issue, particularly in developing countries where prenatal screening and treatment are sporadic (Peeling & Ye, 2004; Saloojee, Velaphi, Goga, Afadapa, Steen, & Lincetto, 2004). The American Academy of Pediatrics, the National Collaborating Centre for Women's and Children's Health, and the Institute for Clinical Symptoms Improvement recommend universal screening for pregnant women early in pregnancy (Kirkham, Harris, & Grzybowski, 2005). Repeat testing should occur later in pregnancy and after delivery in women who are at high risk for syphilis.

EDUCATIONAL IMPLICATIONS OF CONGENITAL INFECTIONS

Students with congenital infections represent a wide diversity of disabilities from no apparent symptoms to multiple and severe disabilities. As with other disabilities, each child will require that his or her educational needs be met on an individual basis.

Meeting Physical and Sensory Needs

Students born with congenital infections are at high risk of having physical and sensory impairments. A multidisciplinary team will be needed to address how to improve physical functioning and make any needed adaptations because of physical impairments. Since sensory impairment is common and may occur after birth, ongoing assessment of vision and hearing is needed to determine if there is any impairment in function. Also, the vision or hearing impairments resulting from the congenital infection can be progressive, necessitating regular ongoing assessment.

In some infections, such as CMV, the young child may continue to be contagious. It is important that the teacher implements proper infection control procedures in the classroom. This includes proper hand washing and cleaning of equipment and environmental surfaces. Infection control procedures should be routinely preformed regardless of whether or not there is a known infection in the classroom.

Meeting Communication Needs, Learning Needs, Daily Living Needs, and Behavioral Needs

Since students with congenital infections exhibit such a wide variety of impairments, educational interventions will greatly vary. Cognitive impairments frequently occur, requiring the use of special instructional interventions. Depending on the extent of physical and sensory impairments, students may require additional instruction on daily living skills, including occupational therapy. Some students will need augmentative communication devices for communication purposes when they have severe physical disabilities (e.g., cerebral palsy). Behaviors vary widely, often requiring behavioral intervention.

SUMMARY

There are several congenital infections that have the potential of resulting in severe disabilities. These include toxoplasmosis, other, rubella, cytomegalovirus, and herpes. These are grouped under the acronym TORCH. The extent of damage caused by these infections varies widely. Educators need to be aware of the severity of the infection and how hearing, vision, and other physical defects can progressively worsen in some cases.

 **Sadaf's Story**

While Rashna was 3 months pregnant, she contracted cytomegalovirus (CMV). The pediatrician informed Rashna that her unborn child could be affected by the infection. When her daughter Sadaf was born prematurely, she was diagnosed with congenital CMV disease. Over time, Sadaf was diagnosed with visual impairments, sensorineural hearing impairment, and motor impairments. Sadaf was treated with ganciclovir and did not suffer significant hearing loss. Despite the severity of her disabilities, Sadaf is doing well in elementary school with a functional curriculum that addresses her individual needs. However, a pregnant teacher has Sadaf as her student. Should she be concerned, and what should she do?

REFERENCES

Arvin, A. M., Fast, P., Myers, M., Plotkin, S., & Rabinovich, R. (2004). Vaccine development to prevent cytomegalovirus disease: Report from the National Vaccine Advisory Committee. *Clinical Infectious Diseases, 39,* 233–239.

Averhoff, F., Zucker, J., Vellozzi, C., Redd, S., Woodfill, C., Waterman, S., et al. (2006). Adequacy of surveillance to detect endemic rubella transmission in the United States. *Clinical Infectious Diseases, 43,* S151–S157.

Bale, J. F., Miner, L., & Petheram, S. J. (2002). Congenital cytomegalovirus infection. *Current Treatments and Options in Neurology, 4*, 225-230.

Barbi, M., Binda, S., Caroppo, S., & Primache, V. (2006). *Journal of Clinical Virology, 35*, 206-209.

Bernstein, D. I., Aoki, F. Y., Tyring, S. K., Stanberry, L. R., St-Pierre, C., Shafran, S. D., et al. (2005). Safety and immunogenicity of glycoprotein D-adjuvant genital herpes vaccine. *Clinical Infectious Diseases, 40*, 1271-1281.

Bonfioli, A. A., & Orefice, F. (2005). Toxoplasmosis. *Seminars in Opthalmology, 20*, 129-141.

Boyer, S. G., & Boyer, K. M. (2004). Update on TORCH infections in the newborn infant. *Newborn & Infant Reviews, 4* (1), 70-80.

Brady, R. C., & Bernstein, D. I. (2003). Treatment of herpes simplex virus infections. *Antiviral Research, 61*, 73-81.

Burdick Harmon, M. (2001). Badfella: The life and crimes of Al Capone. *Biography, 5*(5), 100-107.

Castillo-Solorzano, C., Carrasco, P., Tambini, G., Reef, S., Brana, M., & de Quadros, C. A. (2003). New horizons in the control of rubella and prevention of congenital rubella syndrome in the Americas. *Journal of Infectious Diseases, 187*, S146-S152.

Centers for Disease Control and Prevention. (2005). Achievements in public health elimination of rubella and congenital rubella syndrome—United States 1969-2004. *Morbidity and Mortality Weekly Report, 54*, 1-4.

Centers for Disease Control and Prevention. (2001). Congenital syphilis—United States, 2000. *Journal of the American Medical Association, 286*, 529-531.

Elliman, D. A. C., & Bedford, H. E. (2002). Measles, mumps, and rubella vaccine, autism, and inflammatory bowel disease: Advising concerned parents. *Pediatric Drugs, 4*, 631-635.

Fowler, K. B., & Boppana, S. B. (2006). Congenital cytomegalovirus (CMV) infection and hearing deficit. *Journal of Clinical Virology, 35*, 226-231.

Freeman, K., Oakley, L., Pollak, A., Buffolano, W., Petersen, E., Semprini, A. E., et al. (2005). Association between congenital toxoplasmosis and preterm birth, low birthweight, and small for gestational age status. *International Journal of Obstetrics and Gynaecology, 112*, 31-37.

Frenkel, L. M. (2005). Challenges in the diagnosis and management of neonatal herpes simplex virus encephalitis. *Pediatrics, 115*, 795-797.

Gaytant, M. A., Rours, G. I. J. G., Steegers, E. A., Galama, J. M. D., & Semmekrot, B. A. (2003). Congenital cytomegalovirus infection after recurrent infection: Case reports and review of the literature. *European Journal of Pediatrics, 162*, 248-253.

Gilbert, R., Tan, H. K., Cliffe, S., Guy, E., & Stanford, M. (2006). Symptomatic toxoplasma infection due to congenital and postnatally acquired infection. *Archives of Disease in Childhood, 91*, 495-498.

Gorgos, D. (2006). Trial HSV-2 vaccines show promise. *Dermatology Nursing, 18*, 509.

Gurlek, A., Alaybeyoglu, N. Y., Demir, C. Y., Aydogan, H., Coban, K., Fariz, A., et al. (2005). The continuing scourge of congenital syphilis in the 21st century: A case report. *International Journal of Pediatric Otorhinolaryngology, 69*, 1117-1121.

Heininger, U., & Zuberbuhler, M. (2006). Immunization rates and timely administration in pre-school and school-aged children. *European Journal of Pediatrics, 165*, 124-129.

Heller, K., & Kennedy, C. (1994). Etiology and characteristics of deaf-blindness. *Teaching Research Publications*, p. 47.

Herpes Simplex Blepharitis. (2004). *Review of Optometry, 141*, 7A-9A.

Journal of the American Medical Association. (2006). Brief report: Imported case of congenital rubella syndrome—New Hampshire, 2005. *Journal of the American Medical Association, 295*, 292-294.

Kawada, J., Kimura, H., Ito, Y., Ando, Y., Tanaka-Kitajima, N., Hayakawa, M., et al. (2004). Evaluation of systematic inflammatory responses in neonates with herpes simplex virus infection. *Journal of Infectious Diseases, 190*, 494-498.

Kimberlin, D. W., Lin, C. Y., Jacobs, R. F., Powell, D. A., Frenkel, L. M., Gruber, W. C., & the National Institute of Allergy and Infectious Diseases Collabortive Antiviral Study Group. (2001). Natural history of neonatal herpes simplex virus infections in the acyclovir era. *Pediatrics, 108*, 223-229.

Kirkham, C., Harris, S., & Grzybowski, S. (2005). Evidence-based prenatal care: Part II. Third-trimester care and prevention of infectious diseases. *American Family Physician, 71*, 1555-1560.

Lopes, F. M., Goncalves, D. D., Mitsuka-Bregano, R., Freire, R. L., & Navarro, I. T. (2007). Toxoplasma gondii infection in pregnancy. *Brazilian Journal of Infectious Diseases, 11*, 496-506.

McLeod, R., Boyer, K., Karison, T., Kasza, K., Swisher, C., Roizen, N., et al. (2006). Outcome of treatment for congenital toxoplasmosis, 1981-2004: The National Collaborative Chicago-Based, Congenital Toxoplasmosis Study. *Clinical Infectious Diseases, 42*, 1383-1394.

Meikle, S. F., Steiner, C. A., Zhang, J., & Lawrence, W. L. (2005). A national estimate of the elective primary cesarean delivery rate. *Obstetrics and Gynecology, 105*, 751-756.

Michaels, M. G., Greenberg, D. P., Sabo, D. L., & Wald, E. R. (2003). Treatment of children with congenital cytomegalovirus. *Pediatric Infectious Disease Journal, 22*, 504-509.

Moore, K. L. (1993). *Before we are born: Basic embryology and birth defects* (2nd ed.). Philadelphia: W. B. Saunders.

Ornoy, A., & Diav-Citrin, O. (2006). Fetal effects of primary and secondary cytomegalovirus infection in pregnancy. *Reproductive Technology, 21*, 399-409.

Pass, R. F., Fowler, K. B., Boppana, S. B., Britt, W. J., & Stagno, S. (2005). Congenital cytomegalovirus infection following first trimester maternal infection: Symptoms at birth and outcome. *Journal of Clinical Virology, 35*, 216-220.

Pediatric Alert. (2005). Saying good-bye to rubella and congenital rubella syndrome in the U.S. *Pediatric Alert, 30*(8), 45.

Peeling, R. W., & Ye, H. (2004). Diagnostic tools for preventing and managing maternal and congenital syphilis: An overview. *Bulletin of the World Health Organization, 82*, 439-446.

Peihong, J., Zhiyong, L., Rengui, C., & Jian, W. (2001). Early congenital syphilis. *International Journal of Dermatology, 40*, 191-209.

Petersen, E. (2007). Toxoplasmosis. *Seminars in Fetal and Neonatal Medicine, 12*, 214-223.

Rivera, L. B., Boppana, S. B., Fowler, K. B., Britt, W. J., Stagno, S., & Pass, R. F. (2002). Predictors of hearing loss in children with symptomatic congenital cytomegalovirus infection. *Pediatrics, 110,* 762-767.

Ross, D. S., Dollard, S. C., Victor, M., Sumartojo, E., & Cannon, M. J. (2006). The epidemiology and prevention of congenital cytomegalovirus infection and disease: Activities of the Centers for Disease Control and Prevention workgroup. *Journal of Women's Health, 13,* 224-229.

Rudnick, C. M., & Hoekzema, G. S. (2002). Neonatal herpes simplex virus infections. *American Family Physician, 65,* 1138-1142.

Saloojee, H., Velaphi, S., Goga, Y., Afadapa, N., Steen, R., & Lincetto, O. (2004). The prevention and management of syphilis: An overview and recommendations. *Bulletin of the World Health Organization, 82,* 424-430.

Sever, J. L. (2002). Pediatric cytomegalovirus infections. *Clinical and Applied Immunology Reviews, 3,* 47-59.

Stanberry, L. R., Rosenthal, S. L., Mills, L., Succop, P. A., Biro, F. M., Morrow, R. A., et al. (2004). Longitudinal risk of herpes simplex virus (HSV) type 1, HSV type 2, and cytomegalovirus infections among young adolescent girls. *Clinical Infectious Diseases, 39,* 1433-1438.

Sukonarungsee, S., Bourquin, E., & Poonpit, M. (2006). A first look at children and youths who are deaf-blind in the kingdom of Thailand. *Journal of Visual Impairment and Blindness, 100,* 557-562.

Tiffany, K. F., Benjamin, D. K., Palasanthiran, P., O'Donnell, K., & Gutman, L. T. (2005). Improved neurodevelopmental outcomes following long-term high-dose oral acyclovir therapy in infants with central nervous system and disseminated herpes simplex disease. *Journal of Perinatology, 25,* 156-161.

van der Meijden, W. I. (2005). Strategies for the prevention of neonatal herpes: Just a matter of opinion? *International Congress Series, 1279,* 109-114.

van Schoor, A. N., Naude, H., van Rensburg, M., Pretorius, E., & Boon, J. M. (2005). Cognitive and learning strategies for longstanding temporal lobe lesions in a child who suffered from herpes simplex virus encephalitis: A case study over 10 years. *Early Child Development and Care, 175,* 621-634.

Weintraub, P. S. (2006). Congenital toxoplasmosis treatment: Guarded optimism. *Archives of Disease in Childhood, 91,* 871-873.

Wicher, V., & Wicher, K. (2001). Pathogenesis of maternal-fetal syphilis revisited. *Clinical Infectious Diseases, 33,* 354-363.

Williamson, D., & Demmler, G. (1992). Congenital infections: Clinical outcomes and educational implications. *Infants and Young Children, 4,* 1-20.

CHAPTER 23

UNIVERSAL PRECAUTIONS

Sherwood J. Best

Despite advances in medical technology, children will continue to be born with infections or acquire them after birth. In addition, more children with physical disabilities and health impairments survive to become active participants in their schools, homes, and communities. These children—and the individuals who provide them with educational and therapeutic support—have a right to interaction in environments that promote optimum health and safety. In addition to meeting the academic and social/behavioral needs of students, teachers must also possess the knowledge and skills to meet critical physical, health, and daily living needs. The first step is a thorough understanding of the concept of universal precautions, followed by the ability to implement best practices.

UNIVERSAL PRECAUTIONS

The Centers for Disease Control and Prevention (CDC) is the federal agency that is responsible primarily for the recommendations that are referred to as "universal precautions." In the early 1980s, the CDC responded to the growing incidence of HIV and other bloodborne infections with recommendations for precautions when handling blood and body fluids of infected patients in health care settings. Since then, the CDC updated its recommendations to treat all patients as if they were potentially infected. The resulting infection control guidelines are known as universal precautions (CDC, 1988). In 1996, universal precautions were "expanded to include 'standard precautions', which apply to contact with blood and all other body fluids, secretions, and excretions (except sweat), regardless of whether they contain blood, nonintact skin and mucous membranes" (Chillock & Palenik, 2004, p. 76).

A policy of treating all persons as potentially infected and including expanded standards has several beneficial outcomes. First, it imposes a stricter standard on health care providers by requiring precautions for everyone. Second, it protects the confidentiality of infected persons by providing them with identical care. Third, the universality of these precautions reduces the threat of transmission from infected persons to health care providers to noninfected persons. The federal Food and Drug Administration (FDA) collaborated with the CDC in developing universal precautions that include the following recommendations:

- Use of "protective barriers"—gloves, gowns, goggles, and face masks—when appropriate to reduce the risk of exposure to blood and other potentially infectious body fluids
- Caution in handling needles, scalpels, and other sharp instruments
- Disposal of needles and other sharp instruments in specially labeled, puncture-resistant containers located as close as is practical to where the "sharps" are used
- Use of gloves to draw blood when the health care worker has skin cuts or scratches, when drawing blood from a child, when an inexperienced person is being trained to draw blood, or in any other situation where hand contamination with blood might occur
- Immediate and thorough washing of hands or other parts of the body contaminated with blood or other potentially infectious body fluids (*FDA Consumer*, 1993)

The guidelines also include recommendations for waste disposal and disinfecting or sterilizing nondisposable instruments.

Universal precautions guidelines have been endorsed by major organizations, including the American Medical Association, the American Dental Association, the American Nurses Association, and the Federal Occupational Safety and Health Administration (*FDA Consumer*, 1993). Since 1991, all states are required to adopt the CDC guidelines for universal precautions or a comparable standard.

Teachers may believe that universal precautions do not apply to them since they do not handle sharp instruments such as needles or scalpels. However, their work in educational and other service settings (such as teaching in hospitals or working in day care) necessitates that they be aware of universal precautions and employ appropriate techniques when touching or otherwise interacting with all students. In addition to protecting the teacher, universal precautions protect students with vulnerable immune systems who cannot easily resist infection exposure. The appropriate practice of universal precautions has been associated with decreased incidence of diarrhea (Barros, Ross, Fonseca, Williams, & Moreira-Fiho, 1999) and respiratory infections in health care settings and schools. Several aspects of universal precautions guidelines will now be discussed, including hand washing, diapering, handling blood and other fluid spills, and disposal of contaminated materials.

HAND WASHING

Hand washing remains the most effective means of infection control. The CDC categorizes hand hygiene into routine hand washing, routine hand asepsis, and surgical hand asepsis. Routine hand washing involves the use of nonantibacterial soap and water washing for 15 seconds and should be used

- when hands are visibly soiled or contaminated with material such as blood or other body fluids,
- before and after gloving,
- when touching bare-handed objects known or likely to be contaminated with blood or saliva,
- before replacing defective gloves, and
- before eating or after using the restroom (Chillock & Palenik, 2004)

Routine hand asepsis is used under the same conditions as routine hand washing but substitutes the use of alcohol-based hand rub or medicated soap and water for 15 seconds and includes hand hygiene even when hands are not visibly soiled. Surgical hand asepsis involves an extended scrub for 2 to 6 minutes with an antibacterial agent or use of a nonantibacterial agent followed by drying and use of an alcohol rub.

Routine Hand-Washing Procedure

Although it is not a complex process, proper routine hand washing involves several steps. First, all jewelry, including rings, watches, and bracelets, should be removed. Sleeves should be pushed up above the elbows so that the wrists and lower arms can be properly cleaned. Paper towels for drying should be removed from a dispenser and placed next to the hand-washing area. Using two layers of towels allows the top layer to be used for hand drying, while the bottom layer provides a barrier between the table surface and the top towel. Next, water should be turned on and adjusted to a comfortably warm temperature. The hands should be placed under the water with fingertips pointed down. Next, an adequate amount of soap should be applied. The use of pump soap instead of bar soap reduces the risk of infectious organisms growing on the soap and being transferred to the hands during washing. After wetting the hands and applying soap, all skin surfaces should be washed, including the fronts and backs of the hands, between fingers, and under nails. A "round and round" or "wringing hands" motion can be used to cover flatter skin surfaces such as palms and backs of hands. The fingernails can be "scrubbed" by curling the fingers and rubbing the tips of fingers against the palm of the opposite hand and rubbing vigorously. After washing well with soap, the hands should be rinsed with fingertips pointing up to direct any remaining bacteria away from the fingers. The hands can then be dried with one paper towel and the water turned off by turning the handles with the other paper towel to prevent reinfecting the hands with any microorganism that may have been transferred to the handles. Figure 23–1 outlines the steps for proper routine hand-washing techniques.

Proper hand washing is not limited to adults. Children should also be taught appropriate hand-washing techniques (Gelbwasser, 2007). One strategy for ensuring that all skin surfaces are cleaned is to teach the child to slowly sing the "ABC song" twice while rubbing soap into skin surfaces. It is important that adults monitor hand washing and reinforce children for performing this task thoroughly.

1. Recognize need to wash hands
2. Go to designated area to wash hands
3. Turn on faucet and adjust the temperature
4. Wet hands using running water
5. Put soap on hands
6. Rub hands together, creating lather
7. Wash all skin surfaces, including
   - backs of hands,
   - wrists,
   - between fingers, and
   - under fingernail beds
8. Continue rubbing, counting to 15 slowly
9. Rinse soap off hands well
10. Dry hands with a paper towel
11. Turn off faucet with a paper towel, not with your bare hands

FIGURE 23–1   Proper hand-washing technique.

Soaps and Sanitizers

Antibacterial hand soaps and waterless alcohol-based hand sanitizers have gained in popularity as cleaning agents. However, using a hand sanitizer alone does not substitute for hand washing. In fact, waterless hand sanitizers that kill bacteria may not prevent the spread of viruses, which are likely to be transferred from one person to another by touching, coughing, or sneezing or when objects such as toys or school materials are contaminated and then shared (*Child Health Alert*, 1997). The fresh smell conferred by waterless hand sanitizers may leave the false impression that the hands are cleaner than they actually are, resulting in deferral of hand washing. Soap is the most helpful agent for removing bacteria and viruses from the hands if it is applied in sufficient quantities and is rubbed in thoroughly. While less effective, frequent hand rinsing without soap also removes viruses from the hands. The key is frequent hand washing, followed by application of a hand lotion to keep hands soft and free from cracks or other abrasions.

Unfortunately, teachers do not always achieve strict compliance with hand washing. When hygiene materials are not readily available, sinks are located away from classrooms, and time constraints and children's needs are pressing, teachers may not wash their hands as often as they should. In addition, the hands may become chapped and irritated by frequent washing, reducing the motivation to hand wash. However, since the best mode of prevention is frequent hand washing, every effort should be made to comply with this aspect of universal precautions.

DIAPERING

Infants and young children with physical and health impairments may be eligible for special education and related services before they are toilet trained. Even some older students with physical or health impairments might not have good control of bodily secretions and need to wear diapers. As a result, educators and other service providers must use appropriate precautions when diapering children and/or helping them to be toilet trained. Research in day care settings (Barros et al., 1999) indicates that the incidence of diarrhea among children decreases when they wash their hands before meals and after defecation and when health care providers wash their hands after diapering. It is reasonable to expect that using gloves enhances infection control.

Diapering should occur in an area specifically for that purpose, such as a changing table or mat in a bathroom. The surface of the diaper changing area should be thoroughly cleaned with a bleach and water solution (1 part bleach to 10 parts water) that is mixed and delivered from a spray container. This disinfecting solution should be mixed fresh every day. After spraying the diaper changing surface, it should be wiped with paper towels that are

1. Check to be sure all necessary supplies are ready
2. Place roll paper or disposable towel on diapering surface
3. Lay the child on the diapering surface, taking care that the soiled diaper touches only your gloved hands, not your arms or clothing
4. Remove the soiled diaper
   - Put disposable diapers in a plastic bag or plastic-lined receptacle
   - If clothes are soiled, place in a plastic bag to be taken home
5. Clean the child's bottom and surrounding area with a premoistened disposable towelette or a damp paper towel
   - Dispose of the towelette or paper towel in the plastic bag or plastic-lined receptacle
   - Remove the paper towel from beneath the child and dispose of the same way
6. Wipe your hands with a premoistened towelette or a damp paper towel
   - Dispose of this towel in the plastic bag or plastic-lined receptacle
7. Diaper and dress the child
8. Wash the child's hands and return the child to the group
9. Clean and disinfect the diapering area and any equipment and supplies you touched
10. Wash your hands

FIGURE 23–2   Proper diapering technique.

Source: Adapted from guidelines provided by the Center for Disease Control and Prevention (1988).

then placed inside a plastic bag and sealed shut. Changing areas should be cleaned after each child is diapered. In addition, the floor around the changing area should be cleaned with commercial cleaning solution, using disposable towels or mops. Reusable mops simply spread bacteria from one area to another.

After a diaper is removed, it should be folded so that the soiled area is inside. The diaper should be placed inside a plastic bag, and the bag should be sealed shut. The sealed plastic bag can then be placed into an appropriate container with a lid. Figure 23–2 outlines the steps for proper diapering techniques.

HANDLING BLOOD OR OTHER FLUID SPILLS

Even when caution is used in educational settings, children scrape their knees or elbows, get bloody noses, lose a tooth, or have other accidents that result in a "blood spill." Occasionally, children also become sick and sneeze, cough, vomit, or lose control of their bladder and/or bowels. In all these situations, body fluids contaminate the environment and must be promptly and properly handled to ensure health. The first step in handling blood or other potentially contaminated fluids is proper use of gloves.

Using Gloves

Gloves should always be worn when there is any possibility of contact with blood or other bodily secretions. This form of barrier protection prevents contamination of the person wearing the gloves and the person receiving assistance. Gloves should be selected for proper fit. Remove all hand jewelry before putting on gloves to prevent any punctures or tears.

There is a specific procedure for removing gloves after use. Follow these steps:

- Pinch the left palm of the left glove with the gloved right hand.
- Pull the left glove toward and off the fingers, forming a ball. Hold the ball in the fist of the right hand.

- Place the index and middle fingers of the left ungloved hand under the inner edge of the palm side on the right-hand glove.
- Pull the right-hand glove inside out, over the fingers and over the left glove.
- Both gloves are now inside out and balled together, held in the left hand.
- Dispose of the balled gloves in an appropriate container, such as a biohazard bag or ziplock bag.
- Wash hands (Edens, Murdick, & Gartin, 2003).

Latex Allergy

The use of gloves has done much to prevent the spread of infection. Natural rubber latex gloves were widely used after the CDC issued its universal precautions guidelines because they were durable, comfortable, and affordable and allowed for tactile sensitivity (Sussman, Beezhold, & Liss, 2002). Unfortunately, the proteins contained in latex gloves can cause contact dermatitis. The cornstarch that is used to powder the insides of gloves absorbs latex proteins and releases them into the air when the gloves are removed, adding to exposure (Altman & Keller, 2003). Repeated exposure can result in asthma and life-threatening anaphylactic reactions (Corwin, 2002; Sussman et al., 2002). The person wearing gloves can be at risk for latex allergy, as is the person receiving care who is touched by the glove surfaces. Using vinyl or other nonlatex gloves is the safest solution.

WASTE DISPOSAL

Disposing of waste materials is an important aspect of hygiene in schools and health care facilities. After gloves are on, fluid spills should be mopped up with disposable paper towels. Do not use rags or other materials that would be used again. While wiping up fluid spills, take care not to spread potentially contaminated materials further than the radius of the actual spill. Place the towels in a plastic bag and then clean the contaminated area with soap and water. Wipe the area with more paper towels and then place these in a plastic bag. Finally, decontaminate the area using the 1 to 10 bleach and water solution and allow it to dry. Remove gloves and wash hands, carefully cleaning the faucet and sink with disinfectant after use (Edens et al., 2003).

Tabletops and other work surfaces can also become contaminated with fluids. Regularly sanitize tabletops, especially if they are going to be used as a surface for eating food. Sanitize tabletops before a meal while students wash their hands and again at the end of the school day.

Toys and other washable materials should be cleaned after use. In some daycare settings that provide services to very young children, toys that have been used are placed in a separate box until they are cleaned. This practice prevents the spread of bacteria between children. Soft toys such as stuffed animals cannot always be cleaned by washing. Commercial cleaning products are available that can be sprayed on the soft toys, which are then sealed inside a plastic bag overnight for decontamination to take place.

KEEPING CLASSROOMS CLEAN AND HEALTHY

By practicing a few simple steps, teachers can keep school environments safe and healthy for children and themselves. The first step is basic knowledge regarding universal precautions and their applications. Thinking about the steps in hand washing, gloving, cleaning up contaminated materials and areas, and disposing of waste will prepare the teacher for an actual event. Keep an adequate supply of gloves, paper towels, plastic bags, and cleaning materials readily available. If a bleach and water solution will be used for decontamination, make a fresh solution every day. Store all materials out of the reach of children.

Require regular student hand washing and monitor this procedure. Hand washing before meals and after using the restroom is absolutely necessary. Make hand washing part of the classroom routine and schedule sufficient time to follow through with this important skill.

Model this skill for your students by washing hands together when appropriate. If your classroom is not equipped with running water, use an alcohol-based hand sanitizer, but remember that this option is not as ideal as regular hand washing with soap and water.

Eating areas are especially vulnerable to infectious agents. Children sit close together and may not be careful about sharing utensils and covering their mouths while chewing or if they need to cough or sneeze. Discourage sharing of eating plates, bowls, utensils, straws, and juice/milk boxes or cups. This will require monitoring of the eating area. In addition, train children to cough or sneeze into the crook of their elbows rather than their hands. Directing saliva and nasal secretions away from the hands decreases the potential that infections will be spread. If a child had a very wet sneeze or cough, encourage hand washing before the meal resumes. Make sure eating areas are sanitized before eating.

The final rule for maintaining a clean and healthy school environment is common sense. For example, if a child experiences a nosebleed or falls and scrapes a knee, there is no reason to panic. Using a calm voice, provide comfort to the child while removing other children from the source of potential infection. Put on gloves and provide the child with tissue or gauze pad to cover the bleeding area. Use appropriate techniques to clean the contaminated area, then remove gloves and wash hands. Since accidents can happen outside while children are playing, it is good practice to wear a fanny pack or other portable container in which to put gauze squares, several damp paper towels folded and placed into a ziplock bag, and gloves. This will allow the teacher to render immediate aid without leaving the area for supplies. Everyone will be healthier with some careful thinking and simple precautions.

SUMMARY

In order to maintain a safe, healthy environment, teachers need to practice good infection control measures. It is important for teachers to know the principles of universal precautions, as they apply in the school setting. This includes such areas as proper hand washing, diapering, handling blood and other fluid spills, and disposal of contaminated materials. Keeping classrooms clean and healthy should be a priority for teachers.

REFERENCES

Altman, G. B., & Keller, K. M. (2003). Practice powder-free and latex safe. *Nurse Practitioner, 28*(8), 55-56.

Barros, A. J. D., Ross, A. D., Fonseca, W. V. C., Williams, L. A., & Moreira-Filho, D. C. (1999). Preventing acute respiratory infections and diarrhea in child care centres. *Acta Pediatrica, 88*, 1113-1118.

Centers for Disease Control and Prevention. (1988). Update: Universal precautions for prevention of transmission of human immunodeficiency virus, hepatitis B virus, and other bloodborne pathogens in health-care settings. *Morbidity and Mortality Weekly, 37*, 377.

Child Health Alert. (1997). Handwashing—with or without soap—to prevent the spread of viruses. *Child Health Alert, 15*, 1-2.

Chillock, C. A., & Palenik, C. J. (2004). New CDC guidelines. *RDH, 24*(4), 74-78.

Corwin, A. D. (2002). Latex allergy. *Primary Care Update for OB/GYNS, 9*(4), 144-149.

Edens, R. M., Murdick, N. L., & Gartin, B. C. (2003). Preventing infection in the classroom. *Teaching Exceptional Children, 35*(4), 62-66.

FDA Consumer. (1993). Universal precautions. *FDA Consumer, 27*(3), 12-14.

Gelbwasser, M. (2007). Sniff sniff…*Instructor, 116*(5), 36-38.

Sussman, G. L., Beezhold, D. H., & Liss, G. (2002). Latex allergy: Historical perspective. *Methods, 27*(1), 3-9.

abduction A movement of a body part away from the midline of the body.

acute The short and usually more severe course of a disease process.

adaptations Alterations to a task or materials that provide access to a task or facilitate participation in a task that may include modifications, accommodations, assistive technology, and alternative performance strategies.

adduction A movement of a body part toward the midline of the body.

amblyopia A loss of visual acuity that is not attributable to an organic cause. It can occur as a result of nonuse or visual deprivation or when one eye sees a different image from the other.

ambulatory Describes a person who is able to walk.

anemia A broad term to describe conditions in which the erythrocytes (red blood cells) are decreased in number or quality.

anoxia The absence or a decrease of oxygen in body tissues. Prolonged anoxia results in tissue destruction and ultimately death.

anterior A term used in reference to the forward part of an organ or body, the face side of the body, or ventral (belly) surface of the body.

antibody An immunoglobulin molecule formed in response to a specific antigen. An antibody reacts only with a specific antigen and works to suppress the action of the antigen.

anticipatory grief This is where the individual is grieving for the loss of the ill person before they have died.

antigen A substance that produces an immune response and stimulates the production of antibodies. Antigens include toxins, foreign substances, bacteria, and tissue cells.

aphasia The loss of the ability to use written or spoken language (expressive aphasia) or to comprehend written or spoken language (receptive aphasia) due to damage to specific areas in the brain responsible for speech and language.

arthritis Inflammation of joints characterized by pain, heat, redness, and swelling, which may lead to disuse and/or deformity.

arthrogryposis A congenital condition characterized by multiple contracted and malformed joints (arthrogryposis multiplex congenita).

articular Refers to something that has joints or describes something pertaining to a joint.

asphyxia A severe lack of oxygen that can result in coma or death. Asphyxia is typically a more sudden and significant decrease in oxygen supply as compared to anoxia, although either can have the same sequelae if prolonged.

aspirate See *aspiration*.

aspiration Inhalation of foreign matter into the lungs.

assistive technology Any item, piece of equipment, or product system, whether acquired commercially off the shelf, modified, or customized, that is used to increase, maintain, or improve the functional capabilities of a child with a disability.

asthma A lung disease with acute attacks of shortness of breath and wheezing secondary to airway inflammation and airway obstruction due to allergies or infection.

asthma attack An acute episode of asthma in which the airways constrict and the person usually has shortness of breath, wheezing, and other respiratory symptoms.

astigmatism A condition in which there is an unequal curvature of the cornea or lens, resulting in blurred or distorted images.

ataxia The inability to coordinate muscular control smoothly.

ataxic cerebral palsy Type of cerebral palsy with ataxia.

atelectasis When an air passage is blocked, the air in the small air sacs of the lungs (aleveoli) is absorbed into the bloodstream, and with the inability to receive more air due to the blockage, the air sacs shrink or collapse.

athetoid See *athetosis*.

athetosis A movement disorder caused by a brain lesion characterized by involuntary, slow, writhing movements that are nearly constant (i.e., athetoid movements).

atonia A decrease in muscle tone from normal tone or a lack of muscle tone.

atopy Predisposition for hypersensitivity to environmental allergens.

atrophy The decrease in size or wasting away of a cell, muscle, or tissue.

autonomic dysreflexia A complication with spinal cord injuries that are above the T6 level in which there is a rapid, dangerous elevation of blood pressure due to a noxious stimuli such as a distended bladder.

autonomic nervous system Regulates the functioning of internal organs as well as the internal environment (blood pressure).

brain stem The anatomical designation of the base of the brain that connects the cerebral hemispheres with the spinal cord and controls many autonomic vital functions (respiration, circulation, and alertness).

cancer A variety of diseases in which the cells have the unique trait of unregulated, excessive growth, and have the ability to invade local, or sometimes distant, tissue which can lead to tissue or organ damage.

cataract Any clouding of the crystalline lens of the eye, either partial or complete.

catheter A tube used for withdrawing or inserting fluids into the body; most frequently used to describe the tube inserted through the urethra into the bladder to withdraw urine.

central nervous system Consists of the brain and spinal cord.

cerebellum The portion of the brain below the cerebral hemispheres and behind the brain stem that functions to coordinate movements.

cerebral hemispheres These hemispheres form the cerebrum, the major portion of the human brain.

cerebral palsy A nonprogressive disorder of voluntary movement caused by damage to the motor centers of the brain before or during birth or within the first few years of life.

cerebrospinal fluid The clear fluid that surrounds and helps protect the brain and spinal cord. It originates from ventricles in the brain and circulates between the meninges.

cerebrum Consists of the two cerebral hemispheres and makes up the main portion of the brain.

chemotherapy The treatment of a disease by chemical agents, often the use of antineoplastic medication, to treat cancer.

chest physiotherapy Removal of respiratory secretions (mucus) from the lungs through physical means.

chorea The nearly constant occurrence of involuntary, jerky movements seen in a number of disorders.

chronic illness A disease process that lasts a long period of time (usually more than 3 months to a year) or results in continuous hospitalizations for more than a month.

chronic renal failure A condition in which the kidneys are damaged and cannot function normally.

clean intermittent catheterization A clean procedure in which a catheter (a long, thin tube) is placed through the urinary opening (or an opening made through the abdominal area into the bladder) to allow urine to be released from the bladder and then the catheter is removed. Often used by individuals with myelomeningocele and spinal cord injures.

congenital A condition present at birth, but may be detected prior to birth, at birth, or years later.

congenital heart defect Refers to a variety of conditions in which the heart is structurally impaired at birth.

congenital rubella Rubella that is transmitted to the unborn fetus and is present at birth.

contracture A shortening of a muscle so that motion is limited.

coping A specific effort aimed at reducing or managing a demand on the individual or family system and bring resources to bear to manage the situation.

cornea A transparent membrane that forms the anterior one-sixth of the outer covering of the eye.

cystic fibrosis An inherited disease of the exocrine glands affecting the pancreas, respiratory system, and sweat glands; glandular secretions are increased in amount and consistency, causing obstructions and infections.

cytomegalovirus A virus that results in few or no symptoms in healthy individuals, but can cause severe birth defects when transmitted from the pregnant woman to the developing fetus. It is one of the TORCH infections.

degenerative The process of becoming less functional.

developmental disability A severe, chronic disability of an individual that (a) is attributable to a mental or physical impairment or combination of mental and physical impairments, (b) is manifested before the person attains age 22 months, (c) is likely to continue indefinitely, or (d) results in substantial functional limitations in three or more areas of major life activity.

diabetes mellitus A condition in which there is an abnormally high amount of glucose (sugar) in the bloodstream (hyperglycemia) due to impaired secretions of insulin.

diplegia Affecting both legs, as in diplegic cerebral palsy; complete or partial paralysis of both legs.

diplegic See *diplegia*.

diplopia Double vision that can occur when one eye deviates from correct alignment.

dislocation The displacement of any body part, most typically the relationship of bones at a joint.

distal Far from the point of reference, as opposed to proximal, which means close to the point of reference.

distention The state of being enlarged.

dorsal A term used to denote a position more toward the back (posterior) surface.

dysarthria Poorly articulated speech that may be difficult to understand (dysarthric speech).

dyskinetic cerebral palsy Type of cerebral palsy affecting the basal ganglia, resulting in movement disorders (such as athetosis or dystonia).

dystonia Extremely high muscle tone found in dyskinetic cerebral palsy that can be accompanied by abnormal posturing.

electrolyte A substance that separates into ions when in a solution and then can conduct electricity.

encephalitis An inflammation of the brain.

epilepsy A chronic condition in which the person has recurring seizures (sudden, involuntary, time-limited disruptions in the normal function of the central nervous system).

equilibrium A state of balance or maintaining balance.

esotropia An impairment in eye muscle movements in which one or both eyes turn in toward the nose. Esotropia is a type of strabismus.

etiology The knowledge or study of the causes of a disease.

exotropia An impairment in eye muscle movements in which one or both eyes turn out away from the nose. Exotropia is a type of strabismus.

extension Refers to a body part being in a straight position (e.g., the elbow being straight).

febrile Pertaining to fever.

fetus An unborn baby after the embryonic period, which is the first 7 to 8 weeks of gestation.

flexion Refers to a body part being in a bent position (e.g., the elbow being bent).

fracture A break or disruption in a bone.

Friedreich's ataxia An inherited disease beginning in childhood or youth characterized by a hardening of the dorsal and lateral columns of the spinal cord. Symptoms include ataxia, problems with speech, scoliosis, paralysis (especially of the legs), and swaying, uncoordinated movements.

gastroesophageal reflux This occurs when the stomach contents escape back up the esophagus (the passageway connecting the back of the throat to the stomach), resulting in frequent vomiting and potential irritation.

gastrostomy button A skin level device that may be used instead of a gastrostomy tube for feeding. See *gastrostomy tube*.

gastrostomy tube A tube is inserted into either the stomach or small intestine and brought through the abdominal wall. Liquid nutrients may then be introduced directly into the stomach or intestine, bypassing the oral cavity.

genetic Pertaining to birth or origin. It may also be used to indicate a condition that is inherited. Genetics is the study of heredity.

glaucoma An abnormal increase in intraocular pressure in one or both eyes that can damage the eye.

Gowers's sign A classic indication of Duchenne muscular dystrophy in which children use their hands to push up on their legs in order to get up from the floor to standing.

hearing loss The term encompasses a wide range of disorders and diseases that may cause a variety of deficits in hearing and possibly communication.

hemarthrosis Bleeding in the joints—a common characteristic of hemophilia.

hemianopsia A visual field deficit in which one-half of the visual field is missing.

hemiplegia Affecting the arm and leg on one side of the body, as in hemiplegic cerebral palsy; partial or total paralysis of the arm and leg on one side of the body.

hemiplegic See *hemiplegia*.

hemophilia A hereditary bleeding disorder in which there are inadequate amounts of clotting factor in the blood.

hip dislocation A hip dislocation refers to a complete separation of the bone ends that normally form a joint. The ball of the femur (thighbone) is not properly positioned in its socket (acetabulum).

hip dysplasia An abnormality of development of the hip.

hip subluxation An incomplete or partial dislocation of the hip joint from the socket.

hydrocephalus A condition characterized by an abnormal accumulation of cerebrospinal fluid in the brain, which may result in an enlarged head and pressure on the brain, leading to brain damage.

hyperglycemia An abnormally high amount of sugar in the bloodstream, usually associated with diabetes mellitus.

hyperopia A deficit in visual acuity caused by a refractory error affecting near vision (farsightedness).

hypertension Abnormally high blood pressure.

hypertonia A condition of increased muscle tone (spasticity).

hypoglycemia An abnormally low amount of sugar in the bloodstream. This is a complication of diabetes mellitus, in which there is too much insulin and too little glucose.

hypotonia A condition of decreased muscle tone and decreased resistance of muscles to passive stretch.

hypoxia When the oxygen content of the blood and lungs is too low.

idiopathic Of unknown origin or unto itself.

incontinent The inability to control secretions, most typically bowel and bladder functions.

inflammation A localized, protective response that occurs after injury or tissue destruction; characterized by pain, redness, swelling, and heat.

insulin The pancreatic secretion responsible for transporting glucose from the bloodstream to the cells in the body.

insulin reaction Insulin reaction is an emergency complication of diabetes in which there is too much insulin in the body and too little glucose (hypoglycemia).

intellectual disability A newer term meaning mental retardation.

intracranial Positioned within the cranium or skull.

intracranial hemorrhage Bleeding within the cranium or skull.

intrauterine Within the uterus.

joint A point of junction between two or more bones, also called an articulation.

juvenile rheumatoid arthritis A chronic arthritis disease (joint inflammation) present in a child before the age of 16. Several different subtypes exist with differing characteristics.

kyphoscoliosis A combined kyphosis and scoliosis (see *kyphosis* and *scoliosis*).

kyphosis An abnormal posterior curvature of the spine; when occurring in the upper back, it appears as a hump.

lateral Pertaining to a side or away from the midline.

lazy eye An impairment in eye muscle movements (strabismus) that occurs primarily when the person's eyes are fatigued so that one eye deviates from correct alignment.

learned helplessness A lack of persistence at tasks that could be mastered.

Legg-Perthes or Legg-Calve-Perthes disease A degenerative disease affecting the head of the femur.

leukemia A progressive malignant disease of the blood-forming organs, in which blood is characterized by an increase in leukocytes (white blood cells).

ligament A band of fibrous tissue that joins bones or cartilage and gives more support to the junction.

limb-girdle muscular dystrophy A type of muscular dystrophy that initially manifests as deterioration at the shoulders and pelvis.

lordoscoliosis When a lordosis occurs with a scoliosis.

lordosis An abnormal anterior curve of the spine; when occurring in the lower back, it appears "sway-backed," in which the normal curvature of the spine in the lower back is increased.

lower motor neurons Neurons (cells of the nervous system) located in the spinal cord that receive messages from the upper motor neurons in the brain and send out impulses to the body to cause a body part to move.

lymphoma A general term referring to cancer of the lymph tissues.

malaise A nonspecific feeling of discomfort.

malignant Becoming progressively worse; often used in reference to tumors describing one that is growing and has a tendency to spread and recur (cancer).

medial The middle, or toward the middle.

meninges Three membranes that form a covering of the brain and spinal cord: the dura mater, the pia mater, and the arachnoid.

meningitis An inflammation of the meninges (membranes surrounding the brain and spinal cord).

metabolize The process of chemically breaking down substances to provide nutrients.

metastasis The transfer of a disease from one body part to another part that is not in direct contact.

motor cortex See *primary motor cortex*.

multiple disabilities Two or more disabilities that significantly affect the person's ability to learn and function.

muscular dystrophy Any of a group of inherited diseases characterized by progressive weakness due to the degeneration of muscle fibers. Duchenne muscular dystrophy is one of the most common types.

musculoskeletal system Consists of the muscles, bones, tendons, and ligaments of the body and the systems that involve any of these entities.

myelin A substance that surrounds part of some neurons that aids in transmitting information and maintaining the electrically charged environment of the neurons.

myelination The process of taking on myelin; also called *myelmization*.

myelomeningocele A form of spina bifida in which the meninges and spinal cord are pushed out through the malformed vertebrae, usually resulting in some degree of paralysis, sensory loss, or both.

myopathy A pathology or abnormal condition of the muscles.

myopia A deficit in visual acuity caused by a refractory error affecting distance vision (nearsightedness).

neonate A newborn infant. Infants are called neonates for the first 4 weeks of life.

neuron A cell of the nervous system that transmits electrical energy.

neuropathy A pathology or abnormal condition of the nervous system.

neurotransmitter A group of chemicals that are released from the ends of neurons (at the axon terminal) and travel across small gaps (synapse) to the next neurons to either facilitate transmission of the impulse (excite) or decrease the likelihood that the impulse will continue (inhibit).

nonsymbolic communication The use of movements, gestures, or sounds to communicate.

nystagmus The ocular movements consisting of involuntary, rhythmic eye movements (typically in the horizontal plane).

opportunistic infections Infections (e.g., toxoplasmosis) that typically have no significant consequence to healthy individuals, but if they are acquired by a person with an impaired immune system (e.g., AIDS), they may have devastating results such as blindness, seizures, encephalitis, and death.

orthopedics A category of surgery that deals specifically with the musculoskeletal system.

orthoses Bracing or other types of external supports used to correct deformities, provide support, and increase function (*orthotic* refers to use or application of orthoses).

osteogenesis imperfecta Brittle bone disease.

otitis media An inflammation of the middle ear.

pathological A biological process that is not normal and causes injurious changes in body tissues or function.

pathology The changes in body tissues or structures that are caused by a disease process.

pelvis The large ring of bones at the base of the trunk that forms joints with the femur (hip joint) and sacrum (end of the vertebral column).

perinatal The general period of time just before, during, and after birth.

peripheral nervous system Consists of the nerves that connect the spinal cord to the rest of the body.

plasma The fluid part of the blood in which blood components are suspended.

pneumonia An acute inflammation of the alveoli of the lungs.

posterior A term used in reference to the back part of an organ or body, the backside of the body, or the dorsal (back) surface of the body.

postnatal The period of time after birth.

postural reaction The automatic movement a person makes in order to keep an upright position.

postural tone The normal tension in the muscles that provides the background for normal movement.

prenatal The period of time before birth (during gestation).

primary motor cortex Part of the brain that works in association with other motor areas to cause motor movement throughout the body. It contains large neurons that have long axons that descend down the spinal cord (also known as somatomotor cortex or motor strip).

prognosis The estimate as to the probable outcome or chance of recovery from a disease or process that is based on the symptoms, response, and current knowledge.

proprioceptive Receiving stimuli from sensory receptors in the muscles, tendons, joints, and inner ear that detect motion or position of the body or limb; the sense of the relative position of parts of the body in space. The term can also include providing information about the rate and timing of movements, the amount of force the muscles are exerting, and how much a muscle is being stretched.

prosthesis An artificial substitute for a body part.

proximal Close to the point of reference, as opposed to distal, which means far from the point of reference.

pseudohypertrophy An increase in size without an increase in muscle tissue; observed in the calves of boys with Duchennes muscular dystrophy.

quadriplegia Affecting all four limbs, as in quadriplegic cerebral palsy; paralysis (total or partial) of all four limbs.

quadriplegic See *quadriplegia*.

reflex An automatic, involuntary response to a stimuli.

relapse Used to note a recurrence of a condition after a period of improvement or stability.

remission A period in which the symptoms of a disease become much less significant or may abate entirely.

respiratory system The organs and structures concerned with air intake, output, and gas exchange. The lungs, bronchi, trachea, alveoli, nose, and mouth make up the respiratory system.

rigidity An abnormal increase in muscle tone in which resistance to passive movement is noted throughout the entire range of movement.

rubella Is also known as German measles and was the most common viral cause of birth defects until a vaccination was developed.

sclera The white outer covering of the eye.

scoliosis An abnormal side-to-side curvature of the spine, typically in an S or a C pattern.

seizure A sudden, involuntary, time-limited disruption in the normal function of the central nervous system that may be characterized by altered consciousness, motor activity, sensory phenomena, or inappropriate behavior.

seizure threshold A threshold of excitation that will result in a seizure under certain circumstances.

sensorineural hearing loss A type of hearing loss involving damage to the inner ear or auditory nerve.

shunting The process of providing an alternate route for the flow of body fluid.

sickle cell anemia A chronic, inherited anemia occurring primarily in the African American population, characterized by sickle-shaped red blood cells.

sickling crisis Painful episodes occurring in individuals with sickle cell anemia due to the blockage of small blood vessels in the body, resulting in localized tissue hypoxia. Also known as vaso-occlusive crisis.

somatosensory cortex Part of the brain that receives information from the body regarding simple sensations from the body (also known as somatosensory strip).

spastic cerebral palsy Type of cerebral palsy resulting in spasticity.

spasticity The abnormal increase in muscle tone (hypertonia) often observed with persons who have neurological impairments. It is characterized by a hyperactive stretch reflex.

spina bifida A defective closure of the bony vertebral column that may or may not also involve part of the spinal column with resultant motor and/or sensory impairment.

spinal cord The part of the central nervous system contained in the vertebral column.

spinal cord injury Damage to the spinal cord caused by disease or trauma that results in symptoms ranging from weakness to total paralysis.

spinal muscular atrophy A group of degenerative diseases characterized by progressive weakening and atrophy of the skeletal muscles due to deterioration of motor cells in the spinal cord.

status epilepticus Status epilepticus is a continuous seizure, or recurrent seizures that occur without regaining consciousness.

strabismus The condition of one or both eyes deviating from correct alignment.

symbolic communication Communicating through the use of specific symbols to represent an object, action, or thought.

teratogenic Producing abnormalities during formation, as when a substance produces a defect during gestation.

terminal condition A condition that ends in the person's death.

TORCH Acronym referring to a group of congenital infections—toxoplasmosis, other, rubella, cytomegalovirus, and herpes—that, when acquired during pregnancy, can result in significant birth defects.

toxoplasmosis An infection that is caused by a parasite (*Toxoplasma gondu*) transmitted by infected raw meat and cat feces and, although it causes mild symptoms in a healthy adult, it is potentially very dangerous to a fetus. It is one of the TORCH infections.

trauma Any accident or abnormal occurrence that causes damage.

traumatic brain injury A diagnosis that encompasses many types of injury to the brain; may also be referred to as head injury. Includes both open head injuries in which the skull has been penetrated and closed head injuries in which the skull has not been fractured.

tube feeding Feeding that is given through a tube (e.g., gastrostomy tube or button) that goes directly into the stomach or small intestine in which liquid nutrition is delivered. This is used for individuals who can not eat food orally.

upper motor neurons Neurons (nerve cells) located on the primary motor cortex in the frontal lobe of the brain that have axons descending within the spinal cord.

uveal tract Part of the eye consisting of the iris (colored part of the eye), ciliary body (located behind the lens and helps control the lens and produces aqueous), and choroid (layer of the eye between the retina and the sclera that provides nutrients to the eye).

vaso-occlusive crisis Painful episodes occurring in individuals with sickle cell anemia due to the blockage of small blood vessels in the body, resulting in localized tissue hypoxia. Also known as a sickling crisis.

vertebral column The bones of the spine containing and protecting the spinal cord.

vertical transmission Transmission of an infection from the mother to the fetus.

visual impairment Encompasses many types of vision loss, including deficits in acuity, field loss, ocular motility, or color perception.

Bradding, P., 324
Bradford, S., 47
Bradley, J. S., 371
Brady, M., 46
Brady, N. C., 41
Brady, R. C., 393, 394
Braun, C., 125
Bremer, D. L., 197
Brenner, R. E., 184
Brent, J. L., 30
Brent, S. B., 282
Bresnan, M. J., 245
Bresolin, N., 245, 252
Brewer, D. M., 29
Brichta, L., 250
Bridwell, K. H., 105
Briggs, A., 289
Brightling, C. E., 324
Brineman, D. G., 27
Brinton, B., 43
Britt, W. J., 388
Brodie, M. J., 306, 308, 309, 311
Brodin, J., 44
Brodsky, M. C., 193
Broome, M. E., 289
Broste, S., 177
Broström, E., 177
Browder, D., 46, 47
Brown, E., 29
Brown, F., 46, 47
Brown, L., 45, 46
Brown, R., 104
Brown, R. T., 287
Bruce, S., 126
Bruner, J., 111
Bryant, B. R., 140, 220, 221
Bryant, D. P., 140, 220, 221
Bryson, E. A., 262, 267, 272, 273, 274
Brzustowicz, L. M., 252
Buckingham, S. C., 374
Burack, J., 38
Burden, S. K., 192
Burdick Harmon, M., 395
Bureau, M., 303
Burns, I. T., 371, 372, 373, 374, 375
Burns, J., 185
Burton, R., 22, 24, 121, 122, 123, 124, 129
Bushby, K., 241
Butler, F., 48
Butler, K., 380, 381

Cabanela, M. E., 178
Cakmak, A., 177
Camacho, F., 29
Cameron, D., 252
Camirand, G., 240
Campbell, J., 37
Campbell, P. H., 143, 145, 220
Campbell, S. K., 52, 60
Campo, J., 377
Campos, J., 145
Candy, R., 192
Canne, J., 27
Cannon, M. J., 390
Cannon, S., 48
Cano, J., 377

Cardenas, D., 102
Cardosa-Martins, C., 42
Carius, A., 296
Carlson, D., 30
Carlson, R., 22
Caroppo, S., 393
Carr, E., 45
Caruso, J. F., 255
Casey, A. T., 96
Cassella, J. P., 182
Cassidy, J. T., 173, 175, 176, 178
Castillo-Solorzano, C., 392
Castro-Rodriguez, J. A., 318
Celeste, M., 25
Celum, C., 377
Centers for Disease Control and
    Prevention, 378, 379, 382,
    395, 400
Cha, K., 37
Chambers, A., 286
Chan, K., 44
Chan, K. G., 236
Chang, D., 194
Chapman, R. S., 42, 43
Chari, A., 250
Chen, S. M., 252
Chen, Y., 296
Chevrie, J., 295, 304
Chiafery, M., 109, 111
Chiang, B.-L., 177
Chiarelli, F., 86
Child Health Alert, 372, 402
Chillock, C. A., 400, 401
Chin, R., 304
Chng, S., 161
Chow, J., 296
Christ, S. E., 27
Christenson, S. L., 8
Christian, C. W., 120
Christoffel, K. K., 120
Chu, S. Y., 375
Chuang, Y., 299
Cihak, D., 230
Cioni, G., 194
Clancy, C. C., 23
Clancy, J. P., 267, 272, 273, 274, 276
Clark, R., 276
Cliffe, S., 391
Cocozza, S., 355
Coe, K., 199
Collins, B., 46
Colver, A. F., 31
Conaway, M., 23
Conboy-Ellis, K., 317, 321, 323
Connolly, B. H., 65
Connors, F. A., 47
Connors, P. M., 265, 275
Cook, A. M., 145
Cook, D. G., 318
Cook, E. H., 355, 356, 357
Cook, M. J., 299
Corn, A. L., 192, 200, 209, 215
Cornoldi, C., 39
Corr, C. A., 285
Corti, S., 257
Corwin, A. D., 404
Cotton, S., 235

Coulter, D., 207
Covar, R., 324
Cox, A. H., 282
Craft, S., 27
Crawford, A. H., 177
Crawford, M., 236
Crawley, S., 44
Crisp, J., 286
Crockar, J. H. A., 96
Cron, R. Z., 174
Cronin, A., 55
Cross, D., 48
Cullinan, P., 318
Cunningham, C., 44
Curtiss, G., 128
Cutting, G. R., 262, 265

D'Angelo, M. G., 245, 252
D'Avignon, J., 245
D'Souza, W. J., 299
Dabney, K., 165
Daigneault, S., 125
Dalkilic, I., 233
Danks, D. M., 183
Dannetun, E., 373
Darbee, J. C., 272
Davis-McFarland, E., 376, 378, 380
Day, J., 241, 242
de Gans, J., 371
Deacon, J., 39
Deaton, A., 135
del Romero, J., 377
Delaney, C., 236
Delgado-Escueta, A., 297
Demissie, K., 318
Demmler, G., 391
Dempsey, P., 47
Denckla, M. B., 26
Dennis, C. W., 52, 57
Dennis, M., 27, 109
Denny, R. K., 230
DePompei, R., 124, 125, 126, 131, 134
Derlacki, D. J., 197
DeSimone, G., 382
Desnoyers, H., 245
Devereux, G., 317
DeVivo, D., 235, 245
Dias, M., 108
Diav-Citrin, O., 393
Diaz, C. C., 250
Dicara, J. A., 120
Dickson, G., 240
DiScala, C., 119, 120, 129
Dixon, T. M., 119, 123, 129
Docherty, S., 173
Doja, A., 372
Dollard, S. C., 390
Dominov, J., 241
Doring, G., 274
Dorman, C., 245
Dorman, K., 351, 352
Dorsey, M., 45
Dryden, D. M., 100, 101, 102
Dubowitz, V., 245
Ducharme, M., 240
Duche, B., 305
Duchenne, Gullaume, 233